THE VICTORIA HISTORY
OF THE
COUNTIES OF ENGLAND

A HISTORY OF
OXFORDSHIRE

VOLUME VII

THE VICTORIA HISTORY
OF THE
COUNTIES OF ENGLAND

EDITED BY R. B. PUGH

THE UNIVERSITY OF LONDON
INSTITUTE OF
HISTORICAL RESEARCH

Oxford University Press, Amen House, London, E.C.4

GLASGOW NEW YORK TORONTO MELBOURNE WELLINGTON
BOMBAY CALCUTTA MADRAS KARACHI LAHORE DACCA
CAPE TOWN SALISBURY NAIROBI IBADAN ACCRA
KUALA LUMPUR HONG KONG

PRINTED IN GREAT BRITAIN

INSCRIBED TO THE

MEMORY OF HER LATE MAJESTY

QUEEN VICTORIA

WHO GRACIOUSLY GAVE THE TITLE TO

AND ACCEPTED THE DEDICATION

OF THIS HISTORY

THAME HIGH STREET FROM THE WEST IN 1858

A HISTORY OF THE COUNTY OF

OXFORD

EDITED BY MARY LOBEL

VOLUME VII

DORCHESTER AND
THAME HUNDREDS

PUBLISHED FOR

THE INSTITUTE OF HISTORICAL RESEARCH

BY THE

OXFORD UNIVERSITY PRESS

AMEN HOUSE, LONDON

1962

CONTENTS OF VOLUME SEVEN

LIST OF ILLUSTRATIONS

Thanks are due to the Librarian of the Bodleian Library, the Keeper of the Ashmolean Museum, the Trustees of the British Museum, the Committee for aerial photography of Cambridge University Museum, the National Buildings' Record, and *Country Life* for permission to reproduce material in their respective collections, to Mr. W. Guest and Mr. P. H. Newitt for the loan of three prints and photographs, and to the Royal Archaeological Institute for the loan of the block of Dorchester Barn.

LIST OF ILLUSTRATIONS

LIST OF MAPS AND PLANS

The maps of Dorchester, Drayton, Great Milton, South Stoke, and Thame are partly based on the Ordnance Survey and are published with the sanction of the Controller of H.M. Stationery Office, Crown Copyright reserved.

The historical work on the maps was done by Mary Barran, Marjorie Jones, and Mary Lobel.

The hundred maps were drawn by G. R. Versey and the rest by Mary E. Potter. All the plans of houses and churches, except Camoise Court, were dated by H. M. Colvin, and all were drawn by J. G. Roberts.

EDITORIAL NOTE

THIS volume, the sixth to appear in the Oxfordshire set of the Victoria Histories, is a further outcome of the partnership between the Oxfordshire Victoria County History Committee and the University of London. The local committee, under the chairmanship of Sir Charles Ponsonby, has been responsible for the preparation of the text, and the University of London for the final editing and publication. To the local committee, whose members are named below, the thanks of the University are due for their valuable subsidies. Gratitude must also be expressed to many private subscribers whose names are also printed here.

Work on this volume has been going on since 1950: it was finally written and edited between January 1958 and March 1959. Much is owed to the kindness of the governing bodies of several Oxford Colleges, the incumbents of the Oxfordshire parishes included in this volume, the Bishop and the Dean and Chapter of Lincoln, the Archivist of the Lincolnshire Record Office, the Dean and Chapter of Westminster, private owners, and others, who have given permission to use documents in their care or have lent them to the local committee. Footnotes throughout the volume testify to their considerateness.

Particular mention must be made of the help given by the staff of the Bodleian Library, especially by Dr. Molly Barratt and Dr. W. O. Hassall, and by Mr. H. M. Walton, the County Archivist, and his assistant Mr. S. G. Baker.

In writing the history great help has also been given by Mr. H. M. Colvin, who has revised all the architectural sections, by Mr. P. S. Spokes, who gave information on heraldry, by Dr. Joycelyne G. Dickinson, and by many others, namely the Revd. E. P. Baker, Mrs. H. M. Colvin, Miss C. L. M. Hawtrey, the late Revd. R. A. Ker, Mrs. D. Long, Miss Kathleen Moore, Miss Katharine Price, Miss Ethel Savill, Miss Mary Savill, and Mrs. A. Selwyn, who have freely given of their time. Their public spirit is here thankfully acknowledged.

OXFORDSHIRE
VICTORIA COUNTY HISTORY
COMMITTEE

as at 16 June 1961

President and Chairman

†*Col. Sir Charles Ponsonby, Bt., t.d., d.l.

Vice-Presidents (*ex officio*)

The Rt. Rev. the Lord Bishop of Oxford

The Vice-Chancellor of the University of Oxford

The Rt. Worshipful the Mayor of Oxford

The Rt. Hon. the Earl of Macclesfield, Her Majesty's Lieutenant and Custos Rotulorum for the County, and Chairman of the Oxfordshire County Council

Representatives of the Oxfordshire County Council

Major A. G. C. Fane, m.c.

*C. J. Peers, Esq.

Miss J. M. Shelmerdine

Representatives of the University of Oxford

E. F. Jacob, Esq., f.b.a., Chichele Professor of Modern History

†*Miss L. S. Sutherland, c.b.e., d.litt., f.b.a., Principal of Lady Margaret Hall

Representatives of the City of Oxford

Councillor M. Maclagan

Councillor P. S. Spokes

Councillor N. Whatley

Representatives of District Councils in Oxfordshire

Banbury	The Worshipful the Mayor of Banbury *ex officio*
Chipping Norton	Councillor S. D. Wykes
Henley	Councillor G. H. J. Tomalin
Woodstock	R. B. Ramsbotham, Esq.

Urban Districts

Bicester	Councillor E. T. Clothier
Thame	Miss J. E. M. Fanshawe
Witney	Councillor E. S. Wood

Rural Districts

Banbury	The Revd. C. Browne
Bullingdon	Lt.-Col. C. R. C. Boyle, d.s.o.

Chipping Norton	V. C. Ponsonby, Esq.
Henley	The Hon. Mrs. S. Stonor
Ploughley	Miss A. Deeley
Witney	Miss G. M. Smith

Representatives of Learned Societies

Oxfordshire Archaeological Society
R. T. Lattey, Esq.

Oxford Record Society
R. V. Lennard, Esq.

Oxford Historical Society
W. A. Pantin, Esq., f.b.a.

Oxford Architectural and Historical Society
P. S. Spokes, Esq.

Co-opted Members

The Revd. Canon R. F. Bale

E. R. C. Brinkworth, Esq.

Sir George Clark, d.litt., litt.d., ll.d., f.b.a.

Thomas Loveday, ll.d.

*Miss K. Major, d.litt., Principal of St. Hilda's College

*J. N. L. Myres, Esq., ll.d., Bodley's Librarian

*R. B. Pugh, Esq., Editor, *Victoria History of the Counties of England*

Area Finance and General Purposes Committees

†Sir Basil Blackwell

*H. M. Colvin, Esq.

*H. J. Habakkuk, Esq., Chichele Professor of Economic History in the University of Oxford

*W. O. Hassall, Esq.

*W. G. Hoskins, Esq.

*Lawrence Stone, Esq.

*Miss M. V. Taylor, c.b.e.

*Sir John Wheeler Bennett, k.c.v.o., c.m.g., o.b.e.

†*Col. the Hon. E. H. Wyndham, m.c.

together with the persons marked with an asterisk and/or dagger.

Hon. Treasurers: †The Hon. N. T. A. Fiennes
†R. S. Jenkinson, Esq.

Secretary: †*Mrs. M. D. Lobel

* A member of the General Purposes Committee.

† A member of the Area Finance Committee.

LIST OF SUBSCRIBERS

JANUARY 1949—JUNE 1961

UNIVERSITY, COUNTY, CITY, AND COLLEGES

Oxford University Chest
Oxfordshire County Council
Corporation of Oxford
Henley Borough Council
All Souls College
Balliol College
Brasenose College
Christ Church
Corpus Christi College

Exeter College
Hertford College
Jesus College
Keble College
Lincoln College
Magdalen College
Merton College
New College
Oriel College

Pembroke College
The Queen's College
St. Edmund Hall
St. John's College
Somerville College
Trinity College
University College
Wadham College
Worcester College

PRIVATE SUBSCRIBERS

OXFORD CITY

Miss Cecilia Ady, D.Litt.
Miss Peter Ady
Mrs. Percy Allen
The Ancient and Modern Club
Barclays Bank, Ltd.
Basil Blackwell, Ltd.
Mrs. G. G. Buckler
Mrs. E. W. Burney
Miss C. V. Butler
Sir George N. Clarke, D.Litt., F.B.A.
A. D. M. Cox, Esq.
Dr. A. R. N. Cross
The Dragon School
A. B. Emden, Esq., D.Litt., F.B.A.
Mrs. E. Ettlinger
Sir Charles Fawcett
Miss H. E. Fiedler
Miss H. E. Fitzrandolph

Sir Alan Gardiner, D.Litt., F.B.A.
W. R. Gowers, Esq.
Mrs. R. H. Sturge Gretton
Miss C. L. M. Hawtrey
Miss D. C. S. Hole
Mrs. Arthur Hunt
Professor E. F. Jacob, F.B.A.
H. R. Leech, Esq.
Miss W. Lickes
Mrs. Edgar Lobel
R. S. Loomis, Esq.
The Rt. Revd. D. G. Loveday, Bishop of Dorchester
Professor May McKisack
Miss K. Major, D.Litt.
Miss J. de Lacy Mann
Canon R. R. Martin
N. R. Murphy, Esq.

A. C. Nielsen and Company, Ltd.
The Nuffield Press
Sir Michael Oppenheimer, Bt.
The Oxford Times
W. A. Pantin, Esq., F.B.A.
Sir Karl Parker, C.B.E., F.B.A.
L. C. W. Phillips, Esq.
A. L. Poole, Esq., D.Litt., F.B.A.
Miss E. E. S. Procter
G. D. Ramsay, Esq.
C. J. Rees, Esq.
Miss V. I. Ruffer
Mrs. C. M. Snow
Mrs. J. E. Soulsby
P. S. Spokes, Esq.
A. L. B. Stevens, Esq.
G. H. Stevenson, Esq.
L. Stone Esq.
H. D. Wilson, Esq.

BANBURY BOROUGH

Banbury Co-operative Industrial Society Ltd.
Banbury Historical Society
Mrs. Mary Cheney

Messrs. Cheney & Sons, Ltd.
Messrs. Hunt, Edmunds & Co., Ltd.

Miss C. H. Mackay
Northern Aluminium Co., Ltd.
Messrs. Thornton & Thornton

HENLEY BOROUGH

A. J. Crocker, Esq.
Professor A. M. Hind, O.B.E.

C. Luker, Esq.

C. Cecil Roberts, Esq.

WOODSTOCK BOROUGH WITH BLADON AND BEGBROKE

Dame Henrietta Barnett, D.B.E.
F. A. Bevan, Esq.
Miss F. N. Budd
A. J. Henman, Esq.
Col. A. J. Kerry
Mrs. N. M. Lambourn, M.B.E.
The Revd. H. A. McCann

His Grace the Duke of Marlborough
The Marlborough Arms Hotel
R. C. Morley, Esq.
C. Morris, Esq.
R. B. Ramsbotham, Esq., M.B.E.

Dr. A. H. T. Robb-Smith
Sir John Russell, O.B E., F.R.S.
The Rt. Revd. Bishop Shedden, D.D.
Miss J. M. Shelmerdine
Dr. H. Tothill

BICESTER URBAN DISTRICT

Bicester Local History Circle
Mrs. M. R. Coker
N. Collisson, Esq.

T. G. Curtis, Esq.
R. A. Evans, Esq.
F. T. Hudson, Esq.

Dr. G. N. Montgomery
Rotary Club of Bicester

THAME URBAN DISTRICT

Lt-Col. J. L. Ashton
Col. S. E. Ashton, O.B.E., T.D.
Messrs. Austins of Thame
A. S. Baker, Esq.
Dr. A. Sharman Beer
F. Bowden, Esq.
K. Cartwright, Esq.
A. J. Castle, Esq.
Miss M. I. Claridge

C. M. Cox, Esq.
Arthur G. Enock, Esq.
Miss J. E. M. Fanshawe
The Four Horseshoes (Mrs. A. Baverstock)
C. A. Goodger, Esq.
Messrs. Jenner, Blackburn & Co.
F. W. Jessup, Esq.

Mrs. A. A. Lester
B. M. Letts, Esq.
Messrs. Lightfoot & Lowndes
J. Nelson, Esq.
Peter H. Newitt, Esq.
Sir Ralph Pearson, C.I.E., LL.D.
Messrs. Pursers, Ltd.
H. Rose, Esq.

LIST OF SUBSCRIBERS

WITNEY URBAN DISTRICT

Canon R. F. Bale
Dr. W. Dalgliesh
Messrs. Charles Early & Co., Ltd.

R. E. Early, Esq.
F. W. Marriott, Esq.

Capt. Sidney Smith
E. S. Wood, Esq.

BANBURY RURAL DISTRICT

L. Bagratuni, Esq.
Mrs. J. Berkeley
Miss Monica Bradford
Mrs. A. Browning
Capt. and Mrs. W. H. Carter
H. F. Chamberlayne, Esq.
Lady Dugan of Victoria
Lord Elton
L. C. M. Gibbs, Esq.

J. S. W. Gibson, Esq.
R. P. T. Gibson, Esq.
Lady C. E. V. Hohler
Thomas Loveday, Esq., LL.D.
A. J. Morris, Esq.
Lt.-Col. H. E. du C. Norris
W. L. Pilkington, Esq.
G. B. Randolph, Esq.
Lord Saye and Sele, M.C., D.L.

Lady Saye and Sele
Lt.-Col. A. D. Taylor, D.S.O., M.C.
R. S. Thompson, Esq.
A. W. C. Thursby, Esq.
Lady Wardington
J. Webber, Esq.
Major S. P. Yates

BULLINGDON RURAL DISTRICT

B. G. K. Allsop, Esq., M.C.
Mrs. L. A. R. Anstruther
The Revd. E. P. Baker
J. Barclay, Esq.
Mrs. S. Barry
Miss Bell
Capt. L. H. Bell, R.N.
D. P. Bickmore, Esq.
Lt.-Col. H. T. Birch Reynardson, C.M.G.
F. G. Bonham Carter, Esq.
Miss Edith Bousfield
Lt.-Col. E. C. Bowes
Lt.-Col. C. R. C. Boyle, D.S.O.
Mrs. D. H. Burra
Chalford Property Co., Ltd.
N. M. Clark, Esq.
Miss Clerke Brown
Lord Conesford, Q.C.
Cdr. Coventon
Miss R. H. Coventon
Cuddesdon College
E. Hayes Dashwood, Esq.
Cdr. P. W. Dimsdale
Col. A. V. G. Dower, T.D.
Mrs. Ducat-Hamersley
Mrs. S. C. Evans
F. J. Fane, Esq.
B. Feilding, Esq.
Mrs. M. J. Fisher
Miss S. M. Fry
Mrs. E. E. H. Gallia
G. E. H. Gallia, Esq.
The Hon. Sir Geoffrey Gibbs, K.C.M.G.
H. Gilbert, Esq.

Professor Gillaume
Major John Glyn
Capt. I. I. Goodwin
The Hon. Mrs. Charles Gore
Brigadier-General C. A. L. Graham, D.S.O., O.B.E., D.L.
Brigadier Lord Malise Graham, C.B., D.S.O., M.C.
G. Hastwell Grayson, Esq., F.R.I.B.A.
Capt. G. S. Greene
P. D. Gresswell, Esq.
Clarence Hailey, Esq.
Lt.-Col. R. Hardcastle, D.S.O.
W. O. Hassall, Esq.
The Hon. W. Holland-Hibbert
The Hon. Mrs. W. Holland-Hibbert
The Misses Hoskyns
Mr. and Mrs. A. D. Hough
Mrs. R. L. L. Ingpen
Dr. Leo Jacobi
N. D. G. James, Esq.
Capt. R. F. Kershaw
Major D. A. Litchfield
D. F. Lodge, Esq.
The Earl of Macclesfield, Lord Lieutenant
The Countess of Macclesfield
Major Alastair G. Mann
Philip B. Mansel, Esq.
Major A. A. Miller
Mrs. Ethel M. Miller
Miss F. C. Mitchell
Professor D. Mitrany
E. B. Montesole, Esq.

Lt.-Col. C. L. Mould
Mrs. M. Naish
S. Nowell Smith, Esq.
Herbert Orpwood, Esq.
J. A. C. Osborne, Esq.
J. W. G. Payne, Esq.
Col. H. S. Pearson
C. J. Peers, Esq.
Mrs. D. G. Pott
Sir Stanley Pott
Mrs. V. Powell
C. H. Priestley, Esq.
J. S. Puttock, Esq.
R. N. Richmond-Watson, Esq.
R. Roadnight, Esq.
K. E. Robinson, Esq.
Bernard C. Rowles, Esq.
J. C. Seward, Esq.
Mrs. E. Shepley-Shepley
The Rt. Hon. Lord Somervell of Harrow, O.B.E.
F. Speakman, Esq.
Lt.-Col. A. V. Spencer, D.S.O., D.L.
H. V. Stammers, Esq.
Mrs. G. B. Starky
H. H. Stevens, Esq.
J. Stewart Thomson, Esq.
R. C. Surman, Esq.
Lt.-Col. John Thomson, T.D.
Susan, Lady Tweedsmuir
Sir John Wheeler-Bennett, K.C.V.O., C.M.G., O.B.E.
Lady Wheeler-Bennett
Major G. C. Whitaker
Lady Wilson

CHIPPING NORTON RURAL DISTRICT

The Hon. Michael Astor
Miss H. L. Bailey
A. Balfour, Esq.
Col. J. A. Ballard, D.L.
Capt. R. N. Bevan, R.N.
Miss C. G. Boulton
Major N. B. Brooks, M.C., T.D.
Mrs. N. B. Brooks
Mrs. A. Browning
Miss J. E. Bruce
J. Bullocke, Esq.
H. D. Campbell, Esq.
Mrs. J. A. Chaffers
Mrs. D. H. Chamberlayne
H. F. Chamberlayne, Esq.
Mrs. H. Clutterbuck
Col. G. M. Cooper
Major R. W. Cooper, M.C., O.B.E.
The Hon. Elsie Corbett

T. Cottrell-Dormer, Esq.
Sir Henry Dashwood, Bt.
R. Dodds, Esq.
A. D. Dodds-Parker, Esq., M.P.
E. F. Evetts, Esq.
Eynsham Historical Society
H. F. Fitt, Esq.
Major P. Fleming
H. M. Gaskell, Esq.
A. P. Good, Esq.
W. C. Green, Esq.
Messrs. Groves & Sons, Ltd.
Heythrop College
Cdr. E. G. Heywood-Lonsdale, D.S.C.
Bernard Hunt, Esq.
Miss J. Hutchinson
Miss L. M. Jenkinson
Major E. N. F. Loyd, D.L.
N. Mavrogordato, Esq.

Mrs. T. More
F. P. Nicholson, Esq.
C. H. Norris, Esq.
M. P. Parker, Esq.
Harald Peake, Esq.
Dame Felicity Peake, D.B.E.
Mrs. F. H. Peel
Stephen Peel, Esq.
The Revd. L. Perfect
Col. Sir Charles Ponsonby, Bt., T.D., D.L.
V. C. Ponsonby, Esq., M.C.
G. B. Randolph, Esq.
Ian Robertson, Esq.
J. W. Robertson Scott, Esq., C.H.
L. W. Robson, Esq.
The Rt. Hon. Lord Roche
Mrs. E. Rose
J. S. Ross, Esq.
The Hon. A. G. Samuel

LIST OF SUBSCRIBERS

Chipping Norton Rural District (*cont.*)

Miss N. Sanders
Lord Sandford, D.L.
Sir George Schuster, K.C.S.I.,
K.C.M.G., C.B.E., M.C.
The Hon. Lady Schuster
J. B. Schuster, Esq.
J. W. Shilson, Esq.
Messrs. S. G. Shilson & Sons, Ltd.

Mrs. H. M. Sitwell
Miss O. M. Snowden, O.B.E.
A. S. W. Stonebridge, Esq.
Lord Strang, G.C.B., G.C.M.G.,
M.B.E.
Mrs. E. M. Stubbs
A. N. Sword, Esq.

Eric W. Towler, Esq.
M. B. Watts, Esq.
E. D. Welford, Esq.
B. Whitaker, Esq.
Mrs. V. Wickham Steed
H. D. H. Wills, Esq.
Lady Wyfold

Henley Rural District

J. P. C. Bridge, Esq.
Sir Felix Brunner, Bt.
C. W. Christie-Miller, Esq.
Lt.-Col. F. A. L. Cooper
The Viscount Esher, G.B.E.
Col. Peter Fleming, O.B.E.
Mrs. R. B. Goyder
Mrs. George Hamilton
The Rt. Hon. Lord Justice
Hodson, M.C.

Lt.-Col. Lord John Hope, M.P.
Col. E. Janes, O.B.E.
Mrs. Eric Kennington
Mrs. Melville
Sir Everard Meynell, O.B.E.,
M.C.
Miss L. R. Mitchell
D. Nicholas, Esq.
Col. Guy de Pass, D.S.O., O.B.E.

G. F. Peel, Esq.
The Dowager Lady Rathcreedan
Miss A. Riddell Blount
W. N. Roe, Esq.
Daphne, Lady Rose
Evan John Simpson, Esq.
Sir John Stainton, K.B.E., Q.C.
The Hon. Mrs. Stonor

Ploughley Rural District

Lord Bicester
Vivian Hugh, 1st Lord Bicester,
Lord Lieutenant
The Hon. Mrs. L. Bowlby
Lady Brooke-Popham
Mrs. H. M. Budgett
The Revd. C. L. Chavasse
Mrs. Ellis Chinnery
T. G. Curtis, Esq.
Major A. G. C. Fane, M.C.
Brigadier W. T. Hodgson,
D.S.O., M.C.
G. A. Kolkhorst, Esq.
Brigadier B. C. Lake, D.S.O.

Mrs. Lake
Lt.-Col. P. J. Luard, D.S.O.,
O.B.E.
Lt.-Col. A. G. Lyttelton
The Revd. H. A. MacCann
Canon H. D. A. Major, D.D.
G. T. Morton, Esq.
Major M. Lloyd Mostyn
Dr. G. D. Parkes
J. Pennybacker, Esq., F.R.C.S.
Lt.-Col. Sir Algernon Peyton,
Bt., D.L.
Mr. and Mrs. C. F. L. Piggott
Mrs. E. P. Pinching

John S. Purbrick, Esq.
Mrs. Douglas Stewart
Major H. G. Temple
Col. Sir P. Vickery, C.I.E.,
O.B.E.
A. C. Wall, Esq.
J. Warner, Esq.
Dr. A. Q. Wells
Professor J. H. C. and Mrs.
Whitehead
Mrs. A. B. Whiteley
Col. the Hon. E. H. Wyndham,
M.C.

Witney Rural District

Harold Abraham, Esq.
Major-General W. E. V. Abra-
ham, C.B.E.
Major B. G. Barnett, O.B.E.
The Bay Tree Hotel, Burford
(Miss S. M. Gray)
Miss H. B. Bryce
Lt.-Col. Sir John Burder
Major R. A. P. Butler
Dr. C. T. Cheatle
H. E. Conway, Esq.
The Countryman
John Cripps, Esq.

Mrs. M. F. Davey
W. Freund, Esq.
J. S. Furley, Esq.
Sir William Goodenough, Bt.,
D.L.
Brigadier J. H. Gradidge
F. A. Gray, Esq.
Lt.-Col. W. H. Green
The Viscount Harcourt,
K.C.M.G., O.B.E.
Capt. D. Mackinnon
Michael Mason, Esq.
Mrs. M. Montague

The Hon. Henry Parker
Major P. H. Parker
The Hon. Mr. Justice Phillimore,
O.B.E.
Lord Piercy, C.B.E.
Miss M. Pollard
Lt.-Col. J. J. Powell
Capt. the Lord Redesdale,
D.S.O., D.L., R.N.
C. H. Scott, Esq.
G. F. Smith, Esq.
H. A. Smith, Esq.
Witney Historical Club

Subscribers from outside the County

Miss M. K. Ashby
D. T. Bailey, Esq.
Sir Henry Blackall, Q.C., LL.D.
(Cyprus)
A. E. Bye, Esq. (U.S.A.)

W. C. Clark, Esq.
J. Firth, Esq.
C. Foster, Esq.
J. L. Grassi, Esq.
John Hay, Esq., M.P.

W. Keigwin, Esq.
The Revd. G. Tyndale-Biscoe
P. I. Venables, Esq.
Mrs. Hugh Walker
P. J. H. Whiteley, Esq.

LIST OF THE CLASSES OF PUBLIC RECORDS

USED IN THIS VOLUME
WITH THEIR CLASS NUMBERS

Chancery

C 1 Proceedings, Early
C 2   ,,   Series I
C 3   ,,   Series II
C 5   ,,   Six Clerks' Series, Bridges
C 47 Miscellanea
C 54 Close Rolls
C 60 Fine Rolls
C 66 Patent Rolls
C 78 Decree Rolls
C 93 Proceedings of Commissioners for Charit-
      able Uses, Inquisitions and Decrees
      Inquisitions post mortem, Series I:
C 132   Hen. III
C 133   Edw. I
C 134   Edw. II
C 135   Edw. III
C 136   Ric. II
C 137   Hen. IV
C 138   Hen. V
C 139   Hen. VI
C 140   Edw. IV and Edw. V
C 141   Ric. III
C 142 Inquisitions post mortem, Series II
C 146 Ancient Deeds, Series C

Court of Common Pleas

C.P. 25 (1) Feet of Fines, Series I
C.P. 25 (2)   ,,   Series II
C.P. 40 Plea Rolls
C.P. 43 Recovery Rolls

Exchequer, Queen's Remembrancer

E 134 Depositions taken by Commission
E 150 Inquisitions post mortem, Series II
E 164 Miscellaneous Books, Series I
E 178 Special Commissions of Enquiry

E 179 Subsidy Rolls, &c.
E 210 Ancient Deeds, Series D

Exchequer, Augmentation Office

E 317 Parliamentary Surveys
E 326 Ancient Deeds, Series B

Exchequer, Lord Treasurer's Remembrancer

E 368 Memoranda Rolls
E 372 Pipe Rolls

Exchequer, Office of the Auditors of Land Revenue

L.R. 2 Miscellaneous Books

Home Office

H.O. 107 Various, Census Papers, Population
      Returns
H.O. 129 Various, Census Papers, Ecclesiastical
      Returns

Justices Itinerant

J.I. 1 Assize Rolls, Eyre Rolls, &c.

Court of Queen's Bench

K.B. 27 Coram Rege Rolls

Special Collections

S.C. 2 Court Rolls
S.C. 6 Ministers' Accounts

Court of Requests

Req. 2 Proceedings

Court of Star Chamber

Sta. Cha. 4 Proceedings, Mary

LIST OF PRINCIPAL
BODLEIAN LIBRARY MANUSCRIPTS
USED IN THIS VOLUME

d.d. Ashhurst   Papers about the Ashhurst family and its estates, 16th–20th centuries

d.d. Bertie   Papers about the Earl of Abingdon's estates, 15th–19th centuries

d.d. Bullingdon   Rate books and valuation lists of Bullingdon R.D.C.

d.d. Hobbs   Miscellaneous Oxfordshire deeds

d.d. Par. Culham   Churchwardens' and overseers' accounts and other documents, 18th–19th centuries

d.d. Par. Thame   Churchwardens' accounts, 15th–16th, 18th–19th centuries; parish register, 1665–1756

Oxon. Dioc. Pp.

b 6–18   Parochial returns to bishop's queries, 1793–1824

b 20   Petitions, plans, and correspondence

b 21–23   Oxford diocesan registers, 1737–1868

b 38, 39, 41   Bishop's visitations, 1831, 1834, 1838

b 70   Returns of church, rectory, and school buildings, 1860

c 18   Thame peculiar acts, 16th–17th centuries

c 21–31   Attestations and depositions in ecclesiastical courts, 1570–1694

c 155   Value of livings, 1675–1874

c 264   Oxford diocesan register, 1604–23

c 266   Oxford diocesan register, 1699–1736

c 327   Diocese book, 1778–1808

c 332, 341, 344   Bishop's visitations, 1866, 1875, 1878

c 428   Notifications of absence from clergy, 1815

c 429   Miscellaneous non-residence papers, 1804–27

c 430   Returns of recusants, 1682–1706

c 431–2   Returns of Papists, 1767–80*

c 433   Return of schools, 1815

c 434–5   Register of faculties, 1737–1827

c 441   Return of places of worship, 1810

c 446   Papers about Queen Anne's Bounty

c 448–9   Terriers, early 19th century

c 454–6   Faculty papers, *c.* 1660–1850

c 643–7   Certificates of dissenting meeting houses, 1731–1852

c 649–64   Episcopal correspondence, 1635–1854

c 1692–2086   Oxfordshire parish boxes, 19th–20th centuries.

c 2115   Leases of Culham rectory, 1615–1860

d 13   Dorchester peculiar acts, 1591–5

d 14–16   Depositions and attestations in ecclesiastical courts, 1543–93

d 105–6   Oxford diocesan register, 1543–69, 1660–1702

d 178   Bishop Wilberforce's diocese book, 1854–64

d 179   Bishop's visitation, 1857

d 549   Diocese book, 1807–12

d 555–65   Bishop's visitations, 1759–74

d 566–81   Bishop's visitations, 1802–23

d 707   Return of schools, 1808

d 708   Bishop Fell's diocese book, *c.* 1685

Oxon. Archd. Pp. Oxon.

b 22–27   Miscellaneous papers about Oxfordshire parishes

b 40–41   Terriers, 17th century

b 81   Dorchester visitation processes, 1627–1824

c 2–27   Liber actorum of archdeacon's court, 1566–1761

c 35–44   Archdeacon's articles of enquiry, 1837–68

c 46–115   Churchwarden's presentments, 1730–1844

c 118   Depositions in ecclesiastical courts, 1616–20

c 141–2   Terriers

c 158–61   Dorchester peculiar records, 17th–19th centuries

c 162–4   Thame peculiar records, 17th–18th centuries

d 13   Archdeacon's visitation book, 1756–9

d 14   Dorchester peculiar acts, 1581–91

MS. Gough Oxon.

22, 43   Collections about Great Haseley by Thomas Delafield, *c.* 1740–50

48   History of Great Milton by Thomas Delafield, *c.* 1740–50

MS. Top. gen.

c 43–45   Court rolls of the Earl of Abingdon's estates, 17th–18th centuries

f 19   Sketch book of R. C. Hussey, *c.* 1850

MS. Top. Oxon.

a 46   Accounts of the Earl of Abingdon's estates, 1796–7

a 64–69   Drawings by J. C. Buckler and J. Buckler

* This class number was altered in 1961 to b 101.

NOTE ON ABBREVIATIONS

Among the abbreviations and short titles used the following may require elucidation:

Manuscript Sources

Cal. Q. Sess.	Calendar of Quarter Sessions
Ch. Ch. Arch.	Archives of Christ Church, Oxford
Compton Census	William Salt Library, Stafford, MS. 33, 'The census taken in 1676 in the province of Canterbury giving an account of inhabitants, papists and other dissenters in the various dioceses'.
d.d.	Bodleian Library, MS. d.d.
Dunkin MS.	Collections of John Dunkin (London Guildhall MSS. temporarily deposited in Bodleian Library)
Gamekprs' Deps.	Gamekeepers' Deputations
M.I.	Monumental Inscription
Magd. Coll. Arch.	Archives of Magdalen College, Oxford
MS. Top. Oxon.	Bodleian Library, MS. Top. Oxon.
Oldfield, Clerus	Bodleian Library, MS. index to clergy by W. J. Oldfield, 'Clerus Diocesis Oxoniensis, 1542–1908'
O.R.O.	Oxfordshire County Record Office, Oxford
Oxf. Archd.	Bodleian Library, Oxfordshire Archdeaconry Papers
Oxf. Dioc.	Bodleian Library, Oxfordshire Diocesan Papers
Par. Rec.	Parish Records
Queen's Coll. MSS.	Manuscripts of the Queen's College, Oxford
Rousham Arch.	Archives belonging to Mr. T. Cottrell-Dormer, Rousham Park
Victlrs' recog.	Victuallers' Recognizances
W.A.M.	Westminster Abbey Muniments
Wills Oxon.	Bodleian Library, MS. Wills Oxon.

Printed Sources

Archdeacon's Ct.	*The Archdeacon's Court, Liber Actorum 1584,* ed. E. R. Brinkworth (O.R.S. xxiii, xxiv, 1941, 1942)
Arkell, *Oxf. Stone*	W. J. Arkell, *Oxford Stone* (Oxford, 1947)
Bacon, *Lib. Reg.*	John Bacon, *Liber Regis* (London, 1786)
Baker, *Northants.*	George Baker, *History and Antiquities of the County of Northampton* (2 vols. London, 1822–41)
Berks. Arch. Jnl.	*Berkshire, Buckinghamshire and Oxfordshire Archaeological Journals,* 1895–1930, and *Berkshire Archaeological Journal,* 1930–59
Billing, *Dir. Oxon.*	M. Billing, *Directory and Gazetteer of the Counties of Berks. and Oxon.* (Birmingham, 1854)
Boarstall Cart.	*The Boarstall Cartulary,* ed. H. E. Salter (O.H.S. lxxviii, 1930)
Brewer, *Oxon.*	J. N. Brewer, *A Topographical and Historical Description of the County of Oxford* (London, 1819)
Bridges, *Northants.*	John Bridges, *History and Antiquities of Northamptonshire,* ed. Peter Whalley (2 vols. Oxford, 1791)
Brown and Guest, *Thame*	J. H. Brown and W. Guest, *A History of Thame* (Thame, 1935)
C.R.S.	Catholic Record Society
Calamy Rev.	A. G. Matthews, *Calamy Revised* (Oxford, 1934)
Ch. Bells Oxon.	F. Sharpe, *The Church Bells of Oxfordshire* (O.R.S. xxviii, xxx, xxxii, xxxiv, 1949–53)
Ch. Ch. Arch.	*Cartulary of the Medieval Archives of Christ Church,* ed. N. Denholm-Young (O.H.S. xcii, 1931)
Chant. Cert.	*The Chantry Certificates and the Edwardian Inventories of Church Goods,* ed. Rose Graham (O.R.S. i, 1919)
Char. Don.	*Abstract of the Returns of Charitable Donations made by the Ministers and Churchwardens,* 1786–8, H.C. 511 (1816)

Chron. Abingdon	*Chronicon Monasterii de Abingdon*, ed. J. Stevenson (2 vols., Rolls Series, 1858)
Clutterbuck, *Herts.*	Robert Clutterbuck, *History and Antiquities of the County of Hertford* (3 vols. London, 1815–27)
Coll. Top. & Gen.	*Collectanea Topographica et Genealogica* (Lond. 1834)
Davenport, *Oxon. Sheriffs*	J. M. Davenport, *Lords Lieutenant and High Sheriffs of Oxfordshire, 1086–1868* (Oxford, 1868)
Davey, *Catholic Family*	E. C. Davey, *Memoirs of an Oxfordshire Old Catholic Family* (London, 1897)
Davis, *Oxon. Map*	Richard Davis, *Map of the County of Oxford* (1797)
Dom. of Incl.	*The Domesday of Inclosures, 1517–1518*, ed. I. S. Leadam (2 vols. London, 1897)
E.E.T.S.	Early English Text Society
Educ. Enq. Abstract	*Education Enquiry Abstract*, H.C. 62 (1835), xlii
Educ. of Poor	*Education of the Poor*, H.C. 224 (1819), ix (B)
Elem. Educ. Ret.	*Elementary Education Returns*, H.C. 201 (1871), lv
Emden, *O.U. Reg.*	A. B. Emden, *A Biographical Register of the University of Oxford to A.D. 1500* (Oxford, 1957–9)
Evans, *Ch. Plate*	J. T. Evans, *The Church Plate of Oxfordshire* (Oxford, 1928)
Eynsham Cart.	*The Eynsham Cartulary*, ed. H. E. Salter (O.H.S. xlix, li, 1906–8)
Eyton, *Salop*	R. W. Eyton, *Antiquities of Shropshire* (12 vols. London, 1854–60)
Farrer, *Honors*	William Farrer, *Honors and Knights' Fees* (3 vols. London, 1923–5)
Fines Oxon.	*The Feet of Fines for Oxfordshire, 1195–1291*, ed. H. E. Salter (O.R.S. xii, 1930)
Foedera, ed. Rymer	*Foedera, Conventiones, Literae . . . Acta Publica inter Reges et alios quosvis Imperatores etc.*, ed. T. Rymer (1704–35)
Fosbrooke, *Glos.*	T. D. Fosbrooke, *History of Gloucestershire* (2 vols. Gloucester, 1807)
Foss, *Judges*	Edward Foss, *The Judges of England* (9 vols. London, 1848–64)
Foster, *Alumni*	J. Foster, *Alumni Oxonienses, 1500–1886* (8 vols. Oxford, 1887–92)
Gardner, *Dir. Oxon.*	R. Gardner, *History, Gazetteer and Directory of Oxfordshire* (Peterborough, 1852)
Gen. Digest Char.	*General Digest of Charities*, H.C. 292 (2) (1871), lv
Goring Chart.	*A Collection of Charters Relating to Goring, Streatley, and the Neighbourhood, 1181–1546*, ed. T. R. Gambier-Perry (O.R.S. xiii, xiv, 1931–2)
Hasted, *Kent*	Edward Hasted, *History and Topographical Survey of Kent* (4 vols. Canterbury, 1778–99)
Hearne, *Remarks*	*Remarks and Collections of Thomas Hearne*, ed. C. E. Doble and others (11 vols. O.H.S. ii, &c. 1884–1918)
Hearth Tax Oxon.	*Hearth Tax Returns for Oxfordshire, 1665*, ed. Maureen Weinstock (O.R.S. xxi, 1940)
Hunt, *Dir. Oxf.* (1846)	Hunt & Co's *City of Oxford Directory, including the . . . residents . . . in Abingdon . . . Thame etc.* (Lond. 1846)
Kelly's Handbk.	*Kelly's Handbook to the Titled, Landed and Official Classes*
L.R.S.	Lincoln Record Society
Lamborn, *Arm. Glass*	E. A. Greening Lamborn, *Armorial Glass of the Oxford Diocese, 1250–1850* (London, 1949)
Land Utilisation Survey	*The Report of the Land Utilisation Survey of Britain*, part 56: *Oxfordshire*, by Mary Marshall (London, 1943)
Lascelles, *Dir. Oxon.*	Lascelles & Co's *Directory and Gazetteer of the County of Oxford* (Birmingham, 1853)
Lee, *Thame*	F. G. Lee, *The History . . . of the Prebendal Church of . . . Thame* (London, 1883)
Lipscomb, *Bucks.*	George Lipscomb, *History and Antiquities of the County of Buckingham* (4 vols. London, 1847)
List of Sch.	*List of Public Elementary Schools*, C. 3182, H.C. (1906), lxxxvi
Luke, *Jnl.*	*Journal of Sir Samuel Luke*, ed. I. G. Philip (O.R.S. xxix, xxxi, xxxiii, 1947–53)

Lunt, *Val. Norw.*	The Valuation of Norwich, ed. W. E. Lunt (Oxford, 1926)
Lupton, *Extracts*	H. Lupton, Extracts from the Accounts of the Proctors . . . of the Prebendal Church . . . of Thame (1529–1541) and of the Church-wardens, beginning . . . 1542 (Thame, 1852).
Lupton, *Thame*	H. Lupton, The History of Thame and its Hamlets (Thame, 1860)
Lyon Turner, *Rec. of Nonconformity*	G. Lyon Turner, Original Records of Early Nonconformity (3 vols. London, 1914)
Macnamara, *Danvers Family*	F. N. Macnamara, Memorials of the Danvers Family (London, 1895)
Macray, *Magd. Reg.*	Register of Magdalen College, Oxford, N.S. ed. W. D. Macray (8 vols. London, 1894–1915)
Nichols, *Leics.*	John Nichols, History and Antiquities of the County of Leicester (4 vols. in 8 parts, London, 1795–1811)
O.A.H.S. *Proc.*	Proceedings of the Oxford Society for Promoting the Study of Gothic Architecture, 1839–47 Proceedings of the Oxford Architectural Society, 1847–60 Proceedings of the Oxford Architectural and Historical Society, 1860–93
O.A.S. *Rep., Trans.*	Reports and Transactions of the North Oxfordshire Archaeological Society, 1853–86, and of the Oxfordshire Archaeological Society, 1887–1949
O.H.S.	Oxford Historical Society
Orr, *Oxon. Agric.*	J. Orr, Agriculture in Oxfordshire (Oxford, 1916)
O.R.S.	Oxfordshire Record Society
Oseney Cart.	The Cartulary of the Abbey of Oseney, ed. H. E. Salter (O.H.S. lxxxix–xci, xcvii, xcviii, ci, 1929–36)
Oxf. Jnl.	Jackson's Oxford Journal
Oxon. Chart.	Facsimiles of Early Charters in Oxford Muniment Rooms, ed. H. E. Salter (Oxford, 1929)
Oxon. Fines	The Feet of Fines for Oxfordshire, 1195–1291, ed. H. E. Salter (O.R.S. xii, 1930)
Oxon. Peculiars	The Churchwardens' Presentments in the Oxfordshire Peculiars of Dorchester, Thame, and Banbury, ed. S. A. Peyton (O.R.S. x, 1928)
Oxon. Poll. 1754	Poll of the Freeholders of Oxfordshire taken at Oxford on 17th April, 1754 (Bodl. G. A. Oxon. 4° 346)
Oxon. Visit.	The Visitations of the County of Oxfordshire taken in the Years 1566, 1574, and 1634, ed. W. H. Turner (Harl. Soc. v, 1871)
Par. Coll.	Parochial Collections made by Anthony Wood and Richard Rawlinson, ed. F. N. Davis (O.R.S. ii, iv, xi, 1920–9)
Parker, *Eccles. Top.*	J. H. Parker, Ecclesiastical and Architectural Topography of England: Oxfordshire (Oxford, 1850)
Parker, *Guide*	J. H. Parker, A Guide to the Architectural Antiquities in the Neighbourhood of Oxford (Oxford, 1846)
Pigot, *Dir. Oxon.* (1823)	Pigot and Co.'s, London & Provincial New Commercial Directory for 1823–24
Pigot, *Nat. Com. Dir.* (1842)	Pigot and Co.'s, National and Commercial Directory and Topography of . . . (Lond. 1842)
Pigot, *Dir. Oxon.* (1844)	I. Slater, Pigot and Co's Royal National and Commercial Directory and Topography of . . . Berkshire (&c.), Oxfordshire (Lond. &c. 1844)
Plot, *Nat. Hist. Oxon.*	R. Plot, The Natural History of Oxfordshire (Oxford, 1677)
P.N. Oxon. (E.P.N.S.)	Margaret Gelling, The Place-Names of Oxfordshire, pt. i (English Place-Name Soc. xxiii, 1953)
Poor Abstract	Abstract of the Answers and Returns relative to the Expense and Maintenance of the Poor, H.C. 175 (1804), i
Pub. Elem. Sch. Ret.	Return for Each Public Elementary School . . . for the Year Ended 1st August, 1893 [C. 7529], H.C. (1894), lxv
Regesta	Regesta Anglo-Normannorum, i, ed. H. W. C. Davis Regesta Anglo-Normannorum, ii, ed. C. Johnson and H. A. Cronne.
Reg. Antiquiss.	The Registrum Antiquissimum of the Cathedral Church of Lincoln, ed. C. W. Foster and Kathleen Major (8 vols. L.R.S. 1931–58)

Reg. Univ.	*Register of the University of Oxford, 1449–63, 1505–71, 1571–1622,* ed. C. W. Boase and A. Clark (O.H.S. i, x, xi, xii, xiv, 1884–9)
8th Rep. Com. Char.	*8th Report of the Commissioners for Charities,* H.C. 13 (1823), viii
Ret. of Sch.	*Return for Public Elementary Schools,* H.C. 403 (1890), lvi
Rot. Graves.	*Rotuli Ricardi Gravesend, 1258–79,* ed. F. N. Davis (Cant. and York Soc. xxxi, 1925, and L. R. S. xx, 1925)
Rot. Grosse.	*Rotuli Roberti Grosseteste, 1235–53,* ed. F. N. Davis (Cant. and York Soc. x, 1913, and L.R.S. xi, 1914)
Rot. Welles	*Rotuli Hugonis de Welles, 1209–35,* ed. W. P. W. Phillimore (Cant. and York Soc. i, ii, iv, 1905–8, and L.R.S. iii, vi, ix, 1912–14)
St. Frides. Cart.	*The Cartulary of the Monastery of St. Frideswide at Oxford,* ed. S. R. Wigram (O.H.S. xxviii, xxxi, 1895–6)
Salter, *Oxon. Recusants*	'Recusants in Oxfordshire, 1602–33', ed. H. E. Salter, O.A.S. *Rep.* 1924
Sandford Cart.	*The Sandford Cartulary,* ed. Agnes M. Leys (O.R.S. xix, xxii, 1937–41)
Saxon Oxon	G. B. Grundy, *Saxon Oxfordshire* (O.R.S. xv, 1933)
Sch. Bldg. Grnts.	*Statement . . . of Public Elementary Schools which have Received Building Grants* [Cd. 1336], H.C. (1902), lxxviii
Schools Enq.	*Schools Enquiry Commission Reports* 3966–XI, H.C. (1867–8), xxviii (10)
Schs. and Chars.	*Digest of Schools and Charities for Education* [435], H.C. (1843), xviii
Schs. Ret.	*Return . . . of Number of Children in Inspected Schools in Year Ending 31st August, 1867,* H.C. 58 (1867–8), liii
Secker's Visit.	*Articles of Enquiry Addressed to the Clergy of the Diocese of Oxford at the Primary Visitation of Dr. Thomas Secker, 1738,* ed. H. A. Lloyd Jukes (O.R.S. xxxviii, 1957)
Skelton, *Oxon.*	Joseph Skelton, *Illustrations of Principal Antiquities of Oxfordshire* (Oxford, 1823)
Stapleton, *Cath. Miss.*	Mrs. Bryan Stapleton, *Oxfordshire Post-Reformation Catholic Missions* (London, 1906)
Subsidy 1526	*A Subsidy Collected in the Diocese of Lincoln in 1526,* ed. H. E. Salter (O.H.S. lxxiii, 1909)
Summers, *Congreg. Chs.*	W. H. Summers, *History of the Congregational Churches in the Berkshire, South Oxfordshire and South Buckinghamshire Association* (Newbury, 1905)
Thame Cart.	*The Thame Cartulary,* ed. H. E. Salter (O.R.S. xxv, xxvi, 1947–8)
Thoroton, *Notts.*	Robert Thoroton, *History of Nottinghamshire,* ed. J. Throsby (3 vols. Nottingham, 1790–6)
Top. & Gen.	*The Topographer and Genealogist,* ed. J. G. Nichols (Lond. 1846–58)
Venn, *Alumni*	J. and J. A. Venn, *Alumni Cantabrigienses* (10 vols. Cambridge, 1922–54)
Visit. Dioc. Linc. (1420–49)	*Visitations of the Religious Houses in the Diocese of Lincoln,* ed. A. Hamilton Thompson (L.R.S. vii, xiv, xxi, 1914–29)
Visit. Dioc. Linc. (1517–31)	*Visitations in the Diocese of Lincoln 1517–31,* ed. A. Hamilton Thompson (L.R.S. xxxiii, xxxv, xxxvii, 1940–7)
Vol. Sch. Ret.	*Voluntary Schools Returns,* H.C. 178–xxiv (1906), lxxxviii
Walker Rev.	A. G. Matthews, *Walker Revised* (Oxford, 1948)
Wilb. Visit.	*Bishop Wilberforce's Visitation Returns for the Archdeaconry of Oxford, 1854,* ed. E. P. Baker (O.R.S. xxxv, 1954)
Wood, *Athenae* } Wood, *Fasti* }	*Athenae Oxonienses, to which are added the Fasti,* ed. P. Bliss (5 vols. London, 1813–20)
Wood, *Life*	*The Life and Times of Anthony Wood, Antiquary, of Oxford, 1632–95, described by Himself,* ed. A. Clark (O.H.S. xix, xxi, xxvi, xxx, xl, 1891–1900)
Young, *Oxon. Agric.*	Arthur Young, *General View of the Agriculture of Oxfordshire* (London, 1809 and 1813)

THE HUNDRED OF DORCHESTER

IN the 19th century the hundred covered 11,280 acres which were almost entirely devoted to agriculture. In 1841 the population numbered 3,571.[1] Dorchester, the site of a Roman town and of the first episcopal see of the West Saxons, was the principal village, and its abbey church is still a notable building. Among the other villages in the hundred, Culham, a place of considerable importance in the Anglo-Saxon

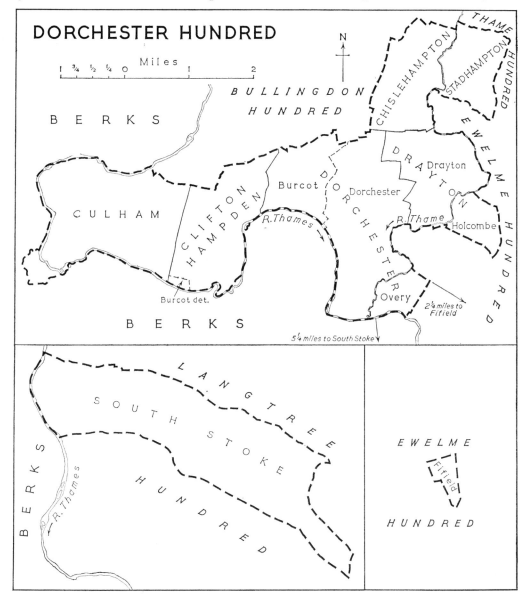

period, has at Culham Manor the remains of a 15th-century grange of Abingdon Abbey; Chislehampton has Camoise Court, also in part a 15th-century house, and the 18th-century mansion of the Peers, which replaced the earlier seat of the ancient family of

[1] *Census,* 1841.

Doyley. South Stoke in the south of the county is historically interesting as a part of the endowment of Eynsham Abbey and later of Christ Church, Oxford.

The hundred is first mentioned in Domesday Book, where most of it forms part of the Bishop of Lincoln's fief.[2] Most of the Oxfordshire estates of the bishop, which clearly represent the pre-Conquest endowment of the see of Dorchester, were grouped in the three hundreds of Banbury, Thame, and Dorchester. In Domesday Book the assessment of the bishop's hundreds of Banbury and Thame is given as 100 hides each;[3] that of Dorchester hundred is only 95, of which 5 lay outside the bishop's fief. It will, however, be argued below that the original assessment of the hundred was 100 hides, and that by the time of Domesday 5 hides, which still formed part of the bishop's fief, had been transferred to the neighbouring hundred of Bullingdon. The arrangement of these estates in three hundreds is strikingly reminiscent of other episcopal triple hundreds. The most famous is the Bishop of Worcester's triple hundred of Oswaldslow and another is connected with the bishopric of Sherborne.[4] These groupings seem to have been made in the 10th century, probably in Edgar's reign, for the provision of ships for naval defence. Traces of similar groups of three hundreds have been noted in Warwickshire, where they are connected with the provision of ships, and in Buckinghamshire and Cambridgeshire.[5] The origin of Dorchester hundred as a grouping of estates which were probably acquired piecemeal over a long period of time explains its scattered nature. It is impossible to determine the constituent parts of the hundred in Domesday but there seems to be no reason for assuming that the 11th-century hundred was very different from the hundred in the 13th century when it comprised the bishop's manor of Dorchester and nearby subinfeudated parts of the bishop's estate, as well as several detached estates at South Stoke, south of Wallingford, Fifield in Benson, and Epwell on the county boundary about 6 miles west of Banbury.

According to Domesday Book, Dorchester hundred consisted of the Bishop of Lincoln's 90-hide estate of Dorchester together with 5 hides at *Hunesworde* which is to be identified with the knight's fee at Chislehampton which formed part of the hundred in 1279, and was then held by Laurence of Chislehampton.[6] There is also warrant for regarding as in some sense part of Dorchester hundred two holdings at Baldon which are described in Domesday Book at the end of the Bishop of Lincoln's fief. These are the 5 hides held by Iseward and the $2\frac{1}{2}$ hides held by Bristeva, and they are readily identifiable with the estates in the Baldons which were held in the 13th century by the bishop.[7] In 1279 five hides in Little Baldon were held of the bishop by William de Baldindon as a knight's fee and $2\frac{1}{2}$ hides in Marsh Baldon were held by the bishop himself. The estate at Marsh Baldon was part of the bishop's Dorchester manor and the virgaters owed suit to the hundred of Dorchester, although they attended the sheriff's tourn at Bullingdon.[8] There seems, however, to have been some confusion about the hundred in which William de Baldindon's fee lay. In 1255 it was definitely described as being in Bullingdon hundred.[9] But in 1279 the two fees held by William in Baldon, Clifton, and Stoke (i.e. South Stoke) were said to be in Dorchester hundred.[10] As one of William's fees certainly lay in Dorchester hundred, and represents the estate of $5\frac{1}{2}$ hides in Dorchester manor held in Domesday by Iseward, the confusion is not surprising.[11] It is more than likely that these 5 hides at Little Baldon were originally, before the

---

[2] *V.C.H. Oxon.* i. 402–3, 411.
[3] For Thame hundred see below, p. 114.
[4] Florence E. Harmer, *Anglo-Saxon Writs*, 266–7, and references given there; E. John, *Land Tenure in Early England*, 116.
[5] *P.N. Warws.* (E.P.N.S.), pp. xix–xx; O. S. Anderson, *The English Hundred-Names*, i, pp. xix, 131–8; iii, p. i.

[6] *V.C.H. Oxon.* i. 411, 428; and see below, p. 9.
[7] Cf. *V.C.H. Oxon.* v. 35, 51.
[8] *Rot. Hund.* (Rec. Com.), ii. 724.
[9] Ibid. 39.
[10] Ibid. 749.
[11] See below, p. 20. For Iseward see *V.C.H. Oxon.* v. 51.

Conquest, part of Dorchester hundred and that together with the 95 hides that Domesday acknowledges as in Dorchester hundred they made up the original hideage. They were certainly held in 1086 by the Bishop of Lincoln and this alone would be an argument in favour of their being regarded as originally part of Dorchester hundred.

The 2½ hides held in 1086 by Bristeva at Marsh Baldon seem at first sight to upset the neatness of this argument and to increase the hideage of Dorchester hundred to 102½. This is not a necessary conclusion. These hides were certainly part of Dorchester hundred in the 13th century and this was presumably the case in the 11th century also. It is, however, quite likely that they are accounted for twice in Domesday and that they formed part of the 20½ hides held *ad firmam* by Bristeva of the bishop's demesne estate at Dorchester. These 2½ hides were certainly part of the bishop's demesne estate in the 13th century and this would be consistent with their being held *ad firmam* in the 11th century. There is nothing surprising in Domesday Book repeating these hides. Such repetition could easily result from the way the information was checked, hundred by hundred, in the Domesday inquiry in Oxfordshire. This meant that any of the bishop's estate of Dorchester that happened to be in Bullingdon hundred would be listed under that hundred even though it was also treated as part of the bishop's estate under Dorchester hundred also. It is therefore likely that Dorchester hundred was originally assessed at 100 hides, of which 7½ lay in the Baldons. Part of this, 2½ hides, were kept in the bishop's estate and remained in the hundred, the rest was subinfeudated and eventually treated as part of Bullingdon hundred. Originally the hundred consisted of episcopal estates alone but by the time of Domesday 5 hides had been alienated from the bishop's fief although they remained within the hundred.

The first detailed description of the hundred was made in 1279.[12] As the beginning of this survey is mutilated it is not possible to reconstruct the whole hundred with certainty. As far as can be seen it then comprised the bishop's demesne manor of Dorchester extending over a wide area, including Overy,[13] Drayton, Burcot, Clifton, Chislehampton, and Stadhampton, and several fees held of the bishop, including Nicholas of Burcot's fee in Drayton (including Holcombe) and Clifton, William de Baldindon's two fees in Clifton, Baldon, Burcot, and South Stoke, Philip le Moyne's fee in Clifton, Burcot, and South Stoke, a 1/10-fee in Burcot held by Geoffrey of Lewknor, and a ½-fee held by Laurence de Louches in Chislehampton and Little Milton. The detached estates, also held by the bishop in chief, were South Stoke and Woodcote, held by Eynsham Abbey, Fifield in Benson, held by Philip de Hoyville, and a fee at Epwell held by Robert Danvers. There was also 1 fee in Chislehampton that belonged to the hundred, but was of the honor of Dudley and not the bishop's.[14] In the 14th-century subsidy returns the hundred is taken to include Dorchester, Drayton, Burcot, Clifton, Chislehampton, South Stoke, Woodcote, and Epwell.[15] In 16th-century subsidies Culham is added to the hundred.[16] The Hearth Tax returns of 1665 show that the hundred remained substantially unchanged, the only alterations being that Exlade, a part of South Stoke, is mentioned separately.[17] By the time of the 19th-century census returns Epwell had been transferred to Banbury hundred although Fifield (in Benson parish) remained in Dorchester hundred until 1881, when it was transferred to Ewelme hundred.[18]

Until the 16th century Dorchester hundred was held by the Bishop of Lincoln. In 1547 at about the same time as the manor of Dorchester was surrendered to the king

[12] *Rot. Hund.* (Rec. Com.), ii. 747–51.
[13] Dorchester and Overy are apparently missing. For this see below, p. 85, n. 80.   [14] *Rot. Hund.* ii. 750.
[15] E 179/161/9. Overy and Fifield are not mentioned by name, but were almost certainly included in the Dorchester list. William de Hoyville, tenant of Fifield, is one of the

contributors and Overy is included with Dorchester in later tax lists.
[16] e.g. E 179/162/341. For the reasons for Culham's earlier exemption see below, p. 30.
[17] *Hearth Tax Oxon.* 52–57.
[18] *V.C.H. Oxon.* ii. 219–20.

licence was given to the bishop to grant the hundred to the king's uncle, Edward, Duke of Somerset.[19] In 1548 the hundred, but not the manor, along with the manor and hundred of Thame, was granted in fee farm to Sir John Williams.[20] Later the hundred of Dorchester, like that of Thame, must have passed to the Norreys family, for in the 17th century it was held by Edward Wray, husband of Elizabeth Baroness Norreys.[21] The manor came to the Berties,[22] and presumably the hundred also, as in the 19th century their descendants held the hundred as well as the manor.[23]

The bishop's rights in his hundred included the return of writs and pleas *de vetito namii*.[24] Three-weekly hundred courts held in 1299 to 1300 dealt mainly with agricultural offences—trespass and purpresture—and breaches of the assize of ale. In February 1300 the whole vill of Stadhampton was fined for concealing the ploughing up of a path. At the same court the Abbot of Dorchester was presented for digging a ditch against Queensford. There were also fines for raising the hue and cry.[25] A later account roll for the hundred in 1520 contains sums for cert money, for view of frankpledge, and for court perquisites.[26]

In the 17th century the hundreds of Dorchester, Bullingdon, and Thame were grouped together for various purposes. For example, in 1634 and 1635 the justices of the peace of the three hundreds are mentioned,[27] and in 1652 the three hundreds had a high collector.[28] This suggests that the division of Thame, Bullingdon, and Dorchester hundreds which it has been argued was created in 1706 had in fact been anticipated in the previous century.[29]

---

[19] *Cal. Pat.* 1547–8, 184.
[20] E 317/Oxon. 6.
[21] B.M. Harl. MS. 843, f. 17.
[22] See below, p. 43.
[23] H. Addington, *Some Account of the Abbey Church of St. Peter and St. Paul at Dorchester* (1860), 124.
[24] *Rot. Hund.* (Rec. Com.), ii. 30; cf. *Cal. Fine R.* 1272–1307, 215.
[25] S.C. 2/197/37.
[26] d.d. Bertie c 24 (uncat.)
[27] *Cal. S.P. Dom.* 1634–5, 446; 1635–6, 136.
[28] Ibid. 1651–2, 252.
[29] Mary Sturge Gretton, *Oxfordshire Justices of the Peace in the 17th Century* (O.R.S. xvi), p. lxxxiv.

CHISLEHAMPTON

SINCE 1932 Chislehampton has been part of the large civil parish of Stadhampton,[1] but for the greater part of its history it has been a small independent parish and township, which contained 939 acres in 1881.[2] Chislehampton appears not to have acquired full parochial status until 1763.[3]

The ancient parish, lying some 5½ miles southeast of Oxford, has no natural boundaries except on the east where the River Thame divided it from Stadhampton. Its southern and eastern parts are low-lying, but northwards the ground rises fairly steeply from 175 feet at Chislehampton Bridge to 290 feet at Hill Farm in the north-west corner.[4] The parish lies mainly on Kimmeridge Clay, with an outcrop of Gault and a small deposit of Plateau Gravel on the high ground to the north-west.[5] Leland's description of the land between Haseley and Chislehampton as 'fruitful of corn and grass, but barren of wood' could also have been applied to Chislehampton itself in the 16th century.[6] It ceased to be quite as true a picture after 1694 when Great Copse was first planted.[7] This wood covered 22·1 acres in 1743 and 23 acres in the 20th century.[8] Until recently, when some of the trees were cut down, it was notable for the largest rookery in the British Isles.

The layout of the roads is much the same as in the 17th and 18th centuries. The principal road runs southwards from Oxford and crosses the Thame by Chislehampton Bridge: it is shown as a gated track on a map of 1628 and the bridge is called Doyley Bridge.[9] In 1664 John Doyley was licensed to inclose part of this road so as to enlarge his mansion provided he made another highway through his lands, and the new 'Oxford Lane', hedged as far as Gotham Hill ground, is shown on an estate map of 1743.[10] The inhabitants were bound to keep it in repair.[11] The road to Abingdon, 'Abingdon Lane', is also shown on the map of 1628 and in 1743 it was hedged and gated at both ends.

Chislehampton Bridge is now 178 feet long and has eight arches and five stone pillars. About 40 feet to the south there is a subsidiary bridge of one arch, which spans a small tributary of the Thame.[12] The main bridge over the Thame has been of importance from an early date. In 1444 the 'good men' of Chislehampton were granted pontage for five years to be applied by the survey and control of Drew Barentine and Richard Quatremain.[13] In 1500 the bridge was described by John Leland. He wrote that he rode over three little bridges of wood and then over a 'great bridge' over the Thame. There were 'five great pillars of stone, upon the which was laid a timber bridge'.[14] As the masonry in the north-east side of the existing bridge seems to date from the late 16th century the timber structure was probably replaced by a stone bridge at that date.[15] Repairs have been frequent: in 1690, for example, John Saunders was employed as mason and repaired it with freestone from Headington Quarry;[16] in 1702 Richard Darling underbuilt one of the main arches at a cost of £14;[17] in 1714 John Saunders was again employed at a cost of about £18.[18] Further work was done at intervals in the following centuries. A John Saunders executed some substantial repairs in 1762. He let cramps into the sixth and seventh arches and rebuilt the west side for a length of 36 feet;[19] in 1800 work costing over £43 was done;[20] in 1823 John Turrill, mason, who was regularly employed until at least 1830, submitted an estimate of over £70 for repairs;[21] and in 1849 George Wyatt of Oxford repaired it at a cost of £234.[22] The firm of Richard Wyatt and Son had already been at work on the bridge in 1821.[23] 'Extensive repairs' were again necessary in 1877 when the county surveyor reported that the masonry was 'in a very critical state'.[24] In about 1899 the bridge was widened by some 9 feet with steel troughing which was shored up with timber in the middle of the spans in 1938; the stonework was repaired in 1938 and 1941.[25]

The siting of the village was evidently dictated by the river crossing: it lies just to the north of it. It was once probably even more of a riverside village than it is now for the first element in its name is derived from the Old English *ceosel*, *cisel* meaning 'gravel, shingle',[26] and its only surviving medieval building, Camoise Court Farm, stands on gravel beside the Thame.[27] The original manor-house and church, moreover, lay close to the river before they were rebuilt at a higher level.[28] The earliest known form of the name, found in 1147, is 'Chiselentona', but 'Chislehampton' occurs in the late 12th century. The colloquial name is 'Chisleton'.

The medieval village was never large and some early inclosure had perhaps reduced its size by the 17th century.[29] An estate map of 1628 marks only the old Doyley mansion and dove-cot, the medieval church, and three farmhouses.[30] These were no

[1] *Census*, 1931. In the writing of this introductory section considerable use has been made of notes by R. M. Haines.
[2] O.S. *Area Bk.* (1882).
[3] For a precise account of the village's ecclesiastical status see below, p. 86.
[4] O.S. Map 6″, xlvi (1881).
[5] G.S. Map 1″ (N.S.) Sht. 254.
[6] Leland. *Itin.* ed Toulmin Smith, ii. 116.
[7] See below, p. 14.
[8] Estate map *penes* C. J. Peers, Esq., Chislehampton House; cf. O.S. Map 25″, xlvi. 2 (1881).
[9] Estate map *penes* C. J. Peers, Esq.
[10] *Cal. S.P. Dom.* 1663–4, 647.
[11] O.R.O. Cal. Q. Sess. viii. 602.
[12] H. J. Tollit, *Oxon. Co. Bridges* (1878), 36.
[13] *Cal. Pat.* 1441–6, 267.
[14] Leland, *Itin.* ii. 116.
[15] Inf. Town and Country Planning Report.
[16] O.R.O. Cal. Q. Sess. v. 47.
[17] Ibid. 22d–23. Freestone and hard stone were bought in Horspath and lime in Garsington.
[18] Ibid. 39–40.
[19] Ibid. 169.
[20] Ibid. 272.
[21] Ibid. 345, 346, 379, 400.
[22] Davenport, *Oxon. Bridges* (1869), 2.
[23] O.R.O. Cal. Q. Sess. v. 327.
[24] *Oxon. Co. Bridges* (Surveyor's Rep. 1878), 36.
[25] Inf. R. W. H. Mellor, County Surveyor.
[26] *P.N. Oxon.* (E.P.N.S.), 155.
[27] G.S. Map 1″ (N.S.) Sht. 254.
[28] Map (1628) *penes* C. J. Peers, Esq., reproduced p. 6.
[29] See below, p. 13.
[30] Map *penes* C. J. Peers, Esq.

doubt the principal houses but there must have been many more for thirteen householders were listed for the hearth tax of 1662 of which five were substantial farmhouses taxed on three or four hearths.[31] The green and the pound are shown on the 1628 map at the junction of Abingdon Lane and Oxford Lane.[32]

farmhouses, Camoise Court Farm and its outbuildings was in very bad repair, and a brick and timber farmhouse and another stone and thatched one were in 'midling' repair. There were also twelve cottages and a good new brick house and malthouse barn, stable, and close. The last is likely to be the present

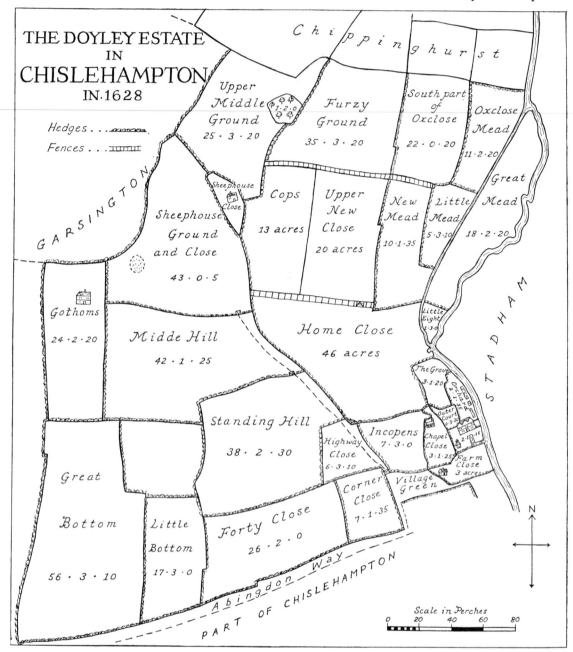

Map showing early inclosure and the sites of the old church and manor-house. Based on a map of 1628 in the possession of Mr. C. J. Peers, Chislehampton House.

Several of these 17th-century dwellings remain. They are timber-framed and have red brick fillings. Many are thatched.

A survey of the Doyley estate in Chislehampton made in 1746 gives a more detailed picture of the village.[33] The manor-house, its outhouses, and its grounds occupied 10½ acres. There were five farmhouses of which two were newly built. Of the old

Coach and Horses Inn, a picturesque public house by the bridge, although the interior of the house is probably earlier than the outside.

Soon after this report the Doyley estate was sold to Charles Peers and a period of building activity followed: the present Georgian church was built in 1763 by Peers and its churchyard was laid out;[34] the old Doyley mansion was pulled down and replaced

[31] E 179/255/4.
[32] In 1746 the green was estimated to be 15 acres:
Brown's Survey *penes* C. J. Peers, Esq.
[33] Ibid.   [34] See below, p. 15.

by Chislehampton House, and Church Farm, a two-storied house with attics of chequer brick, was probably built. Little change, however, seems to have taken place in the size of the village: the Census of 1811 recorded 21 houses.[35] The peak of 28 houses recorded in 1851 was not reached again until the mid-20th century. In 1931, the last census to give figures for Chislehampton alone, there were 27 houses, but there have been additions since.[36] Early-19th-century building included Marylands Farm, a pleasant building of red brick (now roughcast) with wide eaves and a slate roof, and the lodge to the

east angle, which is thought to have been the garderobe; its walls are of medieval thickness. At present there are two stories and attics, but the original house appears to have consisted of a low ground-floor room and a solar above that was open to the roof; a possible hall, west of it, perhaps of timber, has been re-placed. The original wall-plate with roll-mouldings is visible and there is a deeply splayed window of 14th-century date about 8 feet from the ground in the south wall. It is of two trefoiled ogee-headed lights. A window of the same date and on the same level but in the east wall was recently covered

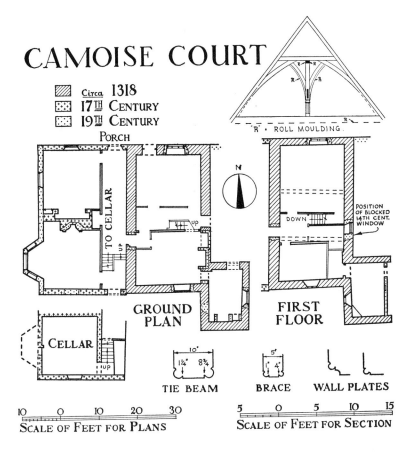

Peers park. In the 20th century six well-designed brick houses have been put up by Mr. Peers and Mr. Chaundy of Camoise Court Farm.[37]

There are two houses of special architectural interest: Camoise Court Farm and the manor-house. Camoise Court Farm is the oldest house in the village. It lies on the Thame 200 yards west by south of Chislehampton Bridge, and incorporates part of a 14th-century house that was once the property of Sir Richard de Louches of Great Milton.[38] He was licensed to crenellate his Chislehampton house in 1318.[39] Later the property passed, as did the Great Milton lands, to the famous Sir Thomas Camoys and so acquired its name. The central block of the present farmhouse is the medieval part,[40] and there are traces of the medieval moat. The house is built of coursed rubble on a north and south axis with gables at each end; it has a square projection at the south-

up. The chamfered entrance to what seems to have been a garderobe also remains. The 14th-century gable above the room contains a cradle roof of three bays of which the two king-posts and curved braces with roll-moulding can be seen.

A straight joint on the north front, to the west of the 14th-century opening (two original jambs remain), marks the building of two stories and an attic, probably in the early 17th century, to the west of the central block. It was built of coursed rubble to match the old house, but the west side was re-built in brick in about 1880. An early-17th-century brick fireplace was discovered in 1956. In the early 19th century a new entrance to the house was made —a Doric porch with fluted columns under a flat roof.

The great house, 'Chisleton' House, is a handsome red-brick mansion standing in its own park on a

[35] *Census*, 1811.   [36] *Census*, 1851–1951.
[37] Inf. Mr. C. J. Peers. The following paragraph is based on notes kindly lent by Margaret Wood and Mr. P. S. Spokes.

[38] See below, p. 11.
[39] *Cal. Pat.* 1317–21, 194. For De Louches see below, p. 123.
[40] For view see plate facing p. 14.

slight eminence overlooking the Thame. It was built, probably between 1766 and 1768, by Samuel Dowbiggin of London, a member of the Joiners' Company.[41] The designs for the house are dated 1766 and the date 1768 can be seen on the rain-water heads of cast lead.[42] Dowbiggin's employer was Charles Peers, who had bought the estate in 1748.[43] The building is rectangular in plan, and has three stories and a basement. Built of locally made red brick,[44] it has an ashlar base, chamfered stone quoins and a stone entablature with bracketed cornice, and a hipped roof covered in slates. All the windows have moulded stone architraves. The west front has a slightly projecting feature of four Ionic pilasters, a low parapet and coping and central pediment with a cartouche of the Peers arms and flanking palms carved in a stone tympanum. The house is entered by steps and through an entrance porch with Doric columns *in antis* added about 1820. An elevation of the east front by Dowbiggin shows balustrades and balls instead of the present plain parapet. That the architect's design was carried out is proved by an old water-colour showing the balustrades. The south front has twin three-sided bays of two stories; the ground-floor windows were altered in the early 19th century when the sills were brought down to floor level.

The interior of the house is interesting: an entrance hall and top-lit staircase hall are run together as a single unit, an unusual feature for the period. The staircase, which is of the cantilevered kind, has delicately turned balusters and handrail and a particularly elegant curve.[45] The balustrading is continued round the hall on the upper floors forming galleries with the rooms opening off them. Some of the early-18th-century furniture that belonged to Sir Charles Peers, a one-time Lord Mayor of London and the father of the builder,[46] has been preserved. There is also a collection of armorial china, specially dispatched from Canton for Sir Charles in 1731.[47]

From the ground floor of the plain east front central steps descend to a wide flat terrace with an orangery to the north. There are the remains of a small formal landscape garden: on the axis of the house there is a short avenue of elms, formerly continued on the west side of the house, which is crossed by another path running from the entrance to the walled kitchen garden towards a statue at its north end. The orangery was built in 1790.[48] It is five-sided with uprights of cast iron and an umbrella roof. The glass consists of small panes. The lodge in the park, standing near the bridge, dates from about the same period or a little later. It has one story and attics, but the two dormer windows are lunette-shaped. The slate roof has wide eaves. The stables lie to the north of the house and the kitchen garden, on the east side near the river, marks the site of the Doyleys' house. This house may have been built at the end of the 16th century when the Doyleys lived

in the parish. Sir John Doyley, sheriff in 1585, who was buried in Stadhampton church in 1623, is the most likely builder of the house.[49] An estate map of 1628 shows its east front as a four-gabled building with a central *porte-cochère*.[50] It faces the river, has an orchard in front and an outer court. Behind the house is a dove-house and the medieval church. According to tradition the mansion was partly destroyed in the Civil War, but in 1665 it was still a substantial house for which sixteen hearths were returned for the hearth tax.[51] An estate map of Stadhampton of 1741–2 has a drawing of the west front of the house,[52] which shows a two-storied building of eight bays and E-shaped in plan. The short gabled wings at each end are of one bay, and there is a central projection of two bays, flanked by two tall chimneys. A map of 1743[53] drawn for Sir Thomas Doyley depicts a façade with four gables and a large stable-yard kind of entrance. It shows formal gardens laid out by the river and Great Orchard Yard, the outer court of 1628. The house has two stories and attics and an irregular arrangement of windows. A survey of the estate made about the same time describes it as 'a very old inconvenient building part brick, part stone'.[54] The surveyor added that the outbuildings were ruinous and that they and the house would 'scarce pay for pulling down and yet were not good enough to keep up'. There was a good new-built double dove-house of brick and a large walled garden. The coppice called Home Ground was 'laid out into walks as a pleasure ground' with ash trees. Part of the house was then occupied by a farmer. Nothing now remains of this mansion, except the bricks in the walls of the present kitchen garden.

Because of the strategic importance of its bridge in the battle for Oxford, Chislehampton was in the centre of the fighting during much of the Civil War. The only alternative route across the Thame was at Wheatley Bridge. By March 1643 both bridges had been provided with gates and there was no passage for man or horse 'but on market days and sometimes in the day time'.[55] The king's forces made great preparation there to prevent parliamentary forces crossing.[56] On 13 June 1643 the bridge was said to be down, though passable on horseback.[57] But a few days later Prince Rupert crossed over it with 1,700 men and returned the same way after his victory at Chalgrove on 18 June.[58] Shortly afterwards the bridge was reported to have been broken down by Royalist forces, which stationed between 60 and 100 men on Chislehampton Hill to command the passage of the Thame. A watch was constantly kept on the bridge by a guard of about 40 men of the forces stationed at Abingdon.[59]

MANORS. Chislehampton is not mentioned by name in the Domesday survey, but the greater part of it is undoubtedly represented by 'Hunesworde' entered in Dorchester hundred, where 5 hides were

[41] H. M. Colvin, *Biog. Dict. of Eng. Architects*, 184.
[42] The following architectural account of the house owes much to the article by A. Oswald, 'Chislehampton House', *Country Life* cxv (1954), 216–19, 284–7.
[43] See below, p. 12.
[44] A brick kiln in 2 acres of ground was part of the Doyley estate in 1749: rental of Chislehampton manor *penes* C. J. Peers, Esq.   [45] See plate opposite.
[46] For Sir Charles see A. B. Beavan, *Aldermen of London*, 121.
[47] The chests in which it was packed and the bills are at

Chislehampton House.
[48] Peers Arch., Pps. *penes* C. J. Peers, Esq.
[49] Par. Reg. For the Doyleys see below, p. 10.
[50] Map (1628) *penes* C. J. Peers, Esq.
[51] *Hearth Tax Oxon.* 56.
[52] O.R.O. Map of Stadhampton by N. Burgess.
[53] Map (1743) *penes* C. J. Peers, Esq.
[54] Peers Arch.: Brown's Survey.
[55] Luke, *Jnl.* 25.   [56] Ibid.   [57] Ibid. 95.
[58] S. R. Gardiner, *History of the Great Civil War* (1897), i. 150; cf. Luke, *Jnl.* 100.   [59] Luke, *Jnl.* 102–3.

THE STAIRCASE OF CHISLEHAMPTON HOUSE BY SAMUEL DOWBIGGIN

THE VESTIBULE OF JAMES WYATT'S ADDITION TO THE GREAT HOUSE, GREAT MILTON

held of the king by William FitzAnsculf.[60] William's widespread fief, later known as the honor of Dudley,[61] included Handsworth (Staffs.) and a scribal error must account for the appearance of this place-name in the Oxfordshire Domesday.[62] The overlordship of the fee in *CHISLEHAMPTON*, which was not named as a manor until the 15th century, passed with the honor of Dudley to the Paynel family and from them to the Somery family.[63] From 1220 to about 1270, however, Chislehampton was part of the dower of Ida Longespée, the widow of Ralph (II) de Somery (d. 1220).[64] She married William de Beauchamp as her second husband[65] and in 1235 he held the Somerys' knight's fee in Chislehampton of the honor of Paynel.[66] After Ida's death in about 1270[67] the fee reverted to Roger (I) de Somery, who died in or before 1273.[68] The male line of the De Somerys died out in 1322 on the death of John de Somery, grandson of Roger (I) de Somery.[69] John's widow Lucy de Somery was assigned Chislehampton and Ditton in Stoke Poges (Bucks.), said to be together worth £4, as dower[70] and apparently held them and other estates until her death some time before 1327.[71] According to a settlement made in 1323, Joan de Botetourt, the sister and one of the coheiresses of John de Somery, had been given the reversion of Chislehampton,[72] but there is no further mention of the overlordship, which may have lapsed.[73]

At the time of Domesday, the tenant of William FitzAnsculf in Chislehampton and Stoke Poges was a certain Walter,[74] whose descendants took their name from Stoke. According to a lawsuit in 1207, a mesne tenancy had been created in Chislehampton by the time of Henry I, when Hugh de Stokes gave the fee of Chislehampton to his younger son Alfred.[75] The mesne tenancy passed to Hugh's son Richard de Stokes and to his grandson Robert, who in 1207

tried to obtain the fee in demesne from Alfred's son Hugh de Chislehampton.[76] He lost his case, however, for his heirs were mesne tenants at the end of the 13th century. Richard de Stokes, his son, succeeded him,[77] but had died by 1254 when his daughter and heir, Amice, was in the custody of Sir Humbert Poges.[78] Sir Humbert's son Robert Poges is said to have married her before 1269,[79] and he was returned in 1273 as the De Somerys' tenant at Chislehampton.[80] He was still the mesne tenant in 1322,[81] but Chislehampton was not mentioned in his inquisition post mortem in 1330[82] and nothing more is heard of his family there.

Alfred, the demesne tenant in Henry I's time, was followed by 1192 by his son Hugh de Chislehampton,[83] the defendant in the 1207 case.[84] In 1235 William de Chislehampton, presumably his son, was the tenant.[85] William was possibly succeeded by a Hugh de Chislehampton and his wife Rose, who occur in 1242,[86] but Laurence de Chislehampton was in possession some time before 1271, when he was said to have already granted a messuage and 2 carucates in Chislehampton to Dorchester Abbey.[87] At that time he was heavily in debt to the Jews, but the king ordered that no distraint should be made on his estate of Chislehampton[88] and he was returned as tenant under Robert Poges in 1279.[89] He was killed in 1283[90] and his son William de Chislehampton succeeded him and held the estate until it was bought in 1315 by Robert de Harewedon.[91] Harewedon was a Chancery clerk, closely associated with Hugh Despenser,[92] and had already contributed to the tax assessment of 1306 in Chislehampton.[93] Later in 1315 he made a settlement with other members of his family,[94] whereby he was to hold the Chislehampton property for life with remainders to his nephew Robert, son of Henry de Harewedon and his heirs, and after to

[60] *V.C.H. Oxon.* i. 411. The suggestion (E. A. Greening Lamborn, *N. & Q.* vol. 187, p. 203) that the Domesday hide in 'Hentone' held by Edward of Salisbury lay in Chislehampton is untenable: see under Chinnor in a succeeding volume.

[61] *Early Yorks. Chart.* vi (*Yorks. Arch. Soc. Rec. Soc.* extra ser. iii), 47.

[62] *V.C.H. Oxon.* i. 428 n; *Dom. Bk.* i. 250.

[63] The descent of the honor of Dudley is discussed in detail in *Early Yorks. Chart.* vi. 47–50; cf. *Complete Peerage*, x. 320; xii. 110–11. There are references to Chislehampton in the pipe rolls: *Chanc. R.* 1196 (P.R.S. N.S. vii), 74; *Pipe R.* 1197 (ibid. N.S. viii), 37, 38; 1199 (ibid. N.S. x), 164.

[64] *Complete Peerage*, xii. 110–11; about 1210 Ida's father William de Longespée held the fee on behalf of Ralph (II) de Somery, then a minor: *Bk. of Fees*, 40. It was evidently an error that the fee was entered as the Bishop of Lincoln's. The bishop had a smaller estate in Chislehampton: see below, p. 12.

[65] *Complete Peerage*, xii. 111–12.

[66] *Bk. of Fees*, 448, 453.

[67] *V.C.H. Bucks.* iv. 415.

[68] *Cal. Inq. p.m.* ii, p. 15.

[69] Ibid. vi, pp. 254–60; *Complete Peerage*, xii. 115.

[70] *Cal. Close*, 1318–23, 623.

[71] Lucy was alive in 1325, but the escheator of Edward II was said to have taken her lands into custody; and Joan de Botetourt held Stoke Poges by 1327: *Cal. Close*, 1323–7, 397; *Cal. Inq. p.m.* viii, p. 274; *V.C.H. Bucks.* iv. 415.

[72] *Cal. Close*, 1318–23, 631–2.

[73] Joan did not claim all of Lucy's dower and Chislehampton may have remained in the king's hands: *Cal. Close*, 1341–3, 458; *Cal. Inq. p.m.* viii, p. 274. Cf. descent of Stoke Poges and Newport Pagnell: *V.C.H. Bucks.* iii. 305; iv. 415.

[74] *V.C.H. Oxon.* i. 411; *V.C.H. Bucks.* i. 254; iii. 305.

[75] *Cur. Reg. R.* iv. 193–4, 258.

[76] Ibid.

[77] *V.C.H. Bucks.* iii. 305.

[78] Ibid.   [79] Ibid.

[80] *Cal. Inq. p.m.* ii, p. 15.

[81] *Cal. Close*, 1318–23, 623, 632.

[82] *Cal. Inq. p.m.* iii, p. 202.

[83] *Pipe R.* 1191, 1192 (P.R.S. N.S. ii), 273; cf. *St. Frideswide Cart.* i. 37; Alfred 'de Chislehampton' occurs as a witness c. 1163–78: *Oxon. Chart.* no. 49.

[84] *Cur. Reg. R.* iv. 193–4. For his daughter see *Fines Oxon.* 76.

[85] *Bk. of Fees*, 448.

[86] In 1242 they paid £1 in the accounts of Beds. and Bucks.: *Pipe R.* 1242 (ed. H. L. Cannon), 112.

[87] *Cal. Pat.* 1266–72, 622–3. For him see also *Ex. e Rot. Fin.* (Rec. Com.), ii. 381.

[88] *Cal. Close*, 1272–9, 389.

[89] *Rot. Hund.* (Rec. Com.), ii. 750.

[90] *Cal. Pat.* 1281–92, 103.

[91] William sold Chislehampton mill in 1315, but in 1346 the fee was described as formerly in the possession of John son of Laurence de Chislehampton: C.P. 25 (1)/189/15/26; *Feud. Aids*, iv. 182.

[92] *Cal. Pat.* 1313–17, 105; ibid. 1317–21, 255. Robert figured prominently in the patent and close rolls, between 1300–18, as justice, attorney, keeper of Winchester bishopric and warden of God's House, Portsmouth; cf. *V.C.H. Hants*, ii. 207. He was a Canon of Lichfield from 1316: J. Le Neve, *Fasti*, i. 595.

[93] E 179/161/10.

[94] They seem to be connected with Harrowden and Finedon (Northants.): cf. *V.C.H. Northants*, iv. 183. It is possible they were connected with the Lewknors for Geoffrey de Lewknor held in Harrowden and a Geoffrey de Lewknor was also demesne tenant in Chislehampton in 1279: *Rot. Hund.* (Rec. Com.), ii. 750; see below, p. 12.

Robert's brother Henry.[95] Robert de Harewedon was returned as lord of Chislehampton in 1316,[96] but had died by December 1318.[97] His nephew Robert evidently succeeded him, for he contributed to the tax of 1327.[98] Either Robert or his son, another Robert de Harewedon,[99] held the fee in 1346,[1] but nothing more is heard of it[2] until 1410, when a 'Beek', perhaps Richard Beke (d. 1418), who left money to Chislehampton chapel, bought it from a certain Hamden.[3] In 1423 John Beke was described as 'gentleman, of Chislehampton',[4] and the same or a son was returned in 1428 as holding immediately the lands 'formerly of Robert de Harewedon' by service of 1 knight's fee.[5] John Beke married Elizabeth, the sister of Richard Quatremain of Rycote,[6] and must have been dead by 1466. His brother-in-law Richard Quatremain was one of the feoffees, who in that year settled Chislehampton manor on John Beke's youngest daughter Sybil and her second husband Robert Poyntz.[7] In 1489 Sybil made another settlement of the manor on herself and her third husband Robert Restwold for life, with remainder to her cousin William Danvers,[8] a grandson of Maud, another sister of Richard Quatremain.[9] By 1500 William Danvers had obtained Chislehampton manor[10] and died in possession in 1504, leaving it to his wife Anne for life and then to his third son William.[11] The widowed Anne did not die until 1531,[12] but her son William covenanted 'to estate' Thomas Doyley of Hambleden (Bucks.) in Chislehampton manor as early as 1524.[13] By 1536 the manor seems to have been finally released to the Doyleys.[14]

Thomas Doyley died in 1545[15] and was succeeded by his son John, who like his cousin and colleague Sir John Williams of Thame founded a fortune in dealings in monastic property.[16] On his death in 1569, Doyley left Chislehampton to his wife Frances for life, afterwards to his son Robert, and to his other heirs male.[17] Frances was persuaded to demise the manor for £300 a year to her younger son John, shortly after he had succeeded to his brother's estates in 1577, and on her death in 1601 he entered into

full possession,[18] though various charges on the manor involved him in a lawsuit with his brother Henry.[19] In 1605 John settled the manor after his death partly on Martha, the wife of his son Cope Doyley, and partly on his own wife Ursula.[20] Sir John died in 1623[21] and, though Ursula lived at Chislehampton until her death in 1635,[22] their son Sir Cope Doyley settled it in 1628 as jointure when his son John married Mary Shirley.[23] John, a sheriff and Member of Parliament for Oxfordshire, succeeded his father in 1633.[24] His widow held the manor as dower for a short time after his death in 1660,[25] but by 1664 it was held by their son John (d. 1709),[26] who became a baronet in 1666. Sir John's son, another Sir John, held it until his death in 1746.[27] In 1748 his son Sir Thomas Doyley sought to revive the declining fortunes of the family by selling Chislehampton to Charles Peers of Olney (Bucks.), the son of Sir Charles Peers, a former lord mayor of London.[28] The Doyleys were also lords of Camoys manor, the second Chislehampton manor, and apparently sold it also to Charles Peers.[29] Henceforth the combined manors were known as Chislehampton manor.

The combined manor has remained in the hands of the Peers family until the present day (1958), descending from Charles Peers (d. 1781)[30] to his elder son Robert (d. 1818) and his grandson Charles, who died childless in 1853.[31] The heir was then John Peers, another grandson of the elder Charles Peers, being the son of his second son John (d. 1835), for many years incumbent of Stadhampton and Chislehampton. In 1855 the younger John was succeeded by his son John Witherington Peers (d. 1876), Vicar of Tetsworth, and he by a son of the same name, who died unmarried in 1891. This last was followed by his brother, the Revd. William Henry Peers, who died in 1921, and he by his son Sir Charles Reed Peers (d. 1952),[32] the father of the present lord of the manor, C. J. Peers, Esq.

In the Middle Ages the estate, later known as CAMOYS or CHISLEHAMPTON manor, formed part of a ½ knight's fee held in Chislehampton and

[95] C.P. 25 (1)/189/15/40. [96] Feud. Aids, iv. 167.
[97] Cal. Pat. 1317–21, 255.
[98] E 179/161/9.
[99] Cal. Pat. 1345–8, 554.
[1] Feud. Aids, iv. 182, where he was erroneously stated to hold of the overlord of the Camoys manor, the Bishop of Lincoln.
[2] A Sir John de Harewedon was knight of the shire and commissioner of array for Oxon. in the late 14th century, e.g. Cal. Close, 1381–5, 291.
[3] Top. & Gen. ii. 343: list of Chislehampton deeds; P.C.C. Marche 42.
[4] Cal. Close, 1422–29, 195; he was possibly connected with the Bekes of Earley (Berks.): cf. V.C.H. Berks. iii. 214.
[5] Feud. Aids, iv. 200.
[6] Lee, Thame Ch. 294; Trans. Mon. Brass Soc. vi. 409; Macnamara, Danvers Family, table facing p. 171: Beke pedigree.
[7] Top. & Gen. ii. 343; C.P. 25 (1)/294/74/34; Beke was probably dead by 1435: Cal. Pat. 1429–36, 448.
[8] Top. & Gen. ii. 343; C.P. 25 (1)/191/31/3.
[9] Macnamara, Danvers Family, 174–9, 214; see also below, p. 127.
[10] Top. & Gen. ii. 343–4.
[11] Macnamara, Danvers Family, 179.
[12] Ibid. 181–3.
[13] Top. & Gen. ii. 344.
[14] Ibid. These prolonged negotiations may have been connected with the marriage of George, William Danvers' son and heir, to Thomas Doyley's daughter Margaret:

see W. D. Bayley, Hse. D'Oyly, 22, 23.
[15] Bayley, Hse. D'Oyly, 23, citing will.
[16] Ibid.
[17] Ibid.; C 3/266/9.
[18] He made a fine on the manor in 1591, apparently in connexion with his marriage to Ursula, daughter of Anthony Cope: Macnamara, Danvers Family, 519; C.P. 25 (2)/197/Mich. 33 & 34 Eliz. See also below, p. 91.
[19] C 3/266/9; a lawsuit with the Perrots was apparently over a claim to the Camoys manor: Bayley, Hse. D'Oyly, 26.
[20] C 142/400/71; C 142/473/51; Cope Doyley's first wife was Martha Quarles, who died in 1618 before her father-in-law: M.I. in Hambleden church; Bayley, Hse. D'Oyly, 28; but cf. C 142/47/5, which cites her death as 1622.
[21] C 142/400/71.
[22] Bayley, Hse. D'Oyly, 26.
[23] C 142/473/51.
[24] Bayley, Hse. D'Oyly, 30–31.
[25] Ibid. 31.
[26] Cal. S.P. Dom. 1663–4, 647; Par. Coll. iii. 286.
[27] Bayley, Hse. D'Oyly, 36.
[28] Ibid. 37; C.P. 25 (2)/1188/Easter 21 Geo. II. Negotiations were apparently begun by Sir John: Parker, Guide, 331, citing Par. Reg. Sir Charles Peers put the manor in trust in 1755: Linc. Dioc. Archives, Mason deposited deeds 2/15.
[29] See below, p. 12.
[30] Burke, Land. Gent. (1846), iii. 257.
[31] M.I. in church.
[32] For the family see Venn, Alumni, and M.I.s in church.

Little Milton of the Bishop of Lincoln's Dorchester manor. Like the main estate, it was not mentioned by name in the Domesday survey, but it is likely that the 2 hides held in 1086 of the bishop's Dorchester manor by a certain James represents the later fee and manor.[33] The overlordship which is last recorded in 1618 followed the descent of the bishop's Dorchester manor.[34]

In the 12th century the Cardunville family were the bishop's mesne tenants: in 1163 Ernald de Cardunville gave 1 virgate there to Dorchester Abbey[35] and in 1166 he was returned as the tenant of a ½-fee of the Bishop of Lincoln.[36] Adam de Cardunville, presumably his son, held the ½-fee by 1191.[37] Adam died before 1210 when William de Boveneye obtained the grant of the wardship and marriage of his heirs.[38] William, therefore, was returned about this time as holding a ½ knight's fee of the Bishop of Lincoln on behalf of the Cardunville heir, of which ¼-fee was apparently in Little Milton.[39] The estate was clearly the ½-fee held by James de Cardunville in Chislehampton and Little Milton in a list of the bishop's knights made after 1225.[40] James died soon after, presumably without heirs, for the estate appears to have escheated to the bishop. In 1225 a certain Alice, claiming to be the widow of James, brought a plea of dower against the bishop[41] for ⅓ of 2 carucates and appurtenances in Chislehampton and ⅓ of land in Milton. She lost her case, for the bishop maintained successfully that she had never been married or dowered at the church door, but only in James's house when he was mortally ill.[42]

There is no further record of the ½-fee either in Chislehampton or Milton until 1279, when it was held by Laurence de Louches.[43] A Laurence de Louches, the same or his son, held the ½-fee of the bishop in 1305.[44] The De Louches family of Chislehampton and Little Milton was closely connected with the De Louches family holding in Baldon St. Lawrence, Wheatley, and Great Milton.[45] Sir Richard de Louches, who was one of the lords of Great Milton, had a grant of free warren in his demesne lands, including Chislehampton, in 1318.[46] In 1322 his estate was in the king's hands because of his support of the Despensers, but he recovered

it in the same year.[47] Though his son John succeeded in 1327 to most of his lands,[48] Elena de Louches, Richard's wife, paid a tax on her Chislehampton land in 1327,[49] which she presumably held as dower. By 1346 John had obtained the ¼-fee in Chislehampton formerly held by Laurence de Louches.[50] In 1353, designating himself John de Louches of Milton, he settled the manor after his death on his son William and William's wife Elizabeth and their heirs.[51] Both John and William had died by 1367, when Elizabeth de Louches, William's daughter, held his land in Great Milton.[52] She brought Chislehampton to the Camoys family by her marriage with Thomas lord Camoys (d. 1421),[53] and in 1416 her son Sir Richard Camoys put it in trust for his wife Joan Poynings.[54] On his death shortly after, it was released to Joan with remainders to their sons, John, Ralph, and Hugh.[55] By 1421 Hugh was the sole survivor.[56] He died in 1426, still under age, and his sisters, Margaret wife of Ralph Radmylde of Sussex and Eleanor wife of Sir Roger Lewknor of Trotton (Suss.), were his heirs.[57]

The Radmylde moiety was held by Ralph Radmylde, who survived his wife, and on his death in 1443[58] he was succeeded by his son Robert (d. 1457).[59] Robert's heir was his only son William, then a minor, and the estate seems to have been put in trust.[60] William died without legitimate children in 1499,[61] when his aunts, Margaret and Isabella Radmylde, were his heirs.[62] It is probable, however, that by this time some arrangement had been made with the Lewknors, as was the case with other Radmylde manors,[63] and that the Radmylde moiety had been taken over by them.

Sir Roger Lewknor, the husband of the coheir in 1426, died possessed of his moiety of the Camoys lands in 1478.[64] His heir was his son Sir Thomas Lewknor, who was an influential supporter of the Lancastrians in Sussex.[65] Before Sir Thomas's death in 1484 his estates were taken into the king's hands for high treason, but his son Sir Roger Lewknor was allowed to hold them during his father's lifetime.[66] In 1498 Sir Roger leased for 60 years 'a certain manor or farm called Cames' in Chislehampton to John Wilmott, a member of the rising class of Oxfordshire yeomen.[67] Later Sir

[33] V.C.H. Oxon. i. 403.
[34] See below, p. 42. In 1618 Sir Barentine Molyns held Chislehampton of Francis Lord Norreys of Rycote: C 142/378/130.
[35] O.A.S. Rep. (1909), 13: text of 1163 bull.
[36] Red. Bk. Exch. (Rolls Ser.), 375.
[37] Ibid. 516. Adam was mainpernor with Hugh de Chislehampton, the under-tenant of the other fee, in 1193: Pipe R. 1193 (P.R.S. N.S. iii), 126.
[38] Pipe R. 1210 (P.R.S. N.S. xxvi), 177.
[39] Bk. of Fees, 40.
[40] Queen's Coll. MS. 366, f. 25. For the date see below, p. 13, n. 94.
[41] Cur. Reg. R. xii. 140, 143.
[42] Ibid. 143.
[43] Rot. Hund. (Rec. Com.), ii. 750. He also held 1 virgate under the main Chislehampton manor paying 1 clove a year to John de Louches for it.
[44] Queen's Coll. MS. 366, f. 34b. In 1316 the bishop was returned as one of the lords (Feud. Aids, iv. 167) and was granted free warren there in 1329 (Cal. Chart. R. iv. 117).
[45] See below, p. 123; V.C.H. Oxon. v. 49, 110.
[46] Cal. Chart. R. 1300–26, 389.
[47] S.C. 6/962/1; in 1322 and 1327 he complained about what trespassers had done to his property in Chislehampton: Cal. Pat. 1321–4, 163, 169, 319; 1327–30, 84.
[48] Ibid. 1327–30, 84, 86; V.C.H. Oxon. v. 50, 110; and see below, p. 123.

[49] E 179/161/9.
[50] Feud. Aids, iv. 182.
[51] C.P. 25(1)/190/20.
[52] Cal. Inq. Misc. iii, p. 250.
[53] Complete Peerage, ii. 510.
[54] Boarstall Cart. 10.   [55] Ibid.
[56] C 138/57/29; Cal. Pat. 1422–9, 91, 173–4.
[57] C 139/28/26; Complete Peerage, ii. 510.
[58] C 139/109/34.
[59] C 139/163/15.
[60] Ibid. One of the trustees was Alice, Duchess of Suffolk, the mother of William's wife Jane.
[61] William left several illegitimate children but none by his wife Jane: Camoys Peerage Claim 1838, 42–49, citing his will and other conveyances.
[62] Ibid. 338; Cal. Inq. p.m. Hen. VII, iii, p. 419.
[63] Cf. V.C.H. Sussex, iv. 35; V.C.H. Oxon. v, 30, 110; cf. Camoys Peerage Claim, 37.
[64] C 140/66/37.
[65] Ibid; Camoys Peerage Claim, 123–4, citing original documents.
[66] Camoys Peerage Claim, 123–4.
[67] E 150/784/16; Wilmott held in Ascot in Grt. Milton (see below, p. 134) and at Stadhampton where members of the family were buried: P. C. C. Horne, 25; in 1517 William Cottesmore held a farm in Chislehampton worth £12 a year and, as guardian of the heir of John Wilmott, another farm worth £6: Dom. of Incl. i. 341.

Roger granted the manor to Edmund Dudley for life and on Dudley's attainder in 1510 the manor again came into the king's hands.[68] Sir Roger, however, recovered it, for in 1541–2 he granted the reversion of certain estates, including the Chislehampton one, to Sir William Barentine of Haseley, who had married his daughter Jane, widow of Sir Arthur Poole.[69] On Sir Roger's death in 1543 his heirs disputed the arrangement made with Sir William Barentine and an Act was required to settle Sir Roger's estates.[70] Sir William Barentine (d. 1550) secured the Chislehampton property for himself with remainder to his son Drew.[71] Drew Barentine held the manor by 1567,[72] but it seems to have come eventually to a descendant of Sir William Barentine's daughter Mary, who with her sister Margaret is said ultimately to have succeeded to the Barentine estates.[73] Mary had married Anthony Huddleston of Millom (Cumb.)[74] and it may be that the marriage of a Frances Huddleston to Sir Michael Molyns of Clapcot (Berks.)[75] accounts for Camoys manor passing to the Molyns family. In 1615 Sir Michael died possessed of 'Chislehampton manor' and a capital messuage called Camoys court (said to be in Dorchester parish) with appurtenances in Chislehampton.[76] His son and heir, significantly called Barentine, had been succeeded in other lands by his own son Sir Michael Molyns by 1631.[77] From this point the descent of Camoys manor is not clear, but it eventually came to the Doyleys, who held the Beke manor in Chislehampton. Sir John Doyley is said to have purchased a farm in the parish about 1673–4,[78] and the Camoys lands were evidently included in the estates sold to Charles Peers in 1748.[79]

OTHER ESTATES. The Bishop of Lincoln held some land in Chislehampton in demesne. His estate was probably included under his 90-hide Dorchester estate in Domesday Book, but there is no specific mention of it until the 13th century when it comprised some 10 virgates let to various tenants.[80] This property followed the descent of his Dorchester manor and was one of the estates surrendered to the king by Henry Holbeach, Bishop of Lincoln.[81] It passed, like other members of the Dorchester manor, to the Norreys family and later to the Earls of Abingdon.[82] In the 18th and early 19th centuries the

Peers family, lords of the other Chislehampton manor, paid a freehold rent of £5 12s. 8d. to the earls of Abingdon for the Chislehampton estate.[83] When the Abingdon estates were broken up,[84] they probably purchased this rent charge.

Some time before 1271 Laurence de Chislehampton, lord of Chislehampton, granted 2 carucates and a messuage, practically the whole of his Chislehampton fee, to the Abbot of Dorchester, who gave them to Geoffrey de Lewknor.[85] In 1269 Geoffrey de Lewknor had obtained a confirmation from Master Moses, a Jew of Oxford, of his right to a meadow in Chislehampton,[86] a transaction which was possibly connected with the debts of Laurence of Chislehampton to the Jews.[87] Geoffrey de Lewknor was still tenant in 1279;[88] in 1315 John de Lewknor sold his holding of 7 messuages and 9 virgates to Robert de Harewedon, who was buying up other property in Chislehampton.[89] There is no further reference to the Abbot of Dorchester's overlordship.[90]

ECONOMIC AND SOCIAL HISTORY.[91] Chislehampton does not appear as an entity in Domesday Book. It was apparently partly surveyed under William FitzAnsculf's fee of 'Hunesworde',[92] and the remainder, which was a part of the Bishop of Lincoln's Dorchester manor, was not surveyed separately, but was included in the survey of his 59¾-hide demesne. On the FitzAnsculf fee in 1086 there was land for 5 ploughs: there were 2 in demesne and 8 *villani* had 1½ between them. There were 20 acres of meadow and a mill rendering 8s. The total value was £4, the same as in pre-Conquest times.[93]

A survey of the bishop's demesne in his Dorchester manor, made in the second quarter of the 13th century, records 10 virgaters at Chislehampton, each of whom paid 5s. 6d. rent. A virgater owed 3 plough services and had to cut hay with 1 man for 3 days until the ninth hour and to gather and cart it until the task was finished. He had to mow for 3 days with 2 men and for ¼-day with 1 man at his own expense, and was to be present for 2 of the bishop's autumn boon-works with all his family and tenants, except his wife. He had to carry corn with one cart until it was all carried and take it to Oxford and Wallingford whence, if the bishop wished, it could be shipped to

---

[68] E 150/784/16; cf. *V.C.H. Oxon.* v. 110.

[69] *Camoys Peerage Claim*, 213, 218, 222. This claim contains much evidence on the Lewknor descent.

[70] Ibid. 218; Jane Poole's marriage to Sir William was disputed by her children of a former marriage and declared invalid in 1540, and therefore her children by him were illegitimate: 'The Divorce of Sir William Barentine', *Sussex Arch. Coll.* lxviii. 279–80.

[71] *Camoys Peerage Claim*, 222. Drew and Charles must have been the two sons referred to in *L. & P. Hen. VIII*, xi, p. 147.

[72] C.P. 40/1251/423.

[73] *N. & Q.* 183, pp. 192, 550. Mary may have been a daughter of Jane Poole, which would also account for the descent of the manor to her descendants by lawsuit quoted in W. D. Bayley, *Hse. D'Oyley*, 26.

[74] Bayley, *Hse. D'Oyley*, 26; W. Hutchinson, *Cumberland*, i. 528.

[75] *Visit. Berks.* (Harl. Soc. lvi), 112. The descent of the Huddlestones in Cumberland is confused.

[76] C 142/378/130.

[77] *V.C.H. Berks.* iii. 548. Sir Michael spent much of his estate in supporting Charles I and it is possible that Chislehampton was one of the manors he disposed of either before or after the civil wars; on the other hand Sir

William Barentine's will (proved 1550) spoke of the sale of Chislehampton premises to John Doyley which was to be confirmed: Dunkin MS. 438/3, p. 217.

[78] O.R.O. Wi I/ii/10 and 11. See also estate map of 1746 *penes* C. J. Peers Esq., Chislehampton House.

[79] Charles Peers was the tenant of the Earl of Abingdon: MS. Top. Oxon. b 192, p. 3.

[80] *V.C.H. Oxon.* i. 402; Queen's Coll. MS. 366, f. 26; and see below, p. 13.

[81] *Cal. Pat.* 1547–8, 133; 1557–8, 408; 1558–9, 437.

[82] See below, p. 42.

[83] See MS. Top. Oxon. b 192, p. 3; b 193, p. 4; b 206, f. 14b; c 383, p. 26; c 385, f. 13. Note that the value of rents in 1551 had been £5 9s. 8d.: L.R. 2/189, f. 8b.

[84] See below, p. 43.

[85] *Cal. Pat.* 1266–72, 522.   [86] Ibid. 370.

[87] *Cal. Close*, 1272–9, 389.

[88] *Rot. Hund.* (Rec. Com.), ii. 750; he also held in Thame.

[89] C.P. 25(1)/189/15/21; and see above, p. 9.

[90] For the descent of Dorchester Abbey's estates see below, p. 43.

[91] This section was written by Mr. R. Haines.

[92] See above, p. 9.

[93] *V.C.H. Oxon.* i. 411.

London. He was also to carry the bishop's provisions to Oxford, Wallingford, and to all the nearer episcopal manors, and was to be allowed food when the bishop was there. When necessary he was to go to Oxford and Wallingford for the bishop's provisions and to carry corn to Kirtlington *cum equo et sacco suo*. He was to carry timber to the bishop's grange from any place where it could be acquired, as well as 1½ cartloads of wood, towards the cost of which he was to give 2*d*. Whenever the bishop came on the feast of St. Martin or Hock Day he was to provide forage, half hay and half straw, for one of the bishop's horses. He owed merchet, heriot, leirwite, a fine on his father's death, and aids when called for by the bishop.[94]

In 1279 there were still 10 virgaters, but the rent of a virgate had fallen to 5*s*. and the services, where they can be compared, seem to have changed slightly. Each virgater who had a plough was to plough 2 acres of the lord's demesne. He had to cut and carry hay until the task was done; to find 2 men to mow for 3 days without food and for 2 days with food provided by the bishop; and to carry hay and corn until it was all carried. He was not to marry his daughter, nor to sell his ox or foal, without licence. He was to carry corn to Fingest (Bucks.), which was part of Dorchester manor, and to the markets at Oxford and Wallingford, and either to cart wood or to pay 4*d*.[95]

On the former FitzAnsculf fee Geoffrey de Lewknor had at this time 2 carucates and 5 tenants, who held 5 virgates in villeinage and paid 25*s*. rent with all customary services, while Laurence de Chislehampton held 1 messuage, a virgate, and part of the River Thame by 'Sepwas' weir. Lawrence de Louches also held part of the river, a messuage, and 1 virgate (the later Camoise farm).[96]

In 1306 16 persons were taxed in the parish, but all except one were assessed at the low rate of 2*s*. and under.[97] The 1344 assessment of £3 0*s*. 3*d*. was the fourth highest in the hundred and may be compared with that of £1 17*s*. 9*d*. for Stadhampton, which had a slightly larger population.[98]

An account for the period 31 January–10 June 1322 has survived for that part of Chislehampton which belonged to the Louches fee (i.e. Camoys manor), then in the king's hand.[99] The assize rents and farm of the mill amounted to £1 18*s*. 2*d*. and the stock was sold for nearly £60. The livestock fetched over £18 and included 5 cart horses, a bull, and 14 oxen. The grain and bean crops were sold for £26 4*s*., while two iron-shod carts realized 20*s*., two dung carts 5*s*., and two ploughs with their equipment 10*s*. The fish in the stewpond were valued at

£4. A century later (1443) this estate was worth £5 6*s*. 8*d*. a year and included 80 acres of arable valued at 4*d*. an acre, 10 acres of meadow at 1*s*. 4*d*., and 60 of land at 6*d*. an acre. The free tenants paid 6*s*. 8*d*. a year and the assize rents amounted to £1 2*s*. 8*d*.[1] In 1422 the rents of the other chief estate in Chislehampton, the Beke manor,[2] amounted to £7 5*s*. 10*d*.; crops of wheat, rye, barley and pulse were grown, and some wheat and barley was sold at Oxford and Watlington. The sale of stock produced £10 15*s*. 3*d*. and included 9 oxen, cows, calves, pigs, hens, and a boar.[3]

There was some engrossment of holdings during the early Tudor period. In 1517 William Cottesmore held two farms, one called *le pasture of Chessyllyngton*, as trustee of John Wilmott, whose father seems to have combined them.[4] A further indication of the increasing concentration of wealth is the small number of nine contributors to the subsidy of 1524 and the amalgamation of virgates in the Dorchester manor: in 1551 four copyholders held its 10 virgates.[5] At this date the rents of this estate amounted to £5 9*s*. 8*d*. or about 11*s*. a virgate. With each yardland went the right to pasture 30 sheep, 2 beasts, and 4 horses, a total of 360 animals. There were 203 trees recorded.[6]

The earliest map of Chislehampton, dated 1638, shows that the Doyley lands (i.e. the former Fitz-Ansculf lands) that lay to the north of Abingdon Lane and comprised 507 acres in Chislehampton and 149 in Chippinghurst were inclosed.[7] In 1694 Sir John Doyley altered some of the inclosed fields so as to make two new closes of 46 acres together and a coppice of 13 acres.[8] The southern part of the parish, comprising the Camoys lands, was inclosed very possibly after they had been acquired by the Doyleys about the 1670's when Stadhampton was inclosed.[9] John Doyley is said, about 1673, to have divided a common meadow with a fence, to have diverted the ancient way to it, and to have taken its first mowth, which the Shirley family claimed to have enjoyed for 100 years as an appurtenance of a yardland in Toot Baldon.[10] The proposal made by Charles Peers in 1743 that local inquiry should be made as to whether 'Sheephouse Leaze' had ever formed part of the common field suggests also that inclosure was of a comparatively recent date. It was supposed presumably that there were old men alive who would remember the layout of the pre-inclosure fields.[11]

In 1746 when Thomas Browne made his survey the whole of Chislehampton, together with part of Chippinghurst in Cuddesdon, formed a compact estate 'all entirely together and within a hedge'. It comprised 1,027 acres, its gross annual value was

[94] Queen's Coll. MS. 366, f. 26. This survey of the lands of the see of Lincoln is written in a 14th-century hand, but it is clearly a copy of a 13th-century survey. There are references throughout (e.g. ff. 2*b*, 4*b*, 25, 27*b*, 33) to a valuation of the bishop's mills made in the 16th year of Bishop Hugh II (i.e. 1225), and there is one reference to an inquisition taken in 1258 (f. 8 *b*). The Oxfordshire part of the survey, however, seems to be based on inquisitions taken soon after 1225. Robert de Vipont is stated to hold knight's fees in various places of the inheritance of his wife Idonea (ff. 16, 19*b*, 23), and he was dead by 1228 (*Cal. Close*, 1227–31, 17, 25, 351). Another of the bishop's knights, James de Cardunville, apparently died just before Michaelmas 1225 (*Curia Reg. R.* xii, 140, 143).

[95] *Rot. Hund.* (Rec. Com.), ii. 749–50.

[96] Ibid. 750.   [97] E 179/161/10.

[98] E 179/161/17. In 1381 there were 63 persons over 14 in Stadhampton and 57 in Chislehampton: E 179/161/41.

[99] S.C. 6/962/1.

[1] C 139/109/34.

[2] See above, p. 10.

[3] B.M. Add. Ch. 41645.

[4] *Dom. of Incl.* i. 341. Leadam calculates that 225 and 112½ acres were engrossed: ibid. 341–2 *n*.

[5] L.R. 2/189, f. 8.

[6] Ibid.

[7] Peers Arch. *penes* C. J. Peers, Esq., Chislehampton House.

[8] Ibid. The alterations were inserted on the map.

[9] The 1743 map (Peers Arch.) gives a number of the furlong names: none survived for the northern part. For the possible purchase of the Camoys estate at this time by Sir John see above, p. 12.

[10] O.R.O. Wi I/ii/11. 1675 was the date of Stadhampton's inclosure: see below, p. 86.

[11] Peers Arch. Letter to Charles Brand.

£1,284 (£1,149 7s. net), and its estimated worth £29,000.[12] There were 9 tenants of more than 40 acres; the remaining 2 held less than 10 acres apiece. The largest farm was that of Henry Swell, an 'extraordinary good tenant', who occupied 192 acres (later 233) and whose farmhouse was 'new built all of stone and tiled'. Camoise Court farm, with 188 acres in the south of the parish, was leased to Jonathan Betteridge, 'a slovenly bad husband'. The buildings were in a bad state, two of the barns needed to be pulled down, and £200 was the estimated cost of the necessary repairs. Another tenant farmed 86 acres, lived in part of Chislehampton Hall, as the great house was called, and occupied a stable, cowhouse, and hogyard there. There were twelve cottages, a dove-house well stocked with pigeons and let for £5 a year, and a kiln which provided bricks for the estate from clay dug in the neighbouring ground. There were 635 acres of pasture, 86 of meadow, and 258 of arable.[13] The preponderance of grass probably continued throughout the century, for the amount of good grass under dairy at Chislehampton was the chief comment made by Arthur Young.[14] The meadow and pasture was leased in 1748 for between £1 10s. and £1 17s. 6d. an acre, the arable for between 17s. 6d. and £1 an acre.[15] Some farms were entirely pasture and only Camoise Court had appreciably more arable than grazing land.[16] This farm also carried a large amount of livestock, and in 1776 there were 136 beasts, including 18 cows, 38 ewes and lambs, 24 wethers, 3 rams, and 20 hogs.[17] It had probably recovered from its former neglected state, for in 1774 the lessee, Paul Smith, had agreed to repair the house and barns, being allowed rough timber for the purpose. In 1776 it was leased to Thomas Cooper at an increased rent. The tenant was to pay £5 for every acre of grass ploughed without the lord's consent and to permit entry on the Lady Day before the expiration of the lease for the ploughing up as a regular summer fallow of a quarter of the arable land. He had also to bring back every year from Shillingford for the lord three wagon loads of coal, each of 1¼ cauldrons, at his own expense.[18]

There were only 30 acres of woodland in the 18th century,[19] but it was of considerable value. Most of it lay in the Great Coppice which John Doyley had made in 1694. In 1746 this coppice consisted of 22 acres well planted with ash stems and laid out as a pleasure ground, the underwood being worth about £150.[20] Contemporary plans show that it was divided into 32 plots with intervening walks. These were cut in intervals between 1748 and 1764, either for the lord's use, or for sale. As many as 500 poles might be cut from a single plot and sold for 6d. to 2s. each.[21] There were also two much smaller coppices and a number of other trees.[22] When cutting hedges the tenants had to preserve all oak, ash, and elm trees.[23] Browne valued the timber on the estate at £1,000, but two years later (1748) another surveyor considered it to be worth £2,316.[24]

In 1703 the fishing rights in the Thame from Wickham's Weir in Cuddesdon parish[25] to the hedge dividing the parish from Drayton field, a distance of over 2 miles, passed with the manor.[26] Browne noted that the fishery was said to be worth £10 a year, but declared that on account of the weirs the expenses on such large estates were always greater than the profits.[27] In 1781 the fishery was leased to William Wigginton for £9 a year, the lord and his friends having liberty to fish. The lord was to be supplied with eels of a good size at 7d. a pound, and other fish at market price.[28]

Between 1795 and 1817 the Court of Sewers made assessments on 48 acres of meadow, valued at either 35s. or 40s. an acre, which were liable to floods. The court ordered the erection of a sluice near the weir, and in 1800 the new gates were found to be of a proper width and the masons were completing their work. At this time, too, the river bed was cleansed throughout the parish.[29]

As in the county generally, the trend during the 19th century was towards the formation of larger farms. In 1886 there were five, two of which, Marylands and Camoise Court, contained more than 300 acres each. The total acreage of the estate was 897 and the gross estimated rental £1,649 5s. 7d.[30] The chief crops were wheat, barley, oats, and beans, but much of the land was pasture.[31] On that account the severe drought of 1893 was a serious matter, for the tenants had no grass for cattle grazing and none to mow for the winter feed.[32] In 1927 the estate was still in the possession of a single owner. There were four tenant farmers, three of whom farmed more than 100 acres each. The principal tenant farmed Church, Lower, and Hill farms, totalling 302 acres.[33] The income from the estate was £1,396.[34] In 1959 the process of amalgamation had been carried still further and the parish was farmed by Mr. Peers and two other farmers.

Chislehampton, despite its greater area, has always been less populous than neighbouring Stadhampton. The 1524 subsidy roll listed only 9 persons there, as against 24 in Stadhampton,[35] and in 1676 there were 53 adults, compared with 85 in the other parish.[36] There is no accurate assessment of population until 1801 when the Census recorded 128 inhabitants. Numbers rose during the early 19th century to a peak of 153 in 1841, but thereafter declined to 85 in 1901. This trend has been reversed during the 20th century and the number of inhabitants rose from 136 in 1931 to 153 in 1951.[37]

---

[12] Peers Arch. Thomas Browne's Survey (1746). John Noble, who surveyed the estate in 1748 for its new owner, Charles Peers, calculated that there were 1,077 acres.

[13] Ibid. 1743 estate map.

[14] *Oxon. Agric.* 11.

[15] Peers Arch. field list, probably by Noble.

[16] Ibid. Browne's Survey.

[17] Ibid. Ann Smith's assignment of stock to C. Peers.

[18] Ibid. copies of details from leases.

[19] Ibid. 1743 map.

[20] Ibid. Browne's Survey.

[21] Ibid. plans of Coppice Quarters, accts., etc.

[22] Ibid. 1743 map.

[23] Ibid. Camoys Ct. lease 1776.

[24] Ibid. Browne's Survey; bill for Noble's Survey.

[25] This is marked on the 1743 map.

[26] Ibid. 18th-century note from original indenture.

[27] Ibid. Browne's Survey.

[28] Ibid. details of lease.

[29] d.d. Ashurst d 4, pp. 123, 163; Peers Arch. assessments for tax. The mill which is mentioned at this time was not part of the estate and is not recorded in the 18th-century surveys or maps.

[30] Peers Arch. valuation list.

[31] Kelly, *Dir. Oxon.* (1887).

[32] Peers Arch. contemporary letter.

[33] d.d. Bullingdon a 5: Rate bk.

[34] Peers Arch.

[35] E 179/161/198.

[36] Compton Census.

[37] *Census,* 1801–1951.

CULHAM MANOR

Showing the 15th-century west wing and Jacobean north front

CAMOISE COURT FARM AT CHISLEHAMPTON

Showing the 14th-century south front with the 17th-century extension to the west

The 18th-century Church in 1821

Interior of the 18th-century Church

CHISLEHAMPTON

CHURCH. Chislehampton church in the Middle Ages was a chapelry of Dorchester and probably had the same original status as the five other chapels, including Stadhampton, confirmed to Dorchester in the papal bull of 1146. Little is known, however, of the early history of the church and as in the post-Reformation period Chislehampton was regarded as a chapelry of Stadhampton, it has been found convenient to combine its history with that of Stadhampton.[38]

The present church at Chislehampton, dedicated to *ST. KATHERINE*, is a small 18th-century structure of stone, built by Charles Peers, the lord of the manor. It is a single rectangular room without structural division between nave and chancel, but

proprieties of church architecture'. Its bell-turret was said to be 'such as is usually placed on stables'.[45] The church was renovated in 1882 and in 1894 the bell-turret was restored and the roof raised at a cost of £165,[46] but these restorations did not destroy its character and it remains one of the few complete Georgian churches in the county. The interior has preserved its Georgian woodwork, high box pews, western gallery, altar rails, and carved altar-piece with the Lord's prayer, the Creed, and the Decalogue. The altar rails are returned westwards on either side, with seats for children behind. It is not known whether they were intended for use by communicants.[47] The elaborately carved pulpit is Jacobean and must have come from the old church,

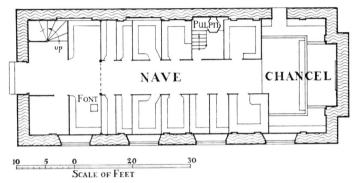

The 18th-century church.

the importance of the altar is emphasized by a recess in the east wall. The exterior is ornamented by carved stone urns and at the west end there is a clock-turret surmounted by a weather-vane pierced with the name of St. Katherine. There are three large round-headed windows on the south side, but none on the north or at the ends. Samuel Dowbiggin, the London architect who built Chislehampton House, may possibly have been employed to design the church.[39] The new building replaced a medieval chapel dedicated to St. Mary, which was first mentioned in 1146 and was situated by the river, close to the old manor-house.[40] Seventeenth-century presentments (1623–1706) record that the chapel was in a good state of repair,[41] but in 1763 when Peers petitioned the peculiar court of Dorchester for permission to pull it down he described it as being in 'so ruinous and decayed a condition that the inhabitants cannot assemble for worship without manifest hazard (to) their lives.'[42] The new church was erected out of the old materials about 200 yards west of the original church and had a churchyard attached; previously burials had taken place at Stadhampton.[43] It was consecrated by the Bishop of Oxford in 1763.[44]

In 1846 this 18th-century church was characteristically described by J. H. Parker, a Gothic revivalist, as being in spite of its neat and trim appearance 'a sad instance of departure from all the

but it is reached by a Georgian staircase and has the 18th-century reading-desk and clerk's seat below it. The font is contemporary with the church building and a space on the opposite side of the aisle has been left where the christening party might stand.[48]

In 1952 an appeal was made for £3,000 to restore the church and verses in aid of the appeal were composed by John Betjeman. By 1954 the extensive repairs advised by the architect, Oswald Brakspear, were completed. All the windows were releaded and one of the angleposts of the bell-turret was renewed. The exterior and interior plaster was renewed and the whole redecorated. The clock face which carries the date 1762 was painted light blue and gold by John Piper. The rafters of the roof, exposed in the 19th century, were again concealed by a coved plaster ceiling.[49] Concealed electric lighting was inserted in the pews in 1956,[50] but the church is still lit mainly by candle light: there are three hanging brass candelabra, of which one is dated 1899, and wall brackets given by Sir Charles Peers some time after 1908.[51]

There are a number of memorials to the Peers family. They include one to Charles Peers, Esq. (d. 1781), the builder of the church, and to his three wives, two of whom were buried in the family vault in the church. The arms and crest of Peers are depicted on the monument. There are tablets to Robert Peers (d. 1818), son and heir of Charles and

[38] See below, p. 87.
[39] For a recent account of the church see article by Arthur Oswald, *Country Life*, 28 Jan. 1954, vol. cxv, pp. 216–18.
[40] *Reg. Antiquiss.* i. 247; Bacon, *Lib. Reg.* 808; for the site of the old church see map of 1628 on p. 6.
[41] *Oxon. Peculiars*, 99–105.
[42] Oxf. Dioc. c 454, f. 154.
[43] See Par. Rec. Reg. and below, p. 87.

[44] Par. Rec. Reg. Note by John Bilstone.
[45] Parker, *Guide*, 330. For a view see plate facing p. 15.
[46] Peers Arch.
[47] Cf. G. W. O. Addleshaw and F. Etchells, *The Architectural Setting of Anglican Worship*, 61.
[48] For a view of the interior see plate facing p. 15.
[49] *Oxf. Mail*, 22 Oct. 1954; Appeal launched by the Church Restoration Committee; inf. Mr. C. J. Peers.
[50] Oxf. Dioc. c 2016.   [51] Inf. Mr. C. J. Peers.

Katherine Peers; to Charles Peers, D.C.L. (d. 1853), heir of Robert; to John Witherington Peers (d. 1876), for 34 years Vicar of Tetsworth; to John Witherington Peers, who died at Wendover in 1891; and one designed by Frederick Etchells to Sir Charles Reed Peers (d. 1952), surveyor of Westminster Abbey, and his wife (d. 1953).[52] Sir Charles was buried in the Islip Chapel, Westminster Abbey, and his wife in Chislehampton churchyard.

A tablet commemorates those who died in the two world wars. The only stained glass in the church is the Peers arms and crest, executed by Kaye & Pemberton in 1953 for the patron and lord of the manor, Mr. Charles Peers.

The church is notable for its fine service of silver-gilt comprising a pair of chalices with paten covers, a pair of enormous tankard flagons, an almsplate, and a small salver, all with inscriptions surrounding coats of arms. On the drum of each flagon is engraved the arms of Peers surmounted by a crest; the inscription on one denoting that it was the gift of the French church, and on the other of the Dutch church in London, to Sir Charles Peers in 1716. Both flagons are also inscribed to the effect that they were pre-sented by the son and surviving family of the late Sir Charles Peers to St. Katherine's Church on Easter Day, 1767, and the names of all these descendants living at that date are inscribed on the base of each vessel. The rest of the plate was given by Katherine Peers, the wife of Charles Peers (d. 1781). It is dated 1749 and must have been given to the old church soon after the family's arrival in the parish.[53]

The registers date from 1763. Previously entries for Chislehampton were made in the Stadhampton register (1556–1762),[54] of which John Bilstone made two copies for the new Chislehampton church.[55]

There are two bells, neither of great antiquity. The old church also had two bells in 1553.[56]

The churchyard is entered by a contemporary stone gateway.[57]

NONCONFORMITY. See under Stadhampton, below, p. 91.

SCHOOLS. See under Stadhampton, below, p. 92.

CHARITIES. None known.

CLIFTON HAMPDEN

THE modern parish of Clifton Hampden dates only from 1819, for until then Clifton was nominally a chapelry of Dorchester.[1] The boundaries of Clifton, however, appear to have remained unchanged from Saxon times until 1932, when they were enlarged by the addition of the civil parish of Burcot.[2] The area was thereby increased from 1,245 acres to 1,924 acres. The only natural boundary of the ancient township and virtual parish, with the history of which this article is concerned, was the River Thames in the south.

At its lowest point, on the Thames, the parish lies 154 feet above sea level, but rises steadily to 250 feet on its northern boundary.[3] At the east end of the village the land rises sharply to form a cliff on which stand the church and the manor-house. The soil consists largely of Lower Greensand, though there is a small patch of Gault on Clifton Heath and a stretch of Alluvium north of the Thames extending from the eastern boundary of Culham to Burcot.[4]

The main Dorchester to Abingdon road runs through the parish from east to west, keeping to the higher ground away from the river. This highway was of great antiquity[5] and was the parish's main means of communication, but it appears to have been neglected in the 16th and 17th centuries and by 1736 was in 'a ruinous state'. In that year an Act of Parliament established a turnpike trust for the area between Henley and Abingdon and empowered it to levy tolls for the maintenance and repair of the road.[6] Further Acts were passed in 1755, 1781, 1802, 1821, and 1841.[7] The trust set up a toll-gate at the eastern approach to the village where the garage now stands. The highway now runs to the north of the lower part of the village, but originally took a loop through it and thence ran up the hill between the present parsonage and churchyard to rejoin the main road after passing through the grounds of the manor-house.[8] It is not clear when exactly the alteration was made: Hucks's estate map of 1786[9] shows only the loop road, but the present main road appears to be marked on Davis's map of 1797.[10] The bulk of the original road through the lower village remained in use in 1958, although the eastern end was blocked up in 1843 and 1882.[11] Two minor roads, Baldon Way, of which part was originally called Watery Lane, and Thame Lane, which crosses Clifton Heath, were probably also ancient roads. Thame Lane formed a cross-country link between Culham and the market town of Thame via Chislehampton. It was in use until the present century, chiefly for the sheep and cattle trade between Oxfordshire and Salisbury.[12] The remaining road, from Long Wittenham, joins the loop road in the lower village by a bridge over the Thames. The bridge, built by Richard Casey, is a red brick structure in the Gothic style, and was

[52] For arms and inscriptions on the monuments see Bodl. G.A. Oxon. 4°. 685, p. 95 (126n.); G.A. Oxon. 4°. 688, p. 94.

[53] The plate is kept at Chislehampton House in 2 cases of contemporary date made to hold it and 2 service books presented by Katherine Peers in about 1753. The plate is fully described in Evans, *Ch. Plate*.

[54] See below, p. 88.

[55] Chislehampton Par. Rec.

[56] *Ch. Bells Oxon.* 92.

[57] For contemporary plan of church and churchyard see Peers Arch.

[1] For an account of the parochial status of Clifton see below, p. 23.

[2] *Census*, 1931.

[3] O.S. Map 6″, xlv (1883); 2½″, 41/59 (1949).

[4] *V.C.H. Oxon.* i, map facing p. 5.

[5] *Cal. Pat.* 1416–22, 33–34.

[6] Turnpike Act, 9 Geo. II, c. 14.

[7] 28 Geo. II, c. 42; 21 Geo. III, c. 97; 42 Geo. III, c. 60 (local & personal act); 1 & 2 Geo. IV, c. 26 (local & pers. act); 4 & 5 Vict. c. 100 (local & pers. act).

[8] J. A. Gibbs, MS. Collections for a Hist. of Clifton Hampden, f. 35, *penes* the vicar.

[9] *Penes* Sir Geoffrey Gibbs, the Manor House, Clifton Hampden.   [10] Davis, *Oxon. Map*.

[11] Gibbs, MS. Collect. f. 35.

[12] Local inf.

erected in 1864 by Henry Hucks Gibbs, lord of the manor, from a design of Sir Gilbert Scott at a cost of £3,617. The bricks used were made in a kiln on Clifton Heath.[13] The construction of the bridge was authorized by Act of Parliament, power to levy a toll being granted.[14] In 1946 the bridge was purchased from Baroness Aldenham by the County Councils of Berkshire and Oxfordshire for £1,850 and freed from toll.[15] The bridge replaced an ancient ferry and ford and lies slightly above the ferry. The ford met the ferry on the Berkshire side of the river and crossed diagonally to the Oxfordshire bank to a point just below the church.[16] The ferry was in existence in the early part of the 14th century when a certain John Broun was ferryman. In 1493 the ferry was demised by Roger Roper of Watlington to Exeter College, Oxford,[17] in whose hands it remained until it was purchased by Henry Hucks Gibbs in 1861.[18] The ferry had a large boat, capable of carrying a man and a horse.[19]

The Thames at Clifton has always been difficult to navigate. There is a hard rock bed full of half-sunken ledges in the neighbourhood of the bridge,[20] and near Long Wittenham the course of the river is circuitous and the stream rapid. A river survey of 1811 refers to the difficulties and dangers of navigation near Slade's Eyot close to Long Wittenham, many disasters having occurred at Wittenham Point.[21] As late as 1826 the Lord Mayor of London, returning from a visit to Oxford, was delayed a long time near Clifton ferry because of the low depth of water.[22] The difficulties of the navigation at Clifton were one of the problems that the Oxford-Burcot Commission had to consider after its establishment by Acts of 1605 and 1624,[23] but it was not until the Thames Navigation Commission was set up in 1751[24] that any serious remedial step was considered.

In 1771 a proposal was made to cut a channel from Clifton ferry to a point just above Culham Pound Lock with the object of by-passing Culham and Sutton Courtenay, but the proposal was dropped.[25] In 1789–90 the towing path from Day's Lock to Culham Bridge was constructed, the path crossing from the Berkshire to the Oxfordshire side of the river at Clifton ferry.[26] The difficulty around Slade's Eyot, however, remained, and in addition there were complaints of exorbitant tolls at the Eyot.[27] A cut through Clifton Mead to avoid the awkward loop in the river opposite Long Wittenham seems to have been first suggested in 1802;[28] and in 1811 it was decided to construct a pound lock at Clifton ferry.[29] Work was begun in 1820 and was completed in 1822, at a cost of £5,420.[30] The weir near the west end of the cut was made in 1835.[31]

The village of Clifton Hampden lies partly to the south of the main Abingdon–Dorchester road and partly on both sides of the lower section of Baldon Way. Its first name means 'tun on a cliff' and is of Anglo-Saxon origin.[32] Its second, for which there is no documentary evidence before 1726,[33] is an unusually late addition to the original name, and it has therefore been suggested that Hampden may really be Hampton, a common ending for villages in the vicinity.[34] There is, however, no real reason to doubt that Hampden is a family name and was added, perhaps, when Miles Hampden was lord of the manor in the 1530's, to distinguish the village from Clifton Ferry on the Berkshire side of the river.[35] It may be noted, however, that Miles Hampden's maternal grandfather is described in a 16th-century pedigree as of 'Clifton Ferris'.[36]

Lord Torrington described the village in 1792 as 'one of the prettiest and flemish-looking villages I ever saw',[37] and in 1958 Clifton was still remarkably attractive and well-kept with a number of timber-framed Elizabethan or early-17th-century cottages and farmhouses. There was much rebuilding in the 18th century and many of the new houses reflect the increased desire for comfort and privacy that characterized the period. An 18th-century house, for instance, adjoining Upper Town Farm, is a brick-built building of two stories. Both it and a neighbouring 18th-century cottage of brick and thatch are screened from the road by a brick and stone wall, overtopped by a large yew hedge. There is also a grass verge in front.

Some of the old buildings appear to have been malthouses in the 17th and 18th centuries: in 1726 there were three in the village, one on the north side of the London road, a second on the east side of the green, and a third on the west side of the green.[38] It is not certain whether the present village inn, the 'Plough', was one of these or not: the building is old, but was first recorded as one in 1821. The 'Fleur de Lys' was mentioned in 1786,[39] and continued as an inn until at least 1864.[40] The third inn was perhaps a house, altered in the late 18th century, near the bridge. It is now two cottages, but is traditionally held to be an ancient hostelry.

Except for the late-18th-century Fullamoor Farm, close to the parish boundary,[41] the three farmhouses are all in the village, but they are now private residences. Two of them date from the 16th and 17th centuries. The oldest is 'Ridges', a timber-framed building with modern extensions. This farm seems to be the one described in a survey of the village in 1726 as the 'capital messuage called the Farm'.[42] Lower Town Farm dates from the 17th

[13] Gibbs, MS. Collect. f. 35; J. A. Gibbs, *Pedigree of Gibbs Family* (1932), 31. The brick-works were abandoned in 1895: local inf.
[14] 27 & 28 Vict. c. 44 (local & pers. act).
[15] O.R.O., C.C.E. 806.   [16] Ibid. P.D. 4/3.
[17] C. W. Boase, *Reg. of Exeter Coll.* (O.H.S. xxvii), 327, 329.   [18] Gibbs, MS. Collect. f. 24.
[19] F. S. Thacker, *The Thames Highway, Locks and Weirs*, 173.
[20] Thacker, *The Thames Highway, General Hist.* 62; John Taylor, *Thame Isis* (London, 1632).
[21] *A Survey of the River Thames* (Oxford, 1811), 16; Berks. R.O. Reading, D/TC 25A; Min. bk. 5th & 6th Dist. Comrs. 1771–1865, f. 40.
[22] R. C. Dillon, *Lord Mayor's Visit to Oxford* (1826), 74.
[23] Act to Clear Passage, 3 Jas. I, c. 20; Act to Make Thames Navigable, 21 Jas. I, c. 32.
[24] 24 Geo. II, c. 8.
[25] Plan in O.R.O. Box 98.

[26] Reading Public Libr. Treacher Papers, Ledger, 1789–97, ff. 78, 93.
[27] Berks. R.O. Thames min. bk. 1771–1865, ff. 29, 34, 41.
[28] Ibid. f. 41.
[29] Berks. R.O. Minutes Thames Nav. Comrs. vii. 22.
[30] Ibid. 28, 126; viii. 201.
[31] Thacker, *Locks and Weirs*, 171–2; Treacher Pps. Copy of expense sheet.
[32] *P.N. Oxon.* (E.P.N.S.), i. 149.
[33] Bodl. MS. Rawl. B 518, f. 59.
[34] *P.N. Oxon.* (E.P.N.S.), i. 149.
[35] Parker, *Guide*, 375.
[36] W. C. Metcalfe, *Visit. Northants.* 25.
[37] *Torrington Diaries*, ed. C. B. Andrews, iii. 173.
[38] Bodl. MS. Rawl. B 518, ff. 85–86, 93, 99.
[39] O.R.O. Victlrs' recog.
[40] Par. Reg. Marriages, 1864, John Casey, publican.
[41] Davis, *Oxon. map* (1797).
[42] Bodl. MS. Rawl. B 518, f. 90b.

century: a timber-framed wing with brick filling survives at the back. A south wing of two stories with attics was added in the 18th century, the initials A.R. and E.P. and the date 1771 being inscribed on the brickwork. The picturesque farm outbuildings, consisting of large weather-boarded barns with half-hipped roofs, also date from the 18th century.

The church, manor-house, and Vicarage stand on the cliff at the east end of the village. The manor-house was built between 1843 and 1846 as a parsonage and was used as such by the incumbent until 1905, when it became the residence of Alban, 2nd Baron Aldenham.[43] Built from the designs of Sir Gilbert Scott at a cost of £3,900, it is a grey, stone building in the revived Gothic style of the Victorian period. Additions were made in 1864–5 by the incumbent, the Revd. J. L. Gibbs.[44] From 1939 to 1943 the building housed a private nursing home evacuated from London, but has since reverted to its former status, and in 1958 was the residence of Sir Geoffrey and Lady Gibbs. The Vicarage has a longer history than the manor-house, the succession of the property being traceable from 1755. The house was largely rebuilt in 1923–4, but its south side dates back to about 1780.[45] It was purchased, together with 8 acres of land, by Anne Noyes, lady of the manor, in 1831; in 1832 she conveyed the house and land to the Bishop of Oxford and the Revd. Joseph Gibbs for use as a parsonage.[46] It was used as such until 1843 and became again a parsonage in 1905.

The parish hall, opened in 1896, was built by Henry Hucks Gibbs to commemorate his elevation to the peerage as Baron Aldenham. In 1898 it was adapted as a reading-room.[47]

To the north-west of Watery Lane is a substantial early-18th-century house built of brick with horizontal fascias of stone. Behind the house were stables and a coach-house; these have been converted into cottages. The house is apparently not mentioned in the survey of 1726, but is shown on Jefferys's map of Oxfordshire of 1767. After serving as a school and a nursing home it became once again a private residence. Nineteenth-century and modern cottages on the road leading from the church to the Abingdon–Dorchester road are of the same general character as the rest of the village. They are of one story or of one story and an attic, and are built of brick and stone and are thatched. Eight post-war council houses have been built outside the village.

The Civil War of the 17th century saw some military activity in the neighbourhood. After the occupation of Abingdon by roundhead troops in May 1644 the parliamentarians began to make sorties into the Dorchester area to raid royalist communications with Oxford.[48] On 6 May 1645 the roundhead commander at Abingdon, Major-General Richard Browne, marched to meet Cromwell at Dorchester,[49] at which time some parliamentary soldiers were quartered in Clifton.[50] Early in 1646 a minor engagement took place near Clifton when a force of roundheads from Abingdon clashed with some of the royalist garrison of Wallingford who had been drawn away from their headquarters by a stratagem. Some 50 cavaliers are said to have been captured.[51]

The Second World War led to the establishment of the Royal Naval air station. It was closed in 1956, but was re-opened in the same year as an Admiralty Storage Depot, covering 592 acres and extending into the parishes of Culham and Nuneham Courtenay.[52]

Henry Hucks Gibbs, first Baron Aldenham (1819–1907), financier, antiquarian, and a benefactor to the village, has been perhaps the only resident of importance. A devoted churchman, he is said to have possessed the finest collection of copies of the Book of Common Prayer in English hands.[53]

MANORS. Clifton was not mentioned by name in Domesday Book, but there can be little doubt that it was surveyed under Dorchester, and was a part of the endowment of the Bishopric of Dorchester. When the bishopric was transferred to Lincoln in about 1070 Clifton was also transferred.[54] The bishop, however, was compelled to enfeoff much of his Oxfordshire land, including Clifton, to meet the heavy burden of providing 60 knights for the king's service and retained only the overlordship of Clifton. This followed the descent of Dorchester manor when in the 16th century Dorchester passed to the Norreys family and later to the earls of Abingdon.[55]

During the medieval period Clifton was divided amongst three of the bishop's knights. The Le Moine fee, or CLIFTON or HAMPDEN manor as it became later, descended from the fee which a Robert Monachus held of the Bishop of Lincoln in 1166.[56] Robert le Moine, probably a son if not the same person, held the fee by 1201, and William le Moine had succeeded him by about 1212.[57] Either he or a son of the same name was in possession soon after 1225.[58] Details of succeeding tenants are not recorded, but the fee clearly remained in the family and in 1279 Philip le Moine was the bishop's tenant. His fee included property in Burcot and South Stoke and seems to have comprised about one-third of Clifton parish itself. He paid scutage to the bishop and owed suit to Dorchester hundred court.[59] By 1300 John le Moine had inherited the property,[60] and he or a son was returned as one of Clifton's lords in 1316 and paid the highest tax contribution for the parish in 1327.[61] In 1346 John, son of John le Moine, held his father's lands in Clifton, Burcot, and South Stoke.[62]

In the 1350's, however, John le Moine seems to have granted John Loveday of Goring rights in the reversion of Clifton manor, as it was now called. He and Loveday were jointly concerned in transactions over Clifton, Burcot, Holcombe, and Drayton in

43 Bodl. MS. Rawl. B 518, f. 3; Gibbs, *Pedigree*, 31.
44 Gibbs, MS. Collect, f. 3.
45 Ibid. f. 18; J. A. Gibbs, *Hist. of Anthony and Dorothea Gibbs*, App. v.
46 Gibbs, MS. Collect. f. 18.   47 Gibbs Pps.
48 E. Walsingham, *Alter Britanniae Heros* (Oxford, 1645), 21; F. J. Varley, *Siege of Oxford*, 68.
49 *A Perfect Diurnal* (London, 1643–9), 6 May, 1645.
50 Dunkin MS. 438/4, f. 85*b*.
51 Hist. MSS. Com. *13th Rep. App. I*, 340; Bodl. Gough Gen. Top. 180: A true relation of a late victory obtained by Maj. Gen. Browne his forces about Clifton.
52 Inf. Civil Engineer-in-Chief, Admiralty.

53 J. A. Gibbs, *Hist. of Ant. and Dorothea Gibbs*, *passim*; Gibbs, *Pedigree*, 31–32; *D.N.B.* 1901–11.
54 *V.C.H. Oxon.* i. 378, 403.
55 See below, p. 43.
56 *Red. Bk. Exch.* (Rolls Ser.), 375.
57 *Rot. de Ob. et. Fin.* (Rec. Com.), i. 155; *Pipe R.* 1201 (P.R.S. N.S. xiv), 213; *Bk. of Fees*, 40; *Red Bk. Exch.* 514.
58 Queen's Coll. MS. 366, f. 25. For the date of this survey see above, p. 13, n. 94.
59 *Rot. Hund.* (Rec. Com.), ii. 749.
60 Queen's Coll. MS. 366, f. 24*b*.
61 *Feud. Aids*, iv. 167; E 179/161/9.
62 *Feud. Aids*, iv. 182.

1358.[63] Loveday died in 1361, and in 1362 his heir Elizabeth and her husband Henry de Aldrynton granted various estates, including land in Clifton and the reversion of Clifton manor, to Thomas de Aldrynton and others;[64] Le Moine still had a life interest in the manor.[65] Some time before 1380 Sir Hugh de Segrave, a former Treasurer of England, had acquired the Aldrynton rights in Clifton manor. He had also purchased other property in Clifton, for example, that of Ralph son of Thomas Cook. In 1380 Segrave granted much of his land to William of Wykeham; amongst the grants were £11 rent from Clifton manor, 'sometime of John Moyne', properties which had once belonged to John de Louches of Garsington, Thomas Cook, and Adam de Shareshull, and the reversion of Clifton manor, at that time held by Robert Maundeville and his wife for life.[66] At the same time Thomas de Aldrynton gave up his rights in the property,[67] and in 1382 Nicholas Drayton of Dorchester, who was related to Sir Hugh de Segrave, released his rights in Clifton and Burcot manors and property.[68] William of Wykeham seems to have intended to endow New College, Oxford, with the property, and in 1381 was granted a licence to alienate Clifton and other manors to St. Mary's College, Winchester.[69] The college administered the manor, which was still farmed by the Maundevilles, until 1390, but seems to have disposed of it about that time. It is likely that both Burcot and Clifton manors were acquired by Sir John Drayton of Kempston (Beds.)[70] and later of Nuneham Courtenay. Drayton, a soldier of fortune, was the son of the Nicholas Drayton who had had rights in the manor in 1382, and he certainly possessed land in Clifton in 1405.[71] He died in 1417, leaving two daughters and coheirs, Joan and Elizabeth.[72] The latter, who married first Christopher Preston of Slapton (Northants.), and second John Wenlock of Wenlock (Salop), who was created Baron Wenlock in 1461, apparently acquired Clifton as a result of a division of the Drayton lands in 1432.[73] Three years later she and Wenlock made a grant of the manor for life to John Delabere, clerk, later Bishop of St. David's (1447–60).[74] When he died the manor reverted to Elizabeth, and on her death about 1461 passed to Richard Preston, doubtless her son by her first marriage.[75] He died, an idiot, in 1489, holding the manor of the Bishop of Lincoln 'as of the manor of Dorchester'.[76] His daughter and heir Elizabeth, said to have been feeble-minded since birth, was

thrice married: to Richard Danvers, Edward Hampden, and Nicholas Lovett.[77] After Elizabeth's death in 1521[78] her third husband retained the manor during his lifetime.[79] By 1535 her heir Miles Hampden was lord of the manor, but the Yonges, who held Bradleys manor in Clifton, had a lease of it from Lovett.[80] Miles Hampden was succeeded by his son Richard and grandson Thomas.[81] About 1599 Thomas Hampden sold Clifton manor to Sir Michael Molyns of Clapcot (Berks.), who was also lord of a Chislehampton manor.[82] At his death in 1615 Sir Michael was said to hold the manor of Francis Lord Norreys of Rycote as of Dorchester manor.[83] In about 1618 his son Sir Barentine Molyns conveyed the manor to Edmund Dunch, lord of a second manor in Clifton.[84] Thereafter, the two manors followed the same descent.[85]

The Burcot fee, known as *CLIFTON* manor in the 16th century, formed a second estate in Clifton. It belonged in the 12th and 13th centuries to the Burcot family, who were mesne tenants of the Bishop of Lincoln's fee in Clifton, Holcombe, and Drayton, and apparently only under-tenants in Burcot itself.[86] In 1166 the fee cannot be identified with certainty among those listed as belonging to the bishop.[87] By 1201 Nicholas son of Bartholomew, perhaps the Bartholomew de Clifton who occurs in 1176,[88] held land in Clifton and was also returned as tenant of the bishop's fee at the same time.[89] In 1212 he was termed Nicholas de Burcot.[90] Either he or a son, also Nicholas de Burcot, held the fee by at least about 1225,[91] and another Nicholas, presumably of the next generation, was in possession in 1279. As chief lord of the fee under Dorchester he then held in Drayton, Holcombe, and Clifton, but he was also under-tenant of 7 virgates of the Le Moine fee in Clifton, Burcot, and South Stoke, and of 2 virgates of the De Baldindon fee in Burcot.[92] His property passed to a son John,[93] but by 1346 the Abbot of Dorchester was returned as tenant of the fee.[94]

Dorchester Abbey had been under-tenant of the Burcots' Clifton property since 1279 at least, when the whole estate save for a ½-virgate was either in its farm or paid rent and scutage to the abbey as mesne tenant.[95] The property remained in the abbey's hands until the 16th century.[96] The abbey also paid a quitrent to Miles Hampden in 1535, which suggests that the abbey's estate still included his manor, perhaps as successors of the 13th-century under-tenants, the Burcot family.[97] The king seized

[63] Bodl. MS. ch. Oxon. 147*b.; cf. *Goring Charts.* 125.
[64] *Goring Charts.* 176–7; cf. p. lvii: Loveday family tree.
[65] *Cal. Close,* 1364–8, 192; and see below.
[66] *Cal. Close,* 1377–81, 375–7. [67] Ibid. 376–7.
[68] Ibid. 1381–5, 239; for the Drayton–Segrave connexion see *V.C.H. Oxon.* v. 240; *V.C.H. Berks.* iii. 400.
[69] *Cal. Pat.* 1381–5, 63.
[70] New Coll. Arch.: bursars' accts. 1381–90. Cf. *V.C.H. Berks.* iii. 454: a similar descent for Aston Tirrold.
[71] Cf. *V.C.H. Beds.* iii. 299; *V.C.H. Oxon.* v. 240. For his possession of lands in Clifton in 1405, see copy of deed of 1405 in the Gibbs Pps. at the Manor House, Clifton Hampden.
[72] C 145/296/59; *V.C.H. Beds.* iii. 299; cf. Aston Tirrold in Berks.: *V.C.H. Berks.* iii. 454. Clifton was apparently in the custody of Robert Bradley in 1428: *Feud. Aids,* iv. 200.
[73] *Cal. Close,* 1429–35, 224–5; Clifton was apparently not divided into moieties as happened with Kempston and Aston Tirrold: *V.C.H. Berks.* iii. 454; *V.C.H. Beds.* iii. 299.
[74] C.P. 40/699, m. 144d; C.P. 25(1)/191/27/71.
[75] See *V.C.H. Beds.* iii. 299.
[76] *Cal. Pat.* 1485–94, 112; *Cal. Inq. p.m. Hen. VII.* i, p. 210.

[77] *Cal. Inq. p.m. Hen. VII,* i, p. 210; iii, p. 333; C.P. 25(2)/51/362/Mich. 12 Hen. VIII.
[78] C 142/37/110.
[79] Req. 2/2/114; 2/3/42.   [80] Ibid.
[81] C 3/235/3; W. C. Metcalfe, *Visit. Northants.* 25.
[82] C.P. 25(2)/198/Hil. 41 Eliz.; cf. C.P. 25(2)/262/East. 37 Eliz.; and see above, p. 12.
[83] C 142/378/130.
[84] C.P. 25(2)/340/East. 16 Jas. I: C 142/402/150.
[85] See below.
[86] See below, p. 67.
[87] *Red Bk. Exch.* (Rolls Ser.), 375.
[88] *Pipe R.* 1176 (P.R.S. xxv), 32.
[89] *Rot. de Ob. et Fin.* (Rec. Com.), i. 155; *St. Frides. Cart.* ii. 363; *Sandford Cart.* ii. 210.
[90] *Bk. of Fees,* 40; *Red. Bk. Exch.* (Rolls Ser.), 514.
[91] Queen's Coll. MS. 366, f. 25.
[92] *Rot. Hund.* (Rec. Com.), ii. 748–9.
[93] *Feud. Aids,* iv. 182.
[94] Ibid.
[95] *Rot. Hund.* (Rec. Com.), ii. 749.
[96] Dugdale, *Mon.* vi. 324.
[97] *Val. Eccl.* (Rec. Com.), ii. 167.

the lands on the dissolution of the abbey, and they were retained by the Crown until 1560 when Elizabeth I granted them to John Doddington and John Jackson.[98] By 1592 William Dunch of Little Wittenham (Berks.) was in possession,[99] and he held the manor on his death in 1597.[1] His son Edmund (d. 1623) was succeeded by a grandson, another Edmund (d. 1678), and Edmund's son Hungerford (d. 1680). Hungerford's heir Edmund, a celebrated Whig politician of the 18th century, squandered his patrimony.[2] On his death in 1719 he bequeathed to his three daughters and coheirs not only his lands in Oxfordshire and elsewhere, but also debts amounting to £26,000, and to meet these debts a private Act of Parliament permitted the sale of lands.[3] In 1726 Clifton manor was purchased from Dunch's trustees by Robert Hucks (d. 1745), a London brewer and M.P. for Abingdon.[4] The estate remained in the hands of the Hucks family until 1814 and was enlarged by various purchases.[5] On the death of Robert Hucks's son and successor, another Robert, who had become a lunatic, it passed by inheritance to Anne and Sarah Noyes, nieces of Robert (II).[6] By a deed of partition of 1815 the manor and lordship of Clifton became the property of Anne Noyes.[7] When Anne died in 1841 she left the estate to her sister Sarah, and after her to her cousin, the banker George Henry Gibbs, heir-at-law to the Hucks family.[8] On the death of Sarah in 1842 G. H. Gibbs succeeded to the property under the terms of Anne's will;[9] he died at Venice in 1842 and was buried at Clifton.[10] His son Henry Hucks Gibbs (d. 1907), created 1st Baron Aldenham in 1896, still held the manor in 1891, but gave it to his son Alban, 2nd Baron Aldenham, who was returned as chief landowner in Clifton in 1903. He died in 1936 and his son, the 3rd baron, died in 1939. Lillie Lady Aldenham, widow of the 3rd baron, held Clifton manor until her death in 1950, when she was succeeded by Sir Geoffrey Gibbs, nephew of the 2nd baron.[11]

A third fee in Clifton, later known as *BRADLEYS* manor, developed from the estate of an Adelinus de Clifton—a successor of the Domesday Iseward—who held 2 fees of the Bishop of Lincoln in 1166.[12] The 2 fees must have included, then as later, land in Burcot, the Baldons, and South Stoke as well as in Clifton.[13] By 1201 Richard, son of a William, who was probably the heir of Adelinus, held the 2 fees and was still in possession about 1212.[14] As in Marsh Baldon he was succeeded by his daughter Agnes, who held the fees in about 1225, and they later passed

to a family called De Baldindon, probably by marriage.[15] William de Baldindon held Clifton property by 1247[16] and in 1279 he or a son held the 2 fees in Clifton, Baldon, and South Stoke in chief of the bishop and for scutage and suit at Dorchester hundred court. Apparently the Baldon property formed one fee and the Clifton and neighbouring lands another.[17]

It may be assumed that the Clifton property descended to the Bradleys in the same way as the Baldon estate, but details are lacking. In 1316 John 'de Bradele' was returned as one of the lords of Clifton and Burcot.[18] His successor can perhaps be identified as the John de Bradecote (? Bridecote or Burcot) who held a ½-fee in Clifton and Burcot in 1346, although nothing has been found to link Geoffrey of the Chamber (*de Camera*), the previous tenant of the ½-fee, with the Bradleys.[19] It is not clear what happened to the Bradleys' estate over the next 70 years. It seems to have come into the hands of the Le Moines, the other Clifton-manor tenants, but reverted to the Bradleys. In 1428 Robert 'de Bradele' held a ½-fee in Clifton and Burcot, which had previously belonged to John le Moine.[20] He also held the Le Moines' ½-fee in Clifton, Burcot, and South Stoke, but this was perhaps a temporary arrangement.[21] His son John seems to have succeeded him in the same year.[22] Thereafter there is a gap in the descent until 1512, when John Lewes and his wife Agnes conveyed the manors of Baldon and Clifton to Robert Froston,[23] and in 1513 Bishop Audley purchased both Little Baldon and Clifton for his chantry in Salisbury Cathedral.[24] Clifton was evidently not retained, for in 1530 William Yonge of Basildon (Berks.) and Little Wittenham held a messuage and farm called Bradleys.[25] In 1543 his son Roger sold Bradleys manor, said to be worth £10 19s. a year, to Sir John Pollard of Nuneham Courtenay,[26] who had also acquired the Baldon estate.[27] The estates passed to his brother Sir Anthony Pollard in 1557; his Clifton manor was described as Bradleys manor held of Lord Norreys as of his manor of Dorchester.[28] Pollard had also acquired lands in Clifton, which had belonged to Littlemore Priory.[29] The Clifton property must have descended like Little Baldon to Anthony's kinsman Lewis Pollard,[30] who in 1636 made a will saying that his executors should sell Broadlease manor (i.e. Bradleys) to pay his debts.[31] The manor was sold soon after, perhaps before his death in 1640;[32] but by 1726 it had apparently been absorbed into the Hucks

[98] *Cal. Pat.* 1558–60, 467; cf. 1549–51, 85.
[99] C 3/253/3.   [1] C 142/249/84.
[2] *V.C.H. Berks.* iv. 382.
[3] 6 Geo. I. c. 10 (priv. act).
[4] Bodl. MS. Ch. Oxon. 2978.
[5] d.d. Cooper & Caldecott c 56 (17).
[6] Ibid.
[7] Ibid.; Gibbs Pps. at the Manor House, Clifton Hampden.
[8] J. A. Gibbs, *Hist. of Anthony and Dorothea Gibbs*, 278.
[9] Ibid.   [10] Burke, *Peerage* (1952).
[11] Debrett, *Peerage* (1958); *Kelly's Dir. Oxon.* (1891, 1903, 1939); and local inf.
[12] *Red Bk. Exch.* (Rolls Ser.), 375.
[13] See p. 67; *V.C.H. Oxon.* v. 35, 51.
[14] *Rot. de Ob. et Fin.* (Rec. Com.), i. 155; *Bk. of Fees*, 40; *Red Bk. Exch.* (Rolls Ser.), 514.
[15] Queen's Coll. MS. 366, f. 25*b*; *V.C.H. Oxon.* v. 35.
[16] *Fines Oxon.* 134; cf. *Bk. of Fees*, 827, 840, for tenure of Baldon in 1242.
[17] *Rot. Hund.* (Rec. Com.), ii. 724, 749.

[18] *Feud. Aids*, iv. 167; cf. B.M. Add. Ch. 26342: mentions John de Bradele's land in Clifton in 1319.
[19] *Feud. Aids*, iv. 182.
[20] Ibid. 200.
[21] See above.
[22] See *Feud. Aids*, iv. 199; cf. *V.C.H. Oxon.* v. 51 for a probable descent of the Bradleys.
[23] C.P. 25(2)/34/225 Mich. 3 Hen. VIII.
[24] Ibid. East. 4 & 5 Hen. VIII; Trin. 9 Hen. VIII; see *V.C.H. Oxon.* v. 52.
[25] O.R.O. Wi IV/iii/1.
[26] Ibid. iii/2–4; C 54/438; this states also that the Pollards sold it to Sir William Essex in 1544, but this was probably part of some legal transaction.
[27] *V.C.H. Oxon.* v. 52.
[28] Ibid.; C 142/182/40.
[29] *Cal. Pat.* 1547–8, 276; B.M. Add. Ch. 20366.
[30] For further details see *V.C.H. Oxon.* v. 52.
[31] O.R.O. Wi I/i/43; cf. IV/iii/7.
[32] Ibid. I/i/44–48: a lawsuit ensued in 1648 over his will when it was claimed he had sold the manor.

estate of Clifton Hampden, for in an estate survey of that date 5 acres described as 'Bradleys Piece' were freehold of the manor.[33]

LESSER ESTATE. About 1487 the Abingdon Guild of the Holy Cross acquired land in Clifton from Joan Hopkins *alias* Yonge of Clifton, and it later passed to Christ's Hospital, Abingdon, successor to the Fraternity of the Holy Cross. The property consisted originally of strips in the Middle and Lower Fields together with meadowland; but after inclosure it comprised 6 acres of meadow, south of the London road, and 17 acres of arable, north of the road. In 1866 Henry Hucks Gibbs, lord of Clifton manor, bought the property from the hospital for £2,500.[34]

ECONOMIC AND SOCIAL HISTORY. Crop markings near Fullamoor Farm may indicate a Romano-British site, but continuous settlement probably dates from the Anglo-Saxon period. The place was undoubtedly colonized by early Saxon settlers who gave it its name of Clifton,[35] but there is little information about the village's layout and system of landholding until the 13th century. In 1086 it was included in the lands of the Bishop of Lincoln's Dorchester manor and is therefore not described in detail in Domesday, although a number of its tenants must have been counted in the population of the bishop's lands, and its meadow land must also have been included in the survey.[36] The village may have shared in the general prosperity of the bishop's estates, which rose in value after the Conquest, but presumably then as later there was much waste land.

An early-13th-century record shows that Clifton was a typical open-field village. When Bartholomew de Clifton granted St. Frideswide's Priory a ½-virgate of arable and 2 acres of meadow the ½-virgate was made up of 11½ acres distributed in strips (6 × 1 a. + 2 a. + 3 a. + ½ a.) throughout the fields or furlongs: on 'Sandhilla', 'Scanland', in 'Shorthmede', and other places; the meadow was in strips too (1 a. + ½ a. + ½ a.).[37] Clifton docs not appear in the survey of the bishop's Dorchester estates made in the second quarter of the century,[38] for the bishop had divided it all between three of his knights and kept no land to farm himself;[39] and although Clifton was surveyed in 1279, it is difficult to be certain how much land was under cultivation, as the Le Moine estate extended into other parishes and the account is far from clear. Moreover the meadow is not mentioned and it is unlikely that this was not important then. Sir Philip le Moine's estate was the largest with about 13 virgates, 17 acres.[40] William de Baldindon had 8 or 9 virgates and Nicholas de Burcot had about 3 virgates besides being under-tenant of about 4 virgates of the Le Moine fee in Clifton. These mesne tenants had let out all their land, a fact which prob-

ably accounts for the comparative freedom of Clifton's population. Only 8 tenants were said to do customary works, of which 2 were cottagers. Most of the tenants paid only rent and scutage for their holdings.[41] The most important lay under-tenant was Geoffrey de Lewknor, lord of Harrowden (Northants.) and a landowner in many parishes in the neighbourhood of Clifton. His 10 virgates of the Le Moine fee are entered twice under both Burcot and Clifton, and must have been divided between the two parishes.[42] The Abbot of Dorchester was another substantial under-tenant with rights over most of Nicholas de Burcot's estate and over 1 virgate of the Baldon fee. At least 3 free tenants and 1 customary tenant held under him. Some of Clifton's tenants had the virgate or ½-virgate holdings typical of many open-field villages, but this was by no means universal: a Nicholas le Carter had 5 virgates, but had let out 3, and there were 2 holdings of 2 virgates and 1 of 1½ virgate.[43]

In the 14th century Clifton supported only a moderately prosperous community, considering its extent, which in modern times was 1,245 acres, and it is likely that even more of it was sandy waste than is the case today. Its contributions to early-14th-century taxes were comparatively small. In 1306 the Abbot of Dorchester contributed 6s. 7d., and in 1327 John le Moine, one of the lords, paid a high contribution of 10s. 1d., but otherwise the contributors seem to have been of modest means. Most of the 16 assessed paid under 2s. in 1306; in 1327 out of 33 assessed 10 paid 2s. to 4s., and 22 others under 2s.[44] The only clue to the size of the community in the late Middle Ages comes from the poll-tax returns of 1377, when 79 adults paid the tax.[45]

The land in the 14th and 15th centuries still continued to be divided between the three estates, although in the case of the Burcot land the lordship had passed to Dorchester Abbey. The Le Moine estate was farmed out and in 1389 Robert Maundeville and Cecilia his wife paid £16 3s. 4d. for the yearly rent of the manor.[46]

By the 16th century Clifton was one of the more valuable of Dorchester's estates, yielding £7 2s. 10d. a year in assized and customary rents.[47] Bradleys estate, consisting of the manor and a messuage and farm called Bradleys and other land in Clifton and Burcot, was leased by a Clifton husbandman for £4 a year in 1530, and the property was sold for £210 in 1543.[48] The Hampden estate was also leased for a term of years and stocked 300 sheep about this time.[49] From the 1523 subsidy list it appears that besides Dorchester Abbey and Abingdon Hospital there were 15 other contributors. The total contribution was a modest one of 32s. 6d.[50]

By the end of the 16th century most of Clifton had become part of the Dunch estate, which extended across the river to Little Wittenham, and the

[33] Bodl. MS. Rawl. b 518, f. 101.
[34] Cal. Christ's Hosp. deeds, 201; 1006 b, c, d; 1033, xiv; Gibbs Pps. at the Manor House, Clifton Hampden.
[35] *V.C.H. Oxon.* i. 334; *P.N. Oxon* (E.P.N.S.), i. 149.
[36] *V.C.H. Oxon.* i. 403.
[37] *St. Frides. Cart.* ii. 362.
[38] Queen's Coll. MS. 366, f. 25 sqq. For the date see above, p. 13, n. 94.   [39] See above, p. 18.
[40] Twenty-two acres to the virgate have been reckoned as in *St. Frides. Cart.* ii. 362. Philip le Moine's virgates are calculated by assuming that 2 of the 7 virgates held by Nicholas de Burcot lay in Burcot and one in South Stoke and that 6 virgates, 3 acres of the 10 virgates held by

Geoffrey de Lewknor were in Burcot: *Rot. Hund.* (Rec. Com.), ii. 749, 751.
[41] *Rot. Hund.* (Rec. Com.), ii. 749; and see below, p. 85, n. 80.
[42] Ibid; see also below p. 177 for Sir Geoffrey de Lewknor.
[43] *Rot. Hund.* (Rec. Com.), ii. 749.
[44] E 179/161/8, 10, 17.
[45] E 179/161/41.
[46] New Coll. Arch. bursars' accts. 1381–90.
[47] Dugdale, *Mon.* vi. 324; cf. *Cal. Pat.* 1558–60, 467.
[48] O.R.O. Wi IV/iii/1, 2, 3.
[49] Req. 2/3/42.
[50] E 179/161/198.

successors of the Dunches gradually acquired rights over the whole parish. The Dunch family lived at Wittenham and the Pollards leased Bradleys estate, so there was no resident squire in the village.[51] The Richard Keate who was occupying a five-hearth house in 1665 may have been the tenant of the manor.[52] The 17th-century hearth-tax returns indicate that apart from half a dozen husbandmen or yeoman farmers who had substantial houses with three to five hearths each, the rest of the inhabitants were of comparatively modest means, if not actually poor. For the tax of 1662 the collector reported that 24 'with only one hearth apiece will not pay' and that he could find nothing in the village on which to distrain.[53] In 1665 12 householders were listed, but 3 were discharged on grounds of poverty.[54] That there were only 9 taxpayers in 1665 is particularly significant when contrasted with the record of the Compton Census of 1676 which gives 130 adult inhabitants (i.e. of 16 years and over).[55]

Clifton was an open-field village until the late 18th century. In the 15th century there were three fields called East, Down, and Ham Fields,[56] which by 1726 had become respectively Upper Field (243 a.), Middle Field (210 a.), and Lower Field (266 a.).[57] Their furlong names, e.g. Moor and Fullamoor, indicate their state before being brought into cultivation.[58] It is possible that at one time more land had been under the plough than in 1726, for the surveyor said that part of the Heath called the Breach appeared to have been tilled formerly. There was practically no inclosure except for closes in the village and little consolidation of lands. Twenty-three of the 45 manorial tenants held land in the common fields, and their separate strips rarely contained more than 1 or 2 rods and at the most 2 acres. Clifton Mead meadow (117 a.) consisted of furlongs of between 1 and 10 acres, and was divided annually by lot according to the number of yardlands held. The crop from Burcot mead (21 a.) was taken by Burcot tenants, but commonage belonged to Clifton. Three tenants had rights over the Moors and the Church's Ayte (19 a.), which were presumably grazing land. Fully one-sixth of the parish (288 a.) was common, waste, or road.[59]

The River Thames played an important part in the village economy. The tenants of the manor had fishing rights in half the stream from Burcot to the Knapps (a small area by the ferry on the south bank of the river), in the whole stream from the Knapps to the Fortys, and from there in half the stream up to Slade's Eyot. Tenants also had the right in summer to drag stones from the stream along the under side of the cliff for the purpose of building fences and walls or for mending roads.[60]

About twelve of the 46 houses and cottages in the village in 1726 were freehold. Two or three cottages only seem to have been held by copy and the rest

were held by lease normally for three lives, although in some cases for twelve years or a term of years.[61] Twenty-two tenants (i.e. nearly half the total number of householders) had only small closes with less than an acre of land attached and no land in the fields, and nine had less than 10 acres. Abingdon Hospital with 10 acres and the lord of the manor with 26 acres were among the eight farmers with holdings of 10 to 30 acres; there were four medium-sized farms with 40 to 80 acres and only two large farms. The Sawyers had 153 and the Dunches 173 acres.[62] The Dunch property was probably let to a tenant farmer and was known as The Farm or Clifton Farm House, part of which had been settled on Elizabeth Dunch in 1713. In 1765, when it came completely to the Huckses, it comprised about 290 acres of which 50 were furze and heath.[63]

Clifton Hampden was inclosed by Robert Hucks about 1770, and Richard Davis's map of 1797 shows the whole parish under plough save for land near the meadow.[64] In 1793 two of Hucks's tenants, Thomas Latham of Fullamoor farm and another, said in their replies to the Board of Agriculture that the inclosures were very large ones and that the farms also were large. They listed as the advantages of inclosure an increased rent, greater quantity and quality of produce, and improved stock, and maintained that the long leases helped.[65] Both these returns and Arthur Young's survey in 1809 show that Clifton farmers were quite progressive, particularly the Lathams of Fullamoor farm. Turnips and clover were said to 'answer exceedingly' and a flexible rotation of crops was in use—wheat with rye-grass, fallow for turnips or vetches, barley or oats, and clover. Latham was experimenting with potatoes in 1809, a crop which was to do very well later. He also cultivated 'a remarkably fine' crop of swedes. Sheep were reared, a cross between the Berkshire and Leicestershire breeds being favoured, and Thomas Latham was quoted as an authority on them by Young. Since inclosure Latham had carried out a good deal of drainage and had laid underground drains of wood and bushes. The method of manuring was to spread dung and coal ashes, or to fold sheep on the land. The farmhouses were described as good and well situated.[66] Over this period there were three, and after about 1816 four, tenant-farmers on the Hucks (later Noyes) estate.[67] The farms—Fullamoor, Lower Town, Upper Town, and Ridges—having 250 to 300 acres each were comparatively large for the county.[68] The manor and lordship of Clifton Hampden, which was in fact these four farms, amounted in 1815 to 1,093 acres and was valued at £1,492 a year, and between 1785 and 1832 it was assessed for land-tax purposes at £70 a year.[69] There were nine other small proprietors paying together another £10 of the tax.[70]

There is no evidence that inclosure resulted in de-

[51] See above, p. 20; O.R.O. Wi/IV/iii/7.
[52] *Hearth Tax Oxon.* 54.
[53] E 179/255/4.
[54] *Hearth Tax Oxon.* 54; some details in the printed version are inaccurate.
[55] Compton Census.
[56] Gibbs Pps. at the Manor House, Clifton Hampden: copy of 1405 deed.
[57] Bodl. MS. Rawl. B 518, f. 59b.
[58] Ibid. ff. 68b, 75.
[59] Ibid. ff. 59b–108.   [60] Ibid.
[61] Ibid.; d.d. Cooper & Caldecott c 56(17).

[62] Bodl. MS. Rawl. B 518, ff. 59b–60.
[63] d.d. Cooper & Caldecott c 56(17).
[64] Arthur Young writing in 1809 says 39 years before: Young, *Oxon. Agric.* 91; Christ's Hospital deed 1006 d; J. A. Gibbs, *Hist. of Anthony and Dorothea Gibbs*, 39.
[65] O.R.O. Wi IX/3.
[66] Ibid.; Young, *Oxon. Agric.* 132, 154, 165, 176, 185, 243, 300–1.
[67] O.R.O. Land tax assess.
[68] Gibbs Pps.
[69] Ibid.; O.R.O. Land tax assess.
[70] O.R.O. Land tax assess.

population, although precise population figures are not available for the 18th century. In 1793 the principal farmers maintained that population had increased rather than diminished[71] and the Census Reports show a steady rise between 1801 and 1871.[72] The parish registers suggest that many families mentioned in 1726 had died out or removed and had been replaced by others.[73] There may have been some emigration in the 1830's, for there was much unemployment in the village: expenditure on the poor rose from £88 in 1803 to £177 in 1835.[74] By 1854 expenditure had fallen to little over £100.[75] Agricultural wages, as elsewhere in Oxfordshire, were low: the standard rate in 1793 for dayworkers was 1s. 2d. a day, 1s. 6d. at haytime and 2s. at harvest; many, however, worked at task rates.[76] To provide work a brickworks was started on the Heath by H. H. Gibbs, the lord of the manor,[77] and two bricklayers were recorded in the 1851 census. Other trades included carpenters (one the keeper of the Plough Inn), a builder, who kept the 'Fleur de Lys', four shoemakers of the same family, three blacksmiths, again of one family, a basket-maker, a dress-maker, a baker, and a grocer. The railway provided some work to labourers and porters, and there were the four farms employing labourers.[78]

In 1867 the condition of cottages in the village was described in a government report as 'fair', and the principal owner was said to have 'every desire' that it should be good; all the cottages had gardens and some farm labourers had allotments for potatoes. The supply of water to the cottages was under examination and by 1868 some improvements had been made in sanitation after an outbreak of typhoid had been caused by an open ditch carrying the sewage of a large boarding school and some adjacent cottages.[79] At this period the Gibbs family were steadily buying up houses and land in the parish. In 1879, for example, H. H. Gibbs bought the holding (63 a.) of the Parsons family,[80] and by 1904 only three houses, one being the Vicarage, were not owned by the lord of the manor. As elsewhere farms were being amalgamated: one tenant occupied two of the parish's four farms, Upper and Home farms, and so farmed 473 acres. There were 50 cottages and 13 houses besides the farmhouses; the brick-kiln and smithy were still in use and a Co-operative Wholesale Society shop had been opened.[81] At the last census (1901) there had been 290 inhabitants. The population continued to fluctuate around this figure in the first three decades of the century. By 1951 it had dropped to 271.[82]

In 1939 and in the 1950's there were two farmers, Home, Upper Town, and Lower Town farms being occupied by one tenant, Fullamoor farm by an-

other.[83] Mixed farming remained characteristic of Clifton in the 20th century, although the bias lay towards arable farming and there was little increase in the number of cattle kept. Sheep were kept, 50 and under for every 100 acres. The main arable crops were wheat, barley, beans, and oats, and in 1914 potatoes were considered to be highly successful.[84]

CHURCH. The chapel of Clifton was a daughter chapel to Dorchester Abbey and formed part of the abbey's endowment. The main endowment of the abbey consisted of churches of the hundred of Dorchester, the endowment no doubt going back to Saxon times. Until 1140 the abbey was a foundation of secular canons, but about that time the canons were suppressed by Bishop Alexander and the endowments transferred to Augustinian canons.[85] It is likely that there was a building on the site of the present church in Saxon times and that it was served by the prebendaries of Dorchester.[86] The first mention of the chapel seems to be in 1146 when Pope Eugenius III confirmed the possessions of Dorchester Abbey. The confirmation mentions six daughter churches, including Clifton.[87] The chapel is again mentioned in 1163 when the abbey's right to Clifton with its tithes along with the abbey's other chapels was confirmed.[88] Unlike most of Dorchester's 'chapels', Clifton apparently did not have full parochial rights until the 19th century. It is called a parish in the mid-16th century; it had its own churchwardens then,[89] and in 1578 its parish registers begin. But in the 16th century its church is, also, called a chapel, in 1714 a chapel-of-ease of Dorchester, and in 1817 'a chapel for the tenants' of the manor.[90]

In 1625 Clifton is recorded as having no churchyard,[91] and apparently baptisms and burials took place at Dorchester, as it was agreed they should still do in 1797.[92] In 1819, when Clifton got its own churchyard, full parochial status was probably attained.[93] In the Middle Ages Clifton was subject only to the abbey's jurisdiction and was exempt from episcopal and archidiaconal control. The Reformation inevitably affected the administration of the chapel. After the dissolution of the abbey Dorchester church and its daughter churches retained their separate jurisdiction as the peculiar of Dorchester, which held its own court, dealing with wills, administrations, marriage licences, presentments, and the like.[94] The peculiar probably ceased to exist about 1847, when Clifton became part of Cuddesdon deanery, but earlier in the century, because the living had been augmented by Queen Anne's Bounty (see below), Clifton came under the jurisdiction of the bishop, although not that of the

[71] O.R.O. Wi IX/3.
[72] V.C.H. Oxon. ii. 219. The 1851 and 1861 figures were swollen by the residents of a private boarding-school.
[73] Par. Recs.
[74] Young, Oxon. Agric. 53; 2nd Rep. of Poor Law Commrs. H.C. 595-II, p. 294 (1836), xxix (2).
[75] Poor Law Unions, H.C. 81, p. 5 (1854), lv.
[76] O.R.O. Wi IX/3.
[77] Local inf.
[78] H.O. 107/1688/4.
[79] Agriculture (Employment of Women and Children), app. pt. ii, H.C. 4202-I, p. 353 (1868-9), xiii.
[80] Gibbs Pps.
[81] d.d. Bullingdon b 33; cf. b 34, a 3: 1912, 1924 lists.
[82] V.C.H. Oxon. ii. 219; Census, 1921, 1931; 1951 (Eccl. Areas).

[83] Kelly, Dir. Oxon. (1939); local inf. Upper Town Farm ceased to be a farm about 1920.
[84] Orr, Oxon. Agric. 27, 204, maps between pp. 196-7, 200-1, 211-12, 219-20; Kelly, Dir. Oxon. (1939).
[85] V.C.H. Oxon. ii. 87.   [86] O.A.S. Rep. 1909, 15.
[87] Reg. Antiquiss. i. 247.
[88] O.A.S. Rep. 1909, 11-12.
[89] Chant. Cert. 29, 120.
[90] Ibid. 102; Hearne, Remarks, iv. 355; J. A. Gibbs, Hist. of Antony and Dorothea Gibbs (1922), 320. See ibid. 447-50, for history of the church.
[91] Oxon. Peculiars, 107.
[92] Gibbs, op. cit. 449.
[93] Gibbs, op. cit. Further Additions and Corrections (1927), p. xvi (11).
[94] Oxon. Peculiars, p. x; see below, p. 53.

archdeacon. It was visited by the bishop in 1802, and again from 1834 onwards,[95] and he began to license its curates in 1830.[96]

From its foundation the church was appropriated to Dorchester and there never was an endowed vicarage. The living in the post-Reformation period was thus apparently a pure donative, i.e. the patron could appoint to the living without presentation of his nominee to the bishop.[97] This remained so until the early 19th century. By 1808, after being augmented by Queen Anne's Bounty, it had become a perpetual curacy.[98] Since 1868 it has been called a vicarage.[99] Dorchester retained the rectory, that is all the income from the church and the responsibility of appointing and paying the chaplain, until the dissolution of the abbey in 1536. It appears that the abbey had begun to grant leases of the rectory in the early 16th century, for in the 1520's it was in the hands of William Yonge of Little Wittenham.[1] In 1535 the parish was farmed for £9.[2] At the Dissolution the rectory was acquired by the Crown, but in 1542 was granted to the Cathedral Church of St. Mary, Oseney, Oxford, as an endowment for the new bishopric of Oxford.[3] The scheme to make St. Mary's the cathedral church of the new diocese did not, however, materialize, and the Crown consequently retained the rectory. In 1545 the Crown sold it to John Pollard and George Rythe.[4] About 1591 Pollard granted a 21 years' lease of the rectory to Robert Baker and John Cox, to begin in 1593,[5] but in 1604 Pollard and his son Lewis Pollard gave a 21 years' lease to John Cox of Abingdon, yeoman. Cox was to pay a fee of £250 and a rent of £25 a year. He was to receive all tithes, but had to provide a curate.[6] In 1615 James I licensed Lewis Pollard to sell the rectory to Anthony Peisley and Richard Allam;[7] but Pollard did not dispose of the rectory and the advowson to Peisley until 1629. The price was £500, the yearly value being stated as £38.[8] Yet in 1663 the yearly value of the rectory was put at £85.[9] The Peisleys, a yeoman family of Clifton, retained possession of the rectory until 1727, when Robert Hucks purchased it from another Anthony Peisley, an Oxford bookseller. The Hucks family kept it until 1814, when it passed by bequest of Robert Hucks (II) to Anne Noyes, and similarly to the Gibbs family, in whose hands the rectory and advowson remain.[10] Tithes were extinguished by a deed of merger under the Tithe Act of 1836.[11]

The value of the living has varied greatly from time to time, and to some extent has depended upon the whim of the impropriator. In 1526 it was worth £5 6s. 8d.[12] In 1656 the curate received £12,[13] but this was the highest sum paid until the end of the

18th century, for by the grant of 1545 the impropriator was required to pay only £5 6s. 8d.[14] About the beginning of the Hanoverian period the impropriator paid the curate a pittance of £6 10s. a year; in 1739 rather more than £10 was paid.[15] George Powell received £30 when appointed to the curacy, and this was increased to 50 guineas in 1806; in 1815 the stipend was further augmented to £80 a year.[16] The increased income was obtained by various means. In 1801 Queen Anne's Bounty set aside £200 for Clifton; in 1819–21 £2,100 more to meet benefactions mainly from the patrons,[17] whilst Anne Noyes made the stipend of £80 a permanent charge on Fullamoor farm. Other benefactions brought the funds of the living to £3,170 by 1830. After 1850 the funds were further enlarged by bequests from the Gibbs family[18] and by the difference in the value of the two houses exchanged in 1905. The result was that in 1913 the funds stood at £11,907, together with a rent charge of £100, bringing the gross income to £457.[19] After 1920 the vicar's stipend was further increased by the yearly interest from £100, bequeathed by a former vicar, N. C. S. Poyntz, in trust to the Oxford Diocesan Board.[20]

Before about 1140 Clifton was supposedly served by one of the prebendaries of Dorchester.[21] After the abbey's refoundation until the Reformation the chapel was probably often served by canons from the abbey, a fact that explains the almost complete absence of names of pre-Reformation curates.[22] In 1343 there is a reference to a grant to Nicholas, clerk of Clifton; in 1526 Hugo Bunting was curate.[23]

After the Reformation there was no resident minister, the parish being served by whoever was available. Thus at the end of the 16th century the curates of Drayton served Clifton.[24] In the 17th century it was served at different times by the incumbents of Culham, Long Wittenham, and Dorchester. In 1714, because of the smallness of the stipend offered, the minister had 'deserted' and there were said to have been no services for six months. The patron finally prevailed upon George Parry, a Fellow of Oriel College, to take the services, for having married 'foolishly one that hath nothing' he was forced to 'take up with small inconsiderable incomes'.[25]

After Robert Hucks bought the village the chapel was served for a time by the Vicar of North Moreton (Berks.), but later the parish registers from 1754–97 give the names of no fewer than 24 different clergy. In the 1790's only one service a month was being held.[26] However, this was changed after 1797 when George Powell, Fellow of Balliol, began a 33 years' ministry. He lived in Oxford and came over to

---

[95] Oxf. Dioc. d 566, b 39.
[96] Ibid. b 22, f. 134b.
[97] Gibbs, op. cit. 448.
[98] Acct. of Benefices, H.L. (1818), xviii; Oxf. Dioc. b 41.
[99] By 31 & 32 Vict. c 117.
[1] Reg. 2/3/42; P.C.C. 5 Thower: will of Wm. Yonge, proved 1531.
[2] Valor Eccl. (Rec. Com.), ii. 170.
[3] 10th Dep. Kpr's. Rep. App. ii. 250; L. & P. Hen. VIII, xvii, p. 491.
[4] L. & P. Hen. VIII, xx (2), p. 446.
[5] C 28 /T/73.   [6] O.R.O. Wi IV iii/6.
[7] Dunkin MS. 438/1, f. 258.
[8] C 5/405/160.
[9] Oxon. Peculiars, 108.
[10] Gibbs, op. cit. 448–9.
[11] Gibbs, MS. Collect. f. 18.

[12] Subsidy 1526, 252.
[13] C 5/405/155.
[14] Hearne, Remarks, iv. 355–6; vii. 28.
[15] Ibid. 356; Gibbs, Hist. 448–9.
[16] Gibbs, op. cit. 449.
[17] Ibid.; C. Hodgson, Acct. of Queen Anne's Bounty (1845), 197, 198, 323.
[18] See above, p. 20.
[19] Gibbs, op. cit. 449–50.
[20] Char. Com. file 99625.
[21] V.C.H. Oxon. ii. 87.
[22] e.g. Visit. Dioc. Linc. 1420–49, ii. 80.
[23] Christ's Hosp. Abingdon Deeds, no. 200; Subsidy 1526, 252.
[24] O.A.S. Rep. 1918, 189.
[25] Hearne, Remarks, iv. 355–6.
[26] Gibbs, op. cit. 449.

Clifton to conduct services. It is said that a bell was rung to warn parishioners that a service was due when his horse was seen crossing Clifton Heath.[27] In 1802 Powell reported that there was morning service every Sunday, and also on Christmas Day and Good Friday; and that the Holy Sacrament was administered three times a year to seven or eight communicants,[28] but in later years the chapel warden complained of his neglect.[29] After 1830, when Joseph Gibbs was appointed to the living, and until 1923 the church was served by several members of the Gibbs family.[30]

The church of *ST. MICHAEL AND ALL ANGELS* is beautifully situated on a cliff at a bend of the Thames and is approached by a flight of some 30 steps. It consists of a nave with north and south aisles, a chancel, a south chapel, a vestry, and a south porch. There is no tower, but a bell turret rises above the west end of the nave. The church was virtually rebuilt in 1843–4,[31] and there were further substantial alterations between 1864 and 1866.[32]

The surviving arcade on the south side of the nave shows that the old chapel dated from the latter part of the 12th century. A north aisle and a south chapel were added in the 14th century, but the building was still of modest size. Sketches made before the 19th-century rebuilding show it as small and squat, with a continuous sloping roof broken by dormer windows and a wooden bellcote.[33] The dormers lighted a west gallery which was a post-Reformation addition.

During the 18th century the church seems to have suffered badly from neglect. Between 1775 and 1779 it was said to be in a ruinous state.[34] In 1779 John Ridge, churchwarden, was excommunicated for failure to have the church repaired.[35] Repairs costing £112 were, however, carried out under the direction of John Wyatt of Oxford in 1779–80. The south side of the church was partly rebuilt; there were minor repairs to the north side and to the bellcote; and the roof was relaid.[36] The south porch was rebuilt in brick in 1819.[37]

The restoration of 1843–4 was undertaken by Sir Gilbert Scott with funds from a legacy of G. H. Gibbs, supplemented by his widow and son. The cost was £1,800. It amounted almost to a rebuilding, and Scott himself described what he did as 'not a strict restoration', for 'we had hardly anything left to restore—it is rather a refoundation (keeping *in the main* to the old plan)'.[38] The style adopted was that of the early 14th century, and Scott designed an elaborate 'Founder's tomb' for Gibbs on the north side of the chancel.

The additions of 1864–6 were also the work of Scott. The north aisle was enlarged and a vestry and organ chamber were added at its east end.[39] The rebuilt north wall contains three imitation Decorated windows and one genuine Early English lancet re-

used from the old building. Low down on the outer wall near the west end is a 12th-century carving representing a boar hunt. It was probably the tympanum of the original doorway.

In 1899 dormer windows were inserted in the roofs of the north and south aisles.

Externally, little of the medieval fabric remains except the 14th-century south chapel. The interior is a mixture of genuine medieval architecture with the revived Gothic of the Victorian era. The south arcade of the nave consists of four transitional Romanesque arches with foliated capitals and moulded bases. There is a piscina in the wall of the south aisle. At the east end of the aisle a 14th-century arch gives access to the small south chapel. The north aisle is separated from the nave by an arcade of four arches with continuous mouldings. There is no chancel arch, a screen only dividing the chancel from the nave.

The furnishings are all Victorian. In 1864 the chancel, previously used for the incumbent's family, was refitted with stalls and the choir placed there; in the same year the pulpit and reading desk were removed and a new pulpit, forming part of the screen, was inserted; an oak screen erected in 1843–4 was replaced in 1864 by a low screen, and in 1867 the upper part of the screen, made in brass by Hart & Son from a design by Sir G. G. Scott, was put up. The figures of St. Michael and the Angels are by J. F. Redfern. The year 1864 saw also the appearance of a new organ.[40] In 1873–4 the reredos and retable were erected (designer C. Buckeridge, constructor Daniel Bell); the mosaics are by Clayton and Bell.[41] Before 1873 a picture of *Ecce Homo* stood above the stone altar.[42] The east window of the chancel, inserted in 1873, is also by Clayton and Bell.[43] There are two stained-glass windows in the south side of the chancel: the first, a small one, is a representation of St. Michael and is by Pace; the second, inserted in 1913, is to the memory of the Venerable Alfred Pott (1822–1908), vicar 1875–82, and his wife, and is by H. W. Bryans, a pupil of C. E. Kempe.[44] Nearby is a brass commemorating John Lomax Gibbs (vicar 1864–74). A sanctuary light, hanging before the altar, is the gift (1921) of his children who made provision for its continual burning.[45] The 19th-century font of early Gothic style replaces a leaden one melted down and used to repair the roof in the early 19th century.[46] The brass candelabra are Victorian; the church is now lit by electric light, which was installed in 1935.[47] The memorials to the fallen of the two world wars are at the east end of the north aisle; they were dedicated in 1920[48] and 1945. In the chancel is the 'Founder's tomb' commemorating George Henry Gibbs (1785–1842). The only other memorials are brass plates to members of the Gibbs family. In the churchyard, however, is a memorial to the first Lord Aldenham, who died in

[27] Alban Lord Aldenham, *Outline Hist. of Clifton Church* (1927) (a pamphlet).
[28] Oxf. Dioc. d 566.
[29] Gibbs, op. cit. 449.
[30] Ibid. 450. In 1832 Miss Noyes gave the living a house.
[31] Parker, *Guide*, 374–5; Alban Lord Aldenham, *Outline Hist. of Clifton Church*.
[32] Gibbs, MS. Collect. f. 32; MS. Top. Oxon. d 93, ff. 57–58.
[33] See plate facing p. 159; S. Ireland, *Views of the River Thames* (1792), facing p. 40.
[34] *Oxon. Peculiars*, 114–15.
[35] Ibid. 115.

[36] Oxf. Archd. Oxon. b 23, ff. 254–7.
[37] Gibbs, MS. Collect. f. 29.
[38] Letter to Edward Freeman (O.A.H.S. Correspondence, no. 205, at the Ashmolean Museum).
[39] MS. Top. Oxon. d 93, ff. 57–58.
[40] *Outline Hist.*
[41] Ibid.
[42] Gibbs, MS. Collect. f. 32.
[43] *Outline Hist.*   [44] Ibid.
[45] Oxf. Dioc. c 1777, Faculty (1920).
[46] *Outline Hist.*
[47] Oxf. Dioc. c 1777, Faculty.
[48] *Outline Hist.*

1907. It is in the form of a cross with an octagonal base and shaft. It was designed by Walter Tower, nephew and pupil of C. E. Kempe.[49]

There is a chime of five bells—treble, second, third, fourth, tenor. The oldest of these is the tenor, made in 1844 and recast in 1907. The others were inserted in 1907 and are by Mears and Stainbank. The former bells were by C. and G. Mears. In 1552 the chapel had two bells.[50]

The church has little plate, none of it old. A chalice, paten and flagon, all silver-gilt and hall-marked 1844, are by I. J. Keith. Another silver-gilt paten is hall-marked 1863. A modern brass almsdish is undated.[51]

There was no churchyard until 1819, burials taking place at Dorchester. In that year Anne Noyes gave ground for the purpose.[52] A lychgate of carved oak stands at the north entrance to the graveyard; it was erected in 1843–4.

The registers begin in 1578.

NONCONFORMITY. Roman Catholicism was fairly strong in Clifton until about the middle of the 17th century. Lists of recusants in the reigns of James I and Charles I give fourteen names.[53] Most of these belonged to the Princes, a yeoman family which intermarried with the Days of Dorchester, another papist yeoman family, who were widespread in the neighbourhood.[54] In the 1620's George Prince served as churchwarden, but this may have been a case of co-operation between the churches,[55] and in 1641, of the twelve recusants listed in Clifton, nine were members of this family.[56] Until the 1670's they were constantly presented by the churchwardens for not attending church;[57] the Compton Census of 1676 listed four papists; and in the late 17th and early 18th centuries several members of the family were Roman Catholics.[58] The last record found of the recusancy of this family in Clifton was in 1720, when George Prince and his son John were stated to be Roman Catholics.[59]

There is no record of Protestant dissent until the 19th century: in 1802 there was said to be none,[60] but in 1833 the house of James Styles was registered for nonconformist worship,[61] and in about 1846 dissent was strengthened by the foundation of Crake's school, whose master and pupils were mainly nonconformist.[62] The farmer who owned the buildings was also a nonconformist, and in 1854 his family, another family, and the school were said to contain about 100 dissenters.[63] There continued to be a large group of dissenters until the school was removed in 1868. By 1878 only eleven were left.[64]

SCHOOLS. There is no record of any school in Clifton before the beginning of the 19th century, although the register of marriages shows that a fair number of people were able to write. In 1802 there was a school where children learned the catechism,[65] and in 1808 it was recorded that the poor 'upon such terms as suit them'[66] sent their children to a dame to learn to read.[67] By 1818 there were two schools, one for 15 children and the other for 6 or 7 infants.[68] The first lapsed and was restarted later. In 1833 it had 20 pupils and there were 12 in the infant school.[69] A Sunday school had been begun in 1828.

Crake's school, a private academy, seems to have been opened in 1846. It occupied the 18th-century house in Watery Lane, the stables and coach-house being converted into dormitories. In the 1850's it was known as a commercial school and was managed by a dissenter with about 30 pupils.[70] In 1866 it was called a grammar school and had about 30 boys, most of them dissenters.[71] About 1868 the school removed from the village because of a fever outbreak.[72]

The present village school for boys and girls was established in 1847,[73] under a trust deed dated 15th October. It was affiliated to the National Society. A new schoolroom for 100 children and a master's house were erected at the expense of William Gibbs, brother of G. H. Gibbs, the late lord of the manor.[74] In 1854 there was one room for boys and girls and another for infants, where girls were taught needlework in the afternoons.[75] There was also an evening school in winter, which it is said had not the desired effect, partly for want of an efficient master.[76]

In 1871 there were 75 children attending the National school,[77] but this number decreased to about 60 between 1887 and 1906.[78] The lighting and ventilation were improved in 1894,[79] and in 1909 an infants' room was added on the south side.[80] The attendance had increased to 70 by 1929[81] and in the autumn of 1934 the school was reorganized as a junior school for children up to the age of 11 years, the senior children being transferred to Dorchester.[82] There were 30 children in 1938 including some from Burcot. In 1948 children from Culham junior school went to Clifton and there were 54 children on the school-roll in 1954. The school was changed from aided to controlled status in 1951.[83]

CHARITIES. Leonard Wilmott, by deed of 1608, gave a rent charge of £1 issuing out of lands in Clanfield to be distributed on Good Friday to the unrelieved poor of Clifton Hampden. The gift was regulated by a charity decree of 1617, and was being

[49] *Outline Hist.*
[50] *Ch. Bells Oxon.* 96–97.
[51] Evans, *Ch. Plate.*
[52] Gibbs, op. cit. *Further Additions and Corrections* (1927), p. xvi (11). For Noyes see above, pp. 20, 24.
[53] Salter, *Oxon. Recusants, passim.*
[54] See below, p. 62; *V.C.H. Oxon.* v, 237, 248. For Princes and Days see Davey, *Catholic Family,* 16–20.
[55] *Oxon. Peculiars,* 106–8.
[56] E 179/164/482.
[57] *Oxon. Peculiars,* 105–12.
[58] Stapleton, *Cath. Miss.* 245; O.R.O. Cal. Q. Sess. ix. 602.
[59] O.R.O. Cal. Q. Sess. ix. 466, 476, 779.
[60] Oxf. Dioc. d 566.
[61] Ibid. c 645, f. 214.
[62] See below.
[63] *Wilb. Visit.*
[64] Oxf. Dioc. c 332, c 344.
[65] Ibid. c 327, p. 245.
[66] Ibid. d 707.
[67] Gibbs, MS. Collect. f. 3.
[68] *Educ. of Poor,* 721.
[69] *Educ. Enq. Abstract,* 744.
[70] H.O. 107/1688/4; *Wilb. Visit.*
[71] Oxf. Dioc. c 332.
[72] Gibbs Pps. at the Manor House, Clifton Hampden.
[73] Kelly, *Dir. Oxon.* (1887).
[74] J. A. Gibbs, *Pedigree of Gibbs Family* (1932), 27.
[75] *Wilb. Visit.*
[76] Ibid.
[77] *Elem. Educ. Ret.* 318.
[78] *Vol. Sch. Ret.* 19; Kelly, *Dir. Oxon.* (1887).
[79] Gibbs Pps.
[80] Plan at Sch. Ho.
[81] Min. of Educ. Sch. file.
[82] Ibid.
[83] Inf. Oxon. Educ. Cttee.

regularly administered in 1823.[84] Since 1865 the money has been distributed with the Noyes charity,[85] and since 1933 a single body of trustees has administered it with the Noyes and Talbot charities.[86]

Mrs. Anne Noyes, of Gloucester Place, Marylebone (Lond.), by will proved 1842, left £1,000 to be distributed in clothing, coal, or bread to the poor of the parish.[87] In 1931 and in 1955 the income of this and Wilmott's charity (£25–£26 together) was spent on coal.[88]

The Revd. Joseph Gibbs, a former perpetual curate, by will proved 1864, left £556 stock, the interest to be applied to the salary of an organist in Clifton Hampden church.[89] The income (£14) was so spent between 1926 and 1931, but in 1953–5 was devoted to church expenses.[90]

Anthony Talbot, of Catford Bridge (Lond.), a native and sometime a sergeant-major in the 2nd Foot Guards, by will dated 1888, gave £15 stock, the interest to be applied to six aged and needy parishioners at Christmas. He desired that the recipients should maintain his parents' graves in the churchyard.[91] In 1905 and again in 1953–5 the income was being applied to graveyard maintenance, but in 1926–31 to six or fewer needy persons according to the terms of the benefaction.[92]

CULHAM

THE parish lies some 7 miles south of Oxford in a bend of the River Thames, which forms its chief boundary, and is of special interest on account of its importance in the Anglo-Saxon and early Norman periods.[1] Geographically the parish divides into three distinct sections: the bulk of it lies between Clifton Hampden and a backwater which branches off from the Thames some 2 miles below Radley and rejoins the main stream at Culham Bridge; Andersey Island, which comprises the area between the backwater and Abingdon; and the Otneys, an area largely meadow land on the right bank of the Thames adjoining the west side of Sutton Courtenay (Berks.). The acreage of the parish is 2,051 and its boundaries appear to have changed but little since late Saxon times when a survey of the parish was made in 940 in the time of King Edmund.[2] The survey mentions the ford where Abingdon Bridge now stands, and refers to 'barrows' at some point along the parish's eastern boundary, but no traces of these remain. The beating of the bounds of the eastern end of the parish was regularly carried out during the Middle Ages and led in 1416 to the institution of legal proceedings by the Abbot of Abingdon against Sir John Drayton of Nuncham. The abbot complained that the Vicar of Culham and his parishioners had been shot at by Sir John and his men, and further that Sir John had erected a fortalice on Culham territory and used it to prevent the vicar and parishioners from making their procession.[3]

The only recorded change of boundary occurred in 1894 when some eyots in the river near Abingdon were transferred to the new civil parish of St. Nicholas, Abingdon.[4]

At its lowest point, in the south east, the parish is 159 feet above sea level, but almost immediately the land rises sharply to 175 feet, thus forming a kind of escarpment along the river bank. Just east of the backwater the ground rises steadily to form Culham Hill, which at its peak is 250 feet above sea level. From the top of the hill the land descends once more

until it meets the Thames again 170 feet above sea level.[5]

The soil is mainly Lower Greensand; but between the Dorchester–Abingdon road and the Thames there is a good deal of Gault, whilst Andersey consists largely of Kimmeridge Clay and Alluvium.[6]

The main Dorchester–Abingdon road runs through the parish from east to west. This highway is said to have existed from 'time immemorial'.[7] It crosses into Andersey Island via Culham New Bridge, erected in 1928 by the Oxfordshire County Council. Until then, Culham Old Bridge, which lies slightly to the south of the present bridge, was in use. The old bridge, now scheduled as an ancient monument, was part of a considerable scheme for improving communications between Abingdon and Dorchester.[8] Between 1416 and 1422 Abingdon Bridge, Culham Bridge, and the causeway across Andersey were erected by the Abingdon Guild of the Holy Cross.[9] Culham Old Bridge, built across the site of an ancient ford known as Culham Hythe,[10] is of stone and has five Perpendicular arches. It has been much altered and repaired during the passage of the centuries and was chiefly maintained by Christ's Hospital, Abingdon.[11] During the Second World War two concrete pill boxes were built on the bridge and part of the parapet was taken down to make room for a concrete platform. These have now been removed and the parapet restored. The causeway also was maintained by the Guild of the Holy Cross and its successor, Christ's Hospital,[12] yet the expenditure of money was insufficient to keep the road in good condition. In fact, during the 16th and 17th centuries the whole of the road from Dorchester to Abingdon was badly neglected. In 1736 it is described as being in a ruinous state; but in that year the first of a series of Acts was passed (1736, 1755, 1781, 1802, 1821, 1841) establishing a turnpike trust for the area between Abingdon and Henley and empowering it to levy tolls for the repair and maintenance of the roads.[13] The trust set up toll-gates at

[84] *8th Rep. Com. Char.* H.C. 13, p. 493 (1823), viii; *10th Rep. Com. Char.* H.C. 103, p. 358 (1824), xiii.
[85] Char. Com. Clifton Hampden G. file; Accts. file.
[86] Ibid. Clifton Hampden G. File.
[87] Ibid. file 8867.   [88] Ibid. Accts. file.
[89] Ibid. file 32201.   [90] Ibid. Accts. file.
[91] Ibid. file 83838.   [92] Ibid. Accts. file.
[1] See below, pp. 30, 31.   [2] *Saxon Oxon.* 22–24.
[3] *Cal. Pat.* 1416–22, 79–80; C 1/6/219; *Chron. Abingdon,* ii. 231.
[4] Order of Local Govt. Board, no. 31930 (21 Nov. 1894).
[5] O.S. Map 6″, xlv (1883); 2½″, 41/49, 59 (1949).

[6] *V.C.H. Oxon.* i, Geological map.
[7] *Cal. Pat.* 1416–22, 33–34.
[8] For the Dorchester section of this road see below, p. 40.
[9] J. Townsend, *Hist. of Abingdon,* 52–53; *V.C.H. Berks.* iv. 435, 439.   [10] Townsend, *Abingdon,* 52.
[11] Inf. the late Miss Agnes Baker of Abingdon from the Hospital's deeds. For a view see plate facing p. 93.
[12] Inf. Miss Baker.
[13] 9 Geo. II, c. 14; 28 Geo. II, c. 42; 21 Geo. III, c. 77; 42 Geo. III, c. 60 (local and personal act); 1 & 2 Geo. IV, c. 26 (loc. & pers. act); 4 & 5 Vict. c. 100 (loc. & pers. act). Cf. below, p. 40.

Culham Bridge and at the junction of Thame Lane with the main highway. The toll-houses are still standing. Most of the highway was freed from toll in 1873,[14] but the section between Culham and Abingdon remained liable to toll until 1875.[15] The highway is joined near one of the old toll-houses by Thame Lane, which after crossing Clifton Heath used to enter the parish near its north-east corner. This road, which is also probably very old, was cut by the creation in 1941 of the Royal Naval Air Station[16] and terminates at a small railway bridge. The highway is also joined by a road connecting the village with Sutton Courtenay. This road crosses the Thames by a bridge erected in 1807.[17] The bridge had been suggested in 1802 as part of a scheme for a new turnpike road from Culham to Streatley via Didcot and Hagbourne;[18] but the opposition was powerful, existing turnpike trusts objecting strongly to the proposal.[19] When the bridge was at last authorized by Parliament the Act stipulated that it should be built 'at or near' Culham Ferry, empowered the proprietors to raise from £4,000 to £7,000 for building costs, and fixed toll rates.[20] The bridge, built by Edward Clarke of Barrington (Glos.), cost only £1,765,[21] although more money may have been spent on the approaches. It has three arches over the main stream and is made of rubble with ashlar dressings. In 1809 it was extended to cover the new Culham Cut.[22] In 1939 the bridge was purchased from the proprietors for £4,500 by the Oxfordshire and Berkshire County Councils in equal shares.[23] When the bridge was made the road to it from Culham village was constructed also.[24] This previously ran to the ferry and was slightly to the west of the present road. Before the building of the bridge the ferry was the only means of direct contact with Sutton Courtenay. The main village street is part of a long loop beginning at the Waggon and Horses Inn and ending at Culham Bridge. The section linking the village green with the bridge is relatively new; it was provided for in the inclosure award and seems to have been first planned in 1808.[25] Before its construction a road running close to the west side of Culham House linked the green with the main highway and thence continued north-east behind Thame Lane and across country to Nuneham.[26] This road too was stopped,[27] but traces of it can still be seen.

The Thames has always been an important means of communication for Culham though little is known with certainty about its history before the Tudor period. Until the early 11th century the arm of the river between Andersey Island and Culham was apparently the main route for transport; but the flow of water is said to have been diverted by Abingdon Abbey into the branch or branches of the river by Abingdon

so that the stream ran closer to the abbey.[28] Leland when writing of this noted that the 'other arme' of the Thames that flowed under Culham Bridge was then the lesser of the two streams and that at floodtime the old bottom of the Thames was filled and that there were then three streams.[29] Obstructions on the river rendered navigation increasingly difficult in the Middle Ages and probably increased the use of the highway. Stone from Taynton quarries, for instance, for the building of Eton College passed through Culham by road and was not loaded upon barges until it reached Henley.[30] In the 16th century the river was certainly navigable from Henley to Burcot; and from there, although with some difficulty, to Culham. The wharfage for Abingdon, in fact, was at Culham,[31] for the passage from Culham to Abingdon via Sutton Courtenay was very tricky. Stones and lead from the dissolved abbey of Abingdon were brought by road to Culham wharf for loading upon barges.[32] But the increased size of barges during the Tudor period meant that the Thames between Oxford and Burcot was virtually innavigable by the end of the reign of Elizabeth I. Hence the establishment of the Oxford–Burcot Commission by Acts of 1605 and 1624 to improve the river between these two places.[33] The commission did not make use of the present course of the river via Abingdon; instead the barge traffic was carried along the backwater between Andersey and Culham Hill, known in early Tudor times as Purden's stream,[34] and from late Tudor times until the early 19th century as Swift Ditch. This passage was deepened, and a pound lock was built about 1636 in a new cutting at the north end.[35] The old lock can still be seen. There was a flash lock about half way along Swift Ditch, which is mentioned about 1585.[36] The passage along Swift Ditch, however, seems to have been difficult near Culham Bridge, and in 1641 there was talk of constructing a lock or weir there.[37] The project never materialized, perhaps because of the outbreak of the Civil War in 1642. Swift Ditch remained the main navigation channel until 1790, when the present route through Abingdon was brought into use by the Thames Navigation Commissioners.[38] Extensive alterations were made in 1790 involving the construction of a pound lock near Abingdon, the building of a towing path along the Thames and the consequent blocking of several streamlets and eyots, and the dismantling of the tackle at Swift Ditch lock.[39] The water passage through Culham was further improved by the construction of the Culham Cut and lock in 1809, which enabled the difficult route through Sutton Courtenay to be avoided.[40] The Cut was made partly along the line of the old Speel Ditch, a straggling channel that

[14] 36 & 37 Vict. c. 90.
[15] 37 & 38 Vict. c. 95.
[16] See below, p. 31.
[17] 47 Geo. III, sess. 2, c. 43 (loc. & pers. act).
[18] Bodl. G.A. Oxon. b 113(27).
[19] Ibid. (28).
[20] 47 Geo. III, sess. 2, c. 43 (loc. & pers. act).
[21] Inf. Mr. P. Walne, Berks. archivist.
[22] F. S. Thacker, The Thames Highway, Locks and Weirs, 170.
[23] O.R.O. Copy of deed of conveyance.
[24] Ibid.
[25] O.R.O. Cal. Q. Sess. ix. 649.
[26] Davis, Oxon. Map.
[27] O.R.O. Incl. award.
[28] Chron. Abingdon, i. 480.

[29] Leland, Itin. ed. Toulmin Smith, v. 76.
[30] D. Knoop and D. P. Jones, The Building of Eton Coll. 1442–60, 15, reprint from Trans. Quatuor Coronati Lodge, xlvi (1933).
[31] Inf. Miss A. Baker from the Hospital deeds.
[32] L. & P. Hen. VIII, xiii (1), pp. 375–6.
[33] 3 Jas. I, c. 20; 21 Jas. I, c. 32. See also below, p. 65.
[34] S.C. 6/109, m. 8d.
[35] Wards 10/55 (pt. 2); F. S. Thacker, The Thames, A General Hist. 67, 77–78.
[36] Thacker, Locks and Weirs, 147.
[37] Ibid.; Bodl. MS. Twyne-Langbaine 1, ff. 71–71b.
[38] Thacker, Locks and Weirs, 144.
[39] Reading Public Libr., Treacher Papers, Ledger 1789–97, f. 111.
[40] Thacker, Locks and Weirs, 167.

left the Thames at the head of the present cut and turned south near the site of Culham lock to rejoin the river close to Sutton Mill.[41] The Cut was first suggested in August 1801.[42] In 1806 the estimated cost was £5,485, but the actual amount spent was £9,000.[43]

The railway line from Didcot to Oxford runs through the eastern fringe of the parish. The railway, first considered in 1833,[44] was not constructed for some years, largely owing to the opposition of the University and City of Oxford.[45] It was completed in 1844. The station, originally called 'Abingdon Road', was renamed Culham in 1856.[46]

Culham village is situated chiefly on both sides of the southern part of the loop road.[47] It got its Old English name (*Cula's hamm*) from its position in a bend of the Thames.[48] The church lies at the west end of the village green and just south of it is the manor-house. The village was rebuilt in 1869–70[49] and therefore contains few old houses or cottages. In fact, only one of the original cottages remains, now the village store. It is of 17th-century origin and was refronted during the 18th century. A new housing estate of 26 houses at the east end of the village was completed in 1952. At the extreme western end of the parish, by the side of the Maud Hales Bridge, Abingdon, are two gabled houses apparently erected between 1685 and 1694.[50]

The oldest building in the village is Culham Manor, which was originally the medieval grange of the Abbots of Abingdon.[51] The house is largely of 15th-century date, but in 1610 the north front was rebuilt by Thomas Bury,[52] who had the date and his initials carved on his new classical central porch. The present north front of two stories is the surviving portion of Bury's façade and ends just to the left of his porch. There was formerly a left wing to match the present 15th-century right wing, and though it was pulled down, perhaps during or after the Civil War, traces of it remain. There is a ground-floor north window of this date in a semi-detached cottage now joined to the main building by a low modern wall, and others of the same date in a garden wall. Whether the medieval grange was as large as the 17th-century house it is now impossible to say, but it seems certain that there was an earlier building on the site of Bury's east wing which may or may not have been connected to the main 15th-century building. Part of the tracery of a Perpendicular window remains. Skelton writing in 1823 said there were 'cruciform openings . . . such as are common in ancient castellated walls', but did not state where these were;[53] and there was no trace of them in 1959.

From the existing remains of the 15th-century building it seems certain that the kitchen was at the north end of the present west wing: its open fireplace and chimney-stack remain. A contemporary hatch leads into what must have been the medieval hall. This was open to the roof. Mortice holes for the

medieval floor joists and the wall-plate of the old roof remain where Bury raised the roof and put in the present first floor. On the first floor behind the porch there is a finely proportioned room with Jacobean panelling which was later used as a court room. The south front and the west wing, once covered with plaster, have been restored to their original 15th-century condition: the structure is stone built up to the first floor and is then half-timbered. The windows of the left wing, although mostly restored, are in their original positions and the wooden mullions of two of them are ancient. According to tradition the abbots of Abingdon used the house as a place of retirement, and the room at the head of a 15th-century ladder staircase, made of rectangular blocks of oak built into the walls one above and beyond the other, is known as the abbot's chamber and once had some heraldic glass depicting the arms of Abbot Coventry (d. 1512).[54] A portion of the linenfold panelling in one of the upper rooms was found in the house, but the rest of the Tudor panelling in the house has been brought from elsewhere.

The walled garden on the north side has a cobbled path leading from the north porch to the church opposite, which is probably contemporary with Thomas Bury's house. There is also an early-17th-century sundial on a stone column which appears to be considerably older than the sundial. On the south side there was once an avenue of walnut trees leading down to the river. In the grounds is a dove-cot, reputed to be one of the three largest in England. It bears the initials C.B. (Cecil Bisshopp) and the date 1685.[55]

When in the 1660's the manor passed from the Bury family to the Bisshopps the manor-house, which in 1665 was assessed on ten hearths,[56] gradually became dilapidated. Until about 1749 it was apparently occupied by the lord's steward; after that it became a farmhouse, occupied in turn by the Welch and Mundy families.[57] The present occupier, Sir Esmond Ovey, has restored it as far as possible to its original state.

Culham House or Rectory, now the largest house in the village, stands to the north of the green. It is a Georgian mansion, and was probably built by John Phillips (1709–75), who was lay rector of Culham and a master builder in London.[58] It is a three-storied structure of red brick with a hipped roof of tiles. It now consists of seven bays, but originally there were only five. The extension took place either at the end of the 18th century or in the early 19th, when the doorway was moved to a new centre bay. The interior has contemporary staircases, overmantles, and doorcases. To the north-east is a stable block. The grounds are surrounded by an early 19th-century brick wall, erected after the inclosure of the parish when the road system was altered. There are traces in the grounds of the old rectorial mansion, presumably demolished by John Phillips;[59]

[41] Ibid. 167–8.
[42] Berks. R.O. D/TC.5: Minutes Thames Nav. Comrs. v. 107.
[43] Ibid. 368; Reading Libr. Treacher Pps. *Rep. of Survey of Thames* (1811), 16.
[44] E. T. MacDermot, *Hist. G.W.R.* i (1), 175.
[45] Ibid. 176, 178, 180.   [46] Ibid. 180.
[47] O.S. Map 25″, xlv. 10, 11 (1875).
[48] *P.N. Oxon.* (E.P.N.S.), i. 150–1.
[49] Dates on houses.
[50] Christ's Hospital, Abingdon, Cal. of leases, nos. 881, 882.

[51] See below, p. 32.
[52] For an account of the house see *Country Life*, 14 July 1950, 132–4; MS. account by Sir Esmond Ovey, Culham Manor. For a view see plate facing p. 14.
[53] Skelton, *Oxon.* Dorchester Hund. 1–2.
[54] *Par. Coll.* i. 109–10.
[55] For Bisshopp see below, p. 32.
[56] *Hearth Tax Oxon.* 54.
[57] d.d. Par. Culham b 3–4.
[58] Cf. *Diary of Mrs. Lybbe Powys*, ed. Emily J. Climenson (1899), 153.   [59] See below, p. 36.

it was not a large house, for it returned only four hearths for the hearth tax of 1665.[60] A pond at one time stood in the grounds before the main entrance.[61] The house was once noted for its collection of china, ancient painted glass, and pictures.[62]

The Vicarage stands between the main highway and the village street. It is said to have been built by Benjamin Kennicott, Vicar of Culham (1753–83), about 1758,[63] and is undoubtedly of 18th-century origin. In 1816 it was reported to be dilapidated, and was accordingly refronted on the south side during that year.[64] It was enlarged in 1849.[65]

The Diocesan Training College for Schoolmasters stands on the main Abingdon–Dorchester highway close to the junction with Thame Lane. Designed by Joseph Clarke of London, it was erected in 1852.[66] The college consisted at first of a three-sided block and a practising school in the grounds, but substantial additions have been made during the present century. The old building, which is in the Gothic style, has been much altered and adapted in recent years.[67]

An old tithe barn was demolished in 1849.[68]

The parish now has three inns. The 'Waggon and Horses' was apparently rebuilt in the early 1800's, but can be traced back to at least 1795.[69] The 'Lion', formerly the 'Sow and Pigs', is a fairly modern building, but it too can be traced back to 1795.[70] The 'Railway Hotel' was built about 1846. A fourth inn, the 'Nag's Head', on Abingdon Bridge, was in Culham parish until 1894 when it was transferred to Abingdon. It was built about 1714.[71] In the later 18th century there were five or six malt-houses in Culham, some no doubt in cottages.[72]

Of the outlying farmhouses Rye Farm is historically the most interesting. Its Old English name means 'at the island', i.e. Andersey Island.[73] Its buildings, except for an 18th-century barn, are of 19th-century date, but it is possible that they are on the site of the palace of the Anglo-Saxon kings (see below). Leland says that in his time there was a barn on the site of this palace and that the common people still called the place the 'Castelle of the Rhae'.[74] The farm's land is mentioned in 1375–6, in 1440–1, and in Tudor times;[75] a farmhouse was certainly in existence by 1633, when it was tenanted by William Bostock, and was probably there in 1614.[76] About 1724, and again in 1766, it suffered severely from fire.[77]

Warren Farm, lying to the north of Thame Lane, is another 19th-century building, but it must have replaced an older house, for about 1752 William Pead was living there.[78] Both Rye Farm and Warren

Farm, therefore, lay outside the village long before inclosure. Zouche Farm, on the other hand, was probably one of the consequences of inclosure. It did not exist at the time of the award of 1813,[79] but is marked on Bryant's map of Oxfordshire of 1823. Its name suggests that it was built after 1815, for in that year Sir Cecil Bisshopp (1753–1828), 8th baronet and lord of the manor, became Baron Zouche.[80]

Culham was an important place in the Anglo-Saxon period and enjoyed special privileges throughout the Middle Ages. Partly because of its close connexion with Abingdon Abbey, partly because of the charm of its situation, and partly because of the excellent sport it provided, the place was especially favoured by the royal houses of Mercia and Wessex.[81] Offa was the first to build a royal residence on Andersey Island and there his son Egfrith died in 796.[82] The sisters of the Mercian king Coenwulf retreated to Culham to lead a holy life,[83] and c. 1050 a church to St. Andrew was built on the island, which thus acquired its name of *Andresia* or Andersey.[84] Although a few Roman remains have been found by the river near Zouche Farm[85] no Saxon remains have yet been found.

After the Conquest both William I and William II used to stay at the royal hunting lodge on Andersey. The Conqueror in particular delighted in the island's green meadows and recuperated there from blood-letting,[86] but Henry I was persuaded by Queen Maud to return the island to Abingdon and to allow the abbot to use the lead from the many houses on the island for the roof of the abbey church. It appears from the chronicler's account that the stone buildings on the island were already in decay,[87] but local memory of them was still strong when Leland visited Culham. He says that there was once a 'fortres or pile lyke a castle in Andersey' and that it lay almost exactly between the old and new courses of the Thames.[88]

In Stephen's reign Culham was plundered by William Boterel, Constable of Wallingford, although he had taken a bribe from Abbot Ingulf in return for a promise not to attack the abbey's property,[89] and despite the privileged position which Culham undoubtedly enjoyed, both on account of its ancient rights of sanctuary and its immunity from royal and ecclesiastical control, other than that of the abbey. This privileged position may be illustrated by the fact that a claim to exemption from taxation in 1291 was successfully vindicated, and that Culham does not appear on later medieval taxation rolls.[90] Its rights of sanctuary seem to have derived from a wide interpretation of the charter of King Coenwulf of

[60] *Hearth Tax Oxon.* 54.

[61] Oxf. Dioc. a 2(R): map of rectorial lands, 1822.

[62] *Diary of Mrs. Lybbe Powys*, ed. Emily J. Climenson, 153 n; Skelton, *Oxon.* Dorchester Hund. 2. The glass was bought by Sir Esmond Ovey and some of it is still at Culham Manor.

[63] Oxf. Dioc. b 70.

[64] MS. Top. Oxon. c 222, pp. 562–3. In Oxf. Dioc. c 435, pp. 76 sqq. there is a description of the 18th-century house with all its measurements. The surveyor was John Hudson of Oxford, the estimated cost £504 16s.

[65] Oxf. Dioc. b 70.

[66] L. Naylor, *Culham College*, 27–28.

[67] See below, p. 38.

[68] MS. Top. Oxon. c 222, p. 568.

[69] O.R.O. Land tax assess.

[70] Ibid.

[71] Inf. Miss A. Baker.

[72] O.R.O. Victllrs' recog. *passim.*

[73] *P.N. Oxon* (E.P.N.S.), i. 151.

[74] Leland, *Itin.* ed. Toulmin Smith, v. 76.

[75] *P.N. Oxon.* (E.P.N.S.), i. 151; S.C. 6/109, m. 10.

[76] Parham House (Suss.) Pps. Culham deeds, nos. 32, 22.

[77] J. Townsend, *News of a County Town*, 59; B.M. Church Briefs, B viiii II.

[78] d.d. Par. Culham b. 4: Overseers' accts.

[79] O.R.O. Incl. award.

[80] *Complete Peerage* xii, pt. ii. 954.

[81] See below, pp. 31, 35.

[82] *Chron. Abingdon*, ii. 273, where Egfrith is given as Egbert.

[83] Ibid. i. 19–20.

[84] Ibid. i. 474; *P.N. Oxon.* (E.P.N.S.), i. 151.

[85] *V.C.H. Oxon.* i. 298, 335.

[86] *Chron. Abingdon.* ii. 49.

[87] Ibid. 50–51.

[88] Leland, *Itin.* v. 76.

[89] *Chron. Abingdon*, ii. 231.

[90] E 179/161/3.

821.[91] By the late 14th century there was evidently popular opposition to these rights: in 1394 the 'Commons' of Essex petitioned the Crown against the abuse of sanctuary both at Culham and at Colchester,[92] and in 1442 Pope Eugenius IV issued a mandate to the Bishop of Lincoln and others to inquire into abuses at Culham and elsewhere.[93] In 1486 Humphrey Stafford and his brother Thomas, after an abortive attempt at insurrection against Henry VII, sought sanctuary at Culham; but Humphrey was later arrested and the claim disallowed.[94] Despite the decision of the court in Stafford's case men still claimed sanctuary at Culham, a case being recorded as late as 1507.[95]

In the 17th century the proximity of Culham to Abingdon and Oxford meant that the village was inevitably affected by the Civil War, for the bridge across Culham ford was of considerable strategic importance. In the spring of 1643 the royalists had an encampment on Culham Hill;[96] but this was abandoned about 12 June when the troops were withdrawn to Oxford.[97] After the king's forces had left Abingdon in May 1644 the parliamentarians seized Culham Bridge, from which they harried royalist food convoys moving into Oxford.[98] An unsuccessful royalist attempt to recapture and demolish the bridge in January 1645 led to a sharp engagement known as the battle of Culham Bridge, in which the king's commander, Sir Henry Gage, was mortally wounded.[99]

On Culham Heath the Abingdon Races were held annually from the early 1730's until 1811, when inclosure compelled their removal to land west of Abingdon.[1] The site of the course was probably in what is now a large field bounded by the railway line and lying immediately to the north of Thame Lane.

In 1941 a Royal Naval Air Station was commissioned as H.M.S. *Hornbill*. It was closed in 1956, but reopened in the same year as an Admiralty Storage Depot. The depot covers 592 acres and extends into the parishes of Clifton Hampden and Nuneham Courtenay.[2]

A few noteworthy men have been associated with Culham: Nicholas of Culham was Abbot of Abingdon (1289–1306) and left some money for the poor of the parish;[3] Benjamin Kennicott (vicar 1753–83) was an eminent Hebrew scholar and librarian of the Radcliffe Camera, Oxford;[4] and three other clergymen of some distinction were curates of the parish for a time in the 19th century. They were Augustus Short, first Bishop of Adelaide;[5] Herbert Kynaston, hymn-writer and High Master of St. Paul's School;[6]

and Henry Octavius Coxe, Bodley's Librarian 1860–81.[7] The blind philanthropist, Elizabeth Margaret Gilbert, was a granddaughter of Robert Wintle, vicar 1797–1848.[8] A 20th-century vicar (1911–17) was the Oxfordshire antiquary W. J. Oldfield.[9]

MANOR. According to tradition the connexion between Abingdon Abbey and the Culham region was already in existence in the late 8th century. The abbey was then in possession of Andersey Island in Culham and exchanged it for Goosey (Berks.) at the wish of Offa (d. 796), King of Mercia.[10] The Mercian kings used the island as a hunting seat and this caused such inconvenience to the abbey that Abbot Rathanus gave King Coenwulf (796–?821) Sutton Courtenay (Berks.) in part exchange for Andersey.[11] The abbey seems later to have lost possession, for both Athelstan, King of Wessex, and the early Norman kings are said to have resided there.[12] It was not until 1101 that a grant by Queen Maud and another by Henry I restored Andersey to the abbey.[13] The account in the Abingdon Chronicle may be inaccurate in detail, but there is no reason to doubt its general content.

CULHAM itself is first mentioned during the reign of Coenwulf. It was then a royal vill and was granted to the king's two sisters who wished ultimately to bequeath the island to Abingdon Abbey.[14] In the Chronicle are two charters, dated 811 and 821, in which King Coenwulf confirmed the abbey's possessions, including Culham: these charters are certainly spurious, but the weight of tradition in favour of the events described is strong.[15] A second charter of 821 is not mentioned in the Chronicle. Yet this second charter of 821—probably as spurious as the first—is really the more important, for it was confirmed by the Crown on several occasions, viz. in 1336, 1380, 1423, 1470, and 1478.[16] In 940 King Edmund is said to have granted Culham for life to Ælfhild, a royal matron. Abingdon Abbey's consent was obtained by the promise to confirm it in its possession of Watchfield (Berks.)[17] On Ælfhild's death Culham was returned to the abbey and Edmund confirmed the grant.[18]

During the Danish invasions of the 10th century Culham was one of the few possessions which Abingdon Abbey retained.[19] The abbey seems to have lost at least part of Culham at or soon after the Conquest, for about this time William I is stated to have imprisoned Abbot Aldred and to have seized properties of the manor.[20] If so, the properties must

[91] Cf. J. C. Cox, *Sanctuaries and Sanctuary Seekers*, 6–7, 205–7. For Coenwulf's charter see below.
[92] *Rot. Parl.* iii. 321. Abingdon Abbey had a cell at Colne (Essex).
[93] *Cal. Papal L.* ix. 282.
[94] K.B. 27/900, m. 8; Hall, *Chronicle* (1809), 427; Holinshed, *Chronicle* (1808), iii. 484. For this revolt see J. D. Mackie, *The Earlier Tudors*, 66.
[95] Berks. R.O. W/JBC 5.
[96] Luke, *Jnl.* 69, 78, 81.
[97] Ibid. 94.
[98] *Perfect Diurnal* (1643–9), 1644–5, *passim*; Edward Walsingham, *Alter Britanniae Heros* (1645), 21.
[99] *Perfect Diurnal*, 14 Jan. 1644/5; Walsingham, op. cit. 21–22; *Mercurius Aulicus*, 11 Jan. 1644/5; B.M. Pamphlets E 24, nos. 14, 20, 21; *Cal. S.P. Dom.* 1644–5, 246–7. For this battle see also John Vicars, *The Burning Bush* (1645 to 1646), 93–95; Lord Clarendon, *Hist. of the Rebellion*, ed. W. D. Macray, iii. 442–3; Wood, *Life*, i. 113.
[1] J. Townsend, *News of a Country Town*, 62 n.
[2] Inf. Civil Engineer-in-Chief, Admiralty.

[3] *Accts. Obedientiars of Abingdon Abbey* (Camden Soc. N.S. li), 50.   [4] *D.N.B.*
[5] Ibid.   [6] Ibid.
[7] Ibid.   [8] Ibid.
[9] *Who Was Who* (1929–40); for his collections for a history of Culham see MS. Top. Oxon. c. 222.
[10] *Chron. Abingdon*, ii. 273.
[11] Ibid. 274.   [12] Ibid. 49, 276–7.
[13] Ibid. 51–52; *Regesta*, ii, no. 550.
[14] *Cal. Chart. R. 1327–41*, 373; cf. *Chron. Abingdon*, i. 18–19; ii. 274–5; see below, p. 35.
[15] For these charters see F. M. Stenton, *Early History of Abingdon Abbey*, 23; Berks. Arch. Jnl. xxv. 24.
[16] *Cal. Chart. R. 1327–41*, 373–4; *Cal. Pat. 1377–81*, 548; *1422–9*, 133; *1466–77*, 136; *1476–8*, 74. See also Berks. Arch. Jnl. xxv. 26–27.
[17] *Cart. Sax.* ed. Birch, ii, no. 759; *Cod. Dipl.* ed. Kemble, v, no. 1135; *Chron. Abingdon*, i. 91–92.
[18] *Chron. Abingdon*, i. 92–93; *Cod. Dipl.* ed. Kemble, v, no. 1135.   [19] *Chron. Abingdon*, ii. 276.
[20] Berks. Arch. Jnl. xxv. 26–27.

soon have been restored, for it was said that Abbot Rainald (d. 1097) was in possession of Culham and that Abbot Faritius got part of it back in about 1101 from Henry I.[21] This part may have been Andersey, which Henry certainly gave back.[22]

The manor remained in the ownership of the abbey until the dissolution of the abbey in 1538, when it was seized by the Crown, John Hyde being appointed bailiff.[23] In 1539 John Wellesbourne of Mixbury was appointed keeper of the site of Abingdon Abbey and of Culham manor.[24] In 1545 William Bury, a London wool merchant and second son of Edmund Bury of Hampton Poyle, received a grant of the manor of Culham in exchange for Calehill in the Isle of Sheppey and £600.[25] It was to be held as a knight's fee at an annual rent of £51 14s.[26] William Bury died in 1563,[27] and was succeeded by his son John. The latter was buried in Culham church in 1572,[28] leaving as his heir a son Thomas, aged four. Thomas, who refronted the manor-house in 1610,[29] died in 1615, leaving half the manor, including the manor-house, to his widow Judith for life.[30] She was the daughter of the well-known Protestant theologian, Lawrence Humphrey, President of Magdalen College, Oxford, and Dean of Winchester;[31] and after Thomas Bury's death she twice remarried, her third husband being Sir Edmund Cary (d. 1637), a member of a prominent official family,[32] who served at the courts of Elizabeth I, James I, and Charles I.[33]

Thomas Bury, Judith's son, died early in 1615, a few months after his father,[34] and was succeeded by his brother William, who died in 1632.[35] He in turn was followed by his son George, at whose demise in 1662[36] the direct male line of the Burys came to an end. The Burys retained possession of the manor until 1666 when by the marriage of George's daughter and heiress Sarah to Sir Cecil Bisshopp, Bt., of Parham (Suss.), Culham passed to the Bisshopp family.[37] The Bisshopps lived part of the time at Culham, at least until Sarah's death in 1680;[38] but in the 18th century they lived at Parham and were mainly connected with Sussex. Sir Cecil, the 4th baronet, died in 1705, and was succeeded in turn by three namesakes.[39] Sir Cecil Bisshopp, 8th baronet, who succeeded to the baronetcy in 1779, successfully claimed the dormant peerage of Zouche de Haryngworth in 1815;[40] but dying without heirs male in 1828 his estates were divided between his two daughters, the younger, Katharine Arabella, wife of Sir George Brooke-Pechell, Bt.,[41] receiving the Oxfordshire lands of Culham and Newington. The deed of partition is dated 1830.[42] An earlier agreement of 1826 declared that if Lord Zouche died without male heirs the entail male on the Bisshopp estates should be cut off.[43]

In 1856 Culham was sold to James Morrell of Headington, in whose family it remains.[44] The price was £72,750, the estate being indebted at the time to the tune of £40,000.[45]

ECONOMIC AND SOCIAL HISTORY. The medieval economic history of Culham is less fully documented than that of other Oxfordshire parishes, for Abingdon Abbey's special rights over it led to its not being included in Domesday Book, the hundred rolls or the tax lists, and few manorial accounts have survived.[46] Part of the manor[47] was granted in the early 12th century by Abbot Faritius to the lignar.[48] An account roll of the lignar for 1355-6 gives some details about farming in Culham: he received £14 13s. 7½d., of which by far the largest part (£12 19s. 11½d.) came from the sale of grain: 13 qrs. of wheat (frumentum), a little over 17 qrs. of rye, 27 qrs. of barley, 11 qrs. of drage, and 5½ qrs. of pulse.[49] The sale of cheese and butter produced 21s.[50] Expenses amounted to £4 6s. 1d., part of which was for salaries: 7s. to John Day (perhaps the bailiff), 3s. to the keeper of the animals, 2s. 6¼d. to the dairy-keeper, and 9½d. to the pig-keeper.[51]

There is no direct evidence that the parish had a mill of its own, and it may well be that the villagers had to take their corn for grinding to the abbey mill in Abingdon. On the other hand, the fishery, which was probably shared with the neighbouring parish of Sutton Courtenay, was of some importance both in medieval and later times. In the 12th century the abbey got 20 sticks of eels from it and a rental of 3s.[52]

Disputes arose with Sutton over the fishery and the mill. Abbot Faritius obtained a declaration in full shire-moot against turves being taken from Culham for the repair of the king's mill and fishery in Sutton. The order, however, was secretly disregarded, the Sutton miller, one Gamel, crossing the river at night to take turves. For this he was fined 30s. in the hundred court. It was more than 100 years before this dispute was finally settled. Between 1230 and 1232 Abbot Robert de Hendreth gave to Robert de Courtenay, lord of Sutton, an angle of an island in the Thames immediately opposite the manor-house in Sutton for digging the required materials.[53] When the abbey was dissolved the fishery was leased to John Wellesbourne for 21 years at £15;[54] whilst in the early 18th century Hearne speaks of numerous large fish being caught just below Culham Bridge.[55]

The manor seems to have comprised the bulk of

[21] *Chron. Abingdon*, ii. 21–23, 288.
[22] Ibid. 52. [23] S.C. 6/109, m. 8d.
[24] *L. & P. Hen. VIII*, xiv (1), p. 594; for Wellesbourne see *V.C.H. Oxon*. vi. 254.
[25] *L. & P. Hen. VIII*, xx (2), p. 223.
[26] Parham House Pps. Culham deed no. 3; for Burys see also *V.C.H. Oxon*. vi. 162.
[27] R. E. C. Waters, *Chesters of Chicheley*, 65.
[28] M.I. in MS. Top. Oxon. c. 222, p. 522.
[29] See above, p. 29.
[30] C 142/350/60. [31] *D.N.B.*
[32] For his father Henry, 1st Lord Hunsdon, and his brother Robert, 1st Earl of Monmouth, see *D.N.B.* and *Complete Peerage*.
[33] For his M.I. see below, p. 37.
[34] C 142/350/31.
[35] Ibid.
[36] Par. Reg.
[37] Parham House Pps. Culham deed no. 50.

[38] She was married there and her first child was born there: Par Reg.
[39] G.E.C. *Baronetage*, i. 156–7. [40] Ibid. 157.
[41] For the Brooke-Pechells see ibid. v. 317.
[42] Parham House Pps. Culham deed no. 51.
[43] Ibid. no. 50.
[44] Inf. F. J. Morrell Esq., Headington.
[45] Ibid. [46] See above, p. 31.
[47] A 14th-century account mentions the abbot's land in Culham: *Accts. of Obedientiars of Abingdon Abbey*, ed. R. E. G. Kirk (Camden Soc. N.S. li), 36.
[48] *Chron. Abingdon*, ii. 321. The lignar was the obedientiary whose main responsibility was the provision of fuel: *Abingdon Accts*. p. xxix. [49] *Abingdon Accts*. 6–7.
[50] Ibid. 6. [51] Ibid. 9.
[52] *Chron. Abingdon*. ii. 149, 308, 322.
[53] *Berks. Arch. Jnl*. xxv. 97.
[54] S.C. 6/110, m. 7.
[55] Hearne, *Remarks*, v. 88.

the land in the parish. It is not possible to calculate the exact acreage from the survey of 1539, but the manorial land was then at least 1,136 acres, and almost certainly more. The value of the manor and appurtenances was £115 13s. 9d. There seem to have been 54 cottages in the village at the time. Freeholders were scarce, but there were 18 copyholders.[56]

In the post-Reformation period the manor was administered in the usual way by the manor court. Seven court rolls of the later 16th and of the 17th centuries survive.[57] They refer to the rights of copyholders and regulate the use of the common land. In 1686 every yardland had customary commons for 5 beasts and 60 sheep. The common called Culham Heath was to be used for horses and cows from 1 May and for sheep from St. Thomas's Day; it was to be hained from 2 February to 1 May. There were similar regulations for other common land; names mentioned are Culham Moor, between the river and the canal, East Mead, North Mead, Barnes Meadow, and Bury Croft, along the river north of the canal. The officials in 1686 were a constable, one or two tithing men, four cowmen ('kerman'), and a hayward;[58] in the 16th century there was also a herdsman.[59] In 1717 the lord of the manor agreed with the tenants to destroy a coney warren in return for the tenants releasing their right to common pasture in certain parcels of pasture-land. The aim was to improve the common.[60] But later in the century manorial rights seem to have been neglected,[61] and copyholding became less common. By the time of inclosure only cottages were held by copyhold.[62] Copyhold tenure was still in existence in 1856,[63] but the important tenants had long ceased to hold their farms by this method. The population seems to have been engaged almost entirely in agriculture, a few families attaining a moderate degree of prosperity as yeomen farmers. In the 16th century the families of Carpenter, Mayott, and Wilmot were of this kind; in the 17th century the families of Mayott, Barnes, Pead, and Reston; in the 18th century the families of Pead, Peck, and Welch; in the 19th century the families of Welch and Mundy. Most of the earlier families appear to have died out or to have left the parish by the 19th century.[64]

The 18th century saw the formation of large farms. During this century it is possible to assess roughly the size of farms from the rating assessments.[65] From 1718 until 1761 rates were assessed on the yardland. The parish was rated at 115 yardlands and until about 1750 between 25 and 30 people were usually rated. In 1731, for example, besides the demesne lands of the manor (about 18 yardlands), there were two large farms, one of 14 and one of 12 yardlands; eleven of between 3 and 9 yardlands, eight of between 1 and 2. Some of the smaller estates may have been held by tradesmen. From the 1750's the number of those rated declined to about 20, and the basis of assessment was changed in 1761 from the

yardland to the pound. In that year the annual value of the parish was estimated at £1,342 5s.; three farms had an average annual value of over £150, four of about £100, and there were three between £50 and £65. This trend towards large farms continued and by 1805 there were three farms of about 400 acres or more and six others of which two were between 150 and 200 acres.[66]

Arthur Young describes some of the farming practices of James Welch, tenant of one of the large farms. He used what was basically a four-course rotation of crops, but with a variation: turnips, barley, clover, wheat, and then, turnips, barley, beans or vetches, and wheat.[67] He kept a cross of Berkshire sheep, the ram being half Gloucester and half Leicester, and he penned them, moving the pens each day, first on his barley land, then on his turnip land, and finally on his wheat land. A pen of 75 hurdles, each 6 ft. long, penned 340 sheep.[68]

There were over 800 acres of inclosed land at this date, but there were still 700 acres in the four open fields; earlier there had been, successively, two and three open fields. The survey of 1539 speaks of Town and Costard Fields, but by the mid-17th century there were three fields. The Parliamentary Survey of 1650 mentions Upper, Middle, and Lower Fields, and in 1685 the vicar's glebe was divided between Culham, Middle, and Cositer Fields.[69] Although in 1810 the glebe was still divided among these three fields (then called Ham, Middle, and Costard),[70] it would seem from Arthur Young's account that during the 18th century there had been a change from a three-course to a four-course rotation. The inclosure award of 1813 mentions Costard, Ham, and North and South Middle Fields. Costard Field formed a triangle between the turnpike and Thame Lane; south of the turnpike, along the river and the Clifton Hampden boundary, was Ham Field; while Middle Field lay to the west of the village. The northern part was mostly above the turnpike and Thame Lane, and the southern part was south of the turnpike.[71] Culham Heath (c. 270 acres) was a large tract of land lying in the north-east of the parish south of Nuneham Park and along the Clifton boundary, where it ran as far south as the turnpike.[72] Together these amounted to about 1,000 acres and there were also about 100 acres of uninclosed meadowland.[73] The inclosure award covered 1,890 acres, so that the area of earlier inclosure, excluding the Otneys, which were also inclosed earlier, was about 790 acres.

The date of the early inclosure is not known, but there was probably some by the mid-16th century. The grant of the manor in 1545 includes a number of meadows and pastures leased to individual tenants,[74] and it is likely that these no longer formed part of the parish's common lands. By the early 19th century the two detached farms, Warren and Rye Farms, were surrounded by small inclosed fields, and there

[56] S.C. 6/109, mm. 8b, 9.
[57] Bodl. MS. Rolls Oxon. 115.
[58] Ibid. Ct. 12 Oct. 1686.
[59] Ibid. Ct. 2 Oct. 1595.
[60] Parham House Pps. Culham deed no. 66.
[61] Ibid. Letters, ii. 123.
[62] O.R.O. Incl. award.
[63] 1856 deed of sale penes J. Morrell, Esq., Headington.
[64] Par. Reg., and M.I.s in the church.
[65] These have been taken from the churchwardens' accts. (d.d. Par. Culham b 1–2). The rectory was not assessed for these rates.

[66] O.R.O. Incl. award.
[67] Young, Oxon. Agric. 133.   [68] Ibid. 302.
[69] Lambeth Libr. Parl. Survey, xiv. 3–5; MS. Top. Oxon. c 222, pp. 542–4.
[70] MS. Top. Oxon. c. 222, pp. 545–6.
[71] O.R.O. Incl. award and map.
[72] Davis, Oxon. Map. The areas can be calculated approximately from the incl. award.
[73] H. L. Gray, English Field Systems, 541, calculates the common as 270 and open-field arable and meadow as 830 acres.
[74] L. & P. Hen. VIII, xx (2), p. 223.

was also inclosed meadowland along the river in the north and south of the parish and along the sides of Swift Ditch.[75]

Inclosure took place under an Act of Parliament between 1810 and 1813.[76] The award covered all the land in the parish, both inclosed and uninclosed, except for the Otneys. The purpose of including the old inclosures was probably to allow for the commutation of the tithes. Sir Cecil Bisshopp, the lord of the manor, received 1,588 acres and a few more for cottages held by life-hold tenure; almost all the rest went to the lessee of the rectory, the vicar, and the poor.[77]

The new rectory and vicarage estates formed by the inclosure award were probably the smallest farms in the parish, for after inclosure the other small farms tended to disappear. According to the Census of 1851 there were five large farms in Culham: the Manor farm of 400 acres, employing 15 labourers; the Home farm of 300 acres, with 16 men; Zouche farm of 400 acres, with 20 men; Warren farm of 300 acres, with 18 men; and Rye farm of 207 acres, with 9 men.[78] Otney farm across the river was not included. In the 20th century farms grew still larger, for in 1958 most of the land in Culham was divided between three large farms.[79]

Before inclosure perhaps about half the parish had been arable.[80] After inclosure the proportion increased, for Culham Heath was turned into large arable fields.[81] In the 20th century land in Culham has been about 60 per cent. arable and the rest meadow or pasture.[82]

The earliest evidence relating to the population of Culham comes from the late 17th century: it was a village of medium size. In 1676 132 adults were returned for the Compton Census, and in 1700 its total population was estimated at about 270.[83] During most of the 18th century there were said to be some 50 houses in the village,[84] but by 1801 there were probably more, for there were 364 inhabitants. Inclosure may have been responsible for a temporary depopulation, although the clearance of land for arable purposes may have increased the demand for labour. Between 1811 and 1821 population fell from 389 to 359, but it then continued to rise steadily until 1871, although the total of 579 included 93 students.[85] It afterwards fell to 344 in 1901, but has since increased slightly. The figure of 1,007 recorded in 1951, however, included 630 naval personnel, but did not include the members of the training college.[86]

By the early 19th century there was a small community of tradesmen in Culham. In 1811, out of the 88 families in the parish, 60 were mainly engaged in agriculture and 19 in trade or handicrafts.[87] In 1851 tradesmen in the village were a blacksmith, with one employee and two journeymen blacksmiths, two tailors, a tilemaker, a wheelwright, a brickmaker, and a carpenter. There were also two rag-dealers

and a 'slop' warehouse, which made clothing and employed seventeen women. Other women worked as dressmakers, laundresses, and hemp-spinners. In all there were 94 houses, 12 of them at Abingdon Bridge.[88] A small brickworks also existed from about the middle of the 19th century until about 1932.

PARISH GOVERNMENT. Various surviving accounts kept by the parish officers, who all regularly levied rates to cover their expenses, throw light on local administration in the 18th century and after. Constables' accounts (1748–67) show that the constable was usually changed every year.[89] His duties included keeping the pound and stocks in repair, and transporting malefactors to gaol. 'Gaol money' is a common item in his expenses account.

There were two highway surveyors, usually prominent men in the parish, such as John Phillips, the lessee of the rectory, and later the vicar, Robert Wintle, and they held office for many years.[90]

The most hard-worked parish officers were the overseers of the poor, who were chosen from among the 'substantial householders' by the vestry.[91] They were elected every year, but because of the small number of suitable men, each one served fairly frequently. There seems to have been a good deal of poverty during the 18th century, especially as the century went on, when rates had to be levied three or four times a year instead of the more normal twice. From 1726 to 1770 the parish supported between about nine and twelve paupers. The number rose in the 1770's and in 1795 and 1796 there was a serious crisis; over £420 was spent in the latter year, as compared with £80 in 1775. There was again a serious crisis in the winter of 1800–1 when there were 40 paupers supported by the parish, and over £1,000 was spent in 1801. In 1815 there were still over 30 paupers.

Outdoor relief normally took the form usual at the time: grants of money and clothing, and the provision of spinning-wheels for the women; but the crisis of the 1790's led to modifications, and flour had to be distributed to the poor on a considerable scale.[92] Apart from the relief of the poor the overseers had the additional burden of paying for militia substitutes if the parish could not provide suitable men and of paying allowances to militiamen's families.[93] Throughout the 18th century there are constant references in the overseers' accounts to medical treatment received by the poor, payment being made for such diverse ailments as smallpox and dog bites.[94] Culham, like other Oxfordshire parishes, made use of the Radcliffe Infirmary in Oxford, and paid 1 guinea and later 2 guineas a year subscription fee. Further, the apprenticeship of pauper children was often an expensive item.[95]

In 1834 the parish came under the Abingdon Poor

[75] O.R.O. Incl. award.
[76] Ibid.; 50 Geo. III, c. 140 (local and personal act): copy in Bodl. L Eng. C 13 c 1 (1810. i(2)).
[77] See below, pp. 36, 39.
[78] H.O. 107/1688/5.
[79] See above, p. 30.
[80] The open fields had covered c. 730 acres, but there had also been some inclosed arable.
[81] O.S. Map 25″, xlv. 11 (1875).
[82] Board of Agric. Returns (1901); Orr, Oxon. Agric. maps opp. 161, 201.
[83] Compton Census; O.A.S. Rep. 1933, 23.
[84] Secker's Visit; Oxf. Dioc. d 564.

[85] V.C.H. Oxon. ii. 219; Census, 1871; Training Coll. reg.
[86] Census, 1911, 1951; see above, pp. 30, 31.
[87] Ibid. 1811.
[88] H.O. 107/1688/5.
[89] Now d.d. Par. Culham b 7. This book also includes the surveyors' accts. 1790–1828.   [90] Ibid.
[91] d.d. Par. Culham b 3–6: overseers' accts. 1726–1816.
[92] d.d Par. Culham b 5–6, 1790–1800, passim, esp. 1795–6.
[93] Ibid. 1792, 1795.
[94] Ibid. b 4–5, 1763, 1779, 1791.
[95] Ibid. 1760, 1789.

Law Union for relief purposes, although local organizations such as the parish clothing-club continued to make provision for the poor.[96] In 1872 the Abingdon Rural Sanitary Council took over the management of Culham's sanitation. As a result of the Local Government Act of 1894 the Culham Rural District Council and the Culham Parish Council were set up.[97] The Culham Rural District Council came to an end in 1932, when it was replaced by the Bullingdon Rural District Council.

CHURCH. Culham's first church may date from the reign of Coenwulf (796–?821), when the king's two sisters retired there from the world so as to devote themselves to the service of God.[98] The proximity of Abingdon Abbey undoubtedly prompted the choice of Culham.[99] There is a later tradition that the royal matron Ælfhild obtained in 940 a grant for life of Culham for a similar purpose. The chapel that she built, dedicated to St. Vincent, and in which she was buried must have been there.[1] Another tradition relates how Edward the Confessor permitted a rich priest, Blacheman by name, to live on Andersey Island and build a chapel there dedicated to St. Andrew.[2] After the Battle of Hastings Blacheman fled from England[3] and in 1101 the chapel, by then no longer used for religious services, was granted by Henry I to Abbot Faritius, who took its materials for rebuilding the abbey church at Abingdon.[4]

Twelfth-century papal confirmations of Abingdon's property do not mention any church in Culham.[5] The tithes of Culham are mentioned in the time of Abbot Hugh (1189–1221),[6] but the first known reference to Culham church is found in a bull of Gregory IX (1227–41), confirming to Abingdon Culham manor with the chapel belonging to it.[7]

By this time Culham formed an ecclesiastical peculiar and was free from the jurisdiction of the bishop. According to the Abingdon Chronicle this freedom had its origin in the grant of King Coenwulf to his sisters, which guaranteed that neither bishop, official, archdeacon, or dean had the right to enter the parish.[8] Coenwulf is also said to have been granted wide ecclesiastical freedom for Culham by Pope Leo III (795–816). The account of these privileges is written at a much later period, but evidently sums up the position of the parish in the early Middle Ages and later. Culham was entirely under the jurisdiction of the abbot, who could hear and decide pleas, both ecclesiastical and criminal. No other ecclesiastical person might try to exercise jurisdiction or claim a pension from the church. The abbot had the right of presentation to the living and did not need to present his nominee to the bishop. If the abbacy was vacant, this right devolved upon the

prior and convent. Finally, the priest serving Culham received the chrism from the sacrist of Abingdon on Easter eve in Abingdon church.[9] Culham remained a peculiar until the abbey's dissolution in 1538, but in the post-Reformation period it was in Cuddesdon deanery and under the jurisdiction of the bishop and the archdeacon.

Because it was a peculiar, no reference to medieval Culham appears in the bishop's records. The church was evidently appropriated to Abingdon by the time of Gregory XI,[10] but it is not clear whether or not there was an endowed vicarage in the Middle Ages. No record of the endowment of a vicarage has been found, but the incumbents from the 14th century at least were known as vicars.[11] Soon after the Reformation there was a vicarage, for presentations were made to it from 1564.[12] On the dissolution of the monastery in 1538, the Crown took over the advowson with the manor; and when the manor was granted to William Bury in 1545 the Crown specifically reserved the advowson and no doubt also the rectory to itself.[13] They were retained by the Crown, although granted to Cardinal Pole for a time,[14] until 1589 when the bishopric of Oxford was endowed with them.[15] The Crown had already granted the right to present for one turn or more to William Hull, who in 1564 presented Richard Maddocke.[16] In 1614 Gregory Slade, a yeoman of Long Wittenham (Berks.), who had been granted the advowson for one turn only by the bishop, presented William Prowse.[17] There is no further instance of the bishop's not collating, the advowson remaining in his hands and being specifically excepted from leases of the rectory.

The rectory consisted of the great tithes, some glebe, and, at least after the Reformation, the Rectory house. It had a customary right to commons for 60 sheep and 5 beasts, but it lost this right in 1656 after a lawsuit between George Bury, lord of the manor, and John Reston, the impropriator.[18]

In the Middle Ages Abingdon Abbey received the great tithes and allocated some of them for specific purposes. Some were used for repair of the abbey buildings; some were given by Abbot Hugh (1189–1221) to the almoner; and in 1272 the tithes of sheaves and hay were given to the lignar.[19] The abbey also received a pension from the vicar of 3s.[20] After the Reformation this pension was charged on the rectory and was paid to the lord of the manor.[21] In 1813 the tithes were commuted at the inclosure award for a fifth of the arable and a ninth of the other land in the parish. The bishop received 167 acres for the great tithes and the rectorial glebe.[22] Tithes continued to be paid on the Otneys until 1847, when they were commuted for a rent charge of £29 5s.[23] The inclosure award did not affect the rector's

96 Par. Rec. Clothing Club Pps.
97 d.d. Par. Culham b 1–2.
98 Chron. Abingdon, i. 19–20.
99 For connexion with Abingdon see above, p. 31.
1 Chron. Abingdon, i. 92.
2 Ibid. 474. For its possible site see O.S. Map 25″, xlv. 10 (1876).
3 Chron. Abingdon, i. 490; ii. 283. For him see E. A. Freeman, Hist. of the Norman Conquest (1876), iv. 143–4, 157.
4 Chron. Abingdon, ii. 50, 52; Regesta, ii, no. 550.
5 e.g. Chron. Abingdon, ii. 192.
6 Bodl. MS. Lyell 15, f. 19.
7 Chron. Abingdon, ii. 293.   8 Ibid. 274.
9 Ibid. i. 20–21.
10 Bodl. MS. Lyell 15, f. 19.

11 e.g. Cal. Pat. 1321–4, 259.
12 Oxf. Dioc. d 105, p. 221.
13 L. of P. Hen. VIII, xx(2), p. 223.
14 C 66/1308.
15 Browne Willis, Survey of Cathedrals (1742), iii. 417.
16 Oxf. Dioc. d 105, p. 221.
17 Ibid. c 264, f. 148b.
18 MS. Top. Oxon. c 222, p. 544.
19 Chron. Abingdon, ii. 329, 293; Bodl. MS. Lyell 15, f. 78b.
20 R. E. G. Kirk, Accts. of Obed. of Abingdon (Camden Soc. N.S. li), 59; L. of P. Hen. VIII, xx(2), p. 223.
21 C 142/469/189.
22 O.R.O. Incl. award; for map of the rectory after inclosure see Oxf. Dioc. a 2 (R).
23 Bodl. Tithe award.

obligation to repair the chancel. The rectorial estate, subject to liability for the upkeep of the chancel, was sold by the bishop in 1869.[24]

Shortly before the Dissolution, if not earlier, the abbey had begun to lease the rectory. In 1535 Thomas Hyde received a lease of it for 35 years at £14 a year.[25] In 1564 Prudence Denton was granted the rectory for 35 years as from 1572;[26] but he died in 1567, leaving his interest in the rectory to Lady Knollys and his cousin Edward Cary in equal shares.[27] By 1587 the rectory had got into the hands of the Reades of Barton, near Abingdon; for in that year Thomas Reade surrendered the letters patent granted to Denton.[28] In return new letters patent were issued conferring the rectory on Mary, wife of Thomas Reade, with contingent remainder to her sons John and Richard;[29] it was in fact held by Richard,[30] apparently until 1615, when the Bishop of Oxford leased it to John Reston[31] for three lives. Leases continued until at least 1860 to be for three lives at the usual rental of £14 a year. A heriot was exacted on the death of a tenant and fines were no doubt paid, although these are not recorded in the leases.[32] From at least 1662 the lessee also paid £10 a year to the vicar. The Restons, a yeoman family, held the rectory until 1732, when the family died out.[33] Later it passed to the Phillips family, who came from East Hagbourne (Berks.), but who also had London connexions.[34] George Phillips, the eldest son of Thomas Phillips, a London carpenter, acquired the lease in 1745;[35] in 1763 it passed to John Phillips (d. about 1775), also a London master carpenter and builder,[36] and then to the latter's nephew John.[37] His descendants held the rectory until 1935.[38]

The value of the living has always been small. Neither the rectory nor the vicarage is included in the usual medieval valuations, although the vicarage was valued at £8 in 1526, when it is mistakenly called a rectory and wrongly associated with Dorchester.[39] The value of the vicarage in the early 17th century was £26 13s. 4d., and in 1739 £32 15s.[40] By 1814, however, the gross value of the living had been increased to £140.[41] In the latter part of the 19th century the Ecclesiastical Commissioners granted £140 a year to the vicarage as from 1877, which was further increased by a grant of £50 in 1927.[42] The endowment of the vicarage consisted of the small tithes and some glebe, and according to a terrier of 1685 the vicar had by custom commons for 60 sheep and 5 beasts,[43] but this right seems to have lapsed during the 18th century, probably during the period of non-resident clergy, for in 1796 the vicar was trying to discover whether he was legally entitled to commons.[44] When tithes were commuted in 1813 the vicarage received some 44½ acres of land in compensation. A piece of land (c. 5 acres) was also set aside for the vicar in lieu of the yearly pension of £10 previously paid by the impropriator.[45] The glebe, which formerly consisted largely of strips in the open fields, was exchanged for 13 acres and reorganized as compact fields.[46] Some of it has since been sold.[47]

The names of only a few pre-Reformation vicars survive: in 1323 the name Walter occurs; in 1358 John Attehalle; in 1416 one William.[48] In 1526 the church was served by a curate who received £5 6s. 8d.[49] In 1738 a curate was paid £20 a year; in 1790 £26; in 1805 £40.[50] The parish was usually served by curates in the 18th century, the vicars living elsewhere; for even Thomas Woods, vicar 1739–53, was as head master of Abingdon School non-resident. Benjamin Kennicott, vicar 1753–83, lived in Oxford; and his successors, George Turner, 1783–97, and Robert Wintle, 1797–1848, were usually absentees, Wintle until 1816. After that non-residence came to an end. Services were held twice on Sundays, and the Sacrament was administered four times yearly during the 18th and early 19th centuries.[51] By 1854, however, Holy Communion was celebrated monthly.[52]

The ecclesiastical parish is slightly larger than the civil parish, for the boundary change of 1894 affected only the civil parish.[53]

The church of ST. PAUL comprises a chancel, nave, north and south aisle, south transept, west tower, and south porch. It is a relatively modern edifice, replacing a medieval Gothic building which stood on the site from the late 12th or early 13th century to the middle of the 19th century.

A statement that the original dedication was to St. Andrew[54] seems to be without foundation. The mistake may have arisen through the confusion of Culham with the chapel on Andersey (i.e. St. Andrew's island), but more probably with Colne (Essex) where Abingdon Abbey had a cell and where the church was dedicated to St. Andrew.[55]

The ancient church was about the same length as the present edifice, but had a narrower nave. The chancel measured 33 ft. 4 in. by 14 ft. 3 in. and was rectangular. The nave was 46 ft. 8 in. long by 15 ft. 2 in. wide; the north transept 15 ft. 2 in. by 13 ft. 7 in.; the south transept 7 ft. by 13 ft. 3 in.; and there was a south aisle 10 ft. 3 in. wide. The chancel, except for the north wall, had been so extensively repaired by 1846 as almost to be new. There was a

[24] Inf. Church Commrs.
[25] S.C. 6/109, m. 8b.
[26] C 66/1308.
[27] Will of Prudence Denton: P.C.C. Stonarde 15.
[28] C 66/1308.   [29] Ibid.
[30] Will of Thos. Reade, 1605: P.C.C. Hayes 24.
[31] Oxf. Dioc. c 2115, no. 1. For litigation of 1626 among the Restons see C 3/413/42.
[32] For leases 1615–1860 see Oxf. Dioc. c 2115, nos. 1–30. The fine paid in 1786 was £350: Oxf. Dioc. (uncat.).
[33] Oxf. Dioc. c 2115, nos. 2–3; Par. Reg.
[34] For their M.I.s see below, p. 37.
[35] Oxf. Dioc. c 2115, no. 4.
[36] Ibid. no. 8. For him and Thos. Phillips see H.M. Colvin, Biog. Dict. of English Architects.
[37] Oxf. Dioc. c 2115, no. 15; for the family see V.C.H. Berks. iii. 281.
[38] For the family in the 19th century see Burke, Land Gent. (1925).
[39] Subsidy 1526, 252.

[40] Dunkin MS. 438/2, f. 166; MS. Top. Oxon. c 222, p. 562.   [41] Oxf. Dioc. c 429, f. 122.
[42] MS. Top. Oxon. c 222, p. 564; inf. Church Commrs.
[43] MS. Top. Oxon. c 222, pp. 542–4.
[44] Ibid. pp. 552–4.   [45] O.R.O. Incl. award.
[46] See terriers of 1685 and 1810 in MS. Top. Oxon. c 222, pp. 542–4, 544–6.
[47] Inf. the Revd. Peter Halewood.
[48] Cal. Pat. 1321–4, 259; Bodl. MS. Lyell 15, ff. 195, 195b; Cal. Pat. 1416–22, 79.
[49] Subsidy 1526, 252.
[50] MS. Top. Oxon. c 222, pp. 561, 562; Oxf. Dioc. d 568.
[51] Secker's Visit.; Oxf. Dioc. d 555, d 566, d 572, d 576.
[52] Wilb. Visit.
[53] See above, p. 27; Census, 1911: Eccl. Areas.
[54] F. Arnold Foster, Church Dedications, i. 57; K. E. Kirk, Church Dedications of Oxf. Diocese, 36.
[55] For Andersey see above, p. 35; Chron. Abingdon, ii. 57–58, 539.

door on the south side with a fanlight over it and a brick chimney. The nave had on the south side five small arches, pointed and recessed, and Early English in style. There was a Decorated window of two lights in the wall of the south aisle.[56] The south transept had a Decorated window of two lights on its east side and another of three lights at the end; above this window was a sundial. A sketch of the south side of the church shows that the original porch added in 1638 was much closer to the south transept than the present porch, and that the line of the roof was lower.[57] The north side of the building seems to have been poorly lit: it had only a single lancet window in the wall, although above was a range of four clerestory windows of two lights. In the north transept, however, in 'a little chapel' was the chief glory of the old church, the east window, which was filled with heraldic glass, the jambs containing chains of heraldic shields with the arms of different families; on each side was a two-light lancet window. This glass was inserted in 1638 and was part of the design of Sir Edmund Cary's monument (see below) erected by his widow. The principal arms were those of Cary and Humphrey.[58] When the church was rebuilt much of the glass was placed in a window of the north aisle, where it now is.

A high window on the north side of the church at one time contained the arms of an Abbot of Abingdon. It is not known when this window disappeared, but it was there when Rawlinson visited the parish in 1717.[59]

The tower arch is described as lofty, well proportioned, pointed but plain. It was boarded up and had a gallery in front of it dated 1721.[60]

In the churchwardens' accounts are constant references to the repair of the fabric, and there seem to have been major repairs in 1792 and 1817,[61] but the building was in such a state of decay in 1852 that there was no alternative but to rebuild it.[62]

The nave was rebuilt in the Early English style in 1852 (architect, Joseph Clarke of London; builder, G. Wyatt of Oxford) at a cost of some £1,600. It could seat 290 persons.[63] The chancel was rebuilt in 1872 (architect R. P. Spiers of London; builder, Groves) at the expense of the lay rector J. S. Phillips.[64] It has an apsidal east end. The tower is the only part of the old church remaining and apparently dates from 1710, this date being inscribed on the leadwork.[65] It is a plain battlemented structure of stone rendered in cement. There was certainly an earlier tower. There is a reference to the steeple in 1552; and in 1704, and again in 1705, the churchwardens were ordered to arrange for the repair of the tower.[66]

The church was refitted after rebuilding. An old communion table dated 1638 and an ancient parish chest survive.

A stone font was given in about 1845 by J. S. Phillips. Before that time a baptismal font of gilded base metal (now used as an alms-dish), resting on a mahogany stand, was used.[67] On either side of the altar there are 19th-century wooden panels with painted figures of saints.

There were once the following memorials to the Bury family: John Bury (d. 1571/2); Elizabeth Wilmot (d. 1607), formerly wife of John Bury; William Bury (d. 1632), son of Thomas Bury, with arms; William Bury (d. 1657/8) and George Bury (d. 1662), under an achievement; Thomas Bury (d. 1671); and Anne Bury (d. 1672/3). There was also the ledger stone of Thomas Rawlins, vicar (d. 1704).[68]

In 1958 the following memorials were in the church: a tablet to Thomas Bury (d. 1614/5);[69] a wall monument with arms to Sir Edmund Cary (d. 1637), the third husband of Judith, formerly wife of Thomas Bury (d. 1614/5); a similar wall monument to Lady Judith Cary, the third wife of Sir Edmund, erected by herself in 1638; a tablet to Sarah Bury (d. 1650), wife of George Bury. A memorial to the Welch family includes John Welch (d. 1807) and his son John (d. 1827). Other memorials are to John Phillips of Culham House (d. 1824); Mary Phillips (d. 1829); Jonathan Peel (d. 1843), signed Godfrey, Abingdon; Robert Wintle, vicar (d. 1848); John Shawe Phillips (d. 1859) and other members of the Phillips family.

A 19th-century tablet commemorates Thomas Bury (d. 1614/5), William Bury (d. 1657/8), Elizabeth Shakespear (d. 1644), John Reston the elder (d. 1675), John Reston (d. 1698), and others.

A war-memorial tablet to eight parishioners killed in the First World War was designed by Denis Godfrey of Abingdon and was erected in 1919. An inscription to those killed in the Second World War was added in 1950.

There are painted-glass windows in the nave and transept to the memory of James Morrell (d. 1863); and one in the chancel to Montagu Phillips (d. 1874), an infant; two painted achievements of the Phillips family are in the chancel and a royal arms of Queen Victoria is over the door.

In 1958 the plate consisted of a silver Elizabethan chalice dated 1575; a silver flagon with heraldic arms given by the Revd. Thomas Woods in 1752;[70] a silver plate, hallmarked 1726, given by the Revd. Benjamin Kennicott in 1761; and a silver paten, hallmarked 1829, given by the Revd. Robert Wintle in 1829.[71]

In 1552 the church possessed three bells and a sanctus bell, and it had a ring of three bells until 1921. These consisted of a tenor of 1597 by Joseph Carter; and two Aldbourne bells, one of 1729 by John Corr and the other uninscribed. These were recast in 1921 by Mears and Stainbank and two smaller bells were added. In 1926 a larger bell was given in memory of G. H. Gillam, vicar. There is a sanctus bell dated 1774 which is hung for chiming. It was cast by Edne Willis of Aldbourne, a noted ringer, and is the only bell known to be by him.[72]

The churchyard was extended in 1887 and again in 1921.[73]

The registers date from c. 1648 for baptisms, 1662

[56] For description of old church see Parker, *Guide*, 367–8.   [57] MS. Top. Oxon. b 220, f. 186.
[58] Parker, *Guide*, 367–8; *Par. Coll.* i. 107–8; Bodl. G.A. Oxon. 4° 685, pp. 107–9; for tricks of the Cary arms see Bodl. 1373 e 65, p. 50a.
[59] Parker, *Guide*, 368; MS. Top. Oxon. b 220, f. 186b.
[60] *Par. Coll.* i. 109; Bodl. G.A. Oxon. 4° 685, p. 109.
[61] d.d. Par. Culham b 2: chwdns'. accts.
[62] Incorporated Church Bldg. Soc. Records (Culham file) at 7, Queen Anne's Gate, S.W. 1.
[63] Ibid.; Oxf. Dioc. b 70; MS. Top. Oxon. c 222, p. 564;

[64] d.d. Par. Culham b 2.
[65] Parker, *Guide*, 367.
[66] *Chant. Cert.* 104; Oxf. Archd. Oxon. c 26, f. 22b; c 25, f. 131.
[67] Parker, *Guide*, 368; Evans, *Ch. Plate*.
[68] *Par. Coll.* i. 107, 109, 110; MS. Top. Oxon. b 220, ff. 186–186b; Bodl. G.A. Oxon. 4° 685, pp. 107–9.
[69] The date is wrongly given as 1624 in *Par. Coll.* i. 107.
[70] For arms see Bodl. G.A. Oxon. 4° 685, p. 109.
[71] Evans, *Ch. Plate*.   [72] *Ch. Bells Oxon.* 110–11.
[73] Oxf. Dioc. c 1790.

for burials, and 1666 for marriages, but the early ones are irregularly kept. There are churchwardens' accounts from 1718.[74]

NONCONFORMITY. There is nothing to suggest that Roman Catholicism was strong in Culham after the religious settlement of 1559. One or two papists are mentioned as living in Culham in the 1620's,[75] but by about 1685 there was apparently only one left.[76] This may have been Mrs. Greenwood. Rawlinson, writing in 1717, says that she was a Romanist, who had founded a charity.[77] In the early part of the 18th century there was a brief revival of Roman Catholic influence, which was centred in the manor-house. Elizabeth Dunch of Newington, wife of Sir Cecil Bisshopp (d. 1725) of Parham, was certainly a convert to Rome, and she had at one time possession of the manor-house,[78] although it is unlikely that she lived there much. The Roman Catholic family mentioned in 1738, with whom the Jesuit Peter Ingleby lived,[79] may be that of Robert Gainsford, who was probably Lady Bisshopp's steward.[80] Earlier in the century John Young had been steward to the family and had lived in the manor-house.[81] He was presented for recusancy in 1706[82] and failed to appear at Wheatley in 1714 to take the oaths of allegiance to George I.[83] When Lady Bisshopp died in London in 1751 Roman Catholic influence in Culham seems to have come to an end.

The growth of Protestant dissent appears to have affected the parish only very slightly. An ejected minister, Maurice Griffith, made his home in the village for a few years and died there in 1676.[84] No application for the licensing of a meeting-house has been recorded; and the 18th-century visitation returns suggest that nonconformity was not strong. In about 1685 only one dissenter is mentioned;[85] and during the next 130 years the returns never give more than nine.[86] Eighteenth-century dissenters are usually referred to as Presbyterians, but there are occasional references to Independents and Baptists. They probably worshipped in Abingdon.[87] In 1854 there were about ten dissenters living in Culham, and in 1878 thirteen were returned.[88]

SCHOOLS. In 1808 there was no endowed school in Culham, but the younger children were taught to read and write in two small schools with about 10 to 20 pupils each.[89] A Sunday school, established in 1815, paid its master from the parish rates while the other expenses were defrayed by voluntary contributors.[90]

By 1818 the dames' schools had disappeared, but two ladies had set up a school for 24 girls, and 60 children were taught in the Sunday school by a poor man of the parish who was paid 2s. 6d. a Sunday. The vicar reported at this time that there were not sufficient means of education for the poor.[91] The situation was distinctly improved in 1833, by which time two day schools had been started, one with 33 children, supported by subscription, and the other with about 20, educated at the expense of their parents. The numbers of the Sunday school had also increased to 75, and this too was supported by voluntary subscription.[92] The vicarage and the rectory gave books to form a parish library the following year.[93]

The village Church of England school was built in 1850 at a cost of £438.[94] It was erected on glebe land and in 1897 the vicar gave more glebe so that additions might be made to the schoolroom and teacher's house. The cost was £300.[95] When the practising school at Culham College was built in 1853 the boys apparently attended there, for in 1854 there were only 38 girls and infants in the village school.[96] In 1890, however, the average attendance was 66[97] and probably included boys since in 1906 the school, with a smaller average attendance of 53, was described as an all-age mixed school.[98] In 1924 it was reorganized for infants up to eight and girls only,[99] but in 1931 the senior girls were transferred to Dorchester. In 1948 the school was temporarily closed, but was reopened in 1951 for children up to the age of eight.[1] In 1954 it had the status of an aided school, and a roll of 26 children.[2]

The practising school was built in 1853 as part of the Diocesan Training College scheme[3] at a cost of £735.[4] From 1853 to 1856 it was a mixed school, but the girls seem to have been excluded in 1856.[5] In 1904 it came partially under the control of the Oxfordshire Education Committee,[6] and in 1924 received senior boys from the village school. The school was closed in 1931, the building being taken over by the college.[7]

An evening school was in existence in 1854 when it was described as 'tolerably successful' and in 1867 there were 11 pupils.[8]

The Diocesan Training College for Schoolmasters is built on glebe land purchased from the Vicar of Culham in April 1851. The foundation stone of the chapel was laid on 28 October 1851 by Bishop Wilberforce and the main building was erected in 1852. The cost was £19,487. There was accommodation for 90 students.[9] The college really dates back to

[74] There is a list and an index of the registers by W. J. Oldfield in MS. Top. Oxon. c 222. The accounts are in Bodl. d.d. Par. Culham b 1–2.
[75] Salter, Oxon. Recusants, passim.
[76] Oxf. Dioc. d 708, f. 70b.
[77] Par. Coll. i. 107. The Greenwoods of Brize Norton were recusants: O.R.O. Cal. Q. Sess. ix. 594–5.
[78] Secker's Visit.
[79] Ibid.; for Ingleby see H. Foley, Records of English Provinces, vii. 391.
[80] d.d. Par. Culham b 1, 1736–48 (chwdns' accts.). He died in 1749: Par. Reg.
[81] Hearne, Remarks, vi. 72; vii. 375; viii. 209.
[82] Oxoniensia, xiii. 80; O.R.O. Cal. Q. Sess. ix. 784.
[83] O.R.O. Cal. Q. Sess. ix. 779; cf. Stapleton, Cath. Miss. 244, where he is wrongly called Charles.
[84] Bodl. MS. Wills Oxon. 27/3/5; see below, p. 144.
[85] Oxf. Dioc. d 708, f. 70b.
[86] Secker's Visit.; Oxf. Dioc. d 555, d 558, d 564, d 566, d 568, d 574, d 576.   [87] Oxf. Dioc. d 566.

[88] Wilb. Visit.; Oxf. Dioc. c 344.
[89] Oxf. Dioc. d 570.   [90] Ibid. c 433.
[91] Educ. of Poor, 722.
[92] Educ. Enq. Abstract, 745.
[93] Oxf. Dioc. b 39.
[94] Min. of Educ. Recs., Bldg. grants, vol. N. 479.
[95] Ibid. Culham File; MS. Top. Oxon. c 222, p. 558.
[96] Wilb. Visit.; and see below.
[97] Ret. of Sch. 213.   [98] Vol. Sch. Ret. 20.
[99] This took effect from 6 Jan. 1925: Min. of Educ. Recs. Culham File.
[2] Inf. Oxon. Educ. Cttee.
[3] L. Naylor, Culham College, 30.
[4] Min. of Educ., Bldg. grants, training colls. 339.
[5] Naylor, Culham Coll. 41; A History of the Practising Sch. (Anon.), 10; Oxf. Dioc. Bd. of Educ. Rep. 1856, p. 10.
[6] History of Practising Sch. 10.
[7] Naylor, Culham Coll. 41.
[8] Wilb. Visit.; Schs. Ret. 337.
[9] Naylor, Culham Coll. 25, 27, 30.

1840, for it is a continuation of a Training Institution established at Summertown, Oxford, by the Oxford Diocesan Board of Education in that year.[10] Until the 20th century building improvements were few. In 1901–2 an assembly room with a laboratory above it was added; in 1907 part of the old building was extended eastwards; and in 1939 a new block was added on the north side of the quadrangle, consisting of a gymnasium and fourteen study-bedrooms. Between 1947 and 1949 extensive alterations were made, three new wings of study-bedrooms and a tutorial block being built to the north of the main structure. The college now has accommodation for 240 students. The chapel was extended in 1954–5. The extension is at the east end and is a tower-like structure of unusual design. The interior has been redecorated and partly refitted.

The college was closed during the First World War and again in 1941. It was reopened in 1920 and 1946.[11]

CHARITIES. In 1606 Joan Whitfield left £10 for the poor;[12] in 1608 John Robinson and William Carpenter gave £5;[13] in the 1640's Maurice Griffith £10;[14] and before 1717 Mrs. Greenwood, a 'Romanist', left a legacy of £20 to be used for distributing 20 twelve-penny loaves to the poor every Good Friday.[15] The churchwardens' accounts, beginning in 1718, speak of this charity and of the Bowles charity, which also appears to have originated in the early 18th century.[16] It was believed in 1738 that the capital value of the charities had once amounted to £50, but by then, thanks to the negligence of the churchwardens, only £20 remained.[17] In the 18th and early 19th centuries the interest on this £20 was distributed in small annual, biennial, or triennial doles to the unrelieved poor.[18] In the 1820's the interest (£1 yearly) was being allowed to accumulate.[19] The charity was lost by 1883.[20]

By the inclosure award of 1813 19 acres in the north-east of the parish were set aside for the poor in place of their right to furze.[21] This area, the Poor's Allotment, was being let about 1820 for £40, and the rent arising spent on coals for the poor.[22] In 1847 the land was sold to the G.W.R., and the proceeds invested in £2,016 stock.[23] Until 1883 the income was distributed in coals, often to all the inhabitants regardless of need.[24] A Scheme made in 1883 stipulated that it should be spent in subscriptions or donations to hospitals or homes on such terms as would secure the benefits of the institution to the objects of the charity, in aid of provident clubs supplying coal, clothing or other necessaries, in purchasing coals for the schools, in contributions towards outfits, and in the supply of clothes, fuel, medicines, or food.[25] By a Scheme of 1932 the objects of the charity were slightly modified.[26] In 1955 the income was £51 and was being distributed for unspecified purposes in 39 separate sums ranging from £1 to £5.[27]

DORCHESTER

THE composition of the ancient parish of Dorchester is somewhat obscure. It may have included the hamlet of Overy as well as Burcot,[1] about 1½ miles north-west of Dorchester, and so have covered an area of 2,263 acres.[2] For centuries, however, Burcot had a separate economic life, and was long recognized as a separate civil parish. For the purposes of this article, therefore, the history of Burcot will not be included except incidentally.[3]

The area of Dorchester and Overy was 1,954 acres.[4] This was still the area of the civil parish in 1959. It then included a new estate of 271 dwellings, made at Berinsfield just north-west of Dorchester and close to the Oxford road.[5]

The River Thames forms the parish boundary to the south and the River Thame for about a mile to the east. To the south-east the boundary crosses the Thame to include the hamlet of Overy. The northern half of the parish has irregular boundaries with the hamlet of Burcot and the neighbouring parishes of Marsh Baldon, Chislehampton, and Drayton St. Leonard.[6]

The parish is low lying and flat, sloping gently from 200 feet in the north to 150 feet in the south.[7] The underlying Gault Clay is covered by gravel[8] and there are large gravel pits, which extended in 1959 to well over 100 acres, to the north-west of the village. There is no woodland in the parish, and apart from the trees of the village and the riverside there is very little standing timber. In 1551 a survey of what had been the Bishop of Lincoln's manor listed 970 timber trees on the copyhold of Dorchester and 785 on those of Overy.[9] Shortly after the Dissolution there were 360 elms and ashes growing on the lands of what had been the abbey's manor.[10]

The oldest known road in the parish is the Roman one leading from Dorchester, where its line is preserved in the main street of the village, to Water Stratford just over the north-east boundary of the county.[11] It is possible that this road continued across the Thame and crossed the Thames by a ford about half-way between Dorchester and Shillingford. It seems probable that the Thame was bridged here in the Anglo-Saxon period but the earliest evidence

[10] Ibid. 8; Oxf. Dioc. Bd. of Educ. Rep. 1840.
[11] Naylor, Culham Coll. 90–91, 99, 106, 122, 124, 128, 131.
[12] MS. Wills Oxon. 193, f. 186; Bodl. MS. Rawl. B 400b, ff. 373b–374. For inquisition of 1615 about this see C 93/6/9.
[13] Bodl. MS. Rawl. B 400b, f. 373.
[14] Ibid. f. 373b.   [15] Par. Coll. i. 107.
[16] Now d.d. Par. Culham b 1; P.C.C. 138 Aston (will of Mary Greenwood, 1714).   [17] Secker's Visit.
[18] d.d. Par. Culham b 2; chwdns' accts.
[19] 8th Rep. Com. Char. 493.
[20] Char. Com. Culham G. file.
[21] O.R.O. Incl. award; Oxf. Dioc. d 572.
[22] 8th Rep. Com. Char. 493.
[23] Char. Com. file 719.   [24] Ibid. file 12514.

[25] Ibid.   [26] Ibid.
[27] Ibid. Accts. file.   [1] See below, p. 69.
[2] O.S. Map 25″, xlvi. 13, 14 (1881); Area Bk. (1878).
[3] For Burcot see below, p. 65.
[4] Census, 1881; earlier Census Reports give less accurate figures.
[5] For an account see Oxf. Mail, 1 Aug. 1958.
[6] O.S. Map 25″, xlvi. 5, 6, 9, 10, 13, 14; xlix. 12 (1881).
[7] Ibid.
[8] Orr, Oxon. Agric. 172; V.C.H. Oxon. i, map between pp. 4–5.
[9] L.R. 2/189, ff. 14–15.
[10] H. Addington, Some Account of the Abbey Church of St. Peter and St. Paul at Dorchester (1845), 172.
[11] V.C.H. Oxon. i. 276–9.

of a bridge is in 1146.[12] In 1381 the bailiffs of Dorchester were granted pontage for three years for the repair of the bridge,[13] and in the mid-15th century more work seems to have been done on it at the expense of two local landowners, Sir Richard Drayton and John Delabere (Bishop of St. Davids, 1447–60),[14] whose benefaction was commemorated in an inscription on a cross which stood on or near the bridge in the 16th century.[15] This cross was removed in or soon after 1781.[16] Leland described the bridge as 'of a good length; and a great stone causey is made to come well onto it. There be 5 principal arches in the bridge and in the causey joining to the south end of it.'[17] In the 17th and 18th centuries it was frequently in need of repair,[18] and by 1781 its condition was so bad that £206 were spent on its repair and widening. In 1808 a grand jury presented that it was again out of repair, narrow, and inconvenient.[19] It was described as a mean and narrow structure, with recesses on one side to enable foot passengers to avoid the real danger threatened by the transit of carriages.[20] A new bridge was, therefore, designed by Mr. Francis Sandys and built about 100 yards above the old structure between 1813 and 1815 at a cost of £23,857.[21] The new bridge is stone built and with its causeway is 1,160 yards long. The old bridge, which led into the green at Bridge End, was demolished in 1816, but the foundations of its piers are still encountered by boats when the river is low. By 1824 the foundations of the new bridge had been so badly washed away that underpinning at a cost of £3,737 was necessary. In 1847 the ladies of Dorchester complained of the nuisances committed on the seats on this bridge which were said to be a disgrace to the parish. The remedy suggested by Mr. William Cobb was 'to slope them up with brickwork . . . so that no person can stand or sit in them'.[22] This was apparently done for the recesses on the bridge are at present 'sloped up' with stone work.

The bridge carries the main Oxford–Henley road which crosses the parish and forms the main street of the village. Since the expiration of the Henley and Dorchester Turnpike Trust in 1873 the maintenance of this road has been the responsibility of the county.[23] The early 19th-century toll-house still stands at the approach to the bridge. This road, probably always the most important through the parish, was used in the 13th century by the Bishop of Lincoln's tenants who were required to cart corn to Oxford and Wallingford.[24] In 1816 Dorchester was said to be chiefly known by it. It ran through to Oxford, Worcester, Gloucester, and South Wales.[25]

A side road of some importance leads via Burcot to Abingdon.[26] There seems to have been a great deal of concern about this road in the 15th century and the Abingdon Guild of the Holy Cross was established to maintain it.[27] The road was turnpiked in 1754–5 and was dis-turnpiked in 1874.[28] In a survey of the Bishop of Lincoln's demesne at Dorchester made in 1348 mention is made of roads or 'ways' to Oxford, Baldon, Drayton, Burcot, and 'Wolden'.[29] In the mid-19th century the River Thame was crossed by three footbridges, one at the confluence with the Thames, another just above the site of the old bridge, and a third leading to Overy via The Hurst.[30] The 'Back Lane' on the west of the village is sometimes known as Watlington Lane and this is most likely a corruption of the name of two holdings of Richard Beauforest in the 16th century, Great and Little Wallington.[31] The track now known as Wittenham Lane was in the mid-19th century called Ferry Road.[32]

In 1580 and 1585 a weir and a lock were owned by Edmund Fettiplace and a weir, which seems properly to have been in Little Wittenham parish, was owned by William Dunch.[33] Both Edmund Dunch and Edmund Fettiplace were members of the ineffective commission set up under the Act of 1605 for improving the navigation of the Thames between Burcot and Oxford.[34] The Dunch interest passed through the Oxendens to William Hallett who in 1789 was given notice to keep the old flashlock shut on the opening of the new poundlock.[35] This was known as Day's Lock and had been staked out in 1788 and completed at a cost of £1,078;[36] it was in utter ruin in 1865 and was rebuilt in 1871.[37] Formerly there was a timber swing-bridge below the lock but an iron bridge was built about 1870 at a cost of £250.[38]

The village of Dorchester lies about 9 miles southeast by south of Oxford on the western bank of the River Thame, about half a mile above the confluence of that river with the Thames. It was one of the two Romano-British 'towns' in the county. The course of its walls, first erected c. A.D. 125, has been determined in part and seems to enclose an area of about 13½ acres, and there is evidence to suggest that at least in origin this 'town' was a military or paramilitary settlement with the civilian settlement outside the walls.[39] It continued to flourish into the 4th century and the recent re-examination[40] of some early Saxon graves from the neighbourhood has led to the conclusion that they are the graves not of invaders but of *foederati* and their dating to the end of the 4th or the early 5th century suggests that life continued in Dorchester to the very end of the Roman period. Indeed it has even been suggested

[12] *Reg. Antiquiss.* i. 247.
[13] *Cal. Pat.* 1381–5, 64.
[14] *D.N.B.*
[15] Addington, *Dorchester*, 135.
[16] O.R.O. Q. Sess. Bridge pps. 71.
[17] Leland, *Itin.* ed. Toulmin Smith, i. 118. Another bridge described by Leland (ibid. 116) is sometimes confused with Dorchester Bridge, but from the context is clearly Chislehampton Bridge.
[18] O.R.O. Cal. Q. Sess. iii, ff. 325, 429; viii, ff. 503, 563.
[19] Ibid. viii, f. 622b; Q. Sess. bridge pps. 71. For an illustration see *Gent. Mag.* 1818, i. 105, reproduced above, plate facing p. 41.
[20] Brewer, *Oxon.* (1813), 379.
[21] For the bridge generally see O.R.O. Q. Sess. Bridge pps. 71; cf. J. M. Davenport, *Oxon. Bridges* (1869).
[22] O.R.O. Q. Sess. Bridge pps. 71 (letter, 1847).
[23] H. J. Tollit, *Oxon. Co. Bridges* (Surveyor's rep. 1878).
[24] Queen's Coll. MS. 366, ff. 25–25b, 26b–27b.
[25] *Gent. Mag.* 1816, ii. 297.
[26] Cf. above, p. 27; below, p. 65.
[27] *Cal. Pat.* 1416–22, 33–34; 1441–6, 36–37; 1476–85, 386.
[28] Turnpike Acts 28 Geo. II, c. 42; 37–38 Vic. c. 95; cf. above, p. 28.
[29] Queen's Coll. MS. 366, f. 60b.
[30] Bodl. Tithe award map.
[31] L.R. 2/189, f. 3b.
[32] Bodl. Tithe award.
[33] F. S. Thacker, *The Thames Highway, general history*, 56, 51.
[34] Ibid. 63.
[35] F. S. Thacker, *The Thames Highway, Locks and Weirs*, 175; for the Dunches see below, p. 43.
[36] Thacker, *Locks and Weirs*, 175.
[37] Ibid. 175–9.
[38] Ibid. 179.
[39] *V.C.H. Oxon.* i. 288–96, 303–6, 336.
[40] Joan R. Kirk and E. T. Leeds, 'Three Early Saxon Graves from Dorchester, Oxon.', *Oxoniensia*, xviii. 63–76.

Air View of Dorchester North of the New Bridge

The Old Bridge in 1818

The High Street in 1961

DORCHESTER

that the continuance of some sort of sub-Roman life in Dorchester was the reason Birinus chose it for his see in 634.[41] The name Dorchester itself would support the theory of continuity. It is first recorded by Bede in the early 8th century in the forms *Dorcic*, *Dorciccaestræ*.[42] The second element is the common Old English *ceaster* meaning a Roman station, but the first is certainly British although its meaning is most uncertain.

Whether or not life continued in Dorchester until the English conquest and after, it is remarkable that both the abbey church, presumably on the site of the earlier church, and the monastic buildings lay outside what seems to have been the line of the Roman walls. The full extent of the Saxon settlement is not known, but after the Norman Conquest and the removal of the see to Lincoln the town may well have declined in importance. William of Malmesbury, writing about 1125, described Dorchester as *exilis et infrequens*, but he added *majestas tamen ecclesiarum [est] magna, seu veteri opera seu sedulitate nova*.[43] Leland, who visited Dorchester in 1542, remarked that 'of old time it was much larger in building than it is now toward the south and the *Tamise* side. There was a parish church a little by south from the abbey church. And another parish church more south above it. There was a third parish church by south west'.[44] This was probably the source of the statements made by such later observers as Hearne and Gough that there were three churches at Dorchester besides the abbey church. Gough, writing in the early 19th century, stated that foundations of one of these churches could be seen 'as you turn up to the bridge in the gardens of the clerk's house'.[45] A few years later J. N. Brewer reported that he could find no trace of such foundations,[46] but he observed what seemed to be the site of one church in Farm Field. There is now no trace of any of these churches. The walls of the town seem still to have been standing in the 12th century.[47] Other lost buildings are the Bishop's Palace and 'The Gyld' and the farmhouse mentioned by Gough, who says it was called Bishop's Court Farm and was in the form of a cross.[48] Bishop's Court is reputed to stand on the site of the bishop's palace. Leland observed old foundations there, and in his time the courts, presumably of the Bishop of Lincoln's manor, were held there.[49]

Apart from post-war development most of the village may be said to be bounded by the rectangle formed by Back Lane to the west and south and Marten's Lane to the north. The only important extension beyond this is Bridge End, which has become a backwater since the construction of the new bridge.

Most of the buildings in the village are basically of the 17th and 18th centuries. The main 19th-century additions are the Vicarage, built in 1856–7 to the design of David Brandon, the Beech House Hotel (originally a private residence), and the former Missionary Training College in Queen Street, which

was formed out of some older buildings by Sir Gilbert Scott in 1877–8.[50] There is also some 20th-century housing in several parts of the village, including an estate called Tenpenny at the south-west end of the village and some varied modern houses at the north-east corner between Queen Street and the river.[51] Most of the earlier buildings have timber frames, generally with brick filling, while buildings of the 18th century and later are generally of brick. Much of the brickwork of all ages is colour-washed. Other building materials are used, including flint and rubble stone, most remarkably in Mollymops cottage in Bridge End, dated 1715, which is built of alternate bands of flint and brick. Most roofs are tiled but some thatch remains, notably in Bridge End and Malt House Lane. Several buildings in the village have been extensively altered from time to time, but still retain many original features. This is particularly true of High Street where a large number of buildings seem to be originally of the 17th century, but have a variety of later frontages. The most striking of these is on Willoughby House, a timber-framed structure of the 17th century, or perhaps even earlier, which has an early 19th-century stuccoed front with a masonry pattern. The Manor House is another good example of an enlarged house in which the earlier building is largely preserved. It is to almost all external appearances an 18th-century house with Gothic windows on the west front and an early-19th-century wing added on the north. It contains extensive traces of an earlier house of the 17th or perhaps even the 16th century. This seems to have been a two-story building and now forms the core of the western part of the house. There are some very fine timbers in the ceilings of the cellar and the ground floor, and the tiled roof may be original. This was the farm-house mentioned by Wood in 1657 as belonging to Mr. Clerk 'which some say was part of the abbey'.[52]

High Street, crossing the village from north-west to south-east, is a most attractive street and contains many groups of buildings of great charm and interest.[53] It winds through the village and is made up of a variety of cottages, houses, shops, and inns with very irregular roof lines. Perhaps the most striking buildings in this street are the inns: the 'Crown', the 'George', the 'White Hart', and what was formerly the Bull Inn but is now three houses. These are all timber-framed buildings and their upper stories oversail, the carved brackets on 'Bullyn' being particularly good. This house also has some fine panelled rooms. All these inns have yards, the best being that of the 'George' with its open gallery.[54]

North-west of the village is Bishop's Court. The central part of the present house is an L-shaped timber-framed structure with brick filling, some of it herringbone, and there are 18th- and 19th-century extensions. The interior contains some fine chamfered beams which may date back to the rebuilding of 1552, which, it is said, is recorded in the title deeds.[55]

[41] *V.C.H. Oxon.* i. 296.
[42] *P.N. Oxon.* (E.P.N.S.), i. 152.
[43] Wm. of Malmesbury, *Gesta Pontificum* (Rolls Ser.), 311.
[44] Leland, *Itin.* ed. Toulmin Smith, i. 117.
[45] Camden, *Brit.* (1808), ii. 28.
[46] Brewer, *Oxon.* (1813), 371 n.
[47] *Reg. Antiquiss.* i. 247.
[48] Camden, *Brit.* (1808), ii. 28.

[49] Leland, *Itin.* ed. Toulmin Smith, i. 118.
[50] W. C. Macfarlane, *A Short Account of Dorchester* (1881), 22.
[51] There are 12 post-war council houses and 14 earlier ones: inf. Bullingdon R.D.C.
[52] Wood, *Life*, i. 224.
[53] For a view see plate facing p. 41.
[54] See also below, p. 51.
[55] Inf. Min. of Housing and Local Govt.

With the probable exception of what is now the school-house at the west end of the church, nothing remains of the monastic buildings. The school-house may have been a guest house. It is a timber-framed building with brick filling, and on the north side the first floor oversails. The south wall, however, is built of stone and in it there is the cusped head of a two-light mullioned window that has been blocked up. There are also traces of other similar windows and of a stone doorway. Wood speaks of the school-house being built about 1654, and this almost certainly refers to the timber-framed structure.[56] When the school-house was built some little underground rooms were discovered, some of them paved with hard white stone, and one of them had a central hearth. Digging at the west end of the church in the 17th century also revealed a small vault which Wood seems to have considered a place of punishment. In the early 19th century there seem to have been the remains of an arched entrance to the monastery at the west end of the church, between this school-house and the church. The main monastic buildings were on the north side of the church, the cloister on the north side of the nave. Nothing now remains of these buildings although substantial remains were described by Wood. To the north of the church there were then some 'great slatted barns, that are supported with buttresses' which were probably the wooden barns forming a quadrangle north of the Manor House.[57] These were recently destroyed to make way for some new houses. Some part of the medieval masonry does, however, still survive.

In the churchyard, close to the south porch, there is a cross, and towards the river there are two ancient cottages.

The hamlet of Overy lies across the river. Its mill, likely to be on the site of one of the two 11th-century mills granted to the abbey,[58] is a timber-framed building with weatherboarding. All the houses at Overy, including the mill-house and the so-called manor-house, are 18th-century brick buildings. The 'manor-house', long occupied by the family of Davey,[59] bears the initials and date WHD 1712.

Queensford Mill, to the east of Dorchester, is partly built of brick, partly timber-framed and weather-boarded. The Mill House and Barn are both brick structures of the 18th century.[60]

During the Civil War, as Dorchester lay so near Oxford and on the main road to Henley, troops were constantly in and about it. Sir Samuel Luke records that in May 1643 Sir John Byron and his forces lay there; that two regiments of the king's foot left it in September, and that the royalists intended to keep garrison there during the winter. In March of the next year all Prince Maurice's foot were said to be at Dorchester as well as some of the king's horse from Oxford. In March 1646 the Committee of Both Kingdoms was informed that 1,000 royalist horse and 500 foot were at Dorchester and intended to quarter there. Colonel Fleetwood was ordered to remove them.[61]

Among residents of interest the 16th-century family of Beauforest[62] and the Roman Catholic Daveys of Overy,[63] who were especially prominent from the 17th to the 19th centuries, may perhaps be singled out. In the 19th century W. C. Macfarlane was a notable curate.[64]

MANORS. The Bishop of Lincoln's great estate of *DORCHESTER*, assessed at 90 hides in Domesday Book,[65] represented a part of the ancient endowments of the see of Dorchester which had been transferred to Lincoln.[66] Of this Domesday estate 59 hides and 3 virgates were the bishop's demesne, the remainder was held by under-tenants.[67] The bishop's demesne and the subinfeudated parts of the estate were almost as extensive as Dorchester hundred and included as well land at Baldon and Little Milton which was outside the hundred.[68]

In the second quarter of the 13th century the demesne manor included lands in Baldon, Burcot, Chislehampton, and Drayton as well as in Dorchester.[69] In 1329 the bishop was granted free warren in his demesne lands in these places[70] and they were still listed as part of the demesne manor in 1551.[71] When the manor was held by the Norreys family and their successors it was reduced in extent[72] and by the 18th and 19th centuries comprised lands in Dorchester, Overy, Drayton, Burcot, and Chislehampton only.[73] Homagers from Dorchester and Drayton attended the courts baron and orders were made for Dorchester, Drayton, Overy, and Burcot.[74]

This complex manor formed part of the temporalities of the bishopric of Lincoln until 1547, when it was surrendered to the Crown by Henry Holbeach shortly after his translation from Rochester.[75] Between 1558 and 1562 the manor with lands to the annual value of £108 in Dorchester, Overy, Burcot, Baldon, Chislehampton, and Drayton was twice used as security by the Crown for loans.[76] Queen Elizabeth granted it to Henry Norreys, later Lord Norreys of Rycote, who was in possession by 1577 at least.[77] He was succeeded in the barony in 1601 by his grandson Francis, who inherited Dorchester manor in 1603 on the death of his uncle Sir Edward Norreys, a younger son of Henry.[78] Francis (cr. Viscount Thame and Earl of Berkshire, 1621) committed suicide in 1622 leaving an only daughter Elizabeth Baroness Norreys as heir.[79] She married Edward

---

[56] Wood, *Life*, i. 224.
[57] For a view see plate facing p. 92.
[58] See below, p. 44.
[59] E. C. Davey, *Memoirs of an Oxfordshire Old Catholic Family* (1898), 22–23.   [60] See below, p. 44.
[61] *Cal. S.P. Dom.* 1645–7, 379; Luke, *Jnl.* 91, 158, 160, 262, 264.   [62] See below, *passim*.
[63] See below, pp. 48, 62.
[64] See below, p. 56.
[65] *V.C.H. Oxon.* i. 402.
[66] Ibid. ii. 4–5.
[67] Ibid. i. 402, 403.
[68] See above, pp. 2, 3, 11; and below, pp. 66, 73; for Baldon, see *V.C.H. Oxon.* v. 35.
[69] Queen's Coll. MS. 366, ff. 25–27b.
[70] *Cal. Charter R.* 1327–41, 117.

[71] L.R. 2/189, ff. 1–18.
[72] See below, p. 83; *V.C.H. Oxon.* v. 35, 51, 52.
[73] e.g. see MS. Top. Oxon. c 381; b 197–205.
[74] MS. Top. Gen. c 43–45; d.d. Bertie b 1 (uncat.).
[75] *Cal. Pat.* 1547–53, 153.
[76] Ibid. 1557–8, 408, 409; 1558–60, 437.
[77] An inquisition of 1577 said that John Pollard (d. 1557) had held Clifton of Henry Lord Norreys as of his manor of Dorchester, but this may have been incorrect: C 142/182/40. A Chancery case maintained that Queen Elizabeth granted it: *Proc. in Chancery, temp. Queen Eliz.* (Rec. Com.), ii. 255. In 1566 a messuage in Drayton was said to be held of the queen's manor of Dorchester: C 142/143/50.
[78] *Complete Peerage*, ix. 643–6; C 142/314/127; C.P. 25(2)/198/Trin. 44 Eliz.
[79] *Complete Peerage*, ix. 646–9.

Wray (d. 1658), a gentleman of the Bedchamber, and after her death in 1645 the courts baron held between 1646 and 1650 were described as of Edward Wray.[80] Their only child Bridget Baroness Norreys was the second wife of Montagu Bertie, 2nd Earl of Lindsey. She died in 1657 and her husband presumably held her Dorchester lands as he certainly did her Thame ones until his death in 1666. Their son James Bertie Lord Norreys, who was created Earl of Abingdon in 1682, succeeded to his mother's lands.[81] On his death in 1699 the manor passed to his son and heir Montagu, Earl of Abingdon,[82] and remained in the hands of the earls of Abingdon[83] until 1876, when it was sold to Sir John Christopher Willoughby of Baldon (d. 1918).[84] The manor and estate, including Dorchester Field Farm (536 a.), was purchased by Guy Nevill Eaglestone Kennett-Barrington in 1915.[85] No lord of the manor was recorded after 1928.[86]

A second *DORCHESTER* manor developed from the estates held in the Middle Ages by the abbey. The nucleus of this estate was the land in Dorchester granted to the canons in the 11th century by Bishop Remigius.[87] In the course of the Middle Ages the abbey acquired estates in the neighbouring parishes of Drayton, Burcot, and Clifton and continued to add to their lands in Dorchester.[88] Like the bishop's manor the abbey's also extended outside the parish, but not over such a wide area. In 1391 the abbot and convent were said to have leased their Dorchester manor.[89] In the 15th century, however, they continued to hold their courts for the property, although they may still have let out the demesne land.[90] After the dissolution in 1536 the 'late monastery of Dorchester' and extensive estates in Dorchester and nearby, including Overy mill, were leased to Edmund Ashfield of Ewelme, and in 1544 this lease was converted into a grant in fee.[91] Sir Edmund Ashfield died in 1578 in possession of Dorchester manor which passed to his grandson, Edmund Fettiplace of Swinbrook, eldest son of William Fettiplace and Elizabeth Ashfield, second daughter of Sir Edmund.[92] The descent of this manor is thereafter the same as the Fettiplace manor of Swinbrook and is given here only in outline. On Edmund Fettiplace's death in 1613 the manor passed to his eldest son, John, founder of the free school at

Dorchester,[93] who died, unmarried, in 1657.[94] He was succeeded by his nephew, Sir John Fettiplace (d. 1672), who was succeeded by his eldest son Sir Edmund, who died unmarried in 1707.[95] The manor passed in turn to his three brothers, Sir Charles who died unmarried in 1714, Lorenzo (d. 1725), and George, the founder of the Fettiplace charity, who died unmarried in 1743.[96] The property then passed to a nephew, Thomas Bushell, who was directed in Sir George's will to take the name of Fettiplace.[97] He died in 1767 and the manor passed to his son Robert.[98] In or shortly after 1777 Robert was 'in distressed circumstances' and conveyed his estates to trustees for the payment of his debts. At this time he was believed to be living in Paris.[99] In 1785 his lands at Dorchester were still in the hands of trustees[1] but by 1787 he seems to have recovered his rights as lord of Dorchester manor,[2] and on his death in 1799 these passed to his brother, Charles Fettiplace of South Lawn Lodge.[3] Charles was succeeded on his death in 1805 by his nephew Richard Gorges, who assumed the name Fettiplace by royal licence of 13 January 1806 and died without issue on 21 March 1806.[4] In May 1808 this Fettiplace manor, with 312 acres of land, &c., was offered for sale by auction and was purchased by George White of Newington.[5] By 1817 he had been succeeded by Thomas Gilbert White,[6] who in 1861 was one of the consenting parties to the inclosure of Dorchester.[7] No mention of his manorial rights was made and there is no further reference to this manor.

LESSER ESTATES. The medieval demesne of the bishops seems to have included Bishop's Court Farm. By the 16th century at least the bishop was leasing this property[8] and at the time when it was handed over to the Crown it was held by Richard Beauforest, a local gentleman.[9] The Crown continued this policy for a time and the lease was granted in 1549 to Roger Hatchman of Ewelme,[10] who also farmed the rectory and leased Overy mills. In 1585 the queen granted Bishop's Court Farm and Queensford mill to William Dunch (d. 1597) of Little Wittenham for £33 16s. 4d. a year, to be held in chief.[11] The property followed the descent of Little Wittenham, passing to Edmund Dunch (d. 1623), to his grandson Edmund (d. 1678), to Hungerford Dunch (d. 1680) and to Edmund

[80] Ibid.; MS. Top. Gen. c 44.

[81] *Complete Peerage*, ix. 649. Records of his Dorchester courts have been preserved from 1675: e.g. Bodl. MS. ch. Oxon. 3846, 3831; d.d. Bertie b 1; Bodl. MS. Rolls Oxon. 144, 146, 150.

[82] *Complete Peerage*, i. 45–47.

[83] For their descent see ibid. 47–49. Records of the Abingdon estate in Dorchester are preserved in d.d. Bertie c 3, c 17; d 1 (uncat.); MS. Top. Oxon. b 121; b 185–205; a 46–47; c 381; c 384–5; c 387.

[84] O.R.O. Wi. I/i/79, p. 95: *Sale cat.* (1914).

[85] Ibid.; O.R.O. C I/iii/9.

[86] Kelly, *Dir. Oxon.* (1928). Kennett-Barrington still lived in the manor-house in 1939: ibid. (1939).

[87] *Reg. Antiquiss.* i, 247; and see below, p. 45.

[88] See above, p. 19; and below, pp. 66, 68. For licences to acquire property in mortmain, see *Cal. Pat.* 1321–4, 416; 1324–7, 196; 1327–30, 263, 464, 493, 504; 1338–40, 210; 1391–6, 100.

[89] C 1/7/258.

[90] For ct. rolls of these estates for 1401, 1461, 1538, 1539, see St. John's Coll., Oxf. muniments.

[91] *L. & P. Hen. VIII*, xix (1), p. 496; cf. H. Addington, *Some Account of the Abbey Church of St. Peter and St. Paul at Dorchester* (1845), 169–72.

[92] C 142/180/1. For this branch of the family see J. Ren-

ton Dunlop, 'The Fettiplaces of Childrey, Berks. and Swinbrook, Oxon.', *Misc. Gen. et Her.* (5th ser.), ii. 204–10; cf. *V.C.H. Berks.* iv. 276.

[93] C 142/333/42; and see *V.C.H. Oxon.* i. 468.

[94] *Misc. Gen. et Her.* (5th ser.), ii. 206; a fine was levied on the manor in 1649: C.P. 25(2)/587/Hil. 1649.

[95] *Misc. Gen. et Her.* (5th ser.) ii. 207–8; *Par. Coll.* iii. 299.

[96] Ibid. O.R.O. H III/a/4; and see below, p. 64.

[97] MS. Top. Oxon. c 120, ff. 54–55.

[98] *Misc. Gen. et Her.* (5th ser.), ii. 209; O.R.O. QSM. II/1, pp. 8, 29; Gamekprs' Deps.

[99] MS. Top. Oxon. c 120, ff. 54–55; O.R.O. QSM. II/1 p. 36.

[1] O.R.O. Land tax assess.   [2] Ibid.

[3] O.R.O. Gamekprs' Deps.; *Misc. Gen. et Her.* (5th ser.), ii. 209.

[4] *Misc. Gen. et Her.* (5th ser.), ii. 210.

[5] *Oxf. Jnl.* 30 Apr. 1808. There is a copy of the sale agreement in Oxf. Dioc. c 1796.

[6] O.R.O. Gamekprs' Deps.

[7] O.R.O. Incl. award.

[8] *Lincs. Chapter Acts*, 1536–47 (L.R.S. xiii), 108–10.

[9] L.R. 2/189, f. 11.

[10] *Cal. Pat.* 1557–8, 102; L.R. 2/189, f. 11b.

[11] C 142/249/84; 402/150.

Dunch (d. 1719).[12] As at Little Wittenham, the three co-heirs of Edmund succeeded, but in 1755 the property was conveyed to the eldest co-heir, Elizabeth Dunch (d. 1779), and her husband Sir George Oxenden (d. 1775).[13] They were succeeded by their son Sir Henry Oxenden, who in 1783 was termed lord of 'Dorchester manor'.[14] Sir Henry had sold his Dorchester property by 1787 to William Hallet, the purchaser of his Little Wittenham estate; and in that year Hallet, as lord of Dorchester manor, appointed a gamekeeper.[15]

MILLS. Queensford mill, first mentioned by name in 1146, was undoubtedly the mill recorded on the bishop's estate in 1086.[16] It remained part of the bishop's estate during the Middle Ages and in 1545 was included with the fishery in the lease of Bishops Court farm to Richard Beauforest.[17] It passed to the Crown in 1547 with the rest of the Dorchester estate, but continued to be leased.[18] In 1585 Queen Elizabeth included the mill in the grant of Bishops Court farm to William Dunch.[19] It followed the descent of the Dunch estate: in 1630, for example, Edmund Dunch leased 'Queeneforde Millnes' and appurtenances for fourteen years for £26 13s. 4d. a year.[20] In the 18th century their successors, the Oxendens, held it.[21] The descent of the mill is not clear after it passed from the Oxendens at the end of the 18th century,[22] but it was in use as a mill at least until the 1870's.[23] At the end of the century it was part of Jabez Balfour's estate of Queensford Mill farm and was sold in 1897.[24] By then it is said to have been used as a store for some time.[25]

There were two water-mills on the abbey's estate in the Middle Ages, said to have been granted to the canons by Bishop Remigius (1072–92),[26] although neither was mentioned in the Domesday Survey. One called Cudicah in 1163[27] was on the Thames, the other was on the Thame.[28] Both were known as Overy mills. They followed the descent of the abbey's Dorchester manor until the Dissolution,[29] when the Crown leased them to Roger Hatchman of Ewelme at first[30] and later included them in the grant of the Dorchester Abbey estate to Sir Edmund Ashfield.[31] Only one mill was mentioned among Sir Edmund's property on his death in 1578,[32] but in the 17th century his successors, the Fettiplaces, received rent from 'the grist mills', presumably the

two Overy mills.[33] At the sale of the Fettiplace estate in 1808, no mention was made of the mills, which perhaps had already been sold.[34] One Overy mill continued to function until the early 20th century;[35] the fate of the other is not known.

FISHERIES AND LOCKS. Fishing rights belonged originally to the bishop.[36] In 1397 he granted all his fishing rights in the Thame and Thames at Dorchester to the abbey.[37] These rights descended to the abbey's successors. In 1538 the Crown leased the Thame fishery to Sir Edmund Ashfield and later included the fisheries in the grant of the manor.[38] Ashfield's heir, Edmund Fettiplace, owned the weir and lock on the Thames in 1580 and 1585,[39] and in the 17th century the Fettiplaces held the free fishery in the Thame and Thames.[40] In 1691 their tenant held the ferry, fishery, and lock for £4 a year.[41] In 1707 Sir Charles Fettiplace released to Edmund Dunch Wittenham Ferry House on an island in the Thames, the ferry between Dorchester and Wittenham, and fishing rights between 'Cowcutt and Feasants Eyot'.[42] The Dunch interest presumably passed to their successors[43] but no further mention of the fishing rights was made.

SOCIAL AND ECONOMIC HISTORY. Dorchester's fields have been occupied from Neolithic times and although many of the prehistoric sites have been excavated, many are only known by aerial photography. Among the more important discoveries made in recent years are an extensive Neolithic complex between the Abingdon and Oxford roads and an early Iron Age site in the same area.[44]

Domesday Book shows that at the end of the Saxon period Dorchester was the chief of a group of estates in this part of Oxfordshire which stood in a special relationship to the town and which supported the bishop and his household.[45] The town had lost much of its former importance by the time of the Norman Conquest and lost more when the bishopric was removed to Lincoln.[46] It retained, however, its position as the centre of the bishop's neighbouring estates. In 1086 the bishop held 59¾ hides on these estates while his knights had 30¼ hides.[47] None of his knights was enfeoffed in Dorchester itself, which was said in 1086 to be entirely in the bishop's own hands.[48] There was a home farm

[12] C 142/402/150; V.C.H. Berks. iv. 382; cf. Bodl. MS. ch. Oxon. 2981–4, for Dunch deeds of Dorchester property.
[13] Bodl. MS. ch. Oxon. 2991; V.C.H. Berks. iv. 382.
[14] O.R.O. QSM II/1, p. 55.
[15] O.R.O. Gamekprs' Deps.; cf. V.C.H. Berks. iv. 382.
[16] V.C.H. Oxon. i. 402; Reg. Antiquiss. i. 247.
[17] Lincs. Chapter Acts, 1536–47 (L.R.S. xiii), 110.
[18] See above, p. 42; L.R. 2/189, ff. 11, 11b.
[19] C 142/402/150.
[20] Bodl. MS. ch. Oxon. 2980.
[21] See above. Sir Henry Oxenden owned it in 1787: C.P. 43/816/no. 303.
[22] See also above.
[23] Pigot, Nat. Com. Dir. (1830); P.O. Dir. Oxon. (1869).
[24] Bodl. G.A. Oxon. c 317(5): Sale Cat.
[25] Ibid.
[26] Reg. Antiquiss. i. 247.
[27] H. E. Salter, 'A charter of Dorchester abbey', O.A.S. Rep. 1909, p. 12.
[28] Ibid.; Reg. Antiquiss. i. 247. The site of the Thames mill has not been established.
[29] See above, p. 43.
[30] L. & P. Hen. VIII, xiii (1), p. 578.
[31] Addington, Dorchester, 170.

[32] C 142/180/1.
[33] Fettiplace estate rental penes Mrs. Buxton, Widford Manor, Burford.
[34] Oxf. Dioc. c 1796.
[35] See O.R.O. Land tax assess.; P.O. Dir. Oxon. (1854, 1869); Kelly, Dir. Oxon. (1887–1920).
[36] See below, p. 45.
[37] Cal. Pat. 1396–9, 73.
[38] L. & P. Hen. VIII, xiv, p. 605; C 142/180/1; and see above, p. 43.
[39] F. S. Thacker, The Thames Highway, Gen. Hist. 51.
[40] e.g. C.P. 25(2)/587/Hil. 1649.
[41] Fettiplace estate rental penes Mrs. Buxton.
[42] Bodl. MS. chs. Oxon. 2987–9.
[43] See above.
[44] See V.C.H. Oxon. i. 263; G. W. G. Allen, 'Marks seen from the air in the crops near Dorchester, Oxon.', Oxoniensia, iii (1938), 169–71; see also other discoveries reported in Oxoniensia, passim; R. J. C. Atkinson, C. M. Piggott, N. K. Sandars, Excavations at Dorchester, Oxon. (1951).
[45] V.C.H. Oxon. ii. 4; and see above, p. 18 and below, pp. 66, 67, 83.
[46] V.C.H. Oxon. ii. 4–5.
[47] Ibid. i. 402–3.
[48] Ibid. 402.

which had land for 4 ploughs and the rest of the land was in the hands of the bishop's peasants, 34 *villani* and 22 bordars. The bishop was himself said to have only 3 ploughs and his tenants had 15 ploughs between them. Some of the English freemen who held of the land of Dorchester may have held in Dorchester itself but the survey does not make this point clear.[49] The estate had almost doubled its pre-Conquest value of £18 and was worth £30 in 1086, together with a number of assets not included in this estimate: the mill rendered 20s., the fisherman paid 30 sticks of eels, and a ½-hide of land brought in 12s. Meadow-land was worth 40s. a year and there was underwood 6 furlongs by three.[50] There is no mention in Domesday of the estate of the Dorchester church, the later abbey, which Bishop Remigius (1072–92) gave the canons on the transference of the see.[51] These lands were described in charters of 1146 and 1163 as the land once held by Hunfredus the priest, i.e. the later Humfrey's mede, *Brademera* with its meadow and pasture, the curtilage and croft which had belonged to Hunfredus the priest, 10 bordars, the episcopal houses and whatever was within the wall. Outside the wall they were granted the land between it and the road going to the house of a certain Dunning, the whole circuit (*ambitus*) of the episcopal granges and the croft beyond them, the garden and furlong beyond it that stretched to Queensford mill and comprised 100 acres, and the meadow bordering the river by this same land and 'suiftlac' meadow on the other side. Most of the meadow and pasture in fact belonged to the two mills which were also granted.[52] The one was undoubtedly Overy mill, described as to the east over the bridge on the Thame. The other, called Cudicah in 1163, was described as on the Thames.[53]

Dorchester's importance as a demesne manor is clearly shown in a survey of the bishop's estates of the second quarter of the 13th century.[54] Not only did the bishop frequently visit the township, but he maintained a demesne farm which was expected to provide for his needs in residence and also supplied produce for him at his other manors. A certain amount was evidently sold, for his tenants had to carry grain to Oxford and Wallingford where it was taken on by boat to London.[55] His demesne land in the whole hundred of Dorchester was 5 carucates, but it is not stated how much lay in Dorchester itself.[56] He must have had a fair-sized farm there for 8 of his Dorchester tenants were required to act as ploughmen, which would mean that he had at least 4 plough-teams.[57] Small parcels of the demesne meadow and pasture were let out to tenants, but no large-scale leasing of the demesne was recorded.[58] The list of labour-services shows that the farm was expected to produce a good quantity of grain and that a number of sheep and pigs were kept on it and neighbouring manors.[59]

The tenants' rents and dues were organized round the needs of the home farm. Only 4 were free tenants, who together held about 2 hides. One, Geoffrey de Verley, held 1 hide, which, however,

the jurors claimed had been customary land in the time of Bishop Robert de Chesney (1148–83).[60] The rest of the bishop's tenants were unfree, holding in all about 31 virgates. All paid merchet, heriot, leirwite, an entry fine for their land, and aid. Working virgaters owed pannage and 'tolsest', four hens at Christmas, and 6d. rent; cottars and groups of *carucarii* (ploughmen) and 'gavelmen' owed the same dues except for the rent. These dues and the whole organization of rents and labour services indicate that the agricultural system at Dorchester was of considerable antiquity. The virgate was the standard holding for about half the tenants, while the cottars held an acre each. Most tenants were expected to attend the autumn boons, but some were completely free of week-work and the more arduous services; others were still liable although arrangements existed for them to pay rent if the bishop did not need their services. Thirteen villeins had no week-work, but paid rent at about 5s. 6d. a virgate and did ploughing and harvest works, usually by ploughing so many acres for the bishop and attending the boons. Six of them owed somewhat heavier services, as well as the same elaborate carrying and carting services which the Chislehampton virgaters owed. They carted the grain from the field until it was all in; carried it to Oxford and Wallingford to be shipped to London, and went on the boat with it if necessary; and also carried the bishop's food to various places. Like the Chislehampton virgater they also owed 'wudeway' and each had to feed one of the bishop's horses whenever the bishop came to the town at Martinmas and Hocktide.[61] There was a group of 7 cottars, 1 half-virgater, and 8 tenants renting small parcels of the demesne who likewise had no week-work. The other tenants of the bishop were liable to week-work. These were 11 villeins with 10 virgates between them, the 8 *carucarii* and 2 half-virgaters, and about 18 of the 28 cottars. The virgaters owed three days a week of farm work and a fourth day when they did carrying and carting services. The ploughmen and cottars did two days a week each with one man. If the land was held at rent or 'farmed' the virgaters each paid 5s. 6d., the *carucarii* 2s. each, and the cottars 1s. or 1s. 4d.; they still had also to perform certain agricultural services.

Their services, whether farmed or not, illustrate the agricultural life of medieval Dorchester. The farmwork on the demesne was divided among the various tenants. The working virgater did ploughing and boon services like the rent-paying virgater. He had to stack and toss the hay ready for his rent-paying fellow to cart; similarly he cut and prepared the wood for carting; stacked and covered haycocks and reaped a half-acre of the bishop's grain each day until it was all reaped. The bishop, when he was at Dorchester, also had his services for two days threshing whether his works were commuted or not. Two works were taken up in making hurdles for the bishop's fold and others were devoted to making the byres and fetching wood from the Abbot of Eynsham's wood at Woodcote for the fencing of the

[49] Ibid. 403.
[50] Ibid. 402.
[51] *Reg. Antiquiss.* i. 246–7.
[52] Ibid.; cf. H. E. Salter, 'A Charter of Dorchester Abbey', O.A.S. *Rep.* 1909, 12.
[53] For mills, see above, p. 44.
[54] Queen's Coll. MS. 366, ff. 25–25*b*, 26*b*–27*b*. For its dating, see above, p. 13, n. 94.

[55] Queen's Coll. MS. 366, ff. 25–25*b*, 26*b*–27*b*.
[56] Ibid. f. 27.
[57] See below.
[58] Queen's Coll. MS. 366, ff. 25*b*, 27, 27*b*.
[59] Ibid. f. 27*b*.
[60] Ibid. f. 25.
[61] For a fuller description of these services see above, p. 12.

bishop's court. When the bishop sent grain to London the virgaters were to steer the boat and help with transport at their own expense. If a man made a quarter of malt from the bishop's grain it was reckoned as two works. The cottars did similar services. Each carried a quarter of a quarter of grain to the ship when it was sent to London, carried eggs, and drove pigs and cattle to neighbouring manors. They helped with the brewing of the bishop's ale. The bishop reserved some of their services for the sheep-shearing which each had to attend. Seven other cottars did no week-work, but among their dues it was stated that if they had sheep they were each to keep 5 in the bishop's fold from Hocktide to Martinmas and to pay 1d. for every 4 in their own fold. One group of tenants was tied closely to the demesne. Eight *carucarii* or ploughmen held 4 virgates between them and were to be the lord's ploughmen. It was also their business to brew the bishop's ale and, with the help of the cottars, they were to guard any thieves and, if necessary, hang them. When the bishop's hay or grain was in the fields they and the hayward were to watch over it nightly. Two others with a ½-virgate each were to be the bishop's shepherd and swineherd, but they could commute this service for rent and lighter services, while a third had in fact commuted his service of being cowherd.[62] The whole tenor of the survey indicates that, even if conditions were changing in the 13th century, the bishop had in the past cultivated his farm by the labour services of his tenants and still expected to use them.

Dorchester's hamlet of Overy was not mentioned by name in this survey, but there were evidently some houses there by this time. Its mill, described as 'beyond the bridge' (*ultra pontem*) was working in 1146.[63] The bishop also had a 13th-century tenant Reginald, distinguished as of *ultra aquam de Dorchester*, i.e. of Overy.[64]

It seems that no survey of 1279 of Dorchester or Overy has survived. The rolls of the hundredal inquest for Dorchester hundred are defective and the first entry concerns Stadhampton.[65]

A survey of the bishop's demesne in 1348 listed about 720 arable acres, 150 acres of meadow, and 40 acres of pasture. Some furlongs lay in townships near Dorchester, but certain of them can be identified as Dorchester lands: the furlong under the Dyke (42 a.), Dyke Furlong (38 a.), Quenford Furlong (9 a.), Whalley Meadow (27 a.) and Horsecroft (in Overy), and 'Erdiche medewe' (later Ardiche).[66] The arable was described in three 'seasons' indicating a three-field system.[67] It is clear that the meadows and pastures of the Thames and Thame played an important part in the bishop's economy. Warborough inhabitants claimed common of pasture in Overy fields, meadows and pasture and there were many disputes over this claim in the 14th century.[68]

No survey exists of the abbey's estate which was administered from its grange. A fire there was mentioned in 1277.[69] In 1298 the lands, rents, and meadows of the abbey were valued at £15 8s. 4½d. a year, and fruits, flocks, and animals at £2 10s.[70] Fourteenth-century records show that the canons continued to build up their estate in Dorchester: in 1397 the bishop granted them the Conynggere (4 a.), pasture called 'Le Hurst' (24 a.), and all the bishop's fishery in the Thames and Thame at Dorchester, together with coneys and other profits, for an annual rent of £2 13s. 6d.[71] At the end of the century, the abbey was leasing its Dorchester estate for a term of years.[72]

The fortunes of the lay people in medieval Dorchester are less well documented. The 14th-century tax lists show that Dorchester paid the largest contribution in the hundred (£3 10s. in 1306),[73] but as Overy and Fifield may be included in the return the figure is of little help in assessing the wealth of Dorchester itself.[74] In 1327 there were 39 contributors to the 20th,[75] but the largest contributor, William de Hoyville, perhaps paid his 13s. 4d. for Fifield in Benson.[76] Except for Hugh Dammory, who paid half this amount, no one in the community had more than very modest wealth. Thirteen paid between 2s. 6d. and 5s., and 25 under 2s., most of them 1s. and under. Neither the bishop nor the abbey were included in the list.[77] The total contribution in this year was £4 9s. 10d., but in 1334 it was reduced to £3 19s. 8d., which remained the standard assessment.[78] In 1354 Dorchester was allowed an abatement of 16s. 8d. perhaps because of the effects of the Black Death.[79] There were 215 adults listed for the poll tax of 1377, the fourth highest figure in this part of Oxfordshire, after Henley, Thame, and Great Milton.[80]

Dorchester remained in ecclesiastical hands until the 16th century when both bishop and canons still had substantial farms. At its dissolution in 1536 the abbey owned 7½ arable yardlands in Dorchester field, an 8-acre close sown with corn, an orchard, and about 80 acres of meadow and pasture. Certain waters and eyots also belonged to it as well as Overy mill, which was farmed for £6 a year.[81] One tenant, Richard Beauforest, a substantial local man, had a large holding for which he paid 76s. 4d. rent a year. The other tenants were 20 cottagers, holding by copy and at rents varying from 3s. for a single cottage to 12s. for a cottage and parcel of meadow. When Edmund Ashfield took up the lease of the lands, rents, and site of the monastery and rectory the total yearly value was stated to be £34 17s. 4d. Herbage and trees—360 elms and ash of 60 to 80 years' growth—were valued at £6.[82] The bishop's farm of Bishop's Court (323½ a.) consisted in 1545 of 95½ acres of pasture, 64 acres of meadow, and 164 acres of arable. Its rent was nearly £20 a year.[83] There were also 23½ virgates held by customary tenants in

[62] Queen's Coll. MS. 366, ff. 25–25b, 26b–27b.
[63] *Reg. Antiquiss.* i. 247.
[64] Queen's Coll. MS. 366, f. 26b; for etymology of Overy see *P.N. Oxon.* (E.P.N.S.), i. 152.
[65] *Rot. Hund.* (Rec. Com.), ii. 747–8, and see below p. 85, n. 80.
[66] Queen's Coll. MS. 366, ff. 60b–61.   [67] Ibid.
[68] *Blk. Prince's Reg.* iv. 298; *Cal. Pat.* 1381–5, 283–4; 1388–92, 439.   [69] *Cal. Pat.* 1272–81, 240.
[70] *Tax. Eccl.* (Rec. Com.), 44.
[71] *Cal. Pat.* 1396–9, 73; cf. 1313–17, 465.
[72] C 1/7/258.   [73] E 179/161/10.   [74] See above, p. 3.

[75] E 179/161/9. No return for 1316 has survived.
[76] E 179/161/9; cf. *Feud. Aids,* iv. 167, 182; *Blk. Prince's Reg.* iv. 7. For the bishop's lordship of Fifield see above, p. 3.   [77] E 179/161/9.
[78] Ibid. 9, 17.   [79] Ibid. 41.   [80] Ibid. 40.
[81] Addington, *Dorchester,* 169–70; *Valor Eccl.* (Rec. Com.), ii. 170.   [82] Addington, *Dorchester,* 152–4.
[83] *Linc. Chapter Acts,* 1536–47 (L.R.S. xiii), 108–9. In 1550 when the bishop's property was leased to Richard Hatchman it consisted of 6 a. of meadow called 'Le Hall', 522 a. arable in Dorchester and Overy fields: *Cal. Pat.* 1557–8, 102.

Dorchester and 7 virgates in Overy, besides other small parcels of land.[84] The bishop's tenants, like those of the abbot, were copyholders and usually took their lands for 2 or 3 lives. Most still had only a single yardland, but four had 3 or 4 yardlands. Their annual rent brought in about £23 a year.[85]

Some local families prospered in the conditions of the 16th century. Out of the total tax from the 47 contributors to the 1523 subsidy Richard Beauforest paid over a third.[86] In 1545 he evidently took over the lease of Bishop's Court,[87] and a few years later he also held of the bishop 3 customary messuages and virgates and a moor called 'Les Tanne house'.[88] Both his sons were termed gentlemen and one had the highest assessment for the 1577 subsidy, paying on £10 worth of goods.[89] Another of the bishop's tenants, Roger Hatchman, a gentleman of Ewelme, who held two cottages and 2 virgates by customary tenure, was able to obtain the reversion of Bishop's Court in 1550 from the Crown for a rent of £14 13s. a year.[90] He had been the Crown's bailiff for the abbey lands and also lessee of the bishop's land for a time.[91] In the subsidy list of 1577 the Cherrills, a yeoman family of Overy, stand out among the sixteen contributors as substantial men.[92]

There is no certain evidence for the medieval and pre-parliamentary inclosure of Dorchester, but some clearly took place. By the 18th century the open fields lay solely in the northern part of the parish and round Overy.[93] It appears that by the 16th century some of the bishop's land was inclosed; it was certainly partly consolidated, for a lease of Bishop's Court in 1545 described land lying in blocks of 50 and 30 acres and of 10 to 20 acres in certain furlongs.[94] The right of the lessee, Richard Beauforest, to hold these lands in severalty was disputed in 1554, when a yeoman and several labourers of Dorchester tore down the gate of Whalley meadow and other inclosed land, including 30 acres of arable. They drove off his cattle and put in their own.[95] In the 17th century tenants claimed that they had once had common rights in Bishops Field and it looks as if the land here had first been consolidated and then later inclosed.[96] The abbey's arable, on the other hand, certainly still lay in the open fields in the 16th century.[97] There is little doubt that much of the meadow and pasture, belonging both to the bishop and to the abbey, lay in separate closes. New close (8 a.), Mill Close (30 a.), and Swannesneste (5 a.) were described amongst the bishop's meadow

and pasture; and amongst the abbey's pasture were the closes Great Mayns (21 a.) and Little Mayns (4 a.), and Connygger (1½ a.).[98] There is no evidence that this arose from any movement to convert arable into pasture in the 16th century. Many of the abbey's pasture and meadow closes are recognizable in medieval grants[99] and the lease of Bishop's Court in 1545 specifically laid down that arable was not to be converted into pasture. This proviso, however, which appears in other of the bishop's leases at this time, may have little special relevance to conditions in Dorchester.[1] Two large pasture closes described in the 17th century as containing 40 and 50 acres respectively indicate that there had been some conversion and inclosure perhaps later in the 16th century.[2]

In the 17th century there were three open fields in Dorchester itself: West Field, Middle Field and East Field were mentioned in contemporary documents.[3] Two can be identified from furlong names as lying in the north of the parish.[4] It is not known how far south the fields extended but in 1728 they were said to 'lye far from home'.[5] In the 17th century a three-course system was probably followed, two crops and a fallow: contemporary court rolls speak of the summertilth (i.e. fallow) field and of the Wheatfield and Lent field.[6] By this time, however, experiments in cropping were being tried. Early 17th-century inventories speak of hitches and it is evident that part of the fallow was being used for growing pulse.[7] By 1728 the fields were said to be 'lately' divided into four and the course was three crops and a fallow.[8] This new system was much criticized by the Earl of Abingdon's surveyor in 1728 on the grounds that the soil was dry and 'burning' in a drought (a modern criticism also), and required constant 'mucking and manuring'; he implied that three crops would exhaust the soil and advocated one part being laid down to permanent grass.[9] Overy had only one field, which in the 18th century was cropped annually.[10] The land was said to be good, but the surveyor thought that a fallow should be incorporated.[11] Later surveys show that his advice was not followed and in 1785 Overy was called 'every year's land'.[12]

Hemp was among the crops cultivated in Dorchester from the 16th century at least, when the hemp crofts or 'Les Hempelands', which lay behind the villagers' cottages, were mentioned.[13]

Although some meadow was inclosed by the 16th

[84] L.R. 2/189, ff. 1b–4: a survey made when it came into the king's hands in 1551. The total number of virgates in the estate was 28 in Dorchester and 7½ in Overy: ibid. f. 13.

[85] L.R. 2/189, f. 4.

[86] E 179/161/198. A Richard Beauforest held land of the abbey as early as 1463: St. John's Coll. Mun. ct. roll 1463.

[87] Linc. Chapter Acts, 1536–47 (L.R.S. xiii), 108–9; and see above for the description of the farm.

[88] L.R. 2/189, ff. 4, 11. His will is Bodl. MS. Wills Oxon. 181.   [89] E 179/162/341.

[90] L.R. 2/189, ff. 3–4; Cal. Pat. 1557–8, 102.

[91] L. & P. Hen. VIII, xiii (1), p. 573; and see above, p. 43.   [92] E 179/162/341.

[93] See below.

[94] Linc. Chapter Acts, 1536–47 (L.R.S. xiii), 110–11.

[95] Sta. Cha. 4/9/53.

[96] C 2/D 14/77.

[97] Linc. Chapter Acts, 1536–47 (L.R.S. xiii), 169; some 16th-cent. field names (e.g. Whalley) were still shown on the 19th-cent. tithe map.

[98] Cf. Valor Eccl. (Rec. Com.), ii. 170.

[99] e.g. the Hurst, Humfreys mede, Swyselake, and Priest moor: Reg. Antiquiss. i. 247; Cal. Pat. 1396–9, 73.

[1] Linc. Chapter Acts, 1536–47 (L.R.S. xiii), 109.

[2] Bodl. MS. chs. Oxon. 298, 363.

[3] Ibid. 3832; MS. Top. Gen. c 44, f. 81b.

[4] Ibid.; cf. Bodl. Tithe award map.

[5] MS. Top. Oxon. c 381, f. 47.

[6] e.g. d.d. Bertie b 1, p. 32; MS. Top. Gen. c 43, p. 179.

[7] In 1604 Thomas Davis of Overy had 40 a. of 'hytchinge' worth £4 presumably in Dorchester and in 1616 Joan Bannister of Dorchester had 20 a. sown with winter wheat, 4a. of summer tilth (presumably fallow), and 11 a. of 'hitchin', and had barley stacked, obviously for the spring field: MS. Wills Oxon. 17, 123. (These references are supplied by Mr. M. A. Havinden.)

[8] MS. Top. Oxon. c 381, ff. 47–48.

[9] Ibid.   [10] Ibid. f. 52.

[11] Ibid.

[12] d.d. Bertie c 3, pp. 11–12.

[13] e.g. L.R. 2/189, ff. 2–4. There are references to hemp in 16th- and 17th-century inventories also, e.g. Bodl. MS. Wills Oxon. 296, 17, 123. The common crops were wheat, barley, and pulses.

century, the records suggest that certain meadows were still common in the 16th and 17th centuries, i.e. Henpoole, Roundel, and Lot meadows and Overy mead.[14] Despite its rivers Dorchester meadows were said to be poor: in 1728 the surveyor maintained that they did not produce 'more than half a turn to an acre'.[15] There were common pasture rights attached to each tenement. In the 17th century the commons were the Moor (probably the common in the north of the parish), the Cow Lease, Bridge Common, the road from Thame to Chislehampton, and the road to Drayton and 'Rundellaway'.[16] The fields also were common when cleared.[17] Regulations about the use of the commons were constantly made by the manorial courts. In 1632 the stint was stated to be 30 sheep and 3 beasts to a yardland and fines of 3s. 4d. per month for every extra gross of sheep and 6d. for every extra cow kept on the commons were imposed.[18] Only lambs which had been lambed on the commons were to be kept on them.[19] In 1634 presentments were made for keeping hogs in the cornfield, sheep in the cow leaze, and beasts from the common herd.[20] Two fieldmen were appointed each year to 'drive' the commons and to impound cattle.[21]

Another of the chief agricultural matters dealt with by the courts were disputes over boundaries of holdings in the open fields. Homagers were frequently called in to settle disputes between tenants, as in 1691 when seven homagers were ordered to meet at the 'Three Cups' in Dorchester and go into Overy field to set out mere or boundary stones 'for the preventing of controversies for the future'.[22]

Dorchester in the late 17th century was evidently rather larger than the average village, and appears to have been a market town. Seventy-nine householders were returned for the 1662 hearth tax.[23] But in 1728 the Earl of Abingdon's estate there was said to consist mainly of small buildings and Dorchester was described as 'a poor town without any manner of trade nor likely much to improve'.[24] The land of the two chief manors, i.e. the Abingdon and Fettiplace estates, was entirely let out to tenants at this period. In 1691 the Fettiplace manor had two tenants at will who held the parsonage house, the demesnes, and tithes for some £285 a year. Three tenants held by lease and their rents brought in £135 a year; 27 tenants were copyholders, paying only small rents. The lord of the manor received only about £19 a year from these tenements as against £169 if he had held them in his own hands. The ferry, mills, and six inns also belonged to him.[25] The Abingdon estate likewise had a preponderance

of copyhold lands held at low rents. In 1728 there were 67 copyholders, 18 leaseholders, and 2 rack-renters in Dorchester, and 15 copyholders and free-holders in Overy.[26] The old value of the estate in Dorchester was £448 15s.; the real value was £564 3s. 8d. and quitrents were £24 10s. 4d. In Overy the old value was £104 16s. 8d. as against £170 12s. real value; quitrents were £4 5s. 3d.[27] On both estates most customary tenants held for a term of two or three lives or on long lease.[28] Resident freeholders were comparatively few: in 1754 only 9 out of 16 40s. freeholders occupied their premises.[29]

A large number of small and medium farms remained typical of Dorchester throughout the 18th century. In 1757 only 4 farmers paid over 10s. to the church rate of 1d. in the £1, while 23 inhabitants paid between 1s. and 6s. and 36 paid under 1s.[30] In 1785 there were again only 5 large contributors to a rate and the land tax for that year shows that there were about 9 medium-sized farms and 32 occupiers of land or cottages assessed at under £2.[31] In 1808 Arthur Young listed 50 rateable farms.[32] Nevertheless the Abingdon estate accounts show that the smaller holders were being gradually eliminated. By 1754 the number of leaseholders and copyholders in Dorchester and Overy had dropped to 75 and by 1813 there were about 9 rack-renters, and 50 lease-holders and copyholders.[33] The sale of the Fettiplace estate further improved the position of the larger farmers. By 1808 four of the largest farms were owned, at least partly, by their occupiers and their farmers were able to buy the tithes in that year and purchase a good part of the 312 acres of the estate which was sold off at the same time.[34] They paid good prices and the sale realized £16,840.[35] The land tax of 1832 shows that some farmers had taken in the holdings of as many as five or six previous tenants.[36] The chief changes in ownership since 1785, when the Earl of Abingdon, the trustees of the Fettiplace estate, and Sir Henry Oxenden had divided most of the parish, was that several of the larger farmers now owned a fair proportion of the parish.[37]

Part of the prosperity of the larger farmer in Dorchester was due to a readiness to experiment with new agricultural methods. The Daveys of Overy were foremost in this. Already by 1757 William Davey (d. 1767) paid the highest contribution to the Dorchester church rate and was clearly farming most of Overy.[38] His farm accounts show that he was producing wheat, beans, and barley for local markets: in one year the wheat crop fetched £438 and the barley £412.[39] In some years dealers

[14] L.R. 2/189, ff. 3–4; MS. Top. Gen. c 43, p. 65; Bodl. Tithe award.
[15] MS. Top. Oxon. c 381, f. 47.
[16] MS. Top. Gen. c 44, f. 81b; d.d. Bertie c 13 (ct. roll of 1625, uncat.).
[17] d.d. Bertie c 13 (ct. roll of 1625, uncat.).
[18] MS. Top. Gen. c 43, p. 65.
[19] Ibid.
[20] Ibid. p. 178. In 1689 4 men were presented for keeping their ewes separate against the custom of the manor: d.d. Bertie b 1, p. 51.
[21] MS. Top. Gen. c 43, p. 66. There was a pound at Overy: d.d Bertie b 1, p. 61.
[22] d.d Bertie b 1, p. 54; for the setting out of boundary stones in Dorchester and Overy fields see ibid. pp. 42, 68, 95; MS. Top. Gen. c 43, p. 179.
[23] E 179/164/504; only 40 names were recorded for the 1665 tax: Hearth Tax Oxon. 52–53.
[24] MS. Top. Oxon. c 381, f. 48.

[25] Fettiplace estate rental penes Mrs. O. Buxton, Widford Manor, Burford.
[26] MS. Top. Oxon. c 381, ff. 38–52.
[27] Ibid. ff. 49, 52.
[28] Ibid. ff. 38–52.
[29] Oxon. Poll, 1754.
[30] Par. Rec. Chwdns' accts.: this does not include the glebe which, however, was not very extensive.
[31] Ibid.
[32] Young, Oxon. Agric. 31–32.
[33] MS. Top. Oxon. b 178; b 207.
[34] Oxf. Dioc. c 1796 contains a copy of the fine dealing with this sale. Other details about it are recorded at the end of the Fettiplace school register (Par. Rec.).
[35] Par. Rec. Fettiplace school register.
[36] O.R.O. Land tax assess.
[27] Ibid.
[38] Par. Rec. Chwdns' accts.
[39] Davey, Catholic Family, 32–33.

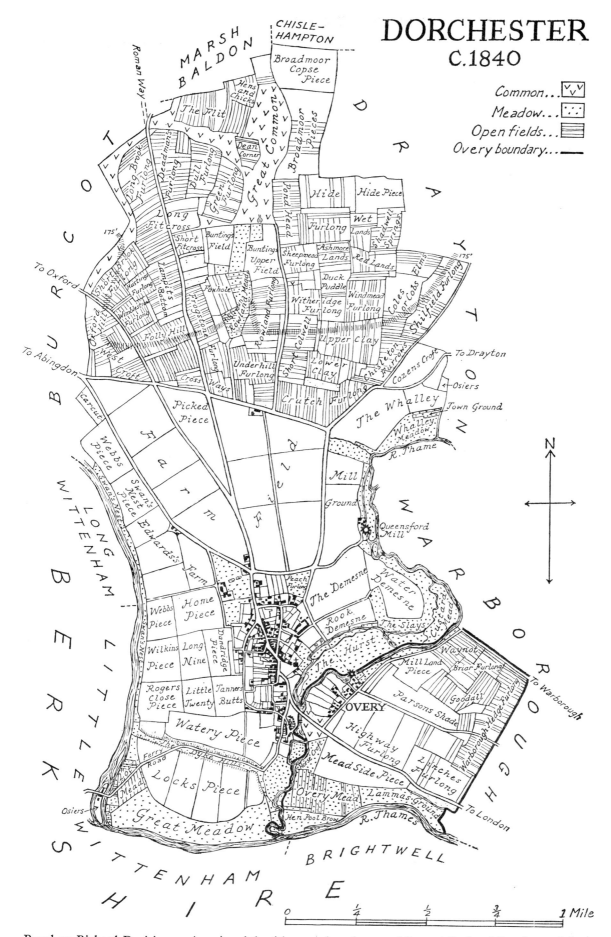

DORCHESTER
C.1840

Common... ⌄⌄⌄
Meadow... ⋰⋰
Open fields... ▤
Overy boundary... ——

MARSH BALDON

CHISLE-HAMPTON

Roman Way

Broadmoor Copse Piece

Hens and Chicks

The Flit

Long Brook Furlong

Deadman's Furlong

Dull Furlong

Green Furlong

Great Common

Broadmoor Pieces

Pond Head

Hide

Hide Piece

Wet Lands

Shadwell Spring

Long Fitcross

Short Fitcross

Buntings Field

Bunting's Upper Field

Bunting Furlong

Sheepmead Furlong

Ashmore Lands

Red Lands

175'

Brook

Short Furlong

Little Furlong

Hustings Furlong

Foxhole

Duck Puddle

Witheridge Furlong

Windmead Furlong

Coles Cross Elms

Shilfield Furlong

175'

To Oxford

Oxford Hill

Wimblestraw Furlong

Lampits Bottom

Frogstone Furlong

Rowland Mead

Rowland Furlong

Short Colwell

Upper Clay

Folly Hill

Underhill Furlong

Lower Clay

Chiselcon Furrows

Cozens Croft

To Drayton

To Abingdon

West Croft

Cross Ways

Crutch Furlong

The Whalley

Osiers

Town Ground

BURCOT

Carcut

Picked Piece

Whalley Meadow

R. Thame

LONG WITTENHAM

Webbs Piece

Swans Piece

Swans Nest

Edwards's

Farm

Field

Mill Ground

WARBOROUGH

To Warborough

Peach Furlong

Queensford Mill

Webbs Piece

Home Piece

Dandridge Piece

The Demesne

Water Demesne

N

Wilkins Piece

Long Nine

Rook Demesne

The Slays

Custard

Rogers Close Piece

Little Twenty

Tanners Butts

The Hurst

OVERY

Waynot

Mill Land Piece

Briar Furlong

Watery Piece

Parsons Shade

Goodall

Ferry Road

Dyke Hills

Horse Croft

Mead Side Piece

Highway Furlong

2 Inches Furlong

Warborough Hedge Furlong

BERKS

Osiers

Mead

Locks Piece

Great Meadow

Hen Pool Brow

Overy Mead

Lammas Ground

R. Thames

To London

LITTLE

WITTENHAM

BRIGHTWELL

SHIRE

0   ¼   ½   ¾   1 Mile

Based on Richard Davis's map (1797) and the tithe awards and maps of Overy (1840) and Dorchester (1847).

came from as far afield as Hereford.[40] His grandson William Davey (d. 1831) paid over £8,000 for land and tithes at the Fettiplace sale in 1808;[41] Davey was a founder of the Oxford Agricultural Society and was highly praised by Arthur Young as 'one of the most intelligent farmers' and 'one of the best' in Oxfordshire.[42] His contemporary Thomas Latham, who farmed at Clifton and Dorchester, was also much quoted by Young.[43] Between them they established such a reputation for Dorchester agriculture that Young advised other farmers to visit the town[44] and George III is said to have driven over from Nuneham to see Davey's model farm.[45] Davey used a varying four-course rotation with the emphasis on beans, peas, and turnips. He was one of the few farmers who, according to Arthur Young, realized that beans should precede wheat and used root crops to clean the ground.[46] Sheep were an essential part of his farming. He had a flock of 600 sheep and lambs, which by 1808 were mainly South Downs.[47] His ploughing was much praised, but it is evident that his success depended on careful husbandry and experiments with crops. Young noted that he had little faith or success with the new drills and horse-hoes.[48] In the next generation his son George Davey was also a noted agriculturalist and a successful exhibitor at Smithfield.[49]

The tithe awards of 1840 for Overy and of 1846 for Dorchester show that most of the land was arable. If Davis's Oxfordshire map of 1797 is accurate the land on the east of the parish had been converted to arable since that date.[50] In the 1840's only about one-eighth of the parish was meadow or pasture; some 1,447 acres were arable.[51] Sixty-four acres in Dorchester and 7 acres in Overy were common lands.[52] Three farms were over 300 acres: George Davey's Overy farm (c. 345 a.), the Lathams' Bishop's Court farm (428 a.) and Vincent Cherrill's Manor farm (312 a.). There were 2 farms of 87 and 112 acres respectively and 6 of 20 to 50 acres. Over 100 people had only cottages and houses and under 10 acres of land.[53] In 1851 four farms over 300 acres were described including James Shrubb's Queensford Mill farm of 600 acres, some of which probably lay outside the parish.[54] One hundred and fifty-seven labourers were employed on these farms.[55] Six hundred and eighty-one acres of Dorchester still belonged to the Abingdon estate, about half held as 'lifeholds' or leaseholds at low rents and the rest held on yearly tenancies.[56] In 1844 it was said that inclosure would greatly increase the value of this land.[57] Nevertheless, there was no inclosure

award until 1861,[58] partly perhaps because most of the land was in the hands of a few farmers. By the award the Earl of Abingdon received the largest allotment of 533 acres in Dorchester and 123 acres in Overy; he was also given 3 acres 3 rod 36 perch for his manorial rights.[59] Vincent Cherrill and Robert Davey received about 60 acres each. There were 22 other allottees in Dorchester and 5 in Overy but most received under 1 acre, 6 of them for cow commons or horse common rights only.[60]

There were considerable changes of ownership at the end of the 19th century, but the larger farms, mostly on the fairly big estates, continued to be a marked feature. The Bertie property was sold and Queensford Mill farm became part of the Jabez Balfour estate which extended into Burcot.[61] The Davey farm in Overy was purchased by St. John's College, Oxford, by 1874 and formed part of their 1,000 acre estate in Overy and neighbouring parishes. One man farmed 550 acres of this estate.[62] By 1916 the six farms in the parish were each under different ownership, two of them being owner-occupied.[63] The rest of Dorchester was divided among a large number of small owners and tenants.[64] By 1959 there had been further amalgamation and there were only four farmers in Dorchester.[65]

A combination of arable and pasture farming remained typical of Dorchester farming in the beginning of the 20th century. When Dorchester Field farm (536 a.) was sold in 1914 over 470 acres of it were arable.[66] Some of the best holdings were to be found between the hills and Dorchester, particularly if sheep were kept to counteract the tendency of the gravel soil to dry out and burn the crops.[67] In 1909 there were over 60 sheep per 100 acres in Dorchester.[68] In the same year Frank Shrubb of Overy farm, who sold 551 sheep off the farm, besides fat beasts and pigs, maintained that sheep breeding was 'his industry'.[69] Following the usual trend in 20th-century Oxfordshire sheep gave way to cattle on this farm and in 1959 beef stock were kept on 70 acres of permanent pasture.[70] Otherwise, little stock was kept in Dorchester, which remained predominantly arable. Over 100 acres have been lost to agriculture in the 1950's by gravel workings in the north of the parish and by the building of the new village of Berinsfield.[71]

The population of the parish rose steadily in the 19th century from 901 in 1811 to 1,097 in 1861.[72] It then declined until in 1901 it stood at only 944 persons.[73] The trend was reversed in the 20th century: in 1951 the population reached 1,500 and

[40] Davey, *Catholic Family*, 33.
[41] Par. Rec. Fettiplace sch. reg.
[42] Young, *Oxon. Agric.* 159.
[43] Ibid. *passim*; the Lathams were 19th-cent. farmers in Thame and South Weston.
[44] Young, *Oxon. Agric.* 159.
[45] Davey, *Catholic Family*, 44.
[46] Young, *Oxon. Agric.* 131, 159, 166, 177.
[47] Ibid. 131, 150.
[48] Ibid. 149, 150, 158.
[49] Davey, *Catholic Family*, 51.
[50] Davis, *Oxon. Map* (1797); Bodl. Tithe awards.
[51] Bodl. Tithe awards.
[52] Ibid.   [53] Ibid.
[54] H.O. 107/1690/125.
[55] Ibid.
[56] Bodl. G.A. Oxon. b 90 (33): *Sale cat.*
[57] Ibid.
[58] For the Act see Dorchester Incl. Act, 22 & 23 Vic. c. 47 (priv. act).

[59] O.R.O. Incl. award.
[60] Ibid.
[61] Bodl. G.A. Oxon. c 317 (5): *Sale cat.*; and see below, p. 69.
[62] St. John's Coll. mun.; *Dorchester Parish Magazine*, Nov. 1909.
[63] d.d. Bullingdon c 94.   [64] Ibid.
[65] The farms are Field farm (part of the Farrant estate, in Drayton, Dorchester, and Burcot), Bishop's Court farm, Overy farm, and Queensford (owned by Amey's, the gravel contractors) and Mount farm, now farmed as one unit: inf. Mrs. Hawken of Mount farm.
[66] Bodl. G.A. Oxon. b 90 (34): *Sale cat.*
[67] Orr, *Oxon. Agric.* 25, 172.
[68] Ibid. plate facing p. 220.
[69] *Dorchester Parish Magazine*, Nov. 1909.
[70] Local inf.
[71] Ibid.
[72] *V.C.H. Oxon.* ii. 220.
[73] Ibid.

has continued to increase because of the settlement at Berinsfield.[74]

The high road has added considerably to Dorchester's prosperity. At the beginning of the 19th century the place was described as 'now humble in buildings and depending chiefly for its precarious resources on the traffic of the high road on which it is situated'.[75] The Census of 1851 shows the predominance of the innkeeper in the small group of shopkeepers recorded,[76] and the names of many of their inns are known from the early 16th century.[77] In 1691 the Fettiplace manor (i.e. the former abbey manor) owned the 'Plough', the 'Saracen's Head', the 'Talbot', the 'Crown', the 'George', the 'Swan', and the 'White Hart'.[78] The 'Bull', first recorded early in the 16th century, occurs again in 1728 and was on the Abingdon estate.[79] Ten inns were recorded in the 18th century,[80] and in 1792 the keepers of the 'George' and the 'White Horse' were important enough to have their own pews in the church.[81] Seven inns were licensed in 1821: the 'Fountain', the 'George', the 'White Hart', the 'Fleur de Lis', the 'Horse and Hounds' and the 'Castle'.[82] A 'Queen's Arms' was mentioned in 1854.[83] Six or seven inns were regularly recorded in the 19th and 20th centuries.[84] Dorchester's inns still flourished in 1959 when the 'George' was one of the leading hotels in the county.

PARISH GOVERNMENT. Only two medieval rolls, those of 1401 and 1463, of the manorial courts held for the abbey's manor are known to exist.[85] They deal with admissions, fines, and heriots, but a court roll of 1539, when the abbey's estate was in the king's hands, contains some open-field regulations.[86] Court rolls and court books for the manor of the bishops' successors have survived for many years between 1624 and 1718 and there is evidence for courts being held up to 1769.[87]

Three courts entered for April 1648, March 1649, and April 1650 were views of frankpledge.[88] In 1649 the view and court baron were held on the same day, each with their separate homage.[89] In the mid-17th century three or four courts baron a year are recorded;[90] in the later part of the 17th century and in the 18th century only one or two a year;[91] and it may be that courts where no business was transacted were not written up. The courts dealt with changes in holdings and with the maintenance of highways and drains and with problems of open-field agriculture.[92] The following points of interest may be noted: a typical heriot paid by a copyholder

was half a year's rent,[93] but in 1685 one tenant gave a horse worth £3 as heriot for 1 messuage and 1½ virgates;[94] in 1625 orders were issued in court forbidding anyone to build cottages on the lord's waste without licence, an indication perhaps of a growth of population;[95] and tenants were constantly admonished to scour ditches and drains in Dorchester street and in the open fields.[96]

There are no surviving court rolls for the Fettiplace manor for this period, but the Fettiplaces were said to have a court leet in the mid-17th century.[97]

In the 17th and 18th centuries the vestry and its elected officers, the churchwardens, constable, and overseers, came to play the predominant part in parish government. Overseers' accounts exist, with some gaps, from 1680 to 1835,[98] vestry minutes from 1733 to 1837, and churchwardens' accounts from 1757 to 1794 and 1824 to 1882. Vestry meetings, of which the Easter vestry was the most important, were held as required. In 1736, for example, there were eight vestries entered in the minute book, but in 1740 there were only two.[99] In the later part of the century, when the problem of poor relief had become serious, it was customary to adjourn the vestry to a later date at the 'White Hart' or at a parishioner's house.[1] Except on rare occasions the vestry was composed only of the minister, the churchwardens, the overseers, and one or two of the 'principle inhabitants and parishioners', such as the Daveys and Cherrills.[2] In 1735 it was definitely stated that besides seven who signed the minutes there was only one other who attended the vestry.[3] In 1738, on the other hand, a proposal to change the way of raising church rates caused an attendance of sixteen.[4] The Easter vestry appointed the three churchwardens of Dorchester. The principal business of the vestry was to authorize the churchwardens' and overseers' rates and to decide the policy about expenditure.[5] Apparently no regular sum could be paid to any pauper without the due authorization of a vestry meeting,[6] and the more frequent vestry meetings called in some years can usually be accounted for by decisions of this kind.

The churchwardens were mainly concerned with the maintenance of the church fabric. They had also the statutory duty of paying for the destruction of vermin and payments for polecats, sparrows, and hedgehogs occur frequently in their accounts.[7] From 1784, however, the charge, save for hedgehogs, was to be met out of the poor rate.[8]

The overseers' accounts present a clearer picture of the problems confronting the vestry.[9] Poverty

[74] Census, 1951; Oxf. Mail, 1 Aug. 1958.
[75] Brewer, Oxon. (1813), 369.
[76] H.O. 107/1690/125. Crafts included a thatcher, basketmaker, and cooper.   [77] Req. 2/12/176.
[78] Fettiplace Rental penes Mrs. O. Buxton, Widford Manor, Burford.
[79] MS. Top. Oxon. c 381, f. 45.
[80] O.R.O. Cal. Q. Sess.
[81] Oxf. Archd. Oxon. c 159, f. 55b.
[82] O.R.O. Cal. Q. Sess.
[83] Billing, Dir. Oxon. (1854).
[84] Ibid.; Kelly, Dir. Oxon. (1854, 1887–1939).
[85] St. John's Coll. Mun. ct. rolls.
[86] Ibid. ct. roll for 1539. There is also a ct. roll for 1538.
[87] d.d. Bertie c 13 (uncat.): 1624–5 ct. roll; MS. Top. Gen. c 43–45: ct. bks. 1632–46, 1646–50, 1712–18; d.d. Bertie b 1 (uncat.): ct. bk. 1685–1706; MS. Top. Oxon. e 302: accts. of fines at manor cts. 1761–70; Bodl. MS. Rolls Oxon. 144, 146, 150, 165: cts. of 1674, 1675, 1676, 1754.
[88] MS. Top. Gen. c 44, ff. 50, 75b, 101b.

[89] Ibid. f. 75, 75b.   [90] Ibid. c 43; c 44.
[91] Ibid. c 45; d.d. Bertie b 1.
[92] For some open-field regulations, see above, p. 47.
[93] d.d. Bertie b 1, p. 32.   [94] Ibid.
[95] Ibid. c 13.   [96] e.g. ibid. b 1, pp. 32, 42.
[97] Par. Coll. ii. 114.
[98] Par. Rec. Overseers' acct. bks. 1680–1744, 1748–68, 1771–1802, 1810–27, 1827–35.
[99] Par. Rec. Vestry min. bk. 1733–1800.
[1] Ibid. e.g. in Aug. 1793, Dec. 1798.
[2] Ibid. Apr. 1791.
[3] Ibid. 17 July 1735.
[4] e.g. in 1728: ibid. Overseers' acct. bk. 1680–1744.
[5] Par. Rec. Vestry min. bk.
[6] Ibid.
[7] Par. Rec. Chwdns' accts.; cf. Tate, Parish Chest, 105.
[8] Par. Rec. Vestry min. bk. 12 July 1784.
[9] Par. Rec. Overseers' acct. bks. 1680–1835. This section is partly based on notes made by Mr. E. G. Thomas.

and unemployment in the parish were not serious in the 17th century and in 1680–1, the first year of the surviving accounts, disbursements totalled only £17 10s. 2d.[10] The War of the Spanish Succession perhaps accounts for the increase in expenditure which at the beginning of the 18th century reached £60 and by the 1740's totalled some £90 a year.[11] There was no remarkable increase, however, until after 1772, and between 1794 and 1801 expenditure reached £1,000.[12] This change was due to the lack of employment and the strain of the wars. In the earlier part of the century the overseers had usually only to support the aged, the sick, and the fatherless families who were given regular allowances. They paid out other miscellaneous sums for schooling, rent, fuel, funeral expenses, and for soldiers or, as in 1732, to help to keep a parishioner out of gaol.[13] In these years there were some 13 to 24 villagers on the rates, receiving fairly regular payments,[14] but by 1818 there were 53 receiving relief.[15] As early as 1740 the vestry was coping with the problem of poverty by making up workmen's wages,[16] a system subsequently known as the Speenhamland system. In the 1780's and 1790's work was often found for able-bodied paupers on the roads, in the gravel pits, and in clearing away snow.[17] In the crucial year 1795 the magistrates ordered that cheap bread should be sold to the poor and at an adjourned meeting of the vestry 'the churchwardens, overseers, and principal inhabitants' agreed to make a 6d. rate in order to give the poor bread at 1s. 5d. the gallon loaf.[18] In 1799 the vestry agreed to make an allowance to the poor who had large families.[19] The roundsmen system was mentioned as early as 1740, when payments of 8d. or 6d. a day were made to various people who were to 'go on their rounds' to everyone paying £10 to the parish rates for 1 day's employment.[20] The system was not mentioned again until 1814–15,[21] but was perhaps adopted more frequently than the accounts reveal. Expenditure on poor relief again reached four figures after 1818 and wages were regularly made up. In the 1820's emigration became a popular way of helping the poor.[22] In 1829 the overseers spent £26 17s. in sending two men to America, the passage itself costing £17.[23] In 1832 a family of seven emigrated at a cost to the parish of £30.[24] There was still extensive unemployment in the parish, however, in 1834: 21 able-bodied men and 16 women were being given regular payments and there were also 52 needy children and 39 infirm or totally disabled people.[25] Nevertheless, the last years of the old poor law were easier ones for the parish and the average expenditure was about £750.[26]

Other aspects of the overseers' work also throw light on contemporary conditions. There were small-pox epidemics in 1741–2, 1753, 1773, and 1774[27] and expenses were heavy. In 1741–2 the parish doctor was given £10 in addition to his normal salary for treating cases of this sort.[28] In 1780 some parishioners were inoculated and many more in 1794. In 1799 it was decided to inoculate the whole parish at a cost of £23.[29] The new vaccine treatment was applied in 1812.[30]

The parish workhouse seems to have been established in 1742 when the parish officers were to be allowed reasonable charges in seeking a workhouse for the poor.[31] The workhouse was managed at first by a woman, who in 1755 was paid by the overseers £33 7s. 4d.[32] In 1764 John Wallis took charge at 30s. a week and the parish paid the rent of the house. He was to maintain the poor in a decent fashion and was responsible for all save smallpox patients, those with broken bones, or bastards. Wallis was to buy three beds and bedding, seven bedheads, and three spinning wheels, the cost of which the parish would refund when he left. He was not to be responsible for the expenses of resettlement.[33] Payments were made for hemp seed and digging up the ground which the town rented: presumably the paupers were set to prepare and spin the crop when grown.[34]

Another aspect of the overseers' work is shown by the payments made for an incurable lunatic. In 1763 the parish paid about £20 for looking after her and transferring her to Bedlam and the vestry agreed to pay 2s. 6d. a week for her maintenance, a charge which recurs in the accounts until 1788.[35] After the establishment of the Radcliffe Infirmary the overseers subscribed 3 guineas a year for which they were entitled to send two in- and two out-patients.[36]

No surveyors' or constables' accounts have survived, but payments to both are recorded in the overseers' account books.[37] In the 19th century, when the constable was appointed by the vestry, he was paid for visiting the public houses on Sundays during services.[38]

CHURCH. Dorchester, which was the seat of a bishopric intermittently from the 7th until the 11th century, is now a vicarage in Cuddesdon deanery. Since 1939 the church has given its name to the Bishop of Dorchester, a suffragan of the Bishop of Oxford. The ecclesiastical parish includes the hamlet of Overy and that of Burcot, which since 1869 has had its own chapel.[39] From the early Middle Ages until the mid-19th century Dorchester was the head of a peculiar jurisdiction which consisted of eleven parishes.

[10] Par. Rec. Overseers' acct. bk. 1680–1744.
[11] Ibid.
[12] Ibid. (1771–1802).
[13] Ibid. (1680–1744).
[14] Ibid.
[15] Ibid. (1810–27).
[16] Ibid. (1680–1744). For other references to this system, see under years 1817, 1823–5.
[17] Ibid. (1771–1802).
[18] Ibid. Vestry min. bk. (1733–1800), 9 Oct. 1795.
[19] Par. Rec. Vestry min. bk. (1733–1800), 2 June 1799.
[20] Ibid. 7 Dec. 1740.
[21] Par. Rec. Overseers' acct. bk. (1810–27).
[22] Ibid.
[23] Ibid. (1827–35).
[24] Ibid.
[25] Ibid.
[26] Ibid.

[27] Ibid. Overseers' acct. bks. (1680–1744, 1748–68, 1771–1802).
[28] Ibid. (1680–1744).
[29] Ibid. (1771–1802).
[30] Ibid. (1810–27).
[31] Ibid. Vestry min. bk. (1733–1800), 4 July 1742.
[32] Ibid. Overseers' acct. bk. (1748–68).
[33] Ibid. Vestry min. bk. (1733–1800) 28 Oct. 1764.
[34] e.g. in 1727; ibid. Overseers' acct. bk. (1680–1744).
[35] Ibid. (1748–68, 1771–1802).
[36] i.e. in the 1780's: ibid. (1771–1802).
[37] e.g. ibid. Oct. 1748, Dec. 1775. The surveyors received very little from the overseers, and probably kept separate accounts. The constables may not have presented a separate account.
[38] Ibid. Chwdns' accts. (1837–43).
[39] For Burcot see above, p. 69.

The history of the church begins at the same time as the ecclesiastical history of Oxfordshire. When St. Birinus began to convert Wessex in 634, he was given Dorchester by Cynegils, King of Wessex, and Oswald, King of Northumbria, as his episcopal seat. He built several churches in the diocese, including that of Dorchester, in which presumably Cynegils was baptized in 635, and his son and grandson soon afterwards, and in which Birinus was buried.[40]

In the late 7th century the West Saxon bishopric was transferred to Winchester, but in the late 9th century Dorchester became the seat of a Mercian bishopric,[41] and Dorchester church for the next 200 years remained a cathedral, Wulfwig, the last Anglo-Saxon bishop, being buried in it in 1067.[42] His successor, Remigius, a Norman monk, had ambitious plans for the church, but he had only begun to carry these out[43] when in 1070 it was decided to move the see to Lincoln.[44]

Before the Norman Conquest the cathedral was served by secular canons, whose prebends were endowed with the chapels of the surrounding villages.[45] After the see was moved to Lincoln, Dorchester and its chapels continued to be served by secular canons until about 1140 Bishop Alexander of Lincoln dissolved them and founded an abbey of Augustinian canons.[46] In 1146, when Eugenius III confirmed the abbey's possessions, he included the church of St. Peter in Dorchester, with its liberties, its tithes, and its chapels.[47] In 1163 there was a similar papal confirmation.[48]

In 1146 six chapels were confirmed: the five which had formed part of the ancient endowment of the cathedral and had been served by the prebendaries (Chislehampton, Clifton Hampden, Drayton, and Stadhampton, in Dorchester hundred, and Toot Baldon in Bullingdon hundred), and Benson, which had recently been given by the Empress Maud to the abbey.[49] By 1163 two more had been added, Pishill and Marsh Baldon,[50] while Nettlebed and Warborough, which later were included among the ten Dorchester chapels, had originally been chapels of Benson.[51]

Except for Clifton Hampden, whose parishioners were buried at Dorchester until 1819,[52] these chapels from the time their records begin had independent ecclesiastical status, that is to say, all the sacraments could be performed in them. Some at least, however, showed their ancient dependence on Dorchester by contributing towards the upkeep of its church build-

ing. In 1625 the wardens of Warborough, Drayton, and Clifton were cited for refusing to pay rates towards it. The wardens of Clifton answered that they had never been compelled to contribute, while the others failed to appear and were excommunicated.[53] At the same period the Dorchester wardens were trying to force the wardens of Warborough and Drayton to keep up their portions of the Dorchester churchyard rails.[54] The wardens of Warborough contributed toward those until the 19th century.[55] In the 18th but not in the 19th century the wardens of Stadhampton made an annual payment of 6s. 8d. to Dorchester church.[56]

From the early Middle Ages Dorchester and its ten chapels (all of those belonging to the abbey in 1146 and all except one of those the abbey held in 1163)[57] formed an ecclesiastical peculiar, which probably had its origin in the 'ancient dignity of the secular minster which at the time of the Norman Conquest had contained the bishop's stool'.[58] The confirmation of 1146 makes it clear that Remigius had allowed the church to preserve some of its liberties after the see had been transferred to Lincoln.[59]

The peculiar, which was in the abbey's jurisdiction,[60] was exempt from that of the archdeacon, although not entirely free from that of the bishop. The bishop did not visit the peculiar[61] but he instituted to Marsh Baldon, the only endowed living there, while inductions were made by the Abbot of Dorchester.[62] The peculiar survived the abbey's dissolution in 1536, and descended with the abbey's manor and the rectory to the Ashfield and then to the Fettiplace family.[63] It is not mentioned in the grant of 1544 to Edmund Ashfield,[64] and at a later date its holders and officials relied on long usage rather than on documentary proof of their rights.[65] By 1581 it had its own seal[66] and its records begin then.[67] From this time at least jurisdiction was exercised by the commissary or official, always a clerk, appointed by the lay rectors.[68] He took the place of both bishop and archdeacon (except that the bishop continued to institute to Marsh Baldon)[69] and he held annual visitations in Dorchester church, which were attended by the ministers and churchwardens of the parishes in the peculiar.[70]

In the late 18th century the Bishops of Oxford were trying to bring to an end all peculiar jurisdictions in their diocese.[71] A case concerning Marsh Baldon, which was heard in 1799 in the peculiar

[40] V.C.H. Oxon. ii. 1; Bede, Hist. of the English Church, bk. iii, ch. 7.

[41] V.C.H. Oxon. ii. 2.

[42] Anglo-Saxon Chronicle, ed. G. N. Garmonsway (1953), 200.

[43] Wm. of Malmesbury, Gesta Pontificum (Rolls Ser.), 312.

[44] V.C.H. Oxon. ii. 4; Regesta, i. 74.

[45] This is inferred from later evidence; in 1291 they were still called 'capellae prebendales': Tax. Eccl. (Rec. Com.), 30.

[46] For its history see V.C.H. Oxon. ii. 87 sqq.

[47] Reg. Antiquiss. i. 246–7.

[48] O.A.S. Rep. 1909, 12–13.

[49] Reg. Antiquiss. i. 247; V.C.H. Oxon. ii. 87.

[50] O.A.S. Rep. 1909, 12–13.

[51] V.C.H. Oxon. ii. 87.

[52] See above, p. 23.

[53] Oxon. Peculiars, 120.

[54] Ibid. 115; Oxf. Archd. Oxon. c 158, f. 41b.

[55] Warborough Par. Rec., Chwdns' accts.

[56] Par. Rec. Chwdns' accts.

[57] By 1163 the abbey held Shirburn, which never formed

part of the peculiar (O.A.S. Rep. 1909, 13). The other churches which remained in ordinary jurisdiction were Bix Brand and Warpsgrove.

[58] Visit. Dioc. Linc. 1517–31, i, p. x.

[59] Reg. Antiquiss. i. 246–7.

[60] No medieval records of the peculiar survive.

[61] Visit. Dioc. Linc. 1517–31, i. 119–40.

[62] V.C.H. Oxon. v. 43. In the 15th century the archdeacon inducted.

[63] See above, p. 43.

[64] L. & P. Hen. VIII, xix (1), p. 496.

[65] Oxf. Dioc. c 649, ff. 90, 97; c 655, f. 24.

[66] Ibid. c 649, f. 100.

[67] Oxf. Dioc. d 14 (1581–91); later records are Oxf. Dioc. d 13 (1591–5); Oxf. Archd. Oxon. c 158 (1625–37, 1662–1721), c 159 (1740–60, 1790–1836), c 160, c 161 (miscellaneous papers).

[68] Oxf. Dioc. c 649, f. 99.

[69] V.C.H. Oxon. v. 43.

[70] In the 18th century the visitations were usually continued at the 'White Hart' and sometimes at the 'George': Oxf. Archd. Oxon. c 159, 9, 41b.

[71] e.g. see below, p. 201.

court, led to an appeal. This gave Bishop Randolph grounds for hope that the whole jurisdiction might be dissolved.[72] The end of the case has not been traced, but the peculiar continued. When in 1808 the Fettiplace estate was split up, instead of following the descent of the advowson or the rectory, it followed that of the manor, being 'appendant' to one of the lots, and was acquired by George White.[73] The peculiar acts continue until 1836,[74] but the next year the last official, George Scobbell, died[75] and no successor was appointed. By 1845 the parish was said to be in an 'extraordinary position', forming a 'sort of ecclesiastical oasis'.[76] As it had been visited by the bishop since 1834[77] the trouble arose from lack of the archdeacon's jurisdiction. The payment of yearly visitation fees, beginning in 1847, probably marks the complete end of the peculiar.[78]

It is evident that by 1146 the parish's ecclesiastical revenue belonged to the abbey.[79] No vicarage was endowed, and the abbey was responsible for seeing that the church was served. After the Reformation the living was a curacy,[80] sometimes called a donative and sometimes a perpetual curacy.[81] Appointments were made by the lay rectors.[82] From 1788 the curates were licensed by the official of the peculiar[83] and from 1838 by the bishop.[84] In 1868 the living became a titular vicarage.[85]

The rectories of Dorchester (to which was attached the serving of the church) and of Overy remained with the abbey until its dissolution in 1536. Overy rectory was granted by the Crown in 1542 to the Dean and Chapter of Christ Church,[86] who still held it in 1840.[87] In 1544 Dorchester rectory, with the right of presentation, was sold with the site of the abbey and its manor to Edmund Ashfield,[88] and then descended with the manor to the Fettiplaces.[89] In the 17th century the Fettiplaces leased it to Sir Edward Clarke of Reading,[90] and after his death in 1638[91] to his widow and then to his son Edward,[92] the 'Mr. Clerk' mentioned by Anthony Wood in 1657,[93] who lived at Dorchester and who married a daughter of Thomas, Viscount Wenman, of Thame Park.[94]

When the Fettiplace estates were broken up in 1808 the rectory and the right of presentation were separated. In 1828 the latter was sold by Diana Frances Gorges, a relative of the Fettiplaces, for £480 to Henry Burrows, a London lawyer.[95] Burrows, who died in 1829, made complicated legal provisions for it in his will and during the 19th century presentations were made by his trustees.[96] In 1883 his nephew, Henry William Burrows, Canon of Rochester, and the Revd. John Burrows, the latter's son, granted the presentation to the Bishop of Oxford.[97] The bishop is still patron.

In 1808 not only was the advowson separated from the rectory but the rectory itself was split up. The tithes were sold in small portions: some (on about 800 a.) became merged with the land, others continued to be paid,[98] until in 1847 they were commuted and a rent charge of £331 9s. 2d. was awarded to a number of holders.[99] When the rectory was divided, the liabilities on it (the payment to the minister and the upkeep of the chancel) were attached to one small lot of 31 acres called the Hurst,[1] formerly part of the abbey demesne,[2] which was bought by William Davey.[3] From this time the Davey family, although they were Roman Catholics,[4] were responsible for the chancel,[5] repairing it as late as 1860.[6] The land later became part of Queensford Mill farm, and when this was sold in the 1890's, in spite of the vicar's protests, the liability for the chancel was repudiated although payments to the vicar continued.[7]

No early valuations of Dorchester rectory exist, for in 1254 and 1291 it was valued with its chapels, first at £20 13s. 4d. and then at £41 6s. 8d.[8] By 1535 this had risen to £134 0s. 6d., of which Dorchester rectory was worth £10 and Overy £3 6s. 8d.[9] The latter consisted of all the tithes of Overy, which were commuted in 1840, Christ Church and its lessee, George Davey, being awarded a rent charge of £96.[10]

Dorchester rectory consisted of all the tithes of Dorchester as well as some land. Litigation of 1665 shows that by then it was worth £200 a year above the 'reserved rent',[11] although a terrier of the same period estimates its value at £140.[12] It is impossible to estimate its value after its division in 1808 (see above).

Before the 19th century the living, as opposed to the rectory, had no settled endowment, the minister being paid by the rectors. In 1526 the abbey paid him £5 6s. 8d. a year[13] and in the 1540's he received

[72] V.C.H. Oxon. v. 43; Oxf. Dioc. c 327, p. 333; c 655, ff. 14-14b.   [73] Oxf. Archd. Oxon. c 161, f. 72.
[74] Ibid. c 159, f. 148b.
[75] Foster, Alumni.
[76] Hist. of Dorchester, pub. Parker & Co. (1882), 85-86.
[77] Oxf. Dioc. b 39.
[78] Par. Rec. Chwdns' accts. 1847-8. The first archdeacon's visitation found is 1868: Oxf. Archd. Oxon. c 38, f. 28.   [79] Reg. Antiquiss. i. 247.
[80] Bacon, Lib. Reg. 808.
[81] Oxf. Dioc. c 651, f. 48; c 446, f. 80.
[82] e.g. Oxon. Peculiars, 132; Oxf. Archd. Oxon. c 161, f. 80.   [83] Oxf. Archd. Oxon. c 161, f. 56.
[84] Oxf. Dioc. b 22, f. 189.
[85] By 31 & 32 Vict. c 117.
[86] L. & P. Hen. VIII, xvii, p. 491.
[87] Bodl. Overy tithe award.
[88] L. & P. Hen. VIII, xix (1), p. 496.
[89] See above, p. 43.
[90] Oxon. Peculiars, 118; d.d. Parker d 2, 1651 indenture.
[91] Par. Coll. ii. 118-19.
[92] d.d. Parker d 2, 1651 ind.; C 5/592/112.
[93] Wood, Life, i. 224.
[94] Hearth Tax Oxon. 52; M.I. in church. For litigation of 1665, in which Viscount Wenman was involved, see C 5/592/112.

[95] Oxf. Dioc. c 1796, Abstract of title.
[96] e.g. ibid. b 22, f. 189.
[97] Ibid. c 1796, Abstract of title; indenture of 1883. For pedigree see M. Burrows, Hist. of Family of Burrows (1877).
[98] Oxf. Dioc. c 1796, 1808 recovery.
[99] Bodl. Tithe award. The largest amount, £106 12s. 9d., went to Vincent Cherrill.
[1] Oxf. Dioc. c 446, f. 80.
[2] H. Addington, Account of the Abbey Church of Dorchester (1845), 169.
[3] Oxf. Dioc. c 1796, 1808 recovery.
[4] See below, p. 62.
[5] Oxf. Dioc. b 41; Oxf. Archd. Oxon. c 38, f. 28.
[6] Oxf. Dioc. c 1796, letter of 14 July 1897.
[7] Ibid. Letters of 12 and 14 July, 17 Sept. 1897; Sale cat. of 1897 in Bodl. G. A. Oxon. c 317/5.
[8] Lunt, Val. Norw. 306; Tax. Eccl. (Rec. Com.), 30. These valuations presumably included the rectories of Burcot and Overy, as was the case in 1535, but there is no specific record of chapels at either hamlet.
[9] Valor Eccl. (Rec. Com.), ii. 170.
[10] Bodl. Overy tithe award. In the second half of the 17th century it had been worth £24: Oxf. Archd. Oxon. b 40, f. 113.   [11] C 5/592/112.
[12] Oxf. Archd. Oxon. b 40, f. 113.
[13] Subsidy 1526, 279.

£8.[14] By the second half of the 17th century he was receiving £26 a year from the Fettiplaces[15] and by the mid-18th century £32.[16] This was still being paid in 1882.[17] From 1716 the curate also received £10 a year from a bequest left by Robert South, Canon of Christ Church. This £42 was increased by the rent of the parsonage (£10) in the early 19th century.[18] In 1813 and 1814 Queen Anne's Bounty augmented the living by £1,200[19] and later augmentations were made in 1842 and in the sixties and seventies,[20] but Dorchester remained a comparatively poor living especially as the minister was expected to help support the schools and local charities.[21]

There were once, according to Leland, three parish churches in Dorchester, two to the south of the abbey and a third to the south-west.[22] No other evidence has been found for these, but Burcot and Overy each had their own rectories and were separately tithed,[23] and it is not unlikely that at one time they had their own churches. They are not recorded, however, in the papal bull of 1146 which confirmed Dorchester's rights in its other churches (capellae).[24] Whatever the history of Dorchester's early churches may have been, the parish was using the nave of the abbey church as its parish church in the late Middle Ages.[25]

The parish was closely associated with the abbey in other ways: it was in its ecclesiastical jurisdiction (see above); and its parish priest was a chaplain appointed by the abbey or perhaps at times a canon.[26] Nothing, not even their names, is known of the clergy before the 16th century. The opening of the tomb of St. Birinus in 1225 and the alleged discovery of his bones must also have affected the life of the parish.[27] The abbey became an official place of pilgrimage and in the next century a shrine was built over the saint's tomb.[28] The offerings at this shrine brought the abbey £5 a year in 1535,[29] but by the 1540's these offerings were 'in decay'.[30]

When the abbey was visited by the bishop in 1441 and 1445 conditions were far from satisfactory[31] and it is unlikely that the parish, which was not included in the visitation, was unaffected. Among the complaints were that the canons spent much of their time in the local taverns, and that parishioners often walked through the cloister on their way to church.[32] At a visitation in 1530 similar conditions were found.[33]

One effect of the abbey's dissolution in 1536

was that the chancel, formerly reserved for the use of the abbey, was acquired for the use of the parishioners.[34] At that time the parish church was not served by canons, for by 1526 Dorchester had its own curate.[35] In the later 16th century there is little doubt that there were resident ministers, one in the 1580's being described as 'no preacher'.[36] At times there appear to have been two priests serving the church.[37]

The peculiar acts, beginning in 1581, tell something of parochial life: besides the usual moral charges, parishioners were accused of not going to church, not receiving communion, and working on Sundays.[38] The 1620's were a troubled time. The parish was a recusant centre;[39] and both the chancel and the church were in a state of neglect,[40] probably partly because the church had become too large for the parish to maintain. Rates of 2s. a yardland in 1624 and 1s. in 1625 were levied for its upkeep, and in 1629 a demand for a 3s. rate produced much opposition.[41] One of the three wardens refused to take part in its collection, for he said he knew it would not be paid;[42] another warden, John Day, also showed himself unco-operative;[43] while a parishioner, when asked to pay the rate, accused the curate, William Winchester, of being responsible for it. Religious differences may have been involved, for he considered as 'baubles' the scripture phrases with which it was planned to adorn the walls.[44] The wardens were ordered to demand publicly the payment of the rate.[45] Troubles continued into the 1630's, Day again being accused of refusing to co-operate with the other wardens and of irreverent behaviour in church.[46]

After the break in the peculiar records in 1637 little is known of the history of the church. Winchester remained as curate until his death in 1655.[47] His successor William Read probably had parliamentary sympathies, for in 1657 the Trustees for the Maintenance of Ministers ordered an increase of £20 in his stipend.[48] By 1662 he had been succeeded by David Thomas, 'a good loyalist',[49] who had come to the parish in the 1650's as the master of the new school, and who, when he became curate, began the custom of holding both church and school.[50] Anthony Wood, a former pupil of his at Thame, visited him at Dorchester.[51]

In the second half of the 17th century the difficulties of the first half were repeated. Recusancy continued and to it was added dissent;[52] the church

[14] Addington, op. cit. 170, 171.
[15] Oxf. Archd. Oxon. b 40, f. 113.
[16] Oxf. Dioc. c 649, f. 21.
[17] Hist. of Dorchester, pub. Parker & Co. (1882), 23.
[18] Oxf. Dioc. (uncat.), Bequest.
[19] C. Hodgson, Acct. of Queen Anne's Bounty (1845), 323.
[20] Return of Augmentations to Poor Vicarages, H.C. 366, p. 8 (1866), lv; Oxf. Dioc. c 1797, Deeds; Lond. Gaz. 22 July 1862, 12 June 1863.
[21] MS. Top. Oxon. c 103, f. 384b; it was worth £100 in 1853 and £180 in 1875: ibid.; Crockford (1876).
[22] Leland, Itin. ed. Toulmin Smith, i. 117.
[23] Valor Eccl. ii. 170; Par. Rec. Chwdns' accts. passim.
[24] They are not included in the confirmation of 1146: Reg. Antiquiss. i. 246–7.
[25] See below, and p. 59.
[26] Some of the abbey's churches were certainly served by canons: V.C.H. Oxon. ii. 87–88.
[27] Cal. Papal L. i. 95, 103; for its history see V.C.H. Oxon. ii. 87.
[28] See below, p. 58.
[29] Valor. Eccl. (Rec. Com.), ii. 170.
[30] Addington, Dorchester, 171, 172.

[31] For these visitations see Visit. Dioc. Linc. 1420–49, ii. 68 sqq., 78 sqq.
[32] Ibid. 68, 69.
[33] V.C.H. Oxon. ii. 89.
[34] See below, p. 59.
[35] Subsidy 1526, 252.
[36] Seconde Parte of a Register, ed. A. Peel, ii. 133.
[37] O.A.S. Rep. 1918, 182–3, where the names of clergy are given.
[38] For the peculiar records see above, p. 53 n. 67.
[39] See below, p. 61.
[40] Oxon. Peculiars, 116.
[41] Oxf. Archd. Oxon. c 158, f. 123.
[42] Ibid. f. 66.
[43] Ibid.; for him see also f. 64.
[44] Ibid. f. 66b.
[45] Ibid. f. 67.
[46] Ibid. f. 86.
[47] Par. Coll. ii. 118.
[48] Cal. S.P. Dom. 1657–8, 168.
[49] Wood, Life, i. 124.
[50] For the school see V.C.H. Oxon. i. 468–9.
[51] Wood, Life, i. 223; for him see also ibid. 108.
[52] See below, p. 63.

rate, apparently 4s. in 1666, was difficult to collect;[53] and the parish clerk had difficulty in collecting his wages, a payment from each householder.[54] Later there was another financial dispute: from 1707 a number of people whose relatives were buried in the churchyard refused to pay the 1s. due claimed by the minister, at this time a local man, Philip Keene (1690–1714),[55] denying that it was the custom of the parish. The decision, which was left to the official of the peculiar, is not known.[56] Church-wardens' accounts (1757–94) show that there were three wardens, as there had been in the 1620's, who changed every year.[57] One was probably chosen by the curate and the other by the parishioners of Dorchester,[58] while the third may have been from Overy. They also received the money collected from Burcot, although the Burcot wardens evidently kept separate records. Most of the wardens' income came from a yearly rate on Dorchester and Burcot; by this time it was levied on the pound instead of the yard-land, and usually ranged from between 1d. and 3d., a penny rate producing £6 17s. 9d. in Dorchester and £1 7s. 9d. in Burcot.[59] Expenditure in the first part of the period usually varied between £8 and £15 although towards the end of the century it often rose to over £20. Almost all the money was spent on the church building.

This pattern continued into the 19th century except that from the 1820's there were only two wardens. The church rate usually continued to vary from 1d. to 3d., but by 1840 the same rate produced about three times what it did in the 18th century. Expenses were usually between about £20 and £40. After the abolition of compulsory church rates in 1868 money was collected by an offertory and the church's income somewhat increased.[60]

In the middle of the 18th century the curate ceased acting as schoolmaster[61] and in the second part of the century he stopped living in the parish.[62] James Roe (1788–1838) never did so, being resident for many years at his Berkshire rectory. In his time the parish was served by a succession of assistant curates, many of whom lived in Oxford,[63] while the 'very small' parsonage was let.[64] Roe paid his curates £50, almost the whole income from the living, and two services were held on Sundays.[65] In the 1820's the assistant curate began to live in the parish,[66] and after Roe's death the ministers were again resident, although the parsonage was no longer used. By 1853 it was 'in ruins'.[67] In the 1830's congregations of 250 in the morning and 350 in the afternoon were reported, with about 100 communicants at Christmas

and Easter, and a Sunday school had been started.[68] By the 1850's daily services were held, with three on Sundays, and there were two Sunday schools and a night school for boys. Nevertheless dissent was strong and congregations, numbering up to 400, were not considered large enough.[69]

In the second half of the 19th century Dorchester had a devoted and generous minister with a private fortune, W. C. Macfarlane (1856–85), who was interested in the church's history[70] and who improved its buildings and extended its activities. He completed the restoration of the church building, which had been begun in 1845, both he and his family contributing towards it.[71] In 1857 the new parsonage was built;[72] in 1869 the chapel at Burcot was opened;[73] and in 1878, largely through his efforts, the Missionary College was founded.[74] He continued holding frequent services, and began the practice of having weekly communions. He placed great emphasis on education, believing that neglect of religion was largely owing to lack of it,[75] and was a liberal supporter of the parish schools. He also built a parish room and a reading room.[76] He belonged to the High Church party, and at once made Dorchester its local headquarters,[77] thus arousing some opposition. The congregation, for instance, had been used to singing the psalms, which in 1861 began to be chanted by the choir.[78] Great emphasis was laid on the choir, which numbered over 100,[79] and choral festivals were often held in the church.[80]

Macfarlane's successor, N. C. S. Poyntz (1886–1920), who began giving daily communion, also met with opposition because of his High Church sympathies, but his devotion to the parish made him much loved.[81] He started the parish magazine[82] and it was probably he who founded the mission in the north of the village.[83] Dorchester has continued to have High Church vicars and some religious differences have continued in the parish.[84]

The church of *ST. PETER AND ST. PAUL* is a large building consisting of a chancel with north and south aisles, a nave with a south aisle, a western tower, and a south porch.[85] Without the tower the church is nearly 200 feet long, and it measures nearly 80 feet across the aisles. With the exception of Oxford Cathedral it is the only surviving monastic church in the county. No trace now remains above ground of the pre-Conquest church founded by St. Birinus in the 7th century, but its foundations presumably exist beneath the floor.

The existing church was built by the Augustinian

[53] *Oxon. Peculiars*, 121, 123.
[54] Ibid. 129, 130; see also 133. For an earlier difficulty of this kind see Oxf. Archd. Oxon. c 158, f. 127.
[55] His will is in Wills Oxon. Peculiar wills (uncat.).
[56] *Oxon. Peculiars*, 131–2.
[57] Par. Rec.
[58] This was the 19th-century custom: Oxf. Dioc. b 39.
[59] Par. Rec. Chwdns' accts. 1757–8.
[60] Ibid. Accts. 1824–82.
[61] Thomas Lancaster (1714–41) was the last to do so.
[62] For names of curates and assistants from 1767 to 1834 see Oxf. Archd. Oxon. b 81, ff. 91 sqq.
[63] Oxf. Dioc. d 705, f. 94; c 428, f. 44; d 549, pp. 70–71.
[64] Ibid. b 9, f. 148b.
[65] Ibid.
[66] Ibid. f. 157.
[67] MS. Top. Oxon. c 103, f. 384.
[68] Oxf. Dioc. b 39, b 41.
[69] *Wilb. Visit.*
[70] He wrote a short history of it (copy in Bodl. G.A.

Oxon. 8° 264). There is an obit. of him ibid. from *Berks and Oxon. Advertiser*, 20 Nov. 1885.
[71] Par. Rec. School reg.: article at back.
[72] Oxf. Dioc. b 70. The plans had been drawn up in 1853: MS. Top. Oxon. c 103, f. 386.
[73] See below, p. 69.
[74] Kelly, *Dir. Oxon.* (1887).
[75] Oxf. Dioc. c 332, c 344.
[76] Obit. in Bodl. G.A. Oxon. 8° 264.
[77] Ibid.
[78] Oxf. Dioc. b 70, Newspaper correspondence.
[79] Par. Rec. School reg.: article at back.
[80] Obit. in Bodl. G.A. Oxon. 8° 264.
[81] Par. Rec. School reg.: Clipping from *Oxf. Times*, 20 Aug. 1920.
[82] Copies from 1904 to 1909 are in the Bodlian.
[83] Kelly, *Dir. Oxon.* (1920, 1939). It was probably the present Red Cottage: local inf.
[84] Oxf. Dioc. c 1797, Correspondence of 1939.
[85] For a view of the exterior see plate facing p. 58.

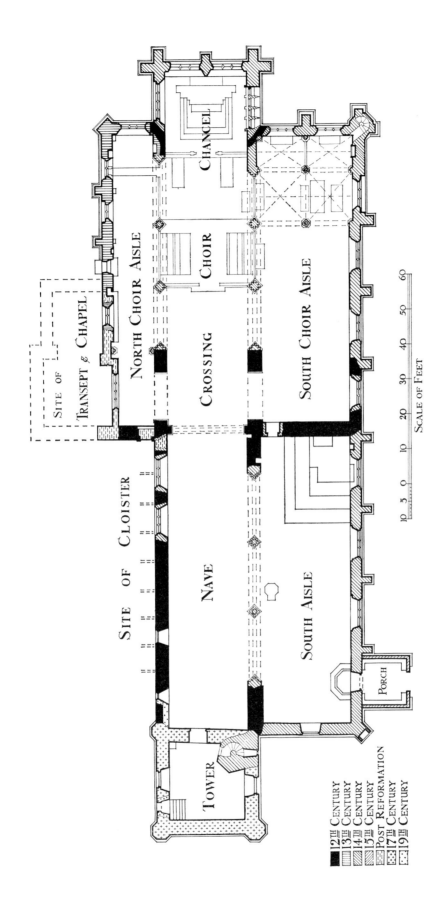

CHANCEL

NORTH CHOIR AISLE

CHOIR

SOUTH CHOIR AISLE

SITE OF TRANSEPT & CHAPEL

CROSSING

SITE OF CLOISTER

NAVE

SOUTH AISLE

PORCH

TOWER

12TH CENTURY
13TH CENTURY
14TH CENTURY
15TH CENTURY
POST REFORMATION
17TH CENTURY
19TH CENTURY

SCALE OF FEET

10 5 0 10 20 30 40 50 60

canons established by Alexander, Bishop of Lincoln, in the middle of the 12th century.[86] Owing to the loss of all the abbey's archives its architectural history before the Dissolution depends almost entirely on structural evidence, which in some respects is not easy to interpret.[87] The earliest portions of the present building date from the late 12th century, and appear to have formed part of a cruciform building without aisles. The north wall of the nave, the western sides of both transepts, the lower part of the south wall of the south transept, the western arch of the crossing, and the eastern angles of the original presbytery all belonged to this late Romanesque church. The western arch of the crossing was probably matched by a similar arch to the east, but appears insufficient to have supported a central tower of any magnitude. The plain unmoulded lateral arches are of uncertain date. As they cut through the string-course which marks the 12th-century work internally they cannot be earlier than the surviving west arch, and in their present form they may even be of post-Reformation date. On the other hand their western responds rest on chamfered bases continuous with those of the western arch, thus demonstrating their 12th-century origin. The east end of the 12th-century church is marked on the north side by a pilaster now partly cut away, but still visible in the angle between the north transept and the chancel, and on the south side by the remains of an ornamental angle-turret, now concealed behind a modern rainwater head, but illustrated by Freeman.[88] The north wall of the nave was originally lighted by a range of tall single-light windows of which one remains complete, and traces of a similar window can be seen at the west end of the south wall. The cloister stood on the north side of the nave, access to it being by a Romanesque doorway (now blocked) in the west wall of the north transept. This entrance appears to have been superseded in the 14th century by another doorway in the north wall of the nave. Adjoining this there are traces of a larger arch or recess of unknown date and purpose. Of the cloister itself nothing now remains, but the ends of its roof-timbers can be seen embedded in the north wall of the nave, and its foundations, seen and sketched by Anthony Wood in the 17th century,[89] were located by excavation in 1882.[90] Some moulded spandrels and capitals preserved with other fragments in the church may well have formed part of the cloisters.

The original plan of the east end of the church is a matter for conjecture. There are likely to have been one or more transeptal chapels north and south of the choir, and the foundations of one such chapel, perhaps of 13th-century date, are known to exist on the north side. The present north aisle appears to represent the eastward extension of the inner chapel on the north side. In its present form it dates from the second half of the 13th century, but externally a fragment of string-course, and internally a series of vaulting shafts with Early English mouldings are evidence that the aisle was begun on a smaller scale early in the 13th century, and later remodelled with its present buttresses and windows. It is not unlikely that a similar aisle formerly existed on the south side, but all trace of the 13th-century arrangements here were destroyed in the following century. The earlier work in the north aisle may perhaps have formed part of a building programme connected with the translation of the relics of St. Birinus, for which papal approval was obtained in 1225,[91] while its later remodelling must have taken place within a few years of the granting in 1293 of an indulgence in aid of the abbey's fabric.[92]

The corresponding aisle on the south side extends to the full width of the transept, and dates from the early years of the 14th century. Its two eastern bays are vaulted, and were probably intended to form the setting for the handsome new shrine in which the relics of St. Birinus were shortly to be placed.[93] At the same time uniform arcades were built on both sides of the choir. The northern arcade at least presumably replaced one of 13th-century date, but it is possible that hitherto the north aisle was separated from the choir by an unpierced wall, for the capitals of the vaulting-shafts in its north wall are placed so low as almost to preclude a normal arcade on the south side. A doorway was also inserted in the former west wall of the south transept, now the west wall of the aisle. This doorway has an external dripmould, thus indicating that at the time it was built there was no aisle on the south side of the nave. It was, however, not long before a broad aisle was added in this position for the use of (and presumably at the expense of) the parishioners, to whom this part of the church was allocated. Externally this aisle forms a continuation of the south choir aisle, and its windows correspond closely in design to those immediately to the east. Its later date is, however, demonstrated both by the existence of the doorway already referred to, and by the difference in the mouldings of the buttresses. The buttress at the south-west angle requires special notice, for it incorporates an early 13th-century niche, with characteristic mouldings and capitals, which must originally have adorned some other part of the church. St. John Hope's suggestion that it stood originally at the south-west corner of the south choir aisle[94] cannot be accepted, as it must antedate that aisle by something like a century, and it is perhaps more likely that it formed part of a 13th-century west front, displaced by the erection of a west tower at about the same time as the building of the aisle. As the construction of the aisle involved a considerable encroachment on the churchyard, a vaulted charnel-house was built beneath the altar in order to receive such bones as were disturbed in the course of the work. Above the altar there is an arched recess in the wall which may represent the blocking of a former window. After the construction of the nave aisle the parish church was separated from the monastic church by a screen, part of which can still be seen in the eastern bay of the nave aisle. In 1530 the bishop directed that the gates between the two parts of the church were to be kept locked at night.[95]

[86] *V.C.H. Oxon.* ii. 87.

[87] For previous accounts of the church see H. Addington, *Some Account of the Abbey Church of St. Peter and St. Paul, Dorchester* (1845), 2nd ed. by W. C. Macfarlane; E. A. Freeman, 'On the Architecture of the Abbey Church of Dorchester', *Proc. of the Arch. Inst. at Oxford 1850* (1854), 228–66; and W. H. St. J. Hope in *Jnl. Royal Arch. Inst.* lxvi. 333–5.   [88] *Proc. Arch. Inst. 1850*, 228–66.

[89] Wood, *Life*, i, pl. ii.

[90] W. C. Macfarlane, *A Short Account of Dorchester* (1892), 22, where it is stated that the cloister-court formed a quadrangle of 81 feet.   [91] *Cal. Papal L.* i. 95, 103.

[92] Linc. Reg. Sutton, f. 65.

[93] For the shrine, see above, p. 55.

[94] *Jnl. Royal Arch. Inst.* lxvi. 333.

[95] *V.C.H. Oxon.* ii. 89.

The Grammar School and Church from the south-west in 1792

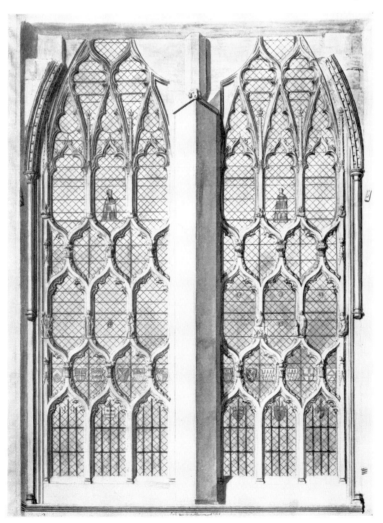

The East Window of the Church

DORCHESTER ABBEY

Somewhat later—probably about 1340—the presbytery was extended eastwards by the addition of a rectangular bay lighted by three large windows of unconventional design. The east window is remarkable both for the unusual character of its tracery,[96] and for its division into two by a central buttress. The north window is so designed as to exhibit the Tree of Jesse, the central mullion representing the trunk of a tree, its branches crossing over the intermediate mullions as far as the jambs. At the base is carved the figure of Jesse, and at each intersection occurs the sculptured figure of one of his descendants, others being represented in stained glass in the intervening lights. The whole composition culminated in a figure of Christ, now mutilated, placed at the point where the central mullion divided. Sculpture and stained glass were similarly combined in the south window to tell what appears to have been the story of St. Birinus. After the south window was in place its cill was cut away to allow the insertion of elaborate sedilia and piscina with crocketted canopies. Behind the seats the wall is pierced by three glazed openings in the shape of spherical triangles. Externally one of the 14th-century buttresses presents a curious architectural anomaly in the form of a niche decorated with 'dog-tooth' moulding in the style of the late 12th century. Unlike the one at the south-west corner of the south aisle, this niche appears to be an integral part of the structure in which it is set, and not an earlier feature re-used. Its presence would seem therefore to be another symptom of the somewhat eccentric taste which is characteristic of the whole east end.

Only two other additions to the fabric are known to have occurred before the dissolution of the abbey. One was the building of a west tower, the other the addition of a south porch. The latter appears to date from the late 15th or early 16th century. Of the medieval west tower only the stair-turret survives. The mouldings of its doorway indicate that it was built in the 14th century.

When the abbey was suppressed in 1536 the chancel was bought for £140 by Richard Beauforest, a 'great rich man' of Dorchester, and the whole building was made available for parochial use.[97] In his will Beauforest left the chancel or abbey church to the parish on condition that the parishioners did not sell or change the 'church implements' without the consent of his executors.[98]

In 1602 a new west tower was built in place of its predecessor, but incorporating the 14th-century stair-turret. It is of traditional design, with octagonal buttresses and flint chequer-work in the style of several late medieval towers in the Thames valley. The date 1602 and the initials J. W. are carved on a stone near the top of the south-west buttress, and an entry in the parish register records 'The tower of Dorchester rebuilt by J. W. 1602.'[99]

This was the only post-Reformation addition to the church, and for the last 300 years the maintenance of so large a fabric has proved a serious problem to successive churchwardens. Evidence of this

is to be found both in visitation complaints about the need for repair,[1] and in the demolition of the greater part of the north transept and transeptal chapel, which seems to have taken place in the 17th century. The truncated transept was incorporated in the north aisle by means of a roughly built wall containing an ill-made 'churchwardens' Gothic' window. In 1633 a double ridged roof was made over the south nave aisle. This involved blocking up the west window of the aisle, and it may have been at the same period that the roof of the porch was raised in such a way as to obscure part of the window behind it. The possibility that the arches north and south of the crossing owe their present unmoulded appearance to post-Reformation alterations has already been mentioned. By the early 18th century the whole church was in serious need of attention, and in 1737 estimates for repairs amounting to over £2,500 were submitted to the Justices with the object of obtaining a brief. This was granted, and resulted in the collection of £714.[2] In 1739 Robert Speakman of Oxford and Benjamin Leasonby of London, carpenters, contracted to repair the roof of the south-east aisle, and Charles Wheeler of Dorchester, plumber, was engaged to cover it with lead.[3] It was probably at this time that the vaulting was taken down and a flat plastered roof inserted in its stead. In 1747 Richard Phillips of Nettlebed, carpenter, engaged to take down and rebuild the roof of the 'middle isle from chancel to the arch'.[4] In 1746 the chancel was repaired at the expense of the Fettiplace family, who owned the great tithes, and a classical altar-piece was set up.[5] The west end of the nave was repaved in 1747, and the north aisle in 1765. No other major repairs appear to have been carried out until the 19th century, and by then the church was 'in some parts in a very unsound and dilapidated state'.[6] The whole of the medieval roofing had been destroyed and replaced by plastered ceilings or 'rough open timber work', the upper part of the east window had been removed in order to accommodate a flat plaster ceiling, and the nave was divided into two by a plastered partition. The south window of the chancel was held together only by iron bands, the sedilia were 'sadly broken and dilapidated', and the whole church was 'far from being in the state of cleanliness and decency in which it ought to be kept.'[7]

In 1844 the Oxford Architectural Society took the initiative in raising money for a general restoration. The fabric was first examined by James Cranstoun, an Oxford architect, who estimated that a complete restoration would cost £3,970. By 1846 £500 had been raised, and the north and south windows of the chancel and the sedilia were repaired under Cranstoun's direction. The restoration of the east window and the re-roofing of the chancel were, however, entrusted to William Butterfield. These works, together with the clearing and reseating of the nave, were accomplished between 1846 and 1852.[8] Between 1858 and 1874 the repair of the church was resumed under the direction of Sir Gilbert Scott,

[96] See plate facing p. 58.
[97] cf. Leland, *Itin.* ed. Toulmin Smith, i. 117.
[98] MS. Wills Oxon. 180, f. 261*b*, printed in Addington, *Dorchester*, 98–99.
[99] Par. Rec.
[1] *Oxon. Peculiars*, 133–6.
[2] Par. Rec. Dorchester Brief bk.
[3] Ibid.   [4] Ibid.

[5] Addington, *Dorchester*, 12, gives the date 1745. The school register gives 1746.
[6] Ashmolean Museum: architect's report in archives of the O.A.H.S.
[7] Ibid. O.A.H.S. correspondence, no. 230. John Carter's drawings of 1793 show the state of the fabric at the end of the 18th century: Bodl. Gough Maps 227.
[8] Ash. Mus.: papers and accounts in O.A.H.S. archives.

who restored all the roofs to their original pitch and rebuilt the vaulting at the east end of the south aisle.[9]

Until the Reformation the most important tomb in the church was that of its founder and patron St. Birinus. Papal authority to translate his body to a more fitting place was obtained in 1225,[10] and a 14th-century chronicler records that a new and magnificently carved marble shrine (*feretrum marmoreum stupende sculpture*) was made in 1320.[11] Large portions of an early 14th-century canopied shrine were found in the 19th century built up into the filling of the blocked doorway in the west wall of the north transept, and are now displayed in the south aisle near the spot where in all probability they originally stood. The lower part of the shrine appears to have been of Purbeck marble, the canopy of freestone, elaborately carved and painted.

There are four medieval effigies, three of stone and one of alabaster. The oldest, one of the stone effigies, is a large recumbent figure of a cross-legged knight dating from the reign of Edward I.[12] It is possible that he may represent 'one Holcum, a knight', who was buried in the church according to a statement by a 16th-century Abbot of Dorchester.[13] A Robert of Little Holcombe held ⅓ hide in Holcombe of the abbot in 1241 and the effigy may represent him or his heir.[14] The abbot told Leland that he thought 'Holcum' was buried in the alabaster tomb, but this supports the effigy of a late 14th-century knight with the lion rampant of Segrave on his breast, and the arms of Segrave and Botetourt were formerly painted on the sides of the tomb.[15] The person commemorated cannot be identified with certainty, but it seems that he must have been a member of the Segrave family descended from a marriage between Segrave and Botetourt.[16] A third effigy, representing a man in legal robes, with the arms of Stonor on the side of the tomb, is probably that of the judge John de Stonor (d. 1354).[17] The fourth effigy is that of a bishop in the style of the early 14th century.[18] It was discovered under the floor in the 18th century and may be the 'image of freestone' with an inscription to Bishop Æschwine (d. 1002) seen by Leland,[19] which had disappeared when Wood visited the church in 1657.[20]

The church once had a large number of brasses and memorial slabs: Wood noted in 1657 that there had been eighteen inscriptions in the south aisle alone and that all but one were defaced.[21] The majority of the memorials have now gone. Of the brasses those that remain are mutilated or have only matrices left. Of the brass of Abbot John de Sutton (d. 1349) the matrices of a man holding a crozier and of the inscription remain.[22] Roger Smith, who resigned as abbot in 1523 and who was also Bishop of Lydda, is commemorated by a much-worn incised alabaster slab with his figure on it.[23] Abbot Richard 'Beweforest' (temp. Henry VIII) has a brass with his figure, a Latin scroll, and an English inscription. His name and crozier are also carved on one of the ends of the choirstall-desks.[24] Abbots are probably also commemorated by two matrices, one of a kneeling figure with a scroll, the other of a floriated cross.[25] Another abbot's brass, seen in the 17th century, has now gone,[26] and so has the inscription to the last abbot, John March (d. 1553).[27] The matrices of brasses to two canons remain: to Brother Ralph, under the north wall of the nave, and to an unknown canon kneeling opposite an angel.[28]

Of the remaining non-clerical brasses or matrices of brasses the oldest is perhaps the indent under a triple canopy in the chancel. The canopy resembles those on the Drayton tombs and the figure may have represented, as Wood thought, a contemporary of the Draytons, Sir Gilbert Wace of Ewelme, who in his will of 1407 provided that the abbot should have services said for him, and may well have been honoured by being buried in the chancel.[29] Leland had earlier identified him as a 'gentleman' named 'Ways'.[30]

The oldest remaining brass is a large one to Sir John Drayton (d. 1417), who asked in his will to be buried in Dorchester church.[31] The figure of his wife Isabella and the arms of Drayton quartering Segrave have gone.[32] Leland and Wood both noted two other Drayton slabs, but were unable to identify them precisely. One must have been to Richard Drayton (d. 1464), who in his will asked to be buried in the abbey between the tomb of William Drayton and the south wall, and the other to William Drayton.[33] Two shields of Drayton and the indent of a man in armour remain and presumably represent one of these Draytons.[34] Of the brass to Margaret Beauforest (d. 1523/4) and her two husbands (one of them named Richard Beauforest, the other William Tanner)[35], and their children, the figures of the woman and a man remain.[36] The shield of Ideley and part of one of Drayton quartering Segrave are all that remain of the brass to Pers[e] Ideley and his two wives, one a Drayton.[37] The

---

[9] For details see W. C. Macfarlane, *Dorchester*, 21. Unexecuted designs for reroofing the north aisle are MS. Top. Oxon. a 24, ff. 102-4.
[10] *Cal. Papal L.* i. 95, 103.
[11] Addington, *Dorchester*, 62, 137. The chronicler, Higden, also refers to the *feretrum mirandi operis*.
[12] See Skelton, *Oxon* Dorchester Hund. plate 1; L. Stone, *Sculpture in Britain: The Middle Ages* (1955),150, 115, plate.
[13] Leland, *Itin.* i. 117.
[14] *Fines Oxon.* 110-11.
[15] For a drawing see Bodl. Gough Map 227 (unfol.).
[16] Addington, *Dorchester*, 129.
[17] Leland, *Itin.* i. 117; Addington, *Dorchester*, 13-14.
[18] For a drawing see Skelton, *Oxon. Dorchester Hund.* plate 1.
[19] Leland, *Itin.* i. 117.
[20] Wood, *Life*, i. 225.
[21] *Par. Coll.* ii. 120. For a full description of brasses and matrices see MS. Top. Oxon. d 195, ff. 307-71; for drawings see ibid. b 220, ff. 120-1; Bodl. Gough Maps 227.
[22] For the opening of this tomb in 1746 see Addington, *Dorchester*, 175.

[23] For inscription see ibid. 15.
[24] For reproductions see ibid. 15-16. For a correction of the statement (*V.C.H. Oxon.* ii. 89-90) that the inscription to this brass belonged to another figure and that no Abbot Beauforest existed see *Berks. Bucks. & Oxon. Arch. Jnl.* xv. 61-62; and *L. & P. Hen. VIII*, i. p. 259, where it is recorded that Abbot Beauforest of Dorchester was pardoned in 1509-10.
[25] For a drawing see MS. Top. Oxon. d 195, ff. 355, 308.
[26] Ibid. f. 316.
[27] *Par. Coll.* ii. 121.
[28] MS. Top. Oxon. d 195, ff. 309, 369.
[29] *Par. Coll.* ii. 116; *Boarstall Cart.* 38.
[30] Leland, *Itin.* i. 117.
[31] *Early Lincoln Wills*, ed. A. Gibbons, 119.
[32] See MS. Top. Oxon. ff. 321-3.
[33] *Oxon. Wills* (O.R.S. xxxix), 25.
[34] For illustrations see Stephenson, *Brasses*, 404; MS. Top. Oxon. d 195, f. 321.
[35] The surname Tanner is uncertain.
[36] MS. Top. Oxon. d 195, ff. 362-3.
[37] Stephenson, *Brasses*, 404 and Appendix. For English verse see *Par. Coll.* ii. 120.

indent of the figures was there until the 19th century.[38]

The only other remaining parts of brasses are an early 16th-century merchant's mark over the matrices of a man, his wife, and two children; and the small figure of a woman, perhaps Jenit Shirrey.[39] The figures of five girls, detached from some brass, though recorded in the 19th century, could not be traced in 1959.[40] There were once memorials to Gilbert Segrave; William Yonge (d. 1430) and his wife Alice with shield of arms; Robert Bedford (d. 1491) and his wife Alice; William Bedford (d. 1516) and Agnes Bedford (d. 1518/19).[41]

There are a number of 17th-century and later memorials, some of them apparently removed from the churchyard. They include those to William Whinchester (d. 1655), pastor for 40 years; Agnes Clerke (d. 1661), wife of Edward Clerke, Esq.; the 'matchlesse' Mrs. Anne Carleton (d. 1669); Francis Dandridge, 'Pharmacop of London' (d. 1714); Jonathan Granger (d. 1774), merchant, citizen and draper of London; Philadelphia Cherrill (d. 1796), daughter of Francis Cherrill; Vincent Cherrill (d. 1807) and his wife Margaret (d. 1791); Mrs. Sarah Fletcher, who 'died a martyr to excessive sensibility' in 1799 in her 29th year;[42] Thomas Latham (d. 1843); and Richard Sheen, Mayor of Oxford (d. 1840).

The church is still rich in medieval painted glass. Four medallions in the openings over the piscina and the sedilia, representing scenes from the life of St. Birinus, date perhaps from the early 13th century.[43] They have been in their present position since 1808 at least, but in 1657 they were in the large south window above.[44] The east window contains a number of panes of 14th-century glass portraying biblical scenes and scenes from the lives of saints, as well as one pane of armorial glass and the figure of a canon, Ralph de Tew.[45] This glass was assembled about 1814 by Colonel or Captain Kennett from other windows and also from a glazier's shop.[46] The glass in the circle at the top was inserted when the window was restored about 1847,[47] and there is later 19th-century glass by Clayton & Bell, placed there in 1874.[48]

Kennett also had placed in the south window of the chancel most of the present collection of armorial glass, part of which had been in the east window.[49] These 21 armorial shields and five in other windows, almost all of which can be identified as those of noble families holding land in the neighbourhood, date from about 1300. They include the

arms of Edward I and of Edmund, Earl of Cornwall, who died in that year.[50] In 1574[51] and certainly as late as 1657[52] most of the armorial glass (more than double the present quantity) was in the east window of the choir and one of the east windows of the south aisle of the choir.

The glass in the north window of the chancel, showing the descent of Christ from Jesse, has probably always been in its present position. Wood noted about 27 figures, some of which had been defaced by the soldiers during the Civil War, and there are now sixteen.[53] They were repaired under the direction of the architect F. E. Howard in 1926.

The modern glass at the east end of the south aisle to members of the Cripps family is said to be by Hardman.[54]

The chancel walls according to Wood were painted 'very gloriously' with all kinds of beasts, of which a lion, a griffin, and a leopard remained.[55] A medieval wall-painting depicting the Crucifixion was restored by Clayton & Bell in 1862-3.[56] It is on the west wall of the nave.

The lead bowl of the font is of 12th-century date. It is decorated with a continuous arcade of eleven semicircular arches, in each of which is a seated figure.[57]

The stall-desks in the choir date from the early 16th century.[58]

In 1552 the church was well furnished with plate and vestments, but by the next year only one chalice remained.[59] In 1929 the silver was all 19th-century.[60]

The Dorchester bells, which are famous for their tone, are unusual in that, with one possible exception, all the original castings have been preserved. The two largest are of the late 14th century: one, the gift of Ralph Restwold (d. 1383), is dedicated to St. Birinus, the other to St. Peter and St. Paul. Except for a sanctus bell and a lych bell these were the only two bells in 1552.[61] Of the other bells, four are dated 1591, 1603, 1606, and 1651. They were described by Hearne in 1711.[62] In 1867 two more were added to make a ring of eight.[63]

The church had a chiming clock in the 1620's.[64] Repairs to it are frequently recorded in the 18th-century churchwardens' accounts and in the parish register.[65] In 1868-9 a new clock, by Moore of Clerkenwell, was put up and quarter chimes were added in 1901.[66]

ROMAN CATHOLICISM. A comparatively large number of Dorchester families remained loyal to the church of Rome. From 1603 the names of many are

[38] MS. Top. Oxon. d 195, f. 350.
[39] Ibid. ff. 359, 370.
[40] Stephenson, *Brasses*, 404.
[41] *Visit. Oxon.* 108, 109, 110. For the probable matrix of William Bedford see MS. Top. Oxon. d 195, f. 360. For other unidentified matrices see ibid. ff. 310-12, 358.
[42] For details of her death by suicide see *Gent. Mag.* lxix (1), 532.
[43] E. S. Bouchier, *Notes on the Stained Glass of the Oxf. District*, 70.
[44] *Par. Coll.* ii. 117; MS. Top. Oxon. b 220, f. 114b.
[45] Bouchier, op. cit. 71-72.
[46] Skelton, *Oxon.* Dorchester Hund. 4n, 7.
[47] *Hist. of Dorchester*, pub. Parker & Co. (1882), 89-90.
[48] Par. Reg. School reg.: Notes at back.
[49] Bodl. Gough Maps 227, Dorch. drawings vii, xiii; Skelton, op. cit. 8. In 1793 there were only two panes of painted glass in this window: Gough Maps 227, Dorch. drawings xiv, xvi.
[50] There are 21 shields in the south window, 2 in the

east window, and 3 in the east window of the north aisle. For these see Lamborn, *Arm. Glass*, 120 sqq. and plates 45-47.
[51] *Visit. Oxon.* 105-8; see also Bodl. Gough Maps 227, Dorch. drawing xvi.
[52] *Par. Coll.* ii. 121; MS. Top. Oxon. e 3, ff. 115-115b.
[53] *Par. Coll.* ii. 118; Bouchier, op. cit. 72. For the window in 1793 see Bodl. Gough Maps 227, Dorch. drawing xii.
[54] Par. Rec. School reg.
[55] *Par. Coll.* ii. 118.
[56] W. C. Macfarlane, *A Short Account of Dorchester* (1881), 16.   [57] Addington, *Dorchester*, 33.
[58] Ibid. 16.   [59] *Chant. Cert.* 101, 119.
[60] Evans, *Ch. Plate*.   [61] *Chant. Cert.* 101-2.
[62] Hearne, *Remarks*, iii. 185.
[63] *Ch. Bells Oxon.* ii. 117-21.
[64] *Oxon. Peculiars*, 118.
[65] Par. Rec. Chwdns' accts. *passim*; Par. reg. 1788-9.
[66] Par. Rec. School reg.: notes at back; Kelly, *Dir. Oxon.* (1939).

known; in 1641 nine were assessed for the subsidy; and the churchwardens made constant presentments of recusants and of people who failed to attend church.[67] From a list of thirteen people who in 1666 failed to receive Easter Communion, almost all can be recognized as members of Roman Catholic families. The figure of six papists given in the Compton Census in 1676 is therefore almost certainly an under-estimate.[68]

Roman Catholicism in the parish has an unusual history in that it centred around several yeoman families. The only members of the gentry listed as recusants in the early 17th century were George Beauforest and a female relative.[69] Of the yeoman families the most important were the Days and the Daveys of Overy. One branch of the Day family appears to have been Dorchester lock-keepers, and the old Wittenham ferry lock was called Day's Lock after them; another branch lived at Burcot.[70] In the early 17th century Walter Day, fisherman, and his wife Grace, and also Richard Day, fisherman, were listed as recusants;[71] from the 1620's to the 1670's members of the family were constantly presented by the churchwardens for absence from church.[72] Six were assessed for the subsidy of 1641, and in the 1666 list of abstainers from Easter Communion five were Days.[73] One member of the family served as churchwarden at about this time, but it is by no means certain that he was an Anglican and this may simply be evidence for the family's predominant influence in the village.[74] Several Days were returned as papists in the late 17th and early 18th centuries,[75] and in 1769 four Days were members of the Britwell Prior congregation to which the Dorchester Roman Catholics belonged at this period.[76] In the early 19th century the Dorchester branch of the family died out.[77]

Other 17th-century recusant families were the Smiths, beginning with Hugh Smith, tailor;[78] the Coldrells (or Cowldwells);[79] the Cherrills, who were not all Roman Catholics but intermarried with Roman Catholic families;[80] and the Princes, who were widespread in the neighbourhood and were sufficiently important in Overy to give their name to a group of buildings.[81] They first appear as recusants in Dorchester in 1666, after the marriage in 1663 between John Prince and Grace Day,[82] but by the early 18th century when two papist members of the family were 'labourers'[83] they had declined in social importance, and the family died out soon after.

No Princes were listed among the Roman Catholic congregation of Britwell Prior in 1769. Many of the family were buried in Dorchester churchyard, where their tombstones can still be seen marked with the Cross as a sign that they commemorated Roman Catholics.[84]

The survival of Roman Catholicism in Dorchester was eventually due, however, to the Davey family. This family had been in Dorchester since at least 1566[85] but Ann, the wife of Richard Davey, was the first of the family to be listed (in 1641) as a Roman Catholic.[86] About 1670 both she and her husband were recusants,[87] and about 1717 William Davey, yeoman, who rebuilt Overy House,[88] registered his copyhold estate as a papist.[89] The family intermarried with other yeoman families of their faith in Dorchester and in neighbouring parishes. Although the community was only intermittently served by a resident priest, it is probable that there were always visiting priests. In the middle of the 18th century mass was being said about seven times a year in a room, fully equipped with altar furniture, in the farmhouse in Overy which had been the home of the Daveys before they moved in 1712 to Overy House.[90] The Jesuit Father Gilbert Wells lived with the Daveys from 1752 to 1758, and Father Bernard Cassidy, S.J., head of the Oxford District, was there in 1773.[91] At other times the congregation was looked after by the priest from Britwell Prior, which was for long a centre of Roman Catholicism. In 1769 Dorchester, with nine members, formed (except for Britwell itself) the largest group in the Britwell congregation.[92] Besides the Daveys and Days the Dorchester group had two members of the well-known local family of Collingridge[93] and it had so prospered by 1780 that it had eighteen members.[94] It was accustomed to be served by a 'missioner', but in about the 1770's there appears to have been some difficulty in finding a priest for it and it was described as 'now destitute'.[95] In the 1790's, however, the community was being served by a French priest living with the Daveys.[96] Later it was served from Thame and in the early 19th century from Oxford, services being held in each place on alternate Sundays.[97]

The increasing prosperity of the Davey family was an advantage to the community. William Davey, a successful farmer and a speculator in government stocks, died in 1831, leaving £20,000.[98] One son, George, was a large-scale farmer, who made his

[67] Salter, *Oxon. Recusants, passim*; E 179/164/482; *Oxon. Peculiars*, 115–28: returns 1621–78, after which there are no further recusancy presentments.
[68] *Oxon. Peculiars*, 120; Compton Census.
[69] Salter, *Oxon. Recusants*, 24.
[70] See below, p. 70. For the family see Davey, *Catholic Family*, 16–17.
[71] Salter, *Oxon. Recusants*, 27, 35, 38, 43.
[72] *Oxon. Peculiars*, 115–28.
[73] E 179/164/482; *Oxon. Peculiars*, 120.
[74] *Oxon. Peculiars*, 130. On the death of John Day (1662) the question of his having church burial was considered: Oxf. Archd. Oxon. c 160, f. 318.
[75] Stapleton, *Cath. Miss.* 245; O.R.O. Reg. of Papists' estates, pp. 60–61; O.R.O. Cal. Q. Sess. ix. 591–2.
[76] Davey, *Catholic Family*, 70.
[77] Ibid. 17.
[78] Salter, *Oxon. Recusants*, 23; *Oxon. Peculiars*, 120.
[79] Salter, *Oxon. Recusants, passim*; E 179/164/482; *Oxon. Peculiars*, 116, 117. Perhaps the same as Cowdry: ibid. 120.
[80] *Oxon. Peculiars*, 116, 120, 121; for them see Davey, *Catholic Family*, 24–26.

[81] For them see Davey, *Catholic Family*, 18–19; *V.C.H. Oxon.* v. 248; and above, p. 26.
[82] *Oxon. Peculiars*, 120, 122–7; Davey, *Catholic Family*, 58.
[83] Stapleton, *Cath. Miss.* 245; O.R.O. Reg. of Papists' estates, p. 64.
[84] Davey, *Catholic Family*, 19n, 70.   [85] Ibid. 6.
[86] Ibid. 7; *Oxon. Peculiars*, 116–17.
[87] E 179/164/482; *Oxon. Peculiars*, 122, 127.
[88] Davey, *Catholic Family*, 21–22.
[89] O.R.O. Reg. of Papists' estates, pp. 63–64; see also O.R.O. Cal. Q. Sess. ix. 591.
[90] Davey, *Catholic Family*, 67, 23.
[91] Stapleton, *Cath. Miss.* 246–7. Father Wells made his will at Dorchester in 1752. See also Oxf. Dioc. c 441, f. 13.
[92] Davey, *Catholic Family*, 67, 70.
[93] Ibid. 40–43.   [94] Oxf. Dioc. c 432, f. 45.
[95] Davey, *Catholic Family*, 67.
[96] Stapleton, *Cath. Miss.* 248. He was buried in Dorchester Abbey, where there is a tablet.
[97] Stapleton, *Cath. Miss.* 248.
[98] For him see Davey, *Catholic Family*, 44–46.

home at Overy House a centre for his co-religionists;[99] another son John built the 'chapel' of St. Birinus at Dorchester in 1849.[1] The chapel's first priest was Robert Newsham, a schoolmaster, who moved his school from Oxford when he settled at Dorchester.[2] In 1851 his congregation was said to average 60, an exaggeration according to the vicar.[3] In 1856 the chapel was registered for marriages and from 1871 it had its own churchyard.[4]

The influence of the Davey family continued to be strong.[5] When John Davey died in 1863 he left his home, Bridge House, to his nephew, Henry Davey, who was priest at the chapel from 1864 to 1878.[6] Henry Davey's brother Robert, who died without children in 1901, was the last of the family to live at Overy. He left £200 to the chapel on which he had also settled 32 acres of land.[7] In the same year Bridge House was settled in trust on the priest serving the chapel.[8] In 1958 it was still being used as the presbytery. The congregation had increased to about 150.[9]

The small church of *ST. BIRINUS* at Bridge End, built in 1849 in the Decorated style (architect W. Wardell),[10] consists of nave, chancel, and south porch, and has a bell-cote. On the west front is a statue of St. Birinus. Inside are brass tablets to members of the Davey family and one to the Revd. Robert Newsham (d. 1859). The chapel possesses a pre-Reformation (c. 1500) chasuble[11] and a small ciborium of much later date, which may have been taken from the chapel in the Daveys' house at Overy.[12] There is another chalice inscribed 'given by Lady Fettiplace to the Oxfordshire Mission for herself and her family'.[13] The cross on the high altar is also old.

The registers date from 1849 for baptisms, 1856 for marriages, and 1871 for burials.

PROTESTANT NONCONFORMITY. The evidence for Protestant nonconformity dates from 1672 when the house of Lawrence Overy was registered as a Congregational meeting house.[14] In 1675 and 1678 the churchwardens presented Stephen Coven as 'a common seducer and leader of a conventicle';[15] he was the ejected Rector of Samford Peverell (Devon), who was licensed to 'teach' as a Presbyterian in London and as a Congregationalist in Watlington. He was described earlier as 'a wandering seditious seminary . . . who goes about from place to place'.[16] In 1680 another preacher at this conventicle, John Coomb, was presented.[17] Most of the thirteen nonconformists returned for the Compton Census of 1676 probably belonged to this conventicle,[18] but in 1668 there had also been a Quaker, Henry Towerton.[19]

In the absence of 18th-century visitations information about the progress of nonconformity is meagre. In 1699 the house of William Thompson, a baker, was registered as a dissenting meeting-place,[20] and in 1796 a labourer's house in West Back Lane.[21] The denomination is not recorded, but it is likely in the case of the last-named registration to have been Baptist, for the next registration in 1820 was of Robert Cox's house,[22] and when a Baptist chapel was finally built it was on land belonging to Sarah Cox.[23] This chapel, next to the Port House, was built about 1837; the 1851 Census recorded its congregation as 75 in the afternoon and 120 in the evening,[24] but the vicar claimed that this was an exaggerated figure due to the special activity of the Baptists at the time of the Census.[25] A Primitive Methodist chapel at Bridge End was built in 1839 and its congregation numbered eighteen in 1851, when it was served by a minister from Wallingford.[26] Both chapels were in use in 1866, but by then dissent was said to be declining[27] and they appear to have been closed by 1882.[28] Both buildings were in use as private houses in 1958.

SCHOOLS. There had been an endowed grammar school in Dorchester since 1652, but by the middle of the 18th century it had ceased to provide effective education.[29] In 1801 a Mr. Paget advertised that he would re-establish 'Dorchester School' which had long been vacant, and offered to board 8 young gentlemen at 20 guineas a year, with dancing and French included in the curriculum.[30] By 1833 the school had 50 pupils.[31]

No record of any elementary education has survived from before the 19th century. In 1815 there were three day schools providing elementary instruction,[32] but these were fee-paying schools and three years later the poor were said to be still 'completely destitute' of the means of education.[33] The first Sunday school was started in 1819. In 1826 a newly established day school, where 7 children were being taught, was recorded, and by 1833 there was yet another school with an attendance of 28 pupils.[34]

[99] Ibid. 51; Bodl. Overy tithe award.
[1] Notes on St. Birinus's Church, Dorchester, *penes* Witham & Co., Orchard House, Wargrave (Berks.).
[2] Stapleton, *Cath. Miss.* 248–9.
[3] H.O. 129/4/125; *Wilb. Visit.*
[4] *Lond. Gaz.* 22 Aug. 1856. Previously Roman Catholics had been buried in the abbey churchyard.
[5] Oxf. Dioc. c 332.
[6] As n. 1 above; Stapleton, *Cath. Miss.* 249.
[7] Davey, *Catholic Family*, 54–55.
[8] Char. Com. file 76886; see also 85284; ibid. unrep. vol. 135, f. 214. The land was later sold for c. £1,775: as n. 1 above.
[9] *Cath. Dir.* (1958).
[10] *Gent. Mag.* 1849, cxxv. 308; inscription in church.
[11] Inf. Victoria and Albert Museum.
[12] Stapleton, *Cath. Miss.* 247.
[13] Inf. the Revd. W. Connick, Bridge House, Dorchester. This Lady Fettiplace has not been identified. For other Roman Catholic Fettiplaces, see Stapleton, *Cath. Miss.* 272–3.
[14] G. Lyon Turner, *Original Records of Early Nonconformity*, iii. 833.
[15] *Oxon. Peculiars*, 127, 128.

[16] *Calamy Rev.* 139.
[17] *Oxon. Peculiars*, 122.
[18] Compton Census.
[19] *Oxon. Peculiars*, 122.
[20] O.R.O. Cal. Q. Sess. viii. 803.
[21] Oxf. Dioc. c 644, f. 27.
[22] Ibid. f. 224. The house of John Wheeler was registered in 1834: ibid. c 645, f. 224.
[23] Bodl. Tithe award.
[24] H.O. 129/4/125. A Baptist room was registered in 1845: Oxf. Dioc. c 647, f. 35.
[25] *Wilb. Visit.*
[26] H.O. 129/4/125. The chapel was registered in 1840: Oxf. Dioc. c 646, f. 135.
[27] Oxf. Dioc. c 332.
[28] Neither is listed in *Return of Churches and Chapels*, H.C. 401 (1882), i.
[29] For the history of this school see *V.C.H. Oxon.* i. 469.
[30] *Oxf. Jnl.* 17 Jan. 1801.
[31] *Educ. Enq. Abstract*, 745.
[32] Oxf. Dioc. c 433.
[33] *Educ. of Poor*, 722.
[34] *Educ. Enq. Abstract*, 745.

The Sunday school had an attendance of 64 boys and 48 girls by 1854.[35]

The National girls and infants school was established in 1836 on land given by the Earl of Abingdon; it was to be a free school and the perpetual curate was to be trustee.[36] It had an attendance of 50 in 1854.[37] In 1872 the present buildings were erected to the designs of Sir George Gilbert Scott; they were enlarged in 1900 to hold 150 children.[38] There was an average attendance of 85 in 1904.[39]

The old grammar school was converted into a boys' National school in 1858 and had an average attendance of 46 in 1887.[40] A new building was erected in 1896–7,[41] and the average attendance was 61 boys in 1906.[42] Later in 1928 it was amalgamated with the girls' National school and was classified as an amalgamated grade III school. It was attended by 219 boys, girls, and infants in 1938. In 1947 the senior department was reorganized as a separate voluntary school, known after 1953 as the Abbey School. In 1954, as a controlled modern school, it had 233 pupils on the roll. It was closed in 1959, when the new school at Berinsfield was opened. The junior department became a primary school in 1947—the St. Birinus Church of England controlled school—with 97 pupils.[43]

Another primary school, the Field Farm Estate County School, was opened in 1952 with 76 children.[44]

A County Secondary Modern School for boys and girls was opened at Berinsfield, a new council estate, in September 1959. It replaced the Abbey School in Dorchester. There was a head master, a full-time staff of twelve, and two part-time staff, and 293 children on the roll.[45]

SS. Peter and Paul's Theological College for Missionary Students was established in 1878, largely through the exertions of W. C. Macfarlane. It trained sons of clergymen and professional men for work in the colonies and mission field and offered a four-year course. By 1881 there were 15 students. Extra accommodation was provided in 1905 by taking over Church House and by 1908 there were 28 students in residence.[46] In 1929 new buildings were provided in Burcot but some students were still in Dorchester in 1939.[47] The number of students fell at the outbreak of war and in 1940 the Burcot premises were let to Bishop's College, Cheshunt (Herts.), and the remaining Dorchester College students went to Launton. In 1942, there being only 4 students, the college was closed. After the war the premises were sold and the proceeds of the sale and existing endowments were formed into a trust, entitled SS. Peter and Paul's Theological Endow-

ment for Missionary Students' under a scheme made by the Minister of Education.[48]

CHARITIES. Hungerford Dunch, by will dated 1680, left £200 to the poor of the parish. In 1698 the money was invested in two closes in St. Clement's, Oxford, and about 1823 the £20 rent from these was given to the poor annually on St. Stephen's Day in sums varying from 1s. 6d. to 6s. according to need.[49] In 1856 the lands were exchanged for 11 acres at Oseney, in St. Thomas's parish, Oxford.[50] In 1898 the income was being distributed in doles to nearly every wage-earner in the parish.[51] A Scheme made in 1906 provided that the income should thenceforth be applied to the maintenance of a nurse to attend poor residents. It stipulated, however, that those who had long been accustomed to receive gifts in money or kind should be entitled to continue to do so. This Scheme was much opposed locally. Accordingly, after a local inquiry by an Assistant Charity Commissioner, a new Scheme was made in 1910 which provided that the income might be applied (i) to subscriptions to hospitals and the like in which the disabled were taught trades; (ii) as grants towards the provision of nurses, midwives, and medicines, in subscriptions to provident societies on behalf of subscribers who through sickness had been forced to allow their payments to lapse, and in providing outfits for those taking up new occupations; (iii) as grants to the sick or distressed; and (iv) in making weekly allowances of from 1s. 6d. to 3s. to persons over 60 wholly or partly unable to support themselves. By a new Scheme of 1912 the distribution of necessaries in kind, in lieu of money payments for the purposes specified at (ii) and (iii), was authorized. In 1934 the lands were sold and the proceeds invested in £1,306 stock.[52] In 1932 £33 of the income was spent in coal, food, and clothing for 30 beneficiaries, and in 1955 a somewhat larger sum, about half the income, in vouchers for goods.[53]

Sir George Fettiplace, by will proved 1743, left a sum of money in trust for charitable purposes in various places. Of the annual income of £200, £10 was appropriated to the poor of Dorchester to be distributed by the vicar and churchwardens in 6d. loaves between Michaelmas and Lady Day.[54] Because of financial difficulties involving the Fettiplace estate, the charity was not distributed for several years in the 1770's, but by 1787 distributions were again being made.[55] In 1908 it was being distributed at the same time and to the same persons as Dunch's charity.[56] In 1931 the income amounting to £10 was being spent in bread.[57]

[35] *Wilb. Visit.*
[36] d.d. Bertie c 17 (uncat.): draft of bargain and sale in 1836 and correspondence about the school.
[37] *Wilb. Visit.*
[38] W. C. Macfarlane, *Short Account of Dorchester*, 22; Kelly, *Dir. Oxon.* (1903).
[39] *List. of Sch.* 526.
[40] Kelly, *Dir. Oxon.* (1887); for details of the schools and their difficulties at the end of the 19th century see Bodl. G.A. Oxon. c 317 (8).
[41] Kelly, *Dir. Oxon.* (1903).
[42] *Vol. Sch. Ret.* 10.
[43] Inf. Oxon. Educ. Cttee.
[44] Ibid.
[45] Ibid.
[46] SS. Peter and Paul's Missionary College *Annual*

Report. There are copies from 1879 in Bodl. G.A. Oxon. 8° 379.
[47] Kelly, *Dir. Oxon.* (1939); see below, p. 66.
[48] Inf. the Ven. H. F. Kirkpatrick, head of the college until 1947 (*Who's Who*, 1959).
[49] *8th Rep. Com. Char.* 494.
[50] Char. Com. file 41866.
[51] Ibid.
[52] For the Schemes see Char. Com. file 116092. For a report of the inquiry see *Ox. Times*, 13 Aug. 1910.
[53] Char. Com. Accts. file.
[54] *8th Rep. Com. Char.* 494–5; *10th Rep. Com. Char.* 384–7.
[55] MS. Top. Oxon. c 120, ff. 37, 58b.
[56] Char. Com. file 86179.
[57] Ibid. Accts. file.

BURCOT

BURCOT lies on the north bank of the Thames, 1¾ miles north-west of Dorchester. Its historical relationship with Dorchester cannot be precisely defined: for long it has been dependent ecclesiastically on Dorchester[1] but independent for civil purposes.[2] In the 18th century it was described as a separate parish, and in the 19th century was placed in a different registration district and rural district from Dorchester.[3]

In 1932 Burcot civil parish was transferred to Clifton Hampden.[4] Its area in 1881 was 679 acres, of which 21·6 were detached meadow (Revell Mead) and lay in Clifton Hampden.[5] The only natural boundary is the River Thames, which has naturally played an important part in the economy.

Burcot's fields lie 169 ft. above sea-level along the Abingdon–Dorchester road, and rise to 210 ft. on Clifton Heath.[6] The soil is mainly Lower Greensand, although there is some Gault in the eastern part of the hamlet.[7]

The highway from Abingdon to Dorchester runs through the parish from west to east. Since the 15th century when Abingdon and Culham bridges were built this road ceased to be of merely local importance and became an important highway carrying traffic from London to Gloucester.[8] The main highway from Dorchester to Oxford also runs through part of Burcot and like the Dorchester–Abingdon road was turnpiked in the 18th century.[9] Another road, running from south to north-east, links the two main highways and practically bisects the parish. It begins in the south nearly opposite Burcot House and runs past Burcot Farm. The smaller tracks in the parish, such as Occupation Row, immediately opposite the church, which were in use until early in the present century,[10] have now largely disappeared. Another track just east of the Chequers Inn ran from the Dorchester–Oxford road south to the Dorchester–Abingdon road, and thence continued south to the River Thames. Large flints for the repair of the surface of the Dorchester–Oxford road were brought by barge along the Thames to Burcot and carried along this track until the present century.[11]

Burcot's position near the River Thames at one time gave it an importance out of all proportion to its size. During the first 30 years of the 17th century the Thames between Burcot and Oxford was virtually innavigable, and consequently goods destined for Oxford had to be unloaded at Burcot and then carried by road into the city.[12] Similarly Headington stone and timber from Shotover and Stowood forests had to be brought by road to Burcot before being shipped to London. The strain on the road system was therefore heavy.[13] Hence the establishment of the Oxford–Burcot Commission by the Acts of 1605 and 1624 to improve the river between Oxford and Burcot.[14] As early as 1606 a scheme of improvements was put forward by James Jessop,[15] but it apparently came to nothing. Although improvements to the river were made during the 1620's,[16] the rate of progress did not satisfy the government, for in 1631 Charles I ordered a fresh examination of the river to be made.[17] The king was concerned with both the cost and the difficulties of shipping timber from Burcot to Woolwich and Deptford.[18] With the opening of the route to Oxford via Swift Ditch about 1636[19] the main difficulties seem to have disappeared, and Burcot lost its temporary importance. Nevertheless, barges continued to stop there until recent times. In 1764 coal was landed at Burcot;[20] and until about 1914 coal and flints were brought by barge.[21]

The village of Burcot lies on both sides of the Dorchester–Abingdon highway.[22] Nearly all the houses are relatively modern, having been built since 1888. The timber-framed and thatched cottages, for instance, once in Occupation Row, were pulled down between 1888 and 1892 by Jabez Balfour and rebuilt on a new site.[23] About 1880 the area began to attract attention as a desirable Thames-side residential district, and this character it still retains. The compactness which the village no doubt possessed in earlier days has therefore tended to be replaced by a more spreadeagled appearance. Yet the core of the village is still the area between the church and the Chequers Inn where the original hamlet seems to have been concentrated.

South of the Dorchester–Abingdon road and near to the river in the west of the parish is a large modern building formerly known as the Croft and now as the Riverside Hotel. Nearby to the east until 1956 was Burcot House. This building, which stood in thickly wooded grounds, dated in part from the 18th century, when it was a farmhouse occupied probably by the Bush family and later, from 1825 to 1886, by the Hannam family,[24] but it suffered greatly from additions and alterations in the late 19th and early 20th centuries. The north front seems to have been built about the mid 18th century. In 1886, when it was bought by Jabez Balfour for use as a private residence, the Georgian building was still apparently intact. It was then a two-storied building, consisting on the ground floor of an entrance hall and four rooms; there were also detached stables and a carriage house.[25] Jabez Balfour between 1886 and

[1] See below, p. 69.
[2] *Census*, 1801, &c.
[3] *Census* 1851, 1901.
[4] Oxon. Review Order, 1932.
[5] *Census*, 1881.
[6] O.S. Map 6″, xlv, xlvi (1883, 1884); 2½″, 41/59 (1949).
[7] *V.C.H. Oxon.* ii, map facing p. 5.
[8] For the highway see above, p. 40.
[9] 9 Geo. II, c. 14.
[10] Local inf.
[11] Local inf.
[12] F. S. Thacker, *The Thames Highway: A History of the Inland Navigation*, 62; see also above, p. 28.
[13] Act to clear passage, 3 Jas. I, c. 20.

[14] Ibid.; Thames Navigation Act, 21 Jas. I, c. 32.
[15] *Cal. S.P. Dom.* 1603–10, 279.
[16] Thacker, *Thames Highway*, 69.
[17] *Cal. S.P. Dom.* 1631–3, 133.
[18] Ibid. 1633–4, 168.
[19] See above, p. 28.
[20] O.R.O. Note on back of printed Orders and Constitutions of Thames Nav. Comrs. Box 98.
[21] Local inf.
[22] O.S. Map 25″, xlvi. 9 (1877).
[23] Gibbs Pps. (at the Manor House, Clifton Hampden); particulars of sale of various properties, 1886; and local inf.
[24] See below, p. 69.
[25] Gibbs Pps. Sale partics. 1886.

1893 erected an ornamental front overlooking an Italian garden, together with other additions.[26] The result was to destroy the symmetry and proportions of the structure. Further additions were made in the 1920's and 1930's, when the house was occupied by Dorchester Theological College.[27] A small chapel was built to the north of the main building and a block of study-bedrooms to the west. In 1940 Cheshunt Theological College was evacuated there. After the Second World War some Serbian refugee-students lived in the building for a time. After standing empty for some years the house and surrounding property were disposed of in 1954 for building purposes. In 1956 the old building and Balfour's additions were demolished. The coach house and the study-bedrooms have been converted into houses, but the chapel remains. The fate of the dovecot is in doubt.

Two other old buildings, lying close together, are situated just south of the Abingdon–Dorchester highway. The Old Cottage, formerly Burcot Cottage, is a timber-framed structure, perhaps dating from Tudor times. The east side was undoubtedly at one time a separate building. It runs from north to south, the original wattle and daub being replaced by red brick. There is a dormer window on the east side. The remainder of the structure runs from east to west and may be two cottages combined. It is timber-framed, with walls of rubble. A modern addition in Tudor style juts out to the north, and there are other modern additions at the west end. Some of the old windows remain. The house was perhaps originally a farm. The Chequers Inn nearby is a timber-framed structure. It seems to be of 16th-century origin and is traditionally held to have been an inn for more than 400 years. The first specific reference to it, however, is in the Victuallers' recognizances in 1791, when John Drake was the landlord.[28] In 1950 it was damaged by fire; the roof and ceiling were destroyed, but the fabric escaped destruction.[29] The building has now been completely restored.

MANORS. Burcot was not mentioned by name in Domesday Book in 1086, but was undoubtedly surveyed under Dorchester manor like the other outlying estates of the Bishop of Lincoln's manor.[30] The bishop subinfeudated most of Burcot, but retained part in demesne and the overlordship of the whole until 1547,[31] when Bishop Henry Holbeche resigned Dorchester and other manors to the king.[32] Burcot was a member of Dorchester manor[33] and its overlordship followed Dorchester's descent, when

it was granted to the Norreys family and later when it passed to the earls of Abingdon.[34]

The bishop's demesne lands also passed to the earls of Abingdon, presumably in the same way as the overlordship, and it was from these that they derived their chief interest in Burcot.[35] Although the property was regarded as part of Dorchester manor,[36] the Earl of Abingdon was called lord of *BURCOT* manor in the inclosure award of 1776.[37] When, however, the estate was put up for sale in 1844 and in 1875, no mention was made of manorial rights.[38] Ultimately the estate went mainly to Jabez Balfour in 1886, and when he went bankrupt in 1893 to a London merchant, George Hooper. As the result of purchases by the Gibbs family of Clifton Hampden, the principal landowners in the 20th century were the Lords Aldenham.[39]

Another manor seems to have descended from the Burcot fee of the Le Moines, who held in Burcot, Clifton Hampden, and South Stoke from the 12th to the 14th century. The mesne tenancy followed the descent of their Clifton holding.[40] During the 13th and 14th centuries under-tenants of the Le Moines held the estate. In 1279 Sir Geoffrey de Lewknor, who held another $\frac{1}{10}$ fee in Burcot directly of the bishop, held Philip le Moine's 6 virgates and 3 acres in Burcot.[41] Geoffrey (d. c. 1282–3) held land in many neighbouring parishes and was lord of Harrowden (Northants.).[42] Sir Ralph de Lewknor held Burcot in 1300, and before 1316 had been succeeded by a Geoffrey de Lewknor and then by Geoffrey's brother John, who was one of the lords of Burcot in 1316.[43] John de Lewknor was still alive in 1325[44] and was apparently succeeded here as elsewhere by his son, another John, described in 1346 as John de Lewknor of Burcot.[45] There is no later record of the Lewknors of Burcot,[46] but their estate was apparently the same as the Burcot manor held in 1380 by Sir Hugh de Segrave. The manor was said to have belonged formerly to a John Frylond, but there is no other record of him,[47] and it is likely that he was in fact the tenant of the Le Moine or Lewknor property. Segrave transferred Burcot manor and John Frylond's other lands in Burcot and Clifton to Bishop William of Wykeham, and they were later, in 1381, transferred to Winchester College for Wykeham's foundation of New College, Oxford.[48] They were kept until 1390 and a John Waryn farmed Burcot during that time.[49] Evidently after 1390 they were sold, like Clifton Hampden, to the Draytons, and followed the descent of Clifton Hampden until the end of the 16th century.[50] In 1597, however, Thomas Hampden sold Burcot

[26] Gibbs Pps. Sale Partics. 1886, 1893.
[27] See above, p. 64.   [28] O.R.O.
[29] *Oxf. Mail*, 3 May 1950.
[30] *V.C.H. Oxon.* i. 403.
[31] See below; cf. C 142/37/110.
[32] *Cal. Pat.* 1547–8, 153.
[33] Ibid. 1558–60, 435, 437.
[34] See above, p. 42.
[35] See below, p. 68.
[36] Cf. L.R.2/189, ff. 5b–6; cf. Abingdon Pps. e.g. MS. Top. Oxon. b 193; c 385.
[37] O.R.O. Incl. award.
[38] MS. Top. Oxon. b 121, f. 209; d.d. Bertie d 1: *Sale cat.* 1844; Gibbs Pps. (at the Manor House, Clifton Hampden): particulars of 1886 sale of Hannam prop.
[39] Gibbs Pps.; and inf. from Sir Leonard Sinclair of Burcot.
[40] See *Rot. Hund.* (Rec. Com.), ii. 748–9; and see above for the Le Moine descent, p. 18.

[41] *Rot. Hund.* (Rec. Com.), ii. 749. The Le Moine fee in Burcot and Clifton Hampden was in all 10 virgates, and the Hundred Rolls give the total figure under both Burcot and Clifton.
[42] See below, p. 177; *V.C.H. Northants.* iv. 179.
[43] See below, p. 178; Queen's Coll. MS. 366, f. 24 b; *Feud. Aids*, iv. 167.
[44] *Cal. Close*, 1323–7, 384.
[45] *Cal. Fine R.* 1337–47, 511; *Feud. Aids*, iv. 182. It is not certain that he is mentioned under Burcot itself. As the holding is a $\frac{1}{2}$-fee this John may be an error for John Bradeley; see above, p. 20.
[46] See also below, p. 177; cf. *V.C.H. Northants.* iv. 179.
[47] *Cal. Close*, 1377–81, 377.
[48] Ibid. 1381–5, 239, 240; New Coll. Arch. Bursars' accts. 1381.
[49] New Coll. Arch. Bursars' accts. 1381–90.
[50] Ibid.; see above, p. 19.

manor and 9 yardlands in Burcot and Dorchester, of which 7 yardlands were in Burcot, to Sir Michael Molyns and his son Barentine Molyns.[51] During the 17th century the property changed hands several times. Sir Barentine Molyns disposed of it to a John Whistler in 1616, who conveyed it in 1627 to a Mr. Mattingley, perhaps the William Mattingley who was dealing with the manor in the 1640's. Mattingley mortgaged the estate to James Yateman in 1633 and in 1641 they both conveyed it to Richard Newdigate; from him it passed to a Roger Styles in 1647.[52] Styles sold the manor and 7 yardlands to the Trustees of the Poor of Great Haseley parish in 1651.[53] At first the trustees leased the manor as well as the 7 yardlands, but after 1754 there is no further reference to the manor,[54] and its fate is obscure.

LESSER ESTATES. By 1201 beside the two main estates there was another small military one which an Alexander of Burcot (*Bridicot*) held of the bishop for $\frac{1}{10}$ fee.[55] He still held *c.* 1209,[56] but by 1212 his son William was tenant[57] and was still in possession in the 1220's. William's immediate successors are unknown, but by 1279 the estate was held by Le Moine's under-tenant, Sir Geoffrey de Lewknor. The military estate was small, only 2 virgates.[58] It was still recorded separately in 1300,[59] but there is no later reference to it,[60] and it may have been merged in the Lewknors' holding under the Le Moines.

In 1166 an estate was held in Burcot by Adelinus de Clifton and formed part of his 2 fees in Clifton and Burcot, the Baldons, and South Stoke, which were later held by the De Baldindon family.[61] Burcot descended with them for a time, and in 1428 was stated to be held by Robert 'Bradeley' who also held the Clifton lands.[62] Part seems to have followed the later descent of Bradleys manor in Clifton, for the Pollards, lords of Bradleys, held a tenement in Burcot in the 16th century;[63] but it is probable that the rest of the estate, which was only 4 virgates, had been divided between under-tenants earlier on. Already by 1279 Nicholas de Burcot held 2 virgates of the De Baldindon property in Burcot,[64] and like his other lands these may have passed to Dorchester Abbey by the mid 14th century.[65] The abbey was twice granted licences in mortmain to acquire land in Burcot in the 14th century and its two surviving 15th-century court rolls include Burcot entries.[66] In 1536 the abbey had rents and farms there, but by 1538 its property had passed to the Crown.[67]

ECONOMIC AND SOCIAL HISTORY. In the Anglo-Saxon period Burcot was probably one of the

villages paying food-rents to the Bishop of Dorchester.[68] Its Old English name, *Brȳda's* cottage, and its position close to Dorchester suggest that it was originally settled from there possibly at an early date.[69] Roman remains have been found at Burcot, but it is unlikely that occupation was continuous there, although it seems to have been so at Dorchester.[70]

In the survey of 1086 Burcot seems to have been included in the account of the outlying parts of the Dorchester estate, by then the property of the Bishop of Lincoln. As later evidence shows that the bishop held part of Burcot in demesne it is likely that some Burcot tenants were included in the 34 *villani* and 22 bordars listed under the bishop's Dorchester manor.[71] It is also likely that the rest of Burcot was held by the bishop's knights, perhaps by the English freemen, who in 1086 held $3\frac{1}{2}$ hides of Dorchester land, for at the end of the 12th century three of the bishop's knights were holding Burcot land.[72]

From a survey of the bishop's estates made in the second quarter of the 13th century it appears that the bishop's demesne estate comprised 28 virgates, and that he had no home farm at Burcot. Seven villein tenants were recorded with unusually large holdings: four had 3 to 5 virgates each, two had 2 virgates each, only one of this group had a single virgate holding. These tenants paid rent at the rate of 5s. 6d. a virgate, and owed services similar to those of the villeins on the bishop's demesne manor of Dorchester. Each was to plough 2 acres at his own cost and 2 at the bishop's; to fallow 1 acre with his own plough, if he had one, and if not by making up a plough-team with others; to go to 2 autumn boon-works at the bishop's cost with all his family except for his wife and daughter, or his nurse if he had no daughter. He was also to carry the bishop's writs, make his distraints and summonses, and accompany the bishop's treasure in transit. His marks of villeinage are seen in his liability to heriot, leirwite, a fine for land on his father's death, and bishop's aids. In addition to these services two of the tenants were to plough an acre of *grascherch*.

Eight other tenants held single virgates at a rent of 5s. 6d. each and services similar to those owed by the villeins of Chislehampton. These included comparatively heavy agricultural and carrying services.[73]

The picture of the bishop's estate presented by the hundred rolls is rather different, and it may be that the survey of 1279 is not complete or that in the earlier survey land of one of the bishop's knights was included. In 1279 eleven virgates were held of the bishop for rent and service. A typical virgater paid 5s. rent a year. He did no week-work, but had

[51] Bodl. MS. Gough Oxon. 22, ff, 89b–90; C.P. 25(2)/198/Trin. 39 Eliz. I.
[52] Bodl. MS. Gough Oxon. 22, ff. 90b–91; cf. C.P. 25(2)/474/Hil. 17 Chas. I; ibid. 22 Chas. I. Burcot deeds of the 17th cent. mention the Whistlers of Brightwell (Berks.) and James Yateman of Middle Temple, London: O.R.O. H 111/f. 2–7.
[53] MS. Gough Oxon. 22, f. 91b.
[54] Ibid. ff. 91b–92; d.d. Par. Gt. Haseley c 4, b 9.
[55] *Rot. de Ob. et Fin.* (Rec. Com.), i. 155.
[56] *Bk. of Fees*, 40.
[57] *Red Bk. Exch.* (Rolls Ser.), 514; Queen's Coll. MS. 366, f. xxv.
[58] *Rot. Hund.* (Rec. Com.), ii. 749.
[59] Queen's Coll. MS. 366, f. xxivb.
[60] e.g. *Feud. Aids*, iv. 182.
[61] See *Rot. Hund.* (Rec. Com.), ii. 724, 749, 751.

[62] See above, p. 20; *Feud. Aids*, iv. 99.
[63] O.R.O. Wi IV/iii/2, 3.
[64] *Rot. Hund.* (Rec. Com.), ii. 749.
[65] Ibid.; and see above, p. 19; *Feud. Aids*, iv. 182.
[66] *Cal. Pat.* 1321–4, 416; 1391–6, 100; St. John's Coll. Mun. Dorchester Abbey ct. rolls, 1401, 1463.
[67] Dugdale, *Mon.* vi. 324; St. John's Coll. Mun. ct. rolls, 1538, 1539.
[68] See above, p. 44.
[69] *P.N. Oxon.* (E.P.N.S.), i. 149.
[70] *V.C.H. Oxon.* i. 333; and see above, p. 40.
[71] *V.C.H. Oxon.* i. 403.
[72] The sokemen mentioned in 1279 in Drayton and Burcot were perhaps the descendants of the English freemen mentioned there: see below, pp. 68, 75.
[73] Queen's Coll. MS. 366, ff. 25b, 26b. For the services owed by the Chislehampton villeins and for the date of the survey see above, pp. 12–13 and n. 94.

to plough 2 acres of the bishop's demesne, to lift hay, to reap for 3½ days in autumn when he supplied his own food, and for 2 days when the bishop provided. He carried grain and carted it to Fingest (Bucks.) and to Wallingford. His marks of villeinage were that he could not marry his daughter or sell his horse or ox without the lord's permission. Seven tenants owed these dues. The eighth, Hugh le Frankelyn, was perhaps a descendant of the freemen of 1086, who had gone down in the social scale: he claimed that his ancestors had been sokemen and therefore free, serving 40 days in war with coat of mail, lance, and helmet (*chapell' de ferro*). He maintained that this service had been taken away by the bishops of Lincoln. Hugh was in any case freer than the others. He paid 17s. a year for his 3 virgates. He still ploughed 2 acres, but only if he had a plough, and was paid 1½d. an acre. All his family except his wife, nurse (*nutrix*), and shepherd were to go to the two autumn boons. He was to carry letters for one day at his own cost and for another at the bishop's, and he was to be at each hundred court of Dorchester. Hugh's under-tenants were not named in the survey, but the bishop claimed services from them: they were to go to the boons and Hugh was to supervise them. Free tenants in Burcot were to be found only on the subinfeudated estates in 1279, a feature which was characteristic of Burcot for many centuries. The Le Moine fee, with over 6 virgates, was the largest of these. It was held by Sir Geoffrey de Lewknor together with the 2 virgates of his own 1/10 fee. William de Baldindon's 4 virgates were held by Sir Richard de la Hyde. None of these tenants had home farms and the estates consisted of rent-paying virgates. Save for the reeve holding 1 virgate in villeinage, the tenants owed no customary services, but paid varying rents and scutage for their part of the fees. Dorchester Abbey was one of the most important tenants with rights over 2 virgates of the Le Moine fee and 2 virgates of the Baldon fee. Two virgates also paid rents to Goring Priory.[74] Burcot was a small township: only 23 virgates were recorded in 1279, and the virgate was probably about 22 acres as in Baldon and Clifton. The village's contributions to the early 14th-century taxes were therefore lower than those of the neighbouring villages of Clifton, Drayton, and Baldon. Only 10 contributors paid in 1306, most making comparatively modest payments of under 2s. to the total of £1 2s. 10¾d. In 1327, when there were 17 taxpayers, one of the larger contributions was the 5s. from John le Frankelyn, probably a descendant of the Hugh le Frankelyn of 1279. The small number of 41 adults who paid the poll tax of 1377 suggests that if there was no evasion the population had declined.[75]

Burcot continued to be divided between three main landowners until quite modern times, but there are few surveys of the village comparable with that of 1279 to give an over-all picture. Between 1381 and 1390 when the chief lay estate (Le Moine-

Lewknor) had come to Winchester College, it was farmed for £5 18s. a year.[76] Dorchester Abbey was receiving £2 10s. 4d. from rents and farms of its estate in 1536.[77] A few years later in 1551-2 the bishop's estate, now in the hands of the Crown, was surveyed. Copyholders were still the only tenants. Four held a messuage and 2 virgates each, one a messuage and a single virgate, and one 4 virgates and a messuage. The total rent was £6 2s. The stint for a yardland was 30 sheep, 3 beasts, and 3 horses, and the surveyor estimated that there were 375 sheep on the Burcot estate. The area was well wooded, for there were said to be 936 trees on the tenants' land.[78] Little is known of the status or life of the villagers, but in 1523 there were 14 inhabitants sufficiently prosperous to contribute to the subsidy.[79] In 1665 there was only one fair-sized house for which a tax on 5 hearths was paid. It belonged to John Day, who was tenant of the Great Haseley charity lands and manor—the old Le Moine estate.[80] He held his 7 yardlands on a 12-year lease for £52 a year.[81] Two other farmers had each paid tax on 3 hearths for their farmhouses, three paid on 2, and one on a single hearth.[82] About half Burcot (the bishop's old estate) belonged to the Earl of Abingdon by this time.[83] His tenants were still copyholders with one or two leaseholders and they attended the Dorchester manorial court. In 1685 2 virgates in Burcot were taken up at the will of the lord for £1 2s. 2d. a year.[84] In 1728 there were 8 copyholders paying rack-rents for holdings ranging from 4 to 93 acres.[85] In 1783 the annual value of the estate, estimated as over 215 acres, was £214 14s. 4d., but rents came to under £7 a year.[86]

An early 18th-century survey of the estate shows that the three-field system of farming, 2 crops and a fallow, was used.[87] Only the name of one field, the North Field, is known.[88] The soil of the manor was described in 1728 as very good, but the meadows as poor and lying far from the homes. It was suggested then that the laying down of part of the land to grass and the drainage of wet land would be a substantial improvement;[89] but there is nothing to indicate that the suggestion was put into operation before the inclosure of the parish. In 1783 part of the estate was described as good corn land, but part as 'burning' land, i.e. liable to drought.[90] The inclosure award shows that Burcot farmers shared their meadow with Clifton Hampden. They took the first crop of Revell Mead (part or all of which was known in Clifton as Burcot Mead),[91] but the aftermath belonged to the Hucks estate of Clifton.

It is clear that there was a movement towards larger holdings before inclosure. Burcot was inclosed in 1776,[92] and the principal landowners then were Willoughby, Earl of Abingdon, whose land was mainly held by copyholders, John Bush, the impropriator and owner of a 7-yardland freehold, and the trustees of the 7 yardlands held for Great Haseley poor. The area inclosed was 616 acres. The effect

[74] *Rot. Hund.* (Rec. Com.), ii. 748–9; and see below, p. 85, n. 80.
[75] E 179/161/9, 10, 41.
[76] New Coll. Arch. Bursars' accts. 1381–90.
[77] Dugdale, *Mon.* vi. 324.
[78] L.R. 2/189, ff. 15b–16.
[79] E 179/161/198.
[80] *Hearth Tax Oxon.* 54; MS. Gough Oxon. 22, f. 91b.
[81] MS. Gough Oxon. 22, f. 91b.
[82] *Hearth Tax Oxon.* 54.

[83] See Abingdon Pps. *passim*: e.g. MS. Top. Oxon. a 46; b 178; c 384, c 385; d.d. Bertie c 3.
[84] d.d. Bertie b 1, f. 35.
[85] MS. Top. Oxon. c 381, ff. 56–57.
[86] d.d. Bertie c 3.   [87] MS. Top. Oxon. c 381, f. 57.
[88] Par. Rec. Dorchester chwdns' accts.
[89] MS. Top. Oxon. c 381, ff. 56–57.
[90] d.d. Bertie c 3.
[91] O.R.O. Inc. award; and see above, p. 22.
[92] Burcot Incl. Act, 15 Geo. III c. 4 (priv. act).

was to change completely the appearance of the countryside: in place of the scattered strips were two large farms, one (c. 236 a.) belonging to John Bush, the other (c. 135 a.) to John Cripps, chief tenant of the Abingdon estate and owner also of 4 freehold yardlands. The Haseley charity lands amounted to about 104 acres. Three tenants of the Abingdon estate were allotted small holdings of 30 to 60 acres and there were 3 small allotments of 1 to 7 acres. Eight inhabitants had no land in the common fields and were to make annual payments in lieu of tithes for their cottages and gardens.[93] The effect of inclosure on the hamlet is hard to assess. The smaller farmers certainly disappeared after the award was made, but not until the Napoleonic Wars. In 1785 there were nine occupants of land; the Bush and Cripps farms and the Haseley charity lands had the highest and almost equal assessments. By 1797 four of the holdings had been absorbed into the Bush and Cripps farms. By 1805 there were only three occupiers of lands:[94] John Bush had taken over the leases of three of the Abingdon holdings and now paid over half the land tax.[95] He apparently farmed the land himself, but in 1807 Gabriel Copland took over the property and let it to a tenant farmer, Charles Tawney.[96] It is likely that this was the property which Arthur Young said was purchased for £13,000 in 1807 by a Mr. 'Tormy'; he said it had a good house and a fishery in the Thames.[97] In 1825 Henry Hannam purchased it and from 1826 or 1827 he farmed the land himself.[98] The Cripps family also increased its lands and by 1805 John Cripps (d. c. 1825) had taken in three other holdings and was paying over a quarter of the total land tax for the parish.[99] From 1807 the estate was occupied by his son James Cripps.[1] The Crippses were agricultural improvers, for in 1809 Arthur Young commented on their experiments in sheep-breeding and noted that they folded in the summer for turnips.[2]

During the course of the 19th century the process of creating larger farms continued and gradually most of the land was absorbed into Burcot House farm. In 1851 Henry Hannam farmed 460 acres, there was a tenant farm (100 a.) belonging to John Cripps, and another small farm (35 a.).[3] By 1856 the Hannams were farming the Haseley charity lands,[4] and in 1879 they purchased most of the Cripps property.[5] By 1889 Jabez Balfour had acquired Burcot House farm and the Haseley charity lands.[6] In 1928 Lord Aldenham owned 500 acres, mainly farmed by the tenant of Burcot farm.[7]

Burcot's farming has been mainly mixed, but with the emphasis on arable, as was necessary in an open-field village: sheep and corn are mentioned in

most of the surveys.[8] In 1801 the village contained 29 families living in 29 houses, 136 inhabitants in all.[9] The only earlier comparable figure is that of the Compton Census which gives 66 adults. The population rose steadily throughout the 19th century. By 1851 there were 40 houses and 189 people and the peak figure of 199 persons was reached in 1881. Numbers of inhabitants have since fluctuated; they were 141 in 1921 with 36 houses and 187 with 38 houses in 1931. The census of 1951 showed a decline in population for the joint parishes of Clifton Hampden and Burcot.[10]

Some record of the village's craftsmen has survived: in the early 18th century there was a tailor,[11] a collarmaker, and a whittayer in the village.[12] The census of 1851 recorded a road labourer (a pauper), schoolmistress, carrier, carpenter, and public house keeper, in addition to the three farmers and their 50 farm labourers.[13]

In spite of its small size there was a good deal of poverty in the late 18th and 19th centuries. In 1783 three cottages on the waste were occupied by paupers who paid no rent.[14] The poor rate of 2s. 8d. in 1803 was higher than that of most villages in the hundred, although naturally much smaller than the Dorchester rate. As elsewhere, the years after the end of the Napoleonic War led to an increase in distress: £117 16s. was spent in 1835 compared with £76 15s. 9d. in 1803.[15] By 1852 expenditure had fallen again to about £76.[16]

CHURCH. No trace of a church or chapel at Burcot has been found either in the medieval or modern period before 1869, when a chapel-of-ease was built. According to local tradition there was a medieval church at Burcot, but excavations of 1857 in 'Church Field', on the north of the road to Dorchester between Clifton and Burcot revealed no traces of it.[17] In the post-Reformation period Burcot had its own rectory (as it had had in the Middle Ages), glebe, and churchwardens. In the 17th century it was considered a part of the 'parish' of Dorchester,[18] but in the 18th-century Vestry minutes refer to the 'parish of Burcot', and Skelton in the early 19th century described it as a parish without a church.[19] It seems, however, to have been generally accepted in the 19th century that Burcot was in Dorchester parish and when its church was built in 1869 its status was that of a chapel-of-ease.[20]

From at least the late 16th century Burcot churchwardens, like those of all the churches in Dorchester peculiar, appeared at the peculiar courts.[21] They made presentments about the township;[22] they levied church-rates for the upkeep of Dorchester church,

93 O.R.O. Incl. award.
94 O.R.O. Land tax assess.
95 Ibid. d.d. Bertie d 1: leases (uncat.).
96 d.d. Bertie d 1: leases (uncat.).
97 Young, *Oxon. Agric.* 17.
98 O.R.O. Land tax assess.; cf. d.d. Bertie d 1: auction catalogue (uncat.).
99 O.R.O. Land tax assess.; d.d. Bertie d 1.
1 Ibid. 2 Young, *Oxon. Agric.* 301–2.
3 H.O. 107/1688/4.
4 O.R.O. Misc. Ay. I/1: the rent was £129, later rising to £160 (after land tax).
5 Gibbs Pps. (at the Manor House, Clifton Hampden).
6 Ibid.
7 d.d. Bullingdon a 3: rate bk.
8 See above; cf. Orr, *Oxon. Agric. passim.*
9 Capper, *Topographical Dictionary.*

10 *V.C.H. Oxon.* ii. 220.
11 O.R.O. Wi IV/ii/2, 3.
12 Ibid.; H 111/g/9.
13 H.O. 107/1688/4.
14 d.d. Bertie c 3.
15 *Poor Abstract,* 402–3; *2nd Rep. Poor Law Com. App. (E),* H.C. 595–II, p. 294 (1836), xxix (2).
16 *Poor Law Unions,* H.C. 451, p. 5 (1854), lv.
17 Parker, *Guide,* 376, and note in Bodl. copy (G.A. Oxon. 4° 697).
18 *Oxon. Peculiars,* 144.
19 Dorchester Par. Rec. Vestry mins. 1745, 1746; Skelton, *Oxon.* Dorchester hund.
20 See Kelly, *Dir. Oxon.* (1864, &c.); *Census,* 1951: Eccl. Areas.
21 Oxf. Dioc. d 13, f. 96.
22 *Oxon. Peculiars,* 139–44.

their mother church, paying about a sixth of the total amount needed each year, but kept their accounts separately from those of the wardens of Dorchester.[23] The curate of Dorchester was their minister.

Burcot rectory, like those of the other churches in Dorchester peculiar, evidently formed part of the early endowment of the canons of Dorchester and then of Dorchester Abbey, which was refounded about 1140,[24] although papal confirmations of the daughter churches of the abbey in 1146 and 1163 do not mention Burcot.[25] The first evidence about the rectory comes from the 1530's when the abbey was farming it for £4 13s. 4d.[26] A description of it then makes clear, what is also shown by later evidence, that the rectory was unusual in consisting of all the tithes, both great and small, and of the church dues of the inhabitants.[27] There was also a small amount of glebe, mentioned in 1663, belonging to the rectory.[28]

At the dissolution of the abbey Burcot rectory was taken over by the Crown, which in 1538 granted it with Drayton rectory to John Danyster of Chobham (Surr.), probably for a term of 21 years.[29] Yet in 1542 it was granted to the new bishopric of Oxford.[30] In 1545 it was sold with Clifton rectory to John Pollard and George Rythe, the former buying out the latter within a few weeks.[31] Its descent then followed that of Bradleys manor in Clifton.[32] The history of the rectory in the 17th century is complicated. In 1615 James I licensed Lewis Pollard to sell it to Anthony Peisley and Richard Allam.[33] In fact Pollard seems to have retained it until 1640, Allam for part of the time being the tenant.[34] In 1640 it was conveyed to Thomas Dennis of Oxford on a 76-year lease at a price of £180.[35] The value in 1663 was said to be £50 a year.[36] In 1666 Thomas Dennis, the younger, and his wife Ursula leased the rectory to Richard Pleydell.[37] Nine years later it had passed into the hands of Richard Nelmes, who conveyed it to the Earl of Leicester and Algernon Sidney as a mortgage for debt. In their hands it remained until the execution of Algernon Sidney in 1683. In 1684 Charles II granted to Henry Sidney all debts due to Algernon; and in 1687 James II gave the rectory to Henry Sidney, who previously seems to have been entitled only to the interest from it.[38] Its history for some time to come is obscure. In 1775 John Bush was the impropriator; and as the Bush family came into Burcot probably as early as 1734, they may have

been possessed of the rectory then.[39] The inclosure award of 1776 commuted tithe, John Bush, who owned both the great and small tithes, receiving substantial compensation (c. 115 a.) in land, the equivalent of one-seventh of the parish. The open-field glebe was exchanged for about 4 acres.[40] The rectory seems to have descended with the Bush property during the 19th and 20th centuries, i.e. through the families of Copland, Hannam, Balfour, and Gibbs, for the title deeds of Burcot Farm, purchased by Alban, Lord Aldenham, in 1919, speak of the rectory or parsonage impropriate of Burcot.[41]

The present chapel-of-ease was erected in 1869 at a cost of about £700 to serve the dual purpose of a chapel and school.[42] In 1878 there was said to be a monthly communion service, and other services twice a week were reported.[43] Since the closure of Burcot school in 1922[44] the building has been devoted solely to spiritual uses.

The chapel, dedicated to *ST. MARY*, is a small brick building, consisting of nave, chancel, and bell-turret. It is in the Gothic style of the Victorian era: the chancel, which is apsidal at the east end, has four single-light windows; the chancel arch is in the Decorated style. A wooden screen with a crucifix above the centre part runs across the entrance to the chancel. The architect was George Gilbert Scott.[45]

NONCONFORMITY. The old faith lingered on in Burcot after the Reformation, although it was less strong than in the neighbouring hamlet of Overy. In the early 17th century two yeoman families, the Tulls and the Philpotts, had recusant members. Agnes Tull, who was frequently listed as a recusant,[46] was in 1624 illegally buried in Dorchester churchyard.[47] Another recusant yeoman couple that appear in 1625 and 1641 were Augustine Ford and his wife.[48]

These families do not appear as recusants after the Restoration, but in the later 17th century there were three recusant families in Burcot: the Bonds,[49] the Nutts,[50] and the Days, a family which also had a branch in Dorchester.[51] Elizabeth, the wife of John Day, was listed as a recusant in 1666,[52] and in the 1670's Robert Day was constantly presented for not attending church.[53] Two branches of the family were listed as recusants in the 1690's.[54] In 1706 John Day and his wife were two of the three recusants in Burcot[55] and in about 1717 Edward Day of Burcot, yeoman and a substantial copyholder, was a Roman Catholic.[56] No further record has been found of the

23 Par. Rec. Dorchester chwdns' accts.
24 *V.C.H. Oxon.* ii. 87.
25 *Reg. Antiquiss.* i. 247; O.A.S. *Rep.* 1909, 11–12.
26 *Valor Eccl.* (Rec. Com.), ii. 170; H. Addington, *Account of Abbey Church of Dorchester* (1882), 166–7.
27 Addington, op. cit. 167; O.R.O. Incl. award.
28 *Oxon. Peculiars*, 141, which mentions 1 glebe land in North Field valued at 3s. a year.
29 *L. & P. Hen. VIII*, xiv (1), p. 607.
30 Ibid. xvii, p. 491. This and the grant of 1545 include the advowson, evidently a formal term, for there was no advowson to Burcot.
31 Ibid. xx (ii), p. 446; O.R.O. Wi IV/iii/5.
32 See above, p. 20.   33 Dunkin MS. 438/1, f. 258.
34 O.R.O. Wi IV/iii/7.   35 Ibid. ii/1.
36 *Oxon. Peculiars*, 141.
37 C.P. 25(2)/708/Hil. 17 & 18 Chas. II.
38 C 66/3291, m. 1.
39 *Oxon. Peculiars*, 135. The Bushes were related probably to John Bush of Abingdon, woollen-draper, who was dealing with land in Burcot in 1692: O.R.O. H 111/g/3.
40 O.R.O. Inc. award. He also received a rent charge of 4s.
41 Gibbs Pps.: MS. Collect. for a hist. of Clifton Hampden, f. 34.   42 MS. Top. Oxon. c 103, ff. 159 sqq.
43 Oxf. Dioc. c 344.   44 See below, p. 71.
45 MS. Top. Oxon. c 103, ff. 159 sqq.
46 Salter, *Oxon. Recusants*, 20 and *passim*. A Mr. Philpott and his wife were returned as recusants as early as 1588 (C.R.S. xxii. 124); Ann, wife of Edward Philpott, was assessed for the subsidy in 1641 (E 179/164/482) and an Edward Philpott, shepherd, was presented in 1623 and later excommunicated (Salter, *Oxon. Recusants*, 43; *Oxon. Peculiars*, 119, 140).
47 Salter, *Oxon. Recusants*, 29; *Oxon. Peculiars*, 139, 140.
48 Salter, *Oxon. Recusants*, 57; E 179/164/482.
49 *Oxon. Peculiars*, 141–3.
50 Ibid. 143; O.R.O. Cal. Q. Sess. ix. 770, 771; Stapleton, *Cath. Miss.* 245.
51 See above, p. 62; and Davey, *Catholic Family*, 16–17.
52 *Oxon. Peculiars*, 120, 141.
53 Ibid. 142–3; cf. the three recusants listed in the Compton Census of 1676.
54 O.R.O. Cal. Q. Sess. ix. 591, 592.
55 Stapleton, *Cath. Miss.* 245.
56 O.R.O. Reg. of Papists' estates, p. 59.

recusancy of the Burcot branch of the family, and in 1769 the only Burcot recusant was Richard Cherrell,[57] probably a relative of the recusant Cherrell family of Dorchester.

Protestant dissent apparently did not exist before the 19th century, but was strong enough in 1803 for the house of Eleanor Frewin to be licensed for religious worship.[58] In 1822 the house of Mary Frewin was licensed,[59] and others in 1830 and 1847.[60] There is nothing to indicate to which denomination these worshippers belonged.

SCHOOLS. There was a day school at Burcot in 1818 where some children were educated at their parents' expense. The poor, it was said, 'would accept any mode of education offered to them'.[61] A Sunday school was started in 1831 where 18 boys and 16 girls were taught at the expense of one of the parishioners.[62] In 1854 the Sunday school had 30 pupils and a dame's school with 15 day pupils was recorded.[63]

A Church of England school for boys and girls was built in 1869. It had 53 pupils in 1871, but the numbers had decreased to 30 in 1887, and to 22 by 1920.[64] The difficulties of the school teacher in early days are well illustrated in the school's log book: it was impossible to enforce attendance and the children were kept at home for weeks on end to work in the fields. The inspector at the end of the century said that the school was taught with kindness, but commented in 1904 that 'much remains to be done to develop the children's intelligence'.[65] The school closed in 1922 and in 1934 the children were walking to Clifton Hampden, and since 1956 they have been going to Dorchester St. Birinus.[66]

CHARITY. Leonard Wilmott, by deed of 1608, gave a rent charge of £2 issuing out of lands in Clanfield, to be distributed on Good Friday to the unrelieved poor of Burcot and like gifts to the poor of other places. The gift was regulated by a charity decree of 1617. About 1823 it was being distributed to some 24 poor according to need. Two further sums of 5s., charged at unknown dates by unknown donors (one of whom, however, appears to have been called Cave) upon lands in Burcot, were distributed at the same time.[67] By 1887 one of the two latter rents had ceased to be paid. After protracted efforts to recover it, G. R. Huggins and Lady Crawford, the second of whom paid the other rent, agreed jointly to redeem the two rents for £10 stock, an arrangement confirmed by Scheme.[68] In 1908 the three charities were placed by Scheme under joint trustees, and provision was made for applying the income to subscriptions or donations to the funds of any nearby club or society capable of supplying the poor with coal, clothing, or other necessaries. The sum of £10, representing the accumulated income of the charities, was invested so that it might be applied, if necessary, to the relief of sufferers in epidemics.[69] Under a new Scheme of 1911 the trustees were authorized to apply the income to subscriptions or donations to hospitals or homes capable of benefiting the poor inhabitants and to clubs or societies supplying coal or clothing, in the provision of nurses and midwives, and in meeting the expenses of poor patients travelling to hospitals or homes. A Scheme of 1937 slightly extended the medical benefits.[70] In 1931–2 £2 14s. was being paid to the Clifton Hampden Nursing Association. In 1953–5 the accumulated income, amounting to £86, was undistributed.[71]

DRAYTON ST. LEONARD

THE ancient parish covered 1,288 acres,[1] but its area was slightly increased in the 1870's as a consequence of the Divided Parishes Acts (1876–1882), and was given in the Census of 1891 as 1,301 acres.[2] The increase is to be accounted for by the inclusion in the parish of Woodmead, the riverside pasture opposite the village, where there had been for centuries several small detached parts of the neighbouring parishes of Newington and Warborough as well as of Benson, Berrick Salome,[3] and Ewelme, which presumably represented early intercommoning arrangements.[4]

Most of the parish lies in a large bend of the River Thame which forms the parish boundary for about 2 miles and separates Drayton from Warborough. Neither the western boundary with Dorchester nor the northern boundary with Chislehampton is marked by any distinctive features. About 300 acres

of Drayton, Holcombe Grange, lie on the opposite side of the river.

Except at Holcombe Grange the underlying Gault Clay is generally covered with gravel[5] and the parish is remarkably flat, the highest point (244 ft.) being on Primrose Hill south of the river.

Apart from the trees of the village, the riverside, and Holcombe Grange, the only woodland is the copse to the north-west of the village and this is recent: it is not shown on the Tithe Award map of 1841 or the Ordnance Survey map of 1881.[6] Holcombe Grange is better wooded than the rest of the parish and its timber is mentioned several times in the visitations made by the President and Fellows of Trinity College, Oxford. In 1769 298 elms and ashes were cut leaving 2,290 trees standing. In 1811 the timber was reported to be in bad order and arrange-

[57] Davey, *Catholic Family*, 70.
[58] Oxf. Dioc. c 644, f. 68.
[59] Ibid. f. 266.
[60] Ibid. c 645, f. 147; c 647, f. 65.
[61] *Educ. of Poor*, 720.
[62] *Educ. Enq. Abstract*, 742.
[63] *Wilb. Visit.*
[64] *Elem. Educ. Ret.* 318; Kelly, *Dir. Oxon.* (1887, 1920); *Vol. Sch. Ret.* 35.
[65] O.R.O. Burcot sch. log bk. 1871–1908.
[66] Inf. Oxon. Educ. Cttee.
[67] *8th Rep. Com. Char.* 492; *10th Rep.* H.C. 103, p. 358 1824), xiii; Char. Com. file 69609.

[68] Char. Com. file 69609 and Burcot G. file.
[69] Ibid. G. file.   [70] Ibid.
[71] Ibid. Accts. file.
[1] *V.C.H. Oxon.* ii. 220; O.S. *Area Bk.* (1882).
[2] Exactly how the increase was brought about escaped the notice of the Registrar General: see *Census* 1891; *V.C.H. Oxon.* ii. 220, 213; O.S. Map 25″, xlvi. 6, 7, 10, 11, 14, 15 (1881).
[3] The Berrick part was mentioned in 1279: *Rot. Hund.* (Rec. Com.), ii. 771.
[4] See below, p. 78.
[5] *V.C.H. Oxon.* i, map between pp. 4–5.
[6] Bodl. Tithe award map; O.S. Map 25″, xlvi.

ments were made for the felling of about 900 trees.[7] In the 14th century 'le Hurst de Draytone' is mentioned and this is probably the same as the meadow to the north-east of the village, which in 1841 was called the Hurst.[8] This suggests that the meaning here was not 'wood' but 'bank'.

The meadows along the river are liable to flooding and the fields of Drayton are traversed by many small watercourses and ditches the 'scouring' of which, or rather the failure to do so, was one of the main concerns of the manorial court in the 17th and 18th centuries.[9]

Two metalled roads lead out of the village, one to Stadhampton across Haywards Bridge, the other west to Dorchester and Burcot. There are also two unmetalled roads, one leading to Chislehampton, the other across the river to Warborough and Newington.[10] The river was formerly crossed by two fords. The lower of these, by the village, remains unbridged but the other, Haywards, was bridged in 1884 by public subscription.[11] Before that there seems to have been a footbridge at this ford, certainly in 1841.[12] There have been at least two other footbridges. The one that remains, just above Lower Grange Farm, is a replacement of the bridge marked at the same place in 1767.[13] The other, just above the ford, was built after 1897 and was washed away after 1948.[14]

The village stands on the right bank of the river about 2 miles north-east of Dorchester. Its double name of Drayton St. Leonard first appears in the Post Office Directory of 1847.[15] Formerly it had been called Drayton by Wallingford. The new name, a natural one to adopt as the church was dedicated to St. Leonard, has been regularly used since 1847.

The village covers a large area for the number of its houses. Apart from the eight council houses built since 1945,[16] most of Drayton lies between the church and the river. There are a remarkable number of old houses. At least fifteen were built in the 16th or 17th centuries, although in some cases there have been extensive later alterations and additions. The Hearth Tax returns of 1665 list 16 houses with 1 to 7 hearths, 5 of them having 5 hearths or more.[17] Most of the old cottages are timber-framed buildings with brick filling, and several are still thatched. The oldest seems to be the 16th-century Garden Cottage by the river south-east of Drayton Manor Farm, but its neighbour, Little Garden Cottage, or Back Cottage, is not much more recent. Other cottages that are particularly worth noting are no. 10 Water Lane, the cottage in the lane south of the former Rectory, Ford Cottage, White Cottage with its five small dormers which in 1841 was divided into three,[18] and a little north of it a cottage with some herringbone brick infilling. Some, like Waterside House Cottage, now called Red Tile Cottage, have old tile roofs. Although timber frame with brick filling is the commonest type of structure for the older cottages there are a few in stone. With the exception of Waterside House and the Old

Rectory all the larger houses in the village are, or were formerly, farmhouses. The two farms in the modern village have houses that were greatly extended in the 19th century. But while Drayton Manor Farm is an enlargement of an old but not very distinguished building, Drayton House Farm is an enlargement of a well-proportioned early-18th-century house of which a chimney stack and a finely panelled room survive. Between these farmhouses is a house, now divided in two, which was formerly called Drayton Farm although it now takes its name, Guys, from a tenant J. H. Guy, who farmed from it in the early part of the 20th century.[19] It is a timber-framed brick building on a rubble base. The White House, also a farmhouse in the mid-19th century, is stone built and consists of a 17th-century block with a wing added in the 18th century. Ford Cottage, a house south of White House which has since disappeared although some of the farm buildings have survived, and Manor Cottage (formerly Nutts) were also farmhouses in 1841. Waterside House was in 1841 a private house and consists of a 16th–17th-century house with modern additions. Its south wall is substantially built of stone but the rest of the old house is timber framed with brick filling. It has fine stone fireplaces, probably 17th century, on the ground and first floors. Opposite its main front there is a large yew tree. The Rectory, now a private house called 'Furlongs', was built by the Revd. A. J. Williams in 1862 at a cost of more than £1,200 and was later enlarged.[20] There are clear traces of an earlier building, shown on the Tithe award Map, but this was not the earlier curate's house, which stood on the road south of the church.[21]

The oldest and most interesting secular structure in the village is the barn which is alternatively called the Haseley Barn, because it was formerly owned by the Great Haseley Trustees, and the Tithe Barn, although there is no evidence, other than its age, to support such a title. It is a timber-framed, weatherboarded building of six bays with a hipped and tiled roof which is carried down over aisles on all four sides. This barn is certainly no later than the 15th century and may have been built towards the end of the 14th. There are several groups of fine farm buildings, some thatched, the most noteworthy being those of Drayton House Farm, Drayton Manor Farm and the cart-shed opposite the White House.

In Holcombe Grange there are two outlying farms, and there were houses on these sites in 1597. In a survey of that year Lower Grange Farm is called the site or capital house of Holcombe Grange.[22] The present house is a timber-framed brick building on a base of stone and brick. To the north a very large stone chimney projects and either side of this there are fine windows, including one of eighteen lights under a pent tile overhang. This house, in many ways the most interesting in the parish, also has a very good south porch and a 17th-century staircase. Upper Grange Farm is basically a 17th-century

[7] Trinity Coll. Oxf. muniments.
[8] d.d. Par. Grt. Haseley d 2 (1); Bodl. Tithe award.
[9] See below, p. 76.
[10] O.S. Map 6″, xlvi (1922).
[11] *Oxon. Co. Bridges* (1878). A tablet on the bridge states that the bridge was erected in 1888 to the memory of Frank Aldworth of Drayton 'by his labourers'.
[12] Bodl. Tithe award map.
[13] Trinity Coll. mun.
[14] O.S. Map 6″, xlvi (1922) (the bridge is not marked on

earlier edns. or on the Tithe award map); O.S. Map 2½″, 41/59 (prov. edn.).
[15] For the etymology of the village's first name, see below, p. 74. [16] Inf. Bullingdon R.D.C.
[17] *Hearth Tax Oxon.* 57.
[18] Bodl. Tithe award.
[19] O.R.O. Wi I/i/79, lot 7 with photographs.
[20] Christ Church Arch. 25 A 53, 81, 83, 84, 89.
[21] Bodl. Tithe award.
[22] Trinity Coll. mun.: 1768 visitation.

building, and has a 17th-century panelled hall. Until it was recently covered there was a dated stone visible bearing the date 1668.

The topography of the village can first be studied in the Tithe Award Map of 1841, and thereafter with the aid of Ordnance Survey maps and the numerous sale catalogues, it would be possible to trace in detail most of the changes in the layout of the village. Before the 19th century it is not possible to do this. There are occasional mentions of particular houses, for example Mr. Yates's house called Pawlings, mentioned in 1574,[23] which cannot now be identified. Nor is it possible to identify the fields and lands mentioned in early deeds and surveys, although the Tithe Award map gives many names. Among those which can be traced back are Lower Shilfield Furlong, which is almost certainly the 14th-century *under schulfull*,[24] and Waterslade which occurs in this form in the 15th century. The village and its fields were in the 17th and 18th centuries divided into two Ends: the eastern part was Town End, the western was Farm End. In the Tithe Award the riverside meadows above the village are described as Town End Mead and those below the village were called Farm End Mead.[25] In the early 17th century the 'whole farme end of Drayton' was presented for failure to observe the ancient custom of perambulation[26] and in 17th- and 18th-century leases lands and houses are often described as being in Town End or Farm End.[27]

There are two public houses in the village, the 'Catherine Wheel' and the 'Three Pigeons'. In 1841 the only licensed house was the 'Catherine Wheel',[28] which was then in what is now called Garden Cottage. In 1805 this house was insured as the 'Catherine Wheel'.[29] Some time after 1841 the licence and name were transferred to what in 1841 was the smithy, and this was probably done by William Townsend who in 1847–8 was both blacksmith and licensee of the 'Catherine Wheel'.[30] The modern house replaced a group of old cottages of which an illustration survives.[31]

MANORS. Drayton was not mentioned by name in Domesday Book but formed part of the Bishop of Lincoln's 90-hide estate of Dorchester.[32] The bishops subinfeudated part of Drayton, but retained part in demesne.[33] Throughout the Middle Ages they treated their *DRAYTON* demesne as part of their Dorchester manor. In 1547 Drayton was surrendered to the crown with other members of this manor[34] and a crown survey of the manor in 1551 included 31 yardlands in Drayton.[35] The estate

remained part of Dorchester manor under the bishops' successors.[36] In the 17th century the courts baron of Dorchester manor were attended by Drayton homagers,[37] and 18th-century surveys of the Dorchester manor of the earls of Abingdon included land in Drayton.[38] At the end of the 18th century and in the 19th century the Abingdon estate in Drayton was described as Drayton manor.[39] It followed Dorchester's descent and was purchased in 1876 by Sir John Christopher Willoughby of Baldon.[40] Drayton manor was sold again in 1916[41] but thereafter manorial rights appear to have lapsed.

A second manor in Drayton, the later *HOLCOMBE GRANGE*, can be traced back to the holding of the Burcot family,[42] who were tenants of 1 knight's fee held of the Bishop of Lincoln in the 12th and 13th centuries. Nicholas son of Bartholomew[43] held the fee in 1201. A Nicholas de Burcot, perhaps the same man, held it in 1212[44] and either he or a son was tenant and concerned in transactions over Drayton land in the 1220's.[45] Another Nicholas de Burcot, presumably a descendant, was in possession in 1279, when the fee was described as being in Drayton, Holcombe, and Clifton.[46] John de Burcot, his son, succeeded, but by 1346 the Abbot of Dorchester was returned as tenant of the fee.[47]

The abbey had been under-tenant of most of the holding in 1279, when it held 4 virgates in Holcombe and 2 virgates in Drayton for scutage, and was under-tenant of the ½-fee with 3 others who were to pay scutage to the abbot when it was demanded.[48] The abbey still held the estate at the time of the Dissolution, when its property in Holcombe was known as Holcombe Grange manor.[49] By 1538 the manor had been granted to Sir Thomas Pope who used it to endow his foundation, Trinity College, Oxford.[50] Most of the estate remained in the possession of Trinity College up to recent times. As lords of Holcombe Grange manor the president and fellows licensed a gamekeeper in 1808,[51] and in 1826 their lessee, Thomas Gilbert White, was described as lord of the manor.[52] Later records make no mention of manorial rights. The farms seem always to have been leased by the college.[53]

The most important estate in Drayton apart from the Abingdon estate was that acquired at the end of the 14th century by Nicholas Drayton (d. by 1402).[54] It was known in the 15th century as *DRAYTON* manor.[55] Nicholas Drayton was either the same as or a close connexion of Nicholas le Naper of Drayton who in 1362 acquired the estate of John Sheepwash in Drayton, Baldon, and Clifton.[56] The connexion between Nicholas le Naper of Drayton and Nicholas

[23] *Oxon. Visit.* 110.
[24] d.d. Par. Grt. Haseley d 2 (2).
[25] Bodl. Tithe award map.
[26] *Oxon. Peculiars*, 145.
[27] Bodl. MS. chs. Oxon. 3866, 3868, 3869, 3872.
[28] Bodl. Tithe award.
[29] Sun Insurance Company plate on the wall of the house and inf. from the Company.
[30] Kelly, *Dir. Oxon.* (1847).
[31] O.R.O. Wi I/i/79, opp. p. 46.
[32] *V.C.H. Oxon.* i. 402.
[33] See below, p. 75.
[34] *Cal. Pat.* 1547–8, 153; 1557–8, 409; 1558–60, 437; and see above, p. 42.
[35] L.R. 2/189, ff. 9–10.
[36] See above, p. 42.
[37] MSS. Top. Gen. c 43–45; d.d. Bertie b 1.
[38] e.g. d.d. Bertie, c 3, p. 28; and see below, p. 76.
[39] O.R.O. Gamekprs' Deps.

[40] O.R.O. Wi I/i/79, p. 95; *Sale cat.* (1914).
[41] Ibid. 83; presumably the purchaser was George Pullen who was one of the principal landowners in 1920: Kelly, *Dir. Oxon.* (1939).   [42] See above, p. 19.
[43] *Rot. de Ob. et Fin.* (Rec. Com.), i. 155.
[44] *Bk. of Fees*, 40.
[45] Queen's Coll. MS. 366, f. 25; *Fines Oxon.* 96; *Sandford Cart.* pp. 210–11.
[46] *Rot. Hund.* (Rec. Com.), ii. 748–9.
[47] *Feud. Aids*, iv. 182.   [48] *Rot. Hund.* ii. 748.
[49] *Valor. Eccl.* (Rec. Com.), ii. 170.
[50] H. E. D. Blakiston, *Trinity College*, 33, 34.
[51] Trinity Coll. Ledger C, pp. 61–62.
[52] O.R.O. Gamekprs.' Deps.
[53] Trinity Coll. mun. Its estate in 1959 was all attached to Upper Grange Farm; see below, p. 78.
[54] d.d. Par. Grt. Haseley d 2 (5).
[55] See below.
[56] d.d. Par. Grt. Haseley d 2 (4).

Drayton is supported by the association of both with Sir Hugh Segrave.[57] Nicholas Drayton's younger son Nicholas succeeded.[58] He had a daughter Elizabeth who married Peter Idle, a minor civil servant.[59] In 1442 Peter Idle and Elizabeth were granted all the estates in Drayton that had been possessed by her father Nicholas.[60] This estate was augmented by grants from Sir Richard Drayton, John Delabere, and others.[61] In 1473 Peter Idle made a will in which he directed his trustees to grant his property in Drayton to his son William and his heirs with reversions to other children of his.[62] Peter died shortly afterwards and in 1475 his son William petitioned Chancery that his father's will be complied with and that Drayton manor and property be conveyed to him.[63] In November 1475 the trustees granted Drayton manor with all lands, &c., in Drayton to William with reversions according to the will.[64] William's step-mother Anne was provided for in Peter's will by an annuity of 5 marks payable out of the estate at Drayton and Dorchester, and she was also to have the use of the parlour, chapel, chambers, and gardens 'within my place at Drayton' until she left them or married.[65] She apparently found employment in the household of Richard, Duke of Gloucester, as Mistress of the Nursery, and it was perhaps in 1479 that the duke wrote to William Stonor and Humphrey Forster asking them to see that William Idle and Elizabeth his sister paid the annuity due to their stepmother.[66] Peter Idle had an eldest son Thomas, to whom his book of *Instructions* was addressed, but neither he nor apparently any of his heirs is mentioned in Peter's will. Nevertheless, Thomas's son Richard claimed, through his grandmother Elizabeth Idle, all the property in Drayton that had once belonged to Elizabeth's father, Nicholas (II) Drayton.[67] Apparently this claim was successful, for in 1481 William Idle aided in person by the Duke of Suffolk used force to eject Richard's mother Alice.[68] Alice petitioned the King's Council for redress and a Privy Seal writ was issued to restore Alice and Richard to Drayton manor and to see that William Idle appeared before the Council.[69] The outcome of this dispute is unknown, but by 1489 the manor seems to have been in the hands of Henry Dene of Drayton.[70] In 1501 it was conveyed to John Yate of Charney Basset (Berks.),[71] and remained with his family during the 16th century. This estate was not treated as a separate manor in later records, but as part of Dorchester manor held in free socage.[72] In 1530 John Yate settled his Drayton estate on his wife Alice and younger son Thomas.[73] Thomas (d. 1565) was the founder of the Yate family of Lyford (Berks.).[74] In the mid-16th century he was one of the most substantial tenants in Drayton, paying 60s. 6d. rent for his land held of Dorchester manor;[75] at his death in 1565 he held 4 yardlands copyhold as well as about 200 acres, 9 yardlands called Drayton Farm, freehold,[76] which was leased to Richard Pawling of Drayton.[77] Thomas Yate's son Francis succeeded him and seems to have lived in Drayton.[78] By 1597, however, Francis's son Thomas had sold the farm to a Robert Doyley of Hambleden (Bucks.) and George Lazenby of Drayton.[79] They divided the property in 1597.[80] The Doyley part (4 yardlands) remained in their hands until the Civil Wars when it was mortgaged and then sold about 1646.[81] The property changed hands several times, but finally, about 1651, it was purchased by the trustees of the Haseley Poor Charity.[82] They continued to lease it to various tenants[83] until they sold it after the Second World War.

ECONOMIC AND SOCIAL HISTORY. Drayton's situation was probably determined by the ford which must have been a convenient crossing of the River Thame, especially before the river was bridged at Dorchester. Its name implies something to do with communications and may mean 'the *tun* where things can be dragged across the river'.[84] It was originally a subsidiary settlement of Dorchester and in Domesday book was treated as part of the Bishop of Lincoln's Dorchester manor.[85] Drayton is first mentioned by name in 1146 as a chapelry of Dorchester.[86]

The main medieval estate in Drayton belonged to the Bishop of Lincoln's Dorchester manor. The first detailed information about it is in a survey made in the second quarter of the 13th century. The bishop's manor then included 23 virgates in Drayton that were held by 18 villeins. Each virgate rendered 5s. 6d. to the bishop in lieu of week-work, the other services owed being the same as those due from the Chislehampton virgaters.[87] In addition to these

[57] Nicholas Drayton the father was a cousin by marriage of Sir Hugh Segrave: G. Wrottesley, 'Pedigrees from the Plea Rolls', *The Genealogist* (N.S. xvi), 167; one of the co-feoffees through whom Nicholas le Naper acquired the Sheepwash estate was Hugh Segrave: d.d. Par. Grt. Haseley d. 2 (3–4). The deeds of the Le Naper and Drayton estates in Drayton are in the same collection: d.d. Par. Grt. Haseley d 2. The connexion is also confirmed by arms in Drayton noted in 1574: *Oxon. Visit.* 106, 110.
[58] His elder brother Sir John Drayton quitclaimed the estate in 1402: d.d. Par. Grt. Haseley d 2 (5).
[59] See *Instructions to his son*, ed. C. D'Evelyn (1935), where his public and private life are fully discussed.
[60] d.d. Par. Grt. Haseley d 2 (6, 8–11).
[61] Ibid. (12). Delabere (Delabert) made a grant to Nicholas (II) Drayton in 1421: ibid. (7). For his connexion with the family see above, p. 19.
[62] d.d. Par. Grt. Haseley d 2 (14, 17).
[63] C 1/50/87.
[64] d.d. Par. Grt. Haseley d 2 (17).
[65] Ibid.
[66] *Stonor Letters and Papers*, ii. (Cam. Soc. 3rd. ser. xxx), 81–82.
[67] d.d. Par. Grt. Haseley d 2 (18).
[68] Leadam, *Select Cases* (Selden Soc. xxxv), 116–17.
[69] Ibid.

[70] d.d. Par. Grt. Haseley d 2 (20–22).
[71] Ibid. (24, 25); C 1/138/55.
[72] e.g. C 142/153/50.   [73] Ibid.
[74] *V.C.H. Berks.* iv. 290.
[75] L.R. 2/189, f. 10.
[76] C 142/143/50; Req. 2/123/14.
[77] Req. 2/123/14.
[78] d.d. Par. Grt. Haseley c 5 (uncat. deed of 1597). In 1574 Mr. Yate of Lyford was said to live in Pawling's House: *Oxon. Visit.* 106.
[79] d.d. Par. Grt. Haseley c 5 (uncat.). This was apparently not the main branch of the D'Oyley family of Hambleden (which inherited Chislehampton and Hambleden): cf. W. D. Bayley, *House of D'Oyley*, 25–27.
[80] d.d. Par. Grt. Haseley c 5 (uncat.).   [81] Ibid.
[82] Ibid.; see also Delafield's 'Hist. of Grt. Haseley': MS. Gough Oxon. 22, ff. 92–93.
[83] d.d. Par. Grt. Haseley c 55 (uncat.); MS. Gough Oxon. 22, f. 93: in 1651 the trustees leased the 4 yardlands. For their estate see O.R.O. Land tax assess.; Inclos. award; Misc. Ay. I/1; Bodl. Tithe award; Kelly's, *Dir. Oxon.* (1887–1939).
[84] *P.N. Oxon.* (E.P.N.S.), 153–4.
[85] *V.C.H. Oxon.* i. 402; and see above, p. 73.
[86] *Reg. Antiquiss.* i. 247.
[87] Queen's Coll. MS. 366, f. 27b; and see above, p. 12.

services which were general throughout the manor most virgaters at Drayton had to plough an acre of land, this service being called *grascherch*.[88] This account may be compared with a mutilated survey of 1279 which shows that the bishop's manor then had 14 villein tenants holding between them 22 virgates.[89] In the earlier survey 5 villeins held 2 virgates each while in 1279 there were 8 holding 2 virgates each.[90] The services due from each virgate in 1279 are described, and there seems to have been no great change since the earlier, more detailed, survey. Each virgater had to plough 2 acres of the bishop's demesne and at the critical times of the year, haymaking and harvest, had to work for $2\frac{1}{2}$ days on the bishop's land at his own expense and 2 days with food provided by the bishop. He had also to cart hay and corn as long as necessary and when required had to cart corn to market. No mention is made of a money rent but this must be a mistake: the commuted week-works had not been reimposed. The virgaters were not freemen: they were unable to arrange the marriage of their daughters or sell their beasts without the bishop's consent.[91] The earlier survey does not mention free tenants, but in 1279 4 tenants, holding 9 virgates between them, claimed that their ancestors had been free sokemen, serving the king in war for 40 days, but that the bishops had withdrawn this service. They owed light boon-dues and ploughed 2 acres if they had a whole plough. They carried the bishop's letters for one day at their own expense and afterwards at the bishop's. They had also to attend Dorchester hundred court. One of them, Walter son of Thomas, held 4 virgates and was evidently a prosperous man with a shepherd and with under-tenants.[92] A fifth free tenant held a messuage and $1\frac{1}{2}$ virgates for 7s. and suit at the hundred court.[93] Both surveys mention a cottager who owed 4s. a year for a fishery in the Thame.[94]

The estate of the bishop's knight Nicholas de Burcot was also described. His $7\frac{1}{2}$ virgates were held by under-tenants. The Abbot of Dorchester was the most important of these, as in the other villages to which the De Burcots' fee extended.[95] The abbot held Holcombe Grange (4 virgates), and several virgates in Drayton proper. Apart from the abbey the most noteworthy tenants of Nicholas de Burcot's fee were Luke le Naper and Robert Sheepwash, the descendants of whom were prominent among the tenants of the 14th century.[96] In 1327, when the total assessment of Drayton was £4 0s. 10d., 25 people contributed, ten of whom were assessed at 4s. or more, including John Sheepwash and Nicholas le Naper.[97] The most conspicuous of the taxpayers of 1327 was, however, John le Wise whose assessment

was 15s. He was probably a descendant of that Richard Wise who appears in both the 13th-century surveys as a virgater on the bishop's manor.[98]

Neither 13th-century survey described the bishop's demesne in Drayton specifically, but it is clear from the services owed that there must have been a demesne and that its routine cultivation must have been by hired labour.[99] The only known survey of the demesne of this manor was made in 1348, when the bishop's Dorchester manor, treated as a unit throughout the whole hundred, was described. Very few of the furlongs recorded can now be identified, but at least 2 were in Drayton, 14 acres in the Hurst, and 30 acres in Waterslade furlong.[1]

There is little evidence for the later Middle Ages, but various surveys, made when Drayton passed out of ecclesiastical hands, throw light on 16th-century conditions. In 1536 the abbey's Drayton lands were held by only 2 or 3 tenants, the largest holding being in the hands of Richard Molyneux who paid £3 2s. rent a year.[2] The abbey held 173 acres in Holcombe in demesne, and these had clearly been inclosed in the Middle Ages for sheep-farming.[3] In 1536 it was stated that 160 acres there were 'partly grown with thorns and fursens'.[4] Holcombe Grange was then valued at £7 8s. 8d. a year, but after the Dissolution the king's lessee paid £8 0s. 3d.[5] In 1597, when it was in the possession of Trinity College, it was divided into Upper and Lower Grange farms and these two farmhouses were the only ones there.[6]

The bishop's former manor was surveyed in 1551, when it was held by the Crown. There were 11 customary tenants, 9 of whom held 21 virgates.[7] One of the others, Thomas Spyer, seems to have held little land although his rent, 10s. 10d. was about the sum due for a virgate. The remaining customary tenant was Thomas Yate, the size of whose holding is not given although his rent was 60s. 6d.[8] The total rental from the customary tenants was £16 5s. 10d. plus a 4d. fine paid by the tenant of 4 virgates for licence to sublet.[9] Thus the Drayton estate constituted a fair proportion of the total rental of Dorchester manor, which was £76 3s. 10d. plus an increment of 60s. 6d.[10]

The survey of 1551 listed in detail the timber on the manor: 424 trees on the Drayton estate;[11] it also described the pasture rights: each of the 31 yardlands was entitled to graze 30 sheep, 2 beasts, and 2 horses.[12]

The prosperity of the Drayton farmer in the 16th century is indicated by the returns for the subsidies: sixteen taxpayers contributed in 1523.[13] In 1577 the total contribution was almost as great as that of Dorchester itself and two farmers paid on £13 and £19 worth of goods.[14] Richard Pawling, one of these,

[88] Queen's Coll. MS. 366, f. 27b.
[89] *Rot. Hund.* (Rec. Com.), ii. 748; and see below, p. 85, n. 80.
[90] Queen's Coll. MS. 366, f. 27b.
[91] *Rot. Hund.* ii. 748.
[92] Ibid.; see also above, p. 68.
[93] *Rot. Hund.* ii. 748.
[94] Queen's Coll. MS. 366, f. 27b; *Rot. Hund.* ii. 748.
[95] See above, pp. 19, 67.
[96] *Rot. Hund.* ii. 748.
[97] E 179/161/9.
[98] Ibid.; Queen's Coll. MS. 366, f. 27b; *Rot. Hund.* (Rec. Com.), ii. 748. The Wise family continued to be prominent in Drayton until the mid-19th cent., see e.g. L.R. 2/189, f. 9b; O.R.O. Incl. award.
[99] The earlier survey gave the bishop's demesne for the whole of Dorchester hundred only: Queen's Coll. MS. 366, f. 27b.

[1] Queen's Coll. MS. 366, ff. 60b–61; cf. Bodl. Tithe award map.
[2] H. Addington, *Some Account of the Abbey Church of St. Peter and St. Paul at Dorchester*, 154 (ministers' accts.).
[3] *Valor Eccl.* (Rec. Com.), ii. 170.
[4] Ibid.
[5] Ibid.; Addington, *Dorchester*, 162–3 (ministers' accts.).
[6] Trinity Coll. mun.
[7] L.R. 2/189, ff. 9–10. Richard Molyneux had taken over 2 virgates formerly held by Richard Fourde, presumably the descendant of the Ateford tenants of 1279; John Banaster held 2 virgates formerly held by John Sugges, perhaps a descendant of John Sug assessed at 18d. in 1327 (E 179/161/9).
[8] L.R. 2/189, f. 10.
[9] Ibid.
[10] Ibid. f. 10b.
[11] Ibid. f. 18.
[12] Ibid. f. 13.
[13] E 179/161/198; 162/341.
[14] E 179/162/341.

farmed the 13 virgates of the Yates's Drayton farm, much of it still open-field land.[15] Shortly after 1565 he had complained that the steward of the queen's manor, Leonard Parret, who was also a tenant of the manor, was overcharging the land with sheep and had so tainted the ground that the previous winter he, Pawling, had lost 9 sheep.[16] Pawling added that Parret as steward was judge in his own cause and 'yet utterly unlearned in the laws of the realm'.[17]

Several court books of the Dorchester manor in Drayton for the 17th and early 18th centuries have been preserved which reveal a little of the working and customs of the manor.[18] Separate orders were made for the two ends, Farm and Town, of Drayton, and although most orders were concerning the scouring of watercourses, there are also regulations about the ringing of hogs and pigs, surcharging the common, and making mounds in the fields. In 1691 the staking of horses on Broad Green before Whitsun was prohibited, as was the penning of sheep on the wheat field after 20 October in 1704. In 1693 the digging of gravel at Church End was prohibited.[19]

The court books also throw a little light on the various freeholds in the manor, no doubt deriving from the estates of Dorchester Abbey and the Yate family.[20] In 1641, for example, John Wise died seized of 3 messuages of the Norreys manor and two messuages freehold.[21] The 1665 hearth-tax return shows that John Wise, assessed on 6 hearths, had one of the largest farmhouses in the village. In that year 10 out of 16 householders paid tax on houses with 6 to 7 hearths.[22]

Evidence in the 18th century for the Drayton estate of Dorchester manor is plentiful. It was then held by tenants of the Earl of Abingdon.[23] In 1728 the earl had 10 tenants in Drayton, excluding one holding of 2 acres, and between them they held 729 acres.[24] The largest holding was that of Henry Wise, 8½ yardlands (171 a.), but there were 3 other tenants holding 111 acres, 122 acres, and 98 acres respectively. Of the remainder 3 held 40 acres or more, and 3 held less than 30 acres.[25] This may be compared with a survey of 1785.[26] In this the earl's estate in Drayton only measured 559 acres, the reduction of 170 acres since 1728 apparently being due to the loss of the lands held then by Henry Wise, whose descendants certainly held about 130 acres freehold in the 19th century.[27] In 1785 the earl had 7 tenants in Drayton. The largest holdings were 151 acres and 131 acres. The two smaller holdings of 1728 (10 a. and 29 a.) remained intact, but the others were amalgamated so that the remaining three holdings were between 74 and 84 acres.[28] The total rental for the earl's land in Drayton was £555, the valuation being 16s. an acre for arable and 35s. an acre for meadow.[29] In 1728 the surveyor reported that the land was good

and that the method of husbandry was two crops to a fallow and that they wanted nothing so much as rest by being laid down to grass for a season.[30] The meadow land was said to be very good and usually let for 30s. to 40s. an acre.[31]

Detailed valuation for tithes was made of the whole parish, apart from Holcombe Grange, in 1799 by Richard Davis of Lewknor.[32] He reported that the parish was rated at 44 yardlands, 24 at Town End, 20 at Farm End, but that the area of each was about equal, the size of the lands being slightly larger at Farm End. The course of husbandry was then 3 crops to a fallow, namely wheat, beans, barley, fallow. The arable of Town End was then divided into four 'seasons', but retained the same names as when formerly divided into three 'seasons', the total measuring 461 field acres. Farm End measured 470 field acres. Davis remarked that the furlongs were short and estimated the area as 620 statute acres. The greater part of Drayton meadow was titheable to Dorchester parish, the other part to Mrs. Ann Ford, but the afterfeed belonged to Drayton parish. He measured it as totalling 30 field acres (25 statute) of which 24 were in Town End Mead. Stint of common was then 1½ cows and 30 sheep to each yardland but less than half that quantity were then kept. The Cow Commons were let at Town End for 15s. each, and at Farm End for 10s. each. The sheep were chiefly wether flocks. The tenant of the tithes provided two bulls for the use of the parish, one for each end. The old inclosures contained about 36 acres of which 16 were arable. His valuation was based on the following crop acreages: wheat 155, beans 155, barley 100, oats 55, clover in fallow field 40, and open-field meadow 25 acres. An average of 120 lambs was bred, 200 sheep sheared, and 30 cows kept.[33] A survey of tithes made in 1812 estimated the common field as 744 acres and recorded that the holdings of the four main tenants ranged in size from 100 to 216 acres.[34] By this time Holcombe Grange was divided into two farms according to a survey made in 1768, although in 1750 the estate had been divided into three farms.[35] A map and survey of 1767 shows that Upper Grange farm was 189 acres, Lower Grange farm 96 acres.[36] Almost the whole was meadow and pasture; only 12 acres of Upper Grange farm in 1768 were tillage, although 50 years previously there had been more.[37] The stock in 1768 on both farms consisted entirely of fatting sheep and milch cows for butter.[38] In 1811 43 cows were milked on the two farms; the butter made was sent to Wallingford market.[39] Generally the Grange seems to have been leased: in 1680 to Mary Spyer, widow; in 1700 to Richard Jones, lessee for over 40 years; and in 1777 to George White of Newington. A Mr. White was still lessee in 1816 and 1826.[40]

---

[15] Req. 2/123/14; and see above, p. 74.
[16] Ibid.
[17] Ibid.
[18] d.d. Bertie c 13; b 1; MSS. Top. Gen. c 43–45. The court books also make it possible to trace the tenurial descent of the main manor and the Great Haseley Charity lands in great detail.
[19] e.g. MS. Top. Gen. c 43, pp. 50, 66; d.d. Bertie b 1, pp. 32, 53, 82, 92.
[20] See above, p. 74.
[21] MS. Top. Gen. c 43, p. 488.
[22] Hearth Tax Oxon. 57.
[23] d.d. Bertie c 3; d 1; MS. Top. Oxon. a 46; 47; b 177–3; c 381; 383–5; 387; e 300–3.
[24] MS. Top. Oxon. c 381, pp. 52–56.

[25] Ibid.
[26] d.d. Bertie c 3, pp. 15–18, 28.
[27] Bodl. Tithe award. The reduction may, of course, be due merely to a more accurate survey.
[28] d.d. Bertie c 3, pp. 15–18.
[29] Ibid. pp. 15–18, 28.
[30] MS. Top. Oxon. c 381, p. 56.
[31] Ibid.
[32] Ch. Ch. Arch. 25 A 3.
[33] Ibid. Rye was evidently grown in the parish at some time, since the Tithe award map has 'Rye lands'.
[34] Ch. Ch. Arch. 25 A 8.
[35] Trinity Coll. mun.
[36] Ibid.
[37] Ibid.
[38] Ibid.
[39] Ibid.
[40] Ibid.; O.R.O. Gamekprs' Deps.

Drayton continued to be farmed by five or six farmers during the first part of the 19th century. In 1785 there were 21 land proprietors and 20 occupiers and owner-occupiers in the parish.[41] The two largest farms, one of them Holcombe Upper Grange farm, were each assessed for about a quarter of the total

there were only three farmers of consequence: Henry Betteridge farmed 350 acres and employed 31 labourers, Abraham Dean farmed 250 acres with 19 labourers, and John Smith of Holcombe Grange farmed 600 acres with 35 labourers.[46] The main landowners over this period were the Earl of Abing-

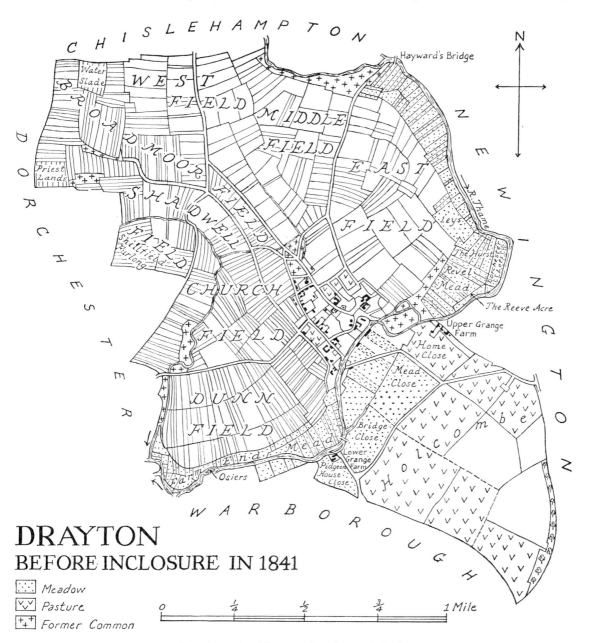

DRAYTON
BEFORE INCLOSURE IN 1841

Meadow	
Pasture	
Former Common	

0   ¼   ½   ¾   1 Mile

Based on the tithe award and map (1841).

tax. Six other farms had more moderate assessments of between £4 and £11. Other inhabitants owned or occupied premises assessed at under £1.[42] By 1816 several farmers had taken over other property and most of the land was in the hands of six farmers.[43] By 1832 there were four chief farmers.[44] In 1841 they had farms of 360 acres (i.e. Upper Grange farm), 221 acres, 219 acres, and 217 acres.[45] By 1851

don and Trinity College.[47] In 1844 the Drayton estate of the Earl of Abingdon comprised some 541 acres.[48] Over half was held on grants for lives or leases and brought in only £4 14s. 8d. a year; the rest was held on a yearly basis, at rents amounting to £356 18s. Much improvement was anticipated from inclosure.[49]

The Haseley Trust and the Betteridge and Wise

[41] O.R.O. Land tax assess.
[42] Ibid.   [43] Ibid.
[44] Ibid.
[45] Bodl. Tithe award.

[46] H.O. 107/1688/4.
[47] O.R.O. Land tax assess.; Bodl. Tithe award.
[48] d.d. Bertie d 1.
[49] Ibid.

families owned smaller areas of 60 to 120 acres in Drayton.[50] Shortly after inclosure in 1861 Henry Betteridge purchased the Wise estate thus bringing to an end their long history as landholders in Drayton.[51] It also marked a significant stage in the growth of one of the main estates in 19th-century Drayton. In 1875, when the Abingdon Estate was finally offered for sale, Henry Betteridge farmed 260 acres as tenant[52] as well as having extensive freehold which when offered for sale in 1901 totalled 372 acres.[53]

The parish to the north of the river remained open-field land up to the second half of the 19th century. At the time of the tithe award in 1841 two-thirds (825 a.) of the parish was arable and just under a third, much of it incorporated in Upper and Lower Grange farms, was meadow and pasture.[54] There were 7 acres of orchards and ozier beds and 37 acres of common. There were then seven fields;[55] one of which, East Field, had been mentioned in the 17th century,[56] while West Field was the old Town End division. The meadow land along the Thame was divided into lots; Woodford Mead, as it was called, was shared by the neighbouring parishes of Ewelme, Benson, and Berrick, and Dorchester had lots farther east.[57] The common was distributed throughout the parish, but in 1841 it was said to be privately owned by the Earl of Abingdon.[58]

In 1861 the whole parish was finally inclosed. As lord of the manor the Earl of Abingdon received just under $1\frac{1}{4}$ acres, equivalent to $\frac{1}{16}$ of the waste. He also received the largest allotment of about 578 acres. Three allottees received between 80 and 120 acres; the six others received only one or two acres.[59]

No precise information about Drayton's population is available before the 19th century. In 1676 an adult population of 128 was recorded by the Compton Census; in 1811 and 1851 there were 287 and 327 persons. After 1861 the population underwent the decline usually found in Oxfordshire parishes, and by 1901 there were 241 inhabitants.[60] This trend continued in the early 20th century, but by 1951 numbers had risen from the 219 recorded in 1931[61] to 314 persons.[62]

No parish records have survived apart from some churchwardens' accounts for 1641–81.[63] The only information that has been found about parish government concerns expenditure on the poor. The poor rate trebled over the years 1776 to 1803, rising from £70 to £220, but the rate in 1803 was still slightly below the county average of 4s. 8d.[64] In 1803 there were 12 adults and 18 children who were permanently maintained by the rates; 23 persons re-

ceived occasional relief.[65] By 1835 expenditure on the poor had reached £342.[66]

Drayton's main business is and always has been agriculture, the cultivation of the plain it shares with Dorchester. In 1914 over 24 per cent. of the crops were wheat and 21 per cent. barley.[67] The soil was said to be easily worked but incapable of withstanding drought.[68] Sheep were a good counter-balance to this type of soil, and there were 60 sheep and over per 100 acres in 1909 and over 40 sheep per 100 acres in 1914.[69] Permanent pasture over the whole parish was under 30 per cent.[70] Most of it was in Holcombe: in 1931 253 acres of Upper Grange farm were pasture.[71] In 1959 this farm (275 a.) was still mostly laid down to pasture.[72] Drayton north of the river was farmed in two units: one consisting of the Henry Betteridge estate together with the Haseley Trust land was a large-scale market garden, farmed from Drayton House farm, the other, Drayton Manor farm, was part of a larger farm, 1,200 acres, belonging to Mr. S. J. Farrant, and was reminiscent of the medieval history of the parish in that it stretched well beyond the bounds of Drayton parish into Burcot and Dorchester, and mainly concentrated on arable farming.[73]

CHURCH. Drayton church is first mentioned in 1146 as a chapel in a list of the possessions of Dorchester Abbey.[74] It was probably one of the chapels appropriated to the abbey which in 1445 were served by its canons, and this is likely to have been the normal arrangement.[75] The chapelry was in Dorchester peculiar.[76]

After the Dissolution the rectory and 'advowson' of Drayton were granted to the Dean and Chapter of Christ Church, Oxford,[77] and they still hold the gift of the living, which was a perpetual curacy until 1870, when the tithes were made over to the incumbent. In the late 16th century the curate of Drayton seems generally also to have served Clifton Hampden[78] and since 1950 Drayton has been held in plurality with Stadhampton and Chislehampton.

In 1526 the curate's annual stipend, paid by Dorchester Abbey, was £5 6s. 8d.[79] and in 1826 this remained the certain annual sum paid by the dean and chapter to the curate.[80] In the early 18th century this payment seems to have been made up to £16 a year[81] and later to £20. By 1778 the dean and chapter also paid the curate a further £10 a year under the terms of Dr. South's will.[82] The living was augmented by the Governors of Queen Anne's Bounty in 1747 and 1758 by £200[83] so that, in 1778 the curate's annual income was £47,[84] including fees

[50] O.R.O. Land tax assess.; Bodl. Tithe award. There are details of the Haseley Trust land in their receivers' accts. 1852–86: O.R.O. Misc. Ay. I/1.
[51] Bodl. G.A. Oxon. b 90 (35): *Sale cat.*
[52] *Sale cats. of Abingdon estate*, 1875 and 1901.
[53] Bodl. G.A. Oxon. b 90 (35, 36): *Sale cat.*
[54] Bodl. Tithe award.
[55] Ibid.; and see map, p. 77.
[56] MS. Top. Gen. c 43, p. 146.
[57] Bodl. Tithe award; and see map, p. 77.
[58] Bodl. Tithe award.
[59] O.R.O. Incl. award. For Drayton inclosure Act see 41 Geo. III, c. 43 (local and personal).
[60] *V.C.H. Oxon.* ii. 220.   [61] *Census*, 1931.
[62] *Census*, 1951.   [63] Par. Rec.
[64] *Poor Abstract*, 402; Young, *Oxon. Agric.* 45, 53.
[65] *Poor Abstract*, 403.
[66] *2nd Rep. Poor Law Com. App.* (E), H.C. 595–II, p. 294 (1836), xxix (2).
[67] Boyd Orr, *Oxon. Agric.*, plates facing pp. 196, 200.
[68] Ibid. 172, 177.
[69] Ibid. plates facing pp. 220, 221.
[70] Ibid. plate facing p. 201.
[71] Trinity Coll. mun.
[72] Inf. Trinity Coll. estate office.
[73] Local inf.; *Land Utilization survey Rep.* 225.
[74] *Reg. Antiquiss.* i. 247.
[75] *Visit. Dioc. Linc.* (*1420–49*), 80.
[76] cf. *Oxon. Peculiars.*
[77] *L. & P. Hen. VIII*, xxi (2), p. 334; cf. xvii, p. 491.
[78] O.A.S. *Rep.* (1918), 189.
[79] *Subsidy 1526*, 279.
[80] Ch. Ch. Arch. 25 A 13.
[81] Oxf. Dioc. c 155, f. 51.
[82] Ch. Ch. Arch. xiv b. 2, p. 10.
[83] C. Hodgson, *An Account of Queen Anne's Bounty* (1845), 323.
[84] Ch. Ch. Arch. 25 A 1.

which amounted then as in 1826 to about £1.[85] In 1801 an estate of 23 acres at Tetsworth was purchased for £900.[86] It yielded varying sums, £29 in 1803, £40 in 1804, £26 in 1831, until in 1876 it was exchanged for £64 16s. rectorial tithes.[87] In 1826 the Governors of Queen Anne's Bounty further augmented the living by a grant of £600 which, together with £200 given by the dean and chapter and a similar sum given by the curate himself, yielded an annual income that raised the value of the living in 1831 to just under £90.[88] In 1865 there was a further augmentation obtained 'not without difficulty'.[89]

In 1535 Drayton chapel was valued at £11 a year[90] and this remained the valuation of the parsonage until at least the beginning of the 18th century. In the 17th century the lessee of the tithes paid £7 6s. 8d. of this in cash, the remainder in kind and although the annual cash payment increased at times in the 19th century to as much as £50 the terms of the render in kind remained unchanged.[91] Apart from this payment the lessee of the parsonage after 1631 also paid the curate's stipend. This may have been the case earlier and certainly in 1553 he was required to provide bread, wine, and wax for the celebrant and to find 'sufficient and honest mansmeate and horsemeate to every preacher coming thither'. The rectory consisted of tithes great and small from the parish north of the river, and an annual rent of 10s. This rent can be traced back to 1552, when the dean and chapter had a dispute with Edmund Ashfield over the first crop from 7½ acres of the *lotte meades* which they claimed should belong to Drayton rectory. It was agreed that Ashfield should have the crop but should pay the dean and chapter 10s. a year or two loads of hay.[92] Thus in 1553 and in 1855 the rectory included this annual payment. In 1799 the rectory was valued at £285 2s. 4d.[93] and the valuations of 1824 and 1834 were almost the same.[94] In 1840 it was £340.[95]

In 1552 the rectory was leased to Richard Pawling and it remained in the Pawling family until the early 18th century.[96] At the end of the 18th century it was held by Edward Tawney and in 1820 by Richard Tawney of Willoughby (Warw.). In 1840 the tithes were commuted and apportionment was altered after the inclosure award of 1861. From the 16th century the tithes of Holcombe Grange were held by the freeholders, Trinity College, Oxford.

Until the 19th century curates seem generally to have been non-resident, although it is probable that John Dunt who was curate from 1625 to 1675 lived in the minister's cottage mentioned in 1641.[97] This cottage may have been the same as the 'parson house, next the churchyard', mentioned in 1778 as having been in the possession of the parish officers who put the poor in it.[98] During the 18th century the church was served for two or three years at a time by students of Christ Church who travelled out on Sun-

days and therefore had no need of a residence. The most famous of these was Phineas Pett, curate from 1787–90. In 1784 the dean and chapter bought a small cottage for the curate's use on Sundays.[99] In 1814 the curate again resided, and this cottage was enlarged in 1830 in a makeshift manner at a cost of £325.[1] In 1858 A. J. Williams, the curate in whose incumbency the extensive restoration of the church was carried out, appealed to the dean and chapter for funds to build a new parsonage house on an acre of land given by the Earl of Abingdon.[2] This house was built in 1862 at a cost of over £1,200 and was enlarged in 1872.[3] As the church has been held in plurality with Stadhampton since 1950 the Rectory has been sold.

In 1778 the curate reported to the dean and chapter that the churchyard was let for 30s. a year which was claimed by the churchwardens for the repair of the church.[4] According to him no one had been buried in the churchyard until about 40 years previously: parishioners were buried in Dorchester. This may not be strictly true because there are some grave-stones in the churchyard dated before 1738, but it is not unlikely that at an earlier time Drayton had no burial ground of its own. The same curate also reported that some land had been let for the repair of the church and this was probably the 2 acres held by the churchwardens in 1841. In the early 17th century there seems to have been an old custom of perambulation or procession about which we know because of failures to observe it.[5]

The church, dedicated to *ST. LEONARD*,[6] is a small stone building, comprising a chancel, nave, and north chapel, with a wooden south porch and a wooden belfry standing at the west end of the nave. The now partly roughcast roof is covered with tiles and the upper walls of the belfry with wooden shingles.

The earliest part of the church is the nave with several 12th-century features, including the doorways in the north and south walls and the traces at the eastern end of the nave in both the north and south walls of windows that have been blocked. In the 13th century the west and north-west windows of the nave were made and the small side chapel added at the north-east end. The chapel has a fine, plain, round Early English pier and two unequal openings in the nave wall. A slightly pointed arch leads to the chancel which seems, judging from the position of the windows, originally to have been lower than the nave, a feature destroyed in the 19th-century restoration.[7]

The tower is a fine timber structure probably earlier than the 16th century: the church certainly had three bells in 1552.[8] The belfry is separated from the nave by 18th-century oak panelling.

In the 16th century the south-west window of the chancel and the south-east window of the nave were altered to admit more light. In 1629 the church and

[85] Ibid. 25 A 13.   [86] Ibid. 25 A 6.
[87] Ibid. xiv. b, 2, pp. 364–5.
[88] Ibid. p. 365.
[89] Ibid. 25 A 94.
[90] *Valor Eccl.* (Rec. Com.), ii. 170.
[91] Ch. Ch. Arch. Drayton rectory box.
[92] Ibid.; Req. 2/17/88.
[93] Ch. Ch. Arch. 25 A 3.
[94] Ibid. 25 A 22–23.   [95] Bodl. Tithe award.
[96] Ch. Ch. Arch. Drayton rectory box.
[97] Par. Rec. Chwdns' acct. bk. s.a.

[98] Ch. Ch. Arch. xiv. b. 2, p. 364; 25 A 1.
[99] Ibid. xiv. b. 2, p. 364.
[1] Ibid. 25 A 15. For plan and description see 25 A 55.
[2] Ch. Ch. Arch. 25 A 53; for appeal to Diocesan Church Building Soc. see MS. Top. Oxon. c 103, ff. 402–3.
[3] Par. Rec. Mortgage.   [4] Ch. Ch. Arch. 25 A 1.
[5] *Oxon. Peculiars,* 144–5.
[6] See Bacon, *Lib. Regis.*
[7] MS. Top. Oxon. d 93, ff. 36–39. For an early 19th-century account of the church see Parker, *Guide,* 326.
[8] *Chant. Cert.,* 103, 120.

tower were reported to be out of repair and subsequently a certain Simon Broadwater was repeatedly presented for not having carried out repairs.[9] Towards the end of that century the condition of the fabric seems to have been fairly good,[10] but in 1721 the roof and windows were 'a little out of repair',[11] and although there are no detailed descriptions of or reports on the condition of the church during the 18th century, it seems likely that the succession of non-resident curates paid insufficient attention to it. In 1817 the chancel was reported to be out of repair, in 1823 the roof, in 1828 two of the three bells were cracked[12] and by 1859 the whole of the church was in very bad condition.[13] The windows of the chancel had had their tracery removed to simplify glazing, the roof was in a bad state and the plaster ceiling was ready to fall. As a result of a report made in that year by Edward Bruton the restoration was undertaken in 1859 by G. E. Street and was completed at a cost of £600.[14] The chancel was partially rebuilt. Its 'common brick floor' was raised. The plaster ceiling was removed and the present high-pitched roof made in place of the old roof, the line of which can still be seen over the chancel arch. The extra weight of this roof and the increased height of the east wall made the angle buttresses at the east end necessary. The tracery of the east window was inserted from new designs, only the mullions being original, and the south-west window was completely renewed. In the nave the ceiling and a western gallery were removed.

This restoration destroyed many features of interest. Apart from those already mentioned, the eastern gable of the nave apparently had a sanctus bell turret on which was a sundial, and the roof of the chancel had an overhanging barge at the east end.[15] A high wooden pulpit was replaced by a stone one which was itself replaced in 1898 by the present brightly coloured wooden one, designed by the Wareham Guild.[16] The seating was completely altered; the new seating was said to be modelled on an old seat still existing in the church. It was intended that the restoration should have been even more drastic, for it was proposed to replace the wooden bell tower with a stone structure thus providing more seating space. Fortunately nothing came of this proposal although it was revived later.

Alterations were, however, made to the tower in 1884 when Bruton reported that it was in need of repair.[17] It was strengthened, its walls were covered with shingles, and a clock was inserted.[18]

In 1930 the chancel floor, raised in 1859 so that there were two steps from the nave into the chancel, was lowered by volunteer labour to its present position of one step at the chancel arch and a second at the altar. At the same time the altar which had been placed against the east wall in 1859 was moved forward into the chancel; the chancel rails were also moved and the choir stalls were rearranged;[19] the sacristy was built in 1932 also by volunteer labour and in accordance with the plans of Mr. Geoffrey Webb.[20]

Electric light was installed in about 1934.[21]

The only medieval glass is in the north chancel window, which is a restoration of a window believed to represent St. Leonard. It has been stated that this window was only discovered in the restoration, but the glass was certainly known in 1846. There is now no trace of the arms mentioned by Lee in 1574.[22] Windows designed by Bucknall and Comper were placed in the east window and in the south-east window of the nave in 1894.[23]

There are memorial tablets to Abraham Deane (d. 1809), William Deane (d. 1846), J. H. R. Mate (d. 1928), H. S. Milford (d. 1952), and to Aston Swindale, M.D. (d. 1952). On the exterior of the south wall of the church there are four 19th-century memorials to members of the Deane and Jackson families.

Apart from the former sundial on the east gable of the nave there are five scratch dials on the south-east wall of the nave and one on the left of the south door which must antedate the porch.

There were three bells in 1552.[24] They were recast in 1884 and another three added. The oldest bell is the former tenor of c. 1470 and inscribed *Sancta Katerina ora pro nobis*. The predecessors of the two other bells were dated 1603 and 1635.[25]

The Elizabethan chalice and paten cover are dated 1575. There is also a large silver paten (hall-marked 1694) and a pewter flagon.[26] At the Reformation the church possessed two chalices with patens 'parcell gylte', two corporal cases, two candlesticks, and a number of vestments and altar clothes.[27]

The registers begin in 1568 and there is a Churchwardens' account book for 1641–81.[28]

NONCONFORMITY. There is no certain record of Roman Catholicism.[29]

After the restoration there was a group of under ten nonconformists in the parish. From 1663 until 1686 there was a steady stream of presentments for non-attendance at church,[30] and six nonconformists were recorded in 1676 in the Compton Census.[31] Their leader was evidently William Lovegrove, tobacco merchant. He was presented in 1678 for holding a conventicle at his house once every month, and although in 1680 he denied this he was again presented in 1681 for the same offence.[32]

In 1808 the incumbent reported that there were in Drayton 'a few Methodists visited once a fortnight by a teacher from Oxford at the house of a small farmer in the village', and by 1816 Drayton was on the Oxford Methodist circuit.[33] In 1834 there were said to be only two families of dissenters.[34] By 1851

[9] Oxf. Arch. Oxon. c 158, ff. 73, 229.
[10] *Oxon. Peculiars*, 150–1.
[11] Ibid. 152.
[12] Ibid. 153.
[13] Ch. Ch. Arch. 25 A 59.
[14] For the restoration and the condition before it see MS. Top. Oxon. c 103, ff. 388–93; d 93, ff. 36–39, and Parker, *Guide*, 326–7; Ch. Ch. Arch. 25 A 59.
[15] Ch. Ch. Arch. 25 A 59.
[16] Oxf. Dioc. c 1800, faculty.
[17] Par. Rec. Report.
[18] Notes in church.
[19] Ibid.
[20] Ibid.
[21] Oxf. Dioc. c 1800, faculty.
[22] *Oxon. Visit.* 106.
[23] Oxf. Dioc. c 1800, faculty.
[24] *Chant. Cert.* 103.
[25] *Ch. Bells Oxon.*
[26] Evans, *Ch. Plate*, 58.
[27] *Chant. Cert.* 103.
[28] Par. Rec. There are transcripts of registers 1662–1816, 1767–1813, 1813–57, in Oxf. Dioc. b 77, c 526, d 273.
[29] John Werott, gent., and Marian Spencer, widow, of Drayton, are mentioned in 1625 (Salter, *Oxon. Recusants*, 40, 46, 56), but may not have belonged to this Drayton.
[30] *Oxon. Peculiars*, 145–50.
[31] Compton Census.
[32] *Oxon. Peculiars*, 149–51.
[33] Oxf. Dioc. d 549, p. 47.
[34] Oxf. Dioc. b 39.

there was a Methodist chapel, said to have been built in 1814;[35] although it only had about twelve members, almost the whole of the 'labouring population' went to some evening services there.[36] In 1879 the present (1958) Methodist chapel was built on land that had belonged to a Drayton grocer and baker. He was one of the four local trustees, the others being labourers.[37] In 1906 the chapel, which is on the Thame and Watlington circuit, was registered for marriages.[38]

SCHOOLS. The first record of any school in Drayton is in 1808, when there was a dame school with 6 children and a day school where 25 children were taught reading, the Testament, the Catechism and sewing.[39] In 1810 two Sunday schools were started with 21 boys and 16 girls and five years later 29 children were being educated in three day schools.[40] Nevertheless, in 1818 it was reported that there were no schools in Drayton although the poorer classes were 'desirous of the means of education'.[41]

By 1833 the Wesleyans had a Sunday school with 46 children, held in their chapel. There was also a day school with 20 boys and girls, which was supported by their parents.[42] The Vicar and other voluntary subscribers were supporting this school in 1854 when there were 35 pupils.[43]

The National School was built next to the Rectory in 1855.[44] The Poor Law Guardians gave the land and premises to Drayton's minister, churchwardens and overseers in 1858 in trust for the education of 'the labouring, manufacturing and other poorer classes in Drayton'.[45] The school had an average attendance of about 40 children until 1906.[46] In 1925 it became a junior school for children under the age of 11 and the seniors bicycled to Dorchester. There was an attendance of 28 in 1943, but in 1947 the school was closed and the juniors have since gone to school at Benson and the seniors to Dorchester.[47]

CHARITY. Mary Spyer by will, in 1697, left a rent charge of £5 on her estate in Huntercombe for the apprenticing of a boy or girl from this parish. The Charity Commissioners in about 1823 reported that for the last 16 or 17 years no application had been made for benefit from this charity, though the owners of the estate did not deny liability to pay the money.[48] The charity was later lost.[49]

STADHAMPTON

THE ancient parish comprised 623 acres.[1] In 1932 Stadhampton was enlarged to 2,426 acres for civil purposes by the addition of Chislehampton, and Ascot, formerly in Great Milton parish, and Brookhampton, formerly in Newington parish and the hundred of Ewelme.[2]

The northern boundary of the ancient parish of Stadhampton followed Haseley Brook from Hangman's Bridge to its confluence with the Thame; the western boundary followed the Thame, the southern Cuxham Brook, which joins the Thame near Chislehampton Bridge. To the east there is no prominent natural feature and the old boundary followed the Milton–Thame road southwards from Hangman's Bridge and then with many indentations, dictated by the field boundaries, ran south to Cuxham Brook.[3]

There are meadows to the north and south along the courses of the brooks, and by the Thame on the west, where the land is liable to floods. The farm land lies, as it must always have done, to the north and east of the village.[4] There is no woodland and comparatively few trees, although in the mid-16th century the parish had been far more thickly wooded than Chislehampton,[5] and a map of 1742 shows that there was plenty of timber in the hedges.[6]

The parish is relatively flat, being mostly below the 200-foot contour line. The greater part of it lies on clay: Kimmeridge Clay in the centre and south west, Gault in the south and east. There is a gravel deposit in the south-west, and a broad belt of Alluvium by the Thame with lesser deposits along the Haseley and Cuxham Brooks.[7]

Since the 12th century the place has been called 'Stodham' or 'Stadham', which may mean 'river meadow where horses are kept'. The 'ton' is a later addition, perhaps influenced by the propinquity of Brookhampton and Chislehampton.[8] The village lies in the south-east corner of the parish. The church fronts the green, and the farmhouses and cottages are spaced round it at widely separated intervals, and along the road to Oxford.[9] The hearthtax returns of 1665 show that in the 17th century there were a number of fair-sized houses: 6 with 5 or more hearths and 5 with either 2 or 3 hearths.[10] The largest with 8 hearths was occupied by Timothy Doyley, one of the chief landowners, but he had been obliged in 1657 to transfer the ownership with other property to his son Robert, who undertook to pay his debts.[11] John Owen, a noted divine and friend of the Doyleys, had the next largest house. When he was ejected in 1659 from the deanery of Christ Church he bought an estate at Stadhampton, his birth-place, and retreated to a 'fair dwelling house' there.[12] A map of 1742[13] gives an exact

[35] H.O. 129/4/123.
[36] Oxf. Dioc. d 179.
[37] Dated stone; Thame Methodist Ch., Conveyance.
[38] Thame Methodist Ch., Registration.
[39] Oxf. Dioc. d 707.
[40] Ibid. c 433.
[41] Educ. of Poor, 722.
[42] Educ. Enq. Abstract, 746.
[43] Wilb. Visit.
[44] O.S. Map 25″, xlvi. 6 (1881); Kelly, Dir. Oxon. (1887).
[45] O.R.O. Misc. Or. I/i.
[46] Kelly, Dir. Oxon. (1887, 1891, 1903); Vol. Sch. Ret. 20.
[47] Inf. Oxon. Educ. Cttee.
[48] 8th Rep. Com. Char. H.C. 13 p. 495 (1823) viii; see also under Nuffield, ibid. p. 523.

[49] Gen. Dig. Char.
[1] Census, 1881. The estimated area in 1841 was 530 acres. For an account of the parochial development of Stadhampton see below, p. 87.
[2] Census, 1931.
[3] O.S. Map 6″, xl (1886), xlvi (1884).
[4] Davis, Oxon. Map.
[5] See above, p. 5; below, p. 85.
[6] O.R.O. CH XII/1: surveyed by W. Burgess 1741/2.
[7] G.S. Map 1″ (N.S.) sheet 254; G.S. Memoir, p. 94.
[8] P.N. Oxon. (E.P.N.S.), i. 154.
[9] O.S. Map 25″, xlvi. 2, 3 (1881).
[10] Hearth Tax Oxon. 56.
[11] Ibid.; Rousham Arch. O 94.
[12] Wood, Athenae, iv. 96–102; and see below, p. 91.
[13] O.R.O. CH XII/1.

picture of the village some 80 years later. It was made for William Ives, a gentleman and an Oxford mercer, and shows his substantial house and some half dozen others, besides cottages bordering the green or lining the lanes leading from it. It shows too that the layout of the ancient village was essentially as it is today. In the middle was the 'towne greensworde', as it was termed in 1619, and which in later times at least amounted to 15 acres.[14] At the end of the 18th century, in 1781 and 1795, it was being let by the overseers for a rent of £28 and £30 respectively.[15] On it were probably the stocks and the pound mentioned in 1798–9, when Richard Hood was appointed hayward to pound the cattle on Stadhampton green and Copsen Lane.[16] The green was reached from the south by the road from Brookhampton and Chislehampton; Milton Lane, which was hedged, led off from the north-west corner, and the Chalgrove road, also hedged, from the east. The Brookhampton–Milton road between 1770 and 1875 formed part of the turnpike which ran from Aylesbury to the Oxford road near Shillingford.[17] One of these, Cat Lane by the manor-house, is mentioned in the 13th century;[18] it or another 'common footpath' was ploughed up about 1300, a trespass for which the village was fined 12d. and a further 6s. 8d. for concealment.[19] Another, Cobstone (or Copsen)[20] Lane, served the fields in the north of the parish. In 1798–9 more than 6s. was expended from parish funds on the repair of its gate and railings.[21] On the south, Mill Lane led down to Cuxham Brook and to the mill, while another lane served 'the Homes', a row of cottages and their gardens which in 1786 formed part of Robert Peers's Chislehampton estate.[22]

During the latter half of the 18th century there was an increase in the number of houses: by 1811 there were 44.[23] Two of the new cottages still stand near the church: one is of chequer brick and has a stone inscribed T.E. 1755, and the other, Vine Cottage, is of rubble stone, has dentilled eaves and late-18th-century gothic windows. Further expansion took place in the first half of the 19th century and there were 78 dwellings in 1851.[24] Many of these were in School Lane as well as in the main street; some were constructed of brick, others of stucco, and most of the cottages were of rubble. The kennels of the South Oxfordshire Hunt were built in 1884 at the north-east end of the green.[25] In the 20th century there was another period of building activity and a council housing estate of sixteen houses now lies between the river and the old main street of the village, where a petrol station has superseded the smithy.[26] Although there had been some recent demolition of the older houses, notably of some 16th-century cottages,[27] a number of ancient buildings dating from a variety of periods, still remained in

1958. Among them is Doyley's early-17th-century farmhouse to the north of the green. It is a stone building of two stories. It has flanking chimneys with diagonal shafts and three gabled dormer windows. The front has been partly modernized in the 19th century, but the gabled back of the house has been little altered. At the east end of the green and approached by a lime avenue is the 17th-century farmhouse, now called a manor-house.[28] It is built of rubble with ashlar quoins and was originally rectangular. It retains some of its original mullioned windows; its three hipped dormer windows have 18th-century casements; over the panelled doorway there is a later hood of moulded wood supported by scroll brackets. The house next to the manor-house has brick and timber construction in its gable ends, but is mainly built of stone with brick dressings. The front was stuccoed in the late 18th or early 19th century. An early-19th-century farmhouse near the church and the early-19th-century Vicarage[29] are the only other substantial houses left on the green, but there are a number of picturesque cottages of the 17th and 18th centuries. They are mostly built of rubble, although some are of colour-washed stucco. Timber framing remains in the gable ends of a few; the infilling is mainly of brick, but some wattle and daub survives. Some thatched and stone-tiled roofs are also to be seen. A group of cottages of this date was pulled down in 1957 to make way for a new road to the council houses. The present village hall, close by the church, is an ancient stone building that may once have been a barn.

In Council House Lane there are other 17th-century dwellings: one, an L-shaped building, is now four cottages; it is timber-framed on a rubble base, and has brick or wattle and daub infilling: the steeply pitched roof is thatched. On the main street there is the 17th-century bakehouse. It is built of coursed stone, bears the date 1658, and is thatched. It was used as a bakery until about 1914. The 'Black Horse' is dated F.G. 1751: it is built of rubble, has brick quoins and dressings and brick dentil eaves. This house may once have been called the 'Wheatsheaf', for an inn of that name was recorded in 1831.[30] The 'Crown', another of Stadhampton's inns, was licensed in 1825 and remained a public house until 1951.[31] In the first half of the 19th century the Baptist chapel (1837) and the school were built and some cottages of this period are distinguished by their red, yellow, and blue bricks.[32] A row of 20th-century houses, built after the First and Second World Wars, have been added to School Lane.

National events impinged on the parish in the 17th century. During the Civil War troops often passed through Stadhampton on account of its nearness to

[14] Rousham Arch. O 82, O 84. Its acreage is first given in the Bodl. Tithe award (1850).
[15] Par. Rec. Parish bill.
[16] Ibid. Overseers' accts.
[17] Acts of 1770 (10 Geo. III, c. 58) and 1875 (38 & 39 Vict. c. xlvi (local & pers.).
[18] Wm. and Hugh de Kattelane (Cathelane): Queen's Coll. MS. 366, f. 26b.
[19] S.C. 2/197: Dorchester hund. ct. rolls.
[20] This is its modern name.
[21] Par. Rec. Parish bill.
[22] Peers Arch. (penes C. T. Peers, Esq., Chislehampton House): Field bk. In a terrier attached to a lease of 1650 Greenway, Cutted Way, and Watchard (or Watchell) Way are mentioned, but it is not possible to identify them now.

More Lane, the gate and rails of which were repaired in 1799, may be the Chalgrove road which ran past 'The Moors' (1850): O.R.O. Misc. Torr. IV/3; Par. Rec.; Bodl. Tithe award.
[23] Census, 1811.
[24] Ibid. 1821–51.
[25] Kelly, Dir. Oxon. (1887).
[26] Inf. R.D.C. Bullingdon. For the smithy see O.S. Map 25″, xlvi. 3 (1881).
[27] Par. Rec. Photographs.
[28] See below, p. 83.
[29] Oxf. Dioc. b 70, f. 713.
[30] MS. Top. Oxon. b 42, f. 91b.
[31] O.R.O. Victllrs' recog.; local inf.
[32] See below, p. 92.

Chislehampton Bridge. Prince Rupert rode through on his way to Tetsworth in June 1643, and returned by the same route after his victory at Chalgrove.[33]

ESTATES. There appears never to have been a manor of Stadhampton in the Middle Ages. At the time of Domesday the township evidently formed part of the demesne lands of the Bishop of Lincoln's Dorchester manor, which were assessed at 59¾ hides,[34] far too large an area for Dorchester alone. The Stadhampton estate and grange were included in a survey of the manor made in the second quarter of the 13th century and they remained in the possession of the bishops of Lincoln until 1547, when Bishop Holbeach surrendered Dorchester manor to Edward VI.[35] The medieval estate appears to have been larger than the 19th-century parish, which covered 623 acres, for 37 virgates were recorded in the 13th century and 39 in 1551.[36] The 3½ virgates with meadow and pasture, which Bishop Burghersh granted to Richard of the Chamber in or before 1333, had presumably reverted to the bishop by 1547.[37] Stadhampton remained with the Crown until Elizabeth granted Dorchester manor to Henry, Lord Norreys of Rycote.[38] He died in 1601, and was succeeded by his grandson Francis, later Earl of Berkshire (d. 1622).[39]

The Norreys family appears soon to have alienated a large part of its Stadhampton property. In the early 17th century the Wilmotts were in possession of 6½ yardlands, 2½ of which were sold by Richard Wilmott in 1637 to Sir Robert Dormer of Dorton (Bucks.)[40] Another messuage and 2½ yardlands had been sold by Henry Lord Norreys in 1586 to John Wise of Drayton. In 1611 this property was conveyed by Robert Doyley and Peter Wilmott, the trustees of John Coale to whom Wise had sold it, to John Cobbet.[41] Cobbet leased it to John Allen of Berwick Prior (Newington) for 99 years in 1621, and in 1632 Sir Robert Dormer, already a substantial landholder in the parish, bought the lease for £800.[42] In the 18th century the property was attached to Studdridge manor in Stokenchurch (Bucks.).[43] In 1732, when it was known as Stadham Farm and comprised about 70 acres, it was mortgaged to Richard Carter of Great Haseley. In 1738 Lt.-Gen. James Dormer (d. 1741) quitclaimed to him all title and interest in the estate.[44]

Terriers of 1619 and 1650 indicate that Timothy Doyley of Chislehampton was a substantial landholder in the parish.[45] In 1657 the latter conveyed his house and lands in Stadhampton, with appurtenances in Brookhampton and Newington, to his son Robert, in consideration of the latter's undertaking to pay his debts.[46] But, as the hearth tax of 1665 shows, he continued to occupy the house.[47] Robert, by his will of 1669, settled his Stadhampton property on his wife Jane (née Loggon) for life.[48] Thereafter its descent is not clear.

By the 18th century the Wises were owners of the greater part of the parish, including Stadham Farm, the former Doyley estates, and some lesser freeholds. In 1740 Robert Wise agreed to sell his property to Oriel College, and a number of draft agreements were drawn up. There was some suspicion that the vendor had fraudulently inflated the value of the estate, and there was talk of repudiating the bargain, but it was eventually carried out.[49] Oriel, however, was unable to purchase the whole of Doyley's farm and part of it was conveyed to Christ Church and to Mrs. Elizabeth Ives. Christ Church, owing to the dispute with Wise, did not receive its share of the property, amounting to nearly 44 acres, until 1749.[50]

In 1785 the land-tax assessments record no less than 15 'proprietors', although some of them, including the tenants of the 44-acre Christ Church estate, were in fact leaseholders.[51] The Jones family owned the tithes and paid the heaviest tax, but the Oriel estate was probably larger, as it was in 1850.[52] Robert Peers of Chislehampton owned 51 acres in 1786 and by 1850 the Peers holding had increased to 81 acres.[53] The only other sizeable freeholds were those of Mr. Aubrey, which by 1832 was in the possession of the Revd. Shaw Hellier, who had 85 acres in 1850; and of Mr. Cripps: in 1850 John Cripps had 89 acres.[54]

At the time of the tithe award (1850) Oriel College and William Jones of Stone Hall, Haverfordwest, owned 138 and 132 acres respectively, the latter being designated lord of the manor. In 1854 Charles Peers was given the title and, in 1887, William and Thomas Franklin. It remained with the Franklins at least until 1920.[55]

Up to 1912 or so the pattern of land ownership had undergone little change since 1850. The Franklins owned the manor-house and about 160 acres, the former Jones's estate. Oriel, which in 1867 had bought a further 43 acres of meadow land for £2,300, now had 181 acres; Christ Church had 34 acres, the Revd. J. W. Peers 81 acres, and R. S. Hellier 85 acres.[56]

In 1921, however, Oriel sold its estate to H. Pether

[33] C. Wilkinson, *Prince Rupert the Cavalier*, 137, 140.
[34] *V.C.H. Oxon.* i. 402.
[35] Queen's Coll. MS. 366, ff. 26, 26b and see above p. 13, n. 94; *Cal. Pat.* 1547–53, 153.
[36] Queen's Coll. MS. 366, ff. 26, 26b; L.R. 2/189; Bodl. Tithe award.
[37] *Cal. Pat.* 1330–4, 438.
[38] See above, p. 42.
[39] *Complete Peerage*, ix. 646–8.
[40] Rousham Arch. (*penes* T. Cottrell-Dormer, Esq.), O 91–92. For the Wilmotts see *Oxon. Visit.* 301–2.
[41] Rousham Arch. O 79. For the Doyleys see above, p. 10.
[42] Ibid. O 78, O 85, O 89, A 25; O.R.O. Fa V/14. See also Rousham Arch. O 82, O 84, for a 99 years' lease by Cobbet to Sir John Dormer of 4 acres of arable. For the Dormer holding in 1650 see terrier: O.R.O. Misc. Torr. IV/3.
[43] O.R.O. Fa V/8, 10–15.
[44] Ibid. Fa V/13. He was the half-brother and heir of Robert Dormer of Dorton, the devisee of John Dormer of

Ascot whose grandfather was Sir Robert Dormer. See the pedigree in *Oxoniensia*, xi–xii, after p. 98.
[45] Rousham Arch. O 82, O 84; O.R.O. Misc. Torr. IV/3.
[46] Rousham Arch. O 94. Cf. W. D'Oyley Bayley, *House of Doyley*, 68: according to whom Timothy Doyley, by indenture of June 1637 [*sic*] demised his Hambleton (Bucks.) estate to Robert for 40 years at £30 a year.
[47] *Hearth Tax Oxon.* 56.
[48] Bayley, *House of Doyley*, 69.
[49] Oriel Coll. Mun. drawer 9. According to the third draft the purchase price was £5,400.
[50] Christ Church Arch. Index to Register of Leases, ii, pp. 405–6.
[51] O.R.O. Land tax assess.
[52] Ibid.
[53] Peers Arch. (*penes* C. J. Peers, Esq., Chislehampton House), Field bk.; Bodl. Tithe award.
[54] O.R.O. Land tax assess.; Bodl. Tithe award.
[55] *P.O. Dir. Oxon.* (1854); Kelly, *Dir. Oxon.* (1887, 1920).
[56] d.d. Bullingdon b 157, b 158; Oriel Coll. Arch. drawer 9.

for £4,600,[57] and four years later the Christ Church property (Manor farm) was purchased by T. W. White for £840.[58] In 1926 and 1927 Magdalen College purchased both properties and the Doyley estate of 215 acres was again united. In 1929 the college bought Church farm (196 a.) from T. Dunn and so became owner of about two-thirds of the parish. The Peers and Hellier lands (c. 200 a.) were in the possession of C. J. Buswell.[59]

MILLS. The parish mills were an important economic asset. When the Bishop of Lincoln's estate in Stadhampton was surveyed in the second quarter of the 13th century there were two mills. The Abbot of Dorchester rented one and 1½ virgate of land for 20s., and the other, 'Heewere', was rented for 10s. by the Prior of Holy Trinity (i.e. Christ Church), Canterbury. Five acres of mill land were leased separately, and among the tenants of 2 virgates was Hugh, miller of 'Stodham'.[60] In 1279 these mills, called 'Brokmellen', were being farmed each year by the bishop for 47s. 4d., but the tenants are not recorded.[61] In 1300 the farm of the mill(s) was increased by 4s.[62] At the time of the 1551 survey Robert Allen was tenant of a water-mill at a rent of 33s. 4d. His copyhold dated from 1537 and obliged him to carry out repairs at his own expense, except for the purchase of wood. There is no mention of a second mill.[63] By 1564, when Dorchester manor was in the hands of the Crown, the mill was so decayed that the manor's overseer declared that it could not be repaired for less than £54 12s. 8d. However, John Doyley, the chief landowner, at the request of the tenants, paid for the repairs and gave £10 for two millstones. In return the mill was farmed to him by the Crown for 60 years at 33s. 4d. a year, with reservation of large trees, underwoods, minerals, and quarries.[64] Before 1608 the tenure of 'two water-mills under one roof' was divided between Dame Elizabeth Peryam, widow of Sir William Peryam, late Chief Baron of the Exchequer, and Lord Francis Norreys of Rycote. In 1608 Lord Norreys sold both to Sir John Dormer of Dorton (Bucks.),[65] who leased them in 1625 to William Kirke, a local miller, for 21 years at £6 a year, with the obligation to pay the original rent of 33s. 4d. to the Crown.[66] William Dormer leased them for 27 years from 1653 to Richard Latham and his son John, on the same conditions.[67]

In 1720 John Dormer mortgaged the mill to John Chambers.[68] Between 1785 and 1832 it was in the possession of the Cripps family, and the Towertons were the lessees until 1829, when they were succeeded by Edward Reynolds, who was still the tenant in 1832. He appears to have sub-leased it for a document of 1830 describes Henry Towerton as the 'miller at Stadham'.[69] As the mill was not situated on the Thame[70] it did not directly concern the Sewers' Commissioners, but in 1801 they ordered part of the Cuxham Brook, which provided it with water, to be cleansed.[71]

The mill itself is not mentioned in the 1850 tithe award schedule, although Christ Church owned the mill close and part of the garden as it had done since at least 1741.[72] At the beginning of the 20th century Mrs. Franklin owned the mill and R. Bobart, whose family had been tenants of Christ Church in 1850, was the tenant.[73] The mill was still working in 1939.[74]

ECONOMIC AND SOCIAL HISTORY. There is no specific information about Stadhampton in Domesday Book as it formed a part of the Bishop of Lincoln's Dorchester manor. The whole was assessed at 59¾ hides and the facts supplied about it are comparatively meagre.[75] The earliest detailed survey of the bishop's estate here that has survived was made in the second quarter of the 13th century.[76] It names 26 virgaters, each paying 4s. 9d. rent and owing the same services as those of Chislehampton;[77] five holders of 2 virgates, each owing double the rent, services and 'wudeway' due from a single virgate; and two tenants, who each held 2½ acres of mill land at rents of 5s. and 4s. with the obligation to mow at two of the bishop's autumn boon-works. In addition, Walter Bunte held a virgate for special services: he took care of the bishop's ploughs and seed, saw that the meadows were properly scythed and gathered, that the corn was duly reaped and collected, and that the ricks and haycocks were properly constructed and covered. If necessary, he was to go to the nearer manors for the provisions of the bishop and the steward, and also to London with corn for sale or delivery to the bishop's barns. The first day he was to travel at his own expense, but afterwards at that of the bishop. It is noteworthy that the manor was producing a surplus for the market, for one of Bunte's services was to accompany the reeve to the markets to sell corn and collect the proceeds. While there he was to purchase everything necessary for the ploughs. When required by one of the bishop's servants he was to be present at episcopal business. He had also to perform occasional agricultural services: he was to plough 2 acres of the bishop's land at his own cost and another 2 acres, the bishop providing his food; and harrow 1 acre if he had his own plough, or if he shared one, he and his partner had to harrow it. He owed 2 boon-works in autumn with his whole family except for his wife and daughter or his mother, if he had no daughter. The bishop provided food at the time of the harrowing service and the boon-works. Walter also owed *merchet*, heriot, *leirwite*, a fine for his land after the

[57] Oriel Coll. Mun. Ledger; Register of Sales. It was first offered to the sitting tenant H. H. Hicks for £5,000.
[58] Christ Church Arch. Register of Sales and Purchases of Estates, p. 16. Smaller properties totalling about 6 acres had been sold in 1919 for £245; ibid. p. A 12.
[59] Inf. the Estates Bursary, Magdalen Coll.; d.d. Bullingdon a 28.
[60] Queen's Coll. MS. 366, ff. 26–26b.
[61] *Rot. Hund.* (Rec. Com.), ii. 748.
[62] S.C. 2/197: Dorchester hund. ct. roll.
[63] L.R. 2/189: survey of Dorchester manor.
[64] Rousham Arch. A 7.
[65] Ibid. O 67, O 68; cf. above, p. 83.
[66] Rousham Arch. O 86, O 87.
[67] Ibid. O 93.

[68] Ibid. O 95–96.
[69] MS. Top. Oxon. b 42, f. 91.
[70] See map by W. Burgess, surveyed 1741/2: O.R.O. CH XII/1.
[71] d.d. Ashhurst d 4, p. 178.
[72] Bodl. Tithe award; 1742 map: O.R.O. CH XII/1. The O.R.O. land tax assess. give Cripps as the 'proprietor' of the mill and lands between 1785 and 1832.
[73] d.d. Bullingdon b 157: valuation bk. 1904; ibid. a 28: rate bk.
[74] Kelly, *Dir. Oxon.* (1939).
[75] *V.C.H. Oxon.* i. 402.
[76] Queen's Coll. MS. 366, ff. 26–26b. For the dating see above, p. 13, n. 94.
[77] See above, p. 12.

death of his father, and an aid to the lord whenever it was demanded.[78]

Of the free tenants, John of the Bridge and Alexander the Smith each held a ½-virgate for 4s. and the abbot of Dorchester held 1½ virgates and a mill for 20s., with the right to pasture 8 cows and a bull with the bishop's animals. Alexander also held 1 virgate for which he owed the service of making at his own cost six ploughs, except for the ploughshare. He was also to have an acre of corn and another of rye, but if he did not perform the services he was to pay 5s. 6d. assize rent.[79]

In the survey made in 1279 16 tenants were said to hold a virgate and a messuage for 5s. and services; 4 held 2 virgates each and a messuage for 10s. and services; 5 held 2½ virgates each and a messuage for a rent of 12s. 5d. and services; 5 held a ½ virgate and messuage for 2s. and services. For their services the tenants had to plough each year 2 acres of the demesne; scythe the meadow and lift the hay; reap in autumn for 3½ days without food being provided and for 2 days with food provided; and cart the corn until it was all carried. A tenant could not marry his daughters or sell his foal or ox without licence; and he had to take the bishop's corn to market at his will. Besides these villein holders of virgates, there was a free tenant, Henry Ferant, who held 4 virgates and a messuage for a rent of 22s. a year and services. He had to carry brushwood for a day on his own land and afterwards on the bishop's; cart for 2 days in autumn with his tenants, the bishop providing food. He also had to do riding service in addition to the autumn boon-work and be present at every Dorchester hundred court. His ancestors, the survey records, used to be free like sokemen and do 40 days' service for the king in wartime. They had to provide their own lance and helmet of iron. This service, however, was withdrawn by the bishop.[80]

This survey appears in some respects to be less thorough than the earlier survey made for the bishop. Only 29 landholders, free and unfree, are listed in 1279 compared with 39 in the earlier survey. The latter number includes the Prior of Canterbury and the Abbot of Dorchester, the lords of the mills, but the others appear to have been resident. The number of inhabitants is high in relation to the small area of the parish, and the 14th-century tax-assessment lists indicate that the community must have consisted of men of comparatively modest wealth.[81] In 1327 there were 28 contributors to the 20th compared with 21 at Chislehampton, but the total tax paid was only a few shillings higher. After the reassessment of 1344 the village was rated at more than a third less than Chislehampton,[82] a decline in prosperity for which

no explanation has been found. If there was any decline in population in the later Middle Ages owing to the engrossment of holdings, it was on a much smaller scale than at Chislehampton. In 1524 there were 24 contributors to the subsidy compared with nine at Chislehampton.[83]

A 1551 survey of Dorchester manor shows that there were then 12 copyholders at Stadham, of whom 1 held the mill only, 7 had 4 or more virgates apiece, and 5 more than 1 messuage. One tenant had 3 messuages and 4 virgates, while another held 1 messuage and 1½ virgates, with 2 cottages and 4 virgates in reversion. A small fee of 2d. to 4d. was required for licence to make a sub-tenant. Each of the 40 yardlands carried right of common for 16 sheep, 2 beasts, and 1 horse, a total of 760 animals. Compared with Chislehampton the parish was well wooded for there were said to be 244 large timber trees and 1,465 altogether.[84]

Six persons had their goods assessed at £3 for the 1577 subsidy, and Thomas Stacy, who was assessed at £12, is clearly the substantial yeoman of that name who was holding 1½ virgates with another 4 in reversion in 1551.[85]

In the mid-17th century there were four open arable fields.[86] Whaddon Field lay in the south of the parish and included Lank furlong on the west and Lillands on the east, part of it abutting on Ascot Field hedge. Forry Field was in the north towards Haseley Brook; but it is impossible to locate Bickwell or Swansey Fields.[87] It is by no means certain that there was a four-field system of cultivation. In 1650, for instance, Robert Bird's holding was unequally distributed, consisting of 6 acres and 6 yards in Whaddon Field, 4½ acres and 1 land in Swansey Field, 3½ acres in Forry Field, and 3 acres and 2 yards in Bickwell Field. He also had 2 acres of meadow ground, the right to cut hay in certain meadows and in Cutted and Watchett Ways, 3½ leys which amounted to 2 acres, and common appropriate to a yardland for 2 cows or other beasts, 2 horses mares or geldings and 20 sheep.[88]

There are some indications that the yeoman farmer here as elsewhere in the neighbourhood was prosperous and respected. John Cobbett, for instance, who in 1615 was claiming an exclusive right to a church pew, which he had built for himself and his family next to the seat of John Doyley, was granted an hereditary right to it.[89] The hearth-tax returns of 1665, moreover, show that yeoman families were occupying substantial houses: Robert Bird and Edward Wise each returned five hearths.[90] Another indication of prosperity and of a fairly populous village at this period is the number of craftsmen: a

---

[78] Queen's Coll. MS. 366, ff. 25b, 26–26b. Walter's agricultural services were the same as those of Robert at the Bridgehead, a Dorchester villein, and are to be found under a Dorchester entry.

[79] Queen's Coll. MS. 366, f. 26b.

[80] *Rot. Hund.* (Rec. Com.), ii. 747–8. The printed edition of the hundred rolls has no entry headed Stadhampton, but a comparison with the original roll (S.C. 5/4b, Tower Ser. Oxon.) shows that the first entry in Dorchester hundred relates to Stadhampton. The original roll of the hundred consists of parts of two rolls, an abbreviated and a fuller one, and possibly of a third roll, which have been sewn together. There is in consequence some repetition. With the object apparently of avoiding this repetition the editor of the printed version has omitted passages here and there. In the case of the first entry he has omitted a passage in the middle of the account which states that 9 hides were held in villeinage of the bishop in 'the hamlet

of Stodham' and repeats, though not in identical words, their general services already given at the beginning of the account. In the original Stodham is also entered in the margin. Although the whole entry is made up from different rolls internal evidence makes it certain that it all relates to Stadhampton.

[81] For table see below, p. 231; E 179/161/10, 9, 17.

[82] E 179/164/7.

[83] E 179/161/198.

[84] L.R. 2/189, ff. 6b–8, 13, 17.

[85] E 179/162/341.

[86] Preamble to Bodl. Tithe award (1850).

[87] O.R.O. Misc. Torr. IV/3 (1650); Rousham Arch. O 82 (1619): terriers attached to conveyances.

[88] O.R.O. Misc. Torr. IV/3.

[89] Oxf. Dioc. b 20, f. 121.

[90] *Hearth Tax Oxon.* 56; many of the names occur in O.R.O. Cal. Q. Sess. i.

cordwainer, blacksmith, malster, and harness-maker are mentioned in 1692, a tailor in 1719.[91]

Inclosure came in 1675, presumably through the initiative of the Doyleys, but no details of the negotiations have been found.[92] The riotous assembly of 1692 in which seven of the Stadhampton yeomen, some of their labourers, and four village craftsmen were involved may have been caused by dissatisfaction with the changes made, particularly as it is stated in the later tithe award that there were 'numerous disputes' at this time.[93]

A map of 1742, which includes most of the present parish, gives a good picture of conditions in the mid-18th century. If the land was not all inclosed in 1675 it certainly was by this date and was held by about eight principal tenants. One of these was William Ives, an Oxford mercer, who had a leasehold estate of some 88 acres.[94] Half of this later formed the estate acquired by Christ Church in 1749[95] and was leased for £2 16s. 8d. up to the middle of the 19th century. The fines for a 7-year lease amounted to £34 between 1757 and 1792, £66 15s. between 1799 and 1806 and thereafter fluctuated considerably, being £114 12s. 4d. in 1824 and £82 4s. 9d. in 1831 and 1838. In 1820 the leasehold estate was valued at £1,345.[96]

A tenant of Stadham farm, part of Oriel College's estate, in the late 18th and early 19th century was the experimental farmer Thomas Smith of Chippinghurst and Stadhampton.[97] He was an expert on the cultivation of flax and he may well have grown it on his land in the parish. In a letter to another well-known farmer, Sir Christopher Willoughby of Marsh Baldon,[98] a member of the Board of Agriculture, he said that flax should be sown about April immediately after ploughing on 'a lively land where there is a depth of soil' and at 2½ bushels to the acre. Before sowing the ground should be harrowed, and the crop hand weeded afterwards and barned in August 'to beat the seed off and water the flax'. It was best sown on land which had not been ploughed for a long time and he considered a moderate crop to be 30 stone an acre and 12 bushels of seed.[99]

In 1793 Smith, in answer to the Board of Agriculture's questionnaire, gave a description of farming in the parish and its neighbourhood. The soil he considered to be rich, dry, and fertile; and capable of great improvement by watering as the meadows by the Thame were extensive and little above the usual height of the water.[1] Very little of the old pasture had been broken up and so grew only natural herbage. There was insufficient woodland. The stock was chiefly cows and sheep with a few breeding mares, but little improvement was made as the calves and lambs were sold off when fattened. The grains were wheat, beans, pease, barley, and oats. As there were many farms of different sizes and tenant farmers of different opinions there was no uniform management, but he divided his own land into eight equal

parts, one, the strongest land near the centre of the farm, he kept in grass as a sheep-walk, sowing rye-grass, broad and Dutch clover. The other seven parts he sowed in rotation with wheat, turnips for spring feed for ewes and lambs, oats, pease for which he dunged the land and after harvest folded it with sheep, wheat, winter vetches, spring vetches, turnips, and barley with broad clover. After the first crop of vetches he manured the land with cart dung and when the vetches were up again spread coal ashes at 30 bushels to the acre. Ploughs used in the district were of two sorts—one with two wheels; the other with none, being generally used for light work. Horses rather than oxen were chiefly used. As a result of inclosure rents had risen, more corn was raised on light soil, turnips, vetches, and clover were cultivated, more stock was kept, and consequently there had been a 'great improvement'. In general he considered that all the uninclosed waste lands would be improved by inclosure, and that nothing would be equal to general inclosure for improving the quantity and quality of stock. He regarded tithes as one of the main obstacles to improvement. For common work wages were 1s. 2d. a day, which was from 6 o'clock in the morning until 6 o'clock at night, and 2s. at harvest, when work continued from sunrise until sunset.[2]

In the late 18th century there were twelve different tenants and two owner occupiers of small holdings. Only two farms, one of them Oriel's, were of any size.[3] By 1850 there were four tenants of more than 80 acres, and William Bobart's farm of 203 acres, leased from three different landowners, was by far the largest. There were 9 acres of small holdings. There was a fairly high proportion of meadow or pasture land, 240 acres as against 340 of arable. There were 19 acres of common or waste in the parish, 1 acre of wood or oziers and the village green comprised 15 acres. There were 20 gardens and buildings.[4]

By the beginning of the 20th century the usual tendency for farms to increase in size is evident at Stadhampton. The three principal tenant farmers held 85, 209, and 203 acres respectively.[5] In 1929 there were two large tenant farmers: a third farmer had purchased the lands he had formerly tenanted and was farming 206 acres on his own account.[6]

Considering the small area of the parish, Stadhampton appears to have always been fairly well populated. In 1676 the Compton Census recorded 85 adults. Because Stadhampton formed part of the peculiar of Dorchester no 18th-century population returns were made to the bishop, but Thomas Smith in 1793 stated that the population would be increased if the land inclosed was not let in too large farms.[7] At the first official census of 1801 the population was 193 and it increased steadily to a peak figure of 401 in 1851. For the remaining decades of the century it declined and was 253 in 1901. Between 1931 and 1951 there was an increase from 277 to 284.[8]

[91] O.R.O. Cal. Q. Sess. i. 46, 199.
[92] Bodl. Tithe award.
[93] O.R.O. Cal. Q. Sess. i. 46; Bodl. Tithe award.
[94] O.R.O. CH XII/1.   [95] See above, p. 83.
[96] Ch. Ch. Arch. Index to reg. of leases, ii, pp. 407, 416; O.R.O. H III h/10.
[97] Oriel Coll. Mun. drawer 9. Cf. O.R.O. Land tax assess. 1789, 1796. He appears in the land-tax assess. for Chippinghurst from 1786 until 1816 as the most substantial tenant and he may have died in the latter year. See also d.d. Ashhurst d 4, p. 28; Par. Rec. Stadham par. bk.
[98] For Willoughby see V.C.H. Oxon. v. 35, 40–43.
[99] O.R.O. Wi IX/2(b).
[1] Many of them were liable to flooding. In 1796 they were worth 35s. to 40s. an acre: Peers Arch. Sewers' tax assess.   [2] O.R.O. Wi IX/3.
[3] O.R.O. Land tax assess.   [4] Bodl. Tithe award.
[5] d.d. Bullingdon b 157: valuation bk. 1904. The farms were Church, Manor, Doylies, Cholsey, Barkers, and Coldharbour.   [6] d.d. Bullingdon a 28: rate bk.
[7] O.R.O. Wi IX/3.
[8] Census, 1801–1951.

PARISH GOVERNMENT. An overseers' account book (1781–99),[9] throws some light on the conduct of local affairs at the end of the 18th century. The annual account of the overseers, which was rendered from Easter to Easter, was allowed at a vestry meeting and later verified on oath before two of the justices. Their income consisted of the rent of the village green, which varied between £24 and £30, a few cottage rents, and the poor-rate. Out of this they paid the 'poor bill', invariably the largest single item, and the 'bills' of the other parish officers: the churchwardens, constable, surveyors, and clerk. There is no clue to what exactly these bills were for. Both the churchwardens and the constable received comparatively large sums, ranging from £3 to £7. In 1798 it was agreed that the two overseers should hold a vestry at Stadhampton church on the first Monday in every month, at 4 p.m. in winter and 6 p.m. in summer. It was still their business among other things to appoint the hayward and regulate the pasturing of animals on Stadham Green and Copson Lane.[10] The hayward was 'to pound all kind of cattle at 2d. belonging to the inhabitants and 4d. to every person out of the parish, geese at the same price, found trespassing'. The owner of unringed pigs was to forfeit 1d. for each.

Expenditure rose steadily from £36 13s. 5d. in 1780–1 to £70 9s. 8¾d. in 1794–5. It jumped to £174 6s. 4¼d. in 1795–6, but then declined slightly, being £143 11s. 8½d. in 1797–8. The poor bill itself, always the largest of the parish bills, increased from £22 1s. 2d. in 1780–1 to £142 13s. 1½d. in 1795–6. In 1781 2d. in the £ on property rated at £821 5s. had realized £6 16s. 10½d.: in 1796 a 2s. 8d. rate produced £134 1s. 2d.[11]

A number of items in the poor accounts are of special interest: in 1791 £1 13s. 4d. was expended on the purchase and spinning of 30 lb. of flax; in 1797, £2 7s. on spinning-wheels. Later accounts record numerous payments for spinning, which was apparently done at home. The able-bodied poor were sent out as 'roundsmen', the parish paying them about 6d. a day. Thomas Smith noted at about this time that there was no employment for the poorer sort of workmen and children in winter and 'they are much to be pitied'.[12] Other sums expended were for the upkeep of the village green, particularly of its ditches, and in 1795, £9 was spent on the repair of two of the parish houses and £1 18s. on coals for the poor.[13] In a visitation return of 1802 Stadhampton Green was declared to be appropriated to the poor.[14]

An incident in 1830 illustrates the discontent among the working population caused by the fear of unemployment. Men from the parish broke a thresh-

ing-machine at Little Milton. In their defence it was argued that they had been over persuaded by neighbours from Drayton, and that the belief among the labouring classes that the destruction of machines was sanctioned by the government had become general.[15] Sickness and old age, however, were the main causes of pauperism: in 1838 there were ten paupers in the parish, three of whom were old and infirm, the remainder sick.[16]

CHURCHES.[17] Stadhampton and Chislehampton, now in Cuddesdon deanery, were once in Dorchester peculiar. In the 11th century like other churches in Dorchester hundred they probably formed prebends for the secular canons of Dorchester, then the cathedral church of the diocese.[18] Although the see was moved to Lincoln in 1092, soon after the death of Bishop Remigius, the canons retained possession of the churches. When Bishop Alexander suppressed the secular canons in about 1140, and replaced them by Austin canons, the endowments of the secular canons were evidently transferred to the new order.[19]

The churches at Stadhampton and Chislehampton are first specifically mentioned in a papal bull of 1146, when Dorchester Abbey was confirmed in its possession of them. The bull states that Bishop Remigius had granted them Dorchester church and its chapels.[20] The abbey retained them until its dissolution in 1536. In 1146 they were described as chapels of Dorchester and in 1291 as *capellae prebendales*, and although during the Middle Ages Stadhampton at least had parochial status, as a sign of dependence on the mother church it paid 7s. a year to the abbey for the right of burial.[21] In the 18th century a similar payment was made to the churchwardens of Dorchester.[22]

It is possible that in the Middle Ages Chislehampton did not acquire full parochial status. It may, for instance, have always buried its dead at Stadhampton. In the post-Reformation period it certainly came to be regarded as in some sense a chapelry of Stadhampton,[23] and did not become a fully independent parish until 1763, when its new church was built. It had, however, a large degree of independence: from the 16th century at least it had its own churchwardens, and in the 18th century, and no doubt earlier, its own overseers and poor rate.[24] Its inhabitants were baptized and married in their own church, but since they had no churchyard were buried at Stadhampton,[25] except that the Peers family built a vault in Chislehampton church in 1749. A payment had to be made to Stadhampton for everyone buried in the churchyard there.[26] In

[9] Par. Rec. There are also two loose sheets for the years 1796 and 1797.   [10] See ibid. 1799.
[11] According to *Poor Abstract*, 402, £80 6s. 9d. was raised by rate for the year ending Easter 1803. If so, there must have been a considerable fall in expenditure since 1796. But the totals in this work should be used with caution. The average of £56 2s. 10d., said to have been raised by assessment during 1783–5, is in fact the average of the total disbursements of the overseers, i.e. including the churchwardens', surveyors', and other bills. This was offset not only by the rate but by other income which at one time had been much greater than the rate itself. If £80 is not the rate but the total sum disbursed, then the rate must have been still smaller.   [12] O.R.O. Wi IX/3.
[13] Overseers' accts. A cottage had been bought in 1772: ibid.
[14] Oxf. Dioc. d 567.

[15] MS. Top. Oxon. b 42, f. 91.
[16] Par. Rec. List of paupers.
[17] The help of Miss Frances Riddell Blount with the later history is gratefully acknowledged.
[18] *V.C.H. Oxon.* ii. 87.
[19] Ibid.
[20] *Reg. Antiquiss.* i. 247.
[21] *Tax. Eccl.* (Rec. Com.), 30; *L. & P. Hen. VIII*, xix (2), pp. 486–7.
[22] Oxf. Dioc. c 653, f. 37.
[23] Rousham Arch. (*penes* T. Cottrell-Dormer, Esq., Rousham), *passim*.
[24] *Chant. Cert.* 102, 104; *Oxon. Peculiars*, *passim*; Oxf. Dioc. c 653, ff. 37–38.
[25] Peers Arch. (*penes* C. J. Peers, Esq., Chislehampton House), 1779 case.
[26] Oxf. Dioc. c 653, f. 37.

practice Chislehampton at this time was so much a separate parish that the curate stated that they formed two parishes 'as separate as Cuddesdon and Garsington'.[27]

In 1763, when the new church at Chislehampton was built, Charles Peers gave the land for a church-yard,[28] and in the same year the Chislehampton registers, which had previously been part of the Stadhampton ones, were started. Since then Chisle-hampton has been in reality a separate ecclesiastical parish. As some Chislehampton families attended service at Stadhampton and continued to be buried at Stadhampton, and as both churches were served by the same curate, the two parishes were, however, usually considered as one.

In the 18th and 19th centuries there was discus-sion as to whether the churches formed separate livings. In 1750 the curate wrote that they had always been distinct and that he was summoned to the visitation at Dorchester separately for the two parishes.[29] Curates were no doubt always licensed separately for each church, even though the nomina-tions were made together.[30] All doubt about the position was removed in 1841 when the livings were formally united as a perpetual curacy.[31] Hitherto the benefices were sometimes called perpetual curacies, sometimes 'impropriate curacies' or donatives.[32] The last two were certainly the more accurate de-scriptions, for the patron was able to appoint and 'turn out' the minister at pleasure.[33] In 1868 the benefice became a titular vicarage.[34]

In the Middle Ages no vicarage was endowed in either church, and therefore their parish priests were not presented to the bishop for institution. They were licensed by the official of Dorchester peculiar until about 1835, when the Bishop of Oxford began to license them.[35]

After the dissolution of Dorchester Abbey the rectory and right of presentation to Stadhampton, with which Chislehampton was evidently included, were granted in 1542 to Christ Church.[36] The college later lost them, for in 1607 the parsonages of Stad-ham and Chislehampton were granted to Cope Doy-ley, the son of the lord of Chislehampton manor, and John Cobbet, a Stadham yeoman, for a rent of £13.[37] In the following year Doyley and Cobbet divided the rectory, which was to be the subject of many legal transactions, into two parts.[38] The first remained with the Doyley family and descended with Chislehampton manor to the Peers family, the present patrons. This part consisted of the 'mansion house' of the rectory, the churchyard of Stadhamp-ton, the obventions and tithes of Chislehampton, and the right of presentation of a minister to say divine service in both churches 'in as large and ample a manner as it has been', and involved responsi-

bility for the chancel of Stadhampton church.[39] Cobbet's share consisted of the tithes of Stadhamp-ton and some glebe land. This part was sold in 1620 to Sir John Dormer,[40] and has since belonged to a number of lay proprietors.[41]

No valuation of the joint rectory has been found before that of 1535, when it was worth £18 6s. 8d.[42] Later the Doyley half of the rectory probably be-came united with Chislehampton manor. In 1746 it was stated that the manor was tithe free.[43] The Stad-hampton tithes were commuted at the inclosure of 1675 for £95, a sum confirmed by the tithe award of 1850 when there were two tithe owners.[44] It is inter-esting to note that the holder of most of the tithes, about eight-ninths, paid a land tax assessment of £8 4s. 6d. out of a total of £78 12s. for the parish.[45]

The curate of Stadhampton, who probably also served Chislehampton, was receiving £5 6s. 8d. a year in 1526 from Dorchester Abbey.[46] The post-Reformation curate, who had no settled endowment, received a stipend from the patron. In the first half of the 18th century this consisted of £26 a year, or 10s. a Sunday, plus Sunday dinner for the curate and the care of his horse. But in 1746 Sir John Doyley, who had been obliged to sell his Chislehampton estate, reduced the stipend to £20 and ceased to 'take care' either of the parson or his horse.[47]

In 1750 Queen Anne's Bounty augmented the joint living by £400, and in 1754 by another £400, while Charles Peers settled on the curate £16 a year for Chislehampton and £12 and a tenement for Stadhampton.[48] In the early 19th century the value of the two livings was about £50.[49] Between 1810 and 1843 Queen Anne's Bounty gave another £1,400 and the Peers family £500.[50] But it still remained a poor living, in 1955 worth only £149, when it was held with Drayton St. Leonard.[51]

During the Middle Ages the churches, which were only a mile apart and probably generally shared a priest, were at times served by the Augustinian canons of Dorchester. This was certainly not so either in 1317, when the chaplain accused the abbot and two canons of opening two coffers of his at Stadham and stealing among other things eight charters and nine bonds,[52] or in the early 15th century, if the evidence of Ralph Carnell can be accepted. He was a young canon who, at the epis-copal visitation of Dorchester Abbey in 1445, com-plained, among other things, that the abbot had sent him against his will to take charge of Stadhampton, which had formerly been served by a secular chap-lain. The abbot described Carnell's violence and sins, including incontinency with a 'Stadham' woman, while Carnell accused the abbot's men of armed assault, of wounding him and imprisoning him.[53]

[27] Oxf. Dioc. c 653, f. 38.   [28] Peers Arch. 1763 deed of gift.
[29] Oxf. Dioc. c 653, f. 38.
[30] For separate licenses in 1767 see Oxf. Archd. Oxon. c 159, f. 47.
[31] Oxf. Dioc. c 436, pp. 526–32. For the curate's belief in 1817 that the livings had always been united see Peers Arch. 1817 letter from J. W. Peers.
[32] *Rep. of Comm. on Eccl. Revenues*, H.C. 54 (1835), xxii; *Account of Benefices*, H.L. (1818), xviii.
[33] Peers Arch. Thomas Browne's survey.
[34] By 31 & 32 Vict. c. 117.
[35] Oxf. Archd. Oxon. c 159, f. 47; Oxf. Dioc. b 22, f. 169.
[36] *L. & P. Hen. VIII*, xvii, p. 491.
[37] Rousham Arch. 1618 exemplification; *Cal. S.P. Dom.* 1603–10, 365.

[38] Rousham Arch. *passim*.
[39] Ibid. Indenture of 13 Apr. 1609.
[40] Ibid. 1620 fine; C.P. 25(2)/340/Trin. 17 Jas. I.
[41] e.g. Bodl. Tithe award.
[42] *Valor Eccl.* (Rec. Com.), ii. 170.
[43] Peers Arch. Browne's survey.
[44] Bodl. Tithe award.   [45] O.R.O. Land tax assess.
[46] *Subsidy 1526*, 252, 279.   [47] Par. Reg. 1746 memo.
[48] C. Hodgson, *Account of Queen Anne's Bounty* (1845), 323; Peers Arch. 1752 indenture.
[49] Oxf. Dioc. c 446, ff. 62, 168.
[50] Hodgson, *Queen Anne's Bounty*, 232, 323.
[51] *Crockford* (1955–6).   [52] *Cal. Pat.* 1313–17, 700.
[53] *Visit. Dioc. Linc. 1420–49*, ii. 79–82; *V.C.H. Oxon.* ii. 88.

When the same priest served both churches, services were held alternately in each. In the late 14th century the people of Stadhampton claimed that when mass was celebrated in Chislehampton, matins and vespers should be said at Stadham, whereas the Chislehampton parishioners wanted those services also in their own church. The dispute was settled by the bishop in favour of Chislehampton.[54]

This appeal to the bishop shows that although Dorchester peculiar was free from archidiaconal jurisdiction, it was not free from the bishop's. After the Reformation it was exempt from both. The churchwardens of Stadhampton and Chislehampton attended the visitations at the peculiar court of Dorchester and made their presentments there until the early 19th century, when they became subject to the bishop's visitation.[55] Although the peculiar survived in some form until c. 1847, Chislehampton and Stadhampton, because they had been augmented by Queen Anne's Bounty, submitted to the bishop's visitation in 1796, 1802, 1823, and 1834.[56]

After the Reformation the churches always had the same minister. One late-16th-century curate named Evans, one of the many Welsh churchmen in the county, got into trouble with the peculiar court, and when excommunicated and prohibited from saying divine service, answered that he would continue to serve and preach until he was removed 'with strong hand'.[57] The next year his successor was summoned before the court for irregularities in the service: he answered that he always said the service according to the Book of Common Prayer except when he preached, and then he said part of it; and that in Chislehampton he could not wear a surplice because there was none.[58] Later curates, such as the early-17th-century Walter Chaundler, remedied this deficiency by wearing the Stadham surplice for service at their other church.[59]

Chaundler (d. 1614) was 'a faithful minister and zealous preacher of God's word', who resided in Stadhampton parish with his family and was buried there.[60] One of his parishioners, for the 'love that he bore him,' built him a tomb in the chancel.[61] Henry Owen, 'a nonconformist all his days', probably followed him as curate. His son John, a prominent Congregationalist minister, was born at Stadhampton in 1616, when he himself is said to have been minister,[62] and from then until 1662 Puritan influence generally prevailed in the two parishes. A note in the register by Robert Morgan, who became curate in about 1641, throws light on the chaos in the administration of the religious life of the village during the Civil War. He says that the register was not found for above two years after his coming so that many names were not registered.[63]

The Puritan sympathies of Sir John Doyley and his wife led to the removal of Morgan and the institu-tion of John Hartcliffe, brother-in-law of John Owen, Henry Owen's son.[64] Hartcliffe seems to have replaced Morgan in the late 1650's, and John Bilstone later noted in his copy of the register that in the time of Cromwell names were 'totally obliterated with a wicked design'.[65] Hartcliffe was in his turn suspended in 1662 and a period of neglect followed.[66] In 1663 the younger John Doyley and his wife were presented for not having provided a minister for the Easter Day service and the churches were reported to be without a settled minister.[67] Robert Morgan was then reinstated, but in 1671 the churchwardens of Chislehampton presented that 'our minister who was constant with us' is now dead and that since then there has been 'not common prayer nor preaching.' The Doyleys continued to take little interest in the church and in 1687 and again in 1694 it was reported to be without a settled minister.[68]

Zeal for the Anglican Church not unnaturally declined among the parishioners: in 1717 the curate presented them at the Dorchester court for refusing to pay the church rate towards the repair of the church.[69] From about 1728 to 1766, however, the parish had the benefit of a resident minister, John Bilstone, and, after 1748, a liberal lord and lady of the manor, Charles Peers and his wife Katherine, who constantly attended the church services with their whole family. Bilstone's interest in his parish is indicated by the beautifully written copy he made of the 'Stadham' register (1567–1772) with the object as he said of preserving 'what may be a very great use in adjusting property amongst posterity'. The differences which arose with his parishioners in the 1760's appear to have been due to zeal rather than to neglect. In 1761 he was accused of not performing the duty according 'to the ancient and accustomed method' and was presented again by the churchwardens in 1764. He retaliated by accusing them of having neglected to present certain 'public offences and enormities' committed in the parish.[70] Bilstone, no doubt, encouraged Charles Peers to provide in 1763 a new church at Chislehampton.[71] When it was consecrated by the Bishop of Oxford, Bilstone preached a sermon in which he praised his patron for his munificence in building this 'sacred edifice' instead of a magnificent pile for his own use. He concluded his eulogy by saying that Peers' liberality and constant attendance at church was a proof that wealth need not always alienate the mind from religion.[72] Bilstone died in 1766 and was succeeded in 1769 by John Witherington Peers, the son of the lord of the manor, who continued to hold the living until his death in 1835. He was a pluralist and never lived in the parish.[73]

In 1797 Thomas Fry, memorable for his work for the neglected parishioners of Toot Baldon, was acting as curate.[74] In 1802 there were 40 communicants at Stadhampton and 30 at Chislehampton.[75]

---

[54] Linc. Reg. Buckingham's Memoranda, f. 138.
[55] Oxf. Dioc. d 13, *passim*; Oxf. Archd. Oxon. c 158–9, *passim*; *Oxon. Peculiars*, 67–79, 99–105.
[56] Oxf. Dioc. c 327, p. 78; ibid. d 567, d 581, b 39. For the peculiar see above, p. 53.
[57] Ibid. d 13, f. 6. See ibid. f. 10b for his absolution.
[58] Ibid. f. 51b.
[59] *Oxon. Peculiars*, 99.
[60] Par. Reg.
[61] Ibid. under 1618. The tomb is now in the churchyard.
[62] *D.N.B.* under John Owen. Owen's name appears in the 1630's: Par. Reg. back page. For John Owen see below, p. 91.

[63] Par. Reg. under 1645.
[64] Morgan was there until about 1657: Par. Reg.
[65] *Calamy Rev.* 251.   [66] Ibid.
[67] *Oxon. Peculiars*, 69, 100.
[68] Ibid. 102, 104, 73.
[69] Ibid. 74.
[70] Ibid. 76–77.
[71] See above, p. 15.
[72] Peers Arch. Printed copy.
[73] e.g. Oxf. Dioc. c 327, p. 78.
[74] Par. Reg. For Fry at Toot Baldon see *V.C.H. Oxon.* v. 54.
[75] Oxf. Dioc. c 327, p. 245.

There was one service every Sunday and four communion services in the year at each church. The children attended a Sunday school recently started at Stadhampton.[76] By 1812 the curate was no longer resident, but came out from Jesus College,[77] and the number of communicants had dropped by 1823 to 16 at Stadhampton, where there were 56 families, and to 12 at Chislehampton, where there were 16 families including the household of the lord of the manor.[78]

After the building of the vicarage house in 1836 at a cost of about £830, largely contributed by the Peers family,[79] the parishes had a permanent resident minister. Services were held regularly and in Stadhampton the congregation so increased that by 1891 it could be called one of the finest in the district.[80]

Chislehampton church, on the other hand, was largely dependent on the tenant of the manor-house as the village was so small. 'If Chislehampton House were empty the church would have to be closed down,' wrote the vicar in 1922,[81] for many of the parishioners preferred to go to services at Stadhampton, and Chislehampton church was considered more as a private chapel, although open to the public.

The church of *ST. JOHN THE BAPTIST* at Stadhampton is a small stone building comprising a chancel, nave, aisles, and 18th-century western tower. The church was considerably altered in the 19th century. The circular font[82] appears to be the only survival from the building that is known from documentary evidence to have existed in 1146.[83] Major alterations were carried out in the early 15th century. The chancel arch was then rebuilt and a north aisle was constructed. The aisle is divided from the nave by an arcade of three arches with plainly moulded capitals. It has an early Perpendicular window of two lights at the east end. The windows in the north wall, which have square heads on the external wall, were perhaps inserted later in the 15th century. The north door is now not used.

There is a record that the church was restored in 1588,[84] and the chancel appears to have been rebuilt early in the 17th century. The priest's door of this period remains, but the windows were altered in the 19th century. The date 1600, cut on the southeast quoin, may possibly commemorate this reconstruction. Presentments at the peculiar court show that the fabric continued to give trouble. In 1623 the belfry, perhaps a wooden one at that period, was reported out of repair, and in 1626 the churchwardens were presented for leaving the pavement of the church in decay.[85] Much interest was taken at this time in the interior furnishings of the church. A reading-desk—inscribed I.P. 1611—and a pulpit were installed.[86] New pews were made in 1636,[87] three years after Sir Robert Dormer of Ascot had

been given permission to build a pew for his family under the pulpit 'at his own proper cost'.[88] The church was probably beautified or repaired after the Restoration, for the date 1663 was at one time inscribed in plaster in the gable of the north aisle.[89]

By 1721 the condition of the tower was serious and in 1727 the churchwardens petitioned to be allowed a 'competent' time in which to repair or rebuild it.[90] It was finally rebuilt, with money raised by subscriptions from the parishioners, by Richard Belcher, a mason of Little Milton. Delafield, writing in about 1740, says that Belcher cut his initials on a stone on the east side of the tower with the date 1731.[91] As it was presented in court that the tower was still out of repair in 1736,[92] it is probable that it was rebuilt in 1737 and that Delafield mis-read the date.[93] It is not shown in Buckler's drawing,[94] and there was no trace in 1958 of the date or initials. The tower is of two stages and is ornamented with urns at each of its four corners. The original west doorway was altered in 1875.

The seating accommodation was increased about the same date by the erection of a west gallery, presumably for the singers. The parishioners of Stadhampton, Ascot, and Brookhampton subscribed £15 for it in 1736.[95] In 1744 a fine royal arms of Queen Elizabeth, carved in oak, was presented by the curate, John Bilstone, and hung over the chancel arch.[96] The arms are blazoned and the supporters, a lion and a dragon, are painted 'in their proper colours'. Beneath is the legend, 'Reginae erunt nutrices tuae, Isai. 49: 23.' In the 19th century the arms were removed to the tower arch.

Minor deficiencies were reported in the second half of the century. In 1750 the chancel floor was out of repair; in 1746 the windows, and the patron, Charles Peers, was asked to mend them. Both were again in need of repair in 1790. In 1809 the roof was mended.[97]

In 1875, however, the state of the fabric and the need to enlarge the church led to a 'thorough' restoration at a cost of £1,309. The architect was E. G. Bruton of Oxford.[98] A drawing of 1821 by Buckler shows that the church then comprised a medieval chancel, nave, and north aisle, and the 18th-century western tower.[99] At the restoration the ritual chancel was extended 'some ten feet further west' by placing the choir stalls, pulpit, &c. in the east bay of the nave.[1] A new east window was inserted and the other chancel windows were restored. A small arch was added at the east end of the north arcade to make room for an organ. A completely new south aisle was built, and the whole church reroofed. The 17th-century pulpit and reading desk and the old box pews were removed. So no doubt was the

[76] Oxf. Dioc. d 566, d 567.   [77] Ibid. d 549, p. 68.
[78] Ibid. d 581.   [79] See above, p. 10.
[80] Oxf. Dioc. c 344; Peers Arch.
[81] Peers Arch.
[82] For an illustration of the font see MS. Top. Oxon. a 68, no. 494.   [83] See above, p. 87.
[84] Oxf. Archd. Oxon. d 14, f. 52.
[85] *Oxon. Peculiars*, 68.
[86] MS. Top. Oxon. d 93, f. 40.
[87] Parker, *Guide*, 329.
[88] Par. Rec.
[89] MS. Top. Oxon. d 93, f. 40.
[90] *Oxon. Peculiars*, 74–75.
[91] MS. Top. Oxon. d 88, f. 57. The date and initials were still visible on 'the upper story' of the tower in the 19th century; ibid. d 93, f. 41.

[92] *Oxon. Peculiars*, 75.
[93] There is no reference to the building of the tower in the original parish register either under 1731 or 1737, but Bilstone, who as an old man made a copy of the register, found an entry, which he states was dated 1731, to the effect that 'Stadham Tower was finished this year and was built by the subscription of several of the inhabitants' (Par. Rec.).   [94] MS. Top. Oxon. a 68, no. 493.
[95] Note in Par. Reg.
[96] Par. Reg.; Parker, *Guide*, 330; Bodl. G.A. Oxon. 4° 687, p. 286. Banbury is the only other church in Oxon. to have a royal arms of this date.
[97] *Oxon. Peculiars*, 76, 77–78.
[98] MS. Top. Oxon. d 93, ff. 40–42; Oxf. Dioc. c 2015, Faculty.   [99] See plate facing p. 120.
[1] MS. Top. Oxon. d 93, f. 40.

west gallery for the singers and the raised large pew in the north aisle, which Parker thought much disfigured the church.[2] New fittings, reading desk, and pews of pitchpine were substituted. The ten commandments, painted on two boards, were placed on the east wall. The 'remarkably sweet toned' organ, made by a former curate, was replaced.[3] In 1882 the chancel was provided with new panelling and a reredos.[4] The last has since been removed and the panelling has been concealed by velvet curtains. In 1924 a faculty to place a cross and candlesticks on the altar was granted. A legacy of £200 left by Mrs. Ellen Lyon was spent in 1910 on a clock for the tower. Electric light and heating were installed in 1933 and 1951 respectively.[5]

There are several brasses (now on the north and east walls of the north aisle): one to John Wylmot (d. 1498) and his wife Anne; another to John Wylmot the younger (d. 1508) and his wife Alys; two to twelve children, apparently Wylmots, but it is not clear to which family they belong; and one to another child, Dorothy Clarke (d. 1654), whose mother was a Doyley. There is a large black marble floor slab behind the altar to Sir John (d. 1709) and Margaret Doyley (d. 1706/7).[6] It bears the arms of Doyley impaling Cholmondely. In the chancel is a marble tablet, signed Henry Westmacott, London, to Sarah Beavis (d. 1783), relict of Arthur Beavis and daughter of Sir Charles Peers. It bears the arms of Beavis impaling Peers.

In the tower there are two large marble wall tablets. One to John Eels (d. 1755), a lieutenant in the Royal Navy, was erected by his nephew James Jones, the son of Ann (d. 1791)[7] and James Jones (d. 1767) of Wrexham, both buried at Stadhampton to whom Eels left his estate. The other one is to Ann, wife of Charles Edward Jones of Great Milton (d. 1784).

An old parish chest remains in the church.

In 1552 there was a chalice and paten of silver gilt, a brass pix, cross, and two candlesticks, and various vestments and altar cloths.[8] The present plate consists of a chalice dated 1712 and inscribed Thomas Wise and Edward Winter, Churchwardens 1713; a pewter flagon of 1840 and two pewter dishes.[9]

In 1552 the church had three bells. A complete new ring of four was cast in 1621 by Henry Knight. Of these two remain but the other two existing bells were cast in 1883 and 1884 by Mears and Stainbank of London.[10]

There is a stone cross in the churchyard, a memorial to the dead in the two World Wars. It was originally designed by H. S. Rogers of Oxford and was erected in about 1920.

The earliest register dates from 1567. There is a gap between 1618 and 1627 and until 1762 Chisle-

hampton entries are included. Bilstone made three copies for the years 1567–1762, one for Stadhampton and two for Chislehampton.

NONCONFORMITY. There was no recorded Roman Catholicism in Chislehampton, and at Stadhampton the only record is of two poor women who were said to be papists in 1708.[11]

There is evidence of strong Puritan influence at Chislehampton and Stadhampton as early as the reign of James I. John Doyley, squire of Chislehampton and 'a great friend to the Gospel,' was a patron of Robert Harris, afterwards a celebrated Puritan preacher and President of Trinity College. When the plague struck Oxford in 1604 he prevailed on the young man to preach at Chislehampton and in the neighbourhood.[12] Doyley's wife Ursula, 'a woman of an extraordinary knowledge and piety', also came from a leading Puritan family and was sister to Sir Anthony Cope of Hanwell, one of the leading anti-episcopalians in the country.[13] Doyley presented to the living of Stadhampton Henry Owen, 'a nonconformist all his days',[14] and father of the Congregationalist minister, John Owen.[15] John Owen was called 'the metropolitan of Independency, the Achitophel of Oliver Cromwell'.[16] When just before the Restoration he was ejected from the deanery of Christ Church because of his moderation, he retired to a Stadhampton house.[17] There he 'called together some of his party to preach and many of his disciples went from Oxon. to hear him . . . but they being several times silenced by soldiers of the militia and sorely threatened that congregation was broken'. There were said to be as many as 30 or 40 of the 'godly party' meeting in his house, and on one occasion in 1661 his house was raided by the militia and six or seven cases of pistols were removed.[18] In 1665 he was indicted at Oxford for holding a conventicle, but he had powerful Royalist friends and was never imprisoned.[19] Although he left Stadhampton in the 1660's and became an outstanding nonconformist preacher in London, he must have kept up his connexion with the neighbourhood, since in 1677 he married as his second wife Dorothy, widow of Thomas Doyley, younger brother of Sir John Doyley of Chislehampton.[20]

The Doyleys were noted for their nonconformist sympathies even after the Restoration. After the suspension in 1662 of John Hartcliffe, Owen's brother-in-law, who had been presented to the living by John Doyley,[21] John Doyley and his wife, and a few others were constantly presented for absence from church and for not receiving communion.[22] Similar presentments continued into the 1670's,[23] and the Compton Census of 1676 gives two dissenters for Chislehampton and seven for

² Ibid.; Parker, *Guide*, 330.

³ Parker, *Guide*, 330.

⁴ MS. Top. Oxon. d 93, f. 40.

⁵ Oxf. Dioc. c 2015, Faculties.

⁶ For the date 1706/7, which is now partly missing, see Bodl. MS. Rawl B 400b, f. 388. The date, however, is wrongly inscribed: Margaret Doyley died Jan. 1704/5 (Par. Reg. and cf. Bayley, *House of D'Oyly*, 34). For the heraldry on the monuments see G.A. Oxon. 4° 687, p. 286.

⁷ It bears the arms of Jones quartering Eeles impaling *gules* three griffins' heads rased argent: Bodl. G.A. Oxon. 4° 687, p. 286.

⁸ *Chant. Cert.* 104–5.

⁹ Evans, *Ch. Plate*.

¹⁰ *Ch. Bells Oxon.* 383.

¹¹ O.R.O. Cal. Q. Sess. ix. 778.

¹² Wm. Durham, *Life and Death of Robert Harris* (1660), 9. For Harris see *D.N.B.*

¹³ Durham, op. cit. 26. For Cope see *D.N.B.*

¹⁴ *Works of John Owen*, ed. T. Russell (1826), i. 4.

¹⁵ For him see *D.N.B.*; Wood, *Athenae*, iv. 97–114; *Calamy Rev.* 376.

¹⁶ Wood, *Athenae*, iv. 101.

¹⁷ See above, p. 81.

¹⁸ Wood, *Athenae*, iv. 100; see also Wood, *Life*, i. 499 n. 3.

¹⁹ *D.N.B.*

²⁰ W. D. Bayley, *House of D'Oyly* (1845), 31.

²¹ *Calamy Rev.* 251.

²² *Oxon. Peculiars*, 69–70, 101.

²³ Ibid. 71–72.

Stadhampton.[24] In 1717 a number of parishioners were presented for not paying their church-rates,[25] but nonconformity seems to have declined during the 18th century for in 1802 there was reported to be none.[26]

The evangelical influence of the Peers family of Chislehampton probably checked the growth of dissent in the two villages in the 19th century. None was recorded in Chislehampton, but in the larger village of Stadhampton it made some progress. In 1810 the house of George Goatley was registered for nonconformist worship.[27] In 1834 no dissenters were returned 'except a few ranters', but a year later the curate of Stadhampton, J. C. Philpot, seceded from the Church of England and later became prominent as a Particular Baptist.[28] He was the minister of the meeting-place licensed in 1835.[29] Two years later a chapel was built[30] that seems always to have been associated with the Particular Baptists. In 1854 it was said to have a congregation of fifteen, most of whom came from a distance.[31] The congregation did not increase[32] and in the early 20th century the chapel was closed.[33] In 1924 the building was sold.[34]

SCHOOLS. No information has been found about children's schooling before the 19th century. A Sunday school was set up in 1800 and in the early years of the century a day-school was established through the generosity of the Peers family.[35] The day-school was held first in the church or in a hired room, but in 1807 Robert Peers restored a coach-house for the use of the school. The new schoolroom was opened with great ceremony in 1808 and 50 children from Stadhampton, Chislehampton, and some neighbouring parishes attended in that year.[36] It must have been one of the two day-schools recorded in Stadhampton in 1815, and was probably the school which was said to be conducted by the Sunday school manager and attended by children from Chislehampton and Brookhampton. The other school consisted of 6 boys and 9 girls.

The Peers school had no endowment at first, but an annual school sermon was preached and a collection afterwards made for the support of the school.[37] In 1818 Mrs. Mary Peers and Mrs. Sarah Stevens Peers gave £100 in Consols to endow the school, and the Peers family became governors of the foundation.[38] The official report of 1833 states that the school was a day and Sunday school supported partly by the Peers charity and the payment of 1d.

a week from each child, but chiefly by voluntary contributions.[39]

A private school was opened in Stadhampton in 1832 and was attended by 46 boys and girls,[40] but it does not seem to have been long-lived for in 1854 only one mixed school supported by endowment and pence existed. About 70 children attended from both Chislehampton and Stadhampton.[41] The Peers school, classified as a Church of England school, continued on the old lines until the 1870's,[42] but in 1878 it was replaced by a Board school, built at Brookhampton with accommodation for 80 children. A School Board of five members for Ascot, Chislehampton, and Stadhampton had been set up and it decided to use the Peers charity for rewards for regular attendance at the new school. Children from these three villages and from Newington attended.[43] The building was enlarged in 1894 and again in 1904 so as to hold 117 children, but the average attendance was 82.[44] In 1931 the school became a junior school for children up to the age of eleven; 58 attended in 1943 and 69 in 1954. The seniors were transferred to Great Haseley. It was known in 1954 as Stadhampton County School.[45]

CHARITIES. At an unknown date one Righton gave £25 to the poor of the parish. Between 1707 and 1750 £1 5s. arising from this charity was paid to the poor and was being paid in the late 18th century. In 1800 £18, presumably drawn from the capital, was applied to the purchase of a cottage to be occupied by a parish pauper. The interest on the residue together with £1, the rent of the cottage, was distributable to the poor. In the early 19th century the distribution was irregularly made but in 1820 £7 15s., representing seven years' accumulated interest, was paid to 136 persons.[46] By 1871 the cottage had been sold and the income of the charity was being applied to the rates.[47] In 1925 280 lb. of flour, purchased out of the income, was distributed to 20 persons and in 1932 the custom was to distribute 6 or 7 lb. of flour to 'certain persons' every two years. It was ruled in the same year that the benefit of the charity should be limited to the inhabitants of the ancient parish.[48] In 1956 the income was 13s. 4d. It was not then distributed nor had it been in the two preceding years.[49]

In 1749 the poor were receiving 6s., the interest on 'Mrs. Ann Wise's legacy'. It appears to have been lost by about 1823.[50]

[24] Compton Census.
[25] Oxon. Peculiars, 74.
[26] Oxf. Dioc. c 327, p. 245.
[27] O.R.O. Cal. Q. Sess. viii. 813.
[28] For his obituary see Gospel Standard, 1 Jan. 1870.
[29] Oxf. Dioc. c 646, f. 11; see also f. 18.
[30] Ibid. f. 50; for its position opposite the church see O.S. Map 25″, xlvi. 2 (1881). It is in Calston Lane: Char. Com. file 99171.
[31] Wilb. Visit.
[32] Oxf. Dioc. c 344.
[33] It is in Kelly, Dir. Oxon. in 1903, but not in 1920.
[34] Under a scheme of the Charity Commissioners: Char. Com. file 99171.
[35] Sch. Enq. 308.
[36] Peers Arch. penes Mr. C. J. Peers, Esq., Chislehampton House; Oxf. Dioc. d 707.

[37] Oxf. Dioc. c 433.
[38] Schs. and Chars. 221.
[39] Educ. Enq. Abstract, 744 under Chislehampton.
[40] Ibid. 754.
[41] Wilb. Visit.
[42] Vol. Sch. Ret. 318; Kelly, Dir. Oxon. (1864, 1869).
[43] Kelly, Dir. Oxon. (1887, 1920); the 1878 visitation stated that it was not intended to transfer either the endowment or sch. bldg.: Oxf. Dioc. c 344; O.S. Map. 25″, xlvi. 3 (1881).
[44] Kelly, Dir. Oxon. (1920); List of Sch. 529.
[45] Inf. Oxon. Educ. Cttee.
[46] Char. Don. ii. 984; 8th Rep. Com. Char. H.C. 13, p. 496 (1823), viii.
[47] Gen. Dig. Char.
[48] Char. Com. file 63948.
[49] Ibid. Accts. file.
[50] 8th Rep. Com. Char. 496.

SOUTH STOKE CHURCH *c.* 1807 BEFORE THE 19TH-CENTURY RESTORATION

DORCHESTER. THE FORMER BARN OF THE ABBEY

South Stoke. Brunel's Railway Bridge of 1840 and the
Extension of 1893

Culham Bridge in 1960

SOUTH STOKE

ALTHOUGH in Dorchester hundred, South Stoke formed an enclave in Langtree hundred in the south of the county.[1]

Like so many of the Chiltern parishes South Stoke is long and narrow, stretching from its short river frontage on the Thames up into the hill land round its hamlet at Woodcote. The ancient parish covers 3,370 acres and is about 5 miles long and a mile wide, except in the south-east corner, where it is as little as half a mile across.[2] The Thames separates it from Berkshire and the Berkshire village of Moulsford; its only other boundary of any importance is the Wallingford–Reading road where it divides Stoke from Checkendon. There have been no recorded changes of boundary until 1952, when Woodcote was made into a separate civil parish and its area was slightly increased at the expense of Goring Heath. The present acreage of South Stoke and Woodcote is 1,898 and 2,167 acres respectively.[3]

The parish lies in the chalk area, but has one small area just south of Woodcote of Reading Beds, which is a mixture of sand and plastic clay.[4] Since Saxon times there have probably been two townships: Stoke to the west, known at times as Below Hill, and Woodcote to the east, known as Above Hill.[5] The latter included Woodcote village and the hamlets of Exlade Street and Greenmoor Hill. The western end of the parish is fairly flat, lying at about 150 ft. above sea level around the Thames, but gradually rises towards the centre to 300 ft. at White Hill and Catsbrain, as these hills have been called since the Middle Ages.[6] The large fields to the east of the village, formerly open fields, and still known as South Stoke Fields, are characterized by an absence of hedges and trees and have a typical downland aspect. The eastern end of the parish reaches 600 ft. at Greenmoor Hill, but drops again near the south-eastern boundary to about 400 ft. It is characterized by its beech woods, part of a large wooded area stretching into both Checkendon and Goring, and its heath land of scrub and bracken, where rare flowers were found by John Sibthorp at the end of the 18th century. As in the Middle Ages it is still a district of isolated farms.

The pre-Roman Icknield Way crosses the parish and forms part of the boundary between Stoke and Woodcote; a parallel road connecting Goring with the Wallingford–Henley road is shown on Davis's map of 1797 and is the Tuddingway of the early 13th century,[7] and the road joining the main road that crosses the eastern end of the parish is yet another medieval road. It was described in 1330 as the high road from Wallingford to Reading crossing Woodcote Heath, and in 1366 as the royal road to Exlade.[8] It probably became less important after 1763–4 when the road from Wallingford to Reading, running

down the Berkshire side of the river, was made into a turnpike. The road joining Stoke to Woodcote is also of great antiquity: it is the 'Barwe' of 1366 and the Barway of 1685 and 1819.[9] A second road running the whole length of the parish was closed when the open fields were inclosed. There is still a footpath running close to the Thames through Cleeve in Goring, where South Stoke's nearest mill used to be in the 19th century, to Little Stoke or Stoke Marmion, where at one time there was also a mill.[10] This path is probably to be identified with the Goringspath of 1366.[11] The nearest bridges across the Thames are at Wallingford and Goring, but in summer there is a small passenger ferry from Stoke to the 'Beetle and Wedge' in Moulsford.

The main railway-line (formerly the G.W.R.) from London to Birmingham and to Bristol crosses the western end of the parish, but the nearest stations are at Goring or across the river at Cholsey. This section of the line, running from Reading to Steventon (Berks.), was built in 1838–40. The bridge over the Thames, known as Moulsford Bridge but locally called 'the Four Arches', consists of four 62-ft. arches of red brick, with Bath stone facings. It was designed by I. K. Brunel.[12]

The ancient village of South Stoke lies on rather marshy meadow bordering the river. The name Stoke means a place, and it was first called Bishopstoke, as it belonged to the Bishop of Lincoln.[13] After it had been transferred to Eynsham Abbey it came to be called Stoke Abbatis or Stoke Abbas. Early in the 14th century the name 'South Abbotestok' is found and South Stoke came to be commonly used to distinguish the village from the nearby North Stoke and Little Stoke.[14] In the 19th century the village expanded towards the Goring road, with which Stoke is connected by three short crossroads running through brick tunnels under the railway line.[15] On the northern cross-road there is a group of houses known by the late 19th century as Newtown.[16] Later a row of twelve houses built about 1900 on the Goring road was added, and more recently houses have been built on the middle cross road. Farther to the south are 22 council houses, twelve of them built since the Second World War.

In the old village, which once consisted of one wide street running parallel to the river, are the church and a number of ancient farmhouses and cottages. All are well preserved and give this part of Stoke great charm. The oldest is Manor Farm on the site of Eynsham Abbey's manor-house (*manerium*) that once stood next to the churchyard,[17] and contained in 1366 a hall, kitchen, and chambers.[18] It stood in over 2 acres of ground and had a grange, houses for the various workmen (*officiorii*) and, according to local tradition, fishponds across the street.

[1] *P.N. Oxon.* (E.P.N.S.), i. 156–7.
[2] O.S. Map. 6″, lii, liii, lvi (1882–3); 2½″, 41/58, 67, 68 (1947–9).
[3] *Oxon. Alteration of Rural Parishes Confirmation Order,* 1952.   [4] Orr, *Oxon. Agric.* map opp. 171.
[5] e.g. O.R.O. Land tax assess.
[6] *Eynsham Cart.* ii. 120, 121.
[7] Davis, *Oxon. Map*; *Eynsham Cart.* i. 193.
[8] *Boarstall Cart.* 25; *Eynsham Cart.* ii. 121, 127.
[9] *Eynsham Cart.* ii. 122; Oxf. Archd. Oxon. b 41, f. 109; see map, p. 102.

[10] *Eynsham Cart.* ii. 109.
[11] Ibid. 120. For an attempt in 1898 to divert this see Bodl. G.A. Oxon. c 317/1.
[12] E. T. MacDermot, *Hist. of the G.W.R.* i (1), 101–2; see plate facing p. 93.
[13] *Eynsham Cart.* i. 152.
[14] *P.N. Oxon.* (E.P.N.S.), i. 156.
[15] The village is on O.S. Map 25″, lii. 6, 10 (1881).
[16] Ibid. lii. 6.
[17] *Eynsham Cart.* ii. 128.
[18] Ibid. 120.

In the post-Reformation period the house was the home of the lessees of the manor, of the Bartons and Palmers in the late 16th century. When William Palmer died in 1598 he provided in his will for the continuation of the old custom 'of freekeeping' in the hall at Christmas.[19] In the 17th century the Wollascotts and the Hannes family lived there, and perhaps Richard Hannes's son-in-law, who was assessed on ten hearths for the hearth tax of 1665.[20] Soon after the house may have been partly pulled down for by 1742 it contained only about four bays of building, and two barns and three stables besides.[21] It was still called the Manor House in 1819[22] and today (1958) is the home of Mr. Bullock, the principal farmer in the village. It is an irregular building of brick, constructed mainly in the 17th and 18th centuries, but inside it retains some oak panelling, moulded beams, and a moulded stone fireplace of an earlier date. In the farmyard its picturesque outbuildings include a square four-gabled dove-cot of brick. It dates from the 16th century, has 1,000 nests and is the largest in the county.

The one-time farmhouse opposite has some modern alterations, but is still mainly a 16th- to 17th-century building. It is roughly H-shaped, is partly timber framed on a brick base and has filling of vitreous brick. Its near neighbour Fulbrooke House, named after a local family,[23] also dates from the 16th century: a brick house of two stories, it stands back from the road behind a small garden with a mulberry tree. Nearby are two timber-framed cottages with brick filling and the 'Perch and Pike', which is mainly a 17th-century house. Its gable-end fronts the street and it is built of flint and has quoins and window surrounds of brick. At the north end of the village there were once three more farmhouses: one, Panters, so called after a farming family,[24] though considerably altered and modernized is substantially a Queen Anne house and has some contemporary panelling; another, College House (formerly College Farm), is an 18th-century building of vitreous brick; the third, now called the Corner House, is perhaps the oldest and least altered of any as far as its exterior goes. It is L-shaped: a two-story 16th-century wing is timber framed and partly encased in rather later brickwork; its overhanging timber-framed gable-end fronts the road. The main wing has two stories of brick; a moulded and bracketed wood cornice, a roof of old tiles, and five 17th-century windows that retain their original wooden window frames with wooden mullions and transoms. Standing well back behind a garden on the east side of the road is a well-preserved late 17th-century house of brick, once called the Warren, but now known as Stoke Abbas House. Like many other houses in the village it has cellars. In the 18th century it was a shop kept by a dealer in coffee, tea, sugar, and rice.[25]

It has not been possible to discover which of the more substantial houses was occupied by the Higgs family. Nicholas Higgs, originally from Gloucestershire, married Mary Barton, the daughter of a lessee

of the manor, and the family were for long the principal residents. In 1589 their distinguished grandson Griffith Higgs was born in South Stoke. He became chaplain to Elizabeth, Queen of Bohemia, and Dean of Lichfield. His loyalty to King Charles lost him his benefices and from 1647 until his death in 1659 he lived at South Stoke. He was a considerable benefactor to the parish and is commemorated in the church by a handsome monument.[26]

The chief 18th-century building in the village is the Malthouse, a house of three bays, which in the early 19th century belonged to the Panters.[27] There have been some 19th- and 20th-century additions at the southern end of the street, but most of the modern building has taken place outside the old village. The chief 19th-century buildings are the Congregational chapel, the red brick school, and the Old Vicarage. The brick chapel was built in 1820 for the Countess of Huntingdon's Connexion, and with its two tall sash windows at the side is not without distinction.[28] The Old Vicarage, a large mansion, was built of stone in 1869 on the site of an older vicarage by the architect Charles Buckeridge;[29] it is set well back from the street behind a brick garden wall built in the mid-18th century by the vicar, Coventry Lichfield.[30] A new and smaller vicarage of glass and wood was built next to it in 1956.[31] Another 19th-century building is the parish hall, built in 1885 on a different site[32] as a temperance hall.

Woodcote hamlet lies about 540 ft. up in a fairly central position in the ancient township.[33] Before the common was inclosed the hamlet used to lie on the western edge of Woodcote Common or Heath and must once, as its name indicates, have been even more closely surrounded by woodland than it is now. The heath is mentioned in the 13th century[34] and until the 19th century played an important part in the life of the parish. Common rights came to an end at the inclosure of 1853 and the common was divided up. The centre of the ancient settlement was around its 11th-century church. James's Farm abuts on the churchyard; Red Lane Farm (now two cottages), and Church or Woodcote Farm are within sight; and the Red Lion Inn, which has been there since at least 1851,[35] is not far distant. They stood at the edge of the heath where the Wallingford–Reading road (known as Red Lane) entered the heath, and it is likely that the road determined their site. Red Lane Farm was originally a rectangular house of three bays, built of brick on a stone base, and probably all timber-framed. The timber-framing can still be seen at the gable-end. The roof is so steeply pitched that it is likely that it was once thatched. Picturesque weather-boarded and thatched barns adjoin it. Woodcote Farm, although it has been recently modernized both inside and out, still retains traces of the original 16th- to 17th-century timber-framed and brick house. A brick barn, which forms a continuation of the house, still retains its timber framing. Another ancient and thatched barn in the farmyard is constructed partly of weather-boarding and is partly

[19] Dunkin MS. 439/2, ff. 324–324*b*.
[20] *Hearth Tax Oxon.* 55. For lessees of manor see below, p. 102. [21] MS. Top. Oxon. c 357, f. 68.
[22] Ch. Ch. Arch. 1819 terrier. [23] Ibid.
[24] Ibid. [25] Title deeds at house.
[26] See below, pp. 96, 108, 110. For his life see *D.N.B.*, *Cal. Cttee. for Compounding*, 1501, and the inscription on his tomb. For the family see W. M. Higgs, *Hist. of Higgs Family* (1933).

[27] Ch. Ch. Arch. 1819 terrier.
[28] See below, p. 109.
[29] Oxf. Dioc. c 2026, Plans and mortgage.
[30] Ch. Ch. Arch. Bk. of Livings, p. 322.
[31] Oxf. Dioc. c 2026, Mortgage.
[32] See below, p. 110; Char. Com. file 61041.
[33] It is on O.S. Map 25″, lii. 12.
[34] *Eynsham Cart.* i. 192.
[35] O.R.O. C.H. SO/II/1; see map, p. 102.

timber framed with brick and flint filling. James's Farm is a 17th-century house, built of flint with facings of red brick, and it has a hipped roof with two dormer windows in it. Opposite the church is the Folly, a Regency house set back behind a low wall and a grass verge. Some way down the hill on the South Stoke road is the old forge and its cottage, dating from the late 17th century. The chief 19th- and 20th-century additions to the old village are the 19th-century school of red brick (recently modernized), the new primary school built in 1957,[36] and the village hall, a well-designed building built on common land and given by the Hon. Algernon Borthwick of Woodcote House as a war memorial after the First World War.[37] The rest of the modern development, which has been considerable, has been mainly in the direction of Greenmoor Hill.[38]

This hamlet lies 600 ft. up near the Goring boundary, and took its name from the pool or 'mere' by which it lay. It was once separated from Woodcote by Woodcote Heath, but because of recent building it is now virtually a part of it.[39] Greenmoor Hill Farm is recorded in the early 17th century, when it was a gentleman's residence,[40] but it is now a modern building. Apart from Upper Shaw Cottage, a 16th-century building of timber, brick, and thatch, and the 'Black Lion', which dates from the early 19th century at least, there is little or nothing left of the ancient hamlet. It now consists of the South Oxfordshire Water Summit Reservoir and Gas Co.'s works, erected in 1906, of new bungalows, red brick villas, a shop, and a garage.

A third hamlet, called Exlade Street, lies on the Reading road towards the eastern boundary of the parish.[41] The second element is *slaed* (valley), and if the first element is derived from the personal name *Ecgi*, as is thought, then the settlement is likely to have been far older than the 13th century, when the hamlet is first recorded.[42] It probably later took its second name, first found in the 18th century, from its position on the main road.[43] It now consists of the Greyhound Inn, said to date from 1625 and recorded in 1787,[44] and a few cottages and houses. The oldest of these is Carter's cottage, a one-story building which probably dates from the 15th century. The centre part of the present cottage is built of three crucks with the main tie beams about 7 ft. above floor level, and with secondary ties near the apex with later vertical struts between the lower and upper struts. There is a 17th-century addition of timber frame and brick filling.

Above the hamlet to the east is Woodcote House, the parish's only large mansion. It is said to have been built in 1733 on the site of an older house, perhaps the manor-house of the lordship of Rawlins.[45] The barn to the south-west of the house, now the school chapel, and the walled garden are much earlier, possibly early Jacobean. The entrance to the big house used to be on the south side at the back of the present building, the house being approached by a long drive lined with elms entered from gates on the

Exlade–Reading road. The two lodges and the gates have disappeared, but the foundations could be seen as recently as 1942.[46] The house was completely re-designed by the architect Detmar Blow in the early 20th century:[47] the present north entrance was constructed; the fine library was made by knocking two floors into one; and the kitchen quarters were switched from one side to the other. The north façade now consists of three stories; it has a central projecting pediment and there are projecting symmetrical side wings of colour-washed brick. The roof is of slate. The chief interest of the interior is the room in the style of the brothers Adam that is said to have been decorated in preparation for a visit of George III and his queen, who are believed to have visited the house on their way to Nuneham. A description of the house in 1800 says that the 'parlor story' had a library; 'a spacious eating room (30 ft. square) with a screen of columns, forming a recess for a sideboard; and an elegant drawing room (30 ft. × 27 ft.) with a modern enriched ceiling, a valuable marble chimney piece of beautiful statuary marble, . . . and a mahogany sympathetic folding door'.[48]

Henry Paget, Earl of Uxbridge, was living in the house in 1759, and later Admiral Sir Charles Hardy, who played a prominent part in the Seven Years War, made it his home until his death in 1780.[49] At the end of the century the Cotton family lived there. Sir Sidney Cotton (1792–1874) of the Indian Army, and Richard Cotton (1794–1880), Provost of Worcester College, and a distinguished Vice-Chancellor of Oxford, were brought up in the house; and in 1827, just after his marriage, Edward Lytton Bulwer rented it and there wrote much of 'Pelham' and 'The Disowned'.[50] Afterwards Woodcote was used as a private preparatory school until 1912. On the outbreak of the First World War it was handed over by the Borthwick family, the then owners, for use as a hospital. Since 1942 it has been again converted into a school for boys. The Oratory School, founded in 1859 by Cardinal Newman, bought the house and grounds from the Borthwicks, moved there from Caversham, and built a new detached wing.

Besides its hamlets Stoke has always had a number of isolated farms. Until the inclosure award of 1853 all the farms at the west end of the parish were in Stoke village, but after the inclosure of the open fields Icknield Farm and Lower Cadley's, both near the Icknield Way, were built. Woodcote, on the other hand, has probably always been characterized by its many outlying farmsteads. Before inclosure there were nine such farms: Broad Street Farm lay on the road between South Stoke and Woodcote, and to the north on the old Wallingford–Reading road, now a woodland track, lay Dean Farm. Payables, Copyhold, Horn's, and New Barn Farms used to lie on the western edge of the common; Greenmoor Hill Farm lay on the eastern edge, and Corker's and College Wood Farms were outposts on the north-eastern and south-eastern boundaries.[51]

The history of some of these farms goes back to

[36] See below, p. 110.
[37] Kelly, *Dir. Oxon.* (1939); inf. Mr. B. Webb, Woodcote.
[38] *P.N. Oxon.* (E.P.N.S.), i. 157.
[39] O.S. Map 25″, lii. 16.   [40] C 142/417/42; 334/54.
[41] O.S. Map 25″, liii. 13.
[42] *P.N. Oxon.* (E.P.N.S.), i. 156–7.
[43] Davis, *Oxon. Map.*
[44] Date painted on side; O.R.O. Victlrs' recog.
[45] Inf. Mr. B. Webb, Woodcote, sometime master at

Woodcote School, see below, p. 97.
[46] Inf. Mr. B. Webb; see also the description of the house with illustrations in *The Life of Edward Bulwer, Lord Lytton, by his son* (1883), ii. 153, 159.
[47] Inf. the Revd. Adrian Morey, O.S.B., Oratory School, Woodcote.
[48] *Sale cat.*: copy in Bodl. G. Adds. Fol. A 266 (45).
[49] D.N.B.; *Life of Edw. Bulwer*, ii. 154, 184, 200, 202, 215.   [50] Ibid.   [51] See map, p. 102.

the 13th century. Nicholas Paiable, Mayor of Wallingford in 1366, was the first recorded owner of Payables.[52] The history of Horn's and Dean's may be even older, for the Horne family were in the parish before 1220 and William de la Dene was recorded as a free tenant in Woodcote in 1279.[53] Dean's Farm is mentioned in 1597 and appears on Davis's map of 1797.[54] The Corkers were in the parish by the 1660's.[55] Upper Cadley's, Quelch's, and Ward's, which appear as farms in the later 19th century, are on the site of buildings in existence in 1819.[56]

The present Payables House (no longer a farmhouse), dates from the 16th to 17th century, but has later additions; Dean's Farm (also no longer a farmhouse) is a long rectangular building dating from the 17th century; it has two stories and cellars. It was originally a flint building, but was refronted with chequer brick on a flint base. Its steeply pitched roof indicates that it was once thatched. The date 1669 on one of the beams may record the year of building. It has two fine barns of weather-boarding, both of exceptional length.

Few persons of distinction, apart from the many eminent residents of Woodcote House, appear to have lived in the parish: the most notable, perhaps, was the 17th-century Dr. Griffith Higgs at Stoke.[57]

MANORS. The pre-Conquest history of *SOUTH STOKE* is not known, but it is likely that it was given to the Bishop of Dorchester before the 10th century.[58] By 1086 the see had been moved to Lincoln and Stoke was temporarily retained by the bishop,[59] but soon afterwards was granted in free alms to Eynsham Abbey under the overlordship of the bishops. During a vacancy of the abbey Stoke came into the hands of the bishop, as patron, and at other times the abbot owed suit to the bishop's hundred court of Dorchester and made an annual payment of 3s. 4d.[60] The actual date of the grant is uncertain, but it may have been in 1094, which is probably the year in which William II ordered Robert Bluet, Bishop of Lincoln, to compensate the abbey for having robbed it of its early endowments.[61] In 1109 Henry I, finding the abbey still *desolata et dissipata*, confirmed its possessions, including Stoke and Woodcote.[62] Eynsham Abbey held the manor until its dissolution in 1539, and in 1546 the king granted the manor and rectory to the new cathedral of

Christ Church.[63] The dean and chapter were still lords of the manor in 1958.[64]

In the 15th century Eynsham began leasing the manor and Christ Church continued this policy until the 19th century,[65] for as in the case of other distant manors the bad state of the roads made direct administration difficult.[66] The lessees played a more important part than the college in the history of the parish: they were known as lords of the manor,[67] they held the manorial courts, and in the 16th and 17th centuries, and again in the 19th, they lived in Stoke.

Henry Doget and John Felowe, officials of the abbot, were the first lessees in 1460,[68] and in 1476 Geoffrey and Morgan Kydewelly, two of the many Welshmen to hold office in the county, received £5 from the rent of the manor and the white robes of a gentleman's livery.[69] In 1536 the Barton family acquired the lease.[70] Walter Barton, who came from Barton in Weobley (Herefs.), also held property in Berkshire, and his brass may be seen in the church of St. Lawrence in Reading.[71] He left his interest in the manor and rectory to his nephew Griffith Barton, the son of Henry Barton of Streatley (d. 1548)[72] and the first member of the family to live in the parish.[73] Griffith was buried in the chancel of Stoke church in 1579.[74] The lease of the manor descended to Margaret, one of his six daughters, and her husband William Palmer, auditor of Christ Church, on whom the manor had been settled at their marriage.[75] Palmer died in 1598, leaving the lease of the manor to one of his sons, Barton Palmer of Cassington.[76] The latter had no sons, and so before his death in about 1605 'for the advancement and maintenance' of his wife Mary and his two daughters, he granted the lease of Stoke for a term of years to Hugh Keate of Hagbourne (Berks.), a relative.[77] But in 1610 the lease seems to have been assigned for 40 years to Henry Arden of Kirtlington, Mary Palmer's second husband.[78] He died in 1622, and was probably followed at Stoke by Edward Wollascott, a younger son of William Wollascott of Shinfield (Berks.), and the husband of Barton Palmer's daughter Anne.[79] He appears as lord of the manor in 1625 and at the visitation of 1634 his was the only armigerous family in Stoke.[80]

By 1642 the manor was in the hands of Richard Hannes, the son of an Oxford brewer and alderman.[81] Although Hannes lived until 1678, the manorial

[52] See below, p. 98.
[53] *Eynsham Cart.* i. 153; ii. 110.
[54] Par. Reg. 1597 petition; Davis, *Oxon Map*.
[55] *Hearth Tax Oxon.* 56; Ch. Ch. Arch. 1669–70 lease.
[56] MS. Top Oxon. c 357, f. 1.
[57] See above p. 94.   [58] See above, p. 1.
[59] *V.C.H. Oxon.* i. 402.
[60] *Rot. Hund.* (Rec. Com.), ii. 750; *Eynsham Cart.* ii, pp. lxix, 118. This may have been the origin of the annual payment of 13s. 4d. which the lessee of Stoke made in the 18th cent. to the Earl of Abingdon, lord of Dorchester manor: MS. Top. Oxon. b 192, p. 4.
[61] *Eynsham Cart.* i. 35. For refoundation of Eynsham Abbey see ibid. pp. vii sqq.; *V.C.H. Oxon.* ii. 65.
[62] *Eynsham Cart.* i. 36. For confirmation of Henry II see *Reg. Antiquis.* i. 83–84.
[63] *L. & P. Hen. VIII*, xxi (2), p. 334.
[64] Inf. Christ Church Bursary.
[65] For conditions of leases see below, p. 101.
[66] Cat. of Manorial Records, Ch. Ch. Bursary (copy in Bodl.), p. iii.
[67] e.g. Bodl. MS. ch. Oxon. 3751.
[68] C 1/54/217; *Eynsham Cart.* ii, p. lxviii.
[69] *Cal. Close*, 1476–85, 36.

[70] *Eynsham Cart.* ii. 241. For lessees in the 16th and 17th centuries see Ch. Ch. Bursary, Bk. of evidence, and from the 17th to the 19th centuries. Index to reg. of leases.
[71] W. M. Higgs, *Hist. of the Higges Family of S. Stoke and Thatcham* (1933), 1–2; *V.C.H. Berks.* iii, 373; iv. 26. His will is P.C.C. 17 Dyngeley, his inq. is C 142/60/84.
[72] Higgs, op. cit. 2; *Berks. Wills* (O.H.S. xxiii), 13. For pedigree of Bartons see Higgs, op. cit. 6.
[73] Higgs, op. cit. 238; E 179/162/341.
[74] Cf. *V.C.H. Berks.* iii. 516, which says 1580. His inq. is C 142/188/4; his will is P.C.C. 10 Arundell.
[75] Dunkin MS. 439/2, f. 328b. For pedigree of Palmers see ibid. f. 327b.   [76] P.C.C. 34, 35 Lewyn, 92 Kidd.
[77] Dunkin MS. 439/2, ff. 326b–327. Palmer called Keate his brother-in-law: ibid. f. 328.
[78] Ibid. f. 327. For a series of transactions between Arden and the Keate family see ibid. ff. 326–7.
[79] *V.C.H. Oxon.* vi, p. 223 for Keate; *Berks. Visit.* i (Harl. Soc. lvi), 147.
[80] Higgs, op. cit. 358, quoting Par. Reg. 1625, 1627; *Oxon. Visit.* 278. See also C.P. 25(2)/473/Hil. 9 Chas. I.
[81] Ch. Ch. Arch. 3. c. 3. 33; Wood, *Life*, ii. 414–15; Wood, *City of Oxford*, iii (O.H.S. xxxvii), 205. For the family M.I.'s in the church see below, p. 108.

courts were being held by 1655 by his son-in-law William Barber of Adderbury,[82] and by 1689 by the latter's son Robert Barber, on whose wife the lease of Stoke had been settled on her marriage.[83] Robert died in 1714 and his son Edward succeeded as lessee.[84] Kemp Harward, M.D., was lessee from 1719 to 1740, and after him his daughter Lucy, the wife of John Head, lord of Hodcott manor in West Ilsley (Berks.). In 1803 Head was succeeded as lessee of Stoke by another non-resident lord, Thomas Williams, Vicar of Stoke.[85] In 1831 the lease was taken over by Isaac King, a freeholder in the parish, who since 1819 at least had been living in Stoke manor-house and renting Manor farm.[86] He was the last lessee of the manor, for in about 1860 Christ Church ceased leasing it.[87]

In the 18th and 19th centuries about two-thirds of the land in the parish belonged to the manor.[88] At different times there were three smaller estates, which probably originated from medieval freeholdings, and were called manors, although it is doubtful if they had manorial rights.

WOODCOTE or *RAWLINS* manor as it was called in 1550 may have originated in the free holding of the 12th-century family which took its name from Woodcote.[89] In the 13th and 14th centuries the family had a house on Woodcote Heath and held in socage 4 and later 5 virgates of the Abbot of Eynsham.[90] The names of different members of the family often appear in local charters, but the last of the family seems to have been Master Henry de Woodcote, who held the property in 1366.[91] In 1443 his 5 virgates were said to belong to the lady of Elvington manor, a small manor in Goring.[92] In 1475 Joan Ralegh, widow of Simon Ralegh of Elvington, died in possession of it.[93]

In the mid-16th century Woodcote manor was stated to have land in the eastern part of the parish, near the present Woodcote House, but it also had lands in Goring and Checkendon.[94] In the 17th century the manor also included land in Rotherfield Peppard and Ipsden.[95]

John Knapp, a yeoman of Whitchurch, held the

manor at his death in 1549, and left it to his son Augustine, a minor, whose elder brother Henry probably held it in trust for him.[96] Augustine Knapp, the founder of Henley school, and of various charities, lived until 1602.[97] He left Woodcote to his brother Henry's son Richard Knapp,[98] a gentleman, who during the late 16th century had already been farming the manor, and was probably the first member of the family to live at Woodcote and be buried in the parish.[99]

He was succeeded in 1611 by his son Henry, who was lord of Woodcote for over 60 years.[1] He was a lawyer, a scholar, and a man of wealth, for in 1665 besides his fair-sized house in Woodcote he had largish houses in Oxford and Wallingford.[2] He died in 1674 leaving Woodcote and half Wyfold Manor in Checkendon to Mary, his daughter by his second wife Hester, the daughter of Sir Edward Clarke of Ardington (Berks.).[3] In 1677 Mary and her husband, Sir Richard Temple of Stowe (Bucks.), held the manor,[4] which passed not to her son but to her nephew Temple Stanyan, the son of Dorothy Knapp and her husband Lawrence Stanyan of Hadley (Mdx.).[5] Temple Stanyan was Under-Secretary of State.[6] On his death in 1752 his widow Grace probably held the manor until her death in 1768,[7] and it then passed to his daughter Catherine, who married Sir Charles Hardy (d. 1780), a distinguished naval officer and a member of a distinguished family.[8]

The Hardys had a son and a granddaughter, Catherine, but in 1787 Woodcote, together with half Wyfold and Checkendon manors, was sold.[9] When it was resold in 1800 the land was split up and during the 19th century only about 50 acres of land belonged to Woodcote House.[10] Henry C. Cotton owned the house in 1801;[11] Adam Duff, a member of a Scottish family, from 1830 until his death in 1870;[12] and in 1912 his grandson, R. Fraser Duff, sold it.[13] He was still called lord of Woodcote or Rawlins manor.

In the Middle Ages there was another freehold in the parish which was later known as *PAIABLES*

[82] Ch. Ch. Arch. 3. c. 3. 41.
[83] Ibid. 3. c. 3. 53; O.R.O. Misc. Pe. II/1: settlement of 1686. See also ibid. 4, 5 for 1691 mortgage.
[84] MS. Top. Oxon. c 165, p. 237, citing Adderbury Par. Reg.; Ch. Ch. Arch. 3. e. 3. 3.
[85] For Head see *V.C.H. Berks.* iv. 35. At this period the lease was sometimes held by trustees, who sometimes held the manorial courts. For details see Ch. Ch. Arch. 3. e. 3, 4, 5 and Ch. Ch. Burs. Index to reg. of leases.
[86] Ch. Ch. Arch. 1819 terrier; for King see below, p. 110.
[87] Ch. Ch. Arch. 3. e. 3. 7.
[88] MS. Top. Oxon. c 357, f. 68; Ch. Ch. Arch. 1819 terrier.
[89] *Thame Cart.* ii. 120.
[90] *Eynsham Cart.* i. 192; *Goring Chart.* i. 107; *Rot. Hund.* (Rec. Com.), ii. 750.
[91] *Eynsham Cart.* ii. 135. For the family see ibid. and *Goring Chart.* index.
[92] Ch. Ch. Arch. 3. e. 3. 1. Stoke land was attached to Elvington manor from the 14th to the 18th cents.: *Goring Chart.* ii. 172 and *passim*; O.R.O. PL I/22, 81.
[93] *Lincoln Diocese Documents, 1450–1544* (E.E.T.S. cxlix), 68.
[94] O. G. Knapp, *Hist. of the Chief English Families Bearing the Name of Knapp* (priv. printed, 1911), 82, quoting C.P. 25(2)/62/493/East. 4 Ed. VI.
[95] C.P. 25(2)/709/Trin. 29 Chas. II.
[96] Knapp, op. cit. 81, citing P.C.C. 25 Lewyn (entered in 1598); C.P. 25(2)/62/493/East. 4 Ed. VI.
[97] *V.C.H. Oxon.* i. 470; see below, p. 111.
[98] Knapp, op. cit. 81–83, quoting P.C.C. 79 Montague and C 142/410/74.

[99] *Par. Coll.* iii. 349; Knapp, op. cit. 83. His will is P.C.C. 32 Fenner.
[1] The manor may have been mortgaged between 1605 and 1631: C.P. 25(2)/339/Trin. 3 Jas. I; 473/Hil. 6 Chas. I.
[2] *Hearth Tax Oxon.* 55; *Oxf. City Documents* (O.H.S. xviii), 91; Knapp, op. cit. 84. For him see Knapp, op. cit. 83–85; for his M.I. in Checkendon *Par. Coll.* i. 86.
[3] Knapp, op. cit. 84, citing P.C.C. 127 Bunce.
[4] C.P. 25(2)/709/Trin. 29 Chas. II; see also ibid. 710/Mich. 33 Chas. II.
[5] Knapp, op. cit. 86–87. For Susannah Newman, another daughter of Henry Knapp, who may have held the manor in her lifetime, see below, p. 110.
[6] *D.N.B.* under Abraham Stanyan.
[7] In 1759 the Earl of Uxbridge was the tenant of Temple Stanyan's widow: Oxf. Dioc. d 557; see ibid. c 434, f. 59b for her burial.
[8] For him see *D.N.B.*
[9] C.P. 43/815/304; O.R.O. Misc. Ou. I/1. For descent of family see Knapp, op. cit. 87.
[10] *Sale cat.* in Bodl. G.A. Fol. A 266 (45). In 1800 Woodcote manor consisted of over 1,000 acres, 285 of which were woodland. Of the 4 farms belonging to it, 3 (Hook End, Checkendon, and Hammond's) were in Checkendon, and New House Farm was in Goring: ibid. 31; O.S. *Area Bk.* For Woodcote House see above, p. 95.
[11] O.R.O. Land tax assess. For the family see *D.N.B.* and above, p. 95.
[12] *Oxon. Poll of Freeholders, 1830.* For the Duffs see Burke, *Land. Gent.* (1937, &c.) under Duff of Fetteresso.
[13] *Sale Cat.* in Bodl. G.A. Oxon. b 92 (38).

manor and in the 20th century as Payables Farm. In 1366, the year in which he was Mayor of Wallingford, Nicholas Paiable held 2 virgates in Woodcote.[14] He was still a free tenant in 1390,[15] but later his estate came into the possession of the Passlew family, another free family which had been in the parish since the 12th century, when the Abbot of Eynsham had granted William Passlew 1 virgate and 21 acres,[16] 20 of them in Goring. The family continued to hold this land throughout the 13th and 14th centuries, and by 1500 had also acquired the house called Payables.[17]

In the 16th century Payables belonged to the Wilders, a prominent yeoman family of Stoke. In about 1530 it was held with 5 yardlands by Thomas Wilder; later in the century William Wilder (d. 1582) who also held 5 yardlands, lived there,[18] as did John Wilder (d. 1657), sometimes called yeoman and sometimes gentleman, in the next century.[19]

The estate seems first to have been called a manor in the late 17th century,[20] and in the 19th century it was known as Payables manor 'within the general manor', attached to which was Payables farm of about 200 acres.[21] By 1688, when it was conveyed to two members of the Justice family, it evidently no longer belonged to the Wilders, and by 1754 it may have been bought by the Claxsons, for John Claxson was returned as a 40-shilling freeholder in that year.[22] It was owned and farmed by members of this family, some of whom were also Reading drapers, until the 1850's.[23]

HYDE manor, which appears in the 16th century, consisted of some 200 acres in Stoke, Woodcote, and Goring.[24] There was a house called Hyde House, and it gave its name to Hyde Lease and Hyde Sheephouse, but the manor cannot be located.[25] It originated in the medieval freehold of the de la Hyde family. The greater part of the estate was not held, like the rest of the parish, of Eynsham Abbey, but belonged to the 2 fees in Burcot, Clifton Hampden, Toot Baldon, and Stoke held of the Bishop of Lincoln in 1279 by William de Baldon or de Baldinton, who was lord of Little Baldon manor.[26] The descent of the overlordship has not been traced, but in about 1545 over three-quarters of the manor was held of the Earl of Derby, who was probably lord of Goring manor.[27] In 1279 a croft and in 1366 a virgate belonged to Eynsham's manor of South Stoke,[28] and in the 16th century 42 acres were held of Christ Church, Eynsham's successor.[29]

By 1227 Roger de la Hyde held land in Stoke.[30] He was probably the same as the Sir Roger de la Hyde who held there and who also had land in Goring in the early 1250's.[31] In 1279 Sir Richard de la Hyde, Sir Roger's son, had an estate of more than 4 virgates in Stoke,[32] as well as land in Burcot and Adwell.[33] He was a prominent local knight, and was still alive in 1305.[34] The De la Hydes were an important Berkshire family, but it has not been possible to trace this branch.[35] Isabella de la Hyde may have been holding the estate in 1366, and at some time in the 15th century it belonged to John Hyde.[36] His grandson Thomas held it until 1503,[37] and it then came into the possession of Sir Bartholomew Rede (d. 1505), goldsmith and lord mayor of London.[38]

Sir Bartholomew's heir was his nephew William, also a London goldsmith, who lived at Oatlands manor in Weybridge (Surr.).[39] He died in 1534[40] and was succeeded by his son John, a minor who died in 1545, leaving a young son likewise named John, who was a ward of the king.[41] The first John Rede and his son had to uphold their claim to Hyde manor against Thomas Hyde, apparently the son of the Thomas Hyde who had parted with it in 1503. The outcome of the two suits brought by Hyde in the 1540's, one in Chancery and one in the Court of Requests, claiming that the Redes had no valid title, has not been found.[42] John Rede sold his Berkshire manors in about 1580, and by the late 16th century Hyde manor belonged to William Palmer (d. 1598), the lessee of the principal Stoke manor.[43] In his will he left Hyde to his son Thomas, to whom he also left his Wigginton manor (Herts.).[44] It is not clear whether or not Thomas Palmer held Hyde at his death in 1608.[45] The last reference to the manor which has been found is in a recovery of 1609.[46]

ECONOMIC HISTORY. Domesday provides the first information about the settlement at South Stoke, which was probably an early one as both the form of the name and the position of the village on the river indicate.[47] The village appears to have prospered in the years after the Conquest under the administration of Bishop Remigius: in 1086 the value of the

[14] *Boarstall Cart.* 264; *Eynsham Cart.* ii. 135–6.
[15] Ch. Ch. Arch. 3.e. 3. 1.
[16] *Eynsham Cart.* ii. 138; *Rot. Hund.* (Rec. Com.), ii. 750.
[17] *Eynsham Cart.* ii. 131; Ch. Ch. Arch. 3. e. 3. 1.
[18] Ch. Ch. Arch. 3. e. 3. 1; Bodl. MS. Wills Oxon. 187, f. 108*b*.
[19] P.C.C. 20 Rutten; Higgs, *Hist. of Higges Family*, 386, quoting C 5/383/78.
[20] C.P. 25(2)/792/East. 4 Jas. II.
[21] O.R.O. CH SO I/7.
[22] C.P. 25(2)/792/East. 4 Jas. II; *Oxon. Poll of Freeholders, 1754.* John Claxson had been churchwarden in 1685: Oxf. Archd. Oxon. b 41, f. 109.
[23] Ch. Ch. Arch. 1819 terrier; O.R.O. CH SO I/9, 10. For their charity see below, p. 111.
[24] Ch. Ch. Bursary, Bk. of evidence; C 1/1012/33.
[25] Dunkin MS. 439/2, ff. 324, 325*b*. Hyde Lease lay north of Stoke village: Ch. Ch. Arch. 1819 terrier.
[26] *Rot. Hund.* (Rec. Com.), ii. 749, 751; *V.C.H. Oxon.* v. 51.
[27] Ch. Ch. Burs. Bk. of evid.; *L. & P. Hen. VIII*, iii (2), p. 1186.
[28] *Rot. Hund.* ii. 751; *Eynsham Cart.* ii. 133.
[29] Ch. Ch. Burs. Bk. of evid.; Bodl. MS. d.d. Ch. Ch. M 88.
[30] *Fines Oxon.* 79.

[31] *Eynsham Cart.* i. 206; *Goring Chart.* i. 15. For his seal see ibid. 17.
[32] *Rot. Hund.* (Rec. Com.), ii. 751.
[33] See above, p. 68.
[34] For him see *Knights of Ed. I*, ii (Harl. Soc. lxxxi), 261.
[35] *V.C.H. Berks.* iii. 420; *Goring Chart.* ii, p. xcv.
[36] *Eynsham Cart.* ii. 133; Req. 2/1/106, where the descent of the family is given. John Hyde's wife was Agnes and their son William.
[37] C.P. 25(2)/191/31/Mich. and Hil. 19 Hen. VII.
[38] Ch. Ch. Arch. 3. e. 3. 1. For Rede see A. B. Beaven, *Aldermen of London*, ii. 19; Compton Reade, *Record of the Redes*, 121; *V.C.H. Berks.* iii. 506; iv. 325.
[39] *V.C.H. Surr.* iii. 477. For pedigree see *Visit. Surrey* (Harl. Soc. xliii), 68.
[40] C 142/57/30.
[41] *V.C.H. Surr.* iii. 477; Ch. Ch. Burs. Bk. of evid.; C 142/72/81.
[42] C 1/1012/33; Req. 2/1/106.
[43] *V.C.H. Berks.* iii. 506; iv. 325; *Par. Coll.* iii. 349.
[44] Dunkin MS. 439/2, f. 324; *V.C.H. Herts.* ii. 315.
[45] His inq. is C 142/304/77, his will P.C.C. 29 Dorset.
[46] C.P. 43/105/36, between Sir Edmund Ashfield and Thos. Moore. Richard Moore was guardian of Palmer's children: *V.C.H. Herts.* ii. 315.
[47] *P.N. Oxon.* (E.P.N.S.), i. 156.

estate—£12 and 12 sticks of eels—was double its pre-Conquest one of £6. The Bishop of Lincoln's estate there was assessed at 17 hides and 1 virgate of land, of which 8 hides were in demesne. Of the 10 ploughs in the parish, only 2 were in demesne, while 8 were shared between 25 peasants.[48]

Neither the hamlet of Woodcote (the name means 'cottage in the wood') or the woods which undoubtedly covered much of the eastern part of the parish are recorded in Domesday, but when Stoke was confirmed to Eynsham by Henry I in 1109 Woodcote with the wood belonging to it was also confirmed to it.[49] Later evidence shows that the boundary between the two townships followed the Icknield Way for the most part and that each township had its own field system, an arrangement which is likely to have come into existence long before the grant to Eynsham. By the mid-13th century Woodcote was large enough to be called *villa* and another settlement at Exlade (the name means 'a clearing in the wood') is recorded.[50] The western half of the parish was commonly called 'below hill' or 'low hill' and the eastern half 'above hill' or 'up hill'. They formed separate tithings.[51]

Eynsham Abbey acquired South Stoke in about 1094, and throughout the Middle Ages the manor was one of its most valuable possessions. In 1269 it was valued at £31 19s. 2d., and in 1291 at £42 6s. 11d.[52] In 1366 the annual value of Stoke and Woodcote was estimated at about £61 10s. This was made up of receipts from rents, works, and tithes from the demesne farm, the fishery, the mill, and the wood.[53] This was not a net figure, for from it had to be paid wages, farm equipment, and the upkeep of the abbey's household in the parish. Accounts of the second half of the 14th century show that total receipts from the manor varied from between about £70 and £90 a year.[54]

Eynsham carried on demesne farming at Stoke until the late 14th or early 15th century. The abbey's demesne in 1269 was said to consist of 12 virgates; in 1279 of 8 or 9 virgates.[55] Since the virgate consisted of 15 field acres, the abbey's demesne of 325 acres of arable land in 1366 seems to have been larger than in the 13th century.[56]

The abbey had a manor-house and other offices in grounds of nearly 2½ acres, and in 1366 these were valued at 6s. 8d. a year.[57] Its regular staff numbered nine or ten. There were slight variations in its composition. In 1396–7 it consisted of a carter, a shepherd, three ploughmen (2 *fugatores* and 1 *tentator*), a woodward, a cowherd, a swineherd, a dairymaid, and an accountant. Wages, totalling £3 9s. 4d., ranged from 12s. for the carter to 4s. for the cowherd and swineherd.[58] Since 1356–7 wages had risen; at that

time they amounted to £2 2s. and in 1372–3 to £2 17s. 4d. The wages of a ploughman, for example, had increased from 5s. to 7s., and then to 8s.; the wages of a carter, 6s. in 1356, had doubled; the woodward, however, still received 5s.[59]

From the extent of the abbey's demesne something can be learned of the topography of the medieval parish. In the early 13th century there was probably a two-field system,[60] but a change to a three-field system seems to have been in progress in 1240 when the abbot was accused by a freeholder of depriving him of his common pasture in Stoke and Woodcote by dividing into three parts land which had always been in two parts.[61] In 1366 there was undoubtedly a three-course rotation in Stoke Field, two fields being sown every year while the third lay fallow. The three fields were the South Field, the Middle Field, to which, because it was the smallest, had been added the Small North Field, and the North Field.[62] The abbey's arable demesne, all of which lay in Stoke and none in Woodcote Field, was divided in the proportion of 136 acres (South Field), 74 acres (Middle Field) and 64½ acres (North Field).[63] There had been some amalgamation of strips, for much of the land lay in holdings of 2 or 3 acres. The value of the arable varied greatly, the land in some places being worth 4d. an acre, and in others as little as 1d. There is no evidence for the arrangement of the fields at Woodcote, but it is unlikely that the common field can have been as extensive as that of Stoke, for much of the upland part of the township probably always consisted of inclosed crofts made on land cleared piecemeal from the scrub or woods.[64] In the south of the parish, along the Goring boundary, the abbey had an arable field of 51 acres called 'Childeslonde', which did not form part of the ordinary field system. In fact, although part of Stoke manor, it was in the parish of Goring.[65] It was poor land, worth only 1d. an acre, but in virtue of this property the abbey had valuable rights of pasture in Goring.[66] This right was disputed in 1345, but it was finally agreed that the abbey's beasts at 'Childeslonde' might pasture in the common fields there, and the monks were allowed to build a house on their estate.[67] In 1366 they had rights of common for 500 sheep in 500 acres of the fields of Goring.[68] In Stoke parish, the abbey's most important pasture land may have been the 60 acres it held in Woodcote Heath.[69] Part of it was inclosed by the mid-13th century.[70] In 1366, however, no part of Woodcote Heath was included among the abbey's separate demesne pasture, which consisted of about 10 acres, and with the meadow after mowing was able to feed 14 cart horses, a bull, and 8 cows and their calves.[71]

There was some meadow in Woodcote, but most

[48] *V.C.H. Oxon.* i. 402.
[49] *Eynsham Cart.* i. 36.
[50] Ibid. 192; *P.N. Oxon.* (E.P.N.S.), 156–7.
[51] Stoke and Woodcote were separately assessed for the land tax: d.d. Wykeham-Musgrave c 33, particular of Stoke; Ch. Ch. Arch. 1819 terrier; O.R.O. Land tax assess.
[52] *Eynsham Cart.* i. 10; *Tax. Eccl.* (Rec. Com.), 45.
[53] *Eynsham Cart.* ii. 118–37. It was stated in 1279 that the abbot held half the Thames in demesne from Stoke Marmion mill to 'Mereway': *Rot. Hund.* (Rec. Com.), ii. 750.
[54] d.d. Ch. Ch. M 91 (1356–7), M 92 (1372–3), M 93 (1396–7).
[55] *Eynsham Cart.* i. 10; *Rot. Hund.* (Rec. Com.), ii. 750.
[56] *Eynsham Cart.* ii. 128, 126.
[57] Ibid. 120, 128.   [55] d.d. Ch. Ch. M 93.

[59] Ibid. 91–93.
[60] For furlong names see *Eynsham Cart.* i. 152–5. These charters (1213–27) granting lands in the fields give names of furlongs only.
[61] *V.C.H. Oxon.* ii. 171; H. L. Gray, *English Field Systems*, 80.   [62] *Eynsham Cart.* ii. 120, 122, 123.
[63] Ibid. 122–5.
[64] For scattered farms and Woodcote heath see below, p. 103.
[65] *Eynsham Cart.* i. 216; ii. 125. For its acquisition see ibid. i. 106, 107, 110–11.   [66] Ibid. ii. 126, 127.
[67] *Goring Chart.* ii. 170–1.
[68] *Eynsham Cart.* ii. 126, 127.
[69] *Rot. Hund.* (Rec. Com.), ii. 750.
[70] *Eynsham Cart.* i. 192, 216.
[71] Ibid. ii. 126–7.

of the meadow lay along the Thames. Here, no doubt, were the 24 acres recorded in Domesday Book.[72] In 1366 the abbey had 17 acres which were separate for the whole year: at the first mowing the acre was valued at 4s. and at 1s. 8d. at the second except in years when there were floods.[73] The total value of meadow and pasture was estimated at £6 8s. 10d., as compared with the £2 9s. 8⅞d. at which the arable land was valued.[74]

The windmill was out of repair at the time of the survey, but when repaired it was worth 30s. a year, and all the abbey's villein tenants of Stoke and Woodcote were bound to grind their corn at it. It is first recorded in 1220–7 and in 1269 was said to be worth 13s. 6d.[75]

The abbey's most valuable source of income was its tenants, who paid money rents and on whose labour the manor was largely dependent. In 1269, of the manor's total value of £31 19s. 2d., £28 came from rents.[76] At the more detailed estimate of 1366, rents amounted to £36 3s. 3d., of which £20 10s. 7d. came from Woodcote, or more than half the total value of the manor (about £61 10s.), while the services of the tenants were valued at another £10 19s. 9d.[77] A small income was also derived from the three-weekly manorial courts, probably held in the hall of South Stoke manor-house,[78] which all tenants from Stoke and Woodcote, free and customary, had to attend. The abbey also held view of frankpledge once a year in June.[79]

In 1279 Stoke, with some 30 landowners, was the larger of the two villages. There were 21 villein virgaters who paid 5s. 9d. rent and owed well-defined labour services for their house and land. In addition 2 villeins held 2 virgates each; 4 cottagers held a few acres for varying rents; and 5 free tenants held in all 3 virgates and 6½ acres, and 20 acres in Goring. In Woodcote in contrast with Stoke, where most of the land was held in villeinage, over half was held freely. Of the 18 free virgates, 4 did not belong to Eynsham and were held by military service by a tenant of William de Baldon. Six tenants held in socage of the abbey, paying rents varying from 3s. 6d. to 14s. a virgate and 1s. for a croft. Twelve villeins held a virgate each and two a ½-virgate. The Woodcote virgater had formerly owed the same services as the Stoke one, but much of his work had been commuted for money. He paid a rent of 13s. 4d., more than double the rent for a Stoke virgate. He still owed certain services, however, principally a plough-service and a boon-work.[80]

In 1279 in the two villages there was a total of about 50 landholders. The population was thus relatively large, as is also shown by early-14th-century tax assessments. In 1306 there were 34 contributors (21 in Stoke and 13 in Woodcote in which Exlade was probably included) and 40 in 1327 in all the parish, a few more than in Watlington or Dorchester.[81] In 1366, when a complete survey of the manor was made, the total number of tenants recorded was higher than in 1279. In Stoke there were

45 recorded tenants: 2 freeholders with a virgate each, 20 villein virgaters, 8 villeins with holdings, larger than a virgate (the largest being of 3 virgates), and 15 villeins (mostly cottagers) with holdings smaller than a virgate.[82] In Woodcote, on the other hand, there were fewer landholders recorded than in 1279, 15 in all. Instead of the 12 villein virgaters of 1279 there were now five. There were 5 other villeins, one of them with 2 virgates, the rest with less than one. The other 5 tenants, with estates of between 2 and 5 virgates, were free.[83]

From this survey it seems clear that the population and the area of cultivation, particularly at Woodcote, had increased after 1279 and subsequently declined: in 1279 some 60 virgates, excluding the demesne, were listed, and in 1366 between 80 and 85, but of these some 15 were vacant at Woodcote; indeed, nearly two-thirds of the virgate holdings there were in the abbey's hands, a consequence perhaps of the Black Death.

All the inhabitants were under obligations to the abbey. Free tenants usually had to do homage and suit of court; the abbey was entitled to wardship, marriage, relief on entry, and a heriot from them. Most tenants had to come in Lent with their ploughs to the spring ploughing (magna precaria) if required, and with their households and families to take part in the harvest (metbedrep).[84] The villein obligations were much heavier. A villein's son might not enter the church or his daughter marry without the abbey's consent, nor could he sell a horse or ox without licence; on taking up a holding he had to pay a fine (40s. was common for a virgate); and on his death his best beast was taken as a heriot.[85] Labour services were heavy and varied according to the amount of land held. The virgate holder in Stoke had to take part in the major farming activities: ploughing, hoeing, mowing the meadow, making and carrying hay, and with his household gathering and carrying away the harvest. He owed various other dues and services: pannage (1d. for a pig); a chicken at Christmas and ten eggs at Easter; Peter's Pence;[86] 'tolcestr' if he brewed at the abbey's inn (2d. or 2 gallons of ale); 'Lodpenny', the payment for carrying a cartload of wood from the abbot's wood at Exlade to the manor-house in Stoke; in November 1d. 'heryngsilver' for carrying herrings from either Stoke or Henley to Eynsham, and in Lent 4s. with his neighbours for 'heryngsilver'; and he also owed an aid each year.[87] The Woodcote virgater was under the same personal obligations as the Stoke one, but his services were much lighter.[88] The value of rents in Stoke amounted to about £15, while services and other dues were valued at £10 6s. 3d. In Woodcote rents were worth £20 10s. 7d. and services only 13s. 6d.[89]

Accounts for the year 1396–7 suggest that the demesne farm was predominantly an arable one: the sale of wool realized £4 9s. compared with £12 5s. 4d. for grain and £12 16s. 4d. for pigs, hay, &c.[90] In the 13th century the crops sown were wheat, mixtillia (a

[72] Eynsham Cart. i. 184; V.C.H. Oxon. i. 402
[73] Eynsham Cart. ii. 126.
[74] Ibid. 126, 127.
[75] Ibid. i. 154, 10.
[76] Ibid. 10.
[77] Ibid. ii. 128–34, 137.
[78] Ibid. 215.
[79] d.d. Ch. Ch. M 91.
[80] Rot. Hund. (Rec. Com.) ii. 750–1; and see above, p. 85, n. 80.
[81] E 179/161/10, 9.
[82] Eynsham Cart. ii. 128–33.
[83] Ibid. 134–7.
[84] Ibid. 131, 132.
[85] Ibid. 128–9.
[86] See below, p. 105.
[87] Eynsham Cart. ii. 128–9.
[88] Ibid. 134–5.
[89] Ibid. 128–34, 137.
[90] d.d. Ch. Ch. M 93.

mixture of wheat and rye), barley, corn cut green (*tramasium*), and oats.[91] The concentration on arable farming, which still prevailed in the 20th century, was likely to have been common at all times owing to the lack of a good water-supply for Stoke Field. There was, however, a sheep fair at Woodcote, which was still being held in 1852. It is first recorded by Rawlinson, but as it was held on the Monday after St. Leonard's Day, the patron saint of Woodcote, it is likely to have been of medieval origin.[92]

The main developments in the 15th century were the end of demesne farming; a continuing decline in the number of tenants; and an increase in the size of farms. In the 1390's Eynsham was still managing its demesne farm through a resident bailiff, but by 1425 the manor-house and land was let for £8 a year, though the bailiff continued to collect dues and rents and hold the courts.[93] In 1460 the abbey leased the entire manor and rectory for 30 years at £34 a year. Some years later the monks claimed that the abbot had charged too low a rent to the lessees, who were his officers, from the 'affection and favour' he felt towards them and that the lessees had broken their contract by selling wood to the yearly value of £10, all of which caused the abbey's 'decay and poverty'.[94] Leasing ceased for some years in the 16th century, but in 1536 Eynsham granted an 80-year lease at £53 6s. 8d.,[95] a sum not far from the manor's 1535 valuation.[96] From this lease the woods were specifically excluded.

The decline in the number of tenants is indicated by the fact that in 1396–7 about 10 virgates were vacant, while by 1424–5 there were more than 13 vacant. Again, in 1396–7 33 customary tenants owed 'Lodpence', while in 1424–5 only 24 did so. In the same period the value of Peter's Pence (1d. per household) declined from 3s. 7d. to 2s. 9d.[97] By about 1530 the pattern of landholding, especially in Stoke, had radically changed. The amount of land under cultivation was approximately the same, but instead of the 45 tenants of 1366, there were now only 17 or 18 tenants. Instead of a virgate being the average holding, there were only 6 farms of a yardland; the rest were larger and 6 of these were of at least 4 yardlands. At Woodcote farms remained small, the largest being of 3 yardlands, while the number of customary tenants was about the same as in 1366. In Stoke rents had gone up, the rent for a yardland now being 8s. or 9s., while services were probably no longer rendered; in Woodcote, on the other hand, where services had been light, rents had slightly decreased.[98]

In the 16th and 17th centuries there were many

prosperous yeoman families. Fifteen people were taxed for the subsidy of 1577, mostly on goods worth between £3 and £5.[99] Thirty-three houses, about half with more than one hearth, were assessed for the 1665 hearth tax, although four of these were discharged by poverty.[1] The principal family which survived from the 16th to the 19th century was the Higgs family: 'the name of Higgs most noted family here', Rawlinson wrote in the early 18th century.[2] By 1819, however, the family had disappeared as landowners, although they continued in the parish as labourers, carters, and carpenters.[3] Other yeoman families which survived from the 16th to the 18th or 19th centuries were those of Wilder and Crutchfield.[4] The Crutchfields seem to have died out by the 19th century, but the Wilders, one branch of which had been freeholders and lived at Payables,[5] were smiths in the early 19th century.[6]

In the 17th and 18th centuries the parish continued to consist largely of small and medium-sized farms, the Manor farm excepted. In 1669–70, for example, there were about 50 copyhold tenants on the manor, with holdings varying from a few acres to 6 yardlands. There were probably about 26 farms of 1 yardland or more; of these 6 were fairly large with 4 or more yardlands.[7] These copyhold estates were usually held for three lives, the rent for a yardland averaging about 10s. Fines were payable on admission, and heriots continued; a £3 or £4 heriot, for example, might be paid for a yardland in the early 18th century. Occasionally the copy was held by someone in another parish, in which case permission to sublet was given.[8]

The manor itself was leased on seven-year leases. These were introduced in about 1660. The rent of the manor and rectory, excluding the woods, was then £35 11s. 1½d. and a specified amount of grain. Fines on the renewal of a lease during the late 17th century, starting in 1669/70, were £200. In the early 18th century they varied between £280 and £350. From 1747, when the fine was £437 10s., they rose to £770 in 1775, £959 in 1796, and £1,323 in 1831.[9] In about 1860 the practice of leasing the manor came to an end; Christ Church took over the land and let it at rack rents.[10] A condition of the lease was that the lessee was to hold a court leet and court baron every year.[11] These courts were held until the 1920's. The later ones dealt only with surrenders and admissions, but at an earlier period the parish officers were chosen. In the early 18th century these consisted of the constable and three tithing men, one each for Stoke, Woodcote, and Exlade Street.[12] In the early

[91] *Eynsham Cart.* i. 8.
[92] *Par. Coll.* iii. 348; Gardner, *Dir. Oxon.* (1852).
[93] d.d. Ch. Ch. M 93, 94.
[94] *Eynsham Cart.* ii, pp. lxviii–ix; C I/54/217.
[95] *Eynsham Cart.* ii. 139–40, 241–2.
[96] The net value of the manor was £34 9s. 8d. and that of the rectory £13 10s. 8d.: *Valor Eccl.* (Rec. Com.), ii. 208, 210.   [97] d.d. Ch. Ch. M 93, 94.
[98] *Eynsham Cart.* ii. 139–40.   [99] E 179/162/341.
[1] *Hearth Tax Oxon.* 55–56.   [2] *Par. Coll.* iii. 274.
[3] For Griffith Higgs see above, p. 102; for the family see W. M. Higgs, *Hist. of the Higges Family of S. Stoke and Thatcham* (1933); on pp. 349–58 is a list of all the Higges entries in the parish register.
[4] *Chant. Cert.* 105; E 179/162/341; *Hearth Tax Oxon.* 55–56; d.d. Wykeham-Musgrave c 33, particular of Stoke.
[5] See above, p. 98.   [6] Ch. Ch. Arch. 1819 terrier.
[7] Ibid. 1669–70 lease. The properties are listed by annual value, but their size can be roughly calculated from this. A farm of 3 yardlands, for example, was valued at

£25: ibid. 3. c. 3. 47. For a list of tenants c. 1740 see d.d. Wykeham-Musgrave c 33, particular of Stoke.
[8] MS. Top. Oxon. c 357, ff. 7, 11, 22 and *passim*.
[9] Ch. Ch. Bursary, Bk. of evidence and Index to register of leases.
[10] Ch. Ch. Arch. 3. c. 4. 43; inf. Ch. Ch. Bursary.
[11] Ch. Ch. Bursary, Bk. of evid. and Index to reg. of leases. At one time it was specified that the college's steward was to hold the courts and the lessee was only allowed to do so on payment of £100. From the 17th century, at any rate, the lessee held the courts.
[12] MS. Top. Oxon. c 357, f. 1. Except for a few excerpts (14th–16th cent.: Ch. Ch. Arch. 3. e. 3. 1), court records before the 17th century have been lost. In Ch. Ch. Arch. there are deeds from c. 1635 arising from the courts, and court books from 1704 to the 20th cent. All are calendared in 'Catalogue of Manorial Records of Christ Church' (copy in Bodl.). MS. Top. Oxon. c 357 is the duplicate of a court book from 1704 to c. 1740. The books were written in Latin until 1734.

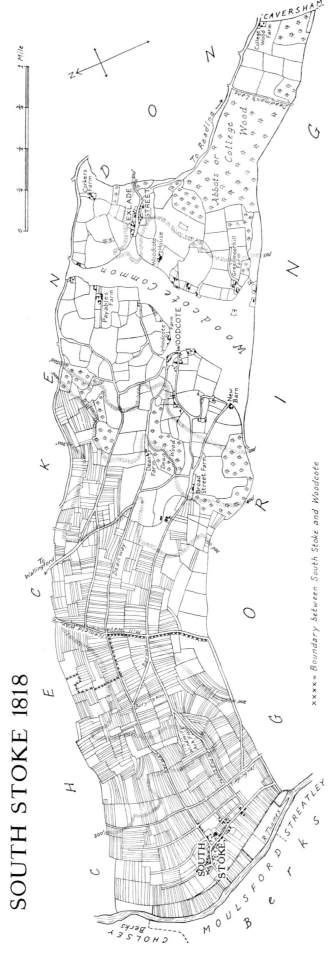

SOUTH STOKE 1818

xxxx = Boundary between South Stoke and Woodcote

Map showing early inclosure in the upland part of South Stoke. Based on a map of 1818 by Frederic Young in the possession of Christ Church, Oxford.

19th century there were two tithing men, two constables, and a hayward.[13]

The lessees of the manor held Manor farm or 'the farm'; it was Eynsham Abbey's old demesne farm and the largest in the parish. In about 1740 it consisted of between 350 and 400 acres of open-field land;[14] in 1819 there were 314 acres.[15] By then its arable strips in each open-field furlong had been consolidated; few were smaller than an acre and many were of several acres.

In the 19th century Stoke was still a parish of small farms. In 1819 Christ Church owned 16 holdings, not counting the Manor farm, compared with 17 in 1740. Of these 6 were of between 50 and 100 acres and 5 of over 100 acres. Outside the manor there were 11 farms of 20 or more acres, and only 4 of them were over 50 acres.[16] These numbers had changed little by the time of inclosure in 1853, when there were still some 15 farms of which 6 were between 100 and 150 acres, and the rest were under 100 acres except for Manor farm (660 a.) in Stoke and Christ Church's Woodcote farm (300 a.).[17]

Before 1853, Stoke was largely an open-field parish. In the 17th century, as in the 14th, Stoke itself had three fields of about 1,000 field acres in all, the Great South Field, the Great North Field, and the Little North Field. The last, which was in the north-west corner of the township, was much smaller than the others. The vicar held 5 strips there, as compared with 31 in the Great North Field and 23 in the Great South Field.[18] Holdings of only a few acres were divided fairly evenly between the two large fields.[19] By 1819 there had been little consolidation, apart from the strips of Manor farm. The vicar's glebe (29½ a.), which had consisted of 59 strips in 1685, was divided into nearly as many in 1819, scattered among some 30 furlongs.[20]

At this time Woodcote had five fields (400 acres in all) of varying sizes—Leasedown, Coombe, Round, and Durley Fields and the Furlong—among which all the Woodcote open-field properties were divided.[21] It is likely that part of its arable may never have belonged to a field system: the presence of isolated farmhouses, some of which go back to the Middle Ages, is an indication of early inclosure. In addition there is a record of 42 acres of closes in the manor of Hyde in 1545, of 95 acres of old inclosures at Payables, and of 70 acres of inclosed arable at Dean farm in 1817.[22] By 1819 at any rate the land on both sides of Woodcote Heath was inclosed. Woodcote Heath (c. 250 a.) itself was uninclosed. It was waste land of the manor and an attempt by Christ Church in the 1650's to inclose it had been either partly or entirely unsuccessful, because the freeholders, including Reading Corporation, had joined in resisting it.[23]

While the parish's common pasture lay in Woodcote, its meadow was mostly along the Thames in Stoke. By the 19th century Woodcote Meadow, still a lot meadow in the 17th century, had gone, and only Great Common and Little Common Meadows remained.[24] Farmers whose lands lay in Woodcote had to cross the parish to reach their meadow.[25] As in the Middle Ages, an acre of meadow went with each yardland of arable.[26]

By the award of 1853 about 1,750 acres was inclosed.[27] The largest allotment (c. 260 a.) went to Christ Church and the lessee of Manor farm, Isaac King, who also received another allotment of 145 acres. There were about 50 other allotments of which 11 were between 50 and 150 acres and all but 3 of the rest were of less than 20 acres, some being of no more than a few perches. Christ Church was awarded 7½ acres for rights on the waste, and the churchwardens and overseers about 14 acres.[28]

Throughout its history the woods have played an important part in the economy of Stoke. Woodcote's wood was confirmed to Eynsham Abbey with the vill in 1109 by Henry I.[29] In 1366 the abbey had at Exlade 348½ acres of wood, which stretched along the road from Reading to Wallingford and was therefore considerably larger than the present College Wood (77 a.). The tenants of Stoke and Woodcote had rights of common there, as did Notley Abbey's grange of Caversham. For this privilege the canons paid two pounds of wax a year to Eynsham.[30] The value of the wood was estimated at £3 13s. 4d. a year, which included housebote and haybote for the manor-house and the rector.[31]

When Eynsham leased the manor in 1460, it provided that no sale of wood was to be made, but the lessees were later accused of selling £10 worth of wood a year, thereby causing the destruction of the woods.[32] At the visitation of 1520 the abbot himself was said to have sold an excessive amount of wood in Stoke and other places, and was commanded not to sell wood without the consent of the monks.[33] When the manor was again leased in 1536, Abbot's Wood and all the other woods 'now being inclosed and copsed' were excepted from the lease of the manor. The lessee was to receive 30 loads of hardwood for fuel, and the woodward was to assign him wood for hedgebote, cartbote, and ploughbote. The customary tenants were to have enough wood to keep their houses in repair.[34] Christ Church continued the policy of keeping the woods in its own hands, but allowing the lessee of the manor and the tenants the same amount as the abbey had allowed.[35] The vicar also was entitled to 8 loads a year and pannage for his swine.[36] In the 18th century all tenants, both freeholders and copyholders, had rights of common in the college woods, but only the copyholders were

[13] Ch. Ch. Arch. 3. c. 3. 27.
[14] d.d. Wykeham-Musgrave c 33.
[15] Ch. Ch. Arch. 1819 terrier.
[16] Ibid.
[17] Bodl. Tithe award; H.O. 107/1690/2.
[18] Oxf. Archd. Oxon. b 41, f. 109: 1685 terrier.
[19] MS. Top. Oxon. c 357, f. 7.
[20] Ch. Ch. Arch. 1819 terrier. No fields are mentioned at this date.
[21] Ibid.
[22] O.R.O. CH SO/I/2; CH SO/III/2.
[23] Ch. Ch. Bursary, Bk. of evidence, quoting an order of 1651 for inclosure of Woodcote and Exlade Heath from Ch. Ch. Chapter bk. f. 44; Hist. MSS. Com. *11th Rep. App. Pt. VII*, 192.

[24] Oxf. Archd. Oxon. b 41, f. 109; Ch. Ch. Arch. 1819 terrier.   [25] Ch. Ch. Arch. 1819 terrier.
[26] e.g. MS. Top. Oxon. c 357, f. 7.
[27] O.R.O. CH SO/I/8. There is a good deal of material about the inclosure in CH SO/I, II, and III.
[28] O.R.O. Incl. award. There are two maps with the award.
[29] *Eynsham Cart.* i. 36.
[30] *Eynsham Cart.* ii. 127.
[31] Ibid.   [32] C 1/54/217.
[33] *Visit. Dioc. Linc. 1517-31*. ii. 143.
[34] *Eynsham Cart.* ii. 241-2.
[35] Ch. Ch. Bursary. Bk. of evidence and Index to reg. of leases.
[36] Oxf. Archd. Oxon. b 41, f. 109.

allowed timber for the repair of their houses.[37] In the late 18th or early 19th century tenants may have lost some if not all of their rights in the woods, for by 1819 College Wood farm, in the south-eastern corner of the parish, had been formed, and its tenant was leasing College Wood (142 a.).[38]

In the hundred years after inclosure, except for its woods, of which there were over 350 acres in 1878,[39] Stoke remained largely an arable parish. In 1914, 70 per cent. of its agricultural land was arable and 29 per cent. pasture.[40] By 1958 arable still predominated, but many farms had been amalgamated. The tenant of Christ Church at Manor farm farmed about 1,000 acres: his farm was mostly arable and was highly mechanized.[41] At Woodcote the largest farm was Woodcote or Church farm (c. 350 a.), which Christ Church had recently sold to the tenant. The land of several of the old farms had been sold off, and some Woodcote land was farmed from Checkendon and Goring. Mixed farming was the general practice in this part of the parish. Pedigree Frisians and Ayrshires were kept on two farms in Woodcote. Reading was the local market, but milk went to Slough and the Milk Marketing Board.[42]

The population of the parish (excluding recent additions) has probably doubled since the 17th century, for Woodcote has developed in the 20th century as a residential area and has grown larger than the mother village of Stoke. In 1676 the adult population of the parish was 232.[43] In about 1718 there were said to be round about 80 houses;[44] in 1759 there were between 90 and 100;[45] from 1768 until 1790 the vicars reported about 100;[46] and by 1811 there were 125, inhabited by 142 families.[47] The population rose from 645 in 1811 to 907 in 1841; it declined to 717 in 1891, but has risen since to 1,025 in 1951.[48]

Stoke and its hamlets were until the 20th century purely agricultural villages. In 1811 out of 142 families 120 were employed in agriculture and 18 in some rural craft.[49] By 1851 the rise in population had led to an increase in both groups of workers. There were the usual village shops, a grocery, at least one smithy, and the post office in Stoke;[50] two smiths and two or three food-shops in Woodcote and Exlade; and three public houses in the parish. Woodcote and its hamlets had more craftsmen and tradesmen than Stoke; they included 2 sawyers, 2 wheelwrights, a cordwainer, a hurdlemaker, 2 lath-renders, a carrier, and a dealer in china and earthenware.[51] The three brickmakers recorded worked no doubt at the Greenmoor Hill brickworks, which had been there since at least 1742.[52] Among the more un-

usual occupations followed at Stoke were those of a straw-drawer, and a twine-spinner. There were also three dressmakers and a laundress in the village, and many Stoke women worked as agricultural labourers.[53]

By the 20th century the old craftsmen had gone. Stoke still had three small shops (one containing the post office), and Woodcote, which was no longer a rural village, had a few shops, a restaurant or two, and two garages. There were five public houses in the parish.[54] A large proportion of Woodcote people in 1920 worked outside the parish, at the R.A.F. station in Goring Heath or in Reading.

CHURCH. The church, with its chapel of Woodcote, is the only one in Dorchester hundred which is in Henley rural deanery. About 1190 it was confirmed to Eynsham Abbey, along with two other churches on the abbey's demesne manors, by Bishop Hugh of Lincoln.[55] It had evidently long been in existence, for ab antiquo it was free from all episcopal dues (ab omni onere episcopali),[56] and may well have been granted with the manor to Eynsham by the Bishop of Lincoln in about 1094.[57] It remained a rectory in the abbey's patronage until 1399, when the abbey appropriated it. In 1397 Boniface IX sanctioned the appropriation of three churches, including Stoke, giving Eynsham permission to serve them with chaplains and to farm all its property, including churches, without the bishop's permission.[58] Royal consent followed on condition that a new altar was set up in the abbey church at which masses would be said for the souls of Richard II and his late queen, Anne of Bohemia, and that vicarages were ordained and distributions made to the poor.[59] In 1399 Bishop Beaufort, who was patron of the abbey, gave his consent,[60] and it was again agreed that vicarages be ordained in order that divine services should be regularly held, the piety of the parishioners encouraged, and the cure of souls not neglected.[61] The church remained in the abbey's possession until its dissolution in 1539. In the 1530's, however, the abbey four times sold the right of presentation.[62] The rectory and advowson were granted with the manor in 1546 to Christ Church, which retained the advowson when it leased the manor.[63] The presentation of 1556 was sold,[64] but the college presented thereafter and was still patron in 1957.

Even before Eynsham appropriated the church, it was receiving a pension of a pound of pepper from it which was valued at 13d. in 1399.[65] Much more valuable were the tithes which the abbey collected in the parish.[66] These, when they were carefully listed

[37] Ch. Ch. Arch. 3. c. 3. 1, 2.
[38] Ibid. 1819 terrier.
[39] O.S. Area Bk. (1878).
[40] Orr, Oxon. Agric. maps opp. pp. 161, 201.
[41] Inf. Mr. Bullock, Manor Farm.
[42] Inf. Mr. Booker, Church Farm.
[43] Compton Census.
[44] Par. Coll. iii. 273.
[45] Oxf. Dioc. d 555. The c. 60 persons given in 1738 is probably an under-estimate; Secker's Visit.
[46] Oxf. Dioc. d 558; c 327, p. 36.
[47] Census, 1811.
[48] V.C.H. Oxon. ii. 220; Census, 1931, 1951. Some of the sharp changes in the later 19th century may be because the members of the boarding school at Woodcote House were sometimes but not always included in the census.
[49] Census, 1811. For examples of earlier craftsmen see MS. Top. Oxon. c 357, ff. 5, 68; Ch. Ch. Arch. 3. c. 3. 49; W. M. Higgs, Hist. of Higges Family, 34.

[50] Billings, Dir. Oxon. (1854).
[51] H.O. 107/1690/2.
[52] MS. Top. Oxon. c 357, f. 68.
[53] H.O. 107/1690/2.
[54] Kelly, Dir. Oxon. (1903, 1920).
[55] Eynsham Cart. i. 45; for Woodcote see below.
[56] Ibid. 47.
[57] See above, p. 96.
[58] Cal. Papal L. v. 13.
[59] Cal. Pat. 1396–9, 361, 464–5; Bodl. MS. d.d. Ch. Ch. M 86.   [60] Eynsham Cart. ii. 180–1.
[61] Ibid. 181–2.
[62] For list of medieval presentations see MS. Top. Oxon. d 460. These four included the presentation of 1549: Oxf. Dioc. d 105, p. 132.
[63] Ch. Ch. Bursary, Bk. of evidence.
[64] Oxf. Dioc. d 105, p. 172.
[65] Eynsham Cart. i. 1, 46, 307; ii, p. lxxvi.
[66] Ibid. i. 4.

in 1270, consisted principally of half the tithes of grain (*garbarum*) in almost the whole parish, and all the tithes on the demesne of Eynsham's Stoke manor.[67] The last at least by 1366 went to the support of the almonry and were collected by the almoner.[68] In 1239 the abbey also had the right to half of some of the small tithes, but it was later agreed that the rector should pay an annual pension of 5s. in place of these.[69] In 1291 Eynsham's share of the tithes was valued at £5 6s. 8d., or nearly half the value of the church (£11 6s. 8d.), and in 1390 they were worth £7 11s.[70]

According to the ordination of the vicarage in 1399, the abbey was to collect all the tithes of grain, hay, and coppice wood in the parish; all mortuaries were to go to it; and it was to have a part of the rector's house and all but 10 acres of the glebe of over 2 virgates. In return it was to be mainly responsible for the church's upkeep.[71] In 1535 the net value of the rectory to Eynsham, after the distribution of £2 in charity, was £13 10s. 8d. a year.[72]

When Eynsham leased the manor in the 15th and 16th centuries, the rectory but not the advowson was included, and this was also true of Christ Church's post-Reformation leases.[73] The lessee undertook to keep the chancel of the church in repair, and as lay rector he kept a bull and a boar for the use of the parishioners.[74] The rectory lands did not form a separate estate. Rectorial tithes in about 1740 were worth £200 and in 1853 were commuted for £765.[75]

As Eynsham took so great a proportion of the tithes, South Stoke, before its appropriation, was rather a poor living: it was valued at £5 in 1254 and £6 in 1291.[76] Part of the rector's income came from his glebe, which in 1366 consisted of 2 virgates and a close of 4 acres. He no doubt had rights of common for this like the other landholders, but he could also keep two cows and a carthorse (*affrus*) in the abbey's pasture, and had the right of housebote and haybote from the abbey's wood.[77]

When in 1399 the living became a vicarage, the incumbent was only allowed a part of the glebe house, a hall and some rooms, and garden,[78] and lost part of the income. He was allowed the small tithes only and the tithes of flax and hemp; his glebe was to consist of 8 acres of arable, including 2 'Lampeacres', and 2 of meadow; and he was to get eight loads of firewood from the abbey's wood, the trees and grass growing in the churchyard, and the offerings of the altar. His responsibilities included keeping a lamp burning in the chancel, and providing bread, wine, and light for church services (on Sundays the parishioners gave a candle) and two processional tapers.[79]

In 1535 the vicarage, valued at £12 16s., was a fairly prosperous one, but by the late 17th century the living had become a poor one: its net value in 1675 was £32 and was about the same in the early 18th century.[80] In the next 100 years it was several times augmented. Christ Church gave £10 a year from Dr. Robert South's benefaction; in 1765 Queen Anne's Bounty and Dr. Stratford's Trustees each gave £200; soon after 1800 Christ Church augmented the living by another £25 on condition that the curate's stipend be increased to £45 and that more frequent services be held; and in 1822 Queen Anne's Bounty gave another £600 to meet benefactions, including one from Christ Church and one from the vicar, John Williams.[81] The value of the living rose from £69 in 1778 to £136 in 1831.[82] In 1853 the vicar's tithes were commuted for £127 15s.[83]

In addition to his tithes, the vicar had eight loads of wood a year from the college's woods, and his glebe. The glebe consisted of about 30 acres, three times as much as in 1399, and was still owned by the vicar in 1853.[84] At the inclosure he was awarded 40 acres.

Because Eynsham had the special privilege of collecting Peter's Pence (a contribution of 1d. from every household) in five parishes, something is known about the collection of medieval church dues in the parish. Eynsham paid the archdeacon, who normally received Peter's Pence, 8s. a year and was allowed to keep any surplus for itself.[85] By the 14th century it was making a profit. In Stoke only those with cattle worth 2s. 6d. were obliged to pay.[86] In 1366 these amounted to about 45 people,[87] and in the 14th century the abbey's bailiff normally collected about 3s. 6d. a year for Peter's Pence.[88] In the 13th century the abbey also collected churchscot, worth 8d a year, a payment normally made to the parish priest.[89]

The first recorded Rector of Stoke, who appears soon before 1200, was named Ralph. He had a chaplain and lived in the parish, for he witnessed local deeds, and his parsonage is mentioned about this time.[90] Two of the 13th-century rectors—Master Osbert de Wycombe (1220–7) and Master Bartholomew de Newenton (1250–?)—were university graduates, and one, Jordan de la Pomeraye (?–1291), resigned the living in order to become a Cistercian.[91] In the 14th and 15th centuries the incumbents were not graduates. After the church was appropriated in 1399 the vicars in accordance with canon law resided, but in the early 16th century Nicholas Asheley (c. 1509–31), who was also Vicar of Aston Rowant, seems to have served Stoke church with a curate.[92]

[67] Ibid. 271, 274–5, where a detailed list is given. There is a list of 1366: ibid. ii. 119–20.
[68] Ibid. ii. 119.   [69] Ibid. i. 4; ii. 119.
[70] *Tax. Eccl.* (Rec. Com.), 30; *Eynsham Cart.* ii, p. lxviii.
[71] *Eynsham Cart.* ii. 183–5.
[72] *Valor Eccl.* (Rec. Com.), ii. 210. The £2 was from all the abbey's appropriated churches.
[73] *Eynsham Cart.* ii, pp. lxviii, 241–2; Ch. Ch. Bursary, Bk. of evid.
[74] Ch. Ch. Burs. Bk. of evid.; Ch. Ch. Arch. 3. c. 3. 2.
[75] Bodl. MS. d.d. Wykeham-Musgrave c 33, part. of Stoke; Bodl. Tithe award.
[76] Lunt, *Val. Norw.* 304; *Tax. Eccl.* (Rec. Com.), 30.
[77] *Eynsham Cart.* ii. 119, 127.
[78] Ibid. 184–5.
[79] Ibid. 183–5.
[80] *Valor. Eccl.* (Rec. Com.), ii. 166; Oxf. Dioc. c 155, f. 21 a; *Par. Coll.* iii. 274; Bacon, *Lib. Reg.* 802. In the post-Reformation period the vicar continued to receive the

small tithes, except those of hay: Oxf. Archd. Oxon. b 41, f. 109. For a case about tithes of firewood, to which he was entitled, see Oxf. Dioc. c 25, f. 226b.
[81] C. Hodgson, *Account of Queen Anne's Bounty* (1845), 166, 198, 199, 324; Oxf. Dioc. c 327, p. 223; Char. Com. file 85345.
[82] Ch. Ch. Arch. Bk. of livings, p. 322; *Rep. of Com. on Eccl. Revenue*, H.C. 54 (1835), xxii.
[83] Bodl. Tithe award.
[84] Oxf. Archd. Oxon. b 41, f. 109: 1685 terrier; Ch. Ch. Arch. 1819 terrier; Bodl. Tithe award; see above, p. 103.
[85] *Eynsham Cart.* i. 2, 67; ii, p. lxii.
[86] Ibid. ii. 129.   [87] Ibid. p. lxii.
[88] d.d. Ch. Ch. M 91–93.
[89] *Eynsham Cart.* i. 10
[90] Ibid. 111, 154, 155.
[91] For list of medieval incumbents see MS. Top. Oxon. d 460.
[92] *Visit. Dioc. Linc. 1517–31*, ii. 68; *Subsidy 1526*. 251.

After Christ Church became the patron, it usually presented its own graduates, and until the 18th century they seem to have lived in the parish. Robert Abbott (vicar 1556–77), for example, was buried in the chancel and left a benefaction to his curate.[93] His successor Hilary Fishwick, a Christ Church graduate, was clearly constantly in residence. The parish register is all written in the same hand until 1614, the year before his death. His name, moreover, is frequently found as a witness to local wills.[94] It was in his time that there was said to have been dancing in the churchyard at Whitsuntide, a charge denied by the churchwardens.[95] No record has been found of disturbances in the parish during the religious changes of the 16th and 17th centuries. The vicar of the Commonwealth period, William Snow (by 1651–63) may have had royalist sympathies, for his son was a godchild of the royalist Griffith Higgs.[96]

In the second half of the 17th century two features of interest in the church life of the period are recorded. There was a church house, probably something like a parish hall, next to the churchyard,[97] and the vicar began the custom, as part of Henry Parslow's charity,[98] of preaching a sermon in Stoke church on the Monday before All Saints' Day (1 Nov.) and in Woodcote chapel on the following Monday. For each sermon he received 10s. and the parish clerk 1s.[99] At this time the parish still had a resident vicar, David Thomas (1663–1701), who was comfortably provided for with a house, which was assessed on four hearths in 1665 and had 'five spaces of good fair building'.[1] He was succeeded by two members of a prominent local family, the Stopeses of Britwell Salome. James Stopes junior was vicar from 1701 to 1706 and his father James Stopes senior from 1706 until 1720.[2]

In the 18th century pluralism and non-residence, caused by the poverty of the living and the smallness and ruinous condition of the vicarage house, were generally the rule. Robert Hughes (1721–43) was the last vicar to live in the vicarage. In 1724 £15 a year was sequestrated from the income of the living for its repair,[3] but his successors had to have much done to it to keep it in a fit state for a tenant. Coventry Lichfield (1743–85) lived at Goring Heath, where he acted as chaplain to Allnut's Hospital in order to supplement his income which, as he complained, was small though his 'flock' was great.[4] However, he tended it conscientiously, for he served Stoke church himself and held two services on Sundays, except on the days when there was a service at Woodcote, catechized the children regularly, and administered communion six times a year to between 20 and 30 communicants.[5]

After 1790 the vicars no longer lived near the parish. Thomas Ellis Owen (1790–5), an opponent of Methodism, lived in Wales,[6] and John Williams (1795–1844), although he held the living for nearly 50 years, during many of which he also leased the manor, was never resident on account of the small value of the living. In order to let the vicarage he spent over £100 on repairs.[7] In the early 19th century the church was served by a curate, who also served Goring.[8] Efforts to see that he resided were unavailing because the house was unsuitable and the farmers refused to give him lodgings.[9] Only one Sunday service could be held, communicants were said to be few,[10] and dissent throve. In order to keep the children and adults from going to dissenting meetings the curate opened an evening Sunday school, and preached an evening sermon.[11]

When P. H. Nind became vicar in 1844 he lived in Woodcote and served its chapel himself, while hiring a curate for Stoke. The Vicarage was enlarged for the latter in 1845 at a cost of £400, but it was still considered only a 'mere cottage' in 1860. Nind moved to Stoke in 1869 when the new Vicarage was built, but he considered Stoke a difficult place because it had many dissenters and Christ Church, the patron, was not interested in the spiritual state of the parish and let the manor to a 'violent opposer of the church', Isaac King. Beer houses were open on Sundays,[12] and most of the parishioners were of the poorest classes, who left home and went to work at a very young age.[13] Evening schools were held in winter for them, but in 1878, out of a total population of 762, there were 25 communicants, and it was even difficult to find people to act as churchwardens.[14] In the 20th century there was no parochial church council.[15]

Architectural evidence shows that Woodcote, which was a separate tithing, had a chapel in the 12th century.[16] It is probably to be identified with the chapel of St. Leonard at Exlade, mentioned in 1406 when Eynsham Abbey paid a carpenter 4d. for repairs,[17] but the first direct reference to it occurs in 1467, when a licence to celebrate services was issued by Bishop John Chedworth.[18] In 1666 the bishop's court decided that the vicar or the inhabitants must keep it in repair and not the lessee of the manor and rectory, who paid for the upkeep of Stoke chancel.[19]

By the mid-16th century the chapel had its own churchwardens,[20] and was probably already licensed for marriages and communion.[21]

In 1597 the Vicar of Stoke was said to be holding services there at Christmas, Easter Day, and on some working days for 'thanksgiving of women and marriages'.[22] As the inhabitants of Woodcote and Exlade were unable to pay someone to serve the

[93] Bodl. MS. Wills Oxon. 185, f. 435b.
[94] Reg. Univ. i. 257; W. M. Higgs, Hist. of the Higges Family (1933), 6, 15.   [95] Archd. Ct. i. 43, 51.
[96] Higgs, op. cit. 40, quoting Higgs's will. For him see above, p. 94.
[97] Oxf. Archd. Oxon. b 41, f. 109.
[98] See below, p. 111.
[99] 4th Rep. Com. Char. H.C. 312, p. 221 (1820), v.
[1] Hearth Tax Oxon. 55; Oxf. Archd. Oxon. b 41, f. 109.
[2] Par. Coll. i. 56; iii. 274. The elder James Stopes by his second wife had another son James who was schoolmaster at Woodcote: ibid. iii. 348; Bodl. MS. Wills Oxon. 207, f. 257b.
[3] Oxf. Archd. Oxon. c 138, f. 47.
[4] Oxf. Dioc. c 652, ff. 63–64. For him see J. R. Bloxam, Magdalen Coll. Reg. ii. 89–90.
[5] Oxf. Dioc. d 557, d 560, c 327, p. 36.
[6] D.N.B.

[7] Oxf. Dioc. c 656, f. 28. For later repairs see ibid. c 435, pp. 296–300.   [8] Ibid. c 327, p. 223.
[9] Ibid. c 656, ff. 28–29.
[10] Ibid. d 567, d 579.
[11] Ibid. d 549, p. 37; c 656, f. 30; b 70.
[12] Wilb. Visit. For the new Vicarage see above, p. 94.
[13] Oxf. Dioc. c 332.
[14] Ibid. c 344.
[15] Oxf. Dioc. c 2026, 1933 faculty.
[16] V.C.H. Oxon. ii. 60.
[17] Eynsham Cart. ii, pp. lxix, lxxxiii.
[18] Linc. Reg. Chedworth memo. f. 86b. For a slightly later reference in 1488 see Goring Chart. ii. 228.
[19] MS. Top. Oxon. c 56, f. 81. In the 1950's no lay rector was known: Oxf. Dioc. c 2026, 1953 faculty.
[20] Chant. Cert. 105–6.
[21] Cal. S.P. Dom. 1634–5, 556.
[22] Par. Rec. Reg. copy of petition to archbishop.

chapel regularly they had been accustomed to go to Checkendon church, when convenient, as well as to their parish church at Stoke, until attempts were made to prevent this by the new rector of Checkendon, Owen Thomas. The chief residents petitioned the Archbishop of Canterbury in 1597 for permission to continue to attend Checkendon as their predecessors had done time out of mind. They stated that Stoke was 2 to 3 miles distant from their dwellings, whereas Checkendon was a ¼- to a ½-mile distant, and that the journey to Stoke twice a day (i.e. 12 miles), particularly in winter, was most burdensome to the strongest of them and intolerable to the impotent, the aged, and to most women and children. For the past two years the Rector of Checkendon had instituted prosecutions in the archdeacon's court against the Stoke parishioners coming to his church. This had involved them 'in great trouble and hindrance from their work' and 'intolerable expenses' for journeys to and lodgings in Oxford and in fees of the court. They added that there were no recusants among them, and that they were anxious not to be compelled to break the laws about church attendance lest their children should lack 'good education and instruction'. They were still willing to communicate at their own parish church and to go there as often as it was convenient, and indeed were supported in their petition by their vicar, Hilary Fishwick, who also made no objection to the parishioners of Checkendon attending his church, if they lived 3 miles or more from their parish church but within ½-mile of Stoke.[23] The archbishop granted the petition as 'the request was reasonable', provided the inhabitants of Woodcote and Exlade attended the parish church at least four times a year.[24]

In 1653 the inhabitants of the hamlets petitioned to have their chapel made into a parish church, licensed for all sacraments, and with a minister of its own.[25] The petition was evidently unsuccessful, for the Vicar of Stoke continued to be responsible for services at Woodcote. By the mid-17th century the chapel no longer had its own churchwardens, though it appears to have become customary for one of the Stoke wardens to be chosen from Woodcote.[26]

During the 18th century there were eight services a year in the chapel, and in the early 19th century one a month.[27] But Woodcote people mostly went to Checkendon until the 19th century and there the owners of Woodcote House had their family vault.[28]

When P. H. Nind became vicar in 1844, he at once rebuilt the chapel, held two Sunday services there, and attempted to get Woodcote made into a separate living.[29] His son H. G. Nind, who succeeded his father in 1887 and who had already been acting as curate of Stoke, left Woodcote to live in Stoke.[30]

The church of *ST. ANDREW* is an ancient building of flint rubble, covered with roughcast, with stone dressings, comprising a chancel, nave, north and south aisles, south porch, and western tower.[31] The original church was evidently rebuilt in the early 13th century, and much of the present building dates from then. The two lancet windows in the north wall of the chancel are from this period. Narrow aisles were probably added on to the original nave at the same time, for there is a restored lancet window at both ends of the north aisle and the south aisle, although partly rebuilt in the 19th century, retains an original lancet window, containing pot-metal glass representing the Virgin and Child, at the east end. The lancet at the west end is 19th-century work. The roof included both aisles under its span.[32] The north aisle is separated from the nave by three Early English arches of two chamfered orders set on heavy round chalk pillars with octagonal abaci. The pillars (now rebuilt) separating the south aisle from the nave were apparently later; with one exception they were octagonal and made of wood, and the arches over them were also wooden, but chamfered and painted.[33]

Much work was done to the church during the 14th century. A Decorated east window of three lights was inserted, also the two windows, with a priest's door between them, in the south wall of the chancel. A new window (the easternmost one) was inserted in the south wall of the south aisle; the south door was rebuilt, and a porch was added. The porch had a pointed roof and a small rectangular window in its east wall.[34] Two Decorated windows and a doorway were inserted in the wall of the north aisle.

It may have been in the late 14th century that a canopied niche was placed in the east wall of the south aisle. It was once painted and traces of colour remained until recently.[35] Of slightly later date is the canopied niche in the north wall of the north aisle. The small piscina which was until recently next to it shows that there was once an altar here.[36]

The battlemented tower was probably built early in the 15th century. Two windows in the south aisle are also Perpendicular work. The two dormer windows, once in the roof over the south aisle, were later additions.[37]

Some work seems to have been done in 1711 and 1712, for Rawlinson noted these dates, with the names of the churchwardens, on the chancel walls.[38] In 1759 a number of minor repairs were ordered: a new north door was to be provided, the chancel door was to be renewed or else walled up, and parts of the floor were to be relaid. Also, the banks of rubbish were to be moved from the walls and specially from the porch.[39] Further repairs were ordered in 1803 and 1822.[40]

In 1857 and 1858 the church was restored at the cost of about £1,000. The architect was J. B. Clacy of Reading.[41] Details of the restoration have not been found, but it was certainly then that the

[23] Ibid. testimony of vicar.
[24] Ibid. licence of archbishop.
[25] *Cal. S.P. Dom.* 1634–5, 556.
[26] W. M. Higgs, *Hist. of the Higges Family*, 44; Oxf. Archd. Oxon. c 103, *passim*.
[27] *Secker's Visit.*; Oxf. Dioc. d 557; c 327, p. 36; d 549, p. 37. After 1813 the marriage entries in the register show that Woodcote was regularly used.
[28] Oxf. Dioc. c 434, f. 59*b*.
[29] *Wilb. Visit.*; Oxf. Dioc. c 332, c 344.
[30] Oxf. Dioc. c 344; Kelly, *Dir. Oxon.* (1891, 1903).
[31] For an account and photographs see C. E. Keyser, 'Notes on the Churches of S. Stoke, &c.', *Jnl. Brit. Arch.*

Assoc. N.S. xxiv; for a pre-restoration description (1849) by the architect R. C. Hussey see Bodl. MS. Top. gen. f 19, ff. 22*b*–24*b*. There are pre-restoration drawings, all from SE.: ibid. f. 24*b*; MS. Top. Oxon. b 165, f. 177; and plate facing p. 92.   [32] Bodl. MS. Top. gen. f 19, f. 22*b*.
[33] Ibid.   [34] See drawing ibid. f. 24*b*.
[35] Keyser, op. cit. 8 and fig. 10*b*.
[36] Ibid. 8 and fig. 10*a*.
[37] See pre-restoration drawings.
[38] *Par. Coll.* iii. 276.
[39] Oxf. Archd. Oxon. d 13, f. 57.
[40] Ibid. c 103, ff. 202, 232; b 51, f. 2*b*.
[41] MS. Top. Oxon. c 103, ff. 326–7; Oxf. Dioc. b 70.

southern arcade separating the nave from the aisle was rebuilt in the Early English style and the south aisle widened, so that now it is nearly 3 feet wider than the north one. The old southern wall, with its windows and doorway was retained, but the ancient clinker-built door was renewed. The south porch, which had been much mutilated, was rebuilt, and the stonework in several of the windows was renewed. The small vestry at the end of the south aisle, joined to the chancel by a new archway, was probably also constructed then.

The plaster ceilings of the nave and chancel were removed, and the roofs of the nave, aisles, and chancel largely renewed. Some of the old roof remains, including a wall plate in the north aisle.[42] The floor of both nave and chancel were tiled and a new pulpit was installed. The buttresses which support both the nave and chancel walls were probably added at this time.[43]

In the 20th century, in 1952, major repairs to the tower, including the replacing of the lead roof with a copper one, were executed.[44]

Other changes and repairs have included the insertion of the clock in the tower after the First World War as a war memorial; the replacing of the small harmonium by an organ (1927); and the installation of electric lighting (1933).[45]

The plain octagonal font is medieval. In 1849 it stood at the western end of the northern arcade,[46] but in 1958 it stood near the south door. Other medieval features are the tiles, assembled at the east end of the north aisle.[47]

The 'ancient, solid, square-ended' seating was retained at the 19th-century restoration and the two seats with 'good plain bold Perpendicular tracery' were placed in the chancel.[48]

The church is noted for the fine 17th-century monument on the north wall of the chancel to the memory of Griffith Higgs, Dean of Lichfield.[49] The figure of the dean is represented in his clerical robes holding a book in his right hand and with his left hand on a skull.[50] There is also a marble tablet in the chancel to James Higgs, gent. (d. 1742), who became Mayor of Wallingford, and to his brother Barton (d. 1722), great nephews of Dr. Higgs. Over the entrance to the south porch is a tablet to Griffith Higgs (d. 1692/3), Dr. Higgs's nephew, with an inscription in which he asks to be buried at the church door.[51] In the tower hangs a large painted pedigree of the Higgs family with heraldic quarterings. There are three monuments in the chancel to lessees of the manor: one to Richard Hannes (or Hanney) (d. 1678) and his wife Jane;[52] and a similar one to his daughter Elizabeth (d. 1657), the wife of William Barber;[53] and one to Lucy Harward (d. 1718/19), wife of Kemp Harward, and to her mother Lucy (d. 1728), the wife of Altham Smith of Grays Inn. This monument,

which is surmounted by three gilded cherubs' heads in a roundel, was erected by Lucy Harward's daughter Lucy, who later married John Head. Other monuments in the chancel are to Henry Hervey of Ipsden (d. 1764); and to Moses Allen, gent. (d. 1770) and his wife Mary.

On the floor of the centre aisle of the nave are four tombstones of members of the Claxson family, who may have lived at Payables:[54] of John (d. 1701); of another John, called John Claxson, senior (d. 1739); of Elizabeth (d. 1743), wife of John; and of William (d. 1748).

Later tablets in the nave are to Sir John Charles Fox (d. 1943) and his wife Mary Louisa; to Lt. David Gordon Dill (killed 1944); and to Thomas Geo. Pither (died as prisoner of war, 1945). There is also a memorial window to Hubert D. Nind (1809–74). The brass noted by Rawlinson to Thomas Walles, his two wives, and eleven children has disappeared.[55]

In the churchyard is the large table tomb of Isaac King (d. 1865), for many years lessee of the manor.

In 1552 the church owned a silver and gilt chalice and paten; a copper and gilt pyx and chrismatory; two brass candlesticks, and two crosses. By the next year only a chalice without a paten remained.[56] The church now owns a very fine silver chalice and paten of 1660, inscribed as being the gift of Griffith Higgs, and bought with the £5 which he left to the church.[57] Both pieces are also inscribed with his arms. There is also a silver flagon of 1869, given by Arthur J. Nind.[58]

In 1552 there were four bells in the church; there should also have been a sanctus bell, but its fate was unknown.[59] Later a fifth bell was added to the ring, for Rawlinson noted a 'ring of 5 good bells'.[60] In the early 17th century four new bells were acquired, three of them the work of Henry Knight I and one of Ellis Knight I. They are dated 1609, 1616, 1622, and 1633. In 1716 another new bell was obtained, and all were recast in 1857. The last was replaced in 1881. In 1920 a sixth bell was added to the ring. It was given by Alfred D'Oily Nind in memory of parishioners who fell in the First World War.[61]

Additions were made to the churchyard in 1884, 1926, and 1941.[62] In 1937 the lych gate was erected. In 1955 the unmarked and untended grave mounds in the west and south-west of the churchyard were levelled.[63] In the churchyard is a stone cross erected as a memorial to the parishioners who fell in both World Wars.

The registers, which also cover Woodcote until 1846, begin in 1557. There are churchwardens' accounts from 1856.

The chapel of *ST. LEONARD* at Woodcote was almost entirely rebuilt in 1845–6. The first documentary evidence for the existence of this chapel dates from the 15th century,[64] but drawings of the

[42] Keyser, op. cit. 8.
[43] The pre-restoration drawings do not show them.
[44] Oxf. Dioc. c 2026, Faculty.
[45] Kelly, *Dir. Oxon.* (1939); Oxf. Dioc. c 2026, Faculties. The organ was given in memory of Eliza, wife of Arthur Simpson of Goring.
[46] MS. Top. gen. f 19, ff. 22b–23.
[47] For example, see W. A. Church, *Patterns of Inlaid Tiles from Oxf. Diocese* (1845), pl. 2; L. Haberly, *Mediaeval English Pavingtiles*, pl. 234.
[48] MS. Top. gen. f 19, f. 23 and drawing on f. 25.
[49] For him see above, p. 94.
[50] The long Latin inscription, which gives his pedigree and details of his life, and mistakenly says he died in 1658

instead of 1659, has been reproduced several times, e.g. in *Par. Coll.* iii. 274–5.
[51] Ibid. 275–6.
[52] For heraldry see Bodl. G.A. Oxon. 4°. 275, 687.
[53] Ibid.
[54] See above, p. 98.
[55] *Par. Coll.* iii. 275.
[56] *Chant. Cert.* 105, 121.
[57] Oxf. Archd. Oxon. b 26, f. 462. For the crest on the chalice see Bodl. G.A. Oxon. 4°. 275, 687.
[58] Evans, *Ch. Plate.*
[59] *Chant. Cert.* 105.
[60] *Par. Coll.* iii. 276.
[61] Keyser, op. cit. 8; *Ch. Bells Oxon.* 391.
[62] Oxf. Dioc. c 2026, Consecrations.
[63] Ibid., Faculties.
[64] See above, p. 106.

old chapel suggest that it was of 12th-century origin.[65] It consisted of nave, apsidal chancel, south porch, and western wooden bell-cot.

Little was probably done to the church in the post-Reformation period. In 1666 the chancel was evidently in need of repair;[66] the date 1692 and the name of the churchwarden once painted on the wall probably indicated some work on the church;[67] and in 1759 the archdeacon ordered several things to be done, including mending the porch door, repairing the reading desk and pulpit, buying a new Bible, and having the Ten Commandments and 'chosen sentences' written.[68]

In 1845–6 the Vicar of South Stoke, Philip H. Nind, who lived at Woodcote, had the chapel almost completely rebuilt in the Norman style at a cost of £1,300.[69] The architect was H. J. Underwood of Oxford. The new building, which is 20 feet longer than the old one, consists, as did the latter, of chancel, nave, south porch, and stone western bell-cot, with the addition of a north vestry. The outside walls of the chancel were retained; the ancient flint-work in its walls is clearly to be distinguished from the new work in those of the body of the church. The old window was blocked up and four new windows and a priest's door inserted. The interior of the church was completely renewed. A gallery was built. Above the communion table the Lord's Prayer, the Creed, and the Ten Commandments were inscribed, and texts were painted elsewhere by Mr. Margetts of Oxford.[70] The gallery remains but the church is now plastered over inside. In 1937 a new communion table, given in memory of H. G. Nind, the vicar, was dedicated.[71] In 1953 about £230 was spent on repairs.[72]

There are three stained glass windows in the chancel by Powell & Sons of Whitefriars in memory of Emily Nind (d. 1902), the vicar's wife,[73] and in the aisle there are memorial windows to Emma Nind (d. 1850) and members of the Ferguson family. In 1872 glazed doors were put in the porch by W. H. Ferguson, a churchwarden. In 1953 they were re-glazed to commemorate the coronation of Queen Elizabeth II.[74]

Rawlinson noted in 1718 that the chapel contained neither 'monument nor grave stone'.[75] When Grace Stanyan of Woodcote House died in 1768 she was buried in the chancel, but two years later her body was moved to the family vault at Checkendon.[76] There are now brass inscriptions to two vicars: Philip H. Nind (d. 1886) and his wife Agnes; and Hubert G. Nind (d. 1936).

The old font (14½ in. in diameter), which is no longer used, is outside the porch door.

In 1552 the chapel owned a silver chalice and paten. In 1958 the plate consisted of a silver chalice, paten, and almsplate, all of 1845.[77] There were two bells in 1552, but the present turret has room only for one. It was made by James Wells of Aldbourne in 1801.[78]

The registers date from 1846. Until then Woodcote was included in the South Stoke registers.

NONCONFORMITY. In 1625 a number of persons, almost certainly papists, were listed as recusants. They included Richard Braybrooke and his wife Christian, one of the daughters of Barton Palmer, a lessee of the manor.[79] There were also several yeomen, including John Prince, a member of a Roman Catholic family that was widely spread in South Oxfordshire.[80] No papists were reported in the Compton Census of 1676,[81] but a husbandman and his wife were returned as such from 1697 to 1720[82] and in the first 20 years of the 18th century there are references to about six others.[83] In 1738 there was one Roman Catholic woman 'of low rank'.[84]

In 1676 there were two Protestant nonconformists[85] and 18th-century visitations mention a few Presbyterians 'of the lower rank'.[86] Dissent evidently increased towards the end of the century, for in 1802 six families of dissenters were being visited every month by a preacher[87] and by 1815 the people were said to be 'generally' dissenters.[88] They went to a chapel of the Countess of Huntingdon's Connexion at Goring, and James Howes, who was minister there from 1814 to 1856, 'founded the cause at South Stoke'.[89] In 1820 the Congregational chapel at South Stoke, which also belonged to the Countess of Huntingdon's Connexion, was built at a cost of nearly £332.[90]

The promoters of the foundation were several of the leading farmers in the parish,[91] and during the 19th century the farmers continued to be largely dissenters. Although in 1851 the Congregationalist congregation was said to number only 35,[92] the vicar reported in 1854 that the whole of Stoke, except for about 20 people, were dissenters, and that Isaac King, the lessee of the manor, was 'a violent opposer of the church'. When King died in 1865 he left £500 to be invested for the benefit of the minister, as long as the chapel should continue in connexion with the chapel at Goring.[93] The vicar had accused Christ Church, the lord of the manor, in 1854 of 'entire want of co-operation and assistance',[94] but it continued to lease to dissenters and in 1866 most of the farms were still rented to them.[95] In 1881 Benjamin Woodward Panter, a member of one of the chapel's founding families, settled £100 on the chapel, and Richard

[65] See drawing from SE. (c. 1806) in MS. Top. Oxon. b 220, f. 213, and plate facing p. 159.
[66] See above, p. 106.
[67] Par. Coll. iii. 349.
[68] Oxf. Archd. Oxon. d 13, f. 57b.
[69] Oxf. Dioc. b 70.
[70] MS. notes on Woodcote, by the Revd. E. A. Elliot, the Vicarage, South Stoke.
[71] Ibid.
[72] Oxf. Dioc. c 2026, Faculty.
[73] Ibid.
[74] Elliot, op. cit.
[75] Par. Coll. iii. 349.
[76] Oxf. Dioc. c 434, f. 59b.
[77] Chant. Cert. 105–6; Evans, Ch. Plate.
[78] Ch. Bells Oxon. 448.
[79] Par. Coll. i. 87: M.I. in Checkendon.

[80] Salter, Oxon. Recusants, 40, 43, 47, 56. Lady Ann Curson, widow of Sir Francis Curson of Waterperry, was also returned as of S. Stoke, but she apparently lived in N. Stoke: Stapleton, Cath. Miss. 291.
[81] Compton Census.
[82] O.R.O. Cal. Q. Sess. ix. 585.
[83] Ibid. 777, 779. In 1706 2 poor women were returned: Oxoniensia, xiii. 81.   [84] Secker's Visit.
[85] Compton Census.
[86] Secker's Visit.; Oxf. Dioc. d 557.
[87] Oxf. Dioc. c 327, p. 223.   [88] Ibid. c 433.
[89] Summers, Congreg. Churches, 109.
[90] Ibid. 110–11; Oxf. Dioc. c 644, f. 222.
[91] William Newell and Thomas and Benjamin Panter can be found in Ch. Ch. Arch. 1819 terrier.
[92] H.O. 129/4/125.   [93] Char. Com. file 38942.
[94] Wilb. Visit.   [95] Oxf. Dioc. c 332.

Pocock King of Reading, who had been the tenant of Manor farm,[96] by will proved 1882, left it £500.[97] The chapel has continued as an out-station of Goring, which is still part of the Countess of Huntingdon's Connexion. In 1958 together they had 26 members.[98]

Closely connected with nonconformity was the village hall. In 1880 Isaac King began collecting money by public subscription for a hall for temperance, religious, and social purposes. By 1885 it had been built on his land; the trust deed of that date describes it as a building of wood and iron called South Stoke Temperance Hall, intended for promoting 'Gospel temperance and religious truth'. Controversy soon developed: King insisted that the hall's use was limited to religious and temperance meetings, while there was local agitation in favour of using it in a less restricted way.[99]

There had been a Primitive Methodist preaching house at Woodcote in the mid-19th century,[1] but no later record of it has been found. The Woodcote Primitive Methodist chapel on the road from Woodcote to Goring Heath is in Goring parish.

SCHOOLS. In 1659 Dr. Griffith Higgs left £600 to buy land to maintain a charity school for 8 poor children. Records show that throughout the 18th century the school had an endowment of £5 a year.[2] By 1808 the endowment had increased to £15 a year and 7 poor children were being taught to read at the school.[3] By 1815 there were 30 pupils.[4] Details of the endowment were given in 1818 when the £15 was said to come from the rent of 22 acres of common field, but the surviving trustee knew nothing of the £600 endowment; the school was also said to have had right of common for 300 sheep, 25 bullocks, and 30 swine on Goring Heath, but the trustees were unable to prove this at the time of the inclosure of the open fields. The school income was paid to a schoolmaster to teach reading to 10 boys and numbers might be made up with girls. The children went to school at an early age and left as soon as they could work.[5] New buildings were erected in 1831[6] and there were 51 daily scholars in 1854.[7] It was a Church school, but in 1877 it was transferred to a School Board of seven members which was formed in 1875,[8] probably as a consequence of the strong dissenting body in the parish. The average attendance at the Board School was 55 in 1890 and 84 in 1903.[9] In 1954 there were only 21 pupils at South Stoke County School, as it was then called, but that was because it had been a Junior school since 1929.

Seniors attended Langtree Secondary School, Woodcote.[10]

There were other schools in South Stoke in the early 19th century. In 1808 there were three small dame schools, one of them kept by a dissenter, and in 1821 Robert Morrell supported the setting up of a school for 30 girls.[11] In 1854 there were flourishing evening schools during the winter months for adults and boys who had left the day school;[12] there is no later mention of these schools. There was also a Sunday school with 70 scholars in 1854.[13]

Woodcote hamlet had a Sunday school from 1708[14] and a day school endowed by Susannah Newman of Woodcote House in 1715, who gave land worth £10 a year to build a charity school for 10 poor children, 6 from South Stoke parish and 4 from Checkendon. A cottage was also provided for a schoolmaster or mistress, who should teach reading, writing, and accounts.[15] The school was held at Woodcote from 1759 or earlier and in 1768 the vicar said that the revenues and the master's house were being carefully preserved and employed.[16] The report in 1808, however, was not good: the house was in disrepair and the master had no scholars and was ill considered.[17] By 1815 the school was again flourishing with 20 boys and 12 girls,[18] and the vicar renovated the school-house shortly before 1818.[19] In 1833 there were 10 free scholars and a further 22 boys and girls were being educated at their parents' expense. New school buildings were erected in 1834.[20] In 1878 the school became a Board school;[21] it was closed in 1899 and a new school was built to hold 120 children.[22] In 1903, however, the average attendance was only 25 boys and girls and 21 infants.[23] It existed up to 1957 as a mixed County School, but was then reorganized as Langtree Secondary School. A new primary school was opened at the same time.[24]

In the 19th century Woodcote House became a high-class preparatory school for boys kept by the Nind family. It was probably opened in 1841 when the vicar, P. H. Nind, leased the house.[25] Of its 44 pupils in 1851, one was a peer and three were members of peers' families.[26] When Nind moved to the new Vicarage at South Stoke in about 1870, his son Hubert Nind kept on the school until he became vicar in 1887. The school was closed before the First World War.[27]

In 1942 the Oratory School, a Roman Catholic public school founded in 1859 at Edgbaston by Cardinal Newman, moved to Woodcote House. In

[96] Kelly, *Dir. Oxon.* (1869).
[97] Char. Com. file 38942. By Scheme of 1942 it was provided that the 3 charities should be administered in accordance with other Huntingdonian trusts as regulated by a Scheme of the High Court of 1899: ibid.
[98] *Congregational Yearbook* (1958). They were in the Central District of the Berks. S. Oxon. and S. Bucks. Union. [99] Char. Com. file 61041.
[1] H.O. 129/4/125.
[2] See *V.C.H. Oxon.* i. 488; *Secker's Visit.*; Oxf. Dioc. d 557; d 563; cf. Gardner, *Dir. Oxon.*: the money was used to buy land which in 1854 yielded £18 a year. For Higgs, see above, p. 94. [3] Oxf. Dioc. d 707.
[4] Ibid. c 433.
[5] *Educ. of Poor*, 730–1; *V.C.H. Oxon.* i. 488; cf. O.R.O. Incl. Award: the trustees received 19 a. 1 r. 31 p.
[6] Oxon. Dioc. b 70, f. 706.
[7] *Wilb. Visit.* It has been taken that the school mentioned in 1833 was at Woodcote: Educ. Enq. Abstract, 754.
[8] *Elem. Educ. Ret.* 319; *Sch. bldg. grnts.* 106; Oxf. Dioc. c 344.

[9] *Ret. of Sch.* 217; *List of Sch.* 529.
[10] Inf. Oxon. Educ. Cttee.
[11] Oxf. Dioc. d 707; *Educ. Enq. Abstract*, 754.
[12] *Wilb. Visit.* [13] Ibid.
[14] Oxf. Dioc. c 433.
[15] *V.C.H. Oxon.* i. 488; *Par. Coll.* iii. 348; the trustees were allotted 21 p. for common rights: O.R.O. Incl. Award. For Susannah Newman see above, p. 97, n. 5.
[16] *Secker's Visit.*; Oxf. Dioc. d 554; d 560.
[17] Oxf. Dioc. d 707.
[18] Ibid. c 433.
[19] *Educ. of Poor*, 731.
[20] Oxf. Dioc. b 70, f. 706.
[21] *Educ. Enq. Abstract*, 754.
[22] *Sch. bldg. grnts.* 106.
[23] *List of Sch.* 529.
[24] Inf. Oxon. Educ. Cttee.
[25] O.R.O. Misc. BRA/viii/1; *Life of Edward Bulwer, Ld. Lytton*, by his son (1883), ii. 154.
[26] H.O. 107/1690/2.
[27] Inf. the vicar.

1959 it had 200 boarders. A new wing was then being built so that numbers could be increased.[28]

CHARITIES. By will dated 1598 William Palmer, the lessee of Stoke manor, left £200 to buy an annuity of £14 for the poor of seven parishes; £2 was for the poor of Stoke, Woodcote and Exlade, to be distributed by the lessee of the manor and the vicar. No land was bought, and in 1610 distributions were not being made.[29] In 1668 William Barber, the lessee, was paying the £2 to the poor, but had bought no endowment. Although ordered to do so,[30] he never did, and by 1786 the charity had lapsed.[31]

In 1602 lands in Rotherfield Grays and Gyldon Dean were charged by the will of Augustine Knapp with the payment of 20s. yearly towards the clothing of 'poor, lame, impotent and needy people' in South Stoke parish. The rent was paid on the eve of All Saints' and was at one time known as 'Waistcoat Money'.[32] In 1877 it was distributed in clothing every three years.[33] In 1881 the rent charge was redeemed for £34 stock,[34] which has since yielded 16s. 8d.[35] In 1926 this was spent on rugs, 3 for Stoke and 3 for Woodcote, but in 1954 in 2 clothing vouchers, each worth 10s., one for each place. The distribution takes place at Christmas.[36]

In 1659 Dr. Griffith Higgs directed his executors to lay out £100 in land and to charge the land with the payment of £5 yearly, £3 to be distributed among 6 poor families of Stoke and £2 among as many from Woodcote and Exlade. Each family at Stoke and Woodcote was to be given 5s. or 3s. 4d. apiece at Christmas and at Easter after morning service. An island in the Thames (c. 1¼ a.), later called 'The Doctor's Gift', was bought for the purpose. Its sale was authorized in 1948, and the proceeds invested in about £334 stock.[37] The income between 1954 and 1956 was about £10 yearly and was distributed at Christmas and Easter in sums of 7s. 6d. to aged, infirm, or sick widows and occasionally to widowers.[38]

Henry Knapp, who died in 1674, left to the poor of Woodcote and Exlade 40s. yearly issuing out of the manor and farm at Rawlins in Woodcote.[39] This charity appears to have been lost before 1820.[40]

Before c. 1820 the owners of an estate in Stoke habitually gave 3 poor women of the parish and 2 of Checkendon blue cloth to make gowns. The charity, if such it was, seems to have been lost thereafter.[41]

Henry Parslow, Paslow, or Pasler, by will proved 1675, charged an estate in Checkendon with the payment of £5 to provide 5 coats for 5 poor men, 1 at

Stoke, 2 at Woodcote, and 2 at Checkendon; and he directed that the Vicar of Stoke should have 10s. for preaching a sermon on the Monday before All Saints' and the clerk 1s.; and that each man receiving a coat should have 1s. and the two churchwardens who should buy the coats 1s. each.[42] In 1937 the rent charge was redeemed for £260 stock.[43] In 1872 only three coats were provided.[44] In 1954 the vicar was still receiving 10s. for preaching. Since 1943 the men from Stoke, Woodcote, and Checkendon have been entitled to 30s. apiece for clothing and 1s. for attending the service. If five recipients are not forthcoming, the value of the vouchers is increased proportionately. In 1957 the value had risen to £3.[45]

Before 1786 an unknown donor had given £40 to the poor of South Stoke. By about 1820 the usual practice was for the interest to be allowed to accumulate for two or three years and then to be distributed in small sums to poor families according to their size.[46] In 1877 the distribution was in coals and both Stoke and Woodcote benefited.[47] Some time before 1877 another unknown donor had given two cottages to the poor. These were burnt down in 1905.[48] The second of these charities and possibly the first also, was regulated by Scheme of 1908 which provided that the interest or rents arising from the land on which the cottages stood and a sum of £183 should be distributed in coal to necessitous residents.[49] Between 1954 and 1956 the income amounted to £6 and was distributed at Christmas in coal to between 8 and 9 recipients.[50]

Mrs. Jane Williams, of Bourton-on-the-Hill (Glos.), by will proved 1831, left £100 stock in trust for the relief of the poor of Stoke parish, together with a like sum for the poor of Chastleton.[51] In 1877 and 1926 the income was spent in blankets.[52] Between 1954 and 1956 the income was £2 10s. yearly, and was usually distributed at Christmas in clothing vouchers of the value of 10s.[53]

William Claxson, of Reading, by will proved 1860, left money, represented by £291 stock, to buy clothing for the benefit of the poor of Woodcote. The legacy was subject to the life interest of his wife, who died in 1873.[54] The charity was first distributed in 1876,[55] and twelve persons were still receiving 12s. each in clothing vouchers in 1954.[56]

By the South Stoke and Woodcote inclosure award of 1853 2 acres were allotted to the surveyors of the highways as a stone and gravel quarry, and a smaller area as a source of chalk and rubble, in each case for the repair of the parish roads.[57] By the same award two plots (5 a.) were allotted to the church-

[28] Inf. the Revd. Adrian Morey, O.S.B., headmaster.
[29] C 93/4/15. The other places in Oxon. were Oxford and Henley.
[30] C 93/30/1.
[31] *Char. Don.* ii. 985. For £20 left by will, proved 1671, of Ann Astell for bread for the poor, which her executors failed to pay, see Bodl. MS. Wills Oxon. 113/2/13, 14; *Char. Don.* ii. 985.
[32] *4th Rep. Com. Char.* H.C. 312, pp. 219–20 (1820), v. For Knapp see above, p. 97.
[33] Char. Com. (S. Stoke) G. file.
[34] Ibid. file 34399.
[35] Ibid. Accts. file and inf. the Revd. E. A. Elliot, vicar.
[36] Ibid.
[37] *4th Rep. Com. Char.* 220–1; C 93/30/2; Char. Com. file 62986; ibid. Accts. file. For Higgs see above, p. 94.
[38] Char. Com. Accts. file.
[39] Char. Com. (S. Stoke) G. file. For Knapp see above, p. 97.
[40] Char. Com. G. file and file 28655.

[41] Ibid.
[42] *4th Rep. Com. Char.* 221. See also Oxf. Dioc. d 560, where the income is said to be derived from the rent of a meadow called Paslow's Butts (£4 2s. 6d.) and from the interest on £40.
[43] Char. Com. file 119442.
[44] Ibid. (S. Stoke) G. file.
[45] Inf. the vicar.
[46] *4th Rep. Com. Char.* 221; *Char. Don.* ii. 982.
[47] Char. Com. (S. Stoke) G. file.
[48] Ibid.
[49] Ibid. S. Stoke. G. file and 62986.
[50] Ibid. Accts. file; inf. the vicar.
[51] Char. Com. Unrep. Vol. 38, f. 174.
[52] Ibid. (S. Stoke) G. and Accts. files.
[53] Ibid.; inf. the vicar.
[54] Char. Com. Unrep. Vol. 38, ff. 172–3.
[55] Ibid. (S. Stoke) G. file.
[56] Inf. the vicar.
[57] Char. Com. Unrep. Vol. 38, f. 82.

wardens and overseers as recreation grounds,[58] two other plots (9 a.) as allotments,[59] and a very small plot as a pound.[60] It was stated in 1896 that the allotment land in Stoke was found useless for cultivation and was subsequently converted into a recreation ground, for which, owing to its swampy character, it was equally useless. It was then let for grazing. The rent arising was first used in aid of the highway rate and later spent on fuel for the poor. The allotment and recreation grounds in Woodcote seem to have been used for their proper purposes.[61] By 1904 these various grounds were being administered by the Parish Council.[62]

The parishioners of Stoke have the right to send an almsman to Allnutt's almshouse in Goring.[63]

[58] Char. Com. Unrep. Vol. 38, f. 84. [59] Ibid. f. 86.
[60] Ibid. f. 88.
[61] Char. Com. file 61041.

[62] Ibid. (S. Stoke) G. file.
[63] *8th Rep. Com. Char.* 203. The history of the alms-house is reserved for treatment under Goring.

THE HUNDRED OF THAME

THE hundred was a comparatively small one: in the 19th century it covered 10,580 acres and had a population in 1831 of 4,734.[1] It was further distinguished by being divided into three detached groups.[2]

The rich pastures of the Thame valley have made the landscape pleasing and the district notable for its dairy produce. Brewer writing in 1813 remarked that no other part of the country was 'more amenable to agriculture'.[3] This richness of soil, the excellence of the stone quarries at the Miltons, and the good communications, particularly

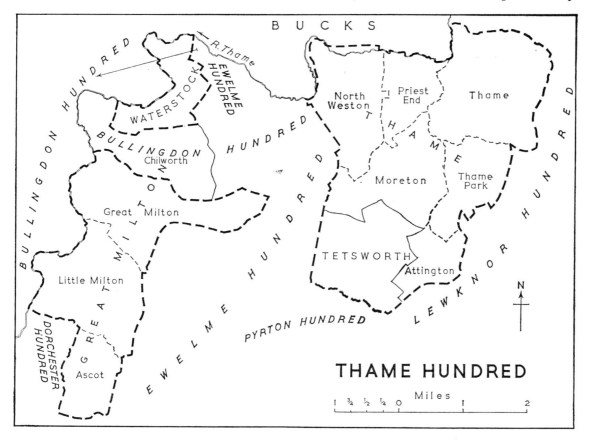

THAME HUNDRED

with the capital, were probably the main factors that attracted so many gentle families to the district both in the medieval and later periods. Chief among them were the Quatremains and Clerkes of North Weston, the merchant Dormers of Thame and later of Ascot, the Wenmans of Thame, the Bruleys, Crokes, and Ashhursts of Waterstock, the Pettys of Tetsworth, and the families of De Louches, Camoys, Radmylde, Grene, Cave, Calfhill (Caulfeild), and others at Great and Little Milton.

The hundred contains no great house such as Nuneham Courtenay, but it has the 18th-century Thame Park which incorporates the remains of Thame Abbey, a number of houses of the gentry, and groups of small dwellings of charm and distinction in the villages, and a market town with a notable High Street.

The creation of prebends of Lincoln at Thame and Great Milton resulted, further-

---

[1] *Census*, 1831.
[2] A. Bryant, *Oxon. Map* (1823).
[3] Brewer, *Oxon.* (1813), 300.

more, in the building of two fine churches. Wood noted that the aisles of the two families of Dormer and Quatremain at Thame make this church 'seem to be a cathedral'.[4]

The hundred is also of interest in that it contains a number of depopulated villages. Attington and North Weston in Thame and Ascot in Great Milton have gone except for a few houses.[5] The two Chilworths and Coombe though in the parish of Great Milton were outside the hundred.[6]

By the time of Domesday Book the hundred of Thame was not a normal hundred composed of contiguous villages assessed at exactly a hundred hides. It consisted of two or, if Waterstock was already in the hundred, of three detached groups of manors belonging to the Bishop of Lincoln. These groups, however, lay fairly close together and not widely separated as was the case with some of the detached parts of Dorchester hundred. Domesday Book says that the bishop had 60 hides in his manor of Thame, of which he held 37 in demesne and his knights the rest, and 40 hides in Great Milton of which he held 31 in demesne and his knights the rest.[7] The holdings of the knights are given in detail in separate entries, but the sum of their hidage does not quite correspond to the 23 hides in Thame and the 9 in Great Milton which they are stated to hold in the preceding entries. It totals 32¾ hides instead of 32 hides.[8] The later history of the fees makes it likely that Robert's 10-hide holding was in Tetsworth.[9] William's 3 hides in North Weston and the 6 hides of Alured and his companions in Attington and Moreton.[10] The 4 hides of Sawold cannot be located with certainty. Of the knights of Milton manor Aluric's 6 hides and William's 3¾ hides seem to be represented by the later fees of D'Oilly and Quatremain in Ascot.[11] It is likely that the William holding 3 hides of Thame manor and the William holding 3¾ of Milton manor are identical, for the Quatremains' holding in the 13th century consisted of 6¾ hides divided between North Weston (3 hides) and Ascot (3¾ hides).[12] The bishop's demesne and the holding of his knights thus form roughly a normal hundred of 100¾ hides. This reckoning, however, is put out by the 5 hides of Waterstock. In the 13th century Waterstock was certainly in Thame hundred and in Thame manor, but it was a detached part and may not have always been so. On the other hand, it is likely that the Sawold, who held 5 hides in Waterstock in 1086 of the fee of St. Mary of Lincoln,[13] is the same as the Sawold already mentioned in the return as one of the bishop's knights holding 4 hides of Thame manor and that there has been some duplication. A further possibility is that these episcopal hundreds were never regular hundreds assessed at 100 or 120 hides, but were aggregations of manors held either in demesne by the bishop or by his knights or by monastic houses holding of the bishop. The artificial nature of Thame hundred is certainly demonstrated by the way it is split up into groups separated from each other by parts of the hundred of Bullingdon. Nor do the hundred boundaries correspond with those of the parishes of which the hundred is composed, although the parish boundaries appear to have been of great antiquity. Sydenham and Towersey, originally in Thame parish,[14] are outside the hundred and so are Chilworth and Coombe, which were hamlets of Milton.[15]

Thame hundred is not mentioned by name in Domesday Book and the entries are in fact entered with places in the hundred of Banbury, also not mentioned by name, under the rubric of Dorchester hundred. Thus, Thame hundred was in all probability once a part of the triple hundred of Dorchester.[16]

4 Wood, *Life*, i. 408.
5 See below, pp. 121, 170.
6 For their sites and history see below, pp. 122, 127.
7 *V.C.H. Oxon.* i. 402-3.   8 Ibid.
9 See below, p. 148.
10 See below, pp. 172, 174.

11 See below, pp. 126, 222.
12 *Cur. Reg. R.* i. 204, 244.
13 See below, p. 222.
14 See below, p. 199.
15 *V.C.H. Oxon.* v. 4.
16 See above, p. 2.

When the hundred is first described in detail in 1279 it consisted of three detached parts. In the first was the town of Thame with its liberties and the hamlets of Attington, North Weston, and Moreton. The liberties, as they were later called, of Thame Park, Priestend, New Thame, and Old Thame are not specifically mentioned, but they are clearly traceable in the account given. A second group comprised the greater part of the parish of Great Milton: this included Little Milton and Ascot, but not Coombe or the two Chilworths which were in the hundred of Bullingdon. Waterstock formed the third detached part.[17] The composition of the hundred continued unaltered throughout its history.[18]

The hundred belonged to the Bishop of Lincoln throughout the Middle Ages. It was worth 40s. a year.[19] When Thame manor was granted to Lord Williams in 1550, the hundred was granted too and thereafter followed the descent of the manor of Old and New Thame which passed to the earls of Abingdon.[20]

Among the bishop's rights in his hundred, the most important was that of return of writs. He could exclude the sheriff, and execute all royal writs through his own bailiffs, who also had the right of hearing pleas *de vetito namii*, normally heard by the sheriff in the shire court. The bishop had also the commoner privileges of view and frankpledge, the assize of bread and ale, and the right of hanging on his own gallows those taken with stolen goods.[21] At the eyre of 1247 the bishop's bailiffs claimed that they had always had the right of making attachments in the hundred to the exclusion of the sheriff and his bailiffs and of hearing pleas *de vetito namii*. They produced no warrant.[22]

If the bailiffs failed in their duty in any way the bishop might lose his privileges. A case of this occurred in 1285 when the privilege of having the return of writs in his three hundreds was taken into the king's hands because of some fault of the bailiff of Banbury.[23]

In addition to his judicial privileges the bishop had a prison though the right to have one is never listed among his other rights. The prison was in Thame and seems to have been in the cellars of the Bird Cage Inn, formerly known as the 'Cage'.[24] It is mentioned only in connexion with the escape of prisoners. In 1247 two cases of escape and flight to Tetsworth and Thame churches were reported.[25] In 1268 a band of armed men broke open the prison and released a man.[26] The prison is last recorded in 1453 when John Benett, bailiff of the liberty, let a man escape who had fled to Thame from Southwark.[27]

From the cases of abjuration of the realm and of inquests recorded on the eyre rolls it appears that the bishop did not have his own coroner.

Occasional references have been found to the activities of the bishop's officers in the hundred. The bailiff played a leading part in the violent affray of 1293.[28] It is known that there was at least one under-bailiff. A Thomas Bocher who held the office in Henry VII's reign was killed, allegedly with the connivance of Prebendary Adrian de Bardis, who was indicted for his murder through the efforts of Edmund Barry, a kinsman of William Smith, Bishop of Lincoln. Adrian's goods were confiscated by the bishop's bailiffs.[29] There was also a steward or seneschal of the hundreds, manors, and demesnes of Dorchester, Thame, Wooburn (Bucks.), and Fingest (Bucks.). The office was held by Sir William Stonor in 1479.[30] The Stonor family had a residence in Thame called the 'Halle Place' as early as 1419.[31] Sir John Daunce was appointed to the office in 1524.[32]

[17] *Rot. Hund.* (Rec. Com.), ii. 820–2.
[18] *Feudal Aids*, iv. 167; *Hearth Tax Oxon.* 43–52; E 179/161/9, 198.   [19] J.I. 1/700, m. 3d.
[20] See below, p. 171.   [21] *Rot. Hund.* ii. 31.
[22] J.I. 1/700, m. 3d.
[23] *Cal. Fine R.* 1272–1307, 215.

[24] See below, p. 165.   [25] J.I. 1/700, m. 3d.
[26] J.I. 1/703, m. 5d; see also *Cat. Pat.* 1354–8, 490.
[27] *Cal. Pat.* 1452–61, 84.   [28] See below, p. 160.
[29] C 1/301 68, 69.   [30] *Cat. Anct.* D. vi. c 5623.
[31] Rousham Arch. N 270.
[32] *Linc. Chapter Acts*, 1520–36 (L.R.S. xii), 47–48.

The rolls of a number of medieval hundred courts have survived.[33] The two great courts were held in June and December on 'Haryndon' Hill (Milton Common) and the three-weekly courts appear to have been held in Thame. The townships of Great Milton, Little Milton, Ascot, Old Thame, Moreton, North Weston, Thame Park, Priestend, Tetsworth, and Waterstock appeared through their constables and tithing men. Great Milton and Little Milton, Tetsworth, Moreton, and Old Thame each had haywards.

The business of the court consisted of the swearing in of the king's jury (20 or more), the swearing in of constables and tithing men, and the payment of cert money. Attington had tithing men and no constable, perhaps because it was already depopulated.[34] On one occasion the Abbot of Thame was presented for his failure to send the two tithing men for Attington and the cert money. Cert money ranged from 1s. for Attington to 6s. for Old Thame. Priestend claimed to owe no cert money because it belonged to the Rector of Thame (i.e. the Prebendary), and at the view of 1473 out of the total sum of 44s. 6d. received 5s. 9d. went to the rector. New Thame was not represented: its port-manmoot acted as a hundred court.[35]

At the great courts presentments were mainly concerned with breaches of the assize of bread and ale, with the excessive toll taken by millers, and obstruction of the roads or flooding caused by unscoured ditches. Presentments of Tetsworth innkeepers were noticeably frequent. At one court a bridge on the foot-road from Thame to Moreton was ordered to be repaired. Occasionally there were presentments for not having men in tithing: in 1473 Thomas Danvers in Waterstock had two outside tithing. The business conducted at these courts was small and the sums received were correspondingly low—at the December views in 1443 and 1472 the total was 16s. 7d. and 18s. 3d. In the second case 10s. of the total came from the free tenants who defaulted in their suit. They included the abbots of Dorchester and Thame.

The ordinary three-weekly hundreds produced sums varying from 10d. to 1s. 10d. in the year 1441–2. In Edward IV's reign business was even less and the sums received varied from nothing to 8d. All these courts appear to have been held at Thame. Their main business was concerned with pleas of debts, and occasional pleas of tresspass and broken contract. In two successive courts held in 1444 there were three and four pleas of debt. In a court of 1450 a man denied five-handed (i.e. supported by the oaths of four friends) that he owed 5s.

Some records for 18th-century views of frankpledge held at 'Harringstone' (or Harrington) hill in June 1786 until June 1794 have also survived.[36] Cert money at the old rates was paid, except that North Weston and Thame Park no longer paid anything. Although there was only one household at Attington at this date[37] it still paid its cert money.

Apart from the holding of courts the bailiff and his officers had much other business. In the 16th century the hundred was the unit for the collection of subsidies,[38] for the administration of the poor law, and among other things for organizing musters.[39] In 1571, for example, they had to make search for rogues and vagabonds;[40] in 1587 they made a return of the quantities of corn and grain preserved in the hundred with the names of the victuallers.[41] Considerable use was made of the hundred in the 17th century, particularly in the matter of relieving the poor: in 1634 and 1635 certificates were returned by the Justices of the Peace for their observance of the king's directions for the relief of the poor in Thame.[42] In 1640 the bailiff of the hundred received a warrant for collecting ship-money.[43]

[33] d.d. Bertie c 16 (uncat.). There are courts for 2, 18, 21, 22, 23 Hen. VI; 12, 13 Edw. IV.
[34] See below, p. 188.   [35] d.d. Bertie c 16 (uncat.).
[36] d.d. Bertie b 3 (uncat.).   [37] See below, p. 191.
[38] *Acts of P.C.* 1556–8, 156; E 179/161/198, &c.

[39] e.g. *Cal. S.P. Dom.* 1547–80, 138; *L. & P. Hen. VIII*, xiv (2), p. 362.   [40] *Cal. S.P. Dom.* 1547–80, 419.
[41] Ibid. 1581–90, 389.
[42] Ibid. 1634–5, 446; 1635–6, 136.
[43] Ibid. 1640–1, 71.

GREAT MILTON

THE ancient parish of Great Milton[1] was large and irregularly shaped: it was 5 miles long by 3 miles broad, lying 9 miles south-east of Oxford and 6 miles south-west of Thame. It comprised the township of Chilworth in the north (1,081 a.), Great and Little Milton in the centre of the parish (1,443 a. and 1,348 a.), and the township of Ascot at the southern end. The parish was thus a large one and covered 4,454 acres.[2] In the 19th century all four tithings were separate civil parishes, and continued to be so until 1932.[3] In that year the civil parishes of Great Milton and Chilworth, except for 13 acres of Chilworth that were transferred to Wheatley, were united to form the civil parish of Great Milton. Ascot civil parish was united with Stadhampton.[4] Little Milton remained a separate civil parish. In 1953, after part of Tiddington with Albury had been transferred to Great Milton and parts of the latter had been transferred to Wheatley and Holton,[5] the civil parish of Great Milton had an area of 2,513 acres.

The ancient parish was bounded on the west and for some way on the north by the River Thame, and one of the tributaries of the Thame formed the short southern boundary. Streams also divided Ascot tithing from Little Milton and formed the hundred boundary separating Chilworth from Great Milton, for Chilworth lay in Bullingdon hundred.

Much of the parish lies between the 200 and 300 ft. contour lines, but it rises to 335 ft. on the London road and drops to 177 ft. at Great and Little Milton meadows bordering the Thame. Most of the eastern side of the parish lies on Portland Beds and has a sandy limestone soil; on the highest parts of the parish there is a thin layer of Gault Clay which also reappears round Ascot at the southern end. There is Kimmeridge Clay in the western part and on Milton Common a belt of Plateau Gravel.[6]

The main Oxford to London road, the 'street' of a charter of 956[7] and apparently a Roman road,[8] crosses the northern tip of the parish. Its importance in the history of Milton may be judged from the interest that was taken in the upkeep of Wheatley Bridge, Harpesford or Herford Bridge, as it was once called after the ford that preceded it. The Anglo-Saxon name was 'herpath' (army way) ford.[9] The bridge is first recorded in the 12th century, when Henry II afforested land extending up to it, and there is record of its repair towards the end of the 13th century.[10] In 1284 a Wheatley man was

granted pontage for two years to enable him to repair the king's bridge. He used local stone from a Wheatley quarry.[11] A similar grant of pontage was made to two men in 1307.[12] In the 16th century Thomas Danvers, lord of Waterstock, bequeathed in 1501 part of £20 for the repair of the bridge and the highway.[13] Another bequest was made in 1631 by Abraham Archdale of Wheatley, who left £10 for its repair.[14] The petition by Milton and other neighbouring villages made about this time to Archbishop Laud gives an idea of the traffic on the road. They complained that Oxford carriers were ruining it by carrying 'unreasonable' loads of 40 to 60 tons each. Laud asked the Chancellor of the University that not more than six horses to a cart should be used.[15]

Leland in 1546 and Ogilby in 1675 recorded that the bridge had eight arches,[16] but repairs to it during the 17th, 18th, and 19th centuries considerably altered its appearance. In 1958 it had three semicircular stone arches, mainly apparently 18th- and 19th-century work. There are numerous records of repairs, e.g. in 1711 William Townsend the elder, mason of Oxford, was to receive £100 for 'surveying' the repair; in 1749 and 1757 Richard Belcher, mason, received £59 odd for his work.[17] In 1809 the bridge was rebuilt and in 1820 the Stokenchurch and Wheatley Turnpike Trust widened the 'little bridge' (presumably part of the medieval bridge)[18] 'adjacent to the main structure' at a cost of £222.[19] The trust considered that the repair of the 'little bridge' should be borne by the county. In 1840 the walls of the embankment adjoining the main bridge were rebuilt. Local stone was probably used as in 1880.[20]

Three secondary roads branch off the London road and run across the parish to the Miltons and their hamlets, and connect with the Shillingford to Aylesbury road. One of these, Swarford Lane, used to run close to Bridge farm, but its route was altered in 1937,[21] so that the farm buildings now stand farther back from the road.

At the time of the inclosure a number of footpaths and field-ways were stopped up or diverted, including one leading from the Wheatley–Little Milton road over the fields by Blagroves to Chippinghurst ford and mill.[22]

The railway from Thame to Oxford, completed in 1864,[23] crosses the tip of the parish and Thame station is 6 miles and Tiddington 2½ miles distant.

Great Milton village stands about 260 ft. up near the eastern boundary of the parish and is well

[1] Throughout this article considerable use has been made of notes and photostats supplied by the late Revd. R. A. Ker, and of notes by Dr. Joycelyne G. Dickinson.

[2] O.S. *Area Bk.* (1882); Map 6″, xl, xli, xlvi (1884, 1885, 1886).

[3] *V.C.H. Oxon.* ii. 218, 222; *Census,* 1851, 1931.

[4] *Census,* 1931.   [5] O.R.O. Review Order 616, 501.

[6] Ibid.; Geol. Surv. Map sheet 237; *V.C.H. Oxon.* i, map between pp. 4–5.

[7] *Cart. Sax.* ed. Birch, iii. 124; cf. *V.C.H. Oxon.* v. 96–97.   [8] Inf. I. D. Margary, Esq.

[9] *P.N. Oxon.* (E.P.N.S.), 142. In the 15th cent. it was called Hertford Bridge: W.A.M. 1634 (Nov. ct.).

[10] V. J. Watney, *Hist. of Wychwood,* 218, citing C 47/11/1/19; cf. W. O. Hassall, *Wheatley Records* (O.R.S. xxxvii), 8, 64, and *passim,* for a history of the bridge.

[11] *Cal. Pat.* 1281–92, 229, 231.

[12] Ibid. 1301–7, 536.

[13] Macnamara, *Danvers Family,* 168: his will.

[14] W. O. Hassall, *Wheatley Records* (O.R.S. xxxvii), 61: his will.

[15] MS. Dunkin 438/4, ff. 16, 20.

[16] Leland, *Itin.* ed. Toulmin Smith, ii. 33; John Ogilby, *Britannia* (1675), map 1.

[17] O.R.O. Cal. Q. Sess. vol. viii; and see also for years 1690, 1694–6, 1729, 1748; and vol. v. for 1712.

[18] It was 'situated within 50 yards of the principal bridge and may be considered part of it': O.R.O. Q. Sess. Bridge Pps. 34.   [19] Ibid.   [20] Ibid.

[21] Local inf.; O.S. Map 6″, xl (1886); 2½″, 42/60, 41/69 (1949).   [22] O.R.O. Incl. award.

[23] E. T. MacDermot, *Hist. G.W.R.* 595.

supplied with springs. It is a large straggling village, built mainly along both sides of a curving street running from the 'King's Arms' and 'The Limes' at the north-west end to the green and the Monkery at the other end. From the Monkery the road descends past the Priory to the 'Red Lion', which ceased to function as a public house in 1959, and to the old Vicarage at the bottom of the hill and then ascends again to the medieval church, standing in a commanding position about a ½-mile from the main part of the village. Near the church are the manor-house, Romeyn's Court (one of the two prebendal manor-houses), and the Great House. It is possible that the medieval village may have once been nearer its church than it is now, but at least by the 16th century it had spread to the ridge road where it is now chiefly concentrated. Although there are a number of 19th-century and later houses in 'Town street' there are still many 16th- and 17th-century buildings constructed of the excellent local stone. Many of these such as the 'King's Head' and the butcher's shop next door have cellars and were probably originally built for tradesmen: these two are L-shaped and although refronted in the 18th century are of 17th-century date and typical of the style of the older houses. The oldest cottages, a group of 16th-century date, lie on the south-east of the green. They form a row of one story and attics: they are built of rubble stone and are now colour-washed, and most have thatched roofs. Most, too, have leaded casements with shutters on the ground floor and have gabled dormer windows. The terrace ends with the Bull Inn, known to have been in the possession in 1684 of Robert Parsons, member of a substantial Great Milton family of that period.[24] The appearance of the group is enhanced by the well-kept grass verge in front. To the west of the green stands the 'Bell' (an 18th-century public house restored in the 19th century), more thatched cottages, and the other of the two prebendal manor-houses, the Monkery. Opposite, standing on the slope of the hill with a terraced approach above the road level, is a row of 17th- and 18th-century stone cottages. They have brick facings, thatched roofs, dormer casements, and also ground-floor casements.

About half-way between the green and the north-western limit of the village stands the 16th-century house of the Pettys,[25] in 1959 the house of the village schoolmistress. It is built of rubble with ashlar quoins. Its gabled front faces the village street, but is set back some way from it. It has stone mullioned windows of four lights on the ground floor, of three lights on the first floor and of two on the attic level. The house is connected to the schoolroom which was added in the same style in 1854.[26]

At the north-west end of the village street is a picturesque group of 18th-century houses and a block of five early 19th-century cottages. They are built of the local rubble stone and have thatched or tiled roofs. The Limes, once a large farmhouse, is in part a Queen Anne house, which was added to and considerably altered in the early 18th century. It stands back from the road behind a low stone wall; its two-storied street front is of five bays with a pedimented porch in the centre. The roof is tiled and there is contemporary panelling inside. A wing of 17th-century date extends eastwards and the detached block of L-shaped stable buildings to the right of the house is probably also of this date.

The early 19th-century cottages and houses are constructed of brick and are usually roofed with Welsh slate; the 20th-century bungalows and houses are mostly roughcast or built of brick.

The parish was singular in the 16th and 17th centuries for the number of gentle families that made their home there, particularly at Great Milton. Its high position, good water, the excellence of the stone from the quarries of Great and Little Milton, Wheatley, or Haseley, which was easily available for building, were doubtless the cause. Signs of these small quarries can still be seen in the Upper Portland beds containing a layer of sandy freestone with a maximum thickness of 6 feet.[27] Plot says that the Little Milton quarries were still of 'considerable use' in the second half of the 17th century.[28]

Among the families that resided at Great Milton in the second half of the 16th century were those of Edgerley, Calfhill (Caulfeild), Grene, Parsons, and Westfalling; and in the 17th century in addition to the Parsons and Grenes, who still appear in the register, there are the names of Astrey, Aldworth, Purefoy, Smith, Petty, Philipson, Cave, and Meetkerke.[29] Sir Herbert Croft's child was baptized in the church,[30] but he does not seem to have been a resident. A number of the houses in which these families lived still survive. They rebuilt or modernized the two ancient prebendal houses and the manor-house, and probably built anew the Priory and the Great House.

The Monkery, as the farmhouse of Milton Ecclesia was called in the 19th century, is mentioned as early as 1318, when Master Gilbert de Segrave, the prebendary, acquired without royal licence a small piece of land for the enlargement of his dwelling.[31] At the end of the 16th century Prebendary John Sled, son of a Great Milton gentleman, lived there. Delafield says that he kept the 'parsonage house in his own hands'.[32] He was one of the richest men in the parish and was buried in Great Milton church in 1601.[33] The Davis family were the next occupants: Martha, John Sled's daughter married William Davis[34] and then the vicar, Richard Attwood.[35] William Davis (d. 1635), her son by her first husband, inherited the lease on her death in 1622 and resided there.[36] His widow Eleanor later took the house to her husband John Cave (d. 1693), a relative of the Waterstock family and later Vicar of Milton.[37] He bought the house for £587 in 1650 and proceeded to enlarge it.[38] Before alteration the house consisted of a parlour, hall, and four bedrooms be-

[24] d.d. Burrows c 1–2 (uncat.).
[25] See below, p. 150.
[26] See below, p. 145.
[27] W. J. Arkell, *Oxford Stone*, 90; 'Stratigraphy and Structures east of Oxford', *Quart. Jnl. Geol. Soc.* pt. 2 (1944), c. 47. Workings at Romeyn's Court can still be seen and stone was quarried at the end of the 19th century at Padding Butts and on the site of the 1957 recreation ground: inf. the late Revd. R. A. Ker.
[28] Plot, *Nat. Hist. Oxon.* (1677), 77.

[29] Par. Reg.
[30] Par. Reg.
[31] *Cal. Pat.* 1317–21, 152.
[32] MS. Gough Oxon. 48, ff. 140, 208–9.
[33] Ibid. f. 140b.
[34] Ibid. f. 141.
[35] C 2/3/40.
[36] MS. Gough Oxon. 48, ff. 141–141b.
[37] C 142/437/101; MS. Gough Oxon. 48, ff. 141–4: Delafield errs in saying that Eleanor was his sister.
[38] C 54/2568.

sides the usual offices of a 17th-century house.[39] A new hall, parlour, and rooms over were built. In 1650 the house was described as having twelve bays of building, eight bedrooms, and three garrets. There were five outhouses, three gardens, an orchard, and three fishponds.[40] Cave died in 1693 in the house, where three of his sons had been born, and was buried in the church.[41] Today (1959) the Monkery is a three-story house built of rubble stone and has a hipped and tiled roof. There are four irregular bays on the road front, a central chimney with three diamond shafts and at the back of the house two large stone chimneys with brick shafts. Parts of the building date from the 15th century, but there have been 16th- and 17th-century additions. To the east there is a 16th-century stone barn of seven bays with

above. On the first floor there are three similar three-light windows and one of two lights, but the ground floor windows are of later date. The central doorway over which is a cartouche with the arms of Boyle gives access to a hall with a wide low-arched Tudor fireplace. The ceiling retains its original oak beams. The chief ground-floor room has a similar fireplace and ceiling. The principal rooms, one above the other, extend the whole width of the house and are panelled in oak. The tradition is that Dr. Westfalling, a vice-chancellor of the University in 1565, originally built the Priory, perhaps as a refuge from the plague in Oxford. He was consecrated Bishop of Hereford in 1585 and presumably left Milton as he died in Hereford in 1601.[45] Later Dr. John Wilkinson, President of Magdalen, bought the house and lived there

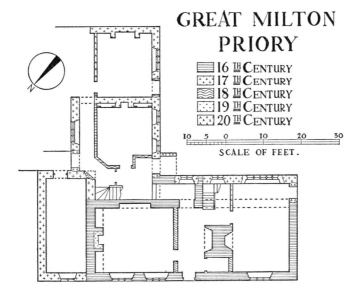

GREAT MILTON PRIORY

▭ 16 TH CENTURY
▭ 17 TH CENTURY
▨ 18 TH CENTURY
▢ 19 TH CENTURY
▨ 20 TH CENTURY

SCALE OF FEET.

a thatched roof, and to the south a 17th-century one of four bays with an old tiled roof. The square dovecot of stone with a louvred dormer head also dates from the 16th or 17th century. The house was modernized when Sir John Aubrey was lessee in 1786–1826.[42]

Isolated from the main part of the village and half-way down the hill leading to the old Vicarage and on to the church lies the Priory, a well-preserved example of a 16th and early 17th-century house. Its name, apparently of 19th-century origin, is a mystery. It is possible that the house was built on the site of Eynsham Abbey's 13th-century barn,[43] or Leland's story that the house was on the site of a cell of Abingdon may have suggested the name.[44] Incidentally there is no evidence that Abingdon had property in Milton, although it had in neighbouring Garsington. Today the Priory has two stories and attics and is built of the local rubble stone with ashlar quoins and dressings. The north elevation has triple gables with moulded copings and small finials. Each gable has a two-light attic casement, stone-mullioned and leaded, and with a drip-mould

with his nephew Henry.[46] The arms of Wilkinson were once emblazoned in a window.[47] A friend and visitor, according to Delafield, was John Thurloe (1616–68), Secretary of State. Thurloe later leased the house; it was said to be his favourite residence, and according to village tradition both Oliver Cromwell and John Milton visited him there.[48] In 1742, when Delafield was writing, William Eldridge (d. 1716) had the house; he was the grandson of another William Eldridge who was the first of the family to have it.[49]

The gardens are disposed in a series of terraces, connected by a flight of wide stone steps leading to a Jacobean door. The house is separated from the road by stone walls in which there are two gateways of late 18th-century date. They have moulded caps and ball finials to the piers.

The 17th-century Vicarage has long been superseded. It was a 'handsome' tiled house of four bays with barn and stables attached.[50] It was replaced first by a house built by the vicar, Richard Cornish (1726–9), and then by one built after the design of Sir Arthur Blomfield in 1867.[51] The Old Vicarage

---

[39] C 142/347/101.
[40] Linc. Regy., Parl. Survey pps. Alnwick tower.
[41] MS. Gough Oxon. 48, ff. 141b–144; and see below, p. 140.   [42] Parker, *Guide*, 319.
[43] *Eynsham Cart.* i. 223.
[44] Leland, *Itin.* ed. Toulmin Smith, ii. 116; cf. Wood, *City of Oxford*, i. 349; Parker, *Guide*, 317 n.

[45] *D.N.B.*
[46] MS. Gough Oxon. 48, ff. 114–22; cf. *D.N.B.*
[47] MS. Gough Oxon. 48, f. 122.
[48] Ibid. ff. 114, 135b.
[49] Ibid. f. 137.
[50] D. & C. Lincoln, Arch. D iv/69.
[51] MS. Gough Oxon. 48, f. 283; Par. Rec.

has been the residence since 1957 of Sir John Sleight, Bt., and a new Vicarage nearby, designed by Thomas Rayson, was completed in 1956 for the Revd. E. P. Baker.[52]

Farther south still and on top of the hill stands the church with the Manor House, the Great House, and Romeyns Court grouped round it. With the well-kept church-yard, their gardens, and parklands they form a striking group and have considerable aesthetic and historic interest. The Manor House stands on the site of a 13th-century house known as Ingescourt and once was occupied by William Inge.[53] In the early 15th-century it seems to have been used as a dower house by Joan, the widow of Sir Richard Camoys, the son of Sir Thomas Camoys of Agincourt fame. The deed giving her possession on her husband's death was executed at Great Milton in 1416.[54] In the 1470's and 1480's, when William Radmylde was lord, some of the old house seems to have been demolished, and a new hall and chamber were erected and repairs were carried out.[55] John Sewy, a mason of Reading, undertook in 1475 to 'new make' the stone work of the hall, making the walls 16 ft. high, putting in a chimney at the upper end, 10 ft. broad, and making two bay windows of freestone, 8 ft. wide, on either side of the hall and another at the upper end. They were to be embattled and be made with 'double story clear lights'. Sewy also undertook to make the stone walls of a new chamber on the south side of the court and to make a number of buttresses including one to support a gallery. Richard Welch, a carpenter of Abingdon, did the carpenter's work on the new hall and chamber and another from Chalgrove was also employed. The freestone was supplied by Thomas Mason of Wheatley from the Wheatley quarries, some of the timber came from Coombe in Great Milton, and the tiles from Nettlebed. Camoys ('Cames') Barn and English Barn, an oxhouse and a hoghouse, were among the outhouses repaired.[56] It was the remains of these extensive buildings, presumably, that Leland saw when he visited Milton in 1548.[57] In 1566 Alexander Calfhill (Caulfeild) leased the house and lived there quietly for fourteen years.[58] Many of his children including Sir Toby Caulfeild, 1st Baron Charlemont, were born at Great Milton.[59] Attempts were made by the Dormers in 1580 to get possession and Calfhill complained that he was obliged to keep a large number of servants at his house to defend his rights.[60] By 1588 Sir William Grene was in occupation of the manor-house.[61] A deed of 1611, which mentions its orchards, gardens, pond, and pigeon-house, states that he was then living there.[62] Apart from some slight remains of the medieval hall the oldest part of the present building probably dates from about 1600 or a little later, and may have been built by the

Grenes or possibly by Sir George Coppin, who purchased the house in 1613.[63] It was considerably extended to the south and north in 1908.[64] The walls surrounding the grounds and the original entrance to the house are 17th-century. There is a contemporary gateway to the road with obelisk finials.[65]

The Great House stands immediately to the west of the church. It was lived in by the Smith family in the first quarter of the 17th century and was presumably rebuilt by them.[66] John Smith was a royalist and a benefactor of Trinity College, who was heavily fined in 1649 for his aid to the king.[67] The house was rated at eight hearths for the hearth tax of 1665.[68] The family intermarried with the Skynner family, of which the most important member was Sir John Skynner, Lord Chief Baron of the Exchequer. He was born at Great Milton, inherited the house from his mother, retired to it in about 1786, and lived there until his death in 1805.[69] After Skynner's death the house devolved to the Rt. Hon. Richard Ryder, Home Secretary, as his wife Frederica Martha was the judge's only daughter.[70]

The present house has an early Georgian front of five bays with a recessed centre. It is built of stone and has two stories and attics. There is a moulded cornice and parapet, and a hipped roof covered with tiles. All the windows have stone architrave-surrounds and the upper ones have apron sills. The central door is in a wide stone doorcase framed by Doric pilasters. The gabled back of the house and the north wing enclosing a small courtyard are the oldest parts. The south front is said to have been added in 1806 though the rainwater heads bear the date 1788. It is on a different level and is faced with ashlar. The front is of seven bays including a two-story segmental bow with three windows to the right hand of the centre. Inside, the rooms have contemporary marble fire-places, and the wing is approached from the old house by three steps and a vestibule framed by Doric columns. Ellis, writing in 1819, records that the architect was 'the late Mr. Wyatt', i.e. James Wyatt (d. 1813).[71]

Romeyn's Court was occupied in Henry VIII's reign by Robert Edgerley (d. 1551), a man of some wealth,[72] and later by his widow Agnes and her second husband Sir Thomas Benger, Master of the Revels to Queen Elizabeth and Visitor of Oxford University.[73] Sir Thomas was leasing the house and manor in 1552[74] and may have been responsible for the oldest part of the present building. In 1650 it was described as an ancient manor-house, consisting of nine bays and eleven rooms in addition to garrets, pantry, milkhouse, and so on. Its outbuildings included two stables, a stone pigeon-house and a gate-house, and there was a garden and an orchard, well stored with fruit trees.[75] The house was originally built in the shape of a U but the centre

[52] Inf. Revd. E. P. Baker.
[53] See below, p. 123.
[54] B.M. Harl. Ch. 54. 1. 34; Parker, *Guide*, 315; and see below, p. 123.
[55] *Jnl. of Br. Arch. Ass.* (vol. xviii. 1955), 42–52, 55–56; a plan is given: ibid. 55.
[56] Ibid. 42–52.
[57] Leland, *Itin.* ed. Toulmin Smith, ii. 116.
[58] See below, p. 124. The name is always spelt Calfhill in the Great Milton registers.
[59] *D.N.B.*; Par. Reg.   [60] Req. 2/111/27.
[61] MS. Gough Oxon. 48, f. 66; and see below, p. 124.
[62] d.d. Hobbes c 15.
[63] Bodl. MS. ch. Oxon. 4029.

[64] Inf. Mr. A. J. Bell, the owner in 1959.
[65] See plate facing p. 121.
[66] Thos. Ellis, *Some Account of Gt. Milton*, 17.
[67] *Cal. Cttee. for Compounding*, 2079.
[68] *Hearth Tax Oxon.* 49.
[69] *D.N.B.*; Thos. Ellis, *Some Acct. of Gt. Milton*, 17–18.
[70] Skelton, *Oxon.* Thame Hundred, 3 n.
[71] Thos. Ellis, *Some Acct. of Gt. Milton*, 18. For an interior view see plate facing p. 8.
[72] MS. Gough Oxon. 48, f. 360; and see below, p. 126.
[73] F. B. Benger, *A Calendar of References to Sir Thomas Benger*; *Visit. Oxon.* 164.
[74] Wood, *Fasti*, 108; and see below, p. 126.
[75] Linc. Regy. Parl. Survey pps. Alnwick tower.

STADHAMPTON CHURCH IN 1821
Before the alterations of 1875

GREAT MILTON. THE SOUTH FRONT OF THE GREAT HOUSE
Designed by James Wyatt

The 17th-century Gateway to the Manor-house in 1821

The Church in 1822 before the Restoration of 1850

GREAT MILTON

has been filled in. It has two stories and is built of rubble stone. The roof is hipped and covered with old tiles. The north-west front has side wings of two bays; the windows are either of 18th-century date or altered in the 19th century. The arched stone doorway in the centre is also 19th-century. A small barn, dated 1868, and group of stable buildings, all stone-built, stand to the north-east of the house.

Little Milton lies in the southern half of the parish at about 190 ft. above sea-level and on a small stream flowing into the Thame.[76] A sale catalogue of 1810 did not exaggerate when it wrote of the village's 'salubrity of air and fine springs of water'.[77] It lies off the main Aylesbury road, but secondary roads radiate from it to the neighbouring villages. It has considerable character and its buildings are noticeably well kept. It is a good example of a nucleated village with several stone-built farmhouses lying along the main street. Although some are no longer used as such the farm buildings in most cases still stand behind them. There are a number of 18th- and late 17th-century houses, such as the 'Three Horse Shoes' and the 'Lamb'; others date from the period of general rural rebuilding, roughly 1570–1640, and these include the manor-house; while at least one house goes back to about 1500. The remains of a medieval village cross were still standing in the early 19th century.[78]

The manor-house has been considerably altered in later periods, but it was originally a 16th-century house. It is a three-storied house built of rubble stone with ashlar quoins. The south front is symmetrical with a slightly projecting feature of three bays with three gables. There is a moulded stone string over the first-floor windows; some stone-mullioned windows and a central doorway dating from the 18th century. It has an arched opening with a fanlight.

Of the smaller ancient houses[79] by far the best preserved stands next to the garage. Built in about 1600 it still has all its original fireplaces and mullioned windows and a restored newel staircase. It has a small cellar and three floors, the top one forming an extensive loft. Its plan is unusual: although the building is roughly T-shaped, the chimney stack is central at the crossing of the T and the staircase is not attached to it as one would expect, but is at some distance from the stack. The south gable has a dovecot built in under the attic windows. The other houses in the village down to the 18th century are either L-shaped or simply rectangular, in nearly every case having entrance doorway, stack, and staircase in a line across the centre of the building. Typical of the L-shaped plan is Greystone Stores, which retains many features of c. 1600 in spite of the drastic alterations to the ground-floor façade. It has upper windows with moulded mullions, a chimney-stack (slightly to the left of centre) with a rectangular stone base, and three diamond shafts of brick with offset and toothed heads, and a cellar with a blocked mullioned window, now well below ground level. Fletcher Farm, lower down the street, was probably originally of simple rectangular plan.

It has a massive central stack, stone-chamfered mullions on the ground floor, and wooden ovolo mullions in the front windows of the first floor. Half of the loft space, reached through a trap-door, seems to have been plastered over at some later date to provide extra sleeping accommodation. The barn nearby has the date 1638 carved on a beam, almost certainly the date of building of both barn and house. Frogmore Cottage, outside the village, is another 17th-century example of the rectangular plan and of a house with a large loft, reached through a trap-door. It is unusual, however, for the way in which a later house has been joined to it at only one corner, a feature which may have been dictated by the marshy nature of the ground.

Although the village is predominantly stone-built there are at least two timber-framed houses which may indicate that this type of construction was common before it was superseded towards the end of the 16th-century by more expensive but more durable building in stone. Well Cottage at the lower end of the main street retains some of its original timbers and wattle and daub; it now occupies only half of the original building which once had a central through passage with a ground-floor room on either side. The other half-timbered house, Hill View, a little below the garage, is of special interest. It is long, high, of rectangular plan, and with a later stone façade with wattle and daub filling and an original window opening. Some very early timber framing can be seen on the first floor at the back. This, together with the curving wind-braces in the roof and the moulded posts and arched braces in one of the bedrooms, suggests that the house was built c. 1500 or even earlier.

The 19th century saw the addition of a church of good design, built in an exceptionally fine position and surrounded by a beautiful churchyard, which has been carefully kept up; of a Vicarage built c. 1850; of a school and schoolhouse; and of a Methodist chapel.[80]

Of Milton's other hamlets Ascot once had a large manor-house, a medieval chapel, and at least three farmhouses.[81] Little is left now except Ascot Farm, an L-shaped, half-timbered and brick house, dating from the 16th and 17th centuries, and a few other survivals of the great house and its appendages. Ascot was the home for several generations of various members of the Great Milton branch of the Dormer family: Sir Michael Dormer acquired it in 1518, and it passed to his son Ambrose (d. 1566).[82] Ambrose's widow Jane, who had a life-interest in the house,[83] took as her second husband William Hawtrey, a London merchant and an original member of the Muscovy company.[84] In her will made in 1581, Jane speaks of her plate and household stuff at 'my mansion house and grounds called Ascott',[85] and it seems probable that the Hawtreys lived at Ascot. There were at least four other Dormer-Hawtrey marriages and William Hawtrey's younger brother Thomas, also a merchant of the Muscovy Company,[86] appears to have stayed in the Ascot house at the end of his life. He made

[76] O.S. Map 6″, xl (1886).   [77] Bodl. G.A. fol. B 71.

[78] For an illustration of 1812 see MS. Top. Oxon. b 220, f. 235b.

[79] The following two paragraphs are based on notes contributed by Mr. D. Portman.

[80] See below, pp. 143, 145.

[81] For its decline see below, p. 134.

[82] See below, p. 127.   [83] P.C.C. 72 Dixie.

[84] Inf. Mr. J. D. A. Barnicot.   [85] P.C.C. 72 Dixie.

[86] J. D. A. Barnicot and J. S. G. Simmons, 'Some Early Printed Slavonic Books', Oxf. Slavonic Papers, ii (1950), 115–17.

his will there, left a bequest of 10s. to the Vicar of Milton, and was buried in Great Milton church.[87] Some details about the building in the time of Sir Michael Dormer, Ambrose's son, have survived. There were at least twelve bed-chambers, including a gate-house chamber, and a long gallery is also mentioned.[88] It is likely that the house suffered from Hampden's raid on Ascot in 1642[89] when he demanded its surrender; it was in any case rebuilt by Sir William Dormer in the 1660's. He was known as William 'the Splendid' and it is evident that his mansion was planned on a large scale, but it was accidentally damaged by fire in 1662 before its completion.[90] It is said that it was 'burnt down',[91] but either some of it was left or it was rebuilt, for William Dormer paid tax on twelve hearths for this house in 1665, and Plot shows it as a four-chimneyed house on his map of 1697.[92] It was evidently used as a dower house until at least 1728.[93] Davis shows a house there in 1797; he also shows the park, the formal inclosed garden, and a chapel in the grounds.[94] Nothing is left now of the house or its outbuildings except for a 17th-century dove-house, granary, and summer-house. The dove-cot has wall faces of vitreous and red brick, with diamond, chevron, and chequer patterns; the eaves string is arched and cusped. The brick granary is octagonal and has a vaulted cellar. The summer-house is built of rubble with ashlar dressings; it is of two stories and has a hipped roof. It is now a dwelling house called Piccadilly Cottage and has been added to and modernized. Seventeenth-century walls of terraces and the gate-posts of the main entrance to the grounds survive. The last have stone piers, cornice heads, and ball finials, and are flanked by avenues of lime trees. A wrought-iron gate of 18th-century date and an early 17th-century gateway of stone, once in the park, are now in the Victoria and Albert Museum.[95]

The chapel, a private one attached to the manor-house, was built probably soon after 1200 and remained until 1823, when it was pulled down.[96] It consisted of chancel and nave, with a central bell-cot over the chancel-arch; both nave and chancel were originally lighted by lancet windows, but two of these on the south side were replaced by two-light Decorated windows in the 14th century. When Powell visited it in 1805 he found it 'in ruins'. There were wall paintings in red in the nave depicting the passion of Christ, scourging, crucifixion, descent into hell, and appearance to Mary Magdalen.[97] A drawing of the chapel from the south was made in 1811 when the building was still entire.[98] Another of 1813 shows it roofless.[99]

Milton's other hamlets, the two Chilworths and Coombe, had disappeared long before Ascot's decline.[1] In 1739 Chilworth Farm, tenanted by Edward Hedges, which was about all that was left of one of the Chilworths, was burnt down with all its outhouses. The landlord, Sir Edward Simeon, Bt., rebuilt the house and Hedges obtained a brief to cover his personal losses.[2] The present Chilworth Farm is mainly of this date, but may incorporate parts of an earlier house. The second hamlet in Chilworth may have centred round the other farmstead in the township, Wheatley Bridge Farm. As the lords of Chilworth Valery and Chilworth Musard each had land in both the hamlets the descent of the property does not help to identify precisely either of the Chilworths.

The approximate position of Coombe is indicated by the field-names compounded with 'combe' recorded from the 15th century and marked on the tithe map to the east of Chilworth farm,[3] where in fact the land forms a natural combe.

The parish has been associated with a remarkable number of interesting persons. Most have already been mentioned in connexion with the houses they occupied, but Thomas Delafield, vicar, though mostly an absentee, should not be omitted. He was educated partly at Milton school, was an assiduous antiquary, and his works included a history of Great Milton.[4]

MANORS. In 1086, the Bishop of Lincoln had 31 hides in Milton and his tenants 9 or 9¾ hides.[5] These lands had apparently come to him from Dorchester when the see was moved soon after 1072.[6] The tenants' hides appear to represent Ascot township and there is no record at this date of the 2 fees in Great and Little Milton (afterwards *GREAT MILTON* manor), first precisely recorded in 13th-century documents, or of the prebendal manor, later known as Romeyn's Court, which came to constitute the two principal manors in Great and Little Milton.

By 1166, the two Milton fees were evidently included in the 8 fees which Roger de Cundi then held under the bishop:[7] he made a grant of land at Milton to Eynsham Abbey;[8] his widow Basilea made a grant of a rent in the parish to Oseney Abbey[9] and was still living in Milton in 1225;[10]

[87] Inf. Mr. Barnicot, from Hawtrey's will (proved 1591) and Gt. Milton par. reg.; cf. F. M. Hawtrey, *Hist. of Hawtrey Family*, i. 22–23, 28–29.

[88] Rousham Arch. L 34.

[89] M. Maclagan, 'Family of Dormer in Oxon.' *Oxoniensia*, xi–xii. 99; G. N. Grenville, *Memorials of John Hampden*, i. 212, 213.

[90] Maclagan, op. cit. 99; Wood, *Life*, i. 458.

[91] Wood, *Life*, i. 458.

[92] *Hearth Tax Oxon.* 51; Plot, *Nat. Hist. Oxon.* frontispiece.

[93] See below, p. 127.

[94] Davis, *Oxon. Map.*

[95] Illustrated in *English Wrought-Ironwork* (H.M.S.O.).

[96] Parker, *Guide*, 320.

[97] MS. Top. Oxon. b 75, f. 52.

[98] Parker, *Guide*, 320. For its site see O.S. Map 25″, xlvi. 7 (1881).

[99] Bodl. G.A. Oxon. 4° 697, facing p. 320; MS. Top. Oxon. b 165, f. 211 (1813); b 220, f. 235 (1812).

[1] See below, p. 134.

[2] d.d. Hobbs c 5. For estimate of rebuilding see O.R.O. Misc. Eve I/2.

[3] See map, p. 132.

[4] For his life see Bodl. MS. Gough Oxon. 48 (Hist. of Milton), ff. 279–81; for his other collections see *Summary Cat. of Western MSS. in Bodl.* Index vol.

[5] *V.C.H. Oxon.* i. 402, 403; and see below, p. 126. For Domesday Book's two versions of the hidage see above, p. 2.

[6] The statement in *V.C.H. Oxon.* v. 4 that Great Milton once belonged to Eynsham Abbey was based on the identification of *Milcetuna* with Milton in *Reg. Antiquiss.* i. 5–7. It is now clear that *Milcetuna* should have been identified with Mickleton (Glos.): cf. *Eynsham Cart.* i, pp. ix. 9, 34, 36, and *passim*. Great Milton was undoubtedly part of the ancient endowment of Dorchester bishopric: see *V.C.H. Oxon.* i. 378; and above, p. 53.

[7] *Red Bk. Exch.* (Rolls Ser.), 375.

[8] *Eynsham Cart.* i. 113; cf. *Reg. Antiquiss.* i. 291.

[9] *Oseney Cart.* vi. 157.

[10] Eyton, *Salop.* v. 157.

finally Agnes, the daughter of Roger and Basilea, married Walter de Clifford, the Marcher lord,[11] who was holding in Milton in John's reign.[12] His son, Walter de Clifford, succeeded him in 1221[13] and in 1236 granted the fees in Great Milton to Walter de Kirkham, Dean of St. Martin's-in-the-Field and later Bishop of Durham, who was then Prebendary of Milton Manor.[14] Walter de Kirkham was to pay £71 and to hold the fees for thirteen years on condition that he performed Walter's foreign service and cleared him of a debt of £155 13s. 4d. to the Jews.[15] In 1279 John de Clifford held the fees.[16] He may have been a member of the younger branch of the Clifford family which had held Frampton-on-Severn (Glos.) under Walter de Clifford in 1235.[17] John de Clifford of Frampton is said to have died in 1299,[18] but his heirs did not hold Great Milton.

By 1305 the Clifford holding was divided: Sir Richard de Louches held a ⅔-fee (later known as *CAMOYS* manor) and William Inge held a ⅓-fee (later known as *INGESCOURT*).[19] Richard de Louches was a member of a widespread family which held lands in both Oxfordshire and Berkshire.[20] He married Elena Wace, daughter of William and Agnes Wace.[21] He was returned as one of the lords of Great Milton at the inquest of 1316[22] and was granted free warren in 1318,[23] but died before 1327 when his son John was in possession.[24] In 1346 John still held his portion of Great Milton,[25] but by 1367 it had passed to Elizabeth de Louches, the daughter of John's son William.[26] She brought it to the Camoys family by her marriage with Sir Thomas Camoys, the commander of the left wing of the English army at Agincourt.[27] Sir Thomas died in 1421, leaving as his heir his grandson Hugh, who was already in possession of the ⅓-part of Great Milton manor, i.e. Ingescourt.[28]

Sir William Inge who held this ⅓-part in 1305 was returned as joint lord of Great Milton with Richard de Louches in 1316.[29] He seems to have been the son of Thomas Inge of Totternhoe (Beds.),[30] and by this time he was a well-known judge (he opened the Lincoln Parliament of 1316) and held extensive possessions in some ten counties.[31] Sir William settled Ingescourt and other lands on his second wife Iseult, the widow of Urian de St. Pierre.[32]

Sir William died in 1322 and his heir was Joan, his daughter by his first wife.[33] She never held the manor, for Iseult (d. 1370) outlived her. Iseult

granted Great and Little Milton to John atte Streete of Little Milton and Robert de Woubourne for the term of her life,[34] and in 1360 Joan's son, William La Zouche of Harringworth, quitclaimed his rights in Great and Little Milton to these two men and to the heirs of Robert.[35] In 1370, soon after Iseult's death,[36] John atte Streete of Little Milton obtained a grant of free warren in his demesne lands in Great and Little Milton for himself and his heirs.[37]

By 1416 Sir Richard Camoys was in possession of Ingescourt. Whether it came to the family by purchase or marriage is not known, but in that year he granted it with all his property in Great and Little Milton to feoffees so as to make provision on his death for his wife, Joan Poynings, daughter of Sir Richard Poynings.[38] By June Sir Richard Camoys was dead and the feoffees released Ingescourt to Joan with reversion to Sir Richard's son John and, if John had no heirs, to the other sons Ralph and Hugh.[39] Both Joan and John died shortly after and Bishop Philip Repingdon of Lincoln had custody of the heir Ralph and of Ingescourt manor.[40] Ralph also died after the resignation of Bishop Philip in 1419 and Bishop Philip and his successor Bishop Richard Fleming both claimed the custody of the child Hugh, who now became heir to Ingescourt.[41] By this time Hugh's grandfather Sir Thomas Camoys had died (1421), leaving Hugh as his heir,[42] and so Ingescourt and Camoys manors were united and Great Milton manor was once again under one lord.

On Hugh's death in 1426, however, his lands were divided between his two sisters Margaret and Eleanor, who had married respectively Ralph Radmylde and Sir Roger Lewknor.[43] There is no record of the descent of the Lewknor portion, although the inquisitions show that the Radmyldes held only half the manor in the 15th century.[44] Some arrangement between the two families had doubtless been made by the end of the 15th century, by which the Lewknors took over some of the Sussex manors of the Camoys inheritance and Wheatley in Oxfordshire and the Radmyldes or their successors took the Milton manors and other Sussex manors.[45] Ralph Radmylde continued to hold after his wife's death and was succeeded by their son Robert in 1443.[46] Robert died in 1457,[47] and his son William, who was a minor in 1457,[48] obtained possession in 1474.[49] Before his death in 1499[50] William disposed

[11] Ibid.
[12] *Bk. of Fees*, 40; in 1201 Walter de Clifford held 5 fees of the Bishop of Lincoln, apparently as Roger's successor: *Rot. de Ob. et Fin.* (Rec. Com.), 153.
[13] *Rot. Litt. Claus.* (Rec. Com.), i. 446b.
[14] *Close R.* 1234–7, 140.
[15] *Cal. Chart. R.* 1226–57, 217.
[16] *Rot. Hund.* (Rec. Com.), ii. 820–1.
[17] *Bk. of Fees*, 441.
[18] R. Atkins, *The Present and Ancient State of Gloucestershire*, 230, gives the Frampton descent.
[19] Queen's Coll. MS. 366, f. 24b: Sir Richard did homage at Dorchester c. 1299–1300.
[20] *V.C.H. Berks.* iii. 547, 549; *V.C.H. Oxon.* v. 110; in 1279 there was a De Louches holding in Little Milton and Chislehampton: *Rot. Hund.* (Rec. Com.), ii. 750.
[21] *Boarstall Cart.* 9–10.
[22] *Feud. Aids*, iv. 167.
[23] *Cal. Chart. R.* 1300–26, 389.
[24] *Cal. Pat.* 1327–30, 84, 86.
[25] *Feud. Aids*, iv. 181.
[26] *Cal. Inq. Misc.* iii, p. 250.
[27] *Boarstall Cart.* 9–10; for Sir Thomas Camoys's career see *Complete Peerage*, ii. 507–8.

[28] C 138/288/29.
[29] *Feud. Aids*, iv. 167.
[30] *V.C.H. Beds.* ii. 336; iii. 430, 449; *Ann. Mon.* (Rolls Ser.), iii. 206–7, 343, 394.
[31] Foss, *Judges*, 366; *V.C.H. Herts.* ii. 188, 307, 366–7; *V.C.H. Hants.* iv. 431; *V.C.H. Bucks.* ii. 361.
[32] *Cal. Inq. p.m.* vi, p. 193; this was probably c. 1313, when he made a similar settlement of Weston (Beds.): *Cal. Pat.* 1307–13, 269, 551.
[33] *Cal. Inq. p.m.* vi, p. 193; xiii, p. 39.
[34] *Cal. Close*, 1360–4, 124.   [35] Ibid.
[36] *Cal. Inq. p.m.* xiii, p. 39.
[37] *Cal. Chart. R.* 1341–1417, 217.
[38] *Boarstall Cart.* 9–10.   [39] Ibid.
[40] *Cal. Pat.* 1422–9, 91, 173–4.   [41] Ibid.
[42] C 138/57/29.   [43] C 139/28/26.
[44] C 139/109/34.
[45] *V.C.H. Sussex*, iv, 6, 9, 35; viii. 81; *V.C.H. Oxon.* v. 50, 110.   [46] C 139/109/34.
[47] W.A.M. 1631.
[48] *Cal. Inq. p.m. Hen. VII*, ii, p. 419.
[49] W.A.M. 1631.
[50] *Complete Peerage*, ii. 510; *Camoys Peerage Claim*, *1838*, 43–44: his will. He left no legitimate children by his wife Jane: ibid. 47.

of various estates. In 1492 he sold Coombe and Chilworth, his other property in Great Milton parish, retaining Great and Little Milton manors.[51] By April 1499 Great Milton had been sold to Sir Reginald Bray, since the court was in that year held in his name.[52] He was the famous Lord Bray who by serving the Tudors had risen from obscurity to found the fortunes of the Brays of Shere.[53] The transaction had been started at least as early as 1497.[54] Leland said that Bray 'bought it off Danvers'[55] i.e. Thomas Danvers of Waterstock, and it may be that Danvers had been an intermediary in some of the numerous negotiations over the manor.[56] On Bray's death in 1503, his nephew Edmund succeeded[57] and in 1510 made a partition of the lands with Sir William Sandys, who had married Margaret, Sir Reginald's niece. Great Milton went to Edmund,[58] and in 1539 to his son John, Lord Bray (d. 1557),[59] who is said to have sold the manor to 'Dormer, Mair of London'.[60] This was Sir Michael Dormer, whose father Geoffrey had obtained the Baldington estate in Little Milton in 1473.[61] Sir Michael himself purchased lands in Little Milton in 1533, and Ascot manor[62] before his death in 1545.[63] Ambrose Dormer his son succeeded him.[64] Ascot became one of the Dormers' seats, and in 1566, the year he leased Great Milton manor for 21 years to Alexander Calfhill,[65] Ambrose Dormer settled the manor on his son Michael, then a minor.[66] Sir Michael, who c. 1580 challenged Calfhill's tenancy,[67] seems to have sold Great and Little Milton manors c. 1588 to Sir William Grene.[68] The Oxfordshire estates of Sir William and his son Michael were the subject of complex dealings arising from their debts.[69] Great Milton manor was bought by Sir George Coppin for £3,000,[70] and he died seized of it in 1619;[71] but his estates also were encumbered by debt,[72] and his son Robert sold the manor for £2,500 to Humphrey Ayleworth,[73] a member of the Gloucestershire and Warwickshire family.[74] By 1634 Thomas Lord Coventry, Lord Keeper of the Great

Seal, who already had the lay fee of Milton manor prebend,[75] had purchased it.[76] He died in 1640 and the Coventry estates were held by his eldest son Thomas (d. 1661).[77] In 1653 Thomas Lord Coventry seems to have settled Great and Little Milton on his younger son Thomas and his wife Winifred.[78] In 1675, however, they conveyed them to Sir William and John Coventry, sons of Thomas's brother, George, Baron Coventry (d. 1680).[79] In 1687 John Baron Coventry died unmarried and the estates went to his uncle Thomas, who became Baron Coventry and was created Viscount Deerhurst and Earl of Coventry in 1697.[80] He seems to have settled Great and Little Milton manors on his second wife Elizabeth Graham. After his death in 1699 they were held by Elizabeth and her second husband, Thomas Savage, who continued to hold them when Elizabeth died in 1724 until his own death in 1742.[81] In 1755 George William, Earl of Coventry (d. 1809), was lord of the manors.[82] In 1773 he sold them to Thomas Blackall.[83] The Blackall family had been established in the neighbouring parish of Great Haseley for several generations,[84] and had leased land in Chilworth in the 17th century.[85] John Blackall died in 1784 in possession of the two Milton manors and of Ascot. The property passed to his cousin John Blackall of Great Haseley (d. 1790), to his cousin's son John (d. 1803) and grandson John. On the last John Blackall's death in 1829, the manors passed again to a cousin, Walter Long of Preshaw (Hants).[86] He was lord of the manors in 1844,[87] but opened negotiations shortly afterwards for their sale to the trustees of the Boulton estate, who purchased the manors of Great and Little Milton, Ascot, Lachford, and Haseley for £184,000 in 1847.[88] Matthew Piers Watt Boulton of Tew Park and Haseley was lord until his death in 1894.[89] His son Matthew Ernest Boulton held the estates until 1914, when his sister Clara Gertrude succeeded to Tew Park and his cousin Lt.-Col. Anthony John Muirhead (1939) to Haseley Court, but there was no

[51] C.P. 40/921, charters enrolled m. 1; W.A.M. 1631.

[52] W.A.M. 1631; in 1503 Edward Lewknor of Kingston Bowsey (Suss.), his wife Sybil, John Goring of Burton (Suss.) and his wife Constance quitclaimed their rights in Milton manor to Sir Reginald Bray and others: *Camoys Peerage Claim, 1838*, 49–51; C.P. 25(1)/294/81/115. They were the descendants of William Radmylde's aunts and heirs, Margaret Radmylde wife of John Goring and Elizabeth Radmylde wife of Nicholas Lewknor: *Complete Peerage*, ii. 510; *Visit. Suss.* (Harl. Soc. liii), 26–30, 45.

[53] *The Ancestor*, vi. 3–7, gives a life of Lord Bray.

[54] *Cal. Close*, 1485–1500, 294.

[55] Leland, *Itin.* ed. Toulmin Smith, i. 116.

[56] In 1503 Bray and others were pardoned for alienations and purchases of land in Milton, late of William Radmylde: *Cal. Pat.* 1494–1509, 304. Milton manor may, like other Radmylde lands, have been conveyed to Westminster Abbey for a time: cf. *Camoys Peerage Claim*, 52.

[57] *Cal. Pat.* 1494–1509, 326, 366; *The Ancestor*, vi. 5.

[58] *Complete Peerage*, ii. 287; C 54/378, m. 30; cf. C.P. 25(2)/34/227.

[59] *Complete Peerage*, ii. 287.

[60] Leland, *Itin.* i. 116.

[61] *Cal. Close*, 1468–76, 321; for the family, see *Oxoniensia*, xi. 90–101; Geoffrey Dormer had owed suit to Camoys manor ct.: W.A.M. 1634; and see below, p. 172.

[62] See below, p. 127.

[63] C 142/143/49; E 150/823/1.   [64] Ibid.

[65] Req. 2/111/27.

[66] C 142/143/49; E 150/823/1.   [67] Req. 2/111/27.

[68] Bodl. MS. Gough Oxon. 48, ff. 66, 362b; d.d. Hobbs c 4, c 5: lists recoveries of 30, 31 Eliz. by Sir William Grene to Sir Michael Dormer; cf. C.P. 25(2)/197/Trin. 27 Eliz.

[69] d.d. Hobbs c 4, c 6 contains many documents about

the Grenes's difficulties in Chilworth. They levied a fine on Great and Little Milton in 1610: C.P. 25(2)/339/Trin. 8 Jas. I. Michael Grene's financial difficulties resulted in his being a prisoner in the Fleet in the 1620's: d.d. Hobbs c 6; cf. *Acts of P.C.* 1618–19, 392.

[70] C.P. 25(2)/340/Hil. 15 Jas. I; C 3/341/86. He laid out a further sum for part of Chilworth.

[71] C 142/384/131.

[72] C 3/341/86.

[73] Ibid.; Bodl. MS. ch. Oxon. c 31, no. 4029.

[74] *Glos. Visit.* (Harl. Soc. xxi), 7; *Warwick. Visit.* (Harl. Soc. lxii), 48. Ayleworth had already bought an interest in Little Milton and Milton manor prebend. For lawsuits and other transactions in the 1620's concerning Great Milton manor see C 3/342/7; Bodl. MS. Gough Oxon. 43, f. 75b; C.P. 43/160/13; C 3/341/86.

[75] Bodl. MS. ch. Oxon. a 21, no. 421; se ebelow, p. 125.

[76] C.P. 25(2)/527/Mich. 9 Chas. I; ibid. Trin. 10 Chas. I.

[77] For the Coventry descent, see *Complete Peerage*, iii. 476–8.

[78] C.P. 43/613/236; C.P. 25(2)/588/Trin. 1659; C.P. 25(2)/708/Mich. 22 Chas. II.

[79] C.P. 25(2)/709/Mich. 27 Chas. II.

[80] *Complete Peerage*, iii. 472.

[81] Ibid.; Bodl. MS. Gough Oxon. 48, ff. 92–92b.

[82] O.R.O. H. IV/1.

[83] C.P. 43/637/209.

[84] d.d. Clerke Brown c 2.

[85] d.d. Ashhurst c 15.

[86] d.d. Clerke Brown c 2.

[87] O.R.O. Incl. award.

[88] O.R.O. Li XX/viii/14: an abstract of the Boulton title.

[89] O.R.O. Gamekprs' Dep. ii. 234; Burke, *Land. Gent.* (1937), 212.

further record of manorial rights in Great Milton parish.[90]

Although the main manor of Great Milton extended into Little Milton township there was also a smaller estate there, known later as *LITTLE MILTON* or *COTTESMORE* manor. By the late 12th century the Bishop of Lincoln had created a ½-knight's fee, held of his Dorchester manor, in Chislehampton and Little Milton. In 1166 Ernald de Cardunville held it.[91] Thereafter the ¼-fee in Little Milton followed the descent of the other ¼-fee of the Cardunvilles in Chislehampton, and presumably escheated to the bishop in 1225, when a certain Alice, who claimed to be the widow of James de Cardunville, failed to establish her right to dower in 10 virgates in Little Milton.[92] By 1279 the Little Milton fee had been granted to Laurence de Louches.[93] He was still the tenant in 1301 and 1305[94] and the estate evidently became merged in the de Louches manor of Great Milton and followed its descent.[95]

In 1279 a William de Bluntesdon was the demesne tenant of most of Laurence de Louches's estate in Little Milton;[96] by 1301 he had been succeeded by a Laurence de Bluntesdon, who died in that year, holding some 9 virgates of Laurence de Louches for ⅛ of half a fee.[97] His daughter Joan was heir, but there is no further record of the descent of the estate in the 14th century. By the early 15th century it is found in the possession of the famous chief justice, John Cottesmore of Haseley and Baldwin Brightwell.[98] He died in 1439[99] and the estate, except for that part of it which formed the dower of his widow Amicia Bruley, passed to his son John. John died before 1474 and his son, also named John, succeeded,[1] but a part again seems to have been assigned as dower, this time to Margaret, widow of John (II) Cottesmore.[2] At this date the estate was also known as Cottesmore manor and was subordinate or partly so to the main Camoys manor of Great Milton, since John (III) Cottesmore (d. by 1519) was frequently fined for defaulting in his suit of court.[3] In Little Milton the Cottesmore possessions included messuages and lands called 'Colrentreves', 'Richemans', and a house 'Bluntesdon', which were undoubtedly part of the 13th-century manor held by Laurence de Louches, but which were in 1487 said to be held of Great Milton manor for payment of 1 lb. of cummin each year.[4] On the death of Cottesmore's son William, Little Milton and Dorton

(Bucks.) were put in trust for John (IV) Cottesmore, the son and heir of William Cottesmore, and of his second wife Florence.[5] In 1533 this John Cottesmore sold the manors to Sir Michael Dormer,[6] who was amassing land in both parishes. In 1554 Little Milton was held by Sir Michael and his heirs of the Bishop of Lincoln as of his 'manor of Dorchester'.[7] Like the other Dormer lands the manor passed to the Grenes,[8] but was bought from them by Sir William Cope of Hanwell, who in 1616 sold Little Milton manor and lordship to Thomas and Paul Ayleworth of Warwickshire for £3,404.[9] It appears from a later lawsuit that they were acting on behalf of their brother Humphrey,[10] who also bought at this time Great Milton manor and an interest in the prebend.[11] Little Milton manor was said to be greatly encumbered by 'sundry leases, annuities, statutes, &c.' made by the Grenes:[12] it therefore changed hands frequently.[13]

It ultimately passed to Lord Coventry, who in 1634 was in possession of both Great and Little Milton[14] manors and it descended thereafter with Great Milton manor. Little Milton manor was offered for sale in 1893 with Little Milton manor farm,[15] but no further reference to it has been found.

Milton manor prebend, known by the 16th century as *ROMEYN'S COURT* and later as the manor of *GREAT* and *LITTLE MILTON* and *THE PREBEND*, was formed, according to the hundred rolls, as a prebend of Lincoln Cathedral by Bishop Alexander of Lincoln (1123–48).[16] It is first mentioned in a papal confirmation of 1146, when it was described as comprising half of Milton.[17] The prebend was sometimes called the manor of Milton and Binbrook, since the appropriated rectory of St. Gabriel, Binbrook (Lincs.) was attached to it.[18] In 1254 it was valued at £25 and at £46 13s. 4d. in 1291; in 1535, when Binbrook was valued separately, Milton was being farmed for £24.[19]

The manor belonged to the prebendary until 1775,[20] when the lessee, Charles Sturgess, Vicar of St. Mary's, Reading, and himself the prebendary from 1727 to 1746, purchased the freehold subject to an annual payment of £24 and £100 or 33 quarters of wheat to the prebendary.[21] The rent-charges were attached to specific parts of the estate in 1803,[22] when Sturgess sold the prebendal manor and estate to William Davey of Dorchester.[23] The estate seems to have been split up by the sale of the Prebendal

[90] Kelly, *Dir. Oxon.* (1903), 145; *Land. Gent.* (1937), 212; *Who Was Who, 1929–40*, 976.
[91] *Red. Bk. Exch.* (Rolls Ser.), 375.
[92] See above, p. 11; *Cur. Reg. R.* xii. 140, 143.
[93] *Rot. Hund.* (Rec. Com.), ii. 750; Laurence de Chislehampton was returned as tenant under Milton (ibid. 821), but the scribe may have confused Laurence de Louches, who held in Chislehampton, with Laurence de Chislehampton who was a different person; see above, p. 11.
[94] *Cal. Inq. p.m.* iv, p. 11; Queen's Coll. MS. 366, f. 25.
[95] See above, p. 123; cf. Chislehampton, above, p. 11.
[96] *Rot. Hund.* (Rec. Com.), ii. 821.
[97] *Cal. Inq. p.m.* iv, p. 11.
[98] W.A.M. 1594: Apr. ct. 1474.
[99] *Par. Coll.* 54.
[1] W.A.M. 1594: Apr. ct. 1474; 1631: Nov. ct. 1487.
[2] Ibid.
[3] Ibid. *passim.*
[4] Ibid. 1631.
[5] C 142/34/6; cf. *Cal. Close, 1485–1500*, 192.
[6] C 146/9420; C.P. 25(2)/34/228/7.
[7] Sta. Cha. 4/6/53.
[8] C.P. 25(2)/339/Trin. 8 Jas. I; C 3/342/7.

[9] Bodl. MS. ch. Oxon. c 65, no. 2517.
[10] C 2/12/72.
[11] See above, p. 124.
[12] Ibid.
[13] C.P. 25(2)/340/Trin. 17 Jas. I; C2/12/7; C 3/342/7; C.P. 25(2)/473/Trin. 2 Chas. I.
[14] C.P. 25(2)/527/Mich. 9 Chas. I; the descent from Cottesmore to Whistler, to 'Greene' and to Astry, given in *Par. Coll.* i. 54, was perhaps of tenants of the manor.
[15] Bodl. G.A. Oxon. b 92a (81), p. 18 (*Sale Cat.*).
[16] *Rot. Hund.* (Rec. Com.), ii. 821.
[17] *Reg. Antiquiss.* i. 199; for other estimates of the prebendal property, see below, p. 159.
[18] *Reg. Antiquiss.* iii. 290.
[19] Lunt, *Val. Norw.* 279; *Tax. Eccl.* (Rec. Com.), 30; *Valor Eccl.* (Rec. Com.), ii. 173.
[20] For lists of prebendaries, see Le Neve, *Fasti.* ii. 189–91.
[21] Act to subject . . . the Prebend Manor of Mych Milton, 15 Geo. III, c 55 (priv. act): copy in Bodl. L. Engl. C 13 c 1 (1774–5).
[22] Bodl. G.A. Oxon, fol. B 71: 1837 *Sale cat.* p. 3.
[23] Oxf. Dioc. b 70, f. 510.

farm in 1806,[24] but the rent-charges continued to be paid to the prebend until 1840 when they were transferred to the Ecclesiastical Commissioners.[25] There is still a prebend of Milton manor in Lincoln Cathedral.[26] The manorial rights were held in 1808 by John Hedges and Benjamin Bennett, but were up for sale in 1810.[27] It is not known what happened to these rights until 1840, when Walter Long, lord of the other Great Milton manors, was also lord of the prebendal manor[28] and perhaps had inherited it from the Blackalls.[29] The manor passed in 1847, like his other property, to the Boulton estate and followed the descent of that estate.[30]

Until 1775 the prebendary usually leased the manor. In the 16th century it was leased from 1516 to Robert Edgerley (Egerley), a prominent parishioner, for 60 years at £24 a year.[31] He married Katherine, possibly a Belson,[32] and there is a brass to their children in Milton church. His second wife Agnes succeeded to the lease on his death in 1551 and took it to her second husband, Sir Thomas Benger.[33] Later, Sir William Grene, lord of Great Milton, and his son Sir Michael were the lessees.[34] By 1616 it was being leased by Sir William Cope of Hanwell, who held the manor courts.[35] From 1628 it was held by Thomas, Lord Coventry.[36] The lords of Great Milton manor were the lessees until 1742, when Ambrose Isted, son of Thomas Isted of London, obtained the lease.[37] In 1765 Charles Sturgess took over the lease and later bought the freehold.[38]

ASCOT is not mentioned by name in Domesday Book, but there are good grounds for supposing that it was represented by the 6 hides and 3¾ hides held in Great Milton by Aluric and William of the Bishop of Lincoln[39] who, as later evidence shows, had 2 knight's fees in Ascot.

The D'Oillys, who held 1 of these fees, were Aluric's successors at Stonesfield.[40] Their holding at Ascot, known in the 15th century as FYNES manor, was first recorded in a charter of William Rufus (c. 1099–1100),[41] which stated that at the king's request Bishop Robert had given back to Nigel, brother of Guy d'Oilly, the land which Guy had held of the bishop and which he had given back

to the church in his lifetime. The land belonged by right to the demesne of the church and the bishop was clearly anxious to keep it as such, for he said that the 6 hides in Ascot were to revert on Nigel's death.[42] Nevertheless, the estate remained in the hands of the D'Oillys for the next century. Guy, probably the Domesday tenant of Wigginton,[43] and Nigel were brothers of Robert d'Oilly, constable of Oxford castle.[44] Nigel was Robert's heir, and in 1166 his grandson Henry (I) d'Oilly held the Ascot fee[45] and Henry's son Henry (II) d'Oilly succeeded him and paid on the fee in 1191.[46] Henry (II) apparently granted the land to his kinsman John d'Oilly (d. c. 1228),[47] for he is found paying on 1 fee held of the Bishop of Lincoln from about 1201 to 1210,[48] after which Henry d'Oilly again answered for the bishop's fee until his death in 1232.[49] The descent of Ascot is not clear for some time after this. Henry left no direct heir and his lands were divided among his kinsmen,[50] but no mention was made of Ascot amongst the lands of the d'Oilly inheritance and it may have reverted for a time to the bishop.

By 1279 the fee was held by Jordan the Forester, who also held land in Lyneham and in Waltham (Berks.).[51] By 1280 Jordan was dead and his property had passed to his daughter Joan, who married John de Fiennes ('Fendus', 'Fienlys'), lord of the honor of Chokes (Northants.).[52] John was returned as holding the fee of the bishop in about 1305, was one of the lords of Ascot in 1316, and contributed to the tax levied in 1327.[53] He probably died soon after.[54] His widow Joan held Ascot and Lyneham in dower and after her death in 1338 her second husband Sir Adam de Shareshull continued as tenant.[55] Adam outlived Joan's son, John de Fiennes (d. 1351), lord of Herstmonceux (Suss.), and John's son William (d. 1359).[56] In 1370, after Adam's death, the estate went in dower to Joan, William's widow, then the wife of Stephen de Valence.[57] On her death in 1378 it reverted to her son Sir William de Fiennes, who had succeeded his brother in 1375.[58] The family had little connexion with the parish, since the centre of their power was at Herstmonceux.[59] Sir Roger Fiennes succeeded in 1403,[60] but either he or his father granted Ascot for life to

[24] Bodl. G. A. Oxon. fol. B 71: 1837 Sale cat.
[25] Oxf. Dioc. b 70, f. 510.
[26] No property is now held in Great Milton by the Church Commissioners.
[27] Bodl. G.A. Oxon. fol. B 71: 1810 Sale cat.
[28] O.R.O. Incl. award.
[29] In 1820 John Blackall was said to be in possession of the united manors, save Chilworth: Gent. Mag. 1820, i. 10.
[30] O.R.O. Li XX/viii/14, p. 11; and see above.
[31] Valor Eccl. (Rec. Com.) ii. 173; C 2/19/318. For the family see Visit. Oxon. 164–5; and above and below, pp. 120, 143.   [32] Par. Coll. ii. 213–14.
[33] Linc. Chapter Acts, 1547–1559 (L.R.S. xv), p. 82; C 3/58/22; C 1/1470/35–6; cf. also C 3/184/40. For Sir Thomas Benger see above, p. 120.
[34] C 2/12/72.
[35] Bodl. ch. Oxon. 420; C 2/12/72.
[36] Bodl. ch. Oxon. 421; see above, p. 124.
[37] O.R.O. H IV/1. For the Isteds see Burke's Commoners, ii. 462.   [38] Ibid.; and see above, p. 125.
[39] V.C.H. Oxon. i. 402, 403.
[40] Ibid. 412; cf. Bk. of Fees, 142, 595; Shaw, Hist. of Staffs. Gen. Hist. appendix, xvii.
[41] Dated by H. E. Salter.
[42] Reg. Antiquiss. i. 13; and also Dugdale, Mon. vi (3), 1272; Cal. Chart. R. 1327–41, 138. The manor is often confused with Ascot under Wychwood (e.g. Reg. Antiquiss. i. 13; P.N. Oxon.(E.P.N.S.), ii. 336), but this did not belong to the bishop.   [43] V.C.H. Oxon. i. 420.

[44] For the family, see W. D. Bayley, The House of D'Oyly; Top. and Gen. i. 368.
[45] Red Bk. Exch. (Rolls Ser.), 375; Henry's death is given as 1168 in Hse. D'Oyly, 11, but as 1163 elsewhere.
[46] Red Bk. Exch. 32.
[47] For John, see Oseney Cart. iv. 476; vi. 151–2, 157; Fines Oxon. 82.
[48] Pipe R. 1201 (P.R.S. N.S. xiv), 212; 1205 (P.R.S. N.S. xix), 148; 1208 (P.R.S. N.S. xxiii), 137.
[49] Bk. of Fees, 40; Queen's Coll. MS. 366, f. 23.
[50] V.C.H. Oxon. i. 440; Ex. e Rot. Fin. (Rec. Com.), i. 231.
[51] Rot. Hund. (Rec. Com.), ii. 743, 744, 821; V.C.H. Berks. iii. 172.
[52] V.C.H. Berks. iii. 172; Baker, Northants. ii. 273–4.
[53] Queen's Coll. MS. 366, f. 34b; Feud. Aids, iv. 167; E 179/161/9.
[54] He is said to have died in 1331: Suss. Arch. Coll. iv. 146.
[55] Cal. Inq. p.m. viii, p. 98; x, p. 495. They levied a fine on the manor in 1337: C.P. 25(2)/190/18/13.
[56] Cal. Inq. p.m. ix, p. 433; x, pp. 495–6.
[57] Ibid. xiii, p. 38; Cal. Close, 1369–74, 145, 157.
[58] Cal. Pat. 1381–5, 190; C 136/54/21.
[59] V.C.H. Sussex, ix. 133; for the Fiennes family see 'The Castle of Herstmonceux and its Lords', Suss. Arch. Coll. iv. 146 sqq.
[60] Complete Peerage, xi. 479, giving William's death as 1403.

his brother Sir James Fiennes, who therefore answered for 1 fee there in 1428.[61] Sir James, created Lord Saye and Sele in *c.* 1447, had a celebrated career as soldier and statesman, but was handed over to Cade's rebels and beheaded in 1450.[62] Ascot reverted then, if not before, to Sir Richard Fiennes, Roger's son, who became Lord Dacre of the South in 1458.[63] He sold the Ascot estate, now called Fynes manor, to Richard Quatremain,[64] whose family had held an estate in Ascot since the early 12th century. Fynes manor was held for a time with the Quatremains' estate, but Richard Quatremain (d. 1477) apparently left a life interest in it to Thomas Boteler, son and heir of Baldwin Boteler, who obtained it in 1484.[65] There were remainders to Richard Grenville of Wootton Underwood, Boteler's nephew, and in 1510 Sir Robert Dormer, who bought the other Quatremain estate, agreed with Richard Grenville to exchange Wootton Underwood manor for Ascot manor and for land in Haddenham (Bucks.), where he had a woolhouse.[66]

The second estate in the hamlet, known by the 15th century as *QUATREMAINS* manor, belonged to the Quatremains from the 12th century at least and formed 1 fee with their land in North Weston in Thame. This was undoubtedly the 3¾ hides in Great Milton and 3 hides in Thame which William held in 1086.[67] In 1166 Herbert Quatremain was holding the fee of the Bishop of Lincoln.[68] By September 1200 he had died, leaving a widow Lettice, who claimed dower of the 6¾ hides in Ascot and North Weston from her son Herbert; it was settled that she should have 5 virgates in Ascot.[69] Her son Herbert was listed as one of the bishop's knights in 1201 and the fee remained until the 15th century in the Quatremain family, who from the 14th century at least resided at Quatremains Place in North Weston.[70] In the time of Richard Quatremain, who succeeded in 1414, part of the fee appears to have been mortgaged and sold. When Thomas Quatremain died in 1398 it had been given in trust for his widow Joan to William Bruley,[71] but it had reverted to Richard Quatremain by 1428.[72] By 1431 Bartholomew Collingridge and his son William, relatives of the Quatremains, were in possession.[73] Later William Collingridge and his wife Sarah were involved in a lawsuit with other grantees, but between 1456 and 1460 the manor, worth £9 a year, was finally awarded to William Collingridge by judgement of the court.[74] The Collingridge title was

thus secured and the manor descended to John Collingridge despite the claims of William Danvers, Richard Quatremain's nephew, who claimed after 1477 that his uncle had promised it to him.[75] John Collingridge died in 1500 in possession of 'Estcote alias Astcote' manor, worth £42.[76] In 1510, however, his heir John Collingridge sold Ascot to Sir Robert Dormer of West Wycombe (Bucks.), to whom he was related by marriage.[77] The two Ascot manors, 'Fynes' and 'Quatremains', thus came into the same hands.

In 1518 Sir Robert Dormer granted the Ascot manors to Sir Michael Dormer, his uncle and a distinguished Mayor of London,[78] and Ascot became one of the seats of the Dormer family for many generations. His son Ambrose (d. 1566) retained this and the family's other property in the parish,[79] but Ambrose's son Sir Michael (II) Dormer ran into debt, and sold the manors in Great and Little Milton,[80] mortgaged Ascot, and sold it before 1609 to his cousin, Sir Robert Dormer of Long Crendon and Dorton (Bucks.).[81] In 1642 Sir Robert settled Ascot manor and other property in Little Milton, Newington, and Stadhampton on his 'youngest son and heir', William.[82] In 1653 William Dormer (d. 1683) settled the manor on himself and on Anna Maria Waller, whom he married.[83] His wife had dower in Ascot, but in 1694 his son John was in possession and settled it on his first wife Katherine Spencer, one of the daughters and coheirs of Sir Thomas Spencer, 3rd baronet of Yarnton.[84] In 1717 John again settled Ascot on his second wife Alice Dighton, and on his death in 1728 he left Ascot House to his wife Alice and his real estate in reversion to his kinsman Robert Dormer of Rousham.[85] Robert Dormer at once mortgaged the estates to his cousin Sir Clement Cottrell-Dormer and sold them later in the same year.[86] In 1760 Sir Charles Cottrell-Dormer of Rousham bought Ascot manor and other estates outright for £20,000.[87] By 1784, however, Ascot had been sold to the Blackalls and thereafter followed the descent of Great and Little Milton.

An estate of 7½ hides in Chilworth was held by Roger d'Ivry in 1086.[88] As his lands passed to Reynold de St. Valery in 1153 this manor acquired the name of *CHILWORTH VALERY.* The St. Valery estates were granted in the 13th century to Richard, Earl of Cornwall, and became part of the honor of Wallingford and later of the honor of

[61] Rousham Arch. L 2; *Feud. Aids,* iv. 197.
[62] *Complete Peerage,* ix. 479–81; *D.N.B.*
[63] *Complete Peerage,* iv. 8.
[64] Rousham Arch. L 7–9: at least 300 marks and probably more were paid.
[65] Ibid. L 12.
[66] Ibid. L 16, 17; A 2.
[67] *V.C.H. Oxon.* i. 403.
[68] *Red Bk. Exch.* (Rolls Ser.), 375.
[69] *Cur. Reg. R.* i. 204, 244.
[70] *Rot. de Ob. et Fin.* (Rec. Com.), 154; see below, p. 173.
[71] Carter, *Quatremains,* 41. Bruley's son John married Maud Quatremain: Macnamara, *Danvers Family,* 224.
[72] *Feud. Aids,* iv. 197.
[73] Rousham Arch. L 6: witnesses in 1456 swear that Richard Quatremain delivered seisin.
[74] K.B. 27/778/mm. 38, 38d, cited in Carter, *Quatremains,* 41.
[75] Carter, *Quatremains,* 56–57; William Collingridge is presumed to have died without issue (*Oxoniensia,* xi. 95), but he apparently had a son John.
[76] *Cal. Inq. p.m. Hen. VII,* iii, p. 400.

[77] Rousham Arch. A 1; L 13, 14; Geoffrey Dormer married Ursula, daughter of Bartholomew Collingridge: *Oxoniensia,* xi. 90.
[78] Rousham Arch. L 18, A 2; *Oxoniensia,* xi. 93.
[79] C 142/143/49. For other property see above, pp. 124, 125 and below, p. 172.
[80] See above, p. 124.
[81] Rousham Arch. L 30, L 32, O 29; cf. L 33; quitclaim of Sir Michael. Sir Michael did not die until 1624; he mortgaged his chattels at Ascot in 1611: ibid. L 34.
[82] Ibid. L 44; in 1632 he had put the manor in trust for himself, with reversion to his son John and remainders to his second son Michael and third son Robert: ibid. L 43.
[83] Ibid. L 49, 51. He was called William Dormer the younger and quitclaimed to William Dormer the elder, perhaps the William Dormer of Combleton who occurs in 1645: ibid. O 34.
[84] Rousham Arch. L 57, 60, 61; *Oxoniensia,* xi. 99.
[85] Rousham Arch. L 62, 64.
[86] Ibid. L 63 and uncat. bill listing 1728 assignment of mortgages from Sir Robert Dashwood to Mr. Cottrell.
[87] Ibid. L 64.
[88] *V.C.H. Oxon.* i. 415.

Ewelme.[89] The overlordship of Chilworth Valery followed the descent of the honor, and as late as 1841 tenants from Chilworth attended the frankpledge courts of Ewelme.[90]

The tenant in 1086 was a certain Hugh, possibly the same Hugh who held under Roger d'Ivry in Stoke Talmage,[91] and who may have been the grandfather of Peter (I) Talemasch.[92] Peter's son Richard (d. by 1205) was the mesne tenant of Chilworth at the end of the 12th century.[93] His son Peter (II) Talemasch sold his estate in Chilworth and Coombe (said to be 1 knight's fee) to Ralph Hareng in about 1223.[94] Ralph, a royal justice,[95] had close connexions with the St. Valery honor and held other land of it in Buckinghamshire and Oxfordshire.[96] The mesne tenancy of Chilworth and Coombe probably followed the same descent as these estates for the rest of the 13th century. Ralph (I) Hareng was succeeded by his son Ralph (II) Hareng by 1230[97] and in 1242 this Ralph still held 1 fee in Chilworth and Coombe.[98] By the 1250's, however, the property had probably already come to the Senlis (St. Lys or 'de Sancto Licio') family, like Holton and the Buckinghamshire estates.[99] In 1279, therefore, Simon de Senlis held the St. Valery fee in Chilworth and Coombe.[1] On his death his estates went to his son Andrew de Senlis, then a minor,[2] who was returned as holding a fee in Holton, Chilworth, and Coombe in the 1300 inquisition into the St. Valery lands.[3] There is no later mention of Andrew de Senlis's connexion with Chilworth and Coombe, though he does not seem to have died until well into the 14th century.[4] Nor is there any further reference to the mesne tenancy of the estate.

Richard Gernon of Coombe was the demesne tenant by the end of the 12th century, and his family, which remained in possession until the 14th century, gave the manor its alternate name of *COOMBE GERNON* (or Garnon). The name Gernon was widespread in south England, but no direct connexion has been found between the Gernons of Coombe and those elsewhere.[5] In 1207 Richard Gernon was involved in a lawsuit over a $\frac{1}{2}$-hide in Stoke Talmage in which it was maintained that Juliana, daughter of Richard Gernon and his wife Lucy, had quitclaimed to Richard Talemasch her rights in the legal part of the fee of 4 knights,

which she claimed of Richard Talemasch in Stoke Talmage and Chilworth. Richard Gernon had been overseas at the time, but was obliged to acknowledge the fine.[6] A Roger Gernon had succeeded him by 1223, when the homage and services of Roger Gernon and his heirs and 1 knight's fee in Chilworth and Coombe were transferred to the Harengs.[7] In 1243 Roger or a son Roger (II) Gernon[8] held the fee in Chilworth and Coombe of Ralph Hareng.[9] A list of Talemasch fees, about the same date, shows that Roger's Oxfordshire holdings included a $\frac{1}{2}$-hide in Stoke Talmage and a $1\frac{1}{2}$ fee in Coombe, of which the $\frac{1}{2}$-fee was apparently in 'Wlfinton'.[10] By 1279 John Gernon, who must have been Roger's son, held the estate which was then estimated as half the total extent of Coombe and Chilworth and had been reckoned as 7 hides in 1255.[11] He or another John Gernon was one of the lords in 1316, and the Gernons were still in possession in 1327, when a John Gernon paid a high tax in Coombe.[12] It is possible that this John Gernon was the Sir John Gernon (d. 1339) of East Lavington (Wilts.), for the manor, or part of it, apparently went in the 14th century to the Rycotes, Clerks, and Englefields, by the marriage of Sir John Rycote to Elizabeth Gernon, daughter and heir of Sir John Gernon of Lavington.[13] Katherine, the daughter of that marriage, married Nicholas Clerk,[14] who in 1398 or 1399 was in possession of '. . . cumbe' by Milton and all lands late of John Rycote of Rycote.[15] In 1428 William Fowler, the husband of Clerk's granddaughter Cecily Englefield,[16] was joint owner of this manor,[17] and in the later 15th century part at least of Chilworth and Coombe was called 'Ricotes'.[18] The other joint owner of the manor was John Beke, who also held at Chislehampton, but no explanation has been found of his connexion, nor of the fact that in 1428 both parts of the estate were said to have been previously in the possession of William of Harpenden,[19] presumably lord of Harpsden, whose lands were in custody in 1378.[20] Beke's daughter Joan married John Rous,[21] who thereby gave the name 'Rous' to part at least of Chilworth.[22] The Beke and Fowler estates may have been united by some family arrangement: Beke's widow, Elizabeth Quatremain, married Nicholas Englefield, Fowler's father-in-law. In any case Thomas Danvers, who

[89] See *V.C.H. Oxon.* i. 440; d.d. Ewelme d 1–3.
[90] O.R.O. CH/E. X, XXIII.
[91] *V.C.H. Oxon.* i. 416.
[92] *Pipe R.* 1131 (Rec. Com.), 3, and see below, p. 149.
[93] *Cur. Reg. R.* v. 110.
[94] *Fines Oxon.* 71.
[95] *Bracton's Note Bk.* (ed. Maitland), ii. 117.
[96] In 1216, he was given custody of Thomas de St. Valery's estates; he held Thornton, Radclive, Hasley, Westbury (Bucks.): *V.C.H. Bucks.* iv. 221, 243–4, 246, 263–4; and in 1242 a Ralph Hareng also held land in Wootton and Bampton hundreds, Oxon.: *Bk. of Fees*, 821, 822.
[97] *V.C.H. Bucks.* iv. 244; *Ex. e Rot. Fin.* (Rec. Com.) i. 194.
[98] *Bk. of Fees*, ii. 826.
[99] *V.C.H. Oxon.* v. 171; see *Cur. Reg. R.* xi. pp. 373, 399, for Hareng and Gernon tenure of Holton; *V.C.H. Bucks.* iv. 220, 243–7, 263.
[1] *Rot. Hund.* (Rec. Com.), ii. 716.
[2] R. Ussher, *History of Westbury*, 116: the estates were held in custody by the Earl of Cornwall.
[3] *Cal. Inq. p.m.* iii, p. 479.
[4] *V.C.H. Bucks.* iv. 221, citing an Andrew de Senlis who was alive until 1328; there was a Simon de Senlis at Holton in 1317: *V.C.H. Oxon.* v. 171.

[5] Cf. Farrer, *Honors*, iii. 203; *V.C.H. Essex*, iv. 262; there were Gernons in 13th-century Wheatley: *Sandford Cart.* i. 80. The later history of Coombe suggests a connexion with Wiltshire.
[6] *Cur. Reg. R.* v. 110; a Richard Gernon occurs in Oxfordshire c. 1197, in 1210, and c. 1221: see *Thame Cart.* ii. 109; *Cur. Reg. R.* vi. 69; *Eynsham Cart.* ii. 174.
[7] *Fines Oxon.* 71.
[8] For the two Roger Gernons see *Fines Oxon.* 94.
[9] *Bk. of Fees*, ii. 826.
[10] *Eynsham Cart.* i. 7–8. 'Wlfinton' seems to be Holton, where the mesne tenants, the Senlis family, held. For the Gernon tenure there in the 1220's see *Cur. Reg. R.* xi. 373, 399.
[11] *Rot. Hund.* (Rec. Com.), ii. 38, 716.
[12] *Feud. Aids*, iv. 168; E 179/161/9.
[13] Lee, *Thame*, 293–4; cf. Carter, *Quatremains*, 15, 61.
[14] Lee, *Thame*, 293–4.
[15] E 210/3142: the deed is mutilated.
[16] Lee, *Thame*, 193–4.
[17] *Feud. Aids*, iv. 199.
[18] C 142/24/626.
[19] *Feud. Aids*, iv. 199. For Beke, see above, p. 10.
[20] *Cal. Pat.* 1377–81, 139.
[21] Lee, *Thame*, 193–4.
[22] So called in 1508: C 142/24/62b.

married Fowler's granddaughter Sybil Fowler,[23] probably came to some agreement with Rous, as he did over Chislehampton,[24] and secured both 'Ricotes' and 'Rous', which descended to his nephew.[25] The fact that Sybil had dower only of Coombe Gernon and not of the Radmylde manor in Chilworth, which Danvers had also obtained, implies that this portion had descended by hereditary right.[26] From this time Coombe Gernon descended with the other Chilworth manor.

In 1086 Hasculf Musard was already in possession of the estate (or part of it) later known as *CHILWORTH MUSARD* manor. A clerk's note added to the entry claimed it to be the land of Roger d'Ivry's wife:[27] if so, it must have been of her inheritance, for it did not pass with the other D'Ivry lands to the St. Valery family, but had for several centuries a different history from Chilworth Valery. The Musards were overlords for about two centuries, and gave their name to their Chilworth manor. Their chief centre lay at Staveley in Derbyshire.[28] A Richard Musard succeeded Hasculf in the early 12th century, and by 1166 Hasculf (II) Musard (d. 1184) had 1 knight's fee of the old enfeoffment (i.e. before 1136) held by a Geoffrey of Chilworth.[29] His successor Ralph (d. 1230) regularly paid on his fees in Oxfordshire,[30] which included Heythrop and Horspath,[31] and his son Robert (d. *c.* 1246) held 1 fee in Coombe in 1235, which was defined more clearly as 1 fee in Chilworth and Coombe in 1243.[32] Robert's brother Ralph (d. *c.* 1271) succeeded him, but the Musard overlordship is not mentioned after 1255[33] and it probably lapsed at the end of the 13th century, when the legitimate male line of the Musards died out.

Geoffrey of Chilworth in 1166 was the first recorded subtenant of the Musard estate.[34] His successors were not noted until 1235, when Alexander of Coombe, a county coroner, held the fee.[35] By 1246 his son William had succeeded him.[36] William had died by 1273, when his wife was assigned dower in Coombe and Chilworth[37] and in 1279 his son John held the fee.[38] The Coombe family apparently continued in possession in the 14th century, for a Richard of Coombe paid a high contribution to the tax assessments of 1306, 1316, and 1327,[39] though he was not returned as lord in 1316.[40] The descent

of the estate in the 14th century cannot be traced, but it probably came into the hands of the Inge[41] or Louches families of Great Milton and ultimately passed to Sir Thomas Camoys by his marriage with Elizabeth de Louches.[42] Like Sir Thomas's other lands it went on his death in 1421 to his grandson Hugh and in 1426 to the Radmyldes and Lewknors.[43] The Radmyldes had the closest connexion with it and their portion was known as 'Radmyll' and consisted of a ½-messuage and 2 carucates in Coombe and Great and Little Chilworth, worth £10.[44] William Radmylde, the last of the family, sold it to Thomas Danvers of Waterstock in negotiations which seem to have lasted from 1492 to 1497.[45] Danvers (d. 1502) appears by this purchase to have rounded off his estate in Chilworth and Coombe which then consisted of the former Musard and Valery fees and the Cottesmore estate.[46]

Thomas Danvers's heir was his brother William (d. 1504),[47] but his widow Sybil (d. 1511) had dower of Coombe Gernon and Chilworth.[48] William's successor, his son John (I), died in 1508 leaving his heir John (II) a minor,[49] who died in 1518 when his property went to his four sisters and coheirs, Anne, Mary, Elizabeth, and Dorothy.[50] By a family arrangement, Dorothy and her husband Nicholas Huband (Hubard or Hubowle), a Warwickshire man,[51] took the Chilworth property.[52] Nicholas died in 1554, and on Dorothy's death in 1558 her son John succeeded,[53] and on his death in 1585, his brother Ralph.[54] Ralph Huband had sold the property to William Grene by 1596.[55] Like the other Grene estates most of Chilworth was mortgaged and eventually sold in the early 17th century to John Simeon of Brightwell Baldwin, a member of a notable Roman Catholic family.[56] A long lawsuit with the Grenes ensued,[57] but the Simeons retained possession. George Simeon, who had been associated with his father John (d. 1617) in the negotiations, held the property until his death in 1664 and settled it on his wife Margaret (Molyneux) in 1660.[58] Sir George's son James (d. 1709)[59] was in possession in 1680, when he mortgaged the property to William Dormer of Ascot for £5,000.[60] His son Sir Edward Simeon held it until his death in 1768.[61] He was unmarried and his estate here and in Britwell Prior consequently passed to Thomas Weld, a younger

[23] For relationships, see Lee, *Thame*, 193–4.
[24] See above, p. 10.
[25] C 142/24/62*b*.
[26] C 142/26/52.
[27] *V.C.H. Oxon.* i. 422.
[28] See *Coll. Top. and Gen.* iv. 2–23, for the following Musard descent.
[29] *Red Bk. Exch.* (Rolls Ser.), 342.
[30] Ibid. 84, 100, 124; *Pipe R.* 1206 (P.R.S. N.S. xx), 124.
[31] *V.C.H. Oxon.* v. 179.
[32] *Bk. of Fees*, 826.
[33] *Rot. Hund.* (Rec. Com.), ii. 38.
[34] *Red Bk. Exch.* (Rolls Ser.), 342.
[35] *Bk. of Fees*, 449; J.I. 1/699, 700.
[36] *V.C.H. Oxon.* v. 5.
[37] *Cal. Inq. p.m.* iv, p. 339.
[38] *Rot. Hund.* (Rec. Com.), ii. 714.
[39] E 179/161/8, 9 and 10.
[40] Richard de Beaufeu, presumably the Richard who was lord of Waterperry, was said to be one of the lords; in 1246 Henry de Beaufeu was lord of a tenement in Chilworth and Coombe: *V.C.H. Oxon.* v. 5. The Beaufeu connexion with Chilworth cannot be traced.
[41] William Inge paid the highest contribution in Coombe in 1306, but paid only in Great Milton in 1327: E 179/161/10 and 9.

[42] C 138/57/29; see above, p. 123. Sir Thomas paid on Chilworth property in 1405: E 179/161/67.
[43] See above, p.123.
[44] C 139/109/34; C 139/163/15.
[45] *Cal. Inq. p.m. Hen. VII*, iii, p. 419; the deeds are printed in *Camoys Peerage Claim, 1838*; by this time the estate extended into Chilworth Valery.
[46] See above; *Cal. Close, 1485–1500*, 142.
[47] Macnamara, *Danvers Family*, 177; C 142/24/12*b*.
[48] C 142/26/52.   [49] C 142/24/62*b* and 63.
[50] C 142/32/36.
[51] Macnamara, *Danvers Family*, 187; *Oxon. Visit.* i.
[52] They obtained possession in 1523; Macnamara, *Danvers Family*, 187. See also C.P. 25(2)/34/227 Trin. 24 Hen. VIII; ibid. 62/494 East. 6 Ed. VI.
[53] C 142/119/139.   [54] C 142/208/202.
[55] C.P. 25(2)/198/Trin. 29 Eliz.
[56] C 2/A 8/1; C.P. 25(2)/339/Trin. 8 Jas. I. Part was sold to the Coppins and eventually came to the Ashhursts of Waterstock: d.d. Ashhurst c 8.
[57] C 3/324/13; ibid. 381/49.
[58] C.P. 25(2)/707/Trin. 12 Chas. II; d.d. Hobbs c 4; see also C.P. 25(2)/473/Trin. 10 Chas. I.
[59] G.E.C. *Baronetage*, iv. 93.
[60] Rousham Arch. O 17.
[61] Stapleton, *Cath. Miss.* 278.

son of his sister Margaret, who had married Humphrey Weld of Lulworth Castle (Dors.).[62] Thomas Weld assumed the name of Simeon, but apparently died soon after, leaving an only daughter Mary, a nun at Bruges. His nephew Thomas Weld succeeded him,[63] and seems to have sold the property in 1794.[64] There is no further mention of manorial rights.

ECONOMIC AND SOCIAL HISTORY. Great Milton was settled at an early date. No trace of British and little of Roman occupation has been found in the neighbourhood, but so favourable a site is unlikely to have been passed over. The surrounding district was occupied in Roman times,[65] a Roman road is thought to have passed through the parish, and the site of a Roman *villa* at Little Milton has been observed from the air.[66] The Domesday place-name 'Middleton', with its ending 'ton' points to an early Saxon settlement. Chilworth, meaning the homestead of *Ceola*, and Coombe were possibly colonizing settlements from Milton, as Little Milton must certainly have been. Ascot may have been named from its position, east of Stadhampton. Other indications of Anglo-Saxon development are the field names: Swarford Ground in Chilworth, the Forty (OE. Forþ—a clearing) and the Breach meadow, another early name for a clearing, in Great Milton.[67]

Before the Conquest the economy of Great Milton with that of other estates composing the endowment of Dorchester bishopric would have been devoted to the support of the bishop's household.[68] After the Conquest and Milton's transference to the Bishop of Lincoln the estate appears to have been drastically reorganized, for by 1086 it had almost doubled its pre-Conquest value of £18. On the bishop's Milton estate, rated at 31 hides and probably including Little Milton, there was the lord's demesne farm, and 24 *villani*, 31 bordars, and a priest occupied the remaining land.[69] The other settlement described under Milton was centred on Ascot, where there were the two estates of the bishop's knights—Aluric's with 6 hides and William's with 3 hides and 3 virgates. Eighteen peasants were recorded—a smaller number than that of the main village.[70] Only part of the settlement in the north of the parish (i.e. at Chilworth and Coombe) was described in 1086: an entry about 7 hides held by Roger d'Ivry was left unfinished.[71] In Hasculf Musard's 2½-hide estate, however, there were 8 bordars, 2 *villani*, and 1 serf. It was worth only £1.[72] There was no recorded woodland or waste. The Domesday commissioners estimated that there was land for 26 ploughs at the Miltons and recorded 24, five on the bishop's farm and

19 in the hands of his tenants. There were 2 ploughs on the demesne farms and the tenants had 4 at Ascot. While there was land for 5 ploughs on the Musard estate at Chilworth there was only 1 plough on the demesne and another belonging to the tenants. There were 23 acres of meadow in Chilworth and meadow valued at 10s. in Milton. There were two mills in the parish.[73]

By 1279 the parish's population had increased and the structure of society had become more complex. The bishop no longer farmed any of the land. There were now two large estates in the Miltons, the Clifford estate and Milton manor prebend, each with 3 carucates in the home farm and with some 30 dependent virgates. There were 2 smaller estates held directly of the bishop, one of 10 virgates belonging to Laurence de Louches and the other of 4 virgates held by the Rector of Milton, another prebendary.[74] There were now some eleven free tenants in the two villages, the most important being Nicholas Marmion and William de Bluntesdon, who had sub-manors of about 10 virgates each.[75] The Abbot of Dorchester was a free tenant in Little Milton: the abbey had held 20 acres and a meadow since 1146 and in 1279 held also 1 virgate by scutage.[76] Customary tenants still formed most of the population as was usual in Oxfordshire: there were 64 recorded customars and 29 cottars. The customary tenants on the two main manors held a standard 1-virgate holding at an assized rent of 5s.; the cottars, replacing the bordars of 1086, paid 2s. to 2s. 6d. for a house and 3 acres. Both classes owed works, for which a virgate paid 2s. and a cottar 6d. There were two small demesne farms on the manors at Ascot: John the Forester had 12 virgates and William Quatremain 4 virgates. The one free tenant held 1 virgate of John the Forester for 5s. and suit of court. As in the Miltons the bulk of the population were customary tenants—there were 11 customars attached to each estate and 4 cottars held of John the Forester and 3 of William Quatremain. There is no mention of the size of their holdings, but the customars paid the same rent and services as the virgaters paid in Milton; the cottars paid less, only 1s. 6d., and those on Quatremain's estate owed 6d. for works. There were also two estates at Chilworth, belonging to John son of William of Coombe and John Gernon. There is no mention of John of Coombe's demesne in 1279, but the record of tenants owing works implied that there was or had been a demesne farm. John Gernon had 2 carucates in demesne with a meadow adjoining. There were 9 small free tenants on the 2 estates—almost half the total number in the parish, but they were still outnumbered by the 28 customary tenants. On the

---

[62] Stapleton, *Cath. Miss.* 278.
[63] Ibid.; d.d. Hobbs c 5.
[64] C.P. 43/845/319.
[65] *V.C.H. Oxon.* v. 100, 108; i. 299, 340.
[66] Inf. I. D. Margary, Esq.; *Oxonensia*, xvi, 80.
[67] *P.N. Oxon.* (E.P.N.S.), i. 141–2, 144; ii. 432, 445.
[68] *V.C.H. Oxon.* i. 378.
[69] Ibid. 402; the name Little Milton first occurs in 1223: *Fines Oxon.* 91.
[70] *V.C.H. Oxon.* i. 403; this entry gives 9 hides 3 virgates, i.e. 3 virgates more than the hidage recorded for the bishop's knights under Milton, but corresponding to the 1279 estimate in *Rot. Hund.* (Rec. Com.), ii. 821. Ascot first occurs by name *c.* 1100: *Reg. Antiquiss.* i. 13.
[71] *V.C.H. Oxon.* i. 415 n. 2.
[72] Ibid. 422.

[73] Ibid. 402, 403.
[74] *Rot. Hund.* (Rec. Com.), ii. 821, 749; and see above, pp. 123, 125, and below, p. 139. This account differs from E. A. Kosminskys (*Studies in the Agrarian History of England*, 78), who did not realize that the Louches (or Chislehampton) estate was held directly of the bishop.
[75] Marmion held about 2 virgates of Clifford, 4 of Bluntesdon, and another 5 held by his own under-tenants; Bluntesdon held the Louches estate. It is not clear whether or no certain virgates were entered twice under different estates, but the acreage of the parish would allow for each being a separate holding.
[76] *Fines Oxon.* 202; *Rot. Hund.* (Rec. Com.), ii. 821; *Reg. Antiquiss.* i. 247. There is no mention of the Abbot of Eynsham's grange, recorded there in 1258: *Eynsham Cart.* i. 223.

Coombe estate there were 10 who held in villeinage. They worked at the will of the lord, paid 25s. a year between them, and were probably ½-virgaters as in Great Milton. There were 6 cottars attached to this estate and 6 cottages were rented for 5s. a year. On John Gernon's land there were 6 virgaters and 4 cottars.[77]

Some light is thrown on the economy of the chief lay estate in the Miltons by the accounts for Richard de Louches's manor (part of the 1279 Clifford estate) rendered in 1322 at the Exchequer. Rent receipts were small and perhaps not all were included. A water-mill and a windmill were farmed out and there was a dove-cot and fish stews on the estate. Most of the goods and stock were sold at the end of the year: these included farm implements and equipment, which fetched over 10s., £3 from hay and forage, £10 from timber, and various sums from barley, dredge, and beans. Fish from the stews sold for £5. Fifteen pigs, 1 cock, and 4 hens were the only stock mentioned.[78]

In the 14th century the parish of Great Milton was, save for Thame, the wealthiest in the hundred and indeed one of the wealthiest in the south part of Oxfordshire. The whole parish paid over £8 to the 20th of 1327 compared with the assessments of £2 to £3 for other parishes in the hundred. The returns of 1306 and 1316 are incomplete, but they give some idea of the comparative number of taxpayers in each of the settlements in the parish and the distribution of wealth. They show that Great and Little Milton were the most important villages: in 1306 the Miltons paid more than twice the amount contributed from Chilworth and Coombe. In 1316 the holders of manorial lands paid high contributions: John de Fiennes 10s. 6d. at Ascot, John Gernon 9s. 6d. in Chilworth, Richard de Combe 7s. in Coombe, and William Inge 8s. in Milton.[79] In 1327 at the Miltons 72 inhabitants contributed. Of these 8 were wealthy, paying between 4s. and 9s. each, and 20 were moderately well off, paying between 2s. and 4s. The 3 small settlements in Chilworth made separate contributions. Seven of the 11 contributors in Chilworth Musard paid 2s. and over. The 9 at Chilworth Valery were less prosperous and paid 2s. or under. The tax for Coombe was paid by only 6 people but 3 of them had manorial rights and together paid £1 of the hamlet's tax of £1 2s. 3d. The amount at which the places were assessed in 1344 shows that the prosperity of Great and Little Milton had slightly increased and that that of the other hamlets was well maintained; Chilworth Musard does not appear on the tax roll. In 1354 both Great Milton and Ascot received a 15s. tax abatement. The Black Death does not seem, however, to have been as disastrous here as elsewhere in the county for in 1377 255 names were listed for the poll tax in the Miltons and Ascot; no record of contributors at Coombe has survived and the decline of the village may date from this period, but about 50 people in the Chilworths were named.[80]

The bulk of the 15th-century evidence concerns the Radmylde (i.e. the 14th-century De Louches and

Camoys) manor in the Miltons and Coombe. William Radmylde did not work the demesne farms himself, but leased them to local men; in 1473 William Colles paid £10 and one load of hay as annual rent for the site of Milton manor, the demesne land, meadow, and pasture, and Thomas Warner had Coombe manor for £8 a year. Rents from virgaters, including £2 to £3 from tenants in Little Haseley, Lachford, and Ewelme amounted to £24, bringing Radmylde's receipts in that year to £43 17s. 4d. This sum varied little in the 1470's and 1480's, the only periods for which documents survive.[81] A 1499 rental lists the manor's tenants. The old pattern of holdings of 1 or 2 virgates or a ½-virgate still persisted and there was no noticeable aggregation of land. In Great Milton 12 tenants held between them some 10 virgates, 7 messuages, 2 cottages, and various acres. Eleven tenants in Little Milton held some 13½ virgates, 6 messuages, 3 cottages, and 3 acres. Most had a messuage and 1 or 2 virgates for rents varying between 5s. and £1 a year. One tenant with a cottage and a garden paid 8s. 4d., another with a cottage and 3 acres paid 3s. 4d. a year. The largest single holding was in Little Milton and consisted of 2 messuages and 3 virgates held for an annual rent of £1 17s. 4d. The rent roll included Ascot mill which together with 1 virgate was rented for £1 4s. a year. Camoys weir, next to Abingdon Abbey's mill in Cuddesdon, was rented for 10s. a year. The total rent of the estate was now only some £17 and apparently had diminished since the 1470's.[82] Courts for the manor were held regularly twice a year, usually in May or April and October or November. The homage of the two villages came separately to present the various misdoings of their fellows. The courts were mainly concerned with transfers of land, the upkeep of houses, and the management of the open fields. A transfer of land in 1472 may be taken to illustrate the custom of the manor: a new tenant, his wife, and son took over a virgate and messuage to hold at will for 12s. a year, relief, and suit of court; he paid an entry fine of 2 capons and on death he was to pay 3s. 4d. as heriot. A wife could succeed to a tenement held jointly with her husband: Thomas and Margery Crede held Ascot mill jointly and when Thomas died in 1482 Margery was admitted as tenant, and later held it jointly with her second husband Thomas Stockham. If a tenement was neglected or a transfer made without licence, the lord could take possession; if a house was burnt down the tenant rebuilt it or forfeited his land.[83] There is no comparable information for Ascot, but a 1463 court roll indicates that tenants were amassing holdings. One of the tenements described in the October court was made up of 1 virgate of demesne, a ½-virgate, 1 messuage and a close, and 1½ virgate and half a messuage; another consisted of a messuage, 3 closes and 3 virgates, and 1 virgate and a close. One capon was paid for relief and 2s. for heriot; tenements were held for one life.[84]

The open-field agriculture of the Miltons is pictured in the court rolls. There were frequent complaints of trespass by people who ploughed up

[77] Rot. Hund. (Rec. Com.), ii. 821, 714–15, 716.
[78] S.C. 6/962.
[79] E 179/161/9, 10. In 1306 William Inge contributed 10s. 7d. in Coombe, but did not appear there in 1316.
[80] E 179/161/8, 9, 17, 30, 40, 41.
[81] W.A.M. 9217.

[82] Ibid. 1596. This was a new rental and presumably brought the position up to date.
[83] Ibid. 1592, 1631, 1632: registers of courts held for Great Milton, Little Milton, and Baldon St. Lawrence, 1472–1500.
[84] Rousham Arch. L 11.

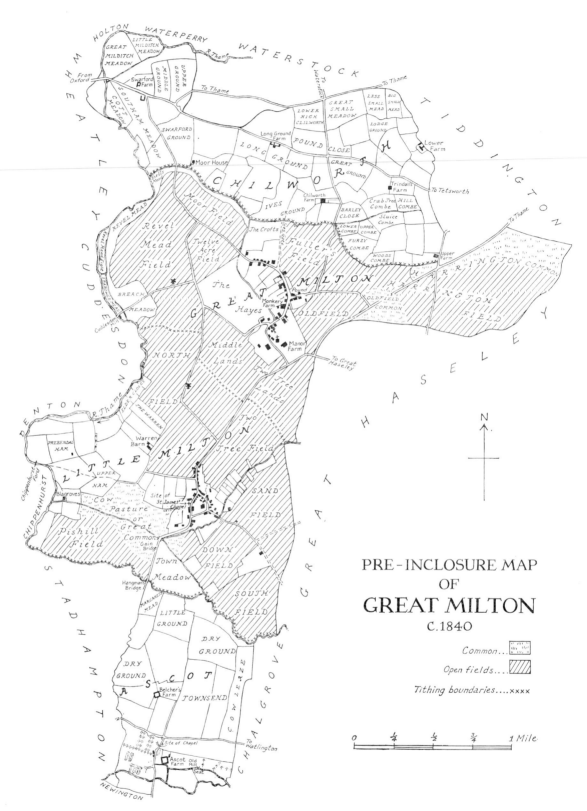

PRE-INCLOSURE MAP
OF
GREAT MILTON
C.1840

Common......

Open fields.....

Tithing boundaries....xxxx

Map illustrating early inclosure and open fields in Great Milton and its hamlets before general inclosure.
Based on the inclosure map (1844), and the tithe awards and maps of the Miltons, Ascot, and Chilworth
(1838–44). Field names printed in capitals are found from the 15th century onwards.

merestones lying between the furlongs and of stray-
ing animals, as in October 1475 when six people
were amerced for allowing horses to wander in the
common fields. In 1487 the court ruled that Great
Milton inhabitants must not allow their foals to
graze at large in the open fields. The hayward took
such animals into the pound at Coombe or Milton:
in 1475 a man was amerced for breaking into the
lord's pound and taking away four distrained horses.
In 1484 a Great Haseley man was presented for
crossing and recrossing Harrington common with
his sheep. The courts were also concerned with the
regulation of the open-field cultivation. In 1481, for
instance, everyone agreed to keep watch over lands
ploughed and sown in the East Field, with a penalty
of 3s. 4d. for disregarding the regulation. At Ascot
the court ordained that animals were not to be kept
on the headlands of the fields when they were sown.
On several occasions in 1497, 1499, and 1500 the
court tried to prevent the overburdening of pastures
and laid down the customary stint: in 1500 it was
said to be 40 ewes, 4 oxen, and 2 horses for each
virgate in Great Milton. The stint was smaller in
Little Milton and was 30 gimmers, 3 oxen. The lord
enforced his own agricultural rights: tenants had to
fold their sheep in the lord's pinfold and were fined
if they tried to remove them. Trees at Coombe were
also valuable assets, and the tenants of the manor
were not allowed to cut them without a licence. The
frequent references to the Thame and the weirs
emphasize the importance of the river to the parish's
economy. One of the chief problems was to keep its
course clear. The Abbot of Abingdon was the chief
offender and the courts frequently presented him
for allowing willows to overgrow and block the
Thame. Sometimes the miller was in trouble: in
1474 John Davy destroyed his meadow, 'Mylledych',
by stopping up his mill weir. The fishing was clearly
of importance and in one 20-year lease of a weir and
fishery the lessee had to promise to keep the lord's
pond stocked with pike, roach, and perch.[85]

There is no clear evidence for the arrangement of
the open fields in the parish in the Middle Ages.
An account of a Great Milton holding in 1473 indicates that there had been little consolidation of
strips: one holding, for example, was distributed in
scattered strips of 3 acres, 2 acres, 1 acre, and ½-
acre in extent. Fields named in the court rolls of
Camoys manor included Southfield, 'Dounnfeld',
Northfield, and 'Sundfeld' in Little Milton, Eastfield, and Harrington Hill field in Great Milton.[86]
There is no reason to suppose, however, that there
were not three 'courses' in Great Milton, as there
evidently were in 1650, when Harrington Hill was
fallow every third year.[87] The common of Great
Milton was in Milton Harrington and in 1484 a
Haseley man was fined for cutting furzes there.
Meadow land by the Thame was important, as
it still is, and there were many references in the

15th century to 'Waywestmede', 'Dranesmede',
'Sparowesmede', and 'Northmede'.[88]

There was a separate field system for the Chilworths in the north of the parish. Eastfield, Moor-
field, and Westfield were named in 1274 and 'Le
Estfelde' and Chilworth Field occur in the 15th
century.[89] These were still uninclosed in the early
15th century: in 1422 a grant was made of lands and
tenements in the village and fields of 'Chilworth and
Chilworth' and in 1462 2 messuages and 2 virgates
were said to be in Chilworth Musard fields.[90] There
must also have been a separate system for Ascot, but
no details of it have survived.

The court rolls show that sheep farming was
extensively practised in the parish and that the
movement towards inclosures had begun at the end
of the 15th century. Large flocks were grazed in
Harrington Field, Milton Common, and on Chilworth Field. Complaints that sheep and cattle overburdened the common and pasture were numerous:
in 1474 Richard Quatremain of Thame, lord of
Ascot, had 400 sheep on Chilworth Field; in 1476
Thomas Danvers, lord of Waterstock, had 300 sheep
and 100 cattle on the lord's common in Chilworth.
The yeoman and husbandmen of the parish as well
as the gentry had flocks. Thomas Eustace, a prosperous yeoman farmer, was presented in 1479 and
1487 for grazing 400 sheep in Great Milton. John
Ives, who held 1 messuage and 1 virgate of the
manor, had 40 sheep more than his due in Chilworth,
and Walter Norreys, holding a close and 4 acres,
had 20 sheep too many in the 1470's and 1480's.
Not all were Great Milton parishioners: John
Burnham of Waterstock had 80 sheep in Chilworth
field in 1473 and the Wixons, yeomen of Tiddington,
had oxen there in 1487.[91] Many of these men, some
gentry and some prosperous yeomen, were responsible for inclosures in the 15th and 16th centuries.
The court rolls mention the lord's inclosed pastures
on Milton Harrington and there were various pasture
closes in Little Milton especially,[92] where there was
good grassland. In 1611 a lease included 5 closes of
pasture and tillage there,[93] and about the same time
the lord of the manor tried to enclose 7 yardlands by
agreement. He said that they were so scattered that
he could not feed or pasture his cattle or draw profits from the property without damage to others.[94]
Good grassland must also account for the siting of
the 18th-century Blagroves farm in Little Milton:
it lay in the fields surrounded by its own closes and
away from the village.[95] The soil, however, was good
for the mixed farming of open-field agriculture; this,
together with the fact that the 15th- and 16th-
century communities were well-established and
large, must explain why the fields of the two villages
of Great and Little Milton remained largely uninclosed until the 19th century in marked contrast
to the other parts of the parish.

Chilworth and Ascot were seriously affected by

[85] W.A.M. 1592, 1631, 1632; Rousham Arch. L 11.
[86] W. A. M. 1592, 1634; some of these fields were named
in the 19th-century tithe award map.
[87] Linc. Dioc. Regy.: Parl. survey. According to Delafield (d. 1749) Oldfield, part of the common fields of Great
Milton, was disputed with Great Haseley: Bodl. MS.
Gough Oxon. 22, f. 61.   [88] W.A.M. 1592, 1634.
[89] Cal. Inq. p.m. iv, p. 338; W.A.M. 1592, 1634.
[90] d.d. Hobbs c 4.
[91] W.A.M. 1592, 1634. For Wixon see V.C.H. Oxon.
v. 8, 12.

[92] W.A.M. 1592, 1634; 'Dykesgrasse', 'Smythesheys',
and 'le Russhe' were other close names. Great Milton
tenants also inclosed in Haseley: in 1476 a man was presented for increasing and inclosing his tenement in Little
Haseley, which was customary land of Milton manor.
[93] d.d. Hobbs c 15; the inclosure in Chilworth called
'Ives his ground' (ibid.) must also date from the 15th or
16th cent.
[94] C 2/G 16/27.
[95] O.R.O. H IV/1, mentions closes around Blagroves
Farm in 1753 when it was described as a dairy farm.

15th- and 16th-century inclosure. They had always been small hamlets and their soil was a heavier clay, suitable for laying down to grass. Progressive farmers of the time were able to buy out the peasant farmers and turn the land over to sheep. Thomas Danvers of Waterstock, mentioned above as a sheep farmer, was one of the foremost of these men in Oxfordshire and bought up the whole of Chilworth and Coombe. In 1499 he took 100 acres of arable and 240 acres of pasture into his demesne and converted '14 arable lands' worth £10 to pasture.[96] The process continued in the 16th century, though there may have been some uninclosed land as late as 1597, for cattle were then said to have been driven off ground called Chilworth Field.[97] By the 17th century all was inclosed, and Chilworth and Coombe were described as 'now being decayed towns and hamlets'.[98] Seventeenth-century deeds show that the land was divided into meadow and pasture closes. These were often large: in 1628, for instance, Coombe Harrington, a pasture close, contained some 80 acres, High Chilworth had 40 acres, and 'Bigger Small Mead' 30 acres.[99] The land was farmed from 4 or 5 farms, which stood in the middle of their own fields, a system which still characterizes this part of the parish.[1]

The same course of events occurred at Ascot. The number of closes in 1463 may indicate that already some land was outside the common-field system and was used for separate pastures. But there were still open-field regulations and the name given to the lord's meadow, 'the mead beneath town', may mean that there was still a hamlet there.[2] In the 17th century Ascot disappeared. John Wilmott of Stadhampton, another of the progressive Oxfordshire farmers, leased two farms from Robert Dormer and in 1516 destroyed a messuage and converted 40 acres of arable to pasture. It has been estimated that he evicted four tenants. Two later complained that they had been evicted for giving evidence at Abingdon. They alleged that Dormer and Wilmott intended to inclose the whole township for pasture, and this was evidently done, for there is no record of parliamentary inclosure in the 18th century. Seventeenth-century deeds show that the land must have been entirely inclosed and list some closes of 50 to 60 acres. At the end of the 17th century there was at least one other farm, Anderson's farm, besides the manor farm.[3]

These changes were reflected in the numbers paying taxes in the 16th century. Chilworth no longer had a separate assessment. In 1524 there were 22 contributors in Great Milton, 15 in Little Milton and still 6 in Ascot. The wealthiest contributors were in Great Milton, where the farmer of the prebendal manor paid on goods worth £50 and 6 others on goods worth £3 to £7; in Little Milton 1 paid on

goods worth £12. In 1542 there were 34 contributors in Great Milton and 3 were men of substance: John Grene, whose family later bought the manor, had goods worth £66, Robert Edgerly, tenant of the prebendal manor, had £50 worth, and John Ives £19 worth. In Little Milton 3 out of 27 contributors had goods worth £10 to £16. In both villages most people paid on goods worth between £1 to £5. There were only 3 contributors at Ascot in 1545: 1 had goods to the value of £20, 2 others to the value of £5. Later 16th- and 17th-century subsidies show a similar picture: Great Milton continued to pay about three times as much as Little Milton; at Ascot the lord and a tenant were usually the only contributors.[4]

The parish as a whole is distinguished by the number of its substantial husbandmen and yeomen and the many well-known Oxfordshire families who had land in the parish. The Ives family, for example, were prosperous inhabitants in the early 14th century and the family is frequently mentioned in 15th-, 16th-, and 17th-century documents.[5] With the Eustace, Wildgoose, and Wiggin families they made up the four families found in the 15th century of which members were still living when Delafield wrote in the 18th century.[6] Another family, the Parsons, was typical of the class of small men who were successful in rising in the social scale in the 16th century. Thomas Parsons rented land worth 12s. 4d. a year in 1499; his descendant Thomas Parsons paid on goods worth £25 in 1577, one of the highest assessments in the parish, and by 1665 Robert Parsons was living in the largest house there, except for the Dormers' house at Ascot.[7] New families came in the 17th and 18th centuries. The Welleses, who also held at Tiddington, were typical of these yeomen. In 1616 Richard Welles married Mary Wildgoose and took over 2 virgates in Great Milton. The family acquired more land in the parish in the course of the 17th century and held Lower Farm by the 18th century; they became substantial tenant farmers in Chilworth as well.[8]

Some documentary evidence for 17th-century farming in Great Milton has survived. A description of the chief lay manor given in 1617 describes it as consisting of 1 messuage, 1 dove-cot, 3 gardens, 220 acres of arable, 6 of meadow, 150 of pasture, and 1 heath. There was common of pasture for 9 horses, 21 cows, and 360 sheep.[9] In a lawsuit over the manor in 1622 some details of stock are given: Humphrey Ayleworth distrained on 200 ewes, 200 lambs, 80 tegs, 17 heifers, a cow, and 2 bullocks, of the value of £300 and upwards.[10] A 1617 tithe case throws some additional light: Sir William Cope, farmer of the prebendal manor, had 20 acres on which he sowed barley, worth £50 at the previous harvest; there were 5 acres sown with woad, each acre worth

---

[96] *Dom. of Incl.* i. 342.

[97] Req. 2/111/27.

[98] d.d. Hobbs c 15.

[99] Ibid. c 4. For other closes, see map on p. 132; cf. d.d. Hobbs c 5, c 6, and c 7; d.d. Ashhurst c 8: other Chilworth and Coombe leases.

[1] Ibid.; Swarford Ground, Dovehouse, perhaps Chilworth, and probably Upper farms existed.

[2] Rousham Arch. L 11; 'Byshoppysclose', 'Gossyppys', were 2 closes.

[3] *Dom. of Incl.* i. 343; cf. M. Beresford, *Lost Villages of England*, 112, 118–19. Robert Dormer (d. 1649) kept cattle and when he put his land in trust he guaranteed not to

diminish 'his stock and sterte': Rousham Arch. L 36; for 17th-century closes see ibid. L 36, L 50 and other deeds in this series.

[4] E 179/161/200, 225; 162/250; and cf. 161/322; 162/258, 341; 163/454; 164/478, 503, 531.

[5] E 179/161/9; d.d. Hobbs c 4, c 9; W.A.M. 1596; Req. 2/6/126.

[6] d.d Hobbs c 9; W.A.M. 1596, 1634, 9217; Bodl. MS. Gough Oxon. 22, ff. 59b–60.

[7] W.A.M. 1596; E 179/162/341; *Hearth Tax Oxon.* 49.

[8] Bodl. MS. ch. Oxon. 420, 421; d.d. Hobbs c 4, c 5; O.R.O. H IV/1; Misc. Eve I/2; and see *V.C.H. Oxon.* v. 12.

[9] C.P. 25(2)/340/Hil. 15 Jas. I.　　[10] C 3/342/7.

8s.; there were 80 acres of warren where he bred rabbits, and in 1616 600 couples, valued at 2s. a couple, were killed.[11]

In 1650 the value of copyhold tenures of the prebendal manor was £19 7s. 8d.; 25 tenants paid between 20s. and 30s. for a messuage and 2 yardlands each. It was the custom to hold for a term of three lives; land was let by the yardland; each yardland had 16 acres of arable, pasture, and meadow, and was valued at £6 6s. 8d. a year. The profits of the court were £19 7s. 8d. Lord Coventry, then the tenant, let the manor-house with its stables, pigeon-house, garden, orchard, and pastures. There was also a manor-house attached to Milton Ecclesia prebend, and 2½ messuages, worth £25 altogether. Pasture rights for both prebends were specified— for the manor prebend, it was 4 cows and 40 sheep a yardland on Harrington Hill; for Milton Ecclesia prebend, it was 30 sheep and 3 cows a yardland on 'Hornston' (Harrington) Hill with the town herd.[12] Details of Chilworth's land appear in Sir James Simeon's account book for 1689 and other years. He owned most of the farms later known as Chilworth farm, Upper and Lower farm, and Trindall's farm. In 1690 he received £235 14s. 7d. for half-yearly rent from eight tenants: Robert Hedges paid nearly £100 rent.[13]

The changes that had taken place in the parish since the late 15th century are reflected in the hearth-tax returns. In Great Milton in 1662 and 1665 44 and 32 families respectively were taxed and four were discharged on account of poverty in 1665. Among those who paid in 1665 the number of farmers living in substantial houses is noticeable. There were seven with five or more hearths. At Little Milton there were also five families who paid on five hearths or more in 1665 but 26 others were less well housed than the Great Milton people. In 1662 35 were taxed. Only four houses, including Sir William Dormer's, were returned for Ascot.[14] It is of interest to compare the figure of 83 households with that of 409 persons listed in the Compton Census of 1676. At Tetsworth, where both the number of families and the number of persons of age is given, the ratio is 2·8 to one.[15] If the ratio was the same at Great Milton there were about 146 families there in 1676.

In 1749 there were some 40 holdings, copyhold and leasehold, in the prebendal manor of Great and Little Milton, and most were valued at well over £5. In 1775 the annual value of the manor was £239 6s. 6d. in rack rents, £20 5s. 7d. in quitrents and £113 3½d. from fines and heriots, reckoned on an average of 12 years. By 1808 there had been changes in tenures: the homage presented that William Davy, the previous lord, had enfranchised various tenements and that John Hedges and Benjamin Bennet, the new lords, had extinguished some copyhold tenures.[16]

The land-tax assessments of 1786 show that besides the large properties there were still many small-holdings in the Miltons. There were 40 landlords and 49 holdings in Great Milton, 13 owner-occupiers and some 35 tenants. There were 40 landlords in Little Milton and 54 holdings, 14 owner-occupiers, and 35 tenants. In Chilworth there were 11 land-owners, 4 owner-occupiers, and 12 tenants. Thomas Weld, the lord of the manor, owned most land here and paid £85 1s. 4d.; he was non-resident and had 4 tenants. Only eight others paid as much as between £10 and £24 in the Miltons and Chilworth, and the majority paid between £1 and £5. By 1816 the Weld interest had disappeared from Chilworth and there was no predominantly large landowner in that part of the parish. In 1785 most of Ascot was owned by one non-resident landlord, who was assessed for eight-ninths of the land tax.[17] By 1832 Edward Franklin was the sole tenant farmer; he had bought the estate by the 1850's and it was one of the centres of progressive farming in Oxfordshire.[18]

In the 1830's the parish still had a high proportion of meadow and pasture land. It amounted to 1,660 acres compared with 2,520 acres of arable; Chilworth had a ratio of meadow to arable as high as 2 to 3 and Ascot had almost as much pasture land as arable.[19] A description of Great Milton meadows some 30 years earlier shows the division of meadow land. Revel Mead with 32 men's math was held by 8 tenants; Breach Mead and the Breach were held by 3 tenants; North Mead was divided into 22 lots and occupied by 6 tenants.[20] Waste land and commons were still important. In 1830 various proprietors and tenants met in a vestry meeting at the Bell Inn to protect their common rights: they agreed not to remove grass or rushes from the commons or waste land or to allow others to do so.[21] Nevertheless the end of the open-field village soon came. Over 902 acres of Little Milton were inclosed in 1839; about 575 acres went to Walter Long, the lord of the manor. Great Milton was inclosed in 1844 when 1,316 acres were affected. The largest allotment of 360 acres went to Walter Long; Charles Couling, owner of the Prebendal farm, received 254 acres and the prebendary of Milton Ecclesia 137 acres. Four acres were allotted for recreation.[22]

The inclosures may have contributed to the drop in population in the second half of the 19th century. The census of 1801 recorded about 1,000 people in the parish, well over three-quarters living in Great and Little Milton. At Ascot the population dropped between the 1830's and 1840's as Franklin brought all the land into his own hands, but there was a steady rise in population elsewhere until the 1840's. Thereafter the population in all parts of the parish declined to 865 in 1901.[23]

Whatever the effect of inclosure on population its encouragement of the larger-sized farm seems certain. Small-holdings decreased in number until in 1882 there were six farms in Great Milton, for example, of between 150 and 200 acres besides the manor farm with 273 acres. The 100 or so cottages and other houses in the village had only their gardens or at most 2 acres of land.[24] The continued growth in the size of farms can be seen at the begin-

[11] Oxf. Archd. Oxon. c 118, ff. 86–88, 118, 174b, 177b, 178, 224b–5, 246. A 50-acre close of pasture, 'the warrene', was said to be worth £30 in 1650: Linc. Dioc. Regy., Parl. Survey.
[12] Linc. Dioc. Regy., Parl. Survey.
[13] O.R.O. Misc. Har. VI/1.
[14] Hearth Tax Oxon. 49–51; E 179/164/504
[15] Queen's Coll. MS. 501, and see below, p. 154.

[16] O.R.O. H IV/1: register of courts for Milton manor prebend and Great and Little Milton manor, 1742–1808.
[17] O.R.O. Land tax assess.
[18] Ibid.; Gardner, Dir. Oxon.; and see below.
[19] Bodl. Tithe award.   [20] d.d. Ashhurst d 4.
[21] Par. Rec. Vestry minutes.   [22] O.R.O. Incl. award.
[23] V.C.H. Oxon. ii. 222, 218.
[24] d.d. Bullingdon c 23.

ning of the 20th century in Little Milton where there were three farms of 257, 300, and 412 acres; at Chilworth where there were five farms of 100 to 200 acres and one of over 300 acres; and at Ascot where there was one large farm of 551 acres and five cottages.[25] This movement has continued to the present day (1957) save in Ascot, where the Oxford County Council purchased the Ascot estate in 1920 under the Small-holdings Act, with the object of assisting demobilized soldiers to settle on the land.[26] By 1922 there were ten cottages each with 30 to 40 acres of land, and by 1931 there were 55 inhabitants, the highest number since the early 19th century.[27]

The parish has always been good mixed farming country. The type of land is well described by Arthur Young: 'Milton field is one of the finest soils . . . in the country: dry, sound, friable loam on gravel'[28] and an agricultural expert in 1917 described it as excellent for the best type of Oxfordshire farming—corn, sheep, and cattle.[29] There have been many changes in the popularity of the various types of farming, but on the whole arable has held pride of place in the Milton economy after the trend of the 15th and 16th centuries towards a pastoral economy. Barley, dredge, and beans were sold off the Louches manor in 1322 and in 1617 barley was grown on Sir William Cope's estate. In 1803 tithes were paid in barley, wheat, maslin and beans, straw, and hay.[30] Turnips and swedes were grown at the end of the 18th century. Arthur Young noted that Milton field had 'the finest show of turnips' he had seen that year (1807) as well as 'very fine and luxurious swedes'.[31] A vestry meeting of 1823 laid down that clover was to be sown in part at least of Milton 'Field', turnips in part of Harrington, and vetches in part of Fulwell Field.[32] Even at Chilworth there had been reconversion to arable: in 1831 Chilworth farm was mainly arable and had only 7 acres of pasture.[33] In 1826 the inventory of crops at Wheatley Bridge farm included oats, barley, beans and peas, spring wheat, and potatoes.[34] When Ashhurst let it out in 1876 he prescribed a five-course rotation.[35] At Ascot Edward Franklin was noted for his good farming and gave a great deal of information to Sewell Read for his agricultural survey of 1854. Franklin practised double-cropping of roots and green crops, and sowed mangolds in the bean quarter.[36]

The introduction of machinery in the parish led to violent opposition. In 1830 rioters from the neighbouring villages of Drayton, Chislehampton, and Stadhampton assaulted James Wells of Little Milton and broke his threshing machines. Six people were indicted and sentenced to 7 years' transportation. The parish itself appears not to have been in sympathy with the attack and 136 parishioners were sworn in as special constables.[37]

Stock farming was still important in all parts of the parish in the 19th century. When Swarford or Wheatley Bridge farm was up for sale in 1814, it was described as mostly consisting of 'very rich grazing land', and in 1815 an inventory of stock included 14 cows and heifers, 212 sheep. There were prize sheep in many parts of the parish.[38] In 1854 valuable Down Cotswold flocks had been kept at Little Milton for twenty years. Read was enthusiastic, too, over the fat lambs at Ascot and the use of a horned Wiltshire ram, but he commented that the lambs 'can only be successfully grazed by those who have a large extent of rich meadow land'. A fine herd of Herefords was kept by Franklin. Read commented that 'the first 30 that were sold averaged £34 each and were excellent in every point being good for the feeder, the butcher, and the public'. The steers were bought at the Hereford October fair, kept throughout the summer, and sold at Christmas.[39] Fruit farming in the parish was not successful: it died out in the early 19th century with the death of its originator, William Speechley.[40]

Throughout most of its history, agriculture and allied crafts have been the parish's main occupation. In both the 17th and 18th centuries the names of wheelwrights, carpenters, cord-wainers, and blacksmiths are recorded. The appearance of a peruke-maker in 1757 was presumably due to the number of gentry living in the neighbourhood.[41] The quarries in Great and Little Milton must have provided the only other industry in the parish. Dr. Plot noted them in 1677 and in 1903 Milton quarries were still worked and provided Portland stone for repairing buildings in Oxford.[42] In 1740 Richard Belcher, a mason of Little Milton, built the tower of Stadhampton church.[43]

The census of 1851 shows that Great Milton was a comparatively self-sufficient community. The majority of inhabitants, some 155 labourers, were employed by 8 farmers, but there were also 4 blacksmiths, 2 wheelwrights, 7 shoemakers, 2 harness-makers, 7 carpenters, 4 or 5 victuallers or innkeepers, a carrier, and a drover, besides the usual trades of shopkeeper, baker, and butcher. There were 2 dressmakers, a milliner, a glover, and 3 laundresses. The professional class was represented by a surgeon and a general practitioner.[44] In Little Milton, Ascot, and Chilworth there were 9 farmers. Little Milton had 3 dealers in livestock, 5 shopkeepers, and a publican. Besides 12 craftsmen of a more common type stone masons still flourished: there was one family of 4 and 2 others engaged in the craft. At Ascot the whole community of 21 centred around Edward Franklin's farm of 1,050 acres.[45] In Chilworth 15 labourers were employed by 3 farmers, and there was a carter and a turnpike keeper.[46] By 1939 only 2 craftsmen were left and in 1957 only about 5 per cent. of the villagers worked on the land, the rest mostly working in Oxford industries.[47]

[25] d.d. Bullingdon c 26, c 7, c 3.
[26] O.R.O. CCE 31, scheme 78.
[27] d.d Bullingdon c 67, c 68; *Census*, 1931.
[28] Young, *Oxon. Agric.* 8.
[29] Orr, *Oxon. Agric.* 19.
[30] S.C. 6/962; Oxf. Archd. Oxon. c 118, ff. 86–88; Oxf. Dioc. c 449, f. 8.
[31] Young, *Oxon. Agric.* 8.
[32] Par. Rec. Vestry minutes.
[33] d.d. Ashhurst c 8; Barley Close, pasture in 1664, was arable in 1838: d.d. Hobbes c 4; Bodl. Tithe award.
[34] d.d. Ashhurst c 9.
[35] Ibid.

[36] S. Read, 'Farming in Oxon.', *Jnl. Royal Soc. of Agric.* (1854), 206, 208, 276.
[37] Par. Rec.; MS. Top. Oxon. b 42, ff. 91–92.
[38] d.d. Ashhurst d 9.
[39] *Jnl. Royal Soc. Agric.* 1854, 223, 230–2.
[40] Inf. the Revd. R. A. Ker.
[41] O.R.O. Cal. Q. Sess.; O.R.O. H IV/1.
[42] Arkell, *Oxf. Stone*, 90; *V.C.H. Oxon.* ii. 267.
[43] MS. Top. Oxon. d 88, f. 57.
[44] H.O. 107/1726/1.
[45] Ibid.
[46] Ibid.
[47] Kelly, *Dir. Oxon.* (1939); inf. the Revd. R. A. Ker.

In the agricultural depression of the late 1860's and 1870's there was so much unemployment and poverty in the Miltons that in addition to the assistance to the poor provided from the rates, special steps were taken by the better-off inhabitants to alleviate distress. An Emigration Fund was set up to help emigrants with their passage to Canada and nearly £50 had been subscribed by 1870 when a group left the parish to join an immigration party going from London to Quebec and Markham, Canada.[48] Free railway journeys in Canada and employment were promised. The letters sent back by the emigrants throw light not only on life in Canada, but also on problems at home and in particular on the close connexion, even in villages, between poverty and excessive drinking of alcohol. One emigrant, for instance, said that he had not touched beer and was better than if he had had a 'gallon a day'. The vicar's comment was that there was hope that the emigrants had 'shaken off the great enemy of the working man in this country'.[49]

A coal club, clothing club, and a Great Milton medical club were also organized. The Christmas morning offertory was used to buy beef for distribution to the poor for Christmas dinners. There were also gifts from individuals, such as 524 lb. of beef given in 1869 by M. P. Boulton.[50] Social and educational activities were encouraged: in 1866 a reading-room was opened in the school and furnished with newspapers, books, draughts, chess, and other games; talks were given; choirs were invited to visit the parish and Milton church choir attended the annual choir-meeting in Oxford.[51] Low wages, however, persisted: in the 1890's Great Milton labourers still earned some of the lowest agricultural wages in England. 'Butchers' meat was seldom seen' in any labourer's cottage and most old labourers were 'on the parish'. Members of the Ancient Order of Foresters were assisted by the Society's Benevolent Club, and also benefited from the social activities of the Order, carried on at the Foresters' Hall behind the 'Bull'.[52]

In 1894 Miss Ellen K. Sheppard built in Church Lane an institute for boys. There during her lifetime they received further education after they had left school. After her death, in accordance with her will (proved 1906), the building, with its lawn, was held in trust for the use of boys of the parish between school-leaving age and eighteen.[53] She also left 'the new institute' with two cottages and a garden for use by the men of the village.[54] The men's institute was falling out of use before the Second World War and after 1944 was used for a time[54] as a boys' club. The social life of the parish was further considerably assisted by the Pott benefactions. In 1923 the Revd. A. P. Pott and his wife presented a village hall, called the Neighbour Hall; in 1929 the Revd. A. P. Pott purchased a recreation ground, as the previous one was inadequate and too far removed; and in 1931 he had a pavilion built for the Sports Club. The village hall stands close to the manorhouse, and is controlled by the Parochial Church Council, which appoints a management committee.[55]

MILLS AND FISHERY. Domesday Book records two mills in the parish, the bishop's mill worth 15s. and the mill of one of his knights worth 8s. a year.[56] The bishop's mill was probably in Ascot on a feeder of the Thame, for this water-mill was always associated with the chief lay manor in Great Milton and followed its descent. It is mentioned c. 1200, when Basilea, the wife of Roger de Cundi, granted 3s. from Ascot mill to Oseney Abbey for the term of her life;[57] in 1279 when John de Clifford held it; and in the time of his successors the De Louches, whose water-mill was described as in Ascot in Milton. In 1322 Richard de Louches farmed it out with 1 virgate for 16s. a year.[58] In the 15th century when the Camoys and then the Radmylde family owned it, it was often described on the court rolls as being in a ruinous condition and in need of repair. In 1484 William and Margery Stockham, the latter being the widow of the previous tenant, were tenants of the mill, 1 messuage and 1 virgate of land, containing 16 acres, for 24s. a year and services; in 1499 William Rede of Ascot was the tenant and also paid 24s. a year.[59] The property passed to Sir Reginald Bray and then to the Dormers and was one of the Ascot water-mills listed in their 16th-century deeds.[60] The other Domesday watermill was on John Forester's estate in 1279 and was held by his successors, the Fiennes, in the 15th century. From them it passed to the Quatremains and Dormers.[61] In 1463 Ascot court said that the path between the two mills should be repaired.[62] One of these was on the 17th-century Anderson's farm and was mentioned as 'the corn mill' in 1728.[63] By the 19th century both were apparently disused; the site of one was marked on the tithe map as 'the old mill seat'.[64]

In 1279 Richard de Sepewas held a third watermill and a ½-virgate in Great Milton for 13s. a year. This may have been the 15th-century mill 'Shittangs' near Millditch Meadow which belonged to the Radmylde manor.[65] There was a fourth water-mill, on the prebendary's estate: in 1500 his tenant was presented for flooding the land.[66] There is no later reference to either of these mills.

There were two other mills in the Miltons in the 14th century and these were probably windmills. The Inge family had one in the early 14th century and in 1322 a windmill on the De Louches' estate

[48] *Milton Magazine*, July, Sept. 1870; Feb. 1871.
[49] Ibid.
[50] Ibid. 1866–73.
[51] Ibid.
[52] Viscount Samuel, *Memoirs*, 15; inf. the Revd. E. P. Baker.
[53] Char. Com. unrep. vol. 139, f. 120; file 85467.
[54] Ibid. Accts. file. In 1946 the property, apart from the two halls, appears to have consisted of only one cottage, which was let.
[55] Inf. the Revd. E. P. Baker, vicar. The hall was designed by Mr. H. Bradfield, A.R.I.B.A., and was vested in the Oxf. Diocesan Board of Finance, as trustees.
[56] *V.C.H. Oxon.* i. 402, 403.

[57] *Oseney Cart.* vi. 157.
[58] *Rot. Hund.* (Rec. Com.), ii. 820; C.P. 25(1)/188/12/74; S.C. 6/962.
[59] W.A.M. 1632, 1596.
[60] Rousham Arch. L 19, L 20, A 8; C.P. 25 (2)/197/East. 29 Eliz.
[61] *Rot. Hund.* (Rec. Com.), ii. 821; Rousham Arch. L 7, L 9, L 12, L 19, L 20.
[62] Rousham Arch. L 11.
[63] Ibid. L 63.
[64] Bodl. Tithe award.
[65] *Rot. Hund.* (Rec. Com.), ii. 821; W.A.M. 1592.
[66] W.A.M. 1634.

was let out for 3s. 4d. a year.[67] There were still two windmills in the parish in 1838 and c. 1900.[68]

Fishing rights in the Thame were attached to the Chilworth manors. In 1274 William of Coombe's widow claimed dower in a fishery extending from her husband's weir to Sir Roger Gernon's weir;[69] and in 1421 Sir Thomas Camoys, who succeeded to the Coombe estate, had a fishery in Chilworth.[70] The Gernon estate had half a fishery also in 1279, which presumably descended with the manor.[71] All the fishing rights must have come by the 16th century to the Hubands, owners of both estates. Thereafter they descended with Chilworth manor.[72] The Milton estate also had fishing rights, held by Lord Coventry in the 17th century and presumably descending with the manor.[73] In 1650 fishing royalties of the prebend manor were worth £26 8s.[74]

PARISH GOVERNMENT.[75] The surviving parish records are the Chilworth overseers' accounts (1691–1819), the Great Milton churchwardens' accounts from 1760, vestry minutes from 1822, and a Great Milton overseers' account book (1826–32).[76]

The records of the Chilworth overseers of the poor give a detailed picture. One overseer was appointed annually, but in fact substantial farmers like the Welleses of Wheatley Bridge Farm and Lower Farm or the Hedges of Chilworth Farm served for many years. Poverty was not a serious problem during most of the 18th century: until 1783 £8 to £15 a year was spent and there were only three or four people a year regularly needing poor relief. The overseers dispensed occasional relief by buying wool to be made into stockings, or by paying for rent and food or medical attention and nursing. From 1785 they rented Moor House as a pest-house, and cases of smallpox were sent to it in 1786. Other payments included the normal ones for resettling paupers in their own parish, for the care of bastards, and for such items as providing militia men for the parish. From 1783 expenditure began to rise, at first to about £40 a year, then to £80 by 1798, to as much as £202 in 1802, and to an average of £150 a year from 1810 to 1819. Both the Speenhamland and roundsman systems were adopted in the parish and large sums were spent on supporting the families of the unemployed and in supplementing wages.[77]

The problem of unemployment was common to all parts of the parish and in 1822 a select vestry was set up. It met fortnightly at the 'Bell', 'Bull', or 'Red Lion'. Relief that year was given at the rate of 8d. a day for a married man and 3d. for his wife, 6d. for a single man, 2d. for boys, and 3d. for women.[78]

Gravel-digging and lacemaking were also subsidized by the parish to provide employment. There were two overseers for Great Milton township and they spent about £330 a year at this time, chiefly on weekly payments to as many as 30 people; a large proportion of the payment was for children.[79] By the 1830's the parish as a whole was spending about £1,000 a year on relief, a quarter the amount paid by Thame. The highest amount was spent in Little Milton: in 1835 £573 17s. on relief in the township, and £20 on removing paupers to the parish from which they came. Ascot spent only £68, since it was the most sparsely populated area.[80]

Vestry meetings were also held to manage the open fields.[81] This function, however, was removed by the complete inclosure of the parish by the 1840's and many of the vestry's other functions by the transfer of poor relief to Thame Union in 1836.[82] Poverty continued to remain a problem: in 1854 Chilworth spent £93 on poor relief, Great Milton £241, Little Milton £249, and Ascot £1.[83]

CHURCH. The church of Great Milton was certainly in existence in 1086 when its priest was recorded, but as Great Milton was part of the endowment of the see of Dorchester there can be little doubt that the history of the church goes back to early Saxon times.[84] In 1086 the church and manor were in the hands of the Bishop of Lincoln and by 1146 two prebends had been endowed from Milton, one of them, Milton Ecclesia, with the church and the appropriated benefice.[85] Until 1844, when Little Milton and Ascot were separated from the ecclesiastical parish, this consisted of the tithings of Great Milton, Little Milton, the medieval chapelry of Ascot, and Chilworth. Like other prebends of Lincoln the parish was until the 19th century an ecclesiastical peculiar, for all prebendal parishes were freed by Bishop Chesney (1148–66) from the jurisdiction of bishop and archdeacon.[86] As in the case of Thame, the prebendary of Milton Ecclesia had archidiaconal jurisdiction and the Dean of Lincoln had the right of visiting every three years.[87] Although the bishop did not visit[88] he instituted to the vicarage and the chapter inducted.[89]

Milton Ecclesia prebend, unlike Thame, was not dissolved at the Reformation, but in the confusion of the period the prebendary evidently lost his jurisdiction, which passed to the dean and chapter. The parish continued as a separate peculiar[90] and visitations were probably held in Great Milton church by the commissary appointed by the chapter, who was almost certainly the commissary for Thame and the chapter's other Oxfordshire peculiars. This

[67] C.P. 25(1)/285/64; S.C. 6/962.
[68] Bodl. Tithe award; d.d. Bullingdon c 23, c 26.
[69] Cal. Inq. p.m. iv, p. 338.   [70] C 138/288/29.
[71] Rot. Hund. (Rec. Com.), ii. 716.
[72] C.P. 25(2)/198/Trin. 39 Eliz.; 707/Trin. 12 Chas. II.
[73] C.P. 25(2)/527/Trin. 10 Chas. I; 708/Mich. 22 Chas. II.   [74] Lincs. Dioc. Regy., Parl. Survey.
[75] For hundred court see above, p. 115. As a member of the honor of St. Valery Chilworth attended the courts of Ewelme honor up to the 19th cent.: d.d. Ewelme Honor d 1–3; O.R.O. CH/E. X/1–53
[76] Par. Rec.; there are also bastardy and other poor relief pps.
[77] Ibid. Chilworth Overseers' bk. 1691–1819.
[78] Ibid. Gt. Milton Select Vestry mins. 1821–2.
[79] Ibid. Gt. Milton Overseers' bk. 1826–32.

[80] 2nd Rep. Poor Law Com. App. (E), H.C. 595–II, pp. 292, 296 (1836), xxix (2).
[81] Par. Rec., Vestry minutes, 1802, 1823.
[82] 2nd Rep. Poor Law Com. App. (E), H.C. 595–II, pp. 292, 296 (1836), xxix (2).
[83] Poor Law Unions, H.C. 81, pp. 248, 249 (1854), lv.
[84] V.C.H. Oxon. i. 402; see above, pp. 113, 124.
[85] See below, p. 139.
[86] H. Bradshaw, Lincoln Cathedral Statutes, revised C. Wordsworth, i. 309–10: V.C.H. Lincs. ii. 80.
[87] See below, p. 201.
[88] Visit. Dioc. Linc. 1517–31, i. 137 n.
[89] Linc. Chapter Acts, 1526–36 (L.R.S. xii), 151.
[90] O.A.S. Rep. 1920, 286; Oxf. Archd. Oxon. c 158, f. 87b. No court records survive until the parish was amalgamated with Thame peculiar.

was the case in the early 1670's,[91] but *c.* 1675 the vicar and churchwardens began to attend the visitations at Thame.[92] From this time the peculiar was formally that of Thame and Milton,[93] although frequently it was called Thame peculiar.[94]

Since the Reformation sometimes the Bishop of Oxford and sometimes the Bishop of Lincoln has instituted to the vicarage.[95] This appears to have been largely a matter of chance. For instance, when in 1782 the prebendary was about to present a new vicar, he was told by the secretary of the Bishop of Oxford to send the presentation to Oxford and by the secretary of the Bishop of Lincoln to send it to Lincoln. After finding out what had been done in the past, he sent it to Oxford.[96]

Soon after 1800 Great Milton, unlike Thame, came under the ordinary jurisdiction of the Bishop of Oxford and in 1802 it began to be visited by the bishop,[97] but like Thame it remained exempt from the jurisdiction of the archdeacon until the middle of the century. Great Milton wills were proved in the peculiar court until 1857.[98]

Bishop Alexander of Lincoln (1123–48), who created Milton Manor prebend, was probably also responsible for appropriating Milton church.[99] The church had been appropriated by 1146, when the endowment in Milton presumably consisted of the advowson of the vicarage, the glebe, and part of the tithes, the bishop's demesne tithes having been granted in 1094 or 1095 to Eynsham Abbey.[1] The appropriated rectory became part of the prebend of Aylesbury, which until the mid-13th century was held by the deans of Lincoln.[2] As a consequence, Milton church was described as a chapel of Aylesbury.[3] About 1260 Eynsham Abbey farmed the demesne tithes for £1 13*s.* 4*d.* to the Dean of Lincoln, as long as he should be Prebendary of Aylesbury, arranging that the abbey's servants should continue to collect them into the abbey's barn;[4] there is no later record of these tithes in the Eynsham cartulary. In 1290 Bishop Sutton created a separate prebend of Milton Ecclesia, endowing it with the appropriated rectory of Milton including, apparently, the demesne tithes.[5]

The first known presentation to the vicarage was made by the Prebendary of Aylesbury in 1268.[6] In the 14th century, when the prebend of Milton

Ecclesia was for many years held by foreign cardinals, their English representatives usually presented.[7] In 1361 the bishop collated, probably through lapse, and in 1375 the farmer of the prebend presented. In the 15th and early 16th centuries the prebendaries themselves presented.

After 1601 the presentation to the vicarage went with the farm of the prebend until the late 18th century, when the prebendary again began to present.[8] In 1840 the advowson was given to the Bishop of Oxford, who has since been patron.[9]

Among the prebendaries of Milton Ecclesia have been many distinguished men, but they had little connexion with the parish beyond drawing money from it.[10] The prebend consisted of the great tithes from the parish, the tithes of wool and lambs, and the land belonging to the church. In 1291 the prebend was valued at £40; in 1535 its net value was £33 18*s.* 6*d.*, and in 1650 it was worth about £250.[11] In 1844 the prebend's tithes were commuted for £850: £274 from Great Milton, £316 from Little Milton, £108 from Ascot, and £152 from Chilworth.[12]

The glebe belonging to the church probably formed the basis of the prebendal estate, known in the 19th century as Monks farm or Monkery farm.[13] It consisted of 120 acres at the time of the tithe award. In 1650, when the estate was surveyed, besides the prebendal house there were two farms of 2 yardlands each, worth £20 each, a small holding of 8 acres, and a cottage.[14] By 1844 these had been amalgamated into one farm,[15] which was exchanged at the inclosure award for 137 acres. In 1840 the property, land, and tithes, was transferred to the Ecclesiastical Commissioners.[16]

Little is known of the administration of the prebend before the Reformation, but it was no doubt farmed,[17] as it continued to be after the Reformation. In 1537 the farmer was Richard Beauforest, who bought Dorchester Abbey at its dissolution.[18] In 1555 the prebend was leased to New College for 60 years.[19] At the end of the century the prebendary John Sled (1575–1601), who had been presented by his father John Sled, gent., of Milton, kept the property in his own hands.[20]

During the 17th century the lease was held by

[91] *Oxon. Peculiars*, 155; Oxf. Archd. Oxon. b 82, f. 10.

[92] *Oxon. Peculiars*, 156.

[93] Oxf. Archd. Oxon. c 162, p. 17; Oxf. Dioc. c 649, f. 105.

[94] Oxf. Archd. Oxon. b 82, f. 18; Oxf. Dioc. c 649, f. 108.

[95] No presentations between 1531 and 1601 have been found. The institution of 1601 by the Bishop of Lincoln does not seem to have taken effect (Linc. Reg. xxx, Chadderton, f. 150); instead there was one by the archbishop during the vacancy of the see of Oxford (Oxf. Dioc. c 649, f. 10*b*). The institutions of 1661, 1693, 1724, 1726, and 1737 were by the Bishop of Lincoln (Linc. Reg. xxxii, Sanderson, f. 6; Oxf. Dioc. c 649, f. 13*b*); those of 1608, 1729, 1749 and later ones were by the Bishop of Oxford (Oxf. Dioc. c 649, f. 10*b*; ibid. b 21, f. 30*b*.).

[96] Oxf. Dioc. c 654, ff. 83–83*b*.

[97] Ibid. d 567; c 327, p. 246.

[98] *Return of Courts Granting Probate of Wills*, H.C. 177, p. 50 (1829), xviii.

[99] *Reg. Antiquiss.* i. 199, 207.

[1] *Eynsham Cart.* i. 36; ii, p. liv.

[2] *Reg. Antiquiss.* iii. 290; J. Le Neve, *Fasti Ecclesiae Anglicanae*, ed. T. D. Hardy, ii. 95.

[3] *Eynsham Cart.* i. 224. For Aylesbury prebend see *V.C.H. Bucks.* iii. 13.

[4] *Eynsham Cart.* i. 223–4.

[5] *Reg. Antiquiss.* i. 231–4.   [6] *Rot. Graves.* 220.

[7] For medieval presentations see MS. Top. Oxon. d 460.

[8] Bodl. MS. Gough Oxon. 48, f. 274 sqq.; P.R.O. Inst. Bks.   [9] Oxf. Dioc. b 70.

[10] For list see Le Neve, *Fasti*, ii. 187–8, and Bodl. MS. Gough Oxon. 48, ff. 154*b*–212*b*, where there are biographical notes by Delafield.

[11] *Tax. Eccl.* (Rec. Com.), 30; *Valor Eccl.* (Rec. Com.), ii. 172. The latter included a payment of £2 to the Vicar of Cholsey (Berks.), for which no explanation has been found.

[12] Bodl. Tithe award. The glebe was tithe free, but there was a contingent charge of £25 on it if it were sold.

[13] Parker, *Guide*, 318–19; *Kelly's Dir. Oxon.* (1939).

[14] Linc. Dioc. Regy., Parl. Survey.

[15] Bodl. Tithe award.

[16] Oxf. Dioc. b 70; ibid. d 178. This was done by 3 & 4 Vict. c. 113, § 50.

[17] e.g. *Cal. Close*, 1377–81, 187; Linc. Reg. x, Buckingham, f. 363.

[18] *L. & P. Hen. VIII*, xii (2), p. 246; xiv (2), p. 320.

[19] Bodl. MS. chs. Oxon. 1297–9, where the college is subleasing various pieces of land.

[20] John Sled, senior, bought one presentation: *Linc. Records in Time of Cooper* (L.R.S. ii), 2, 242, 257; cf. *Cal. S.P. Dom.* 1547–80, 524. For Sled, junior, see Venn, *Alumni*.

local families who lived in the prebendal house.[21] Eighteenth-century lessees had fewer connexions with the parish. Early in the century the lease was held by Sir Nathan Wright, who before his death in 1721 sold it to Richard Carter (d. 1755) of Chilton (Bucks.).[22] It was he who presented Thomas Delafield to the vicarage.[23] Carter's daughter Martha married Sir Thomas Aubrey, Bt., of Boarstall (d. 1786), and in 1844 the lease was held by trustees named in the will of Sir John Aubrey (d. 1826).[24] The rent continued at £40 a year, no doubt on the payment of a large fine, and the usual term was for three lives.

The original ordination of the vicarage has not been found, but by the 16th century, and probably before, the vicar had the small tithes of the parish except those of wool and lambs, which belonged to the prebendary, and a large payment in kind from the rectory.[25] This was still being paid in kind in the 17th century, and consisted among other things of 12 quarters of barley, 5 of wheat, 3 of mixed corn (masley dine) and of beans, and several good loads of hay.[26] In 1291 the vicar was receiving £6 and in 1526 £9 6s. 8d.; in 1535 the vicarage was valued at £15, in 1650 at £60, and in 1808 at £138 10s.[27] By 1808 the payment from the rectory was being made according to the price of grain and in 1929 it was exchanged for an annual payment of £90.[28] In 1844 the vicar's tithes were commuted for £185.[29] In 1842 the living was augmented by about £35 a year, and in 1864 by another £38; in 1867 £800 was given towards a parsonage house; and in 1901 there was another augmentation of £26.[30]

The first evidence about the residence of clergy at Milton comes from Domesday, where it is recorded that the priest had a share in the 19 tenant ploughs;[31] the next in 1228 when a toft near the church suitable for a priest's dwelling-house was obtained. As Milton was regarded as a chapel of Aylesbury at this date the house was said to be for the chaplain. By the 1260's Milton had a vicar: in 1268 James de Frestone was presented on the death of the last vicar.[32] One vicar early in the 14th century became a Franciscan; another died in 1349, probably from the Black Death.[33] In the 15th century several of the vicars were university graduates, and one at least, John Kendall (1443–c. 1463), was a pluralist, as was the 16th-century Master John Fisher (1531–c. 1554).[34]

One of the most distinguished vicars of Milton was John Howson (1601–7), later Bishop of Oxford

and Durham, and a strong opponent of Puritanism. He was a canon of Christ Church and Vice-Chancellor of Oxford in 1602, but it is nevertheless probable that he was often at Milton. He was married in his church in 1605 and his daughter was baptized there in 1607.[35] During most of the 17th century the living was held by two resident vicars, Richard Atwood (1608–58) and John Cave (vicar 1661–93). Cave, who was also the farmer of the prebend, was living at Milton in the 1640's.[36] He may have had Puritan sympathies, for in 1646 he took the place of the dispossessed Rector of Middleton Cheney (Northants.).[37] In 1661 he became Vicar of Great Milton.[38] Like others in the parish he had trouble with his churchwardens, and was presented for not paying part of his church-rate and for not providing rushes and straw for the church.[39] The Dormers of Ascot and several people of Little Milton were also presented for refusal to pay the church-rates.[40]

For the greater part of the 18th century the parish suffered from absenteeism, but between 1693 and 1723 it was fortunate in having John Hinton as vicar. Born in a Great Haseley cottage, he was considered by Delafield to be a 'polite, well-bred, ingenious man, a good scholar, a pious Christian, and a generous friend'. He started a grammar school for the village.[41] In his old age he was assisted by an unreliable curate, 'a licentious unassuming person of little learning'.[42] His successor Thomas Delafield, one of Milton's best-known vicars (1724–6, and 1737–49), was consistently non-resident, even though Richard Cornish (vicar 1726–9) had built a new vicarage.[43] Delafield's successors throughout the century likewise lived out of the parish.

As Milton was not subject to the bishop's visitations, little is known of the religious life of the parish at this time. Early in the 19th century, during the long incumbency of Thomas Ellis (1800–48), frequent services were held, two on Sundays and five communion services a year. Attendance was good; there were at least 50 communicants and the number increased in the early years of the century.[44] Ellis's main complaint was about the under-payment of his parish clerk, who received about £2 a year in fees and £2 for minding the clock, with the result that clerks were often unsuitable or illiterate.[45]

By the mid-19th century congregations of 250 to 300 were reported. Out of 564 adult parishioners, about a third were communicants, a fifth were good

[21] Bodl. MS. Gough Oxon. 48, ff. 140b–141, 144–144b.
[22] Ibid. ff. 145b, 148b. For Wright see D.N.B.; for Carter see Lipscomb, Bucks. i. 144.
[23] Bodl. MS. Gough Oxon. 48, f. 149.
[24] For the family see G.E.C. Baronetage, iii. 94–95; Bodl. Tithe award.
[25] Subsidy 1526, 259.
[26] Bodl. MS. Gough Oxon. 48, ff. 367b–369b: 1632 terrier; Linc. Dioc. Regy. D iv, 69: 1677 terrier.
[27] Tax. Eccl. (Rec. Com.), 30; Valor Eccl. (Rec. Com.), ii. 172; Linc. Dioc. Regy., Parl. Survey; Oxf. Dioc. c 446, f. 124.
[28] Oxf. Dioc. c 449: 1803 terrier; Oxf. Dioc. c 1895–6, 1930 grant.
[29] Bodl. Tithe award.
[30] Lond. Gaz. 1842, p. 1167; 1845, p. 2985; 1864, p. 2027; 1867, p. 4558; Bodl. Par. Box, 1901 grant.
[31] V.C.H. Oxon. i. 402.
[32] Reg. Antiquiss. iii. 290.
[33] For list of medieval vicars see MS. Top. Oxon. d 460.

[34] Cal. Papal L. xi. 570, which reads Rendall; L. & P. Hen. VIII, xxi (1), p. 245.
[35] Bodl. MS. Gough Oxon. 48, f. 267b, citing Par. Reg. For his life see D.N.B., where he is said to have been married at Black Bourton in 1601.
[36] Bodl. MS. Gough Oxon. 48, ff. 275–275b; for Atwood and Cave see above, p. 115.
[37] Calamy Rev. 105; Bridges, Northants. i. 186; Baker, Northants. i. 654.
[38] Wood, Life, ii. 138.
[39] Oxon. Peculiars, 155.
[40] Ibid. 156–9.
[41] Bodl. MS. Gough Oxon. 48, ff. 277b–278b.
[42] Ibid. f. 290b.
[43] Ibid. ff. 281, 283, 287b. Cornish was the brother-in-law of his patron Richard Carter. He was succeeded by his brother Thomas (d. 1737), who was also Rector of Wheatfield: ibid. ff. 283–284b.
[44] Oxf. Dioc. d 549, p. 57; ibid. d 581.
[45] Ibid. d 573, d 581.

attenders, a quarter were 'middling churchmen', and the 20 others dissenters, according to an analysis made by J. H. Ashhurst (1848–56), vicar in Bishop Wilberforce's day.[46]

Before Ellis's death Little Milton and Ascot, which were separate tithings, were in 1844 separated from the parish of Great Milton, which continued to include Chilworth, and were formed into a district chapelry.[47] Little Milton and Ascot had each had a medieval chapel. That at Ascot was a private one

century building, which is likely to have consisted of chancel and nave only. Of this church one deeply splayed window survives in the north wall of the chancel and the outlines of two blocked-up windows can be seen in the spandrels of the north arcade in the nave.

Early in the 13th century the chancel arch was rebuilt and the chancel may have been extended to its present size though this enlargement probably did not take place until the following century. An

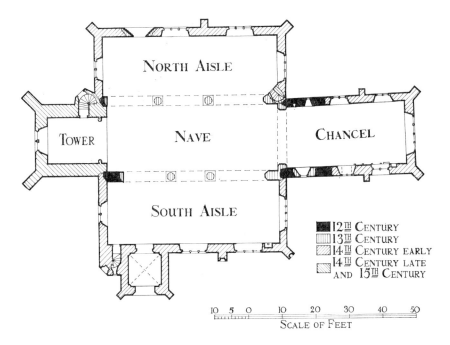

NORTH AISLE

TOWER   NAVE   CHANCEL

SOUTH AISLE

■ 12TH CENTURY
▥ 13TH CENTURY
▨ 14TH CENTURY EARLY
▧ 14TH CENTURY LATE
   AND 15TH CENTURY

10 5 0   10   20   30   40   50
SCALE OF FEET

attached to the manor-house.[48] Of the chapel of St. James at Little Milton little is known. The light endowed with land in Little Milton may have been either in the chapel or in Great Milton church.[49] The chapel had certainly gone by the mid-18th century, when the chapel yard was known as 'chappel heys'.[50] A new district church was built at Little Milton in 1844, and a few years later a vicarage. The patronage of the living, since 1868 a vicarage, belonged to the Vicar of Great Milton for life and then to the Bishop of Oxford.[51] It was endowed by the Ecclesiastical Commissioners with £95 a year in 1845 and in 1864 with a further £150 a year.[52]

As soon as the church was opened, frequent services, two on Sundays and holidays, and daily prayers with a lecture during Lent, were held. The vicar, however, complained that the congregation of about 160 was not large enough for the parish and did not increase. He had to fight indifference and an active Methodist community.[53]

The parish church of *ST. MARY*[54] comprises a chancel, nave, north and south-aisles, south porch with parvise above, and a western tower.[55] In the main it dates from the 14th century, but there are considerable survivals from earlier periods. The earliest parts of the structure belong to a 12th-

original lancet window still survives in the south wall. The nave was enlarged by the addition of aisles, perhaps of about half the width of the present aisles. They are divided from the nave by arcades each of three arches. These arcades exhibit certain peculiarities whose significance in the architectural history of the church is not clear. The circular columns are irregularly spaced, and the western arch of the southern arcade lacks the mouldings of its fellows. In addition the mouldings immediately above the capitals of the eastern column of both north and south arcades are interrupted on the sides facing the aisles in a manner which is difficult to explain. Both arcades appear, however, to be more or less contemporary, for, with the exception mentioned above, the mouldings of their arches correspond to those of the chancel arch with one additional member.[56] It is likely that the richly moulded Early English north doorway, which is certainly not in its original position, was once the 13th-century south door.

It is probable that the 13th-century building was severely damaged by fire, for all the cut stone moved at the time of the restoration of 1850 was found to have Early English moulding on the inside and fresh moulding cut on the reverse side to match the

[46] *Wilb. Visit.*
[47] *Lond. Gaz.* 1844, p. 3553.   [48] See above, p. 122.
[49] *Chant. Cert.* 28, where Little Milton is called a parish and the light and obit are said to be in the parish church.
[50] Bodl. MS. Gough Oxon. 48, f. 286.
[51] Oxf. Dioc. c 1897, Presentation.

[52] Oxf. Dioc. b 70, f. 502; *Lond. Gaz.* 1845, p. 2985; 1864, p. 2027.   [53] *Wilb. Visit.*; Oxf. Dioc. c 344.
[54] This description of the church is largely based on material supplied by the Revd. E. P. Baker, Vicar of Gt. Milton.   [55] See plate facing p. 121.
[56] Cf. Parker, *Guide*, 305.

Decorated work of the 14th century. Every Early English stone found had been burnt.[57]

In the early 14th century the church was largely rebuilt, the material of the old building being re-used. The aisles were widened and new windows with 'Decorated' tracery were inserted. The east window and four two-light windows were inserted in the enlarged chancel;[58] the nave walls were raised and a clerestory of six quatrefoil lights added. A new south door, a vaulted south porch with a carved boss, the room over it, and a staircase turret were built. The buttresses on this side of the church are of the same period; they are ornamented with niches surrounded by crocketed canopies and finials; a parapet with gargoyles runs above. In the south aisle there is a 19th-century copy of the original 14th-century piscina. Perpendicular windows were added in the late 14th or early 15th century, one over the chancel arch and the other at the east end of the clerestory on the south side. Patterned tiles, of which some have been assembled by the present chancel curb, were laid down in the chancel. A corbel in the south aisle with the arms of Camoys (lords of the manor in the reign of Henry V) may give a clue to the date of its roof.

The present tower and tower-arch were built towards the end of the 14th century. The tower is of three stages with deeply projecting angle buttresses. The papal indulgence of 1398 granted to all who visited or gave alms for the conservation of Milton church may have been connected with these additions.[59]

The roof of the nave was restored or rebuilt in 1592, the date being carved on the easternmost tie-beam over the chancel-arch. The chancel roof also appears to have been renewed in the 16th century. Parker dated it as late as the reigns of Mary or Elizabeth I: it had short king-posts and tie-beams resting on plain chamfered corbels.[60] There is no record of any work done to the fabric during the 17th century and little for the 18th. The 'inside of the church was much out of repair' in 1714, the 'sentences' were worn out and the 'church defaced', and arrangements were made for repairs.[61] The date 1735 carved on a beam in the south aisle probably indicates some repairs to the roof executed at that date. The rood screen with turned balusters dividing the nave from the chancel and the box pews, both of which are depicted in a pre-restoration print of the interior of the church, were installed after the Reformation.[62] At some date in the 18th century the west gallery, which is traditionally said to have been built out of the profits of a Whitsun ale,[63] was probably erected. It was presumably removed at the restoration.

By 1850 the church was in need of drastic repair. It was restored at a cost of over £2,000 under the direction of Gilbert Scott. G. Wyatt of Oxford was employed as builder. The roofs of nave, aisles, and tower were newly boarded and in parts releaded; the chancel roof was entirely renewed and the east end of the chancel rebuilt. The church was underpinned all round and an open gutter laid.[64] The rood stairs, the sedilia, piscina, and aumbry were opened up and the piscina in the south aisle was reconstructed.[65] An aperture was discovered in the north wall of the chancel, containing what is thought to have been an acoustic jar.[66] The church was re-pewed in oak, and new choir stalls, copied from those in Dorchester Abbey, were made.

A number of changes have been introduced since the restoration. In 1860 the Dormer monument (see below) was moved from the south aisle and the vestry there was 'taken down' in order that the space made might be used for pews for the children of the parish school.[67] Both monument and vestry were placed beneath the tower at the west end.

Substantial repairs were undertaken in 1926 at a cost of £600. The roof was thoroughly restored and other repairs to the fabric were effected. The architect was H. Bradfield of Great Milton.[68] In 1927 the Revd. A. P. Pott paid for the addition of a vestry at the west end of the north aisle.[69] In 1933 electric light in accordance with the design of the architect H. Grayson of Great Milton was installed. The church had previously been lit by oil and candles.

During 1955–6 repairs to the stonework included a new cross over the east gable to replace the one provided in 1850 as a copy of the medieval cross, and also the repair of the external stonework of some of the windows.[70]

Some wall paintings were discovered at the restoration of 1850, but were obliterated.[71] Traces of one remain over the doorway of the south porch. A few small fragments of medieval glass have also survived in three of the windows of the south aisle, and in the east window of the north aisle there are two quatrefoil lights that are said to illustrate the parable of Dives and Lazarus.[72] Of modern painted glass that in the east window is by T. Willement (inserted in 1850), that at the west end of the south aisle by Castell, and in 1868 glass by O'Connor was inserted in the west window of the north aisle to the memory of A. M. Ellis. In 1915 a memorial window to Margaret A. Sawyer, designed by Heaton, Butler, & Bayne, was placed at the east end of this aisle. Another to Charles Harris Rowles (d. 1947) and his wife Bertha (d. 1954) in the south aisle was made by M. Farrer Bell.

Of the furnishings of the medieval church, the broken pieces of a portable altar of Purbeck marble, found at the restoration of 1850, were incorporated in 1913 in the altar table placed in the Lady chapel in the north aisle;[73] some 15th-century carved bench ends, now in the choir, were preserved at the same time. One has a representation of two cruets, chalice, and wafer. The Jacobean pulpit was a bequest to the

[57] MS. Top. Oxon. d 93, f. 17.
[58] For the drawing by J. Buckler of the 14th-cent. east window, see MS. Top. Oxon. a 67, no. 382.
[59] Cal. Papal L. v. 177.   [60] Parker, Guide, 304.
[61] Oxon. Peculiars, 159–60.
[62] Bodl. G.A. fol. A 139* (70).
[63] MS. Top. Oxon. b 220, f. 235b.
[64] Ibid. d 93, ff. 17–28.
[65] Parker, writing in 1846, observed that the sedilia and the piscina in the chancel were concealed behind plaster and 'much defaced': Guide, 304.

[66] O.A.S. Rep. 1895/6, 23–24; Bodl. 2194 c. 15, 133, 139.
[67] Oxf. Dioc. c 1895–6, Faculty. For a view of the interior before the restoration see plate facing p. 159.
[68] Oxf. Dioc. c 1895–6, Faculty.
[69] Ibid.
[70] Ibid.
[71] Drawings of some are in the church muniment room.
[72] Parker, Guide, 306. For a note on and photographs of this glass see Bodl. 2194 c. 15, 464–6.
[73] Oxf. Dioc. c 1895–6, Faculty.

church made by Thomas Parsons (d. 1640);[74] before the restoration it stood in the angle of the north arcade and the chancel arch.[75] Another 17th-century addition was the clock by Nicholas Harris, which was installed in the tower in 1699.[76] In 1860 an organ was ingeniously disposed, part north and part south of the deep respond of the south arcade of the nave; in 1875 a reredos designed by Arthur Blomfield was erected; in 1889 a brass lectern was presented in memory of Alexander and Elizabeth A. Sheppard.[77] Two brass standards with branching candelabra, now on either side of the altar, were acquired to commemorate the Diamond Jubilee of Queen Victoria in 1897. In the next century six brass sconces were placed in the chancel to the memory of Emily Lovell (d. 1918).

In 1940 oak rails designed by H. S. Rogers of Oxford replaced the rails of oak, brass, and iron which had in their turn replaced between 1862 and 1864 the oak rails designed by Gilbert Scott.[78]

In 1958, owing to the initiative of the vicar, the Revd. E. P. Baker, the royal arms of Elizabeth II were hung over the north door. Panels of the Creed and Lord's Prayer were hung on either side of the east window to replace those removed in the last quarter of the 19th century. The Ten Commandments were painted on the spandrels of the chancel arch to replace those painted there in 1850, which were expunged in about 1932. All this work was done under the direction of E. Clive Rouse and executed by Miss J. T. Lenton.

A key-bugle and an ophicleide, formerly played in the church choir, are preserved with some constables' truncheons in the south aisle. The helm, sword, and orle of Sir Michael Dormer (d. 1624), and two pikes provided for the village's Home Guard in the Second World War are under the tower.

The earliest monuments in the church are the two sepulchral slabs with floriated crosses in relief dating from the 13th century. They were once in the chancel but were removed at the restoration of 1850 to the north aisle. Also in the north aisle are two fragments of a medieval effigy which may derive from the monument of Sir Richard de Louches (d. c. 1320–5) and his wife Elena Wace that was seen by Leland.[79] The only medieval brasses in the church are to the four children of Robert and Katherine Eggerley. Two of the four figures, three of the four shields (the fourth has been recently lost), and the inscription remain. The elaborate tomb of Sir Michael Dormer was placed in 1618, during his lifetime, at the east end of the south aisle, where traces of the railing which fenced it off can still be seen. The effigies of Sir Michael and Lady Dormer lie on an alabaster base and supported on a higher level between them lies that of Ambrose Dormer, Sir Michael's father. At the east end of the base an alabaster panel displays in relief a scene of Sir Michael Dormer engaged in the Spanish wars. Inscriptions recording the lives

of the two Dormers and shields of many quarterings also adorn the base. The monument has been attributed both to Gerard Christmas and to Epiphonius Evesham.[80] It was restored, cleaned, and repainted in 1956 under the direction of E. Clive Rouse.

There are mural tablets to Elizabeth Wilkinson (d. 1654), wife of Henry Wilkinson, Principal of Magdalen Hall; Joan (d. 1695), wife of Adolphus Meetkerke; John Smith (d. 1699); William Eldridge (d. 1716); Richard Cornish (vicar, d. 1729); the Revd. Francis Astry (d. 1754); John Blackall, gent. (d. 1755); Francis Jemmett, Esq. (d. 1784) and his wife Mary (d. 1782) by John Osborne, Oxford; and Capt. Lancelot Kerby Edwards (d. 1867). The first two tablets mentioned were in the chancel until 1875. Among the many inscriptions on the floor of the church the following may be mentioned: John Yong, Esq. (d. 1642/3); Mr. Thomas Yong (bur. 1692/3); Charles Hawkins (d. 1691/2); Anna, wife of William Loe (d. 1681); John Skynner (d. 1729) and his wife Elizabeth (d. 1769); William Loe (d. 1754); John Reeve (d. 1757); William Pease, vicar (d. 1781); William Skynner (d. 1794); Sir John Skynner, Chief Baron of the Exchequer (d. 1805); Paul Wells (d. 1805); Thomas Ellis, vicar (d. 1848).[81] There is a board giving details of Couling's charity and commemorating Charles Robey Couling (d. 1911).

In 1552 the commissioners recorded four bells and a sanctus bell.[82] In 1631 a 'stock' ring of five bells was supplied by Ellis Knight. In 1679 the churchwardens reported that the 'great bell' was broken. In 1684 the bells were again 'in good repair'.[83] Two were recast in 1673 by Ellis and Henry Knight and three were recast in 1771 by Thomas Rudhall of Gloucester. The present (1958) ring of eight are dated 1673 (two), 1771 (three), 1772, 1848, the eighth being an undated bell of the 17th or 18th century. The sanctus bell is dated 1825.[84]

The church possesses some old silver: a silver chalice, perhaps the one listed in the inventory of 1552 with paten cover (1568); a silver tankard flagon and pair of alms plates (1764), given by Joan Smith, wife of Anthony Smith of Little Milton. There are also a pewter plate and tankard with marks of John Shorey (c. 1714).[85]

The registers begin in 1550. There are churchwardens' accounts from 1760.

The church at Little Milton dedicated to ST. JAMES was built in 1843–4 on land given by Walter Long, lord of Great and Little Milton manors.[86] It is in the Decorated style and comprises a chancel, nave, vestry, western tower, and south porch. It has a barrel-shaped wooden roof. The architect was John Hayward of Exeter and the builder George Wyatt of Oxford. Unlike the design of many later churches that were influenced by the Tractarian movement, the entrance to the pulpit

[74] Cal. of Parsons' Wills and Administration (Lond. 1902), p. 67.
[75] See plan of church in Parker, Guide, 302.
[76] Recorded on the clock face.
[77] Oxf. Dioc. c 1895–6, Faculties; cf. report by H. S. Rogers.
[78] Ibid. Faculties.
[79] Leland, Itin. ed. Toulmin Smith, i. 164. For the Louches family see above, p. 123. The arms of Wace were once in a window of the church.
[80] For genealogy of the Dormer family see above, p. 127;

for the sculptors see The Walpole Society, xxi. 16, pl. XXI (a); and MS. notes by the Revd. R. A. Ker, reporting Mrs. Katharine Esdaile's view.
[81] For some of the families commemorated see below, index. For heraldary on the monuments see Bodl. G.A. Oxon. 4° 686, 211–15; G.A. Oxon. 16° 217, 187–9, 192a–b, 193.   [82] Chant. Cert. 117.
[83] Oxon. Peculiars, 159–60.
[84] Oxon. Bells, 209–10.
[85] Evans, Ch. Plate.
[86] Oxf. Dioc. c 1897, Petition for consecration.

was directly from the vestry and not from the chancel.[87] The Lord's Prayer and the Commandments are inscribed on stone on either side of the altar. The cost of £1,500 was met by private subscription and a grant from the Incorporated Church Building Society.[88]

In 1861 a faculty was granted to add an embattled tower with spirelets and a clock. The cost was met from a bequest of £1,200 for this purpose made by Mrs. Catherine Grayson, widow of Anthony Grayson, Principal of St. Edmund Hall.[89] The architect was again John Hayward. In 1958 after one of the spirelets had fallen down the remaining ones were taken down by Simm & Co. of Oxford, and the parapet was repaired at a cost of £280.[90]

In 1901 an oak reredos and pulpit, executed by H. Hems of Exeter, were given in memory of Capt. E. P. Wardlaw (killed 1901); a heating apparatus was installed in 1914; in 1947 the bells were rehung and electric lighting was installed.[91]

In 1854 painted glass was placed in the east window and in two windows in the nave; one of the latter was in memory of Catherine Grayson (d. 1853). In 1869 a third window was installed to Edith M. Sawyer. The west window is in memory of Edward L. Franklin of Ascot (d. 1869). There are two memorial brasses to those who lost their lives in the First and Second World Wars.

The medieval piscina, now in the sanctuary, is the one found in 'Chapel Heys', the site of the medieval chapel of St. James that once served Little Milton.[92]

The church possesses an early Victorian silver chalice with paten and an alms-dish.[93] There is a ring of six bells, all by Mears and Stainbank and dated 1867, and a sanctus bell of 1832.[94]

The registers date from 1844.

ROMAN CATHOLICISM. There were few adherents of the old faith in either of the Miltons. Only one Roman Catholic family was recorded in the early 17th century in Little Milton: Ralph Astry and his wife Anne were presented for not receiving communion in 1616;[95] from 1625 to 1641 Anne Astry was listed as a recusant, and in 1641 she paid the double tax imposed on recusants.[96] In 1671 there were said to be no 'Popish recusants'.[97] In the early 18th century, however, a member of a leading Roman Catholic family, Francis Curson, lived in Great Milton until his father's death in 1727. He also had 'papist' servants.[98] The Simeons of Aston (Staffs.) and Britwell Prior, another prominent Roman Catholic family, who were lords of the manor of Chilworth and Coombe in the 17th century and later, were not resident. In 1700 some local inhabitants maintained that the estate was secretly held for the Dominicans.[99]

PROTESTANT NONCONFORMITY. The influence of the Dormer family of Ascot, which had strong Puritan affinities, and of the Doyleys at Chislehampton, a neighbouring parish, encouraged the growth of Protestant dissent. Throughout the 17th century the churchwardens presented many people for failure to attend church and for non-payment of rates. It is not generally made clear whether the offenders were Papist or Protestant,[1] but the presumption is that they were Protestant, except where there is evidence to the contrary as there is in the case of the Astrys. Among those who appeared in the peculiar court were members of the Dormer family. In 1619 Sir Michael Dormer was presented with three of his servants for non-attendance,[2] and in 1677 and 1685 William Dormer and John Dormer were successively presented for failing to pay church rates.[3] Hearne's view of John Dormer was that he was 'a heathenish irreligious man'.[4] Earlier in the century on leaving Oxford in 1637, John Owen, who later became a noted Independent divine, stayed a short time at Ascot as chaplain to Sir Robert Dormer,[5] and may well have been active in the surrounding villages. Delafield, the vicar (1724–6, 1737–49) and antiquary of Great Milton, reported a tradition that in the mid-17th century Quakers and Anabaptists and other 'field conventiclers' held meetings under a large elm tree between the two Miltons.[6]

A number of offenders against church discipline were presented by the churchwardens later in the century. In 1677 Paul Wildgoose of Little Milton, with three others, appeared in the peculiar court for not attending church and in 1679 Wildgoose was again presented. In 1677 three people were presented for not paying church rates. Richard Wiggin, one of them, was in trouble for the same reason in 1685, together with Thomas Anderson and Thomas Coles of Little Milton. In 1708 William Coles of Little Milton failed to pay the Easter offering and in 1714 fifteen people including two of the Wildgoose family were presented for not paying church rates.[7] In the same year John Brookes (a servant) was indicted at Quarter Sessions for nonconformity.[8] The presentments do not give the whole picture. It is known, for instance, that Maurice Griffith, the ejected Vicar of East Claydon (Bucks.), was living 'on his temporal estate at Milton' in 1665[9] and in 1673 he and his wife endowed a charity at Little Milton (see below), but he appears to have left the parish by the time of his death at Culham in 1676.[10] The original

[87] This entrance to the pulpit is now (1958) blocked up.
[88] Oxf. Dioc. c 1897, Petition for consecration; MS. Top. Oxon. d 93, f. 29.
[89] Oxf. Dioc. c 1898, Faculty.
[90] Inf. the Revd. W. F. Grace, Vicar.
[91] Oxf. Dioc. c 1897, Faculties.
[92] Parker, Guide; and see above, p. 141.
[93] Evans, Ch. Plate.
[94] Ch. Bells Oxon. 210–11.
[95] Oxon. Peculiars, 161. Humphrey Mullins was presented at the same time, and may possibly have been a papist.
[96] Salter, Oxon. Recusants, 51, 52, 54; E 179/164/482. For the family see Bodl. MS. Gough Oxon. 48, ff. 125b sqq.
[97] Oxon. Peculiars, 155.
[98] O.R.O. Cal. Q. Sess. ix. 779; Oxoniensia, xiii. 80;

O.R.O. Reg. of Papists' estates, p. 84. For the family see V.C.H. Oxon. v. 299, 308.
[99] MS. Top. Oxon. d 351, f. 36. No evidence has been found for the statement that the Simeons had a chapel in their Chilworth house, the 'Combe', which was burnt down in 1739: Stapleton, Cath. Miss. 267.
[1] Oxon. Peculiars, 155–61.
[2] Ibid. 154.
[3] Ibid. 156, 158.
[4] Hearne, Remarks, ix. 404.
[5] D.N.B. For Owen see above, p. 91.
[6] Bodl. MS. Gough Oxon. 48, f. 155.
[7] Oxon. Peculiars, 154–60. One of those presented was an Astry, and he may have been a Roman Catholic.
[8] O.R.O. Cal. Q. Sess. viii.
[9] Calamy Rev. 237.
[10] MS. Wills Oxon. 27/3/5.

returns for the Compton Census listed five dissenters.[11]

As the Miltons were a peculiar the visitation returns of the 18th century provide no information about the nonconformity which is likely to have continued there, but by the early 19th century there is evidence of its existence. In 1808 a minister was reported to have come from Thame to make converts,[12] and in the same year a house in Little Milton was registered for Protestant worship,[13] perhaps the house where in 1810 a Baptist minister occasionally preached.[14] In 1811 another house in Little Milton was registered[15] and in 1814 a few parishioners were attending a 'salvationist' preacher there after the church service.[16] In 1811 a house in Great Milton had also been registered.[17]

Later in the century Methodism flourished in both the Miltons. In 1831 the first chapel was built in Little Milton.[18] One of the leading Methodists was Thomas Perkins, a Little Milton grocer from London, and the chapel trustees included another grocer and a labourer of Little Milton, two Great Milton farmers, and tradesmen and labourers from other parishes, including Drayton, Chalgrove, and Watlington.[19] The chapel had a congregation of about 30 that was taught by a shoemaker and a visiting preacher.[20] In 1842 the present chapel was built in Great Milton.[21] According to the census of 1851 each chapel had a congregation of about 40 in the afternoon and 50 in the evening,[22] but there is some doubt about the accuracy of these figures. In 1854 the incumbents reported that there were 20 professed Wesleyans in Little Milton and the same number in Great Milton. They alleged that since many attended services at both chapels, they had been counted twice in the census; also many who were not dissenters occasionally attended the meeting-house in the evening, and on the day of the census special pains had been taken that there should be a full attendance.[23] There continued to be a fair number of Methodists in both places,[24] and in 1890 the present chapel was built in Little Milton[25] on a new site, and the old chapel was sold.[26] Both Great and Little Milton chapels still had trustees (largely tradesmen) from several nearby parishes, but the leading local Methodist was probably Charles Surman, a Great Milton farmer.[27] Both chapels are on the Thame and Watlington circuit.

SCHOOLS. The first notice of a village school occurs in 1641 when Richard Milles, gentleman, was presented in the archdeacon's court for keeping a school in the parish without a licence;[28] at the end of the century the vicar John Hinton kept a grammar school, and one of his pupils was Thomas Delafield, later Vicar of Great Milton.[29] As Milton was a peculiar there are no reports from the vicars in answer to visitation inquiries which might throw light on schooling in the 18th century. Nineteenth-century evidence shows that a Sunday school was started in 1800; that by 1805 there was a charity school for boys and girls, supported by Mrs. Ryder, the daughter of Sir John Skynner, and that there were a number of other small schools.[30] In 1808, besides the charity school, attended by 20 children, and the Sunday school with 88 children, there was a school with 10 children, supported by voluntary subscription. 'Great numbers', however, were said to have no means of education.[31] In 1815 there were five small schools for 80 children, run partly on the National plan, but their pupils left at 7 or 8 years of age to engage in husbandry or lacemaking.[32] In 1818 there were 70 children in three day schools and it was said that many attended other schools in neighbouring parishes.[33] The Milton schools were all short lived: two new day schools were opened after 1818 where 21 children were educated at their parents' expense and in 1835 there were said to be six infant schools in the village besides the day and Sunday school under the vicar's control.[34] There was no adequate accommodation for the church day school: it was held in an Elizabethan house, once the home of the Petty family, which was rented for £15 a year. The vicar, Mr. Ashhurst, considered this an excessive sum and exerted all his energies to obtain a new school.[35] The National Society helped with funds and in 1854 the National Mixed School was opened with accommodation for 150 children.[36] It was enlarged in 1860.[37] The school accounts of 1868 show that it was largely supported by private subscriptions and a government grant although Kent's charity supplied some £21 and rent from the recreation ground another £8 10s.; the greater part of the income went on the stipend of the master, the mistress, and assistant who together were paid some £123. Children paid 2d. a week every Monday morning, and those who were unpunctual or irregular in attendance were not admitted.[38] The average attendance was 80 in 1871, 93 in 1889, and 71 in 1903.[39] In 1930 the school was reorganized as a junior school for children up to eleven years; the seniors walked to Great Haseley at first, but were later transferred to Wheatley where they attended in 1956. The Great Milton school, which became controlled in 1952, had 55 pupils in 1943 and 71 in 1954.[40]

By 1818 there was a separate day school at Little

[11] Queen's Coll. MS. 501.
[12] Oxf. Dioc. d 571.   [13] Ibid. c 644, f. 99.
[14] Ibid. c 441, f. 23.   [15] Ibid. c 644, f. 124.
[16] Ibid. b 39.   [17] Ibid. c 644, f. 123.
[18] Ibid. c 645, f. 189; Char. Com. file 32884. It no longer exists. It was opposite the church and is marked on the 25″ O.S. map, xl. 15 (1880).
[19] Thame Methodist Church, Conveyance.
[20] Oxf. Dioc. b 39.
[21] Dated stone; Char. Com. file 42410. Registered in 1845: Oxf. Dioc. c 647, f. 26.
[22] H.O. 129/5/156.
[23] Wilb. Visit.
[24] Oxf. Dioc. d 179, c 332, c 344.
[25] Dated stone.
[26] Thame Methodist Church, Note on 1831 conveyance; 1890 conveyance.
[27] Ibid. 1890 conveyance; 1885 list of trustees.
[28] Oxon. Peculiars, 154.

[29] Bodl. MS. Gough Oxon. 48, f. 278.
[30] Oxf. Dioc. c 433; c 327, p. 246; d 571; the charity school is said to have been held in Wells Farm: inf. the late Revd. R. A. Ker. For the Skynners see above, pp. 120, 143.
[31] Oxon. Dioc. d 707.
[32] Ibid. c 433.
[33] Educ. of Poor, 727.
[34] Educ. Enq. Abstract, 750; Oxf. Dioc. b 39.
[35] Par. Rec. Correspondence.
[36] Par. Rec.; Oxf. Dioc. b 70. The Committee of the Council for Education is said to have raised difficulties and the school was built without a government grant: Par. Rec. For the building see above, p. 118.
[37] Oxf. Dioc. b 70.
[38] Par. Rec. Sch. accts.
[39] Elem. Educ. Ret. 320; Ret. of Sch. 214; Vol. Sch. Ret. 21.
[40] Inf. Oxon. Educ. Cttee.

Milton attended by 14 children and a Sunday school with 70 children.[41] The day school seems to have closed within a few years, but a second Sunday school with 60 children was started in 1827 by the Wesleyan Methodists.[42] By 1854 three day schools had also been set up: one parochial school with 48 pupils, supported partly by subscription, partly by payments from parents, and two other day schools. Each had 12 scholars who were paid for by their parents.[43] One of the schools was for infants only. The chief hindrance to educational progress was the early age at which children left school. The vicar described this as 'an evil increasing yearly'.[44] An evening class, held in winter, for 20 young men was said to be quite successful.[45] The present school was set up in 1861 with the help of the National Society and replaced the other day schools.[46] It had an average of 62 children in 1889 and was enlarged to hold 90 in 1893 but there were only 50 children attending in 1903.[47] The older children were transferred to Great Haseley in 1931 and Little Milton school became a junior school for children up to eleven years. There were 14 children in 1943 and 27 in 1954.[48]

CHARITIES. William Young (d. 1694), a member of a prominent local family, settled in trust £100, the interest on which was to be laid out in clothing. Sir John Doyley of Chislehampton (d. 1746) became, as a trustee, possessed of the capital, and in the wreck of the fortunes of his family the money appears to have been lost. The charity moneys, at all events, were not payable c. 1820 or subsequently.[49]

John Jony Kent, a Great Milton doctor who died in 1814, left by his will £1,575 stock, the interest of which was to be used for the poor of the parish, a portion of the dividends being retained for the purchase of further stock to be applied to the same charitable purpose. Owing to various legal delays the charity was first distributed in 1819; greatcoats and cloaks for the men and women were provided, and other clothing for the children, and sums of money were given in addition. The Charity Commissioners, when they reported c. 1820, thought that the application of part of the income of the charity to the purchase of further stock for a longer period than 21 years from the testator's death would be irregular.[50] Whatever course the trustees may have taken in consequence of that opinion, the value of the stock had risen to £2,136 by 1891 and so remained in 1931.[51] By 1864 it was the practice to pay out of the income an annual contribution of £21 to the village school and other contributions to the village coal and clothing clubs, and also to use the income in direct purchases of clothing.[52] In 1903 and 1904 the money was distributed in clothing vouchers of varying value to every parishioner, apart from skilled artisans and those 'in higher positions'. Later it appears to have

been spent in gifts of coal to those who did not subscribe to the coal club. After that club 'died out' in 1923 it became the rule to use the money to distribute coal to each family, not being 'property owners', at Christmas.[53] In 1956–7 the distribution mainly took the form of weekly grocery vouchers for the elderly and indigent.[54] The income was reduced from £64 to £59 in 1890 and further reduced to £53 in 1904; it remained at that figure in 1956–7. In 1931 and in 1956–7 a balance was left in reserve after distribution.[55]

Charles Robey Couling, of Romeyns Court, by will proved 1912, left £300 free of legacy duty to form 'Couling's charity'. The proceeds, after investment, were to be applied to the purchase of coal or other fuel to be distributed among the most deserving poor parishioners of Great Milton.[56] The income, £10, was being applied in 1931 and in 1954–6 in the purchase of coal, distributed in 1956 to 33 persons.[57]

Mrs. Kate Elizabeth Couling, of Romeyns Court, by will proved 1925, left £100 free of legacy duty, the proceeds, after investment, to be applied to the upkeep of her own and her late husband's tombs in Great Milton churchyard, 'as an example of tidiness and attractiveness in the churchyard'. The residuary legatees agreed that the legacy should be applied to the general upkeep of the churchyard, special attention being given to the two graves. The money was invested in £98 stock to which in 1931 £20 was added upon the vicar's instructions.[58] The annual income appears to have amounted to c. £5 between 1928 and 1931 and to c. £4 in 1953–5. It was paid in the former period to the treasurer of the churchyard fund and in the latter to the churchwardens.[59]

By deed of 1673 the Revd. Maurice Griffith and his wife Elizabeth gave £10 for the benefit of the poor of Little Milton, 1s. 6d. being given annually to each of the four poorest families and 1s. to each of the six next poorest. By 1786 the sum of £10 with the savings therefrom or from other money given for the poor of Little Milton had accumulated to £24. In 1821 the amount of the dividends, £1 5s., was laid out in bread and distributed to about 20 poor families of Little Milton.[60] Between 1929 and 1931 the income amounted to 13s. yearly and then and subsequently seems to have been distributed with the Grayson charity (see below).[61]

Catherine Grayson, widow, of St. Giles' parish, Oxford, by will dated 1853, left £400 stock in trust to be laid out in fuel and clothing to be distributed on or within ten days of Christmas between six poor men and six poor women of good character selected by the incumbent of Little Milton, preferably those aged 60 or above. The legacy was invested in 1861 in £360 stock.[62] Between 1954 and 1956 the income was £9, and was distributed, with the Griffith charity, in coal and clothing to the six oldest men and six oldest women of the parish of Little Milton.[63]

[41] Educ. of Poor, 727.
[42] Educ. Enq. Abstract, 750.
[43] Wilb. Visit.
[44] Ibid.
[45] Ibid.
[46] Vol. Sch. Ret. 23.
[47] Ret. of Sch. 215; Kelly, Dir. Oxon. (1903); Vol. Sch. Ret. 23; cf. Sch. Bldg. Grants, 106.
[48] Inf. Oxon. Educ. Cttee.
[49] 8th Rep. Com. Char. 547; Bodl. MS. Gough Oxon 48, ff. 110b–111.
[50] 8th Rep. Com. Char. 545–6.
[51] Char. Com. file 23902; Accts. file.

[52] Par. Rec. accts.
[53] Char. Com. file 19532.
[54] Inf. the Revd. E. P. Baker, Vicar of Great Milton.
[55] Char. Com. file 23902; Accts. file; inf. the Revd. E. P. Baker.
[56] Ibid. file 90325.
[57] Ibid. Accts. file.
[58] Ibid. file 106278.
[59] Ibid. Accts. file.
[60] 8th Rep. Com. Char.; Char. Don. ii. 990–1.
[61] Char. Com. Accts. file.
[62] Ibid. Unrep. Vol. 26, f. 407; Little Milton G. file.
[63] Ibid. Accts. file; inf. the Revd. E. P. Baker.

TETSWORTH

TETSWORTH was one of the ancient chapelries of Thame and did not become an independent ecclesiastical parish until 1841. It was administratively separate from Thame from an early date, however, and covered 1,179 acres in 1932, when the civil parish was enlarged to 2,618 acres by the addition of Attington and part of Thame to the west.[1] The ancient boundaries followed Haseley Brook in the south, and the old boundary on the east used to run from the Wheatfield road to Horsenden Hill, some way to the west of the modern boundary. On the north and east, where Tetsworth touched Attington and Thame, the boundary line made numerous right-angled turns indicating that it was drawn after the layout of arable strips.[2]

The ancient chapelry lay in the Clay belt,[3] mainly between the 200 and 300 ft. contours: it rose in the centre to over 300 ft. and also at Horsenden Hill at the north-east corner. Tetsworth common lay to the north-west of the village.[4]

The main Oxford–High Wycombe–London road runs diagonally across the parish; it became a turnpike in 1718.[5] The records reveal the importance of the high road in the life of Tetsworth from early times. The village is marked on a mid-14th-century road map of England[6] and in 1447 a licence was granted to found a hermitage at Tetsworth and a chapel of St. John the Baptist for the purpose of repairing the road. The hermit was to labour with his hands for the maintenance of the highways between Stokenchurch and Wheatley Bridge, which had long been a trouble for lack of repair.[7] At the Reformation the hermit disappeared but he was remembered as late as the 19th century by a field called the Hermitage beside the Thame road.[8]

In the wills of medieval inhabitants of Tetsworth and the neighbourhood bequests were constantly made for the upkeep of the highways,[9] and post-medieval documents contain many references to travellers on the Tetsworth road. As the village was 12 miles from Oxford it became a stage on the route from London to Oxford for the postchaises and carriers, and it was there that letters from the capital for the great houses such as Rycote were left.[10]

Plot noted in 1677 that the ways were mended with the local stone called 'maume'. It was so free of sulphur that it slaked in winter like lime and Plot thought the local farmers should much rather 'mend their lands than highways' with it. He left a specimen with the son of the 'ingenious improver, Sir Thomas Tipping', as a 'thing not unworthy of his father's trial'.[11]

That the roads might be dangerous appears from occasional records. A 16th-century Star Chamber case records that an Oxford carrier, taking goods and

passengers to London, was attacked at Tetsworth by four armed men. They wounded the eight occupants of his conveyance and opened valuable chests.[12] In 1681 Viscount Latimer wrote that he had arrived safely at Oxford without encountering highwaymen, having paid a visit to Rycote whilst his coach 'baited' at Tetsworth.[13] Another case is recorded in 1762 of a highwayman robbing one of the Oxford coaches near Tetsworth.[14]

The heyday of the road was after the making of the turnpike in 1718 until the coming of the railways in the 1840's,[15] when road traffic dwindled and one of the principal hostelries, the 'Swan', was partly converted into a post-office and the 'Royal Oak' was pulled down.[16] Hearne records how the Mayor of Oxford and others dined at Tetsworth in 1725 and that Dr. Edmund Hailey of Greenwich, the Savilian Professor of Geometry, designed to lie there on his return journey after a visit to Oxford in 1727.[17] In 1835 Pigot's *Commercial Directory* records that three London coaches went daily via Tetsworth and Wheatley to Oxford. There were two vans and wagons a week from London going by the same route, besides much local traffic.[18]

The chief coaching inn was the 'Swan'. In the 17th century when it was the property of the Sedley family and of Sir Charles Sedley, the dramatist, its name was changed to the 'Sedley Arms'.[19] By 1719 the inn had reverted to its original name.[20]

The present building is of many dates, but the late 17th-century and 18th-century façade of chequer brick conceals a much older and rather smaller building. The original house, probably built c. 1600, consisted of a timber-framed L-shaped building of two stories and attics, with three fine brick chimney-stacks at the back. The range parallel with the road probably contained the hall, with a screens passage and kitchen or buttery to the east and a staircase and parlour to the west. On the first floor is a post which shows that the walls were formerly covered with wall-paintings. About 1700 the whole building was extensively remodelled and enlarged; an eastern projecting wing was added, the existing ranges were encased in brick, a row of rooms was added at the back, and along the eastern side of the western range was added a two-story gallery. The building now consists of a main block of two stories and attics, and of flanking wings projecting towards the road. It has a first-floor string and the cornice of moulded wood and plaster is deeply coved. The roof is hipped and tiled. The south elevation of the centre block has three hipped dormer windows. There are eight bays with mullioned and transomed windows of which the upper ones are original, but the ground floor ones were, until recently, sash windows. The building has

---

[1] *V.C.H. Oxon.* ii. 222; *Census, 1931.*
[2] O.S. Map 6", xli (1885).
[3] *V.C.H. Oxon.* i, map between pp. 4–5.
[4] O.S. Map 6", xli (1885).
[5] An Act for repairing the roads from Beaconsfield . . . to Stokenchurch Hill, 5 Geo. I, c. 1 (priv. act).
[6] *The Map of Great Britain c. A.D. 1360 known as The Gough Map* (O.U.P. 1958).
[7] *Cal. Pat.* 1446–52, 180–1.   [8] Lee, *Thame*, 214.
[9] e.g. in 1529, 1545: Bodl. MS. Top. Oxon. c 47, p. 256.
[10] *Cal. S.P. Dom.* 1598–1601, 437; John Ogilby, *Britannia* (1675).

[11] Plot, *Nat. Hist. Oxon.* (1705), 70.
[12] Sta. Cha. 8/61/1.
[13] Hist. MSS. Com. *14th Rep. App. IX,* 423.
[14] Brown and Guest, *Thame,* 169.
[15] E. T. MacDermot, *Hist. G.W.R.* ii. 595.
[16] H.O. 107/1726/2; Kelly, *Dir. Oxon.* (1854, 1869).
[17] Hearne, *Remarks,* ix. 3, 301.
[18] Pigot, *Nat. Dir.* (1835).
[19] An Act for vesting . . . the estate of Henry Perrot, 3 Geo. II, c. 15 (priv. act). It was then attached to Windbush manor.
[20] O.R.O. Li XIII/i/1.

many contemporary details such as its six-panelled door in the centre block with a rectangular fanlight, divided into four pointed arches, and its diamond-shaped chimney stacks. There is much 16th- and 17th-century panelling inside.

Despite the importance of the London road, the village as a whole does not border it. It is a hill village, lying largely on two lanes that branch off to the south-west of the main road and climb the steep hill to the church at the summit. Davis's map of 1797 shows the 'Swan' and the Pettys' manor-house[21] as the only buildings on the north-east side of the London road, and even by 1839 this was still the case.[22] Fields and the green common (7 a.) lay next to the 'Swan'. Tetsworth was a fair-sized village in the 17th century with at least 43 householders[23] and some timber-framed cottages of this period, many of them thatched, still survive. 'Robertlyn', for example, has one story and an attic, is timber-framed with brick and rubble fillings; and the roof is half-hipped and thatched. Other cottages of the same period are built partly of flint and partly of brick. The farmhouse opposite to the 'Red Lion' is a rubble-stone house of 17th-century date with brick additions. The village has still some 18th-century houses such as the house opposite the 'Swan', which has a characteristic panelled door and a wreathed and enriched fan-light. The present 'King's Arms' is also an 18th-century building, built on a terrace above the level of the road. Rebuilding was sometimes the result of fire as in 1736.[24] Nineteenth-century additions to the village included the church and the Vicarage, built in 1846,[25] the red-brick and Gothic school with a bell-turret, and the Congregational chapel of red brick with stone facings (1890).[26] In the 20th century a council housing-estate of 32 dwellings was built at Marsh End after the Second World War,[27] and in 1952 a village hall was erected.[28]

At one time the most important house in Tetsworth was the manor-house, standing on the site of Mount Hill Farm.[29] It was built early in the 16th century by Maximilian Petty. It is said by Wood that he pulled down the wool storage rooms attached to the 15th-century house in Thame, which he had bought from Geoffrey Dormer and where he had lived for some time. He used the materials to build his Tetsworth house.[30] Here the Pettys lived for several generations. John Petty, grandson of Maximilian, of Tetsworth and Stoke Talmage was granted arms in 1570, and some at least of his ten children were born at Tetsworth.[31] His son Charnell, 'an old puritan', lived at Tetsworth from 1614 to 1634,[32] and in his will, proved 1661, willed that his wife Ellen should enjoy the mansion house.[33] At this time it was a fair-sized house rated at 13 hearths for the tax of 1665.[34] Plot shows it with four chimneys on his map

of 1677 as he does other houses of the gentry such as Dormer's at Ascot, and Doyley's at Chislehampton.[35] Christopher Petty sold the house in 1683 to his kinsman Christopher Wood, a relation of the antiquary Anthony Wood.[36] Later in the century it was divided into a baker's house and three others.[37] The present house, Mount Hill farmhouse, stands on the crown of the hill with its gable-end facing the highway and its north front facing a lane, from which it is approached by a flight of twelve steps. The gable-end has three stories and an attic; the north front has two stories and an attic. A covering of stucco mostly conceals the brick and stone of the old house, and a 19th-century porch and sash windows have been added.

Because of the early inclosure of Tetsworth field some of the parish's farmhouses, Latchford House, Goldpits, and Spencer's, for example, were not in the village.[38] The only one that still has any historical interest is Harlesford farmhouse and its outbuildings. The 18th-century house is built of vitreous brick with red dressings; and the outbuildings are partly brick, partly weather-boarding, and the roofs are covered with old tiles.

Tetsworth's position on the London road and in one of the main battle areas of the Civil War meant that troops were frequently passing through. In 1643 Hampden visited Major Gunter's cavalry which were quartered in and about Tetsworth;[39] Prince Rupert went through on his way to Chalgrove Field, and parliamentary scouts often picked up news there, particularly from travellers from London or Oxford. It was reported in October 1643, for example, that some of the king's foot and horsemen were quartered in the village;[40] in January 1644 that the king and queen themselves were there, and that the French ambassador had also passed the night there, his coach having broken down.[41]

Of its inhabitants the Petty family achieved a local position of some importance and one George Pettie (1548–89) made his mark on literature as a minor writer of romances.[42] Among churchmen Eliezer Williams (1754–1820), historian and genealogist, had a brief association with Tetsworth as curate,[43] and J. W. Peers (vicar 1841–76) was responsible for building the church, Vicarage, and school.[44]

FEES. *TETSWORTH* does not appear by name in the Domesday survey, but its lands were included in the Bishop of Lincoln's Thame manor of 60 hides. It is probable that it was represented mainly by the 10 hides held by a certain Robert, one of the bishop's knights,[45] and that he is to be identified with the Robert who held of the bishop in Banbury, Cropredy, and Wickham.[46] He may very possibly have been the father of Aucher Chevauchesul, who flourished at

---

[21] Davis, *Oxon. Map* (1797). For house see below.
[22] Davis, *Oxon. Map*; Bodl. Tithe award map.
[23] E 179/255/4 (1662).
[24] Britwell Salome Par. Rec. Brief.
[25] See below, p. 157.   [26] See below, p. 159.
[27] Inf. Bullingdon R.D.C.
[28] The land on which it was built was settled in trust in 1952: Char. Com. Tetsworth G file.
[29] The identification of the sites of the two houses is made from a comparison of the field-names of land abutting on the manor, garden and orchard in 17th-century documents with the names on the tithe map.
[30] Wood, *Life*, i. 409; Rousham Arch. (un-cat.)
[31] Par. Rec. Reg.; Wood, *Athenae*, i. 552–3; and see below, p. 150.

[32] Wood, *Life*, i. 32, 36, 37.
[33] P.C.C. 20 Bruce.   [34] E 179/164/504.
[35] Plot, *Nat. Hist. Oxon.* frontispiece.
[36] Wood, *Life*, i. 30–31.
[37] O.R.O. Li XIII/viii/a/1.
[38] See below, p. 153; O.S. *Area Bk.*
[39] Geo. Nugent Grenville, *Some Memorials of John Hampden* (1832), 429.
[40] Luke, *Jnl.* 159.   [41] Ibid. 237, 240.
[42] *D.N.B.*   [43] *D.N.B.*
[44] See below, pp. 157, 159.
[45] *V.C.H. Oxon.* i. 402, 403.
[46] Ibid. 403. His Banbury lands were probably at Epwell, for later evidence shows that Epwell and Tetsworth were held as 2 fees: *Thame Cart.* ii. 198–9.

Tetsworth in the first half of the 12th century,[47] and the grandfather of Robert Chevauchesul. This last was in possession of Tetsworth by *c.* 1146,[48] and Tetsworth must have been included in the 3 fees he was holding of the Bishop of Lincoln in 1166.[49] The date of his death is uncertain, but he appears to have been alive in 1201.[50] At that date he was holding only 1 out of his 3 Oxfordshire fees; the other 2 fees had been for some time in the possession of his two sisters Emma and Maud.[51] Maud had married Peter Talemasch,[52] possibly the son of Hugh Talemasch of Stoke Talmage,[53] and himself lord of Stoke.[54] Peter, however, had died by 1181,[55] and Maud must have died before 1198, for it was their son Richard who was then in possession of half the Tetsworth fee.[56] In this year (1198–9) he and Robert Danvers, the heir to a moiety of the Tetsworth and Epwell fees, were engaged in an assize of mort d'ancestor over two of their Oxfordshire fees, a suit which may have had some connexion with Peter's debts to the Jews recorded in the same year.[57] Richard married Avice Taillard, a sister of Richard Taillard who frequently witnesses charters with him,[58] and appears to have died in or before 1205, when his son and heir Peter is found in possession of a ½-fee at Finstock in Charlbury, a part of his father's property.[59] In 1209–12 Peter Talemasch and Robert Danvers were returned as joint lords of Tetsworth; Talemasch was said to hold a ¾-fee.[60] When a survey of the bishop's Thame manors was made *c.* 1225 Peter Talemasch was still holding.[61] Robert Danvers's share had descended to him from William Danvers of Bourton and Chislehampton, who had acquired it by his marriage with Emma Chevauchesul.[62] William Danvers was one of Henry II's knights, and it has been plausibly suggested that he may have supported the king against Becket, since he was omitted from Thame Abbey's prayers for his family.[63] Robert the son of William and Emma had succeeded by *c.* 1197, and his younger brother Ralph was then holding part of Tetsworth of him.[64] Robert was a man of some standing: he acted as king's assessor in Oxfordshire in 1200.[65] He was still holding the Tetsworth fee in 1209–12,[66] but on the marriage of his eldest son Geoffrey before 1222 he gave 1½ fee, including his Tetsworth fee, as dowry

for Geoffrey's wife Sara.[67] Both Geoffrey and his father were dead by the time of the Lincoln survey (*c.* 1225), when William Danvers, Geoffrey's brother and heir, was recorded as holder of the Tetsworth fee.[68] From a final concord made in May 1225 it appears that Geoffrey died before 1225, for by then Sara had already taken a second husband.[69]

William Danvers seems to have died before 1247.[70] He was followed by his eldest son Robert, who in 1279 held the Tetsworth and Epwell fees including the land once held by the Talemasches.[71] In 1305 it was specifically stated that Robert Danvers was heir to Peter Talemasch's fee.[72] A 14th-century record shows that Robert's son Simon held both the Danvers and Talemasch fees and that each contained property in both Tetsworth and Epwell.[73] Simon had subinfeudated his Tetsworth land which was mainly held by Thame Abbey.[74] In 1316 Simon Danvers and the Abbot of Thame were returned as joint lords of Tetsworth and in that year Simon was summoned for military service as one of the lords of Tetsworth, Epwell and Swalcliffe, Drayton, Stadhampton, and other lands.[75] Simon lived until at least 1327[76] but before his death he disposed of some of his Tetsworth property. In 1321 he gave some 4½ virgates and a ⅔-fee there to Geoffrey de Stokes and his wife Alice, who may have been Simon's daughter, with remainder to their son Geoffrey.[77] In 1336 John de Wheatfield acquired the ⅔-fee from a Geoffrey de Waterbeck,[78] perhaps the same man as Geoffrey de Stokes. He died about 1345[79] and in the following year his son John was returned as holding a ⅓-fee in Tetsworth. His assessment on only a ⅓-fee, John son of Simon Danvers and the Prebendary of Thame each holding another third, may represent some internal arrangement concerning the fee.[80] John de Wheatfield had died by 1361 and his heirs were Joan and Elizabeth.[81] They succeeded to the Tetsworth land, but in 1367 a Nicholas Tetsworth obtained half the property from Reginald de Grey and his wife Elizabeth and in 1374 he obtained the other half from Hugh Streatley and his wife Joan.[82] The descent of the property is not clear after this. In 1428 Walter Cotton, at that time lord of a Bletchingdon manor and of Exning (Suff.), held the Wheat-

[47] *Thame Cart.* ii. 111.
[48] Ibid. 104, 143.
[49] *Red Bk. Exch.* (Rolls Ser.), 375; cf. *Eynsham Cart.* i. 141–3. For Robert see also *Pipe R.* 1163 (P.R.S. vi), 48.
[50] *Rot. de Ob. et Fin.* (Rec. Com.), i. 155.
[51] For the relationship see *Thame Cart.* ii. 105, 111. There was also a younger brother Roger: ibid. i. 96; ii. 106.
[52] Ibid. i. 96.
[53] For Hugh (fl. 1121–50), who became a monk of Gloucester, see *Cal. Doc. France*, ed. Round, 262; *Pipe R.* 1130 (H.M.S.O. facsimile) 3; *Historia et Cartularium Monasterii Gloucestriae* (Rolls Ser.), i. 331–2; *Regesta*, ii. p. 352.
[54] *Thame Cart.* i. 96, 101.
[55] Ibid. ii. 106. Cf. Macnamara, *Danvers Family*, 18 n.
[56] *Thame Cart.* ii. 106; cf. *Bk. of Fees*, 40; *Pipe R.* 1199 (P.R.S. N.S. x), 225.
[57] *Pipe R.* 1199 (P.R.S. N.S. x), 224, 225.
[58] *Thame Cart.* ii. 111. For Richard Taillard see ibid. 173; *Eynsham Cart.* i. 145–6.
[59] *Eynsham Cart.* i. 134. In 1208 Peter granted Tetsworth land to Thame: *Thame Cart.* ii. 113–14; in 1210 Peter was involved in a suit over Tetsworth land: *Cur. Reg. R.* vi. 98. He also inherited half Robert Chevauchesul's holding in Fawler: *Eynsham Cart.* i. 144–5.
[60] *Bk. of Fees*, 40.
[61] Queen's Coll. MS. 366, f. 23; for the date see above, p. 13, n. 94.
[62] For Emma and her children see *Thame Cart.* ii. 110–

[] 11. See also Macnamara, *Danvers Family*, pedigree facing p. 27.
[63] Macnamara, *Danvers Family*, 20–21.
[64] *Thame Cart.* ii. 107, 109. Roger, clk., and William were other brothers: ibid. 106, 110.
[65] Macnamara, *Danvers Family*, 20; *Rot. Cur. Reg.* (Rec. Com.), ii. 132.
[66] *Bk. of Fees*, 40.
[67] *Eynsham Cart.* i. 143–4; Macnamara mistakenly says 1½ fee in Tetsworth: *Danvers Family*, 50.
[68] Queen's Coll. MS. 366, f. 25; *Fines Oxon.* 73; *Eynsham Cart.* i. 144.
[69] *Fines Oxon.* 73.
[70] Ibid. 146.
[71] *Rot. Hund.* (Rec. Com.), ii. 820.
[72] Queen's Coll. MS. 366, f. 34b. Tetsworth was held with Epwell for 2 fees, hence the statement that Tetsworth was held as 2 fees in 1305.
[73] *Thame Cart.* ii. 198–201.
[74] Ibid.
[75] *Feud. Aids*, iv. 167; *Parl. Writs*, ii (3), 752.
[76] Macnamara, *Danvers Family*, 67.
[77] *Thame Cart.* ii. 171; Macnamara, *Danvers Family*, 67.
[78] C.P. 25 (1)/19/18/4.
[79] Ibid.
[80] *Feud. Aids*, iv. 181.
[81] *Blk. Prince's Reg.* iv. 446, 464; cf. *Records of Bucks.* xiii. 396–7.
[82] C.P. 25 (1)/190/22/65 and 76.

field and Danvers property in Tetsworth, but no later reference to the Cotton tenure has been found.[83] It is probable that the land was entirely held by sub-tenants and became merged in other manors. The prebendary's ⅓-fee likewise has not been traced beyond 1428, but it appears to have followed the descent of Thame prebend.[84]

MANORS. From the time of its removal from Oddington to Thame[85] the Cistercian Abbey of Thame began to acquire land in Tetsworth through the gifts of the pious, and particularly from the families of the various holders of fees—Chevauchesul, Talemasch, and Danvers. Its property was later known as TETSWORTH manor. The abbey obtained a hide from Robert Chevauchesul before 1146;[86] in 1197 Ralph Danvers, with the consent of his lord and brother Robert Danvers, gave 2¼ virgates;[87] and in 1199 Alan, clerk of Tetsworth, and his wife Clarissa gave 2 virgates.[88] About the same time Robert Danvers, his brothers William and Roger, and their cousin Richard Talemasch each gave a virgate.[89] Their mother Emma Danvers had already given 2 acres.[90] The charters record in all the gift of 15½ virgates,[91] but from a survey made in about 1225 it appears that Thame Abbey held 8¼ virgates of the Danvers fee and 8¾ of the Talemasch fee, besides 3 virgates at farm and 12¼ acres in small parcels.[92] Its total holding was thus over 20 virgates. In 1279 the jurors declared that the abbot's holding was 9½ virgates held of Robert Danvers's fee by scutage and suit of his court, and 8½ virgates held of Peter Talemasch's fee by scutage.[93] Talemasch was by now dead, having given the abbey his Stoke Talmage manor as well as part of his Tetsworth fee.[94] In 1316 the abbot was therefore returned as joint lord of Tetsworth with Simon Danvers[95] and he held his share as 1 knight's fee.[96] The estate, usually known as the Grange, is first designated a manor in 1365, when the abbot was granted free warren there,[97] and was retained by the abbey until its dissolution in 1539.[98]

In 1542 Thame Abbey's manor along with Stoke Talmage was granted by the Crown to Robert King, the last Abbot of Thame and the first Bishop of Oxford.[99] He proceeded to lease it in 1547 for 99 years at £20 2s. 10d. to Sir John (later Lord) Williams of Thame.[1] The manor was afterwards lost to the bishopric, and the lease to Lord Williams was terminated. In 1558 and 1560 Tetsworth manor was listed among the large sales of land to a number of London citizens,[2] but it was in the hands of the Crown again in 1589, when it was granted in fee simple for £44 5s. to Christopher Petty and his son Charnell, members of an old Tetsworth family.[3] Christopher Petty was already in possession of an estate in Tetsworth, which had been left to him by his father John Petty. This John Petty had been granted arms in 1570; had built up a large Oxfordshire estate;[4] and on his death in 1578 had divided his Tetsworth lands between two younger sons, George and Christopher.[5] In 1589 George Petty died, leaving his share to Christopher.[6]

In 1602 the Pettys were given permission to sell Tetsworth manor to Walter Jones of Chastleton,[7] whose daughter Ellen married Ralph Holt of Stoke Lyne. Since Thomas Holt, the son of Ralph and Ellen, later married Charnell Petty's daughter Susan,[8] it is probable that the manor was returned to the Pettys in some kind of family settlement. Christopher Petty died in 1614, and his son Charnell succeeded.[9] On the latter's death in 1661 he left Tetsworth in trust for his young grandson Christopher, the boy's father Christopher being already dead.[10] Christopher Petty obtained possession in 1674;[11] he married Hester, the daughter of Robert Parsons, a gentleman of Great Milton; but he was a man of 'unthriftiness, folly, and extravagance',[12] and had soon dissipated his estate. In 1680 and 1683 he sold a part of his land to Anthony Wood's brother Christopher, and in 1683 he sold the manor and other land, said to be worth £2,000, to Thomas Phillips, a lawyer of Ickford (Bucks.).[13] Petty's absorbing interest was bell-ringing, and Hearne says that he 'rang away . . . a good estate' and died 'very reduced' at Thame, probably in 1739.[14]

Thomas Phillips died in 1705, having left most of his property to his son-in-law Lenthall Trotman of Bucknell, because his son Thomas had become a Roman Catholic; the property was to revert to the Phillips family in the event of the heir becoming a member of the Church of England.[15] Trotman died in 1710,[16] and in 1717 his two sons Samuel and Thomas were returned as owners of Tetsworth manor.[17] However, by 1733 Thomas Phillips appears to have recovered possession, for in that year he augmented with Tetsworth land the endowment of a charity in Ickford, founded by his father.[18] Thomas Phillips the younger died in 1742 leaving two sons,[19] both Roman Catholics, and the younger one Henry Phillips sold Tetsworth manor with land in Ickford to the Earl of Abingdon in 1756. It then consisted of

[83] Feud. Aids, iv. 191, 197; cf. i. 67, 178; for Cotton, see W. A. Copinger, Manors of Suffolk, iv. 158.
[84] See below, p. 171.
[85] V.C.H. Oxon. ii. 82.
[86] Thame Cart. ii. 104; confirmed by Robert de Chesney, Bishop of Lincoln (1151–66): ibid. 104–5.
[87] Ibid. 108.   [88] Ibid. 106.
[89] Ibid. 107, 110, 111.
[90] Ibid. 111.
[91] Ibid. passim.
[92] Thame Cart. ii. 173–4, dated c. 1225 by writing.
[93] Rot. Hund. (Rec. Com.), ii. 820.
[94] Thame Cart. i. 96, 97.
[95] Feud. Aids, iv. 167.
[96] Ibid. 197.
[97] Cal. Chart. R. 1341–1417, 192.
[98] Valor Eccl. (Rec. Com.), ii. 213.
[99] L. & P. Hen. VIII, xvii, p. 489.
[1] C 66/1344, m. 18.
[2] Cal. Pat. 1557–8, 408–9; 1558–60, 435. The second was surrendered in 1562: ibid. 1558–60, 437.

[3] C 66/1344, m. 18. For pedigree see Wood, Life, i. 32–36.
[4] Wood, Athenae, i. 552–3.
[5] P.C.C. 43 Langley. For George Petty see D.N.B.
[6] Wood, Athenae, i. 552–3.
[7] Dunkin MS. 438/1, f. 243; C.P. 25(2)/198/East. 44 Eliz.   [8] V.C.H. Oxon. vi. 316.
[9] Lee, Thame, 221; Dunkin MS. 438/2, f. 176.
[10] P.C.C. 20 Bruce.
[11] C.P. 25(2)/709/Trin. 26 Chas. II.
[12] Hearne, Remarks, ix. 388; Bodl. MS. Gough Oxon. 48, ff. 132–132b.   [13] Wood, Life, i. 36.
[14] Bodl. MS. Gough Oxon. 48, ff. 132–132b; Hearne, Remarks, ix. 388; Lee, Thame, 669.
[15] Lipscomb, Bucks. i. 286; for Phillips pedigree see Lee, Thame, 603–6.
[16] For him see V.C.H. Oxon. vi. 74.
[17] O.R.O. Reg. of Papists' estates, pp. 12–13.
[18] V.C.H. Bucks. iv. 61; 27th Rep. Com. Char. H.C. 225, pp. 26–28 (1834), xxi.
[19] C.R.S. vii. 396 (Waterperry R.C. reg.).

only about 100 acres of land and a few quit-rents.[20] The manor formed part of the Abingdon estates until about 1810 and brought in an income of £120 odd.[21] It was apparently sold to the Revd. Samuel Ryder Weston, a canon of St. Paul's,[22] who was in possession of the manor-house and land in Tetsworth in 1810.[23] He died in 1821: his heirs were Charlotte Weston, who was lady of the manor in the 1850's, and Frances (neé Weston), the wife of A. H. Matthews (d. 1854), Vicar of Weston-on-the-Green, who owned Manor farm (116 acres).[24] In 1859 the property was in the hands of A. M. Matthews, the Revd. A. Matthews and the Revd. H. S. Ryder Matthews, nephews of Charlotte Weston.[25] In about 1866 the manor and Manor farm were bought by Joseph Cornish, a Tetsworth farmer, from the Matthews family.[26]

During the reign of Edward III a John Windbush built up an estate in Tetsworth of some 9 messuages and about 150 acres with appurtenances.[27] In 1471, when this estate was acquired from a Richard Seymour and his wife Isabel by Richard Fowler, Chancellor of the Duchy of Lancaster, it was called *WINDBUSH* manor and consisted of 8 messuages and 260 acres of land.[28] Fowler owned much other Oxfordshire property, including the recently acquired Moreton manor in Thame,[29] and several manors in Buckinghamshire. He died in 1477,[30] and in 1504 Windbush was in the possession of his widow Joan, sister of Sir Thomas Danvers of Waterstock.[31] She died in 1505,[32] and Windbush was probably sold by her son and heir Richard Fowler (d. 1528), who was a spendthrift and certainly sold much of his other property.[33]

By 1507 the manor seems to have been in the hands of Thomas Bradbury, a London mercer and alderman (d. 1510);[34] it is next recorded in 1540, when George Baldry of Hadley (Suff.), the son of Sir Thomas Baldry, another mercer and Mayor of London, died in possession of both Tetsworth and Moreton.[35] The custody of his infant heiress Elizabeth was granted to Sir Richard (later Lord) Rich, Chancellor of the Court of Augmentations,[36] and in about 1554 she married his son Robert, 2nd Lord Rich, who died in 1581.[37] As her second husband she married Robert Forth, and after her death in 1591 he held Tetsworth and Moreton for life.[38] They

were inherited not by her eldest son Robert, who became Earl of Warwick, but by her second son, Sir Edwin Rich, who in 1601 sold them to Henry Savile, Warden of Merton College and Provost of Eton.[39] At the end of the 16th century the Pettys of Tetsworth had an interest in Windbush and may have been leasing it,[40] and in 1620 Savile seems to have mortgaged it to Maximilian Petty, a Thame lawyer.[41] After Savile's death in 1622 Windbush and Moreton were held for life by his widow Margaret, and were then inherited by their daughter Elizabeth, the wife of Sir John Sedley, Bt. (d. 1638), of Aylesford (Kent).[42] In 1656 the manors passed with the title to their youngest son Sir Charles Sedley,[43] who in 1669 sold Windbush to James Perrot of North Leigh, a member of an old Oxfordshire family.[44] The property descended from the elder James Perrot (d. 1687) to his son James (d. 1725) and to his grandson Henry, who sold Windbush and Moreton in 1730 to Sarah, Duchess of Marlborough.[45] The property brought in an annual revenue of about £450.[46] In 1762 it was settled on Lord Charles Spencer of Wheatfield, a younger son of the 3rd Duke of Marlborough.[47] He died in 1820; his son John in 1831, the same year in which his grandson Frederick Charles, Rector of Wheatfield, died, leaving an infant son. By this time the Spencer estates were so burdened with annuities that in 1835 an Act was passed to sell part of them in order to preserve the Wheatfield estate.[48] Manorial rights had probably long lapsed.

A part of the 37 hides which the Bishop of Lincoln held in demesne in Thame in 1086 was in Tetsworth:[49] in 1279 eight tenants held 8¼ virgates from the bishop direct (*in capite*),[50] and in 1535 his estate in Tetsworth and Moreton was valued at £6 1s. 2d.[51] In 1547 the bishop was licensed to grant his *TETSWORTH* manor, along with other manors, to Edward Seymour, Duke of Somerset.[52] On his execution in 1552 Seymour's lands escheated to the Crown, and Tetsworth and Thame came into the possession of Lord Williams of Thame.[53] This Tetsworth manor was inherited by his daughter Isabella and her husband Sir Richard Wenman and followed the descent of Thame Park until the second part of the 17th century, although some of the land was sold to Charnell Petty in 1614.[54] The last time Tetsworth

[20] C.P. 43/692/433; d.d. Bertie c 20.
[21] Bodl. MS. Top. Oxon. a 46, p. 12; O.R.O. Land tax assess.
[22] For him see Venn, *Alumni*.
[23] O.R.O. Misc. Bea V/3.
[24] Gardner, *Dir. Oxon.*; O.R.O. Gamekeepers deps. For finances of Weston family see O.R.O. Misc. Bea V, *passim*.
[25] O.R.O. Gamekprs' deps.
[26] O.R.O. Misc. Bea V/21; Lee, *Thame*, 226 n.; Kelly, *Dir. Oxon.* (1887).
[27] *Thame Cart.* ii. 170–1.
[28] C.P. 25(2)191/29/15; P.R.O. Harrison, Extracts, viii. 233.
[29] See below, p. 176.
[30] C 140/62/39. From this time until *c.* 1600 Stockholt Barnes in Akeley (Bucks.) followed the same descent as Windbush: *V.C.H. Bucks.* iv. 146.
[31] C.P. 40/968, m. 489. For pedigree see Macnamara, *Danvers Family*, opp. 155.
[32] *Cal. Inq. p.m. Hen. VII*, iii, pp. 306–7; Windbush is not mentioned.
[33] Leland, *Itin.* ed. Toulmin Smith, i. 115; *V.C.H. Oxon.* v. 171.
[34] C.P. 40/982, m. 448. For him see A. B. Beaven, *Aldermen of London*, ii. 20.
[35] C 142/62/72; *Complete Peerage*, x. 777.

[36] *L. & P. Hen. VIII*, xvi, p. 456.
[37] *Complete Peerage*, x. 776–7.
[38] C 142/232/56. For settlement on Forth see C.P. 25 (2)/197/Hil. 29 Eliz.
[39] C.P. 25(2)/198/Trin. 42 Eliz. and Hil. 43 Eliz. For Savile see *D.N.B.*
[40] P.C.C. 43 Langley (will of John Petty, 1578).
[41] C.P. 25 (2)/340/Hil. 17 Jas. I. For Pettys see above, pp. 148, 150.   [42] C 142/397/73.
[43] G.E.C. *Baronetage*, i. 73–74; C.P. 25 (2)/707/Trin. 13. Chas. II.
[44] C.P. 25(2)/708/Trin. 21 Chas. II. For Perrots see E. L. Barnwell, *Perrot Notes* (1867), 103; pedigree ibid. 136.   [45] O.R.O. Li XIII/v/3.
[46] 3 Geo. II. c. 15 (priv. act): copy in Bodl. G.A. Oxon. c 196.
[47] d.d. Bertie b 5, Abstract of title to N. Weston.
[48] 5 & 6 Wm. IV, c. 23 (priv. act): copy in Bodl. L. Eng. C 13 c 1 (1835, no. 23). For family see Burke, *Land. Gent.*
[49] *V.C.H. Oxon.* i. 402.
[50] *Rot. Hund.* (Rec. Com.), ii. 820. Another 3½ virgates probably belonged to the Templars: see below.
[51] *Valor. Eccl.* (Rec. Com.), iv. 2.
[52] *Cal. Pat.* 1547–8, 184.
[53] C 142/182/42.
[54] Dunkin MS. 438/1, f. 257.

was mentioned among the Wenman lands was in 1678.[55] The land was evidently sold, for in 1842 the owner of Thame Park held no land in Tetsworth.[56]

LESSER ESTATES. Early in the 13th century Peter Talemasch granted the Templars, in one of whose churchyards he desired to be buried,[57] in free alms a hide (or 4 virgates) of his Tetsworth land, and added a charter of warranty.[58] One of the virgates belonged to his widowed mother Avice, and by 1210 she had successfully sued the Templars for it.[59] Consequently they sued Peter for the virgate,[60] and in 1211 he agreed to let them have 31 acres in Stoke Talmage in its place during his mother's life.[61] Later he added another 5 acres in Stoke.[62] On Avice's death the virgate returned to the Templars, who before this litigation had already leased their Tetsworth hide to William Coco and his heirs for 2s. a year and 6s. 8d. relief on the death of a tenant.[63]

This hide formed part of the Sandford Preceptory's estate, and like its other property passed in the 14th century from the Templars to the Hospitallers.[64] In 1513 it was being rented from the Hospitallers at 2s. a year by the Fraternity of the Holy Cross in Abingdon.[65] After the dissolution of the Hospitallers in about 1540 and of the guild in 1547, the land probably came into the possession of the Pettys of Tetsworth.[66] A house that had belonged to the Abingdon guild was held by John Petty of Stoke Talmage on his death in 1589.[67] He also held a house which had belonged to the chantry founded in Rycote chapel by Richard Fowler and Richard Quatremain.[68]

In the course of two centuries the Cozens family, yeomen of Thame and Tetsworth,[69] acquired an estate in Tetsworth. Thomas Cozens (d. 1744), who seems for a time before 1731 to have lived at Dormer Leys in Attington,[70] purchased in 1729 a messuage and two closes, called Harlots Ford and Ford Close.[71] His son Thomas (d. 1789), who made further purchases, was known by 1772 as 'of Harlesford'.[72] Succeeding generations continued to buy up land in Tetsworth, one of the largest purchases being made in 1838 by another Thomas Cozens (d. 1857), who paid about £5,000 for land from the Spencers, which included Peesleys Ground and Bandage Way.[73] In 1870 his successor, his nephew John Cozens (d. 1879), bought two farms, the Royal Oak Inn, and the manor-house.[74] By 1894 and 1904 when Cozens's executors tried to sell the estate the family owned 478 acres.[75] By the 1920's Edward Walker was the chief landowner and by the 1930's the former Cozens estates had been divided up.[76]

ECONOMIC AND SOCIAL HISTORY. The early economic history of Tetsworth is obscure, but there can be little doubt that the township, which

from an early date was part of the endowment first of the bishopric of Dorchester and then of Lincoln, was a valuable asset.[77] The London road, bisecting the village and its lands and providing easy communications, and the Thame valley with its rich pastures, had a decisive effect on the development of the place.

The fragmentary evidence for the medieval system of husbandry makes it certain at least that open fields were the basis: there are 12th- and 13th-century references to acres and fractions of acres distributed in furlongs, to meadow (i.e. Estmede) in Tetsworth field, and to pasture for oxen and horses 'in the fields (*intra campos*) of the town', and in the Talemasch demesne land.[78] Nevertheless, its economy had little resemblance to the typical open-field manor of the Midlands. From the account given in the Hundred Rolls of 1279 Tetsworth, compared with many other Oxfordshire villages, is outstanding for the number of its small free tenants and for the comparatively few villein virgate or ½-virgate holders, burdened with labour services. Most of the land was held by the Bishop of Lincoln's knights and subinfeudated, or by the Abbot of Thame, but the bishop kept in demesne about 100 acres.

On Robert Danvers's fee there were said to be 4 virgates in demesne and only 2 customary tenants, one holding a ½-virgate and rendering 5s. for rent and service, and 1 cottar paying 12d. rent. In addition to his customars Robert Danvers had 5 free tenants, of whom the chief, the Abbot of Thame, held 9½ virgates by military tenure. Walter de Dunsden held 1¾ virgate by scutage, suit, and a nominal rent, and had 4 customary tenants holding the land of him for rent and service; Thomas de Worthe held 6 acres for 1d. rent, suit, and scutage. Richard Danvers, another member of the family, had 2 free tenants and 5 cottars, apparently freemen, holding of him: he is not said to hold himself of Robert. One free tenant held a ½-virgate for 3s. 6d., suit, and scutage; another, Henry Danvers, held a messuage and 6 acres of Richard for 12d. and scutage. The cottars paid a total rent of 7s. In addition to this land Richard Danvers held 1 virgate of the bishop for 1d., suit, and scutage.

Most of the abbey's land (i.e. 9½ virgates held of the Danvers fee and 8½ of the Talemasch fee)[79] must have been held in demesne, for its recorded tenants mostly held only a few acres: 9 cottars with a cot and 3 acres each paid a total rent of 48s. 2d.; 12 cottars each with a messuage paid 17s. 4d. There were a number of small free tenants; 3 ½-virgaters paid rents of 5s. to 8s. 6d.; 5 others with a few acres each mostly held for small money rents; 1 virgater paid a rent of 10s. and another 7s. rent and scutage; finally, there was Roger Danvers, who held a small property for 11s. 2d. and suit.

[55] C.P. 43/383/254.   [56] Bodl. Tithe award.
[57] *Sandford Cart.* i. 149.
[58] Ibid. 171–2.
[59] Ibid. 173.
[60] *Cur. Reg. R.* vi. 98, where the suit is for 3 virgates.
[61] *Sandford Cart.* i. 173–4.
[62] Ibid. 152–3.
[63] Ibid. 172–3.
[64] It may have corresponded with the 3½ virgates said in 1279 to be held in chief of the bishop, but owing 3s. rent to the Templars: *Rot. Hund.* (Rec. Com.), ii. 820.
[65] Bodl. MS. C.C.C. 320, f. 11; for its history see *V.C.H. Berks.* ii. 92; iv. 439.
[66] *Cal. Pat.* 1549–51, 375: in the occupation of John Petty when sold to a group of Londoners.

[67] C 142/223/79.   [68] Ibid.; *Chant. Cert.* 139.
[69] See Lee, *Thame*, 226–8.
[70] O.R.O. Li XIV/vi/1: a messuage and land in Attington where John Cozens 'formerly dwelt' was let to the Hesters.
[71] Ibid. Li XIII/i/16.   [72] Ibid. xi/1.
[73] Ibid. v/8–12; other purchases were made in 1799 and 1824: ibid. ii, iv.
[74] Ibid. v/3.
[75] Ibid. x; Bodl. G.A. Oxon. b 92 (20).
[76] Kelly, *Dir. Oxon.* (1920); cf. d.d. Bullingdon c 150: 1926 rate bk.
[77] See above, p. 170.
[78] Bodl. MS. chs. Oxon. 631, 633; *Thame Cart.* ii. 113–14, 173–4.
[79] For the acquisition of this estate see above, p. 150.

A third holding of 3½ virgates was held by Edmund de Burton of the Bishop of Lincoln for suit, scutage, and a rent of 3s. to the Templars. Edmund had 2 tenants, one holding a ½-virgate for 6d., suit, and scutage, the other holding a croft and 1 acre for 3s. 4d. and scutage. Seven other tenants of the bishop held a virgate or less of land for various money rents ranging from 1d. to 8s., usually combined with suit to the hundred, or with suit and scutage. Of these Richard Danvers and William son of Robert were the only virgate holders. The last paid 8s. rent, a pair of gloves and owed suit. He had 3 cottar tenants.[80]

A late 13th- or early 14th-century account of how Thame abbey's land was burdened with scutage shows that there were still the same three main holdings beside the bishop's demesne, which is naturally not included: that of the Danvers family, that of Edmund de Burton, who held 4 virgates of the former Talemasch fee, and that of the Abbot of Thame, who held part of both the Danvers and Talemasch fees. Since 1279 some of the smaller holdings had been minutely subdivided: the virgate, for example, held by the 'heirs of Gunne' was divided between eight tenants, and another virgate held by 'the heirs of Franceys' was divided between nine tenants.[81] A terrier of 1378 of the lands of John Wynbush gives the same picture of Tetsworth's much-divided land. Wynbush had gradually built up a small 'manor' of about 6 virgates and a number of tofts, crofts, 'placea', and messuages from thirteen or so different owners.[82]

From the 14th-century tax lists it appears that Tetsworth was a comparatively large village and prosperous. There were 27 contributors in 1327, of whom half paid 2s. and over, and at the reassessment of 1344 the village's total tax was increased from £2 16s. 10d. for the 20th to £3 19s. 3d. for the fifteenth.[83] The Black Death appears to have inflicted a damaging blow, for in 1354 the village was allowed a tax abatement of 30s., a very high figure compared with those of neighbouring villages.[84] Only the market-towns of Watlington and Thame received higher abatements. The incident reported on the patent rolls of 1349 may perhaps be regarded as one of the consequences of the disaster suffered by the village. Roger le Longe of Tetsworth, one of the Oxfordshire coroners, was assaulted by certain of the villagers at his close in Tetsworth, had his goods carried away, and was hindered in the performance of his duty.[85] The second half of the century appears to have seen recovery, for 110 persons paid the poll tax of 1377.[86]

The abbey farmed out its grange in the 15th century[87] and in the early 16th century. When the abbey was dissolved in 1539 it was receiving £6 13s. 4d. for the grange, and £3 8s. 6d. for rents of

assize compared with the £19 14s. 9d. it had received in 1478.[88] It is likely that, as at Sydenham, the abbey used its Tetsworth grange mainly as a sheepfarm.[89] Some 12th-century evidence suggests that it may not have been difficult for it to inclose its land at an early date. When Robert Chevauchesul granted a hide of land to Thame it seems to have been largely consolidated: it lay in 3 furlongs only and was marked out by stones.[90]

The 16th century as elsewhere was a period of change at Tetsworth. The yeoman family of Petty eventually acquired Thame Abbey's property in Stoke Talmage and in Tetsworth and much of the rest of the village's land.[91] Three Pettys appear on the subsidy list of 1542 and between them paid on £62 of the village's total assessment.[92] With their relations by marriage the Woods of Oxford and the Caves of Great Milton,[93] the family continued to hold the predominant position in the parish during the first half of the 17th century. Although some of the Petty property was sold on the death of Maximilian Petty of Thame in 1639 to pay his debts two members of the family were still being assessed on substantial holdings for the tax of 1641.[94] This predominance of the Pettys and the fact that Thame Abbey's holding may have been long largely inclosed would account for the early inclosure of the open fields. The exact date has not been found, but it took place just before 1631, for a sale in that year of a 24-acre close to a Pyrton yeoman included 'common of pasture for 1½ yardland in the late common fields of Tetsworth, if the land sold was subject to common rights'.[95] There appears to have been protracted opposition, for in 1654 reference is made to the recompense to be made if the buyer of property from Edmund Petty is hindered in his possession 'by reason of the inclosure of Tetsworth being not yet legally settled'.[96] The commons were not inclosed: deeds of the 18th and 19th centuries make frequent reference to common rights on the Common Marshes and Common Green.[97] In 1838 the tithe award recorded about 52 acres of common, and common pasture for beasts was still being leased in the 20th century.[98]

The evidence of the leases points to the predominance of pasture, and so of sheepfarmers, although there are occasional references to arable closes.[99] The large closes on Maximilian Petty's farm, for instance, were all used as pasture in 1639. They were in all probability ancient inclosures made by the monks: Bandage Way and Scholars Bridge Close (80 a.), Latchford Hole (10 a.), and Harlots Ford and Ford Close (34 a.) all lay along the banks of Haseley Brook and were close to the abbey's Stoke Grange in Stoke Talmage.[1] Further evidence of sheepfarming comes from a deed of 1631 which gives the stint

[80] *Rot. Hund.* (Rec. Com.), ii. 820.
[81] *Thame Cart.* ii. 198–201.
[82] Ibid. 170–1. For the size of the virgate see ibid. 199, where 1 acre usually pays ¾d. scutage and 1 virgate pays 1s. 7½d.   [83] E 179/161/9, 17.   [84] E 179/161/30.
[85] *Cal. Pat.* 1348–50, 311. His family was settled in Tetsworth and paid the highest contribution to the tax of 1327: E 179/161/9.   [86] E 179/161/40.
[87] Bodl. MS. Rolls Oxon. 141: in 1478 John Caldon farmer of the demesne paid an annual rent of £5 6s. 8d.
[88] *Valor Eccl.* (Rec. Com.), ii. 213; Bodl. MS. Rolls Oxon. 141.
[89] Sydenham Grange was inclosed and leased out in the 15th cent.: Bodl. MS. Rolls Oxon. 141.
[90] *Thame Cart.* ii. 103–4.   [91] See above, p. 150.

[92] E 179/162/225; cf. 162/341 (1577 subsidy); 162/200 (1523 subsidy). For Christopher and George Petty, who were termed gentlemen by 1583, see Rousham Arch. N 435.
[93] Wood, *Life*, i. 79, 472; ii. 138.
[94] C 142/578/10; E 179/164/478.
[95] O.R.O. Li XIII/ii/1.   [96] Ibid. i/3.
[97] e.g. ibid. viii/b/1; vi/1.
[98] e.g. ibid. viii/b/6: 1907 lease. When the Cozens estate was up for sale in 1904, 11 cow commons were said to equal c. 15 acres: Bodl. G.A. Oxon. b 92 (19).
[99] e.g. O.R.O. Misc. Gr. I ap/1.
[1] C 142/578/10; cf. O.R.O. Li XIII/i/1. Bandage Way and Latchford Hole Mead are on the tithe map of 1838. Harlot's Ford has survived in the name of the farm, Harlesford farm.

for 1½ yardlands as 3 beasts and 60 sheep, and from a lease of 1697 of a large pasture ground (60 a.), which mentions an adjoining sheep-house.[2]

The sale of fleeces was doubtless the chief economic incentive for the conversion to pasture, but the proximity of a market-town at Thame and of Oxford meant a continuous demand for mutton. It may be significant that Thomas Wood, the father of the antiquary, who had acquired land in Tetsworth early in the 17th century, was also landlord of the flourishing 'Fleur de Lys' in Oxford,[3] and that a later purchaser of the Woods' farm at Tetsworth was Henry Jemott, a victualler of Thame.[4] A combination of the victualling or butcher's business with sheep-farming was not uncommon at this period.

Inclosure and the London road, which brought trade to the inns, account for the growth of a prosperous middle class. In 1662 the owner of 'The King's Arms' was assessed on 13 hearths and widow Woodbridge on 10 hearths; the 1665 list contains the names of 4 men with houses of 6 to 8 hearths apiece and of 7 with 3 or 4 hearths.[5] It is of interest that these were new men and that the substantial Elizabethan families—the Pettys, Bowyers, Clacks, Watkyns, Wets, and Grenings—had gone. The Elizabethans, indeed, were themselves new men: two of the leading contributors to the subsidy of 1542, John Adkyns and Ralph Ferme, had disappeared by 1577.[6]

Little is known about the number of inhabitants before the official census returns of the 19th century. For the hearth tax of 1662 there were 43 names listed,[7] and in 1676 there were 122 adults returned for the Compton Census. The original Census returns for this parish have survived: there were stated to be about 42 families of about 119 persons that are of age (i.e. 16 years probably) who conformed, besides three dissenters.[8]

In the 18th century the land continued to be divided into a number of small farms.[9] In 1786, besides the chief property owners, Lord Charles Spencer, John Young, and a Mr. Haydon, there were fifteen smallholders, but they cannot have held much more than their cottages, for they each paid less than 5s. tax.[10] There was a marked tendency for the number of holdings to increase in the early 19th century, partly perhaps because of the rising population and also because of the type of intensive farming practised. In 1786 there had been 39 holdings; there were 49 in 1816 and 1832.[11]

In 1809 Arthur Young commented on the excellent deep loam and noted that they ploughed with four horses at Tetsworth and did an acre a day.[12] The land was still mainly given over to pasture: Davis's map of 1797 shows the parish divided into

hedged fields of which only two were used as arable, and in 1838 there were 1,111 acres of meadow as against 56 of arable.[13] A lease of Manor House farm (117, a.), of which only a few acres were arable, in 1809 to James Lindars, innholder, is of interest in the provision that no rape seed, cob seed, mustard seed, hemp, flax or madder, should be sown or planted.[14]

During the first part of the 19th century sheep on the Tetsworth farms, as elsewhere in the area, began to give way to cattle, and butter- and cheese-making increased in importance. The tendency, noticeable at the end of the century in many neighbouring parishes, for these last two industries to be replaced by milk-production seems not to have affected Tetsworth. Both small and large farmers there found it more profitable to continue to make butter and rear bullocks and heifers.[15] All the farmers were described in 1851 as graziers,[16] and in the early 20th century Goldpits farm (70 a.) was still all pasture, Harlesford farm (156 a.) was described as having 'rich dairy and grazing land second to none in the country', and the rest of the Cozens estate was also mainly pasture;[17] the Berties' Latchford Hole farm (52 a.) was let out for grazing.[18] Grazing has continued to predominate, except during the First and Second World Wars.

The tendency for farms to increase in size was evident in this parish as elsewhere in the region. In 1838 there had been eight small and medium-sized farms, ranging from 52 acres to 145 acres.[19] By 1904 Harlesford farm (145 a.) and Goldpits farm (69 a.) were being farmed together, and Manor farm or Mounthill (293 a.) included two other smaller farms.[20] By 1939 there were four farms each with over 150 acres and two with under that amount.[21]

Tetsworth's population reached its maximum in the third quarter of the 19th century, but has declined since. In 1931 there were 297 inhabitants and only 94 houses as against 501 persons and 112 houses in 1851.[22]

Although agriculture has always been the staple occupation, Tetsworth's position on the London road encouraged the growth of other occupations. Two men called Chapman were tenants in 1279 and another of that trade was recorded in 1403.[23] Fifteenth-century records also mention a barber, maltman, miller, and a tailor, and a number of petty tradesmen occur in 17th- 18th- and early 19th-century records.[24] Noteworthy among them are two masons and a watchmaker, Joseph Kingston, recorded in 1786, and John Bentley of Tetsworth, post-chaise driver, mentioned in 1815.[25] That Tetsworth was rather different from the neighbouring

[2] O.R.O. Li XIII/iii/1.

[3] Wood, *Life*, i. 79, 169.

[4] Henry Jemmott was in possession by 1668 (O.R.O. Li XIII/ii/7, 8); John Jemmott of New Thame, grazier, was in possession in 1688 (ibid. 9). The family gave its name to Jemmott's Close. Bodl. Tithe award and map.

[5] E 179/164/504; *Hearth Tax Oxon.* 44–45.

[6] cf. 1577 tax: E 179/162/341. The name of Clack appears in Clacks Close on the 1838 tithe map.

[7] E 179/164/504.

[8] Queen's Coll. MS. 501.

[9] Cf. C. Sewell Read, 'Farming in Oxon.', *Jnl. Royal Soc. of Agriculture*, xv (1854).

[10] O.R.O. Land tax assess. For Young, see also O.R.O. Li XIII/iii/16.

[11] O.R.O. Land tax assess.

[12] Young, *Oxon. Agric.* 104.

[13] Davis, *Oxon. map*; Bodl. Tithe award and map.

[14] O.R.O. Li XIII/viii/c/3.

[15] Orr, *Oxon. Agric.* 28, 223, 226–9.

[16] H.O. 107/1726/2.

[17] Bodl. G.A. Oxon. b 92 (19, 20): *Sale cats.*

[18] Ibid. (22).

[19] Bodl. Tithe award; the farms can be identified with 20th-cent. farms by means of leases and field names (O.R.O. Tetsworth leases, *passim*).

[20] Bodl. G.A. Oxon. b 92 (19, 20); Kelly, *Dir. Oxon.* (1903).

[21] Kelly, *Dir. Oxon.* (1939).

[22] *V.C.H. Oxon.* ii. 222; *Census*, 1931, 1951; H.O. 107/1726/2.

[23] *Rot. Hund.* (Rec. Com.), ii. 820; *Cal. Pat.* 1401–5, 302.

[24] *Cal. Pat.* 1399–1401, 492; 1452–61, 509; Bodl. MS. ch. Oxon. 632: Thame 100 ct. 21 Hen. VI, June 21; O.R.O. Cal. Q. Sess. ii.

[25] O.R.O. Li XIII/iv/4, 7.

rural villages is revealed by the conviction in 1819 of as many as six shopkeepers for using false weights.[26] The Census return of 1851 emphasizes still more the trading character of the place. There were 5 butchers and grocers and a baker, 7 milliners, dressmakers, and drapers, a tailor, a hairdresser and a shoemaker. Agricultural needs were well served by 4 wheelwrights, 2 blacksmiths and their journeymen, a saddler, a harnessmaker, and a joiner. A letter-carrier and a mail contractor, turnpike gate-keeper, four publicans (one of them a cordwainer and another a butcher), the Swan hotel keeper, who was also the postmaster, and another inn-keeper, once again testified to the importance of the London road in the life of the village, although it was by this time of negligible importance compared with the days before the railway era.[27]

The history of the innkeepers can be traced back to 1482, when two were indicted for selling victuals at an excessive price.[28] In 1485 there is a record of another, a Thomas Preston, who was in a sufficiently large way of business to owe money to a London goldsmith.[29] In 1502 the constable, who was also an innkeeper, paid a fine with another man for licence to brew and bake in their inns.[30] Two inns, the 'Crown' and the 'Swan', were owned by Thame Abbey[31] and in the 1530's their tenants were paying substantial rents of £6 and £4 13s. 4d. Both these hostelries probably came into the hands of the Petty family at the end of the 16th century. A third inn, the 'George', was in existence in 1555–6, when John Bowyer was tenant of both the 'George' and the 'Swan'.[32] Yet another, the 'Catherine Wheel', is recorded in 1644 when it was a private house; it was 'new built' in 1683;[33] the 'Starr' occurs in 1648 as the property of Edmund Petty;[34] 'The King's Arms' in 1651,[35] a 'George' inn, later 'The King's Arms', was again recorded in 1813[36] and the 'Royal Oak' appears in 1792.[37] In 1784 Lord Torrington said that there were 'two goodish' inns, especially the 'Swan', and a third for 'minor travellers'.[38] By 1838 there were at least four—the 'Red Lion', the 'King's Arms', the 'Swan', and the 'Crown'.[39]

From the earliest times the affairs of the township were conducted in the hundred court of Thame. Ordinances about the clearance of ditches, particularly those near the king's highway, i.e. the London road, were made there and the view was held.[40] No record of separate courts for the Tetsworth manors has survived, but there is a little evidence for parish government in the 19th century. The township had its own churchwardens, overseers and waywardens, and after 1841 when Tetsworth became a parish they conducted their business through the vestry. Tetsworth owned a sawpit, two Highway Closes (c. 4 a.), and a Poorhouse. Rents from the closes were used to

repair the footways, although in 1836 the Visitor said in court at the visitation of Thame that these rents should properly be used for the churchways only and should be appropriated by the churchwardens. The closes were let for £11 10s. a year in 1855 and £15 10s. in 1875. There were also four or more parish cottages, presumably let to the poorer parishioners, but in 1852 it was resolved that they should be pulled down. It was decided at the same time to use the house on Nap Hill as a pest house.[41]

Many in Tetsworth suffered from unemployment and poverty in the early years of the 19th century. Between 5 per cent. and 7 per cent. of the population was receiving relief at any one time between 1813 and 1834. Unemployment was most acute in the winter months and large sums were laid out on the roundsmen system at those times, e.g. £31 in December alone in 1833. Other relief included the paying of paupers' rents, distributing coal, and giving allowances to soldiers' wives. There was a smallpox outbreak in 1814 when the overseers paid 1s. for moving people, another 1s. for burying their clothes, and £2. 2s. to the Radcliffe Infirmary for the admission of emergency cases. Expenditure was high for a civil parish of this size, and rose in the 1830's, e.g. £606 was paid out in 1816 and £722 in 1833.[42] Even as late as 1851 26 persons were receiving poor relief.[43]

CHURCH. Since 1841 Tetsworth has been a vicarage in Aston deanery, but like Sydenham and Towersey (Bucks.) it was formerly a chapelry of the prebendal church of Thame, and was, therefore, in the peculiar jurisdiction of Thame.[44] Architectural evidence shows that the church was in existence by the 11th or early 12th century, but its early history is not known. It may not have always been a chapel of Thame, but may once have had an independent ecclesiastical position, for in the late 12th century its priest was called 'presbyter' or 'persona'.[45] Its relationship to the church of Thame is first defined in the mid-13th century (see below). In 1841 Richard Slater, who had bought the advowson of Thame, made its chapelries into separate vicarages and vested their advowsons in trustees known as the Peache Trustees.[46]

The revenue of the three chapelries of Thame was divided according to the ordination of Thame vicarage, made in the time of Bishop Grosseteste (1235–53), between the Prebendary of Thame, the Vicar of Thame, and the chaplains of the three churches or chapels.[47]

The holder of the prebend, who was also a landowner in Tetsworth,[48] collected the great tithes and the tithes of wool and hay; the Vicar of Thame was entitled to the rest of the tithes; and the three chaplains each received what was the smallest part of the

[26] O.R.O. Cal. Q. Sess. 1.
[27] H.O. 107/1726/2.
[28] d.d. Bertie c 16 (uncat.): 100 ct. 1481.
[29] Cal. Pat. 1467–77, 77.
[30] d.d. Bertie c 16: 100 ct. 1502.
[31] Valor Eccl. (Rec. Com.), ii. 213.
[32] d.d. Bertie c 16.   [33] Wood, Life, i. 107.
[34] O.R.O. Li XIII/i/1.
[35] d.d. Par. Gt. Haseley b 9 (uncat.).
[36] O.R.O. Li XIII/viii/d/1.
[37] Ibid. vii/b/2. Cf. ibid. XIII/vii/c 1 where the 'Royal Oak' is described as 'newly erected' in 1818.
[38] Torrington Diaries, ed. C. B. Andrews, i. 119.
[39] Bodl. Tithe award; the 'Royal Oak' was also recorded in 1818 and 1853: O.R.O. Li XIII/vii/c/1; Lascelles, Dir.

Oxon. (1853). The 'Sun' and the 'Four Horse Shoes' were marked on the 1881 O.S. map 25″, xli.
[40] e.g. d.d. Bertie c 16: 100 cts. 1443, 1481, 1502.
[41] Notes by the late Revd. S. J. Nightingale from the vestry mins.; Bodl. Tithe award.
[42] Par. Rec. Overseers accts.
[43] H.O. 107/1726/2.   [44] See below, p. 201.
[45] Thame Cart. ii. 107, 111.
[46] Return of Benefices, H.C. 227, p. 6 (1872), xlvi; Lee, Thame, 148. For list of trustees see Oxf. Dioc. c 2044, Presentations.
[47] Oxf. Archd. Oxon. c 141, pp. 125–6; and see below, p. 202.
[48] See above, p. 149. In 1842 he had c. 40 acres: Bodl. Tithe award.

church income and property, the revenue from his altar and from the house and land belonging to his church. The prebendary was responsible for the up-keep of the chancel; the vicar had the duty of nominating the chaplain and could remove him with the consent of the prebendary; he also had to provide all the books and ornaments needed in the chapel; the chaplain was expected to meet ordinary and extra-ordinary payments, except for certain contributions 'decreed of old in the chapter of Lincoln' or to be decreed in the future, which were to be paid by the prebendary.

After the dissolution of the prebend in 1547, the great tithes belonged to the lay rector, and in 1842 his Tetsworth tithes were commuted for a rent charge of £210, and in 1848 his Attington tithes were commuted for £18 10s.[49] The Vicar of Thame continued to collect the small tithes, which were commuted in 1842 for a rent charge of £115, but he became responsible for either serving Tetsworth church himself or for paying a curate[50] as the chaplain's endowment had practically disappeared: the altar offerings virtually ceased after the Reformation and there is no mention of glebe in Tetsworth except for 20 tithe-free acres which belonged to the Rector of Wheatfield.[51]

When, in 1841, the living was separated from that of Thame, it was endowed with the vicarial rent charge of £115, which was increased in 1848 by a similar charge of £6 10s. from the small tithes of Attington.[52] Between 1842 and 1844 the living was also augmented by £600 from Queen Anne's Bounty, £650 from the vicar, J. W. Peers, and £260 from other benefactors.[53]

The history of the peculiar of Thame is not well documented and little is known of medieval church life. The names of some priests who lived in Tetsworth in the late 12th century are recorded. From about 1180 for some 20 years there was William the priest, who had a house in the village;[54] in about 1200 the parson of Tetsworth was named Roger.[55] One of these may have been married, for a few years later the 'son of the priest' was holding a virgate.[56] Also living in the parish in the late 12th century was another clerk named Alan, whose wife Clarissa was the niece of Robert Chevauchesul, lord of the manor. They were wealthy enough to give 2 virgates of land to Thame Abbey.[57]

The ordination of Thame vicarage makes it clear that in the Middle Ages Tetsworth had its own chaplain, who was supposed to have a clerk to live with him in his house and help him serve the church.[58] The names of a few of these chaplains are known, but nothing more.

In the mid-15th century a hermitage and a chapel dedicated to St. John the Baptist were built in Tets-

worth, but they were independent of the parish priest. When the guild of St. Christopher in Thame was founded in 1447, the wardens were allowed to found this hermitage and build a chapel for the hermit. The latter was permitted to acquire lands to the value of £2 a year; he was to pray for the king and queen and for the members of the guild, and to keep the high road in repair.[59]

By the 16th century, and probably before, Tetsworth had its own churchwardens. They are recorded in the accounts of the wardens of Thame in 1532 as paying 1s. 6d. for Peter's Pence.[60] Judging from the 17th-century churchwardens' presentments in the peculiar court, the parish was well conducted at this period. They usually reported that there were no recusants or any who refused communion, and that the fabric was in good order. On one occasion they said there was no service book and asked for a month's grace in which to get the book.[61]

After the Reformation Tetsworth continued to have its own curate, but as the living was so poor he probably also held another living.[62] The list of curates, however, is incomplete and little is known of the history of the church at this period. The church-wardens' presentments from the 1670's state that the minister, wearing his 'priestly habit', performed the full church service on Sundays and holy days.[63] After 1686, when the last 17th-century curate of Tetsworth died,[64] the church was usually served either by the Vicar of Thame or his curate, and in the second half of the 18th century the vicar complained that he had to serve both Thame and its chapels either by himself or with the help of one other minister.[65] Little record of 18th-century services has been found, but in the middle of the century Tetsworth was known as the only church in the district which had no more than one service on Sundays.[66] Earlier when Samuel Thornbury (1722–51), who was also Rector of Stoke Talmage, lived in Tetsworth, things may have been better. His letter to the bishop in 1745 asking for a gift of tracts to be distributed among his parishioners is evidence of his interest.[67]

A revival of church life took place at the beginning of the 19th century when Henry Campbell, a man with an 'independent fortune', became curate.[68] He said that when he came to the parish in 1804 he found the people very 'discordant among themselves, very profligate, and very ignorant'. Sundays were spent mostly in 'low profligacy' and sport, especially cricket, which he had succeeded in stopping, at least during church services. Among the few who went to church he found 'an old grudge' about seats in the gallery, which the churchwarden had settled. To rid himself of the choir, as he disapproved of its four members, he introduced singing through-

[49] Bodl. Tithe awards: Walter Long still held the Tetsworth part of the prebend, but had sold the parts belonging to Thame and Sydenham. The lay rectory descended with Haseley Court, Major A. J. Muirhead being lay rector in 1923: Oxf. Archd. Oxon. c 44, f. 55b; Oxf. Dioc. c 2044, 1923 faculty.
[50] e.g. Oxf. Dioc. c 656, f. 187.
[51] Bodl. Tithe award.
[52] Bodl. Attington tithe award.
[53] C. Hodgson, Acct. of Queen Anne's Bounty (2nd ed. 1845), 231, 232, 235, 308.
[54] Thame Cart. ii. 104, 107, 108, 109.
[55] Ibid. 111.
[56] Bodl. MS. ch. Oxon. 202; Oseney Cart. vi. 151–3.
[57] Thame Cart. ii. 106.

[58] Oxf. Archd. Oxon. c 141, p. 125.
[59] Cal. Pat. 1446–52, 181; see above, p. 147, and below, p. 203.   [60] Lee, Thame, 56.
[61] Oxon. Peculiars, 169–72.
[62] Anthony Maund, for example, curate in c. 1620 (Oxf. Dioc. c 18, f. 232b), was also Rector of Wheatfield.
[63] Oxon. Peculiars, 171.
[64] Oxf. Archd. Oxon. c 162, p. 64.
[65] See below, p. 205.
[66] Oxf. Dioc. c 659, f. 177.   [67] Ibid. c 652, f. 86.
[68] The correspondence about this is in ibid. c 656, ff. 181–8. Campbell, who was an illegitimate son of Viscount Palmerston (Lee, Thame, 614), died in 1846 leaving £15,000 to charity: Gent. Mag. 1846 (1), N.S. xxv. 549.

out the congregation. The parishioners had then asked for a selection of psalms and hymns, and he had obtained the one in use in Leicester church. One of his special aims was to start a Sunday school so as to draw the children, who spent Sundays 'in all kinds of idleness and vice', into the church. The churchwardens and several others approved of this plan, but it was opposed by others who declared that they would never give a shilling for 'the instruction of the poor'.

Partly by these measures Campbell aroused resentment in the parish, and a complaint made to the bishop stated specifically that he was not using the proper form in the church services and more generally that his services were drawing dissenters away from their own meeting and that there must be some reason for this. Campbell admitted to having two or three times inadvertently omitted a minor part of the service; and he later admitted that he had broken the Act of Uniformity by omitting 'the church service' (no doubt evensong) and had instead gathered the children in the chancel on Sunday evening, catechizing them, explaining parts of the Bible to them, and concluding with two or three collects from the communion service. To justify his conduct, which he agreed was wrong, he wrote that he was trying to draw dissenters back to the church, that some who had gone to the chapel 'from not having something to do' now went to church. Far from being Calvinistic, he said he tried to follow the writings of William Jones of Nayland and Charles Daubeny, two theological writers of repute with High-Church leanings.[69]

The whole story is not known nor is the end of it. At one point the bishop demanded Campbell's immediate dismissal by the Vicar of Thame; he may have later relented, but Campbell did not remain long in Tetsworth (his name does not appear in the parish register) and the parish was returned to the care of Timothy Lee, the Vicar of Thame.

In 1841, when Tetsworth became a separate living, it again had its own vicar. The first was J. W. Peers (1841–76), a member of the Chislehampton family,[70] who took the place in the village of a lord of the manor. He took an active part in parochial administration, taking the chair at vestry meetings, and either beginning or following the practice of naming one churchwarden while the parish named the other.[71] In 1846 he built a 'handsome and commodious' Vicarage,[72] rebuilt the church (see below), and built the school.[73] He held frequent services, with two sermons on Sundays and more than twelve

communions a year, but the number of communicants, sixteen or seventeen, remained small.[74] Towards the end of the century, however, numbers both of communicants and of the congregation increased.[75]

By 1911 the ecclesiastical parish had been enlarged by the addition of Attington, whose inhabitants had long been accustomed to attend Tetsworth church,[76] and the living became formally known as Tetsworth with Attington.[77]

The status of Attington, which was a part of the parish of Thame in the Middle Ages, was somewhat uncertain in the post-Reformation period. Its few inhabitants probably attended Tetsworth church[78] and so 18th-century documents sometimes refer to the parish 'called Tetsworth and Attington', and even to the 'parish of Attington'.[79] In the 19th century Attington was considered extra-parochial.[80] No evidence has been found that it ever had any churchwardens[81] and it does not appear to have paid either tithes[82] or church rates.[83] It may have been exempted in the Middle Ages as it mostly belonged to Thame Abbey.

The present church of *ST. GILES*, which was entirely rebuilt in 1855, is a stone building consisting of chancel, nave, south aisle with tower and spire rising over the south porch, and north vestry. The smaller medieval church which it replaced is stated to have contained some long-and-short work of Anglo-Saxon date in the north-west corner,[84] but the main structure dated from the early 12th century. It consisted of a single nave and chancel, separated by a Romanesque arch, plain and very narrow.[85] The round arch of the south doorway had an elaborate inner moulding.[86] Its tympanum was carved with the figures of a bishop, in pontificals with a crozier in his left hand and giving a benediction with his right hand, and of a priest holding in his left hand an open book and pointing with his right hand to the pascal lamb and banner within a nimbus.[87] The north doorway, destroyed in 1855, was of the same age and character, but simpler in design.[88] There was also a window of the same period in the north wall of the chancel,[89] and a Romanesque piscina which were destroyed at the same time.[90]

The chancel was rebuilt in the 13th century. The three-light east window and the three single lancets in the south wall shown in early 19th-century drawings were of the period. The steeply pitched roof of the chancel was raised to a higher level than that of the nave.[91]

[69] For them see *D.N.B.*
[70] See above, p. 10; for him see Venn, *Alumni.*
[71] Par. Rec. Vestry bk.
[72] Gardner, *Dir. Oxon.*; Lupton, *Thame*, 103.
[73] See below, p. 159.
[74] *Wilb. Visit.*
[75] Oxf. Dioc. c 344.
[76] *Census*, 1911: *Eccl. Areas.*
[77] *Crockford.*
[78] For baptisms and burials of Attington parishioners see Tetsworth Par. Reg. 1834, 1835, 1838.
[79] Oxf. Archd. Oxon. c 30, f. 214; c 33, f. 321b. *Oxon. Peculiars*, 173.
[80] *Census* 1831, &c.; Bodl. Tithe award; Tetsworth Par. Reg. 1834, 1838.
[81] None appear in *Oxon. Peculiars.*
[82] This has been inferred from the evidence of the Tithe award.
[83] This has been inferred from a case of 1713–15 in which the tenant of 3½ yardlands in Attington belonging to the Tippings refused to pay church rates to Tetsworth. George Tipping, he said, had agreed to pay rates on the

land for his own life, but before that they had never been paid. By 1713 the property had passed to William Tipping. For this see *Oxon. Peculiars*, 173; Oxf. Archd. Oxon. c 162, p. 208; c 30, ff. 212–15; c 33, ff. 321–2.
[84] F. G. Lee in MS. Top. Oxon. c 3, f. 273, and *Thame*, 201.
[85] Descriptions in *Gent. Mag.* 1792, lxiii (2), 719; Lee, *Thame*, 200–2; and by G. E. Street in MS. Top. Oxon. c 104, f. 396b.   [86] MS. Top. Oxon. b 220, f. 166.
[87] Described in *Archaeologia*, 1853, xxxv. 487; for drawings see *Gent. Mag.* 1790, lx (1), opp. p. 17; Dr. Lee's in MS. Top. Oxon. c 3, f. 273, which differs slightly from Buckler's drawing of 1823 (see plate facing p. 159). It also shows the ancient iron hinges on the door.
[88] Lee, *Thame*, 201; drawings in MS. Top. Oxon. c 3, ff. 273, 274b.
[89] Lee, *Thame*, 201.   [90] Ibid.
[91] For drawings from SE. see *Gent. Mag.* 1793, lxiii (2), opp. 719, which is inaccurate since it shows no windows in the chancel except at the east end; MS. Top. Oxon. c 3, f. 277, which also shows only the east window in the chancel; and plate facing p. 158.

In the 15th century windows were inserted in the nave, two in the south wall,[92] and perhaps the same number in the north wall. G. E. Street described their architecture in 1851 as more elaborate than those proposed for the new church.[93] The south porch made of oak was also of this period;[94] the square wooden belfry of the dove-cot type, which was in existence in the 19th century was of uncertain date.[95] Almost no record has survived of work done to the fabric after the Reformation until the 19th-century rebuilding. It is recorded that the chancel windows were out of repair in 1681.[96] Between 1708 and 1713 church rates of more than normal amount were raised and repairs were presumably carried out. The church appears to have been in good condition when Rawlinson visited it in 1718: his only comment on the building was that it was 'very ordinary'.[97]

and of Doyley in other windows. Drawings of these were made by F. G. Lee and also of a fragment of an early medieval monumental slab with a floriated cross.[5] The early 16th-century brass effigies of John Gryning, his wife Alys, and their three children were once in the nave.[6] Another ancient brass in the chancel had gone by the early 19th century.[7] There were also memorials to Francis Fosset, senior (d. 1705), and to his wife Mary (d. 1702); to two infants (d. 1708) of Christopher Newell, clerk, and his wife Ann; and to Ann (d. 1773), daughter of Richard Hobday.[8]

In 1958 there were several memorials to the Cozens family: (1) Thomas (d. 1789) and his wife Esther (d. 1806) and Thomas (d. 1834); (2) Robert (d. 1797); (3) John (d. 1879) and his wife Charlotte (1860) and their daughter (d. 1903); (4) Ellen (d. 1915), widow of

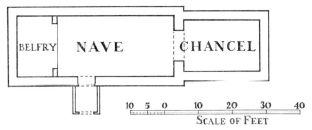

Church of St. Giles before the rebuilding in 1846.

During the incumbency of John W. Peers plans for a new church were considered. The diocesan architect, G. E. Street, reported in 1851 that portions of the fabric of the old church were 'of very considerable merit, and in good preservation' and that the chancel was 'very perfect'. He thought it 'very inadvisable' to allow their destruction.[98]

In spite of attempts by the bishop to save the church it was decided to rebuild on the same site. The architect was John Billing of Reading; the cost was £2,250.[99] The building was consecrated by Bishop Wilberforce in 1855.[1]

The design of the new church was in the Early English style; it has been little altered since and remains a characteristic example of Victorian church building. It figures in the background of a contemporary oil painting of the Revd. J. W. Peers and his family.[2] All the interior fittings were replaced at the restoration, including the pulpit installed in 1626, and the old pews with doors.[3] The Commandments, the Creed, and Lord's Prayer were painted on the east wall of the chancel. An organ was installed in 1877 and a new heating system in 1922; choir desks were presented by S. A. Fane in 1924; and electric light was installed in 1936.[4]

During the restoration many medieval and later memorial inscriptions and all the heraldic glass were destroyed. The glass included the arms of Adrian de Bardis, Prebendary of Thame, in the chancel, and the arms of Peppard of Lachford (Great Haseley)

John Cozens, and Mary Cozens (d. 1920). There were also tablets to J. W. Peers (vicar 1841–76) erected by the parishioners; to W. J. R. Latham, killed in France in 1918; and a stained glass window at the east end to A. E. Hutt (d. 1923), who was people's warden for 33 years. It was designed by Lawrence Willis of London.[9]

In 1552 the church was poorly furnished with only a chalice and a surplice.[10] In 1958 it had a pewter paten, flagon, and alms-plate, dating from the 18th century, and a silver chalice of 1842.[11]

In 1552 there were only three bells, but in 1718 there were five small bells all 'not above 160 lb. weight' according to Rawlinson.[12] Later in the century there were said to be six bells, as there were in 1853.[13] In 1958 there was still a ring of six, which had been recast in 1936 by Mears and Stainbank in their Whitechapel foundry. Three of these had been cast in 1695 by Richard Keene, a fourth in 1702 and the tenor, though 'broken' in 1683, does not appear to have been recast until 1787 and then largely through the generosity of William Hobday. The treble was provided in 1853.[14]

The registers date from 1604 for baptisms, 1625 for marriages, and 1653 for burials. The churchwardens' accounts begin in 1833.

NONCONFORMITY. The churchwardens' presentments throughout the 17th century state that there were no Popish recusants in the parish and no

[92] Ibid.   [93] MS. Top. Oxon. c 104, f. 396b.
[94] Lee, *Thame*, 200, 201.
[95] Drawing in MS. Top. Oxon. a 69, no. 549 (c. 1822).
[96] *Oxon. Peculiars*, 172.   [97] *Par. Coll.* iii. 310.
[98] MS. Top. Oxon. c 104, ff. 396–7.
[99] Ibid. ff. 394–5; Oxf. Dioc. b 70.
[1] Oxf. Dioc. c 2044, Consecration.
[2] *Penes* C. Peers Esq., Chislehampton House.
[3] MS. Top. Oxon. b 220, f. 166.
[4] Oxf. Dioc. c 2044, Faculties; inscription in church.
[5] MS. Top. Oxon. c 3, ff. 273, 274, 277, 277b.

[6] Richard Lee and Wood gave the date as 1523, Matthew Hutton as 1513. By the early 19th century the inscription had gone: *Visit. Oxon.* 28; Bodl. MS. Wood E 1, f. 251; MS. Top. Oxon. b 220, f. 166.
[7] MS. Top. Oxon. b 220, f. 166.
[8] Ibid. f. 166b.   [9] Oxf. Dioc. c 2044, Faculty.
[10] Lee, *Thame*, 203–4. The inventory is not in *Chant. Cert.*   [11] Evans, *Ch. Plate*.
[12] Lee, *Thame*, 204; *Par. Coll.* iii. 310.
[13] Lee, *Thame*, 205; Oxf. Archd. Oxon. c 44, f. 55b.
[14] *Ch. Bells Oxon.* 408–10.

THAME VICARAGE
Destroyed in 1841

TETSWORTH CHURCH
Before the rebuilding of 1855

GREAT MILTON CHURCH IN 1850

S. DOORWAY OF
TETSWORTH OLD CHURCH

WOODCOTE CHAPEL IN 1819

CLIFTON HAMPDEN CHURCH c. 1807
Rebuilt 1843–4

evidence for any Roman Catholicism has been found later.[15]

The Compton Census of 1676 recorded three non-conformists,[16] but otherwise there is no record of Protestant dissent before the 19th century. By 1804 it was apparently flourishing. In that year the house of Robert Caterer was licensed as a dissenting meeting-house.[17] This may be the 'Methodist chapel' referred to in correspondence of 1804 between the bishop and Henry Campbell, who was serving as curate and who claimed to have drawn many dissenters back from the chapel to the church. He considered the chapel to be at a very low ebb and likely soon to be lower. The Methodist preacher is said to have found Campbell's attention to children and young people 'the most formidable opposition'.[18] Campbell, however, did not long remain in Tetsworth, and on his departure dissent may have again increased.

In 1818 the private school kept by Isaac Caterer was licensed as a meeting-house,[19] in 1823 a chapel was built, and in 1824 a Sunday school started.[20] A deed of sale[21] of the newly erected chapel shows that the Caterer family had played a leading part: Mrs. Mary Caterer and Mr. Robert Caterer and others sold it in 1825 to William Wiffen, the minister at Thame,[22] and others. In 1828 Robert Caterer left Tetsworth with his family to become minister of Rotherfield Peppard.

In 1842 Tetsworth came under the care of the Oxfordshire and West Berkshire Congregational Association, but five years later, when a Baptist pastor was appointed, the association withdrew its annual grant.[23] In 1851 the chapel, described as Independent, had about 30 in its congregation.[24] The Wesleyans, who in 1835 had registered a private house as a meeting-place and still had a separate meeting in 1842,[25] may by now have joined the chapel, for in 1854 the vicar described it as 'mongrel', since it had a Baptist pastor and a Wesleyan and Independent congregation.[26] Two more Wesleyan ministers were appointed and in consequence Tetsworth was not readmitted until 1864 to the local Congregational Association. This Association became in 1868 the Berks., South Oxon., and South Bucks. Congregational Association (later Union). Between 1877 and 1886 the church was without a minister, but the appointment of Thomas Scott in 1886 led to the building of the present chapel, next to the old one, in 1890 at a cost of £850.[27] The old chapel continued to be used as a Sunday school.[28] In 1892 the average Sunday congregation was 97, and there were 90 children in the Sunday school. The chapel organized a Young Peoples' Guild, a Band of Hope, a Temperance Society, a Mothers' Meeting and a Coat and Clothing Club. In the early years of the 20th century the chapel was again without a pastor and became a preaching station of Mansfield College, Oxford. Later it was served first by the minister of Benson and then by that of Thame.[29] In 1958 it had only four members.[30]

Mrs. Harriette Tawse, of Child's Hill, London, by will proved 1905, left two cottages for the maintenance of the chapel fabric or the general purposes of the congregation. The cottages were sold and the proceeds invested in £100 stock. The income, c. £4, does not seem to have been paid after 1925. Thomas Deverill, by will proved 1922, left, subject to his wife's life interest, £200 stock, the income on which was to be applied to the maintenance of the chapel services. The money became payable in 1939.[31]

SCHOOLS. There is no record of any school at Tetsworth before the 19th century. Two private day-schools existed in 1815, of which one was kept by Isaac Caterer, who later became the Congregational minister.[32] The dissenters had also established a Sunday school in 1812, and in 1818 there were about 30 children attending it.[33] Only one day school was returned in 1818,[34] but more schools were established in the next decade, a girls' school in 1827 and a mixed infants' school in 1829. The two last had 6 and 28 pupils respectively in 1833.[35] In that year there were also two other day schools which together took 30 boys and 8 girls. All these schools were supported by parents.[36] There is no later record of them, and in 1847 a new school with accommodation for 90 pupils was built in the centre of the village at the cost of J. W. Peers and other contributors. Each child paid 2d. a week and the teacher's salary was raised by subscription.[37] It was a Church of England school and later became affiliated to the National Society. There were 81 pupils in 1854, 25 less than the number attending the Sunday school.[38] By 1871 attendance at the National school was only 51 children.[39] The reduction in numbers must have been at least partly caused by the existence in 1871 of another school, about which nothing is known as it omitted to make a return[40] after its transference in 1879 to the new School Board for Tetsworth and Attington which had been set up in 1877.[41] Attington children in the 19th century appear always to have attended schools in neighbouring parishes, and when the board school for the School Board District of Tetsworth and Attington was opened in 1881 children from both villages attended. The average number of pupils was 74 in 1889 and 69 in 1903–4.[42] The school was reorganized in 1938 as one of the Thame schools for children up to eleven years, and

[15] Oxon. Peculiars, 170, 171. For the Phillips family, non-resident lords of the manor, see above, p. 150.
[16] Queen's Coll. MS. 501.
[17] Oxf. Dioc. c 644, f. 71.
[18] Ibid. c 656, ff. 185–187b; see above, p. 157.
[19] Oxf. Dioc. c 644, f. 199.
[20] Summers, Congreg. Chs. 258–62 for its history. Unless otherwise stated this book is the source for the following account.
[21] At Memorial Hall, Farringdon Street, London, E.C. 4; Char. Com. file 84911.
[22] See below p. 213.
[23] Minute books of the Berks. S. Oxon. and S. Bucks. Cong. Assoc. (now Union), penes the General Secretary, Reading. [24] H.O. 129/5/156.
[25] Oxf. Dioc. c 646, f. 20; Cong. min. bks.
[26] Wilb. Visit.
[27] Cong. min. bks. The site of the new chapel was

settled in trust in 1889: Char. Com. file 84911; Tetsworth G. and Accts. file.
[28] Kelly, Dir. Oxon. (1903, 1920). The old chapel had become dilapidated by 1935 and the site was sold in 1938 by the Congregational Union, to which it had been transferred: Cong. min. bks.; Char. Com. file 84911.
[29] Cong. min. bks.
[30] Congregational Yearbook (1958).
[31] Char. Com. file 84911; Tetsworth G. and Accts. file.
[32] Oxf. Dioc. c 433; Summers, Congreg. Chs. 258–9.
[33] Oxf. Dioc. c 433; Educ. of Poor, 731.
[34] Ibid.   [35] Educ. Enq. Abstract, 756.   [36] Ibid.
[37] Gardner, Dir. Oxon.; Lascelles, Dir. Oxon.
[38] Wilb. Visit.
[39] Elem. Educ. Ret. 320; Sch. Bldg. Grnts. 106.
[40] Elem. Educ. Ret. 320.
[41] Kelly, Dir. Oxon. (1887); Sch. Bldg. Grnts. 106.
[42] Ret. of Sch. 217; List of Sch. 29.

senior children were sent by bus to Thame. In 1955 they were attending the John Hampden School there and Thame Secondary Modern school. Tetsworth school had 30 pupils in 1943 and 68 in 1954, when it was known as Tetsworth County Primary school, and was attended also by children from Stoke Talmage and Wheatfield.[43]

CHARITY. Miss Mary Elizabeth Cozens, of Brighton, by will proved 1920, left to the patrons of Tetsworth church £2,000, duty free, to be applied in augmentation of the benefice, subject to the requirement, so far as the law allowed, that the sepulchral monuments of the Cozens family in church and churchyard should be maintained by the patrons or incumbent. The residue of her estate she left in trust, as 'the Cozens Bequest', the income to be paid once yearly or oftener to needy women of Tetsworth or adjacent parishes, not being Roman Catholics. By Scheme made in 1924 the neighbouring parishes were defined as Thame, Great Haseley, Stoke Talmage, Wheatfield, Adwell (with S. Weston), Lewknor, Aston Rowant, and the benefits defined as cash payments, by loan or otherwise, in cases of sickness or special distress; weekly allowances of between 1s. 6d. and 5s. for those unable to support themselves; and pensions. The capital then held in stock was £5,557. Besides this the sum of £555 was owing on security of mortgages, and there were expectancies on the death of a person then living.[44] In fact, the capital was not fully paid over until 1953 when £405 was added to the original stock.[45] In 1955 and 1956 the annual income was £395 and was distributed in weekly pensions of 6s. or 10s. a head, in Christmas gifts amounting to £9 in the first year and £10 10s. in the second, and in a special grant of £5 5s. in 1956.[46]

THAME

As an ancient market-town on the Buckinghamshire and Oxfordshire border, only 14 miles from Oxford and 46 from London, Thame has from time to time been directly affected by outside influences and by national and regional movements in which its inhabitants have often played no mean part. The area appears to have been little affected by the Romans, though Stukeley says that Thame was a Roman town,[1] but as part of the ancient endowment of the Bishopric of Dorchester[2] Thame played a leading part in christianizing the surrounding district, probably from the 7th century onwards. In the 12th century through its Cistercian Abbey the town was connected with the movement for monastic reform: parishioners of Thame were generous in their grants of land to the abbey, and some of the abbots are known to have been local men.[3] In the 1460's, at least a few townsmen played a part in another religious reform movement, for 'heretics' of Thame and High Wycombe, who were stated to have been influenced by the heretical teaching of the Rector of Chesham Bois (Bucks.), were condemned by Bishop Chedworth.[4]

In the 15th and 16th centuries the Quatremains of North Weston and Lord Williams of Thame were pioneers in the care of the poor and aged and in the promotion of education.[5]

There is some evidence that at least some of the leading townsmen were out of sympathy with the religious changes made by Henry VIII, and the fact that 'two of the most seditious' were ordered to 'suffer at Thame' for their part in the Oxfordshire outbreak of 1549[6] suggests that the Crown may have had a special reason for choosing Thame as the place to stage a spectacle calculated to deter revolt. In the next reign, moreover, the churchwardens of Thame showed a spirited determination to save the wealth of their church and guild from royal confiscation, and they forestalled the chantry commissioners by selling the church goods.[7]

The inclosures of the period certainly met with opposition: the town supplied one of the leaders in the abortive agrarian revolt of 1596.[8]

In the 17th century again there was stubborn opposition to some of the unpopular measures of Charles I: in 1628 the inhabitants refused to billet soldiers,[9] and many of the gentry of the neighbourhood were strongly opposed to arbitrary taxation. Among the 40 in Oxfordshire who refused to pay ship-money in 1636 was Sir Francis Wenman of Thame Park, and the bailiff of Thame hundred refused to have anything to do with its collection.[10]

In the 18th century Thame showed itself equally alive: the Thame troop of yeomanry formed in 1788 was one of the first in the country and in 1803 a volunteer corps of three companies was enlisted by P. T. Wykeham of Tythrop.[11] The only Frenchmen, however, to invade Thame were the 100 or so prisoners on parole who were billeted in the town from 1805 until the end of the Napoleonic War.[12]

The town has twice seen violent conflict in its streets. The first occasion was a local affair, though it had national implications. It resulted from a papal provision to the prebend of Thame. Edward son of Sir John de St. John was provided by Pope Nicholas IV and tried to seize the prebend by armed force from Master Thomas de Sutton, Archdeacon of Northampton, on whom it had been conferred by his uncle Oliver Sutton, Bishop of Lincoln. St. John's supporters occupied the prebendal house and expelled the servants of Master Thomas, and it was alleged that they tried to prevent the celebration of the services in the church by his clergy.[13] Episcopal appeals to the king to remove the 'intruders' were

---

[43] Inf. Oxf. Educ. Cttee.   [44] Char. Com. file 99558.
[45] Ibid. 103133.
[46] Ibid. Accts. file.
[1] For Roman finds see *V.C.H. Oxon.* i. 344; W. Stukeley, *Itinerarium Curiosum* (1776), i. 43 and index.
[2] See below, p. 170.
[3] See below, p. 176. For abbots see *V.C.H. Oxon.* ii. 85–86: Robert of Tetsworth, John of Thame, and Robert King.
[4] Linc. Reg. Chedworth memo., ff. 60, 61, 62b.

[5] See below, pp. 215, 217.
[6] *V.C.H. Oxon.* ii. 35–36.
[7] *Chant. Cert.* 116; see below, p. 197.
[8] *Cal. S.P. Dom.* 1595–7, 317, 344; see below, p. 190.
[9] *Acts of P.C.* 1627–8, 450.
[10] *Cal. S.P. Dom.* 1636–7, 210.
[11] Brown and Guest, *Thame*, 170–1.
[12] Ibid. 171–3.
[13] *Reg. Sutton*, iv. (L.R.S. lii), 47–49, 64, 67, 70–71, 104, 117.

without effect and in August 1293 a climax was reached with an attack by some 200 armed men on the church by St. John's followers: arrows were shot at the priests celebrating mass at the high altar, two clergy were wounded and mass was said in the desecrated building by a priest 'suborned' by the attackers. Solemn excommunication in Lincoln Cathedral, in Oxford, Thame, and other churches of the diocese followed and renewed appeals were made to the king. At the end of January 1294 the bailiffs of Thame and Banbury with other officials of the Suttons and a band of armed men blockaded the church in an attempt to starve out the 'clerks and servants of the church' supporting St. John. The bishop and his agents were ordered to appear before the king to answer for this breach of the peace, and the alleged obstruction of the highways in five places by dykes, the breaking down of Long Crendon Bridge, and the prevention of passage by wayfarers. The bailiff of Thame replied that they had blockaded the church in order to prevent the escape of felons and by order of the coroner, who had viewed the body of a man murdered by the followers of St. John. They had blocked the highways in order to preserve the peace.[14] All those who supported the papal provisor were afterwards solemnly excommunicated in the cathedral of Lincoln and in the churches of Oxford and Thame and in all those of Cuddesdon deanery.[15]

During the Civil War there was again fighting in the town's streets. Thame's position on the Aylesbury–Oxford road at a distance of only 14 miles from the city and its importance as a market meant that both royalist and parliamentary forces were interested in controlling it and were constantly skirmishing in the neighbourhood. The grammar school was forced to close for a time and the ordinary life of the market was interrupted.[16] Early in 1643 attempts were made by the parliamentary forces to obtain a permanent footing in Thame as part of their plan of controlling Oxford. Their companies were reported in the town in March and on 10 June Essex took up his headquarters there.[17] So it was that John Hampden, mortally wounded at the Battle of Chalgrove Field, died at Thame.[18] The reverse at Chalgrove and other successful royalist attacks in the neighbourhood forced Essex to withdraw to Aylesbury in July.[19] In August the royalists were commandeering all the fat cattle bought by London butchers at Thame market; in October they were planning to 'fetch away' all the cattle and stop the passage of provisions to Aylesbury; in January 1644 Prince Rupert made the town his base for an attack on Aylesbury and royalist forces appear to have remained in Thame until the spring of 1645.[20] With the king again at Oxford in November 1645 after his defeat at Naseby, the

parliamentarians decided to occupy Thame in force in preparation for an attack on Oxford and so as to prevent the city from drawing on the Thame area for supplies.[21] A 'great party' of troops under Col. Greaves was quartered in the town, and in December two regiments under Col. Whalley were sent from Fairfax's army to tighten the parliamentary grip.[22] Already as a result of the occupation the town had suffered the raid led by Col. William Legge in September 1645, so graphically described by Anthony Wood. In June 1646 the operations against Oxford ended in the surrender of the garrison, and Wood recorded that on the same day many of the king's foot came into Thame to lay down their arms.[23]

Many persons of note have lived at or visited Thame. Royal visitors included Edward I (as the Lord Edward) in 1264, Edward III in 1365, and Edmund of York, guardian of England, in 1399.[24] The bishops of Lincoln often stayed in the parish[25] and many of the prebendaries, such as Adrian de Bardis, a local benefactor, were distinguished men and were often resident.[26] In the post-Reformation period the manors belonged to families of national importance. Lord Williams, Thame's greatest benefactor, was the first successor of the bishops[27] and he was succeeded by the Norreys family, who had close contacts with the parish until the Earl of Abingdon gave up Rycote House at the end of the 18th century, and by the Wenmans, who inherited Thame Abbey from Lord Williams, and resided there until the 19th century.[28] Thomas Viscount Wenman (d. 1665) who was related by marriage to the Hampdens, was a moderate parliamentarian. He had his house besieged and his estate seized by the royalists, but was later imprisoned by the parliamentarians.[29] He offered hospitality in 1649 to Seth Ward, later Bishop of Salisbury, when he was expelled from Cambridge.[30] Philip, 6th Viscount Wenman (d. 1760), was the unsuccessful Tory candidate in the great election contest of 1754, though he won in Thame by a large majority.[31]

Of those born in Thame the most distinguished is Sir John Holt (1642–1710), Lord Chief Justice.[32] Like many other notable 17th-century men he was educated at the grammar school. Its pupils in the first half of the century included John Hampden, Henry King, Bishop of Chichester, Shakerley Marmion, the dramatist, Edward Pocock, orientalist, and John Fell, Dean of Christ Church and Bishop of Oxford.[33] Others born at Thame were Robert King (d. 1557), the last abbot of Thame and the first Bishop of Oxford;[34] George Etherege (fl. 1550), physician, Regius Professor of Greek at Oxford and a recusant;[35] William Basse (? d. 1653) of Moreton, a poet and sometime retainer of Richard Wenman; Mary Bracey,[36] second wife of the poet Edmund

[14] Select Cases in King's Bench, iii (Selden Soc. lviii), 11–18; Reg. Sutton, iii (L.R.S. xlviii), pp. xxxix–xli. For other references to this affair see Cal. Inq. Misc. i, pp. 459–60; Cal. Pat, 1292–1301, 109; Rot. Parl. i. 101–2.
[15] Reg. Sutton, iv. 44–49, 104–5, 107–9, 117.
[16] Wood, Life, i. 114; Luke, Jnl. i. 69.
[17] Luke, Jnl. i. 27; ibid. v, viii.   [18] D.N.B.
[19] Luke, Jnl. i. 93, 98, 99, 101, 106, 111.
[20] Ibid. 140, 162, 206, 215, 219, 238.
[21] Cal. S.P. Dom. 1644–5, 176.
[22] Brown and Guest, Thame, 115.
[23] Wood, Life, i. 120–4, 128; F. J. Varley, Siege of Oxford, 81.
[24] Cal. Close, 1264–8, 4; Cal. Pat. 1364–7, 164, 165, 167; Cal. Close, 1396–9, 519.

[25] e.g. John Bockington: MS. Top. Oxon. c 3, p. 425b–6; see also Queen's Coll. MS. 366, f. 26.
[26] See below, p. 202.
[27] See below, pp. 171, 217. For his tomb see plate facing p. 208.
[28] See below, pp. 169, 177.
[29] D.N.B.   [30] Ibid.
[31] R. J. Robson, Oxon. Election of 1754, passim; MS. Top. Oxon. c 3, p. 334.   [32] D.N.B.
[33] For them see ibid. and J. H. Brown, Hist. of Thame Grammar School, 76.
[34] D.N.B. For his lodgings see below, p. 169.
[35] D.N.B. and see below, p. 210.
[36] See D.N.B. under E. Waller. For others named see ibid. s.v.

Waller (1606–89); James Figg (d. 1734), a noted prize-fighter; and Richard Powell, M.D. (1767–1834), whose portrait hangs in the committee room of St. Bartholomew's Hospital.

The parish lies along the south bank of the River Thame and on the borders of Buckinghamshire. In 1932 it was reduced in area from 5,229 acres to 3,140 acres: the land south from the Shabbington boundary up to and including North Weston (1,094 a.) was added to Great Haseley, and Lobbersdown Hill with the land round Moreton Field farm (995 a.) was added to Tetsworth.[37] The pre-1932 boundary followed the River Thame on the north and for a short distance on the west, but for the rest it followed an artificial line that once separated the open fields of townships. This line took many right-angled turns, especially by Sydenham where there were some particularly artificial twists as the line turned north-east to skirt Thame Park and include Blackditch farm before going north to form the county boundary, dividing the parish from Towersey on the east.[38] This area included the town, which comprised New Thame and parts of Old Thame and Priestend, and the remainder of the liberties or hamlets of Old Thame and Priestend, together with those of North Weston, Moreton, and Thame Park.[39] The parish, however, had only been limited to these hamlets since 1841, when the chapelries of Sydenham, Tetsworth, and Towersey, formerly in Thame parish, were made independent.[40] Of these villages, Sydenham lay in a different hundred and Towersey in a different county and all three had long developed along independent lines.[41] Their histories, therefore, except incidentally, will not be included in this article. The history of Attington township (444 a.), on the other hand, which was defined as a separate civil parish and as extra-parochial in the 19th century,[42] will be included. It was originally in Thame parish, and its manorial history was closely connected with Moreton and Thame Park.[43]

Most of the land lies between the 200- and 250-ft. contours, rising gently from the river's edge towards the Chilterns. On the south-west it rises more steeply towards Lobbersdown Hill (333 ft.). Occasional low hills, Barley Hill, Christmas Hill, and Horsenden Hill surmount the general rise.

Geologically the land is composed of Portland Beds, Limestone, and Calcareous Sands round about Thame, Clay and Lower Greensand along the banks of the Thame, and Gault in the south.[44] These variations have considerably affected the agricultural history of the district.

There is an ample water-supply. Apart from the Thame and its two tributary brooks there is the Cuttle Brook, which roughly bisects the parish. All are often in flood even today, and at one time the floods could be dangerous. In the great flood of 1798 a wagon was swept off the Crendon causeway, and by another in 1894 Thame Bridge on the Crendon road was destroyed.[45] Both the river and the brook were at one time full of a variety of fish.[46]

Round North Weston and in the north-east of the parish the landscape retains something of the treeless character of open-field land, but the roads are well lined with trees and Thame Park in the south-east is well wooded. The deer park is one of the most ancient in the county: it covered about 420 acres in 1852, but, if Davis surveyed it accurately, was somewhat smaller at the end of the 18th century and in the 12th century covered about 300 field acres (3 carucates).[47] It was once the property of the bishops of Dorchester and later of the bishops of Lincoln. There is documentary evidence for its enlargement in Henry I's reign when the king licensed before 1131 an exchange of land with Richard de Vernon, as the Bishop of Lincoln needed it for his park.[48] Soon after this augmentation, at latest before 1141, it was given to the Cistercian monks of Ottley in Oddington as a site for their new abbey, later known as *Sancta Maria de Parco Thame*.[49] Throughout the Middle Ages, therefore, the park was devoted more to sheep than to deer.

Thame is at the centre of a network of roads coming into it from the surrounding villages of Buckinghamshire and Oxfordshire. Most of them are ancient roads, but some have increased their relative importance and others have declined in value. The present road from Oxford, for instance, was comparatively little used and remained a bridle road on the Thame side of North Weston as late as 1823.[50] The old road from Thame to Sydenham on the other hand has long gone out of use. It is first recorded in 1317 as a way running from Thame east of the abbey to 'parts of the Chilterns'.[51] The abbey was allowed to enclose part of it provided the abbey made another of the same size on its own soil. Davis shows on his map of 1797 a way running along the east of Thame Park to Sydenham and a way some way to the west of it that peters out in the park: these are very probably the old and the new roads. After the Inclosure award in 1826 the park road only continued in use.[52]

The most important through road from earliest times until the mid-18th century was the way from Aylesbury to Tetsworth, passing through Thame, along Moreton Lane and over Horsenden Hill. This took the Wallingford traffic and was also used by travellers to Oxford or London. Its early importance is apparent from the fact that Thame, Tetsworth, and Wallingford are three of the towns shown on the earliest English road map (c. 1360).[53] The bridge at the north end of this road over an arm of the Thame was therefore of some importance. A manorial court in 1444–5 reported that the bridge at Cottesgrove (i.e. Scotsgrove) End was in decay and that the Bishop of Lincoln and the Prior of Rochester ought to repair it.[54] The bridge at Priestend over the Cuttle Brook was even more important and appears to have

[37] O.R.O. Oxon. Review Order, 1932.
[38] O.S. Map 6″, Bucks. xxxvi; Oxon. xli (1885).
[39] Bodl. Tithe award (1848). In the 1851 Census New and Old Thame are described as townships, and Priestend as a hamlet.
[40] See below, p. 200.
[41] For Tetsworth see above, p. 156; for Towersey see V.C.H. Bucks. iv. 105–7.
[42] Census.
[43] See below, pp. 174, 199 n. 59.
[44] V.C.H. Oxon. i, map between pp. 4–5.
[45] Lupton, Thame, 2; Brown and Guest, Thame, 2.
[46] Lupton, Thame, 2.
[47] Gardner, Dir. Oxon. (1852); Davis, Oxon. Map (1797); Rot. Hund. (Rec. Com.), ii. 820.
[48] Regesta, ii, no. 1707.   [49] V.C.H. Oxon. ii. 83.
[50] A. Bryant, Oxon. Map (1823).
[51] Cal. Pat. 1313–17, 651.
[52] O.R.O. Incl. award (1826).
[53] The Map of Great Britain c. A.D. 1360 known as The Gough Map (O.U.P. 1958).
[54] d.d. Bertie c 16 (uncat.).

been kept up by the parish. It undertook its repair certainly in 1836 and widened its approaches, the county contributing £50.[55] The old Aylesbury–Tetsworth route gave way in 1770 to the turnpike from Aylesbury to Shillingford via Thame, which ran south of North Weston along the present Rycote road and on to Little Milton. Rycote Way had long been of importance, for as early as 1345 a stone causeway from Thame to Rycote had been begun at his own cost by a Thame merchant, Edward le Spicer.[56] The other principal road in the 18th century ran along the High Street of the town, skirted Thame Park and passed through Attington before joining the London road 3 miles to the south of Thame. The road to Chinnor and the Icknield Way, which ran 4½ miles to the south-east, must always, however, have been of local importance, and the road connecting Thame with Long Crendon and other Buckinghamshire villages in the north by way of Thame Bridge was certainly much used.[57]

The upkeep of this bridge was a constant burden: in 1309 Bishop Dalderby granted an indulgence for its repair; in 1335 it was again broken down and a commission was appointed to find who was responsible for the upkeep and compel them to discharge their duty.[58] Liability for its repair was in dispute as late as 1829.[59] As owner of the prebend the Baroness Wenman was declared responsible for the Oxfordshire section of the bridge and an indictment having been preferred against her the fine was spent on repairs. After its destruction by floods in 1894, the bridge was reconstructed in 1896 at a cost of £4,600.[60]

The roads about Thame were in a bad state before the turnpikes were made towards the end of the 18th century. Defoe noted that no provision was made for the repair of the roads in the vale of Aylesbury and beyond it into Oxfordshire; later Lord Torrington complained of the state of the cross roads round Crendon and Thame, declaring that for the most part they were impossible to tour in chaises or phaetons and 'would *tame* the fiercest horse'.[61] Great improvements had been made by 1813 when Brewer stated that the 'majority of parochial roads or cross ways are much better than the great thoroughfares were a century ago'.[62] The coming of the turnpikes made it possible to run a coach from Burford via Oxford and Thame to London in 1773, and by about 1830 there was a coach from Thame to London three times a week until 1860.[63] But Thame never became a coaching centre: with Tetsworth so near it was not too inconvenient to join the London coach there. Four Thame roads were turnpiked. The first from Aylesbury to the turnpike between Shillingford and Benson was opened in 1770.[64] There were gates at

Thame Mill, and Priestend, and the receipts at these in 1802 were £110 and £342 respectively.[65] The road from Thame to the Oxford road between Tetsworth and Postcombe was turnpiked in 1785 with a gate at Brick Kiln Lane at which the receipts in 1802 were £194.[66] In 1833 a turnpike trust was set up for a road from Thame to Bicester.[67] In 1881 the United Trust with a debt of £2,650 and assets worth £1,549 was wound up.[68] A proposal, made in 1823, to carry the Oxford–London road through the parish almost along the line of the present railway failed owing to the objections of certain landholders.[69] Existing lanes were used instead and the present Oxford–Thame–Risborough road by way of Kingsey Field resulted.

In the 20th century the Chinnor road has been increasing in importance owing to the growth of the Chinnor cement works and since 1929 has carried more traffic than either the Postcombe or Rycote roads.[70]

The railway came to Thame in 1858 when an extension of the line from High Wycombe via Princes Risborough, authorized by Parliament in 1857, was built. The line was taken over by the G.W.R. in 1867, the connexion between Thame and Oxford having been completed in 1864.[71]

The town of Thame lies in the extreme north of the parish just to the south of the River Thame, from which it took its name. The word is probably a corruption of the Celtic root *teme*, meaning dark.[72] The town's site must have been determined by the strong defensive position of the river and its two tributaries which lie on three sides of it and by the sandstone island that emerges here out of the surrounding clay.[73] The geological conformation also largely determined the present lay-out of the town. Along a gently sloping ridge running north-west to south-east runs the long and remarkably wide High Street with the parallel Wellington Street to the north-east and Southern Road to the south-west.[74]

The original town of Old Thame lay at the west end of the High Street along the roads which encircle the church—the Oxford road to the north-west and Bell Lane to the south-east. Here in Church Road was the Bishop's Court House. When the church was made a prebend of Lincoln in about 1140 a prebendal house was probably built and from this time, no doubt, dates the liberty of Priestend which lasted as a unit of local government up to the 19th century. Development eastwards and the creation of New Thame probably took place in the 12th century, and in the first quarter of the 13th century the centre of the High Street itself, where Middle Row now is, began to be built on.[75] The early 13th century was undoubtedly a period of great building activity: the

[55] H. J. Tollit, *Oxon. Co. Bridges* (*Surveyor's report, 1878*), 77; Brown and Guest, *Thame*, 241.

[56] *Cal. Pat.* 1343–5, 549.

[57] Davis, *Oxon. Map* (1797); and see below, pp. 179, 184, *passim.*

[58] Linc. Reg. xlvi, Dalderby, f. 119; *Cal. Pat.* 1334–8, 199.

[59] J. M. Davenport, *Oxon. Bridges* (1869), 8.

[60] O.R.O. Q. Sess. Bridge Pps. 23; *Oxon. Co. Bridges* (1895); Brown and Guest, *Thame*, 241.

[61] D. Defoe, *A tour through England and Wales* (1725), ii. 179; *Torrington Diaries*, ed. C. B. Andrews, i. 211–13.

[62] Brewer, *Oxon.* (1813), 41; Brown and Guest, *Thame*, 166–8.

[63] Brown and Guest, *Thame*, 168 citing *Oxf. Jnl.* 1773; Pigot, *Nat. Com. Dir.* (1830–60).

[64] Act to amend road from Aylesbury . . ., 10 Geo. III, c. 58. There is a minute bk. of the turnpike trustees for 1789–91 in d.d. Hobbes c 22. [65] *Oxf. Jnl.* 1802.

[66] Ibid.; Act for repairing the road from Aylesbury . . . through Thame, 25 Geo. III, c. 127.

[67] Act for repairing the road from Aylesbury . . . to Thame . . . and Bicester, 3–4 Wm. IV, c. lxxxvi.

[68] O.R.O. Q. Sess. D.T. 2.

[69] Lupton, *Thame*, 20–21.

[70] Inf. the Clerk, Thame U.D.C.

[71] E. T. MacDermot, *Hist. G.W.R.* iii. 6; Brown and Guest, *Thame*, 227–9 (citing *Oxf. Jnl.*).

[72] *P.N. Oxon.* (E.P.N.S.), i. 141, 146.

[73] O.S. Map 25″, xli. 2, 3.

[74] See below, pp. 164, 179.

[75] See below, p. 179; and map, p. 164.

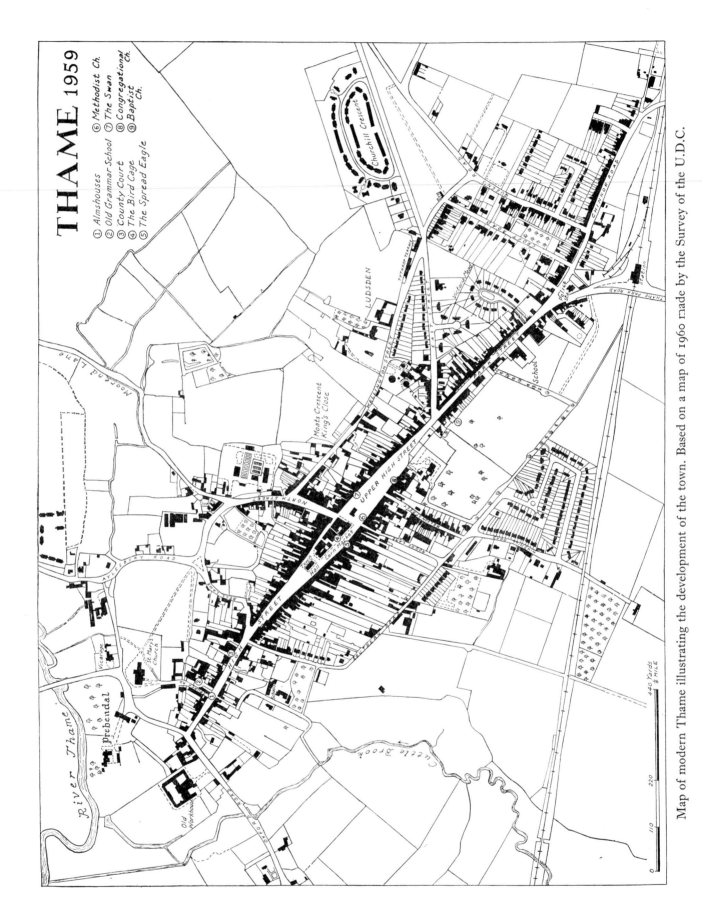

Map of modern Thame illustrating the development of the town. Based on a map of 1960 made by the Survey of the U.D.C.

parish church was newly built on a large scale, and so it seems was the abbey church and the prebendal chapel and one-time hall.[76] By the mid 15th century, if not earlier, the town had extended to Friday Street (North Street) and partly along it.[77] By 1700 houses extended as far as the White Hound Pond and by 1823 were almost continuous to that point and along much of Pound Lane (Wellington Street).[78] But Ludsden was still a hamlet and the land between it and the east end of Brick Kiln Lane (Park Street) was open field. Even in 1860 Ludsden still consisted of three farms with cottages.[79] After 1850 the freeing of land by the inclosure award (1826), the growing population, and later the opening of the railway station and the increased powers of the Urban District Council, led to the development of the town to the south-east and south.[80] By 1880 the gas works (now pulled down) and a row of artisans' houses at the beginning of East Street had appeared; also Tythrop Terrace and Railway Terrace.[81] These were followed by over 60 new houses built between 1880 and 1890 along Chinnor Road and in Pickencroft (Queen's Road). These were mostly vitreous-brick and red-brick villas for artisans. At about this date too All Saints' Church, a corrugated iron structure, was erected in Chinnor Road and a row of two-story houses in the Gothic style in Thame Park Road; between 1900 and 1910 came Croft Road and Nelson Street; and after the two World Wars there was further expansion. Between 1919 and 1939 an estate of 178 houses was built off Windmill Road and between 1945 and 1959 Victoria Mead and Moat Crescent were laid out besides 172 Council houses in Churchill Crescent and other estates on the north side of Thame.[82]

Apart from dwelling houses several schools and other public buildings have been erected in Thame since 1827 when the Congregationalist Chapel (now the Masonic Hall) was built.[83] In 1835 came the Workhouse, designed by G. Wilkinson of Witney, who was afterwards asked by the Poor Law Commissioners to design similar buildings for Ireland.[84] Next came the National school and the British school; in 1861 the County Court, built of local bricks and embellished with a shield of arms; and in 1878 the new buildings of Lord Williams's Grammar School on the Oxford Road.[85] In 1959 a new secondary modern school was begun.[86]

The most striking feature of the town today is still its wide High Street, stretching for over ¾-mile from the Oxford Road to the police station. In the mid 19th century Billing's *Directory* stated with much truth that if Middle Row was taken down 'it would make this noble street second to none in any market town in England'.[87] Hotels, public-houses, shops,

and residential houses lie on either side. All periods of architecture from the 15th century (or possibly earlier) to the present day, are represented, and though about 1900 many of the old houses were re-fronted and the shops acquired plate-glass windows, the general effect is still one of beauty and dignity.

Among the oldest buildings, the 'Bird Cage' is one of the best preserved and most interesting. The main structure dates from the 15th century, but its stone cellar may be earlier. The house is timber-framed and has lath and plaster filling, now rough cast. The west end is a three-story building with its top story oversailing all round and supported on long and very heavy curved brackets on corner posts. On the first floor are two 15th- to 16th-century rectangular wooden bays with traceried lights, shaped and curved aprons, and small tiled roofs. The centre of the house is of two stories and the east end has one story and an attic, but part of the original east end has been replaced by the International Stores. There is a pent-roof projection across the ground floor. The house has been an inn for some years, but the local tradition is that it was once the town prison and it seems likely that it is identical with the 'tenement called the cage' which was the property of the guild of St. Christopher in 1529.[88] Another secular building, partly of 15th-century date and worth noting, is the house called the 'Cruck'. It has 16th-century timber-framing with plaster filling and stands on a rubble base. There is a fragment of Elizabethan wall-painting inside. One gable-end has the remains of a cruck built in to the lower story that was apparently part of an adjoining cottage now destroyed.

Most numerous are the 16th to 17th-century, 18th-century and Regency houses, though many of them were altered later. The chief characteristics of the 16th–17th-century houses are their irregular gables, cut barge-boards, timber-framing, oversailing top stories, and diamond-shafted chimneys. Some have plaster filling, some rubble and plaster, and others have brick. An important building material in the 16th century and earlier was white earth, later known as 'witchert'.[89] Some have been refronted in the 18th century and their earlier characteristics are observable only at the rear of the building or inside. Some are still thatched. The 18th-century houses or those with 18th-century fronts are usually built of brick and are on the whole rather plain Georgian houses, with the usual characteristics of the style.[90]

The best examples of the 16th century are Lord Williams's almshouses and his grammar school. The almshouses were apparently built after 1550 when Lord Williams succeeded to the chantry property and before his death in 1559.[91] They replaced the original Quatremain Hospital which Leland said

[76] See below, pp. 167, 169.

[77] e.g. letter about medieval house: MS. Top. Oxon. c 3, p. 423; d.d. Bertie c 16 (uncat.): ct. rolls, *passim*.

[78] Architectural evidence.

[79] Lupton, *Thame*, 6.   [80] See below, p. 183.

[81] O.S. Map 25″, xli. 3 (1880); d.d. Bullingdon c 36 (valuation list).

[82] Brown and Guest, *Thame*, 239; inf. the Clerk, Thame U.D.C.   [83] See below, p. 213.

[84] Lupton, *Thame*, 24–25; see below, p. 196.

[85] For the schools see below, p. 215.

[86] Inf. the Clerk, U.D.C. For a map of modern Thame see opposite.   [87] Billing, *Dir. Oxon.* (1854).

[88] d.d. Bertie c 16 (uncat.): roll of guild of St. Christopher, 1525–6.

[89] The following 16th- or 17th-century houses may be

noted: High Street, nos. 20, 21, 24, 28, 50, 78, 85, 87; Upper High Street, nos. 6, 7; 'Stonecroft', nos. 33, 92. White earth is frequently mentioned in court rolls and leases.

[90] The following are among the 18th-century houses: Corn Market, nos. 12, 18; High Street, nos. 4, 5, 15, 41, 42, 43, 45, 46, 47, 51, 52, 53, 54, 72, 73, 81, 81a (originally one house), 82, 83, 90, 91, 92, 93, 94, 99, 100, 102, 108; Butter Market, nos. 3, 4; Upper High Street, nos. 1–5, 39, 105 and 106. For houses with 18th-century fronts to older buildings see Upper High Street, nos. 8, 10–13, 16, 26, 31, 40.

[91] An account roll of the guild of St. Christopher for Michaelmas 1548–50 mentions repairs each year for the almshouses, which in August 1550 became the property of Sir John Williams. This suggests that the Quatremain building was still standing. For Lord Williams see below, p. 171.

stood close by the church and which Camden, writing in 1586, said no longer existed.[92] The present building (now partly private cottages and partly store-rooms) is a picturesque range of timber-framed, two-storied cottages set at right angles to the High Street. The top-story oversails and is supported on carved brackets. There is a central angular bay on each floor. There were once six cottages of two rooms each.[93] Externally except for some 19th-century windows they have been little altered. Buckler's drawing of 1821 shows them when they were still six almshouses.[94]

The grammar school, now used by Messrs. Pursers as offices and store-rooms, was built in 1569.[95] It is a two-storied building with attics built of rubble with dressed stone copings. It consists of rooms for the master and usher, facing west on to Church Row, with attics above for the boys and a lofty school-room behind (50 ft. by 20 ft.). Over the central door-way is set a carved panel containing the arms of Lord Williams. The forecourt is now entered from High Street, but the school was originally separated from the almshouses by a wall.[96]

The building suffered during the Civil War, but was repaired by 1661 when Warden Woodward of New College found it 'new mended, lathed and tiled'.[97] At one time the windows of the schoolroom contained the royal arms and those of Lord Williams and his connexions.[98] The master had a garden and orchard, at the corner of which was the privy.[99] Various 19th- and 20th-century additions have been made to the old building, including the staircase and bandstand bought from Lord Rothschild's house at Halton near Aylesbury, when the school building was used as a dance-hall and café between the two World Wars.[1]

Among the best preserved 16th to 17th century houses is Corner Cottage in Bell Lane, a picturesque thatched building of brick, plaster, and timber. Another is no. 1 Butter Market and 'The George' which were originally one building. This house consists of two stories and an attic, is timber-framed, and part has a double-gabled front oversailing at first-floor level with heavy bracket supports, in their original carved form, and the other part (now 'The George') has a similar oversail, but without gables. A massive central chimney with four diamond shafts remains. The 'Saracen's Head', although it has a 17th-century gabled exterior, is really a much older house. It is timber-framed, but the inside timbers appear to be of 15th-century date and are set in a massive and elaborate symmetrical pattern with curved braces in the panels. The house had a vaulted medieval cellar, mutilated in the course of modern alterations.[2] Other 16th-century buildings are the 'Nag's Head' with its

three oversailing gables, the 'Rising Sun', the Swan Hotel, which has an 18th-century front of brick,[3] and the 'Abingdon Arms', though the last has been very much altered at later dates. It was once a five-bay building, of which the main part was timber-framed with brick filling in the front and lath and plaster and some rubble at the rear; it has been reduced in size and converted into shops. No. 109 Lower High Street is another 16th-century structure and is typical of many houses in this part of the High Street. It is a timber-framed house with brick filling, a central chimney stack, and a side entry to the rear of the premises. Inside there are spiral staircases and 17th-century corner fireplaces. It has been refronted in the early 18th century and has an early-19th-century shop front.

Five buildings of interest dating from the 16th and 17th centuries are known through prints or documents only. They are two successive market-halls, the old Vicarage, the Court House, and the Place House. The 16th-century market-hall was a timber-framed building of two stories with open spaces for shops below. On the top story there was ornamental pargetting. The roof was tiled and surmounted by a short weather-vaned turret.[4] It was this building that John Verney, writing to Sir Ralph on 6 October 1679, said had fallen down.[5] A new market-house built at the expense of the Abingdon family in 1684 stood on large stones embedded in the ground which supported oak pillars.[6] About 1850 the building was repaired and improved and was used for the monthly Petty Sessions.[7] As it accommodated barely 80 people it was replaced in 1888 by the present Town Hall.[8]

The old Vicarage, where Anthony Wood boarded as a schoolboy, lay near the site of the present Vicarage, but closer to the road. It was replaced in 1842,[9] but 19th-century prints show it as a two-story house of two builds with picturesque gables and timber-framing.[10] It was assessed on four hearths in 1665.[11] The 16th-century fireplace in the hall of the present Vicarage may have come from the old house.

The Court House, said to have contained early Tudor timbering and oak panelling, stood, until 1891, at the east angle of the churchyard and Church Row.[12] This was the manor-house of Old Thame and presumably replaced the 'Hall' of the Bishop of Lincoln, which was the administrative centre of his demesne in the early Middle Ages. Bishop Hugh de Welles was granted 30 pieces of timber in 1219 for making it, and one of the services of the bishop's villeins in the 13th century was to carry timber to his 'hall and grange'.[13] The bishop's courts were held there: Court Close is still the name of a field to the south of the church, and the large barn, standing on

[92] Leland, *Itin.* ed. Toulmin Smith, i. 115; Camden, *Britannia* (1695), 263; and see below, p. 217.
[93] Char. Com. file 70169; and see below, p. 217.
[94] See plate facing p. 166.
[95] J. H. Brown, *Short History of Thame School*, 29.
[96] Ibid. 36. For views of the school see plate facing p. 166 and MS. Top. Oxon. a 69, no. 555; ibid. a 42, p. 44. For a description see *Sale cat.* 1876 (MS. Top. Oxon. c 3, p. 369) and accounts in Brown and Guest, *Thame*, 90–93; Lupton, *Thame*, 112–15; *V.C.H. Oxon.* i. 475–6.
[97] Brown, *Thame School*, 81–82, 102–3.
[98] Wood, *Life*, i. 409.
[99] *Some account of Lord Williams* . . . (Thame 1873), 54, 108.
[1] Lupton, *Thame*, 113; and inf. Messrs. Pursers.
[2] Lee, *Thame*, 497 n.
[3] For deeds (1714–1811) of the 'Rising Sun' see d.d.

[4] See plate facing p. 178.
[5] Hist. MSS. Com. *7th Rep. App. I*, 476.
[6] Brown and Guest, *Thame*, 232; Lupton, *Thame*, 10. See above, frontispiece.
[7] Lupton, *Thame*, 10; Billing, *Dir. Oxon.* (1854).
[8] Lupton, *Thame*, 10; Brown and Guest, *Thame*, 232.
[9] For the new Vicarage, see below, p. 205.
[10] For 19th-cent. views see Lee, *Thame*, facing p. 632; MS. Top. Oxon. c 3, p. 97; ibid. a 112, pp. 43, 97. There is a plan in ibid. d 41, f. 415. See also plate facing p. 158.
[11] *Hearth Tax Oxon.* 43.
[12] Brown and Guest, *Thame*, 13.
[13] *Rot. Litt. Claus* (Rec. Com.), i. 399; Queen's Coll. MS. 366, f. 24; *Bill for settling part of the estates of Robert Barry, &c. . . . 1699* (a copy is Bodl. G.A. Oxon. c 197).

For Hall's Brewery c 39. For the 'Swan', see below, p. 184.

Lord Williams's Grammar School in 1822

Lord Williams's Almshouses in 1821

THAME

Before restoration in 1837

As restored by Charles Stone in 1837

THAME. THE PREBENDAL HOUSE AND CHAPEL

the opposite side of the road and now called Church Barn, was in the 15th and 16th centuries called Court Barn.[14] When the Wrays had the lordship in the 17th century Edward Wray leased in 1626 the manor-house to Vincent Barry, his steward,[15] and it was from the Barrys' house that Anthony Wood watched the royalist attack on Thame in 1645.[16] The capital messuage and Court Close were leased to Robert Barry in 1691.[17] The barn is a long low building with a brick base supporting a timber-framed upper part with herring-bone brick filling. A dove-cot of brick with a hipped roof also remains. It adjoins the churchyard, and was ordered to be rebuilt in 1526 when leased by the bishop to Richard Rey.[18]

The most important lay house in Thame in the Middle Ages was almost certainly the 'Place House'. It was the manor-house of Baldington manor, and belonged first to the Baldingtons and then to the Dormers.[19] It lay in Friday Street (i.e. North Street) on the east side and at the High Street end in Lee's Close.[20] In 1473 Geoffrey Dormer, senior, acquired it from Thomas Baldington's daughter and apparently used it as one of his residences until 1498 when he leased it to John Hall for life.[21] In 1484 it was described as having glazed and latticed windows, all shuttered.[22] The arms of the Mercers' Company are said to have been in the window of the house and were perhaps placed there in the time of Geoffrey's son Sir Michael, who was a London mercer.[23] In 1592, when John Dormer leased it to John Symeon (d. 1619) of Pyrton, it was occupied by a yeoman farmer,[24] and in 1611 was described as 'lately his [Dormer's] dwelling house'.[25]

A fifth house, once the 'Mansion House' of the Knollys family in the High Street, has been largely destroyed. It was erected at the close of the 16th century by Sir Francis Knollys (d. 1629), and was later rebuilt and inhabited by Francis Knollys, M.P. (d. 1757), and by Sir Francis Knollys, Bt., M.P. (d. 1772). In the 19th century it was used as a school.[26]

Priestend at the west end of the High Street also still has a number of ancient houses including Castle's Farm, a 16th-century timber-framed building of lath and plaster with a central chimney; some 16th-century cottages that retain in their cruck construction the remains of earlier cottages; and the oldest of all Thame's houses, the Prebendal. The earliest reference to the prebendary's house occurs in 1234 when Ralph de Wareville, Canon of Lincoln, received a royal grant of wood for his house in Thame.[27] The existing chapel must have been built at about that date: it has two lancets in the north and south walls and one at the west end. The east window is a triple lancet with moulded rear arches supported by detached shafts with foliated capitals. The chapel has an undercroft. The original stone house was built round a quadrangular courtyard.[28] The dormitory and undercroft still adjoining the chapel extend almost the full length of the south range; the original 13th-century hall, now destroyed, lay on the east side of the quadrangle with the chapel projecting eastwards from its south-east corner. The building seems to have been used as a great chamber when a new hall with a porch to the north of this building and a two-storied block still farther to the north were built in the 15th century.[29] The north-western range of buildings dates from the 14th century and the whole of the former western range no longer exists. The rebuilding may have followed on the inspection made by the proctor of Nicholas, Cardinal Prebendary of Thame, who was appointed in 1380 to survey and repair the houses and the property of the prebend lately held by a rebel cardinal.[30] When the prebend was dissolved the house passed with the part of the prebend known as the rectory to the Thynne family and was ultimately sold to Baroness Wenman. Anthony Wood noted that the hall and chapel were standing in 1661, but were in ruins and that there were the ruins of other rooms half round the quadrangle.[31] Early 19th-century drawings show that the place was being used as a farmhouse.[32] In 1836 Charles Stone of Thame bought the building from Baroness Wenman, and converted it into a dwelling-house by dividing the great hall into two floors and small rooms. His architect was H. B. Hodson.[33] Since then the house had been continuously used as a private dwelling and has been carefully restored. The chapel was first restored by Col. Harman Grisewood and W. W. Seymour in about 1912.[34] The restoration of the chapel has been completed by Mr. and Mrs. H. G. Keppel-Palmer, who have also modernized the house and at the same time restored many of its ancient features. Professor Dickie of Manchester University supervised these alterations in 1938–9. The 19th-century ceiling of the hall was removed and a 16th-century roof of carved oak from Essex has been inserted at a height of 17 to 18 ft. The remains of the moat, which once surrounded the house on three sides, the river being on the fourth side, have been filled in.[35]

In its present form the house is L-shaped and of two stories with an irregular east front. The 15th-century hall is to the left of the projecting entrance porch. It is lighted by two tall mullioned and transomed two-light windows with cusped heads. There is a two-light window with stone mullions and cusped heads to the lights on the first floor. The gabled

[14] d.d. Bertie c 16 (uncat.): receipts of guild of St. Christopher, 1550.
[15] *Bill for settling . . . estates of Robert Barry, etc. . . . 1699.*
[16] Wood, *Life*, i. 122; C.P. 25(2)/473/Trin. 2 Chas. I.
[17] See *Bill for settling . . . estates of Robert Barry . . . 1699.*
[18] See also *Country Life*, 21 Nov. 1952, p. 1659; *Linc. Chap. Acts 1520–36* (L.R.S. xii), 72–73.
[19] See below, p. 172.
[20] Brown and Guest, *Thame*, 48.
[21] Rousham Arch. N 382*.
[22] Ibid. N 437.
[23] MS. Top. Oxon. d 88, f. 112. Elizabeth, widow of William Dormer, and her second husband Hugh Hollinshed lived there in 1566: Rousham Arch. N 430.
[24] Rousham Arch. N 447; C 142/372/162.
[25] Rousham Arch. N 458.
[26] See below, p. 216.

[27] *Close R.* 1231–4, 490, 492.
[28] *Archaeol. Jnl.* (1910), lxvii. 367.
[29] For chapel see O.A.H.S. *Proc.* v (1886), 36. For a case about the house between the Prebendary, Adrian de Bardis, and others in the reign of Henry VII, see C.P. 40/897.
[30] *Cal. Pat.* 1377–81, 582.
[31] Wood, *Life*, i. 409. In 1553 it had been occupied by a Robert Cope: d.d. Bertie b 6 (uncat.).
[32] e.g. MS. Top. Oxon. a 69, no. 558; a 39, ff. 136–44; a 42, ff. 42, 45; and see plate opposite.
[33] Caption to lithograph (1850) in MS. Top. Oxon. a 39, pp. 137b, 138b; d.d. Hobbs c 24 (uncat.): additional abstract of title; cf. c 25 (uncat.).
[34] Inf. Mr. Harman Grisewood.
[35] Inf. Mrs. Keppel-Palmer, The Prebendal, Thame. The chapel was rehallowed in 1955 by the Bishop of Dorchester and is sometimes used for Communion.

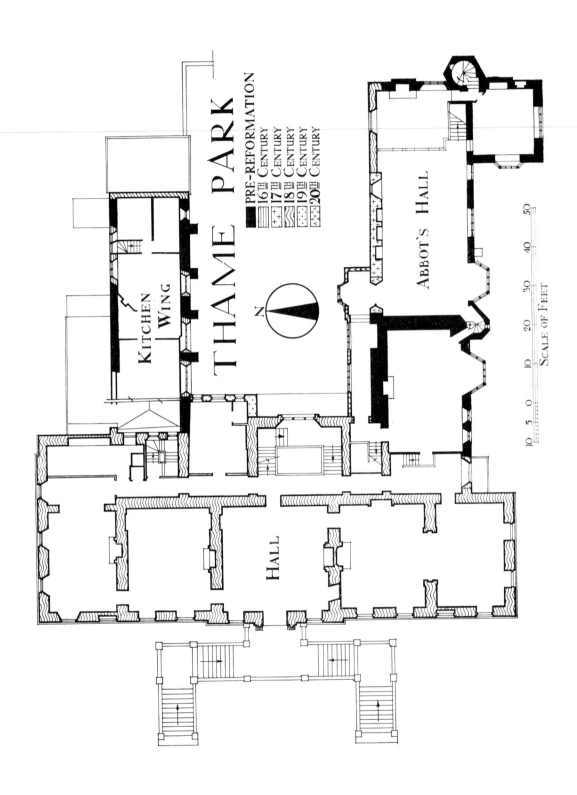

THAME PARK

PRE-REFORMATION
16TH CENTURY
17TH CENTURY
18TH CENTURY
19TH CENTURY
20TH CENTURY

N

KITCHEN WING

ABBOT'S HALL

HALL

SCALE OF FEET

10 5 0 10 20 30 40 50

extension to the right of the porch contains a tall similar two-light window on the first floor and a later (probably 16th-century) three-light window on the ground floor with three-centred heads to the lights. The present tracery has been added at a later date, for a print of 1837 shows the house with mullioned windows and plain lights.[36] All the windows have drip moulds. The roof rests on a stone corbel table dating from the 15th century. It used to be part tiles and part thatch before the 19th-century restorations.[37] The joining wall shown in 19th-century drawings was probably used for rebuilding the house in the 1870 restoration. It was built up again on the old foundations by Mrs. Keppel-Palmer.

Outside the town, in the hamlets, the chief ancient building is Thame Park, the site of Thame Abbey. Except for the abbot's lodgings, which were built early in the 16th century, and the 13th-century range to the north, nothing now remains of the monastic buildings or of the abbey church. The buildings appear to have been in a bad state of repair early in the 16th century, 'in ruins' according to Bishop Longland,[38] and on the dissolution of the monastery the greater part of them including the abbey church were apparently either pulled down or used as farm buildings. In about 1840 the site was examined by William Twopenny, who made drawings. He calculated that the church had been 230 ft. long by 70 ft., and that it had a Lady chapel extending a further 45 ft. at the east end. The bases of fourteen piers of the nave, seven on either side, were still visible. There were traces of a detached rectangular building on the south, which he supposed might have been the chapter house, and also traces of other monastic offices.[39] A report made about 1507 by William Wood, a monk of Thame, to Pope Julius II corroborates Twopenny's calculations of the size of the church. He said that the abbeys of Furness and Thame were of almost equal dimensions.[40]

The original church was consecrated in 1145 and the building was presumably begun about 1140.[41] Fragments of the old building, however, found in walls in the 19th century all had Early-English mouldings, and a stone lavatory with Early-English carving of birds and flowers existed in 1841.[42] Such documentary evidence as there is supports the view that the chancel at least was rebuilt in the early 13th century. In 1232 Henry III gave the monastery timber for making the stalls of the choir, and in 1236 30 oaks to make a kiln in order to rebuild the chancel which had fallen down.[43]

When the Wenmans obtained the site of Thame monastery,[44] they preserved the abbot's lodgings and part of the monastic buildings. The lodgings, which form the south front of the present house, were built at three separate dates and are an 'excellent' specimen of the late phases of domestic Gothic. The earliest part of the range dates perhaps from about 1500 and comprises a small upper and lower hall

with bay windows at the east end; an extension was added later, embodying a larger hall, on the ground floor, of five bays with an upper hall and a second room beyond. Lastly, a low tower of three stories in height covering the original external south door was built after 1530 when Robert King became abbot. The second building has a large south oriel and a projecting stair. The stone entrance door has a four-centred arch within a square frame. The whole range was formerly covered with stone slats. The western upper apartment has a late 16th-century stone fireplace, but the moulded beams are early 16th century and may have been put in in Abbot Warren's time (d. 1529). The parlour on the first floor of the tower retains its original linen-fold panelling with an internal porch and carved wooden frieze showing Italian influence.[45] On the ceiling of the ground floor room are the arms of numerous benefactors of the abbey. The kitchen wing to the north is older than the Tudor wing. The sixth Lord Wenman pulled down part of the old abbey in 1745 and added a Palladian west front: his architect was said by Lee to have been Smith of Coventry, but it seems probable that Smith of Warwick was intended, that is William Smith (1705–47), the son of Francis Smith of Warwick.[46] The architecture is 'simple and restrained'. The reception rooms on the *piano nobile* were probably altered by the last Lady Wenman (d. 1870), who entertained William IV here.[47]

Extensive alterations were made about 1920 by W. H. Gardiner under the supervision of G. Berkeley Wills of London and in accordance with his designs.[48] All the 19th-century decoration, much of it in the style of Louis XV, was removed. Ionic capitals replaced the 'badly modelled' Corinthian ones of the original columns in the dining room.

The Wenmans also preserved as a private chapel a medieval chapel lying to the north-west of their house. It was presumably a chapel built just outside the gates of the abbey for travellers and others. A 19th-century engraving of it by F. Mackenzie shows that it dated from the 14th century.[49] It was then as it is today: a parallelogram in shape with a high-pitched roof, a western bellcote and a west doorway. The building was restored in 1836 by Sophia Baroness Wenman.[50] Lee complained that too many of the ancient characteristics of the chapel were then marred or destroyed. High pews, 'ugly to a degree', a 'cumbersome and vulgar' pulpit and reading pew, and an organ were installed. The floor was laid partly with tiles (some 15th and some 16th century) from the ruins of the abbey. The restoration was begun by 'Mr. Harris' and completed by 'Mr. Abraham'. It seems likely that Harris was Daniel Harris of Oxford and that Abraham was Robert Abraham of London (1774–1850), who had a Roman Catholic connexion.[51] The following monumental inscriptions were recorded by Lee:[52] Thomas Wenman (d. 1665), eldest son of Sir Francis Wenman, Bt.,

[36] See plate facing p. 167.
[37] See drawings cited above in n. 32.
[38] *V.C.H. Oxon.* ii. 85.
[39] Article by F. G. Lee in *Building News*, 30 Mar. 1888, 455.
[40] Ibid.; *Recs. of the Eng. Province*, ed. H. Foley, vi. 546.
[41] *V.C.H. Oxon.* ii. 83; *Country Life*, 17 July 1909, 90.
[42] *Building News*, 30 Mar. 1888, 455 n.
[43] *Close R.* 1231–4, 38; 1234–7, 245.
[44] See below, p. 177.
[45] For accounts of the building see *Country Life*, 17 July 1909, 90; T. Garner and A. Stratton, *The Domestic Archi-*

tecture of England during the Tudor Period, ii. 201–2. For a plan of the Tudor part see W. H. Godfrey in *Archaeol. Jnl.* 1929, lxxxvi. 59.
[46] For the Smiths see H. M. Colvin, *Biographical Dictionary of English Architects*, 556–7.
[47] For Sophia Elizabeth Baroness Wenman see *D.N.B.*
[48] *Architect. Rev.* 1922, li. 17–19. This includes a plan and photographs.   [49] See plate facing p. 171.
[50] For a critical account of the restoration see F. G. Lee in *Blding. News*, 30 Mar. 1888, 457.
[51] Colvin, *Biog. Dict.* 27, 266; Lee, *Thame*, 456 n., 457.
[52] Lee, *Thame*, 398–400.

Seymour Wroughton (d. 1736), Philip, 6th Viscount Wenman (d. 1760), Sophia Viscountess Wenman (d. 1787), who was interred in an open vault in a small projecting sanctuary at the east end, Father Bernard Stafford (d. 1788), Philip, 7th Viscount Wenman of Tuam and Baron Tuam (d. 1800), by Westmacott, and Sophia Elizabeth Baroness Wenman of Thame Park (d. 1870). Lupton records a memorial in the chapel-yard to the Countess de Roubion (d. 1854).[53]

At the hamlet of North Weston, now consisting only of the Manor Farm and a few cottages, the chief house of interest was once the manor-house, which was largely pulled down in the early 19th century.[54] In the 14th century it was the home of the Quatremains and was called Quatremains Place,[55] and after it had passed to the Clerkes it was probably rebuilt by Sir John Clerke out of the proceeds of the ransom of the Duke de Longueville, whom he had captured at the Battle of the Spurs.[56] A sketch of the old house shows that it was a picturesque two-storied and gabled building, composed of a central range of rooms and two projecting wings at each end.[57] It was taxed on sixteen hearths in 1665.[58] Lupton, writing in the mid-19th century, says that he saw a beam taken from the hall on which was cut the date 1527.[59] The present farmhouse and outbuildings represent part of the east wing and the kitchen offices of the old house. The house is built partly of brick and rubble, partly of timber, and has a massive outside chimney stack with brick chimney shafts set diagonally.

The red-brick walling of an 18th-century garden also survives. The end facing south is rounded and contains a stone alcove with Ionic columns and a pediment above with the arms of Clerke.[60] A medieval chapel lying to the west of the house was pulled down about 1810 or 1820.[61] The date of its construction is unknown, but a new window had been inserted towards the end of the 14th century when Guy Quatremain was baptized. The baptism took place before his father's death in 1399.[62] The chapel was used for a baptismal service as late as 1750 and in the mid-19th century the pillars of the nave were still to be seen supporting the roof of a cart-shed.[63]

Moreton lies on the Cuttle Brook and is still a sizeable village with a number of ancient cottages and farmhouses, as well as a 19th-century Primitive Methodist chapel, a former National school, and a number of 20th-century council houses.[64] Its appearance was completely altered by the inclosure award. The large green in the south-west was inclosed and though some of the oldest houses are still in this area, the modern village has spread north-eastward. An older part of the village where there are timber-framed and thatched cottages is grouped round a small green to the north-east of the old one. Moreton never had a manor-house or a church.

No trace has been found of the medieval village of Attington, *Eatta's* hill,[65] but it is probable that it lay on the Thame road over 300 ft. up and where the ordnance survey map of 1885 marked a well.[66] This position would agree with the references to the village and various adjoining closes in a mid-15th-century terrier: 'South Close' lay between Attington and Copcourt, 'West Close' between the west end of the village and London Way towards Tetsworth, and 'North Close' lay between Attington and Horsenden Hill.[67]

By the time of the hearth tax of 1665 only Dormer Leys farmhouse in the north-west of the parish was listed, and Davis's map of 1797 shows only this house and the house later called Attington House, in the south-west of the parish.[68] Attington House is a two-storied building with attics of 18th-century date. It is built partly of brick and partly of ragstone with brick quoins and dressings. It has two hipped dormers and a tiled roof.

MANORS.[69] In the Anglo-Saxon period *THAME* was among the endowments of the bishopric of Dorchester, and with the bishop's other demesne manors in Oxfordshire—Banbury, Cropredy, Dorchester, and Great Milton—formed 'a great episcopal estate of immemorial antiquity'.[70] However, the earliest specific evidence for the connexion between Thame and the bishop is the death of Oscytel, Bishop of Dorchester and later Archbishop of York, at Thame in 971.[71] When in 1070 it was decided to move the See of Dorchester to Lincoln,[72] its possessions were transferred to the Bishop of Lincoln, who in 1086 was holding Thame of the king.[73] The manor then consisted of 60 hides, of which the bishop held 37 and his knights 23 hides. The 37 hides held by the bishop represented not only Thame itself, but the bishop's demesne lands in Moreton, North Weston, and Tetsworth, while the 23 hides held by his knights represented land in Attington and Moreton, North Weston, Tetsworth, and possibly Waterstock.

From 1126 onwards Honorius II and successive popes confirmed to the bishops their lands at Thame with its liberties and appurtenances,[74] and Henry II granted to Bishop Robert de Chesney free warren there, as his predecessors had had it in the time of Henry I.[75]

The demesne manor, consisting of Old Thame and the town of New Thame, with lands in Moreton, North Weston, and Tetsworth,[76] was kept in the bishop's hands throughout the Middle Ages. In 1279 he was returned as holding the hundred and the manor (which included its subinfeudated parts) of the

[53] Lupton, *Thame*, 57.
[54] Ibid. For the decline of the hamlet see below, p. 190. There are air photographs of the site at the Ashmolean Museum (Dr. St. Joseph's Collection).
[55] C 137/71/70; see below, p. 173.
[56] See below, p. 173.
[57] See plate opposite.
[58] *Hearth Tax Oxon.* 48.
[59] Lupton, *Thame*, 105.
[60] See plate opposite.
[61] Ibid. Gardner, *Dir. Oxon.* (1852).
[62] MS. Top. Oxon. c 3, pp. 425*b*–6.
[63] Lupton, *Thame*, 105.
[64] O.S. Map 25", xli. 2; and map, p. 189.
[65] For its decline see below, p. 190.

[66] O.S. Map 6", xli.
[67] *Thame Cart.* ii. 174, 179, 183.
[68] *Oxon. Hearth Tax*, 52.
[69] The history of the manors in Thame is based on notes made by J. Grassi and W. Guest.
[70] F. M. Stenton, *Anglo-Saxon England* (1947), 432; see also *V.C.H. Oxon.* i. 378.
[71] *Anglo-Saxon Chron.* ed. G. N. Garmonsway (1953), 119.
[72] *V.C.H. Oxon.* ii. 4.
[73] Ibid. i. 402, 403. For the components of the manor see above, pp. 114, 148; below, pp. 172, 174.
[74] *Reg. Antiquiss.* i. 188–9, 191, 194, 196, 203.
[75] Ibid. 69.
[76] For these demesnes see pp. 152, 174, 176.

The Former 16th-century Manor-house

The 18th-century Garden-house at North Weston Manor, showing the arms of Clerke

NORTH WESTON

The medieval Chapel of Thame Abbey and the 18th-century front of Thame Park in 1823

The Church from the north-east in 1821 before the 19th-century restorations

THAME

barony of Banbury for the service of 5 fees,[77] and in 1316 he was described as lord of Old and New Thame.[78] In the early Middle Ages, during a vacancy of the see, the possessions of the bishopric came into the king's hands. The long vacancy between 1166 and 1183 explains the fact that in 1182 the episcopal manors, including Thame, were held by the king.[79] Because Hugh de Welles, although consecrated in 1209, did not receive the temporalties of his see until 1213, Thame is again listed in about 1212 as in the king's hands.[80] In the early 14th century the policy changed, for the Dean and Chapter of Lincoln bought from Edward II for £1,000 the right of having the custody of the possessions of the see during a vacancy,[81] and from that time Thame, like the other episcopal manors, was evidently administered by the chapter between the death of a bishop and the accession of his successor.

In 1547 Henry Holbeach, soon after being translated to Lincoln, sold for 'certain great sums of money' to Protector Somerset the greater part of the possessions of his see, probably as the price of the bishopric. Included in the sale was the valuable Thame manor, including the bishop's lands in Moreton, North Weston, and Tetsworth,[82] which had been assessed at £71 10s. 2¾d. in 1535.[83] By 1550 Somerset had transferred it to Sir John Williams,[84] who at about the same time acquired the site and lands of Thame Abbey.

Williams, a younger son of Sir John Williams of Burghfield (Berks.), was from about 1530 a royal official who built up a large estate from monastic lands. In 1554 he was created Lord Williams of Thame by Queen Mary.[85] He lived at Rycote in the neighbouring parish of Great Haseley and had many associations with Thame.[86] By his first wife Elizabeth, granddaughter of Thomas Bledlowe, a London grocer and alderman,[87] Lord Williams had three sons, who died in their father's lifetime, and two daughters, Isabella, the wife of Richard Wenman, and Margaret, the wife of Henry Norreys (later Lord Norreys),[88] who became their father's heirs on his death in 1559. As far as the property in Thame was concerned, the land which had belonged to the bishop descended to the Norreys family, while that which had belonged to Thame Abbey went to the Wenmans.[89]

The bishop's manor after the Reformation was sometimes described as New and Old Thame manor, and sometimes considered as two manors, *NEW THAME* and *OLD THAME*.[90] Norreys died in

1601 and the manor passed to his descendants.[91] James Bertie, Lord Norreys, who inherited in 1666,[92] was created Earl of Abingdon in 1682 and was followed in 1699 by his son Montagu, who died childless in 1743.[93]

In the 17th century the manor-house and demesne lands of Old Thame manor were leased to the Barry family. Vincent Barry, the son of Francis Barry of Thame and the nephew of Vincent Barry of Hampton Gay, who may have first acquired the lease from the Wrays in 1626,[94] was a J.P. and a prominent Thame resident. He died in 1666,[95] leaving a son Vincent (d. 1680), who in 1657 had obtained the lease for 99 years at £20 a year.[96] Vincent's eldest son Vincent inherited Hampton Gay,[97] but the lease of Thame went to another son Robert, later Vicar of Northfleet (Kent), who in 1706 sold part of the estate to pay his debts.[98] Thereafter the family disappears from Thame.

Montagu Bertie was followed as lord of Old and New Thame by his nephew Willoughby Bertie (d. 1780); by his son Willoughby Bertie, the 4th earl (d. 1799), and then by his grandson Montagu, the 5th earl (d. 1854). The latter in 1844 offered for sale his property in Thame parish, including the manors of Old Thame, New Thame, Priestend, and North Weston, with nearly 2,400 acres of land.[99] Priestend was successfully sold, but not the Thame manors, for the earls of Abingdon continued to be lords of the manor and the chief landowners.[1]

On the death of Montagu, the 6th earl, in 1884, his Thame property passed to his younger son, Francis Leveson Bertie, a distinguished diplomat, who was created Viscount Bertie of Thame in 1918.[2] On his death in 1919 he was succeeded by his son Vere Frederick, the 2nd viscount, who lived at Shirburn Lodge and died in 1954, when the title became extinct.[3]

PRIESTEND, a separate part of Thame, had its own field system, and there presumably lay the property of the prebendaries during the Middle Ages.[4] In the mid-16th century other property there passed to William, Lord Windsor, who held courts for Priestend manor, as it was then called. The manor was still held in 1573 by his son Edward, Lord Windsor, who had succeeded in 1558,[5] but it appears to have been held by the Norreys family by about 1600.[6] It descended to them and their heirs, the earls of Abingdon, with the main manor of Thame, but remained a separate manor with its own courts and tenants.[7] In 1844 the Earl of Abingdon sold his

[77] *Rot. Hund.* (Rec. Com.) ii. 820.
[78] *Feud. Aids*, iv. 167.
[79] *Pipe R.* 1182 (P.R.S. xxxi), 59.
[80] *Bk. of Fees*, 40. For this vacancy see *V.C.H. Lincs.* ii. 21.
[81] *Cal. Pat.* 1361–4, 350.
[82] *Linc. Chapter Acts, 1536–47* (L.R.S. xiii), 150–3; *Cal. Pat.* 1547–8, 184; E 210/D 10440.
[83] *Valor Eccl.* (Rec. Com.), iv. 1.
[84] *Cal. Pat.* 1549–51, 427.
[85] For him see *D.N.B.*; Lee, *Thame*, 415 sqq.
[86] See below, pp. 204, 215, 217.
[87] For him see A. B. Beaven, *London Aldermen*, ii. 14.
[88] C 142/126/150. His will is printed in *Acct. of Lord Williams . . . with his will* (Thame, 1873): copy in Bodl. G.A. Oxon. 80958.
[89] C.P. 25(2)/259/East. 3 Eliz.; see below, p. 177.
[90] C.P. 25(2)/198/Mich. 44 & 45 Eliz. For whether it was one or two manors see MS. Top. Oxon. c 381, f. 79; d.d. Bertie b 1, pp. 261, 337.
[91] C 142/399/153. The manor followed the descent of Dorchester manor until 1876: see above, p. 42 and C.P.

[91] 25(2)/387/East.'21 Jas. I; ibid. 526/Hil. 4 Chas. I; Bodl. MS. Top. gen. c 44, f. 44. [92] d.d. Bertie b 3.
[93] For Earls of Abingdon see *Complete Peerage*, i. 45 sqq.
[94] C.P. 25(2)/473/Trin. 2 Chas. I. For pedigree see *Visit. Oxon.* 326; Wood, *Life*, ii. 481. He acted as steward of the courts of the main manor: d.d. Bertie b 3.
[95] Wood, *Life*, ii. 81; M.I. in Lee, *Thame*, 115.
[96] C 78/1305/6. [97] *V.C.H. Oxon.* vi. 155.
[98] *Bill for settling estate of Robert Barry, 4 & 5 Anne*, c. 60 (priv. act): copy in Bodl. G.A. Oxon. c 197. He had obtained a 99-year lease from the Earl of Abingdon in 1699 on payment of a £400 fine. For Barry see Foster, *Alumni*.
[99] Bodl. G.A. Oxon. b 92(21): *Sale cat.*
[1] Gardner, *Dir. Oxon.* (1852); Kelly, *Dir. Oxon.* (1887).
[2] Kelly, *Dir. Oxon.* (1903). For him see *Complete Peerage*, xiii. 203 and E. Gaskell, *Oxon. Leaders* (priv. printed, c. 1907).
[3] Kelly, *Dir. Oxon.* (1939); *The Times*, 31 Aug. 1954, p. 8. [4] See above, p. 162; and below, p. 199.
[5] C 3/2/203/4.
[6] C.P. 25(2)/198/Mich. 44 & 45 Eliz.
[7] d.d. Bertie c 16, b 1; MS. Top. Oxon. c 381, f. 66.

Priestend manor, with over 700 acres of land, to William Keppel, Viscount Barrington, and Joseph Henley of Waterperry.[8] No later record has been found of the manor, but by the 1880's the Earl of Abingdon was again the chief landowner in Priestend.[9]

From at least 1577 the Wenmans also held an estate in Priestend which is listed among their lands as a manor until the late 17th century.[10] After this it disappears.

The first mention of *BALDINGTON'S* or *BALDINGTON* manor in Thame occurs in 1419. It was then held of the Bishop of Lincoln,[11] and probably continued to be,[12] although the overlordship is not mentioned after the middle of the century. The manor-house and probably much of the land belonging to the manor lay in Old Thame, but there were appurtenances in New Thame, Moreton, and North Weston.[13] Land in other parishes—Great Milton, Denton in Cuddesdon, Garsington, and Toot Baldon —which were held by William Baldington in 1419[14] were said later in the century to form part of the manor, as was also land in Long Crendon and Ickford (Bucks.).[15] In the late 16th century the manor still included appurtenances in New Thame, Moreton, and Priestend, but not land outside the parish.[16]

John Baldington of Thame, probably a member of the family which had held Little Baldon in the 13th century,[17] was an important man who often served on commissions of the peace.[18] He acquired Albury manor,[19] and may have been the first of his family to own Thame property. His son William, who lived at Albury,[20] died in 1419 holding Baldington's manor.[21] His heir was his son Thomas. He left a widow Agnes, the daughter of John Danvers by his first wife and therefore a half-sister of Sir Thomas Danvers of Waterstock, and three young daughters, Agnes, Alice, and Isabella.[22] Thomas's widow, who married as her second husband Sir John Fray (d. 1461), probably held the manor until 1454, when she granted it to her two elder daughters.[23] By that time Isabella was dead; Agnes, the wife of William Brome of Holton, received Albury as her inheritance;[24] and Baldington was evidently Alice's share of her father's lands. She was already the widow of John Wakehurst and in 1473 she and her second husband,

Henry Tracy of Toddington (Gloucs.),[25] sold the manor to Geoffrey Dormer for £313 13s. 4d.; he was, however, to pay them a yearly rent of £9 14s. less 3s. 4d. for the steward who held the courts.[26]

Dormer, a merchant of the Calais Staple, was an important man in Thame.[27] He died in 1503, but in 1498 he had settled Baldington on his son Geoffrey,[28] who also lived in Thame and was probably the Master Dormer who was buried there in 1537.[29] The younger Geoffrey left no children, so his heir was his younger brother Sir Michael Dormer, a London mercer and in 1541 Lord Mayor of London.[30] The latter bought up much property in Oxfordshire and Buckinghamshire. Some of his manors he left to his elder sons,[31] but Baldington, Attington, and Dorton (Bucks.) he settled on a younger son William and his wife Elizabeth.[32] William Dormer, Old Thame's richest inhabitant,[33] used Attington and Dorton to obtain ready money,[34] and in 1560, in return for £450, he granted Thomas Sackville (later Earl of Dorset) a yearly annuity of £53 6s. 8d. out of Baldington.[35] Before his death in 1563 he settled the manor for life on his wife Elizabeth and then on his son John.[36]

Dormer's widow married as her second husband Hugh Hollinshead of Thame and in 1566 they were able to reclaim from Sackville all his rights in Baldington.[37] She was probably dead by 1584 when her son John, who lived at Dorton and was to become a prominent Buckinghamshire knight, was in possession of Baldington.[38] In 1586 he settled the manor on his wife Jane, the daughter of John Giffard of Chillington (Staffs.).[39] No mention has been found of the manor after 1586 and it is probable that some of the lands were sold. Sir John Dormer's heirs, the Dormers of Ascot, and their successors, the Dormers of Rousham, held land in Thame until at least the early 18th century.[40]

In the Middle Ages *NORTH WESTON* fee or manor as it became later, was held of the Bishop of Lincoln as of his manor of Thame.[41] The overlordship was last mentioned in 1625, when the manor was held of Edward Wray and his wife,[42] the lords of Thame manor.

The tenant of the fee in 1086 was a certain William, one of the bishop's knights. His fee con-

[8] Bodl. G.A. Oxon. b 92(21): *Sale cat.*; d.d. Bertie c 5, p. 33; ibid. b 5, declaration of merger.
[9] d.d. Bullingdon c 36, p. 40.
[10] C 142/182/42; C.P. 43/383/254.
[11] C 139/15/22. [12] C 139/80/28.
[13] C.P. 25(1)/191/28/43.
[14] C 139/15/22.
[15] *Cal. Close*, 1468–76, p. 322; Rousham Arch. N 336.
[16] Rousham Arch. N 436.
[17] *V.C.H. Oxon.* v. 51.
[18] *Cal. Pat.* 1381–5, *passim*; for him see also *Cal. Fine R.* 1369–77, 209.
[19] *V.C.H. Oxon.* v. 9.
[20] e.g. Rousham Arch. N 293.
[21] C 139/15/22.
[22] C 139/80/28; ibid. 105/10. For Danvers pedigree see Macnamara, *Danvers Family*, opp. 103. For Agnes's 4 husbands and her monument in Long Melford (Suff.) church see ibid. 143–54.
[23] P.R.O. Harrison, Extracts, vii. 278; C.P. 25(1)/191/28/43.
[24] *V.C.H. Oxon.* v. 10.
[25] For Tracys see S. Rudder, *Gloucs.* (1779), 771.
[26] Rousham Arch. N 337 (also 339); C.P. 25(1)/191/29/16. No later record has been found of the rent. For releases by Agnes Fray and William Tracy, Alice's son, see *Cal. Close*, 1468–76, p. 322; Rousham Arch. N 336, 344, 354.
[27] For pedigree see M. Maclagan, 'Family of Dormer in

Oxon. and Bucks.', *Oxoniensia*, xi–xii, between pp. 98 and 99. Dormer's father is said (ibid. 96) to have married Judith, daughter and heiress of Robert Baldington, lord of Baldington, but no evidence has been found in the Rousham archives for the existence of either Robert or Judith.
[28] Rousham Arch. N 467 (also 382); C.P. 25(1)/191/31/Mich. 14 Hen. VII.
[29] Lee, *Thame*, 521.
[30] For him see A. B. Beaven, *London Aldermen*, ii. 27.
[31] See above, pp. 124, 127; *V.C.H. Bucks.* ii. 275, 300.
[32] Rousham Arch. N 468; *V.C.H. Bucks.* iv. 47.
[33] E 179/161/258. For his part in Lord Williams's funeral see Lee, *Thame*, 428. For his acquisition of Long Crendon manor see *V.C.H. Bucks.* iv. 40. His London connexions are illustrated by, e.g. his mortgaging Baldington to John Peers, a London fishmonger: Rousham Arch. N 426–7, 470, 472–3, 477.
[34] See below, p. 175.
[35] Rousham Arch. N 420 (also 469).
[36] Ibid. 474 (also 476).
[37] Ibid. 430; see also 442.
[38] Ibid. 436, 479, 480; C.P. 43/6/61.
[39] Rousham Arch. N 481. Their tomb is at Long Crendon.
[40] Ibid. N 464, 465.
[41] *Rot. Hund.* (Rec. Com.), ii. 822; *Cal. Inq. p.m. Hen. VII*, iii, pp. 306–7.
[42] C 142/420/89.

sisted of 3 hides in Thame (i.e. North Weston) and 3¾ hides in Great Milton (i.e. Ascot).[43] From at least 1166, when Herbert Quatremain held a fee of the bishop,[44] until the 15th century North Weston and Ascot formed the two halves of the fee known in the 15th century as 'Quatremains manor'.[45] Herbert Quatremain died before September 1200[46] and was followed by his son Herbert, who was listed as one of the bishop's knights in 1201 and still held in about 1230.[47] His son and heir William Quatremain succeeded, but had died by 1279 when his heir William was a minor.[48] Thomas, the son of William II, was returned as lord of (North) Weston and Ascot in 1316. He married Katharine, the daughter of Guy Breton, and both he and his wife died in 1342.[49] The Thomas Quatremain who was in possession in 1346 was their son.[50] He considerably increased the family estates, and numerous properties in Wiltshire and Oxfordshire were recorded in the inquisition on his death in 1398.[51] The family was settled at North Weston.[52] Thomas Quatremain was followed successively by his three sons John (d. 1403), Guy (d. 1414) and Richard, a London merchant, who succeeded at the age of twenty-two.[53] Richard became a man of high standing in the county, being connected by marriage with many of the leading families, representing the county in parliament in 1432 and 1433, and acting as high sheriff in 1436.[54] In the 1450's the family lost Ascot, but Richard Quatremain held North Weston until his death in 1477.[55] He also acquired another property there, called Hall Place, which had once belonged to William Baldington of Thame.[56] Quatremains manor, and probably also Hall Place, were held by Richard's widow Sybil, the heiress of Rycote, until her death in 1483.[57] Since the Quatremains had no children, North Weston had been settled on Richard Fowler and his wife Joan Danvers, who was the granddaughter of Richard Quatremain's sister Maud and John Bruley of Waterstock.[58] Richard Fowler had died in 1477, but Joan lived until 1505, holding at her death the manor and Hall Place.[59] Her heir was her son Sir Richard Fowler, who sold most of his property.[60]

By 1519 John Clerke, to whom Fowler had sold

Shabbington manor (Bucks.),[61] was holding the North Weston manorial courts,[62] and in 1520 or 1521 the manor was conveyed to him.[63] Clerke, a younger son of William Clerke of Willoughby (Warws.), had gained fame and money by taking prisoner Louis, Duke of Longueville, at the Battle of the Spurs in 1513.[64] He died in 1539, leaving a widow Agnes, formerly the wife of Nicholas Pynchon, sheriff of London, and a son Nicholas.[65] In 1542 Agnes and Nicholas, who was in debt to Sir John Williams, leased Shabbington and North Weston to him for 60 years.[66]

In the 1550's, however, Sir John leased the manor back to the Clerkes.[67] Nicholas Clerke died in 1551[68] and was succeeded by a son William, who held North Weston in 1572, probably the year in which he married Margaret, the daughter of Sir John Bourne, Secretary of State to Mary I.[69] On Sir William Clerke's death in 1625 Weston was inherited by his son William,[70] who died childless the next year,[71] and then by a younger son Francis on whom it had been settled.[72] Sir Francis only lived until 1632 and left a young son John,[73] who was made a baronet in 1660 and died in 1667.[74] North Weston was again left to a younger son Francis,[75] M.P. for the county, who died childless in 1715, having put the manor in trust for his nephew Francis Carr Clerke, the son of his brother Richard.[76] The trustees were to choose for Francis a 'sober and discreet' wife, by whose fortune he could clear the estate, for in 1720 unpaid debts and legacies amounting to £6,000 were still owing.

Francis Carr Clerke married Katherine, the daughter of Henry Bertie of Chesterton, who brought him £2,000. Their young son Francis also married a member of a prominent local family, Susannah Ashhurst of Waterstock, but her marriage portion of £1,000 was not large and in 1748 Francis, who had succeeded his father in 1730, began mortgaging North Weston. By 1753, when the mortgage amounted to £9,000, he was forced to sell the estate, thus bringing to an end the family's long connexion with Thame. The manor was sold in 1755 for £31,000 to the Duke of Marlborough,[77] who in 1762

[43] V.C.H. Oxon. i. 403.
[44] Red Bk. Exch. (Rolls Ser.), 375; cf. Fines Oxon. 17.
[45] Cf. above, p. 127.
[46] Cur. Reg. R. i. 204, 244.
[47] Rot. de Ob. et Fin. (Rec. Com.), 154; Queen's Coll. MS. 366, f. 23.
[48] Rot. Hund. (Rec. Com.), ii. 822.
[49] Feud. Aids, iv. 167; brass in church.
[50] Feud. Aids, iv. 187; brass in church.
[51] C 136/106/39.
[52] C 137/170/71; cf. Cal. Close, 1461–8, 143; Carter, Quatremains, 11, 12.
[53] C 137/71/20; C 138/8/32; Carter, Quatremains, 34.
[54] For him see Carter, Quatremains, 29–43.
[55] The conveyance of 1449 to Sir John Fortescue and others is no doubt only a settlement: Cal. Close, 1461–8, 143.
[56] Ibid. where Quatremain is said to have bought it of Abingdon Abbey.   [57] C 141/3/33.
[58] Ibid. For relationship see Carter, op. cit. 58–59.
[59] Cal. Inq. p.m. Hen. VII, iii, pp. 306–7.
[60] A proposed sale by Fowler to John Spencer, to whom the manor had been mortgaged and to whose daughter Fowler's son George, an idiot, was betrothed, came to nothing, although it involved the families in litigation: C 1/310/16; ibid. 487/10. For Fowler pedigree see Lee, Thame, 295.
[61] V.C.H. Bucks. iv. 102–3.
[62] d.d. Bertie c 13.
[63] C.P. 25(2)/34/226/East. 12 Hen. VIII.

[64] Brass in Thame church; for pedigree see Lee, Thame, 310.
[65] C 142/82/123; for his will see Lee, Thame, 321; for Weston manor-house see above, p. 170.
[66] d.d. Bertie b 6, 1542 indenture; C.P. 25(2)/34/229 Mich. 34 Hen. VIII. In his will Lord Williams left the rest of the lease of North Weston to his stepson Christopher Edmonds, who had apparently been living there: Lee, Thame, 307.   [67] Lee, Thame, 307.
[68] V.C.H. Bucks. iii. 232. For the Clerke tombs at Hitcham see Lipscomb, Bucks. iii. 283–5.
[69] C.P. 25(2)/196/Mich. 14 Eliz. (probably a marriage settlement). It is not clear what happened to the manor in the 1550's and 1560's. It seems at one time to have been held by Roger Alford, who married Nicholas Clerke's widow Elizabeth (Lee, Thame, 307).
[70] C 142/420/89. For a 17th- and 18th-cent. pedigree see Lipscomb, Bucks. i. 446–7.
[71] C 142/430/170.
[72] C 142/420/89; see also C.P. 25(2)/526/Hil. 5 Chas. I.
[73] C 142/483/69; see also C.P. 25(2)/474/Mich. 21 Chas. I: John Clerke to John Alford and John White.
[74] G.E.C. Baronetage, iii. 80. For his wife see Lee, Thame, 100, 101.
[75] C.P. 25(2)/865/Hil. 10 Wm. III.
[76] d.d. Bertie b 5, abstract of title, from which most of what follows is taken. The original deeds are ibid. b 7, c 22, d 2.
[77] d.d. Bertie b 5, abstract pp. 31, 37, 40; C.P. 25(2)/1189/Mich. 29 Geo. II.

settled it, together with other Oxfordshire property, on his younger son Lord Charles Spencer.[78] It remained with the Spencers of Wheatfield, until the manor (about 585 a.) was sold in 1836 to the Earl of Abingdon,[79] who already owned some land in North Weston which had been bought by the 1st earl in 1684.[80]

From that time North Weston followed the descent of Thame manor[81] until 1913, when Sir Francis Bertie sold his land there (about 685 a.) and the estate was broken up.[82]

A second estate in Weston, about 9 virgates, was a part of the Bishop of Lincoln's demesne manor of Thame in the Middle Ages.[83] In 1535 the estate, valued at £6 13s. 4d., was farmed to Sir John Clerke of North Weston,[84] and in 1547 Bishop Longland leased 4 yardlands, Bishop's Weir, and some quitrents for 99 years to Sir John Williams, who acquired the rest of the bishop's demesne manor of Thame in the same year.[85]

Until the Reformation Attington and Moreton, whose medieval history was closely connected, were members of the Bishop of Lincoln's manor of Thame.[86] Land in each township formed the two halves of one knight's fee,[87] known in the 13th century as the 'fee of ATTINGTON and MORETON'.[88]

It is probable that the 6 hides belonging to the bishop's knights, Alured and his companion, at the time of Domesday Book lay in Attington and Moreton and represented this fee.[89] In the second quarter of the 12th century Fulk de Fontibus appears to have held it.[90] He had a son and heir Hervey de Fontibus,[91] but a part of his land in Oxfordshire and Leicestershire was left to his two daughters Alice, the wife of Hugh, the Constable of the Bishop of Lincoln,[92] and Parnell, the wife of Hugh de Braimuster. They divided it so that Alice had 'Blaweston', i.e. Blaston (Leics.),[93] and Parnell had 'Attington' (i.e. Attington with part of Moreton).[94]

That this fee was so often described as Attington is probably to be accounted for by the fact that only part of Moreton belonged to the fee; the rest was a part of the bishop's demesne manor.[95]

The de Braimusters were a Norman family, who took their name from Brémoy (Calvados),[96] and held

among other lands in England Bledlow manor (Bucks.), not far distant from Attington. In 1158 Hugh de Braimuster leased Attington to Hervey de Fontibus for six years in return for being made Hervey's heir and for an annual rent of 40s.[97] When Hugh de Braimuster went on pilgrimage to Jerusalem (c. 1160–80), he divided his Norman and his English lands between his sons Hugh and Odo.[98] Hugh, whose interests were probably entirely Norman, granted his share of Attington (and Moreton) to Odo in about 1192, and confirmed the arrangement whereby Odo had granted the estate to Thame Abbey[99] (see below). In 1192 Odo wrote to Bishop Hugh of Lincoln saying that since he had to spend more time in Normandy than in England, the abbey would perform the military service of his fee.[1] He remained in Normandy after King John had lost the duchy to the French,[2] and his Oxfordshire fee, described for the first time as lands in 'Attington and Moreton', was in the meantime returned to the bishop by the king. In 1207 the sheriff was ordered to restore these lands to Odo,[3] who immediately subinfeudated them for £23 6s. 8d. to Henry de Coleville. Henry was to pay 72s. a year to Odo and perform the knight's service.[4] Shortly after (1209–12) Henry was duly returned as one of the bishop's knights and as holder of a fee in Attington (i.e. in Attington and Moreton).[5] He is also recorded as holding the Attington fee in a survey of the bishop's estates made in the second quarter of the 13th century.[6] There can be little doubt that he was the Henry de Coleville who was Sheriff of Cambridgeshire and Huntingdonshire in about 1250,[7] and who died in or before 1256.[8] A Philip de Coleville, one of Edward I's knights, is later found holding land in Cambridgeshire and Huntingdonshire, and had rights in Attington in 1262. It is likely that he was Henry's son.[9] There is no further record of the family's connexion with Attington and the fee must have been taken into the bishop's hands. In the inquest of 1276 it was reported that the bishop had enfeoffed the Abbot of Thame with the fee in Attington and in Moreton. It was alleged that this had been done in prejudice of the king's rights, since the king thereby lost the wardship of the fee.[10] The abbey nevertheless retained the lordship until its dissolution. In 1279 it

[78] d.d. Bertie b 5, abstract pp. 81–82.
[79] See above, p. 171; 5 & 6 Wm. IV, c. 23 (priv. act); d.d. Bertie b 5, 1836 Sale cat.
[80] d.d. Bertie b 5, 1676 indenture.
[81] See above, p. 171.
[82] Bodl. G.A. Oxon. b 92(22): Sale cat.
[83] Rot. Hund. (Rec. Com.), ii. 822.
[84] Valor Eccl. (Rec. Com.), iv. 1.
[85] Linc. Chapter Acts, 1536–47 (L.R.S. xiii), 130, 131; see above, p. 171.
[86] Rot. Hund. (Rec. Com.), ii. 821; C.P. 40/876, m. 444; Valor Eccl. (Rec. Com.), ii. 213.
[87] e.g. Fines Oxon. 39; Rot. Hund. ii. 31.
[88] Thame Cart. i. 59.
[89] V.C.H. Oxon. i. 403. In the 15th cent. Attington had 400 a. of arable land (i.e. about 5 territorial hides).
[90] Thame Cart. i. 54. He appears to have been dead by 1158: ibid. 53.   [91] Ibid. 53.
[92] For Hugh the Constable as witness see Reg. Antiquiss. ii. 17; iii. 263.
[93] For the identification of 'Blaweston' see Red. Bk. Exch. (Rolls Ser.), 587; Nichols, Leics. ii. 445; for the form of the name, V.C.H. Leics. i. 308.
[94] Thame Cart. i. 54. As Attington was worth less than Blaston it was arranged that part of Blaston should be added to it to equalize the shares.
[95] See above, p. 170 and below, p. 187. That the Attington fee at this date included part of Moreton is demonstrated

by the fact that Geoffrey de Moreton, tenant of a Moreton estate, is described in about 1150 as Hugh de Braimuster's man. [The charters make it clear, moreover, that Moreton land was at one time part of the inheritance of both Alice and Parnell, and it was presumably because of Alice's one time rights that her husband confirmed the grant of 1½ hide in Moreton to Thame Abbey made by Hugh de Braimuster's man: Thame Cart. i. 43, 44.]
[96] It was called Brémoest in the 14th cent.: C. Hippeau, Dictionnaire Topographique du Calvados (Paris, 1883). For the family's connexion with Bledlow see V.C.H. Bucks. ii. 248.
[97] Thame Cart. i. 53–54.
[98] Ibid. 53.
[99] Ibid. 58.   [1] Ibid.
[2] Rot. Norm. (Rec. Com.), 142; Rot. Lit. Claus. (Rec. Com.), i. 79b.
[3] For him see also Reg. Antiquiss. ii. index; Pat. R. 1216–25, 71, 81, 127.
[4] Fines Oxon. 39.
[5] Bk. of Fees, 40.
[6] Queen's Coll. MS. 366, f. 23; and see above, p. 13, n. 94.
[7] Cal. Pat. 1247–58, 42.
[8] Close R. 1254–6, 258.
[9] Fines Oxon. 189. For family see Knights of Edward I (Harl. Soc. lxxx), 223–4.
[10] Rot. Hund. (Rec. Com.), ii. 31.

was said to hold it of the bishop by scutage,[11] but by 1346 it was holding in free alms.[12]

At the end of the 12th century Thame Abbey was the demesne tenant of that part of Attington which was known as *ATTINGTON ABBOT* in the 16th century. In 1192 Odo de Braimuster granted the abbey for 40s. a year, the half of Attington which his brother Hugh had held.[13] In 1207 the abbey's share was reckoned as ¼-fee.[14] When Attington was granted to Henry de Coleville the abbey's rent of 40s. and its foreign service were transferred to the new lord. When the De Coleville mesne tenancy ended in the second half of the 13th century the abbey held this ¼-fee directly of the bishop.[15]

After the dissolution of the abbey in 1539 Attington Abbot was acquired by Lord Williams of Thame and like the abbey's other lands was inherited by his daughter Isabella Wenman[16] and followed the descent of Thame Park.[17] Manorial rights may have survived into the 19th century, for in about 1830 Miss Wykeham was known as lady of the manor,[18] but they were not mentioned when the estate was sold in 1917, and had presumably lapsed.[19]

The demesne tenant of the other ¼-fee in Attington, later known as *ATTINGTON* manor, at the beginning of the 13th century was Richard de Turri, for several years under-sheriff of Oxfordshire and a bailiff of the Earl of Cornwall.[20] He paid a rent of 33s. 4d. and performed the foreign service.[21] It is probable that the John de Turri who granted a rent in Attington to Thame Abbey in the 1180's was his father and was already tenant of the ¼-fee.[22] The De Turris' holding appears to have passed by marriage to the De Hampden family, lords of Great Hampden (Bucks.), for in 1271 Alexander de Hampden had a rent in Attington in the right of his wife Marina.[23] In 1279 his estate in Attington was the largest freeholding,[24] and his son Reginald[25] was returned in 1316 as one of the lords of Attington.[26]

The De Hampdens' estate passed, perhaps by marriage, to the branch of the De Lewknor family which held Wormsley in Stokenchurch and Heythrop in the 1270's.[27] In 1306 John De Lewknor paid the largest contribution to the 16th in Attington,[28] and was presumably already the De Hampdens' tenant there. Robert de Lewknor, his successor at Wormsley and Heythrop,[29] similarly paid the highest contribution in 1327,[30] and John de Lewknor of

Wormsley and Heythrop was granted free warren in Attington and his other Oxfordshire lands in 1337.[31]

The descent of this ¼-fee is obscure until 1384, when Sir Reginald de Malyns of Henton died in possession of half 'Attington manor', as it was then called, which he held of the Abbot of Thame.[32] This half followed the descent of Henton until the late 15th century.[33] On John Barantyne's death in 1474[34] his widow Elizabeth, who married as her second husband Sir John Boteler, may have held it for life, but in 1481 it was being claimed by Geoffrey Dormer,[35] merchant of the Calais staple and already lord of Baldington's manor in Thame.[36] He probably acquired Attington at about this time and like Baldington's it descended to his grandson William Dormer of Ascot. In 1552, when the latter sold Attington and Dorton (Bucks.) to Henry Gray and his wife Anne, but leased them back at an annual rent of 100 marks,[37] a complicated series of financial transactions began. In 1557 Dormer sold the reversion of the manors for £513 6s. 8d. to Henry Reynolds,[38] whose widow, after Dormer's death, sold them back to Dormer's widow Elizabeth Hollingshead.[39] After a Chancery suit over Attington manor, the Dormers regained possession, and William Dormer settled it on his son John in 1563.[40] In 1591 John Dormer sold it, together with some pasture land which had been leased to John Petty (d. 1578) of Tetsworth,[41] for £1,150 to George Tipping (later Sir George) of Wheatfield,[42] the eldest son of Thomas Tipping of Draycott and the grandson of William Tipping of Merton.[43]

On Tipping's death in 1627[44] Draycott and Attington were inherited by his second son William, a theological writer of some repute, who lived at Draycott.[45] In 1639 Tipping sold part of the manor for £301 10s. to Richard Cornish, an Adwell yeoman,[46] but left the rest of the estate to his son George, also of Draycott.[47] The last known record of the connexion of the Tippings with Attington was in 1727, when Bartholomew Tipping of Draycott was party to a fine levied on Attington.[48] No further reference to the manor has been found.

The demesne tenants of the *MORETON* part of the fee in the early 12th century were the De Moretons, a family which took its name from the village. Osmund de Moreton had been succeeded before 1146 by his son Geoffrey,[49] who had at least two sons, William

[11] Ibid. 821.   [12] *Feud. Aids*, iv. 181.
[13] *Thame Cart.* i. 56, 58.   [14] *Fines Oxon.* 39.
[15] *Rot. Hund.* (Rec. Com), ii. 821; *Feud. Aids*, iv. 181. For its economic history see below, p. 187.
[16] C.P. 25(2)/196/Mich. 14 Eliz.
[17] See below, p. 177. For fine of 1621 see C.P. 25(2)/340/Trin. 19 Jas. I: Sir Rich. Wenman to Sir Thos. Denton and Wm. Basse.
[18] O.R.O. Gamekprs' deps.; Kelly, *Dir. Oxon.* (1869).
[19] Bodl. G.A. Oxon. b 92 (23): *Sale cat.* (lots 41–44).
[20] Davenport, *Oxon. Sheriffs*; *Oseney Cart.* v. 50. For his manor and chapel at Aston Clinton (Bucks.) see *Rot. Grosse.* 349–51; *V.C.H. Bucks.* ii. 315.   [21] *Fines Oxon.* 39.
[22] *Thame Cart.* i. 56–57. Like his lord Odo de Braimuster John held land in Bledlow: *V.C.H. Bucks.* ii. 248.
[23] *Fines Oxon.* 199–200, 204. In the 15th cent. the Hampdens held a manor in Bledlow: *V.C.H. Bucks.* ii. 247.
[24] *Rot. Hund.* (Rec. Com.), ii. 821.
[25] *V.C.H. Bucks.* ii. 288.   [26] *Feud. Aids*, iv. 167.
[27] *Fines Oxon.* 201; *Rot. Hund.* ii. 786.
[28] E 179/161/10.
[29] *Boarstall Cart.* 297 ,306; *Fines Oxon.* 224.
[30] E 179/161/9.
[31] *Cal. Chart. R.* 1327–41, 387. His other lands were Heythrop, Wormsley, and Shirburn. He does not appear

to be the same John de Lewknor who was Sheriff of Oxon. and Berks. in 1333: *Cal. Fine R.* 1327–37, 381.
[32] C 136/36/9.
[33] See under Chinnor in a succeeding volume.
[34] C 140/50/36.
[35] C.P. 40/876, m. 444. For Barantyne pedigree see O.A.S. *Rep.* 1909, 31.
[36] See above, p. 172. He held land in Attington by 1485: Rousham Arch. N 370.   [37] C 78/44/3.
[38] Ibid.; Rousham Arch. N 418, 419.
[39] C 78/44/3; ibid. 58/3. This is a Chancery suit brought by Sir Thomas Sackville and Ralph Sheldon against Henry Gray. See also C 146/9445.
[40] Rousham Arch. N 475.   [41] P.C.C. 43 Langley.
[42] Rousham Arch. N 442; C.P.25(2)/197/Trin. 33 Eliz.
[43] For family see *Oxon. Visit.* 151, 274.
[44] Ibid. 275.
[45] Ibid. 274. For him see *D.N.B.* which, on the basis of Wood, *Athenae*, ii. 243, wrongly states that he became Vicar of Shabbington (Bucks.) and died unmarried. The Vicar of Shabbington was John Tipping: *Walker Rev.* 76–77.   [46] Bodl. MS. ch. Oxon. 2715.
[47] P.C.C. 35 Fairfax; *Hearth Tax Oxon.* 34.
[48] C.P. 25(2)/1090/East. 13 Geo. I.
[49] *Thame Cart.* i. 41; ii. 143.

and Walter.[50] William was still living in Moreton in about 1180.[51] Although his family retained land in Moreton until the 13th century,[52] the ½-fee seems to have passed to the Bixtrops by about 1190, for Walter de Bixtrop, a nephew of Geoffrey de Moreton,[53] then granted land to Thame Abbey, which was apparently identical with that once held by the abbey of the De Moretons.[54] It is established beyond doubt that in 1207 Matthew de Bixtrop, the son of Walter,[55] had been holding for some years the ½-fee in Moreton of Odo de Braimuster. In 1207, when Henry de Colville became Braimuster's tenant for the whole fee, it was agreed that Matthew de Bixtrop should hold of Henry by the service of a ½-knight as before he had held of Odo.[56] Matthew was to become prominent in early-13th-century Oxfordshire.[57] He was still alive in the 1230's.[58] He appears to have had no heirs and in 1279 the jurors stated that the Abbot of Thame held ½-knight's fee in chief of the Bishop of Lincoln through the good offices (per medium) of Matthew de Bixtrop.[59]

The abbey, however, had long had an estate in Moreton. Before 1146 Geoffrey de Moreton gave it a hide in free alms on condition that during his life or until he became a monk the abbey should give him every year a certain amount of grain, 2s. 2d. for his hose and shoes, and allow him a cow and a calf.[60] Hugh the Constable gave ½-hide, which he had received from Geoffrey as a relief, but insisted on receiving the service due from Geoffrey's hide.[61] When Robert de Chesney, Bishop of Lincoln (1148–66), later confirmed the gift of this 1½ hide to Thame, he freed the abbey from all service due to him.[62] In about 1180 Ralph, son of Roger and his wife Adeliza, gave another ½-hide;[63] there were also other smaller grants;[64] and by 1279 the abbey had rounded off its estate by acquiring Matthew de Bixtrop's ½-fee.[65] It then held by military service, but by 1346 it had been freed of this burden and was holding in free alms.[66] After the dissolution of Thame Abbey in 1539 its Moreton lands, which were valued in 1535 at £46 16s.[67] and included the manor known as SHEPECOTTS or SIBCOTTS, were granted with many of the abbey's other possessions in 1542 to Sir John Williams,[68] and passing to his heirs, the Wenmans, followed the descent of Thame Park.[69] Sheepcot appears among the Wenman lands until the late 17th century;[70] it probably later became absorbed in Moreton manor (see below), which comprised about 250 acres altogether. In 1823 Sophia Elizabeth

Wykeham was called the lady of Moreton manor,[71] but there is no later reference to manorial rights.[72]

The largest estate in MORETON was held of the bishop in 1279 by military service by Sir Nicholas de Segrave.[73] Segrave was a member of an important Leicestershire family which had some association with the De Colevilles, holders in the 13th century of the knight's fee in Attington and Moreton.[74] Although no later reference has been found to any Segrave connexion with Moreton,[75] the land evidently descended in the family to the Lord Segrave (d. 1353) who married Margaret, daughter and heiress of Edward I's brother Thomas of Brotherton, Duke of Norfolk.[76] Their daughter Elizabeth, Baroness Segrave, married John de Mowbray, Lord Mowbray, and among the lands inherited from his mother by their second son Thomas, who became Duke of Norfolk,[77] were lands in Moreton. In 1397 he leased these for life to Nicholas Hall.[78]

Thomas de Mowbray died in exile in 1399 and his second son John, Duke of Norfolk, in 1432, leaving a widow Catherine Neville. Moreton evidently formed part of her dower, for she and her third husband John Viscount Beaumont held it in 1458, when it is first called a manor.[79] Before Catherine's death,[80] however, Moreton had passed to her son John de Mowbray, Duke of Norfolk, who held it at his death in 1461.[81] He had granted it for life to Richard Southwell, a Norfolk man who was in his service.[82] The next duke may have granted it permanently to Southwell, for in 1469 it was acquired from the latter by a group which included Richard Quatremain and Richard Fowler.[83] Fowler held it at his death in 1477,[84] and from this time it followed the descent of Windbush manor in Tetsworth,[85] passing in the 18th century to the Spencers of Wheatfield, who still held it in 1835.[86]

A third estate in Moreton was the Bishop of Lincoln's demesne. In 1279 he held 9 virgates in villein tenure,[87] and in 1535 his lands in Moreton with those in Tetsworth were valued at £6 14d.[88] They passed with the bishop's Thame manor to Lord Williams of Thame and his heirs, the Norreys, and after to the Bertie family, who in 1682 became earls of Abingdon.[89] A holding called MORETON manor, which in the 16th century seems to have had its own courts,[90] was listed among their lands until the early 19th century.[91] In the 18th century the earls' 4 yardlands (about 140 acres) in Moreton formed part of their manor of New and Old Thame.[92]

50 Thame Cart. i. 42.   51 Ibid. 45–46.
52 Sandford Cart. i. 119; see also Fines Oxon. 165.
53 Thame Cart. i. 42.
54 Ibid. 47.
55 Eynsham Cart. ii. 173.
56 Fines Oxon. 39. For the Braimusters see above.
57 V.C.H. Oxon. v. 130, 290.
58 Oseney Cart. ii. 559 n. 2.
59 Rot. Hund. (Rec. Com.), ii. 821.
60 Thame Cart. i. 41; ii. 143.
61 Ibid. i. 43–44.
62 Ibid. 45.   63 Ibid. 47.
64 Ibid. 48, 51–52.
65 Rot. Hund. ii. 821.
66 Feud. Aids, iv. 181, 197.
67 Valor Eccl. (Rec. Com.), ii. 213.
68 L. & P. Hen. VIII, xvii, p. 103.
69 See p. 177.
70 C.P. 25(2)/196/Mich. 14 Eliz.; C.P. 43/383/254.
71 O.R.O. Incl. award.
72 e.g. see Bodl. G.A. Oxon. b 92(23), lots 31–36: 1917 Sale cat.
73 Rot. Hund. (Rec. Com.), ii. 821.
74 Philip de Coleville acted as surety for Nicholas de Segrave in 1276: Cal. Close, 1272–9, 427; see also Reg. Antiquiss. iii. 221.
75 In 1325 their only Oxfordshire property was some rent in Henton, held of Reginald de Hampden: Cal. Inq. p.m. vi, pp. 427, 431. In 1316 John Paynel was listed as one of the lords of Moreton and Attington (Feud. Aids, iv. 167), but no other record of this family has been found.
76 For Segraves see Complete Peerage, xi. 603–10.
77 Ibid. ix. 383–4, 601–8 for the Mowbrays.
78 Cal. Pat. 1396–9, 66.   79 E 210/D 4142.
80 Complete Peerage, ii. 62.
81 C 140/5/46.
82 For him see Cal. Pat. 1467–77, 26, 352.
83 C.P. 25(1)/191/29/13; see also ibid. 74/64.
84 C 140/62/39.   85 See above, p. 151.
86 5 & 6 Wm. IV, c. 23 (priv. act).
87 Rot. Hund. ii. 821.
88 Valor Eccl. (Rec. Com.), iv. 2.
89 See above, p. 171.
90 d.d. Bertie c 16.
91 C 142/399/153; C.P. 43/467/47; ibid. 894/464.
92 MS. Top. Oxon. c 381, ff. 73–74, 79, 80.

Another manor was formed, probably in 1139, when the Cistercian Abbey at Otley in Oddington was moved to Thame and endowed by Alexander, Bishop of Lincoln, in free alms with 3 carucates of land there.[93] After the Reformation the property was called *THAME PARK*.[94] Robert King, the last abbot, surrendered the abbey in 1539, and in March 1542 the Crown granted many of the monastic lands in and around Thame, including the demesne farm, called Home Grange, to Sir John Williams at an annual rent of £84 6s. 8d.[95] Sir John, who was related by marriage to King, had been acting as the abbey's receiver and leasing part of its Thame property.[96] In September 1542 the site of the abbey, including no doubt its buildings and the £84 rent, was given to King, who had been made the first Bishop of Oxford, as part of the endowment of the see.[97] They were later lost to the bishopric, for in July 1547 Edward VI granted them with some abbey lands to the Duke of Somerset, who immediately transferred them to Sir John Williams,[98] who thus acquired all the abbey's Thame property. On his death in 1559 his daughter Isabella and her husband Sir Richard Wenman inherited the abbey lands in Thame, Moreton, Priestend, Attington, and Tetsworth.[99]

The Wenman family were wool merchants, settled at Caswell manor near Witney.[1] Sir Richard Wenman's grandfather Richard and his father Sir Thomas were merchants of the Staple of Calais.[2] With the marriage of Richard Wenman to Lord Williams's daughter the family acquired large new estates and was henceforth to play an important part in Oxfordshire history. It lived at Thame Park until the 20th century.

On Sir Richard Wenman's death in 1572[3] Isabella, who married as her second husband Richard Huddleston of Little Haseley, held the Thame Park property until her own death in 1587,[4] ten years after her eldest son Thomas had died.[5] The Thame property descended to Thomas's son Richard,[6] who in 1596 was knighted for gallantry at the taking of Cadiz. He served as M.P. for the county, and in 1628 was created Viscount Wenman of Tuam in the Irish peerage.[7] He died in 1640, having settled Thame Park on his son Thomas and his wife Margaret, daughter of Edmund Hampden[8] and a coheiress of her uncle, Sir Alexander Hampden of Hartwell (Bucks.).[9]

Thomas Wenman, the 2nd viscount, was a moder-

ate parliamentarian who was reduced to poverty by the royalist seizure of his estates.[10] He died in 1665, being succeeded in the title by his younger brother Philip, who died without children in 1686.[11] Thomas Wenman, however, had left several daughters; one of them, Mary, married her distant cousin, Sir Francis Wenman, Bt., of Caswell (d. 1680),[12] and their son Sir Richard Wenman, created Viscount Wenman in 1686,[13] inherited the Thame Park property. He died in about 1690, leaving an idiot son Richard, the 5th viscount (d. 1729). According to Thomas Delafield Richard's son Philip, the 6th viscount, was 'of a not much greater capacity'.[14] He was succeeded in 1760 by his son Philip, also an M.P. who married a daughter of the 3rd Earl of Abingdon, and died without children in 1800, when the title became extinct. His heirs were the descendants of his sister Sophia, the wife of William Humphrey Wykeham of Swalcliffe (d. 1783).[15] The Thame Park estate descended to Sophia, the daughter of Sophia Wykeham's eldest son, William Richard Wykeham (d. 1800).

Sophia Wykeham, described by the diarist Greville as 'a half-crazy woman of large fortune', was a friend of the Duke of Clarence (later William IV), who in 1818 was planning to marry her. The marriage was forbidden, but in 1834 he created her Baroness Wenman.[16] She lived at Thame Park and died unmarried in 1870.[17] Thame Park passed to her cousin, Philip Thomas Herbert Wykeham, the eldest son of Philip Thomas Wykeham. He was succeeded in 1879 by his nephews, the sons of his brother Aubrey Wenman Wykeham-Musgrave (d. 1879), who married Georgiana, the daughter of Sir James Musgrave, Bt., of Barnsley (Gloucs.), and the heiress of her brother, Sir William Augustus Musgrave, Rector of Chinnor and Emmington.[18] Their elder son, Wenman Aubrey Wykeham-Musgrave, who inherited Thame Park, moved to Barnsley in 1914 and died in 1915.[19] His son, Herbert Wenman Wykeham-Musgrave, put up for sale in 1917 about 3,300 acres of the Thame Park estate[20] and manorial rights lapsed.

LESSER ESTATES. In the early 13th century a ⅕-fee was held of the bishop by Mabel, a widow.[21] By about 1225 she had been succeeded by William son of Osbert.[22] By 1279 this fee was held by Sir Geoffrey de Lewknor, a royal justice and lord of Great Harrowden (Northants.), for a rent of 9s., scutage, and

[93] *Rot. Hund.* (Rec. Com.), ii. 820; for the abbey's history see *V.C.H. Oxon.* ii. 83–84; vi. 279.

[94] For the name see above, p. 162.

[95] *Foedera*, xiv. 661; *L. & P. Hen. VIII*, xiv (2), p. 185; xvii, p. 103.

[96] Lee, *Thame*, 385, 410–11; *Valor Eccl.* (Rec. Com.), ii. 213, 214; see also *L. & P. Hen. VIII*, xiv (1), p. 586.

[97] *L. & P. Hen. VIII*, xvii, p. 490.

[98] *Cal. Pat.* 1547–8, 121, 208.

[99] C.P. 25(2)/259/East. 3 Eliz.; C.P. 25(2)/196/Mich. 14 Eliz.; C 142/182/42.

[1] For pedigree see Lee, *Thame*, 433 sqq.; *Visit. Oxon.* 178–9.

[2] For history see Lee, *Thame*, 433, 439; *V.C.H. Bucks.* iv. 255.

[3] See Lipscomb, *Bucks.* iii. 135–6 for 16th- and 17th-cent. Wenman tombs at Twyford.

[4] C 142/182/42; *Complete Peerage* (orig. edn.), viii. 141 note.

[5] C 142/182/42.

[6] The grant of 1608 is evidently a confirmation: C 66/1759, no. 5.

[7] For him see *D.N.B.*; for family see *Complete Peerage* (orig. edn.), viii. 91 sqq.

[8] C 142/492/49.

[9] *V.C.H. Bucks.* ii. 257, 278; see Lipscomb, *Bucks.* ii 302 for pedigree.   [10] For him see *D.N.B.*

[11] Lipscomb, *Bucks.* iii. 136.

[12] For him see *Complete Baronetage*, iii. 267.

[13] For grant of title see Burke, *Extinct Peerage*, 624.

[14] MS. Top. Oxon. d 88, f. 59b. His wife Sophia was the sister and coheiress of Philip Herbert of Tythrop, M.P. for Oxford. For his M.I. at Thame see Lee, *Thame*, 113; and see above, p. 161.

[15] For Wykeham pedigree see Lee, *Thame*, 437; Burke, *Land. Gent.* under Wykeham-Musgrave.

[16] *Greville Diary*, ed. P. W. Wilson, i. 259; *Letters of George IV*, ed. A. Aspinall, ii, no. 739 and notes.

[17] *Complete Peerage* (orig. edn.), viii. 93–94. For the division of her estate see Lee, *Thame*, 404 n. 10. For her see also Brown and Guest, *Thame*, 198–200.

[18] *Complete Baronetage*, ii. 436 for family.

[19] Brown and Guest, *Thame*, 268. For him see E. Gaskell, *Oxon. Leaders* (priv. printed, c. 1907). For his younger brother Philip James Digby Wykeham see Burke, *Land. Gent.*   [20] Bodl. G.A. Oxon. b 92(23).

[21] *Bk. of Fees*, 40.

[22] Queen's Coll. MS. 366, f. 23.

suit at the hundred court.[23] He was succeeded at Thame in about 1300 by his son Ralph.[24] Both Ralph and his eldest son Geoffrey were dead by 1316.[25] The latter's brother John held the ⅛-fee in Thame in 1346.[26] Although John de Lewknor had a son John and a grandson Robert, by the end of the century the family had lost Harrowden,[27] and there is no later record of any connexion with Thame.

From the late 14th century the Stonors of Stonor Park had an estate in Thame; Sir Ralph de Stonor (d. 1394) held it by 1390,[28] and it descended in the family to Sir William Stonor, who in 1479 was appointed hereditary steward of several of the Bishop of Lincoln's manors, including Thame and Dorchester.[29] He died in 1494 and his eventual heir was his daughter Anne, the wife of Sir Adrian Fortescue. Part of the Stonor lands, however, were claimed by Sir Walter Stonor, a nephew of Sir William's.[30] By a royal award of 1536 the property was divided between them.[31] The Thame estate is not mentioned, but it probably went to Fortescue, who was holding it in 1536.[32] No later record of it has been found. Fortescue, who was executed in 1539, left two daughters by Anne Stonor. One of them married Sir Thomas Wentworth, Lord Wentworth, and their daughter Margaret was the second wife of Lord Williams.[33] It is possible that through her the Stonor property in Thame became united to Lord Williams's Thame manor.

TRADE AND INDUSTRY. The early history of Thame is obscure, but there can be little doubt that it was a place of importance in the early Anglo-Saxon period. Its well-protected position on the bend of a navigable river and its good communications favoured its rise.[34] Ancient roads such as the Icknield way and London way passed within a few miles, while others from Tetsworth on the London road, Aylesbury, and Chinnor converged on it. The traditional belief that it was fortified by the Danes and retaken by Edward the Elder in 941 has arisen from a confusion with Tempsford (Beds.),[35] but that Thame was once a royal vill is not improbable. The slight indications in the surviving charters that Old Thame enjoyed a special kind of free tenure allied to the later burgage tenure lends some support to the belief.[36] That the town became the centre of a group of episcopal estates belonging to the Bishops of Dorchester is generally accepted.[37] It may be that the Mercian king Wulfhere, who was certainly in the town in

675,[38] endowed the Mercian bishopric of Dorchester, established between 675 and 685,[39] with Thame and its dependent villages. If so, this was perhaps no more than a restitution of property first granted by the West Saxon kings when the bishopric of Dorchester was founded in 635.[40] The importance of the place may be further seen in its relations with the surrounding district: it was the mother church of three others and gave its name to the hundred.[41] It is likely that it already had an episcopal residence, as it did in later days, for Oscytel, Bishop of Dorchester and later Archbishop of York, died there in 971.[42] In short, the status of Anglo-Saxon Thame was very different from that of the ordinary rural village.

The town's importance was increased in the time of Bishop Alexander when the church was made a prebend of Lincoln and a Cistercian monastery was established just outside Thame.[43] Perhaps at this time, too, the new town, *novus burgus de Thame*, was laid out to the east of old Thame.

Precisely when New Thame and its market were founded is uncertain, but all the evidence points to its being a post-Conquest creation and a 'planned' seignorial borough cut out of the bishop's demesne and paying all dues to him. Such ventures by lay and ecclesiastical lords were common in the 12th century and later, the object being to increase profits from market dues and courts and raise the value of rents by attracting new tenants.[44] The earliest evidence for the new town dates from the end of the 12th century, but the 1140's would have been a likely time for its foundation, for Bishop Alexander was then in the course of decreasing the extent of his demesne farm at Thame.[45] Moreover, the establishment of the prebendal household at Priestend and of the abbey would both have encouraged the growth of the market, though as the Cistercians were exempt from the payment of toll and dues in all markets and fairs the bishop's dues would not have been increased in their case.[46]

The earliest record of the Tuesday market and by implication of the new town, since Tuesday has always been market-day in New Thame, dates from the time of Bishop Walter de Coutances (1183–4).[47] The market was then well established and was held by prescriptive right. A royal charter granting a market at Thame was not obtained until 1215,[48] and in 1219 a licence was obtained by Bishop Hugh de Welles to divert the Oxford–Aylesbury road so as to make it pass through 'his town of Thame'. The

---

[23] *Rot. Hund.* (Rec. Com.), ii. 820. For him see *Knights of Ed. I*, iii (Harl. Soc. lxxxii), 31.
[24] Queen's Coll. MS. 366, f. 34*b*. Geoffrey was alive in 1300: *Cal. Inq. p.m.* iii, p. 480.
[25] See Farrer, *Honors*, ii. 325–6 for family.
[26] *Feud. Aids*, iv. 182.
[27] *V.C.H. Northants.* iv. 179; *Genealogist*, N.S. xiv, 253.
[28] *Cal. Close*, 1389–92, 290; 1392–6, 113.
[29] *Cat. Anct. D.* vi, C 5623. For pedigree see *Stonor Letters*, i (Camden Soc. 3rd ser. xxix), opp. p. vii. See ibid. 30, 141, for references to Thame property.
[30] C 1/505/54.
[31] Stat. 28 Hen. VIII, c. 36.
[32] *L. & P. Hen. VIII*, x, p. 461.
[33] *Complete Peerage* (orig. edn.), viii. 96, 140.
[34] See above, pp. 162–3. Early topographical works stress the importance of the river, which was navigable by barges until the 18th cent., as a means of communication: e.g. *The Agreeable Historian*, London, 1746.
[35] e.g. by Plot, *Nat. Hist. Oxon.* 350; P. Russell, *England Displayed by a Society of Gentlemen* (1769).
[36] Rousham Arch. N 15. A free tenement in Old Thame

was granted for a money rent with the right 'to give, sell, or bequeath'.
[37] F. M. Stenton, *Anglo-Saxon England*, 432.
[38] *Cod. Dipl.* ed. Kemble, v. 987–8.
[39] Stenton, *Anglo-Saxon England*, 68.
[40] Ibid. 35; *V.C.H. Oxon.* ii. 1.
[41] See above, p. 113 and below, p. 199.
[42] *Anglo-Saxon Chron.* ed. G. N. Garmonsway (1953), 119.   [43] See above, pp. 171, 177.
[44] *British Borough Charters*, 1042–1216, ed. A. Ballard, 19–36.
[45] Leland reported what was presumably the local tradition that the town was given by the king for a fee-farm rent to the bishops of Lincoln about the time of Bishop Alexander (*Itin.* ed. Toulmin Smith, ii. 110; iv. 34–35).
[46] *Cal. Chart. R.* 1226–57, 14.
[47] Brown and Guest, *Thame*, 33.
[48] This was a general grant permitting the Bishop of Lincoln to hold markets and fairs in all his manors. Thame is specifically mentioned in a confirmation of 1227: *Cal. Chart. R.* 1226–57, 33. The grant was confirmed again in 1229: ibid. 105.

The Former 16th-century Market-house

The High Street and Pig Market in 1935

THAME

THAME HIGH STREET FROM THE WEST

Showing the lay-out of New Thame on the south side and the 13th-century encroachments on the high-road

object of the diversion was to oblige travellers to pass through to the market-place and so increase and facilitate the collection of tolls.[49] The old route was by Lashlake and Priestend, following the course of the river. The new route was the present one—along Friday Street (now North Street) and into the High Street.[50]

Whatever the date of the creation of the borough it is evident that it was prosperous and expanding in the first half of the 13th century. According to the hundredal inquest of 1255 Bishop Hugh de Welles had erected houses in 1221 in the king's highway in Thame in order to increase his rents, and these were occupied in 1255 by Geoffrey Taylor and five others.[51] At the same inquest the jurors of the *burgus* said that eighteen stalls were erected in the market-place in the royal way, and that Bishop Robert Grosseteste had been the first offender in 1251/2 and that he was followed by Bishops Henry Lexington (1254–8) and Richard Gravesend (1258–79) and their bailiffs who 'augmented the encroachments from year to year'.[52] These encroachments evidently marked the beginning of the erection of permanent stalls and houses in the market-place, the modern Middle Row. An earlier account of New Thame, included in the survey of the Bishop of Lincoln's estates in the hundred made in the second quarter of the 13th century,[53] records that there were already 63 burgesses, and that the rents of assize in Thame brought in 75s. plus a new increase of 4s. 9d., while the issues of the borough (i.e. from courts, markets, and other dues) totalled £17 4s. 1½d.[54] The increment of 4s. 9d. must refer to new burgage tenements laid out after the creation of the borough and presumably to the buildings in the market. At the time of the survey a few burgesses held more than or less than 1 burgage: Alexander the carpenter has 3½ burgages, another has 3, another a ½-burgage, but the majority held 1 burgage apiece. The uniform rent of 1s. for a whole burgage puts Thame among the many post-Conquest foundations that had this rent and whose customs may have been modelled on those of the Norman town of Breteuil.[55] The rent here as elsewhere was a ground rent—1s. for each plot of burgage land.

The survey itself and many later 13th-century charters show that the original burgages were field acre-strips.[56] At the time of the tithe award of 1826 the township of New Thame covered 50 statute acres,[57] and in view of the well-known permanence of township boundaries it must be supposed that this was the original amount of land cut out of the bishop's demesne. The acres were soon subdivided into half-acre and quarter-acre burgages: their pattern is still clearly visible between Southern Road and Brook Lane on the 25-inch ordnance survey.[58] It looks as if uniform burgage strips may have once extended as far east as Park Road. The southern

boundary is formed by Southern Road and the footpath which continues it. The houses on the High Street almost all have long narrow gardens, of uniform length but varying width, and their boundaries, by analogy from other ancient towns, can confidently be assumed to be identical with those of many of the 13th-century burgage tenements. The length of the present strips is about 700 ft.

The pattern is less clear to the north of the High Street and may never have been so regular. The area immediately north of the market is circular in shape and can never have contained more than a few burgages of 700 ft. long; at present most tenements are 300 ft. or less in length. The permanent houses and stalls erected in the king's highway have already been mentioned. Today Middle Row, with some of its houses fronting on the Butter Market and some on the Corn-market, extends 100 yards along the middle of the town's main street. Here probably was 'le shop rew' with stalls in it recorded in 1345, and 'le Bocher rew' of 1377.[59]

There is little direct evidence about the development of the town and its trade in the later Middle Ages, but a pointer to its growth is the subdivision of tenements. There is evidence that this subdivision was well advanced before the third quarter of the 13th century. There were then many burgages with several houses built on them, and half- or quarter-acre of burgage was frequently being sold.[60] The new tenants came largely from neighbouring towns or villages, and sometimes from further afield. Men from Berkshire and Buckinghamshire as well as Oxfordshire were among them. Out of seven witnesses to a mid-13th-century charter five came from Abingdon, Chinnor, Hughenden, Tusmore, and Upton.[61] Other burgesses came from Aylesbury, Oxford, Attington, Fritwell, Mapledurham, Sydenham, and Tetsworth.[62] The town's development was threatened by the setting up of a rival market at Haddenham (Bucks.), only 3 miles north-east of Thame, but on the petition of Bishop John Dalderby the charter granting a market was withdrawn in 1302,[63] and in the tax-assessment lists of the early 14th century Thame appears as a prosperous small market-town, easily outstripping its rural neighbours in wealth and population. At the beginning of the century New Thame and Old Thame (which included Priestend) were roughly equal in wealth, the New Town paying £6 3s. 2d. in 1306 and the Old Town £6 1s. 10d.[64] The returns for 1327 suggest that New Thame, where there was greater space for development and where all the land was freely held, was expanding: there were 50 contributors in Old Thame and 67 in New Thame.[65] Their combined assessment was £11 11s. 5d. compared with £10 10s. 11d. from the Miltons and their three hamlets, an exceptionally large and populous rural parish. If the assessments of Moreton and North Weston hamlets are added to

---

[49] *Rot. Litt. Claus.* (Rec. Com.), i. 402.
[50] See map, p. 164.
[51] *Rot. Hund.* (Rec. Com.), ii. 31.
[52] Ibid. 37.
[53] For the precise dating see above, p. 13, n. 94.
[54] Queen's Coll. MS. 366, ff. 23b, 25.
[55] Mary Bateson, 'The Laws of Breteuil' (*E.H.R.* xv), 73–78.
[56] There are over 400 medieval charters in Mr. T. Cottrell Dormer's archives at Rousham Park.
[57] Bodl. Tithe award.
[58] O.S. Map 25″, xl. 3. See also plate facing p. 179.
[59] Rousham Arch. N 124, N 204. There were permanent

stalls which could be bought and sold: e.g. ibid. N 51, N 56.
[60] e.g. ibid. N 7, N 60, N 63, N 66. Small closes were apparently attached to the burgages; there are references in the 14th cent. to 'Borgage croftes' (e.g. ibid. N 43, N 80, N 309).
[61] Ibid. N 2.
[62] e.g. ibid. N 66, N 93, N 99, N 101, N 169, N 200, N 260.
[63] *Cal. Chart. R.* 1257–1300, 461; MS. Top. Oxon. c 3, p. 403.
[64] E 179/161/10.
[65] E 179/161/9.

that of Thame, and it seems certain that at Moreton[66] at least some of the villagers were partly living on Thame market, the total assessment comes to £16 19s. 10d. When the tax assessments were revised in 1334 New Thame's tax was steeply increased.[67] This and the disastrous effects of the Black Death on the neighbourhood may have been responsible for the Bishop of Lincoln's efforts between 1351 and 1361 to enforce the payment of toll in his Thame market by traders from villages in the honor of Wallingford and so check a decline in his revenues.[68]

The poll tax of 1377 clearly reveals the comparative density of population both in Old and New Thame, and emphasizes once again Thame's outstanding position in relation to the ordinary rural village.[69]

The documents throw some light on the trade and crafts carried on from the 13th to the 15th centuries. For the most part the occupations appear to be those commonly found in other towns. Among the various middlemen recorded were spicers, fishmongers, horsemongers, and victuallers (vyneter); among the crafts were those of fuller, weaver, skinner, couper, tanner, sadler, tailor, lorimer, leadbeater, napper, cordwainer, glover, chandler, goldsmith, parchmentmaker, and baker of white bread.[70] In a small market-town the brewers and bakers must always have been preponderant, but there is no direct evidence for this until the 15th century. One craft, however, early gained a lasting reputation. William the glazier of Thame is believed to have supplied much of the painted glass for Merton College chapel.[71] He received £10 2s. in 1307 and 1310 for his painted glass. He also supplied Notley Abbey where fragments of glass similar to the Merton glass have been found.[72] An Alice and a William the glazier occur in 1309 and 1317.[73] The tax roll of 1327 lists four glaziers, John the glazier, Adam and another John, all living in New Thame, and a Henry the glazier in Old Thame.[74] Adam was alive in 1332 when he witnessed a charter, and Thomas Glazier, who was living in 1353, may have been his son.[75] Although so pre-eminent for glass-painting Thame was far from being able to supply all the skilled hands required, and still less could the materials needed for such enterprises as the church restoration be obtained in the market. When the aisle of St. Mary's was being rebuilt in 1443 lead, for example, was obtained from Aylesbury.[76] In 1449 a carpenter from Chilton was engaged to make the seats and at a later date William Holden, a smith of Bicester, to repair the clock. In 1502 two men from Abingdon were obtained to mend the bells.[77]

The most influential of the burgesses, however, from the start were naturally the merchants. A ruling hierarchy on a small scale, composed of men whose wealth seems to have been partly based on land and partly on merchandising, is clearly in existence in the 13th century. The names of Thomas Elys, William Pyron, Richard Basset, Richard Dereman, and William Surman constantly appear in the records of New Thame as witnesses.[78] The Elys family were certainly engaged in the wool trade, and Pyron may have been too. He owned, as 'mesne tenant', part of the land of the new borough: burgages are constantly said to be in his 'fee'.[79] The merchants and innkeepers stand out as the leaders of the town in the following centuries also. The early 14th-century Edward le Spicer, for example, who was rich enough to begin making a causeway between Thame and Rycote, was a mercer.[80] But the Elys family was for some generations perhaps the most outstanding of the merchant families. Its wealth and influence was apparently based on land and trade combined, and although members of the family owned many burgages this was probably by way of investment and in order to acquire the freedom of the market. Most of them appear to have lived in North Weston. Richard Elys of North Weston and his son Thomas were among the most frequent witnesses to the surviving charters of the second half of the 13th century.[81] Thomas Elys, who was accumulating burgages in the town and acres in the field at the end of the century sold in 1311, just before his death, round 400 acres with messuages.[82] Robert Elys, wool merchant of Thame, was perhaps a younger son. Knowledge of his connexion with the wool trade has been preserved by chance. His sixteen sarplers of wool, shipped in 1316 on the 'Petite Bayard' of London, were lost with the ship to the Admiral of Calais who made an armed attack on it in the channel.[83] Elys's cargo, valued at £160, was the second largest consignment on the ship which was carrying the goods of sixteen merchants. It is significant of the family's interest in the trade of Thame that when the daughter of Thomas Elys married William Cray of Long Crendon (Bucks.) her parents gave a burgage tenement with her.[84] Elys' son John Elys[85] was also an influential man, who almost certainly combined the keeping of sheep flocks with town interests. Like his father, he lived at North Weston. He served on a commission of oyer and terminer in 1351 and was appointed justice to keep the Statute of Labourers in Buckinghamshire in 1359.[86] In the next century one of the Elys family, a citizen and mercer of London, is found buying wool at Watlington in 1476 in company with Richard Gardener, a mercer and alderman of London.[87]

The burgess aristocracy of the first half of the 15th century was a select group consisting chiefly of the families of Elys, Benett, King, Wendelborough, Manyturne, Bate, Bonste, and Hall. It was they who gave the largest sums for the reconstruction of the north aisle in 1443 and for the making of the church seats when a collection was made in 1449.[88] From their ranks came the churchwardens and the bailiffs.[89]

[66] See below, p. 187.   [67] e.g. E 179/161/17.
[68] Blk. Prince's Reg. iv. 7, 277, 298, 378.
[69] See below, p. 188.
[70] Rousham Arch. N 10, 17, 50, 51, 71, 94, 112, 134, 135, 149, 152, 262. For the record of a weaver in 1284–5 see C 47/79/85.
[71] H. W. Garrod, The Ancient Painted Glass in Merton College, Oxford, 43.
[72] Brown and Guest, Thame, 74.
[73] Rousham Arch. N 33, N 62.
[74] E 179/161/9.   [75] Rousham Arch. N 85, N 152.
[76] Berks. Bucks. and Oxon. Arch. Jnl. ix. 120; x. 22.
[77] Lee, Thame, 41, 27.   [78] Rousham Arch. N 61.

[79] e.g. ibid. N 56, N 274, N 381.
[80] Cal. Pat. 1343–5, 549.
[81] e.g. Rousham Arch. N 30, N 31, N 48.
[82] Ibid. N 45, N 47.   [83] Cal. Pat. 1313–17, 546.
[84] Rousham Arch. N 32.
[85] For relationship see ibid. N 123.
[86] Cal. Pat. 1350–4, 161; 1358–61, 216.
[87] The Stonor Letters and Papers, ii. (Cam. Soc. 3rd ser. xxx), ed. C. L. Kingsford, 1.
[88] Lee, Thame, 13–15, 42. For Bennetts see Lupton, Extracts, 3, 14, &c.
[89] Lee, Thame, 152–3; Rousham Arch. N 325*, N 330, N 345.

William Bate, to take one example, who was the second highest contributor, was a draper, and his son John Bate was later to acquire gentle rank.[90]

Relations at this time between Thame and the capital were evidently comparatively close. Grants of land or of burgages in Thame were sometimes made by Thame men to Londoners and vice versa,[91] and many sons of Thame families went to London and prospered there. Sir John Daunce of London, for instance, was the son and heir of John Daunce of Thame and the owner of burgage land in Thame.[92] Thomas Wells, citizen and tailor of London was the cousin and heir of John Wells (d. 1488) of Thame;[93] and Sir Michael Dormer, lord mayor of London, was the son of Geoffrey Dormer (d. 1503) of Thame.[94] There is some record too that as in later centuries trade was done by Londoners in Thame. Direct evidence for this, however, is only found when bad debts were incurred. A Thame baker was sued by a London citizen, a London fishmonger was owed £2 by a Thame plough-maker, and a London mercer had a debt of £5 10s. owing from a Thame chapman.[95]

In the 15th century there were two merchants resident in the parish whose importance far outstripped the normal small trader of Thame, though the increasing wealth and importance of some of these is reflected in their brasses in the church. The first was Richard Quatremain, a younger son of Thomas Quatremain of Rycote and North Weston, who had been brought up to trade and was employed in the customs in London before he succeeded to North Weston and became an M.P. and Sheriff of the county.[96] His experience of trade and connexions with London can hardly have failed to have been useful to the town. He was certainly its benefactor, for he founded six almshouses.[97] In the last quarter of the century by far the wealthiest and most influential of the Thame merchants was Geoffrey Dormer, member of a family long settled in Thame, and a merchant of the Calais staple.[98] He bought Baldington's manor-house, 'the Place House', with the manor in 1473 and lived in it until a few years before his death in 1503.[99] The importance of the family in the town is reflected in the church. The earlier Quatremains and Baldingtons, who were both large landowners in the neighbourhood, had in turn given their name to the south transept, and similarly the north transept, where Geoffrey Dormer's stone table-tomb may still be seen and where later Dormers were buried, was known as Dormer's aisle in the 16th century.[1] Besides Sir Michael, Geoffrey's second son, his youngest son William Dormer, a benefactor to the church and active in town affairs, seems also to have been engaged in trade and to have had close connexions with the city of London. He was associated, for example, in his dealings over Baldington with John Peers, fishmonger of London and ancestor of the Peers family of Chislehampton.[2] After his death his widow Elizabeth married Hugh Hollingshed, a London merchant and no doubt another of his London associates.[3] Hollingshed too made Thame his place of residence.[4]

Another local family, widespread in the neighbourhood but of less importance, which was said to have been also engaged in trade as well as farming, was the yeoman family of Hester.[5] Vincent Hester, a cordwainer, left over £64 worth of goods at his death in 1605.[6] The family was to acquire gentle rank and considerable wealth in the 17th century.[7] From the time of Henry VII the Hesters were often churchwardens, and under Edward VI and Elizabeth they supplied the church with new service books.[8]

The price revolution and the religious changes of the 16th century had a far-reaching effect on the town. As elsewhere the century was a period of great prosperity for the yeoman farmers in the Thame area, and Thame market and its tradesmen must have benefited from their prosperity. There is little direct information about the town's development, but there is enough to indicate that considerable progress was made during this century and the next. Early-16th-century subsidies indicate to what a great extent New Thame had already developed: it contributed almost four times as much as Old Thame. In 1523–4 £15 15s. 6d. was paid by New Thame householders compared with £4 18s. 10d. at Old Thame[9] and £9 4s. 4d. altogether from the rest of the hamlets.

Thame Abbey then consisting of an abbot and twelve monks was surrendered to the king in 1539, and town tradesmen may have suffered some temporary loss, for Bishop Longland had recently complained of the elaborate feasts at taverns indulged in by the young monks and of the reckless extravagance of Abbot Warren;[10] but in the long run the material gain to the town was great. The abbey's lands went to Sir John Williams who also acquired the bishop's lands.[11] To this moderate and humane man the town perhaps owed during the religious changes of the Reformation period more than appears on the surface. One obvious benefit was the grammar school, founded one must suppose in response to local desire.[12] Another was the refoundation of the almshouses.[13]

Evidence for the arrangement of the market place is fuller in this century. The market or moot hall is first recorded in 1509. It had shops underneath it, four of which were leased by Geoffrey Dormer for

---

[90] Rousham Arch. N 333, N 349; P.R.O. Harrison, Extracts, v. 1069. For the Bates family as benefactors of the church see Lee, *Thame*, 44 n.
[91] Rousham Arch. N 231, N 266.
[92] Ibid. N 399.
[93] Ibid. N 372.
[94] See above, p. 172.
[95] *Cal. Pat.* 1429–36, 159; 1441–6, 119, 214. For relations in the 16th cent. see Thomas Bonse, citizen and upholsterer of London, who was the son of Thomas Bonse of Thame (Rousham Arch. N 408, N 409), and a case in 1588 of a Thame mercer who owed £64 to a London haberdasher and granted the end of his lease of 2 yardlands in Thame in payment (ibid. N 440).
[96] For him see A. F. Carter, *The Quatremains of Oxfordshire*, 29 sqq.
[97] See below, p. 217.
[98] A Geoffrey Dormer, Gent. held land in Thame in

[1430]: Rousham Arch. N 287. A Robert le Dormer occurs in 1324: ibid. N 72.
[99] See above and below, pp. 167, 208.
[1] See below, p. 207.
[2] Rousham Arch. N 426, N 473.
[3] For Hollingshed see *Cal. S.P. Dom.* 1566–79, 301.
[4] They were living at Baldington manor in 1566: Rousham Arch. N 430. Elizabeth was widowed again by 1576: ibid. N 432. Cf. E 179/162/341.
[5] Lee, *Thame*, 231.
[6] Bodl. MS. Wills peculiars, 41.
[7] For pedigree of Hester see Lee, *Thame*, 76 n.
[8] Lee, *Thame*, 154, 157.
[9] E 179/161/192; 162/341.
[10] *V.C.H. Oxon.* ii, 85.
[11] See above, pp. 171, 177.
[12] See below, p. 215.
[13] See below, p. 217.

20s. from the Bishop of Lincoln; and a clock is mentioned in 1543.[14] As one would expect, special parts of the market were devoted to the sale of particular wares. Cock Row, the Drapery, and Sheep Row are recorded in 1509; the Butter Market, the Cornmarket, and the Hog Fair, although not recorded until the 17th century, were no doubt in existence.[15] The market cross stood between the moot hall and the head of Middle Row, with the Drapery 16 ft. to the north.[16] To the south of the cross was the common well: both were recorded in the 15th century.[17]

The market brought large numbers into Thame from outside and inns and victuallers must have thriven. One of the innkeepers, John Benett, appears to have been one of the richest men in the community in the first half of the century.[18] For several generations his family had been a leading one in the town, and like so many Thame people their wealth may have been partly based on their farms: the John Benett who was arrested for debt and pardoned in 1456 was described as a yeoman.[19] In 1587 there were 20 victuallers in the town, amongst them the Stribblehills, one of the leading families in the town, and the owners of the 'Swan'.[20]

References to the Michaelmas fair at Thame occur in 1577, when the inhabitants of Aylesbury, where plague had broken out, were forbidden to go to it, and in 1592, when the fair was postponed on account of the queen's visit to Rycote and the fear that London merchants would bring the plague to the Thame neighbourhood.[21] The growing importance of the cattle-market in this century may be assumed from our knowledge of the increase in pasture farming that took place in the surrounding district during the century.[22] Its importance in the next century is vouched for by a letter written from Henley in 1644 by Sir James Harrington.[23] He commented on a proposal of the king to fortify Shirburn saying that this would 'cut off all our provisions from Thame which is our best market for cattle'. It is clear from this letter that Thame market continued during the war despite the fact that the town lay in a disputed area. Anthony Wood, who witnessed many skirmishes in the streets, wrote 'you cannot imagine what disturbances they [the people of Thame] suffered by the soldiers of both parties, sometimes by the Parliament's soldiers of Aylesbury, sometimes by the King's from Boarstall House and at Oxford and at Wallingford Castle'.[24]

The woollen-draper, the linen-draper, and the mercer are among the most influential tradesmen in this century, and the next.[25] There is no evidence, however, to suggest that there was anything approaching a clothmaking industry in Thame: the wool seems mostly to have been sold to be made up elsewhere. In 1606 when Lord Norreys obtained a confirmatory grant of the Tuesday market it was called a wool-market. The date fits in well with the conversion of much land in the neighbourhood to sheep farming.[26] A variety of crafts are also recorded in this period, furrier, capper, armourer, gunsmith, fletcher, cordwainer, and chandler,[27] but as far as one can tell from the fragmentary evidence there seems to have been no specialization in any particular craft. The milliner and the apothecary are first recorded about this time and the brickmaker also.[28] In the 1640's if not earlier it was obligatory to have brick or stone chimneys: a man was presented at the view in 1648 for not pulling down an old chimney in his house and having a new brick or stone one made according to the order of the court.[29] The industry developed and ultimately gave its name to Brickkiln Lane (the modern Park Street).[30]

The town seems to have made a good recovery from the setback of the Civil War. The climate of religious and political opinion during the commonwealth was favourable to the small and medium trader, and new families were attracted to the town. The Reynolds, Wollastons, and Burrows, for instance, were said to have come from Leicestershire. The Burrows were woolstaplers as well as drapers; they had a business in London with a branch at Thame and were clearly substantial people. George Burrows (d. 1693) is entitled 'marchant' in the parish register.[31]

The hearth-tax returns of the 1660's show that many of these traders lived in substantial town houses and that New Thame had developed considerably. In 1662 149 householders were listed in New Thame and seven in Old Thame and Priestend.[32] Some 30 years later there were said to be 1,300 adult persons in Thame and its two hamlets of Moreton and Weston.[33] Many of the inhabitants of New Thame were farmers, a reminder of how much a market-town of this kind was dependent on the surrounding countryside, and several of the richest were innkeepers. The keeper of the 'Red Lion', whose substantial hostelry was rated on ten hearths for the hearth tax of 1662, was one of the Thame tradesmen to issue tokens between 1653 and 1669.[34] Other tokens that have survived were issued by 3 grocers, 2 chandlers, 2 hatters, 2 mercers, 1 draper, and 3 post innkeepers.[35]

There are many testimonies to the importance of the market in this century, and in the early 18th century. Its prosperity had been threatened in 1657 by a petition for a chartered market at Aylesbury, but Thame traders petitioned against it with success.[36] The market evidently served a wide area, for it was decided in 1683 that the 'hair' market and horse fair at Thame relieved the necessity of one at Oxford.[37] 'The New State of England' (1691)

[14] *Thame Gazette*, 21 May 1889: manorial accounts 1509; Lupton, *Extracts*, 15.
[15] See 17th-cent. ct. rolls, *passim*: d.d. Bertie, b 3, c 14, c 15; MS. Top. Gen. c 43–45.
[16] *Thame Gazette*, 21 May 1889.
[17] d.d. Bertie c 16 (uncat.): ct. rolls, *passim*.
[18] E 179/161/200; E 179/162/250, 258.
[19] *Cal. Pat.* 1452–61, 327. Possibly the same as the John Benett who was bailiff in 1453: ibid. 84.
[20] *Cal. S.P. Dom.* 1581–90, 389 (no. 56); Req. 2/42/110.
[21] *Acts of P.C.* 1577–8, 36; ibid. 1592, 195.
[22] See above and below, pp. 133, 190.
[23] Brown and Guest, *Thame*, 126.
[24] Wood, *Life*, i. 114.
[25] e.g. Rousham Arch. N 401, N 438, N 445; Bodl. MS.

chs. Oxon. 3912, 3913, 4393; O.R.O. Thame deeds V/ii/c/2, 3, &c. [26] C 66/1678.
[27] d.d. Hobbs c 17, *passim*; Rousham Arch. *passim*. The inventory of William Smith, gunsmith, totalled over £74 in 1644: Bodl. MS. Wills peculiars, 51.
[28] Bodl. MS. ch. Oxon. 3913; Oxf. Archd. Oxon. c 164, ff. 83, 85. [29] MS. Top. Gen. c 44, f. 68.
[30] For other references to bricklayers see d.d. Hobbs c 17, c 18 (uncat.).
[31] Lee, *Thame*, 243; Par. Rec. Reg. [32] E 179/255/4.
[33] Queen's Coll. MS. 501; see below, p. 212, n. 58.
[34] E 179/255/4.
[35] Ashmolean collection of tokens. For illustrations see Lee, *Thame*, 585–90. [36] *Cal. S.P. Dom.* 1656–7, 308.
[37] *Cal. S.P. Dom.* 1683–4, 310.

summed up the general opinion when it noted that the market was 'eminent chiefly for the buying of cattle, which makes it much frequented by graziers and butchers from London and other parts'.[38] Defoe described it in 1722 as 'a great corn market', and in 1746 it was said to be 'well furnished with live cattle and all other provisions and necessaries'.[39] The solid Georgian houses that today line the High Street, the monuments in the parish church, and the charitable foundations still bear witness to the prosperity of the upper-class townsman in the first half of the 18th century.[40] Disputes over pews are also significant: Mrs. Frances Stribblehill, for example, was presented in 1701 for trying to make several seats into one large pew and keeping it locked for her sole use although it would hold at least twelve persons.[41]

New trades and professions appear: those of an attorney, a bodice-maker, and a hat-band maker were among those who had wall monuments in the church to commemorate them,[42] and an apothecary Richard Callis, who sold his practice in 1771 to his journeyman apprentice for £200, described himself as having a 'very considerable business'.[43] There was also a group of clock-makers—William Lawrence flourished from c. 1740–1770 and a Thomas Lawrence (? a son) was apprenticed to him in 1759 for seven years. Joseph Stockford, also a bell-hanger, made the clock for Ewelme Church; and Thomas Stockford, who was established at Great Haseley in 1764, later transferred to Thame.[44] Finally, three members of the Stone family were clock-makers. This family was one of the most influential in the second half of the 18th century and the 'Spread Eagle' is said to have been built as their private house. Edward Stone's will (proved 1765) shows that he was a sadler, and that of his three sons one was a sadler, another a watch- and clock-maker, and a third a silver-smith and whip-maker.[45] The clock-maker was Richard Stone, apprenticed in 1761 to Charles House in London, but after of Thame. One of his clocks is now in St. Nicholas Church, Marston. A John Stone was also making clocks at Thame from about 1760 to 1795 when he seems to have been succeeded by Thomas Stone. A certain Tomlinson was making long-case clocks at the end of the century, but he was not apparently John Tomlinson, watch-maker and gunsmith, who had a shop in the High Street in the mid 19th century.[46]

As there was no staple trade and the craftsmen and shopkeepers were entirely dependent on the prosperity of the surrounding agricultural area the last decades of the 18th century and particularly the period of depression between 1815 and 1818 were far from prosperous ones for the town. There had been food riots as early as 1766 when the mob attempted to have the prices of bread, cheese, butter, and bacon reduced.[47] The war bore hardly on the town: between 1786 and 1820 the poor rate increased

alarmingly.[48] In 1785 Lord Torrington found Thame 'a mean and gloomy town' and in 1809 Arthur Young spoke of the 'very depressing poverty' of Thame.[49] Various local factors, however, assisted in the recovery which was marked in the third quarter of the 19th century. The improvement in the roads and ease of communication after 1800 was great and the inclosure award of 1826 was also beneficial since it allowed greater concentration on grazing and dairy farming, for which the area was particularly suitable and so increased the importance of the cattle market.[50] The project, mooted in 1828, to build a canal from Aylesbury to Thame[51] would, if carried through, have done much to relieve poverty, for, as Young noted, the high price of coal, high because of the necessity of bringing it 13 miles by land, was 'greatly against the comforts of the poor'.[52] Rising population added to the difficulties of the town: it rose from 2,293 in 1801 to 3,053 in 1851, mainly as a consequence of immigration from the neighbouring villages of Oxfordshire and Buckinghamshire, though some immigrants came from as far afield as Scotland and abroad.[53] Nevertheless, in 1860 Lupton could write of shops well stocked with goods of great variety from poplins to ploughs and of well-to-do graziers doing 'great business' in the streets.[54] Business was encouraged by two banks that had offices in the town: the London and County Joint Stock Banking Company and the Thame and Aylesbury Old Bank, drawing on Praeds & Co., were open on the Tuesday market day and by 1887 the London & Co. Bank was opened on two days a week and on fair days.[55] Although the population of the parish remained at about the 1851 level for the rest of the century, the numbers of inhabitants in the town was increasing slightly at the expense of that of the hamlets.[56]

Although there was no staple trade there were several small local industries in the 19th century.[57] These were family businesses and though some have declined and disappeared, others have continued until the present time (1959). Chief among them was the wool-stapling business of H. & C. Pearce. In 1860 Henry and Charles Pearce, who had a small business in Bell Lane, took over the business which had been carried on since 1750 by the Payne family at Lashlake.[58] In 1779–80 Paynes handled 3,376 tods, valued at £2,476; in 1790 4,838 tods, valued at £5,530; in 1800, 6,504 tods valued at £10,118.[59] H. & C. Pearce purchased wool from the local farmers and in 1939 they handled their maximum amount (including skin wool), for any one year, 1½ million lb. weight at an average price of 1s. a lb. In that year besides local wool (about ½ million lb.) they bought from other English districts, from Ireland and New Zealand. The firm was still thriving in 1958.

The ancient trades of fell-mongering and tanning

[38] G. Miege, *The New State of England* (1691).
[39] D. Defoe, *A Tour through England and Wales* (1725), ii. 23; *The Agreeable Historian* (1746).
[40] See below, pp. 209, 218.
[41] MS. Top. Oxon. c 3, p. 143.
[42] See below, p. 209. Cf. d.d. Hobbs c 17, &c. (uncat.). For the attorney John Stribblehill (d. 1692), a rich man, see Wood, *Life*, i. 400.   [43] d.d. Hobbs c 21 (uncat.).
[44] Inf. Dr. C. Beeson, Banbury.
[45] d.d. Hobbs c 21 (uncat.).
[46] Inf. Dr. C. Beeson; Gardner, *Dir. Oxon.* (1852).
[47] MS. Dunkin, 438/4, p. 224.
[48] See below, p. 196.

[49] *The Torrington Diaries*, ed. C. B. Andrews, i. 213; Young, *Oxon. Agric.* 328.
[50] See above, p. 163, and below, p. 192.
[51] MS. Dunkin 438/5, p. 383.
[52] Young, *Oxon. Agric.* 328.
[53] *Census*, 1801–51. Only 67 per cent. of the population was registered as 'natives' in the census. The figure 3,053 excludes 206 paupers in the workhouse: H.O. 107/1726/2.
[54] Lupton, *Thame*, 17–20.
[55] Gardner, *Dir. Oxon.* (1852); Kelly, *Dir. Oxon.* (1887).
[56] *Census*.   [57] Hunt, *Dir. Oxf.* (1846).
[58] Inf. Messrs. H. & C. Pearce; d.d. Hobbs (uncat.).
[59] Ledgers of H. & C. Pearce & Sons, Thame.

were still being practised in 1823. In 1857 H. C. Pearce purchased Winchello's tan-yard and it is now used for fell-mongering. Under recent marketing controls this firm, now associated with the Midland Hide and Skin Co., collected from eleven widely scattered abbatoirs from Oxford to London and employed fifteen workers. The nearest fell-mongering centre is Charlbury.[60]

Another old trade which was flourishing in the 19th century was brewing.[61] In 1857 Benjamin Field was using the 'malthouse with enclosed kiln etc.', in the High Street, and the Bell Yard opposite for malting and brewing.[62] Plot declared in his *Natural History of Oxfordshire* that Thame well-water was unsuited for brewing and that 'their beer will stink within fourteen days', and that if the town were not supplied by the adjoining rivulet, 'the place must needs be in a deplorable condition'.[63] Certainly the trade never acquired a reputation comparable to Bicester breweries,[64] and Field's had ceased by about 1880. Malting came to an end in 1904.[65]

Basket-making and chair-making were successfully carried on for many years by Hunt and Staples of Middle Row. Hunts were basket-makers at least as early as 1804, for in that year William Hunt took as apprentice a poor boy from the workhouse.[66] In 1823 the two businesses each employed eight or ten men making baskets, parts of chairs, and wooden bowls. Hunt used 8,000 bundles of osiers a year from the Old Town Meadows, Kingsey Bottom, and Thame Park. In 1890 osiers were obtained from Somerset, in 1935 from Algeria, but there was still a local supply for in 1921 the Moreton osier bed had been planted.[67] The baskets were mainly 'butter flats', and the industry slowly declined after 1865 when rinder pest first caused the local farmers to change over from butter-making to milk production.[68]

Chairs of beech wood were also made by Fenner of Park Street and Newitt of High Street. The last were making complete chairs and polishing them in 1874 when the business was closed.[69] Thame chairs had long had a good reputation in the Midlands.

Howlett's coach-building business flourished from 1843 until the beginning of the 20th century. It cut and carried its own timber and even manufactured its own springs.[70]

The Thame Park brick kilns were opened in the early 19th century and bricks for the county court were made there in 1869. Those for the new Town Hall in 1887 were made at the Christmas Hill works started in the mid-19th century. Both businesses were ultimately killed by cheaper bricks from Peterborough, but in 1934 the Christmas Hill works were restarted as the result of a boom in building, only to be closed on the outbreak of war in 1939.[71] The kilns and yard were then used for storing war material.

The chief 19th-century representative of generations of earlier carriers was Howlands. Carriers are known to have been going regularly to London in 1600,[72] and Howlands claimed that they had been doing so since 1676. They delivered to London agricultural produce from the surrounding villages and the markets of Marlow, Wycombe, and Thame. The firm still (1959) flourishes and deals mainly in hay, corn, and fertilizers.[73]

Lace-making was never so important in Thame as in the surrounding villages, particularly the Buckinghamshire ones,[74] though some pillow lace was made in the 19th century and purchased by London dealers.[75] Young, writing at the beginning of the century, observed that 'a very few' at Thame made lace and that 'there is nothing flourishing in the fabric'.[76] The Napoleonic prisoners continued the trade, but it was dwindling away by 1860, and by 1884 it was almost extinct.[77] In 1905 there was an exhibition of the Thame lace industry at the Albert Hall, but there were no lacemakers left in 1958.[78]

Since 1856, when the *Thame Gazette* was first published, printing has been among the leading Thame trades. It was first printed by Charles Ellis, then by Meers, and in 1910 the business came into the hands of F. H. Castle, the brother of the present owner. The firm of Castle & Sons now has 30 employees of whom 24 are engaged in printing.[79] In the 1880's the *Thame Observer* and the *South Oxfordshire News* also began to appear.

Since the earliest times inn-keeping has been one of the town's chief occupations. The port-moot rolls of the 15th century have many references to overcharging by the victuallers and in one case overcharging for horse fodder as well as for the man's food is specifically mentioned.[80] These inns depended entirely on the market and the country people and traders that it brought into the town. They provided stabling and accommodation for the night—the 'Swan', for example, still has the remains of stabling for 30 or 40 horses—and not one was a coaching inn. Fifty-nine different names of inns have been traced,[81] but this does not necessarily mean that there were 59 different hostelries. Inns often changed their names: the 'Spread Eagle', for one, was stated in 1882 to have been formerly the 'Oxford Arms'.[82] However, the number of inns must always have been great: in 1906 there were 35 and 30 in 1914, nearly three times the average for the county in relation to the population.[83]

[60] Inf. Messrs. H. & C. Pearce; d.d. Hobbs (uncat.); Pigot, *Lond. Dir.* (1823).
[61] One of the manorial mills was a malt mill in the 16th cent. d.d. Bertie c 16 (uncat.).
[62] Brown and Guest, *Thame*, 189; *Oxf. Jnl.* 1756.
[63] Plot, *Nat. Hist. Oxon.* 36.
[64] *V.C.H. Oxon.* vi. 35.
[65] Brown and Guest, *Thame*, 189.
[66] Par. Rec. Misc. pps.
[67] Brown and Guest, *Thame*, 187.
[68] Orr, *Oxon. Agric.* 27–28.
[69] Brown and Guest, *Thame*, 188. Cf. Lupton, *Thame*, 13, who states that beechen chairs were the chief manufacture in 1860.
[70] Brown and Guest, *Thame*, 188.
[71] Ibid. 190; Kelly, *Dir. Oxon.* (1900); local inf.
[72] J. Taylor, *The Carrier's Cosmographie* (Lond. 1637).

In 1854 there were 29 carriers in Thame: Billing, *Dir. Oxon.*
[73] Inf. Messrs. Howland & Bush Ltd.
[74] Mrs. Bury Palliser, *History of Lace* (1902), ed. M. Jourdain and A. Dryden, 378–83.
[75] Brown and Guest, *Thame*, 183–5; *V.C.H. Oxon.* ii. 253.
[76] Young, *Oxon. Agric.* 328.
[77] Lupton, *Thame*, 13.
[78] Brown and Guest, *Thame*, 185; local inf.
[79] Inf. Mr. Castle; Brown and Guest, *Thame*, 195.
[80] d.d. Bertie c 15, *passim*.
[81] By Mr. W. Guest.
[82] d.d. Hobbs c 23: lease.
[83] Kelly, *Dir. Oxon.* 1906; U.D.C. Rate Bk. 1914. Since 1915 licences have been curtailed, and in 1952 there were 22 licensed premises.

The chief inn in Tudor and Stuart days was the 'Red Lion'. It stood opposite the Market-house on the south side of the High Street. The officials of the peculiar held their courts there.[84] In the 18th century its reputation was poor: in 1785 Lord Torrington called it a 'bad inn'.[85] Nevertheless, the turnpike trustees held their meetings there and it was the chief posting house and social centre in the early 19th century.[86] It closed in 1860: it was in 1959 the offices of Messrs. Lightfoot & Lowndes.[87] Its position as principal inn had been usurped by the 'Greyhound' since at least the beginning of the century. In 1816 with the 'Bull', 'Crown', 'Anchor', and 'Swan', the 'Greyhound' was one of the five inns at which the churchwardens were to hold their feasts in rotation.[88] The inclosure commissioners put up there in 1823–6, but by 1852 it had become a shop and the 'Spread Eagle' was the leading hostelry.[89] Until the Town Hall was built in 1888 most of the town's public functions and festivities were held in its large assembly rooms.[90]

There were also many people whose livelihood depended on the market and fairs. Besides the regular Tuesday market there had long been two fairs.[91] In the 19th century there appear to have been at least three.[92] The statute fair for the hiring of servants was on 11 October and was continued on the two following Tuesdays. This fair was also noted for the sale of horses and fat hogs. Other fairs, held on the Tuesday in Easter week and the first Tuesday in August, were principally for cattle. In 1852 the wool market is said to have been discontinued for several years,[93] but a Christmas fatstock market, held on the first Tuesday after 6 December had come into existence, certainly by 1849.[94] Among the tradesmen and business men listed in Gardner's Directory of 1852 were two auctioneers, three corn dealers, a cattle dealer and a horse dealer.

During the last third of the 19th century and the beginning of the 20th the market was carried on under many difficulties: rinder pest broke out in November 1865 and no cattle were brought to the market for a year. Many later closures were necessary on account of outbreaks of rinder pest in 1877, of foot and mouth disease in 1883, and of swine fever in 1894.[95] The Board of Agriculture threatened to close the market in 1903 unless accommodation was made for cattle on a surface impermeable to water, so that it could be efficiently washed and disinfected. The right of the market authority, Sir Francis Bertie, to break up the highway for the necessary paving was denied by the Council, but eventually the work was carried out by him with their approval. An area 100 × 6 yds. was paved along the north of the High Street for cattle, a piece 60 × 4 yds. opposite the Fox Inn for sheep and two areas for pigs in the centre. In 1904, when the paving was complete, posts and chains were erected to keep cattle off the pavement.[96] There were never pens or stalls for cattle. Throughout the 20th century Thame market has ranked third

in the county in general importance. Until 1939 livestock was auctioned, and dairy produce, corn, eggs, hay, straw, hides, poultry, and wool were sold wholesale by private treaty. There was also a small retail market. Average weekly figures were: cattle 40–120 (150–200 in best weeks); sheep 120–700; pigs 150–400; calves 60–160. During 1934 2,234 cattle, 19,135 sheep, 15,221 pigs, and 4,342 calves were entered for sale. Supplies came from the Vale of Aylesbury, the Chiltern Hills, South Oxfordshire, and North and Mid-Bucks. Nearly all fat beasts were disposed of for export to other districts, buyers coming from Aylesbury, Reading, London, and the central Midlands. In 1919 a 100 horses would be auctioned, but in 1935 not more than three or four, and by 1959 none.[97]

After the Marketing Acts of 1931 and 1933 the method of distribution was changed greatly. Store stock was not controlled, but no fat stock was auctioned; it was only graded. When the areas for the marketing of fat cattle were determined Oxford gained at the expense of Thame. There are now no private sales of hides and wool, the sales of hay have diminished, and none is now exported to London. During the First World War the production of fat cattle was discouraged in favour of wheat, but in 1950 a distinct return to fat-stock production was noted. In 1949 the Thame Fat Stock Show was resuscitated, and the keen interest in it revealed a desire to return to pre-war conditions as regards fat-stock. With the diminution of auctioning, attendance at the market decreased.[98]

After many years of controversy an enclosed market has been established on a site of about 4 acres in North Street at a cost of £35,000. It is equipped to deal with fat-stock and dairy cattle: there are a sales ring, auctioneers' rostrum, and offices. For dairy cows and calves there is a covered building containing 40 stalls and there are sheep and pig pens and accommodation for poultry. The retail market has moved from the Cornmarket to the old site of the pig and cattle market. Average annual stall tolls between 1945 and 1952 totalled £450. Cattle tolls during the same period averaged £80 per annum, to which must now be added £1,100 per annum from the auctioneers for the rent of their offices.[99]

But since the Second World War Thame has become far less dependent on its market. It remains the natural centre for the surrounding area of about 6 miles in radius, though its services have been modified by modern manufacturing and marketing methods and transport. It has become more than ever a residential town: in 1952 140 people worked at the Cowley Pressed Steel and Morris Motor Works and some in Oxford, Aylesbury, and Haddenham.[1] Rateable properties, excluding dwelling houses and farm land, numbered: commercial 162, inns 22, industrial 10, public utility 6, educational and cultural 6, entertainments 3, and miscellaneous 14.[2] There were few industries in the town, but the total number

[84] Oxf. Archd. Oxon. c 162, pp. 100, 115.
[85] *Torrington Diaries*, ed. C. B. Andrews, i. 212.
[86] Minute Bk. (1789–91) of turnpike trustees (d.d. Hobbs c 22); *Thame Gazette, passim*.
[87] Brown and Guest, *Thame*, 151.
[88] d.d. Par. Thame c 5.
[89] Gardner, *Dir. Oxon.* (1852).
[90] *Thame Gazette, passim*.
[91] See e.g. P. Russell, *England Displayed by a Society of Gentlemen* (1769).

[92] Pigot, *Dir. Oxon.* (1823); Gardner, *Dir. Oxon.* (1852).
[93] Gardner, *Dir. Oxon.* (1852).
[94] Seymour Diary cited by Brown and Guest, *Thame*, 211–12.
[95] *Thame Gazette, passim*; Brown and Guest, *Thame*, 225.
[96] Brown and Guest, *Thame*, 225.
[97] From Mr. W. Guest's MS. notes.
[98] Ibid.   [99] Ibid.
[1] Ibid.   [2] Ibid.

employed in them was relatively high. Thame Mill Laundry employed 200, mostly women, and four or five other firms including agricultural machine repairing, printing, and building 30 to 35 each, and four others including fell-mongering, agricultural merchanting, and light-engineering 10 to 15 each.[3]

Of the commercial firms 84 are shops doing the normal country-town business. The fifteen bespoke tailors of 1846 have been replaced by two, the six iron smiths by one, but the last in addition to shoeing has a local reputation for ornamental iron work, particularly gates and signs. Garages, electrical and wireless shops are comparatively new ventures. The British Fan and Electric Co. Ltd. in Park Street deals in fume and dust extraction and employs about fifteen in staff. The latest arrival is Shell Mex and B.P. Ltd. which opened its offices in 1958 for the distribution of petroleum products in Oxfordshire and Buckinghamshire. There are about 45 employees. Almost all businesses are privately owned.[4]

Population has increased rapidly in recent years. The decline which followed 1891, the peak year for the 19th century, was arrested after 1918 and numbers rose rapidly after 1945. The population in 1951 of the Urban District, a much smaller area than the ancient parish, was 4,171.[5]

The town has an active social and sporting life. There is a public recreation ground of nearly 9 acres under the control of the Urban District Council. A sports' club, and cricket and football clubs flourish.[6] The town had a cricket pitch certainly by 1825 when seven men were convicted for using it for bull baiting.[7] A rifle club, instituted in 1908, has declined,[8] but hunting is still popular. The town lies in the country of the South Oxfordshire Hunt: the Earl of Abingdon first hunted this country from at least about 1770, but he limited himself to the area between Thame and Tetsworth and kept his pack at Rycote.[9]

The great annual event of the year is the Thame Show. It is claimed that it is the second largest single-day show in the country.[10] It was instituted in 1855 when the Thame Agricultural Society was founded.

AGRARIAN HISTORY.[11] Although Thame was undoubtedly the centre of a large estate supplying food rents in the early Anglo-Saxon period to the Bishop of Dorchester, there is no direct evidence for its economic life before Domesday Book.[12] It may be noted here, however, that its economic ties with the villages of Towersey in Buckinghamshire and Sydenham in Lewknor hundred, both daughter churches of Thame, may once have been much closer than they were by the 11th century, and that though Thame's dependent villages of North Weston, Attington, Moreton, and Tetsworth are not mentioned in Domesday, there is no reason to suppose that they were not already in existence. The fertility of the soil would encourage early settlement[13] and the form of the names of the villages and the number of plough-lands recorded in 1086 supports this view. Attington derives from Eatta's hill (O.E. *Eattan dun*), Moreton from *Mor-tun*, Tetsworth from *Tætel's worþ* and Weston is the *west tun*, i.e. west of Thame, with North added to distinguish it from South Weston, a Domesday village.[14]

In 1086 there were 37 hides in the bishop's demesne manor of Thame and land for 34 ploughs, but only 24 were in use. The bishop had 5 in demesne and 5 serfs, and his customary tenants, 27 *villani* and 26 bordars, had 19 ploughs. There was a mill, worth £1, and the meadowland, always highly prized in the rich Thame valley, was worth £3, a tenth of the value of the whole manor. The pre-Conquest valuation of Thame was £20, but when received by Bishop Remigius the estate had so suffered that its value had fallen to £16.[15] Of the 23 hides held by the bishop's knights, it is said that there were 10 ploughs in demesne, and that 16 *villani* with 21 bordars and 8 serfs had another 10 ploughs. These holdings were in an area that included North Weston, Moreton, Attington, and Tetsworth.[16]

The size of the bishop's manor was diminished in the 12th century by a number of grants: first, Thame Abbey received 3 carucates on its refoundation in 1139 or 1140, when Bishop Alexander gave his park at Thame so that the Cistercian monks of Ottley in Oddington might have a more favourable site;[17] second, the new prebend of Thame was endowed with 4 carucates by Bishop Alexander by 1146,[18] and possibly about this time part of the bishop's demesne was set aside for the foundation of the *burgus* of New Thame.[19] The remainder appears to have continued as a demesne manor, administered by the bishop's servants, probably until 1509, when it was farmed to Geoffrey Dormer.[20] Details, however, are lacking except for a few scattered notices. Apart from an account of the sale of corn in 1181–2, entered on the pipe roll as the manor was in the king's hands during a vacancy,[21] there is no further information until the detailed description given of the manor in the survey of the bishop's estates made in the second quarter of the 13th century. The bishop then had 7 free tenants, 5 at Thame and 2 at North Weston, holding between them 14½ virgates and paying assised rents of 73s. 2d. The Thame tenants were also bound to do carrying services: Roger, son of Lete, for example held 3 virgates for 18s. rent and carried the lord's writs as far as Banbury, Buckend (Hunts.), Biggleswade (Beds.) and Wooburn (Bucks.); he also carried, with the bailiff, the bishop's money. Of the customary tenants of Thame,[22] 10 held 10½ virgates, 21 half-virgates and 4 tofts; 16 were cottars. There were 16 villein virgaters in North

---

[3] Ibid.
[5] *Census.*
[6] Inf. the Clerk, U.D.C. and local inquiry.
[7] MS. Dunkin 439/3, p. 270; 438/5, p. 284.
[8] Brown and Guest, *Thame*, 252.
[9] *V.C.H. Oxon.* ii. 351. For the later history of the hunt see ibid. 351–4.
[10] Inf. the Secretary, Thame Show Cttee.
[11] The help of Mrs. Moira Long with the writing of this section is gratefully acknowledged.
[12] See above, p. 170.
[13] Cf. R. Lennard, *Rural England*, 1086–1135, 1 sqq.

[4] Ibid.

[14] *P.N. Oxon.* (E.P.N.S.), i. 99, 143, 144, 146.
[15] *V.C.H. Oxon.* i. 402.
[16] Ibid. 403; and see above, pp. 148, 172, 174.
[17] *V.C.H. Oxon.* ii. 83–84.
[18] *Rot. Hund.* (Rec. Com.), ii. 820; and see below, p. 199.
[19] See above, p. 178.
[20] *Thame Gazette*, 21 May 1889: manorial accounts.
[21] *Pipe R.* 1182 (P.R.S. xxxi), 59.
[22] There is no separate entry for the Moreton tenants, who appear to be included under the heading of Thame. For the bishop's demesne lands in Tetsworth see above, p. 151.

Weston. No comparison can profitably be made with the number of tenants in 1086, for the manor had been reduced in size. The account of the rents and services given illustrates the transitional period when the villein might be doing either week-work or paying a money rent and doing an agreed amount of boon-work, presumably according to the lord's needs.

The bishop had 5 plough-lands in demesne and could have 200 sheep and 20 cows. He drew some of his permanent as well as seasonal labour from his customary tenants. Two of the half-virgaters were to be the lord's ploughmen if he wished and for this were quit of all other services. Two others were liable to keep the lord's cows and his sheep, and one of the cottars was the lord's gardener and was quit of the services which the other cottars owed. Another virgater was not liable for week-work, because he made the ironwork for 4 ploughs, providing the iron himself. Some of the tenants may have been *famuli*, who had been provided with some land, for 2 men who held tofts were called ploughmen (*carucarii*). Since the time of Bishop William (1203–6) the cottars had been allowed to rent a certain meadow for 3s. in lieu of the hay they used to receive from the bishop at mowing time. All customary tenants paid dues to the bishop when they succeeded to a holding or married a daughter, and they paid fines for fornication and gave an 'aid' when the lord wished.

The North Weston villeins owed much the same services, but paid only 5s. when they held a virgate at farm.[23]

The hundredal inquest of 1279 reveals a number of developments on the bishop's manor and in its dependent hamlets. The bishop had 4 plough-lands in demesne with a mill and two weirs, and 38 recorded tenants as against 46 in the earlier survey. The half-virgater class of tenant was not mentioned as such and there were now 21 virgaters and 17 cottars, who held 4 acres each. No services are recorded and the whole entry is of the briefest kind, since the king had little interest in the bishop's manor. The amount of customary land under cultivation had remained much the same. The holders of 1 virgate paid a rent of 5s. and their services were valued at 3s. As at the time of the earlier survey some 50 years before, the bishop had 4 free tenants in Thame besides Geoffrey de Lewknor, tenant of ¼-knight's fee, but the jurors made no mention of services other than scutage and suit to the hundred of Thame. Others holding of the bishop in Thame were the rector, i.e. the prebendary, who had 16 virgates in villeinage, and the abbey, which had 3 carucates in alms. The 4 carucates assigned to the church seems to be an error and simply a repetition of the prebendary's holding.[24]

More detailed accounts are given of the bishop's property in the hamlets of Attington, Moreton, and Weston. The bishop had 9 virgaters in Moreton, although most of the manor's land there had been subinfeudated: Nicholas de Segrave held 10 virgates by military tenure, and had 7 virgater and 6 half-virgater tenants paying a rent at the rate of 12s. a virgate.[25]

Thame Abbey was the other chief tenant, holding Moreton (and Attington) for ½-knight's fee. In Moreton it had 32 tenants, but only 5 of these, including the smith and the miller, held as much as 10 acres to a virgate. The rest of the 21 tenants had only a messuage or a cottage, with a few acres attached, and may have been craftsmen, partly dependent on the market at Thame for their livelihood. Among them were at least one weaver and two carpenters. In Attington the abbot had an estate of 6 virgates and 12 tenants, of whom 1 held 3 virgates for 30s., scutage, and suit of court; and 3 others held 2⅝ virgates between them and paid rent at the rate of 10s. a virgate. The abbot also had 8 cottagers paying rents ranging from 2s. to 5s. On a second estate in Attington of over 4½ virgates, belonging to Alexander de Hampden, there were no cottagers. The virgaters held from 1¼ virgates to ½-virgate each and likewise paid rent at the rate of 10s. a virgate (24 a.).[26]

In North Weston William Quatremain held the manor to which were attached 15 virgates in Ascot, in Great Milton parish. His 7 demesne virgates and fishery, however, were certainly in North Weston, and he had there 2 customary tenants and 5 free tenants who owed small-rents, scutage, or suit of court. William son of Henry held 8 virgates and a fishery of the bishop, but had granted them to subtenants. John Basset, who held a hide in socage of the bishop, had done likewise. The bishop himself had 8 customary tenants and 2 tenants besides John Basset. These too held in socage and owed suit of court for a virgate and ½-virgate respectively. The bishop's customars held on the same terms as his Moreton ones, but Quatremain's 2 customars paid 5s. rent and did services worth 3s. for 1 virgate. The 3 customars of William, son of Henry, owed the same rent and services; his 3 cottars paid 4s. and their services were worth 1s.[27]

The early years of the 14th century as elsewhere seem to have been disastrous for the farming community at Thame. The abbey, more able than most to cope with adversity, was heavily in debt, perhaps owing to bad seasons and murrain among the sheep.[28]

A record of a sale of a farm and stock in 1311 for £104 5s. provides interesting information both about farming practice at this time and on the way in which a rich Thame landholder, who had invested in land in the fields and town alike, seems to have got into financial difficulties. The property, which included burgage tenements, belonged to Thomas Elys of Thame and North Weston, a son of Richard Elys, clerk, a leading man in the town and parish.[29] Thomas Elys had 38½ acres sown with corn and wheat; 36½ acres of barley, drage (barley mixed with corn), beans, and oats; and there must have been a certain amount lying fallow. He also had 142 acres of meadow and 55 acres of pasture. There were considerable stocks of grain, malt, and hay in his three granaries, 16 head of cattle, 131 sheep and lambs, as well as poultry and pigs. His farming equipment was extensive and is listed in detail.[30] In the same year he sold another 92 acres and 7 messuages and tofts,[31]

[23] Queen's Coll. MS. 366, ff. 23b–24. For the date of the survey see above, p. 13, n. 94.
[24] *Rot. Hund.* (Rec. Com.), ii. 820; and see below, p. 199.
[25] *Rot. Hund.* ii. 821.
[26] Ibid. ii. 821–2. The size of the virgate is deduced from the fact that the normal rent for a virgate was 10s. and that

13s. 4d. was paid for 1 virgate and 8 acres.
[27] Ibid. 821–2.
[28] *V.C.H. Oxon.* ii. 84.
[29] See above, p. 180.
[30] Rousham Arch. N 45.
[31] Ibid. N 47.

but as his son John continued to hold land in Old Thame and North Weston[32] it is evident that only a part of the family property was sold.

Although small flocks of sheep, like Elys' or the flock of 200 that the Bishop of Lincoln might keep,[33] may have been common form the main emphasis at this period appears to have been on arable farming. The lands of the Cistercian abbey were possibly an exception. The order's addiction to sheep-farming is well known, and the abbey's interest in the wool trade is exemplified in 1224 by the grant of a licence to export wool despite the general prohibition in force.[34] Although Thame Abbey had other property besides its Thame lands, it is likely, particularly in view of the evidence there is for the consolidation of its open-field land, and because of the large extent of its park land, that much of its wool came from Thame, where the soil was so well suited to grazing.[35]

Some light on the relative wealth of the hamlets in the 14th century is thrown by the tax-assessment lists. New Thame and Old Thame with 67 and 50 taxpayers respectively in 1327 easily take the lead. North Weston has 27, Moreton 20, and Attington 16 contributors. The respective totals paid are £6 7s. 11d., £5 3s. 6d., £3 2s. 11d., £2 5s. 6d. and £2 2s. 4d.[36] The reassessment of 1334 led to a somewhat drastic change: the respective totals were then £9 2s. 8d. for New Thame, £3 7s. 9d. for Old Thame, and £2 14s. 6d. for North Weston.[37] Developments at Moreton and Attington cannot be gauged as they were taxed together in 1344.[38] Whether these reductions should be attributed to the influence of the bishop or to a real decline in production is a matter for speculation. In 1354 the comparatively high abatement of 6s. for Attington compared with 6s. for Weston, 3s. for Moreton and 40s. for Old Thame and Priestend may indicate that Attington's population was already declining.[39] The poll tax of 1377 shows that both Attington and Weston with 27 and 49 adults respectively were small hamlets compared with Moreton with 69 adults. At Priestend and Old Thame there were 211 tax payers and 325 at New Thame.[40]

Contemporary evidence for the field system is slight, but it seems that the arable fields were divided into five groups, those of Old Thame, North Weston, Moreton, Attington, and Priestend. Four of these sets of fields, those of Old Thame, North Weston, Moreton, and Attington are apparent from the account in the hundred rolls[41] and references in the charters, but the first explicit mention of Priestend is in a document of 1412 which deals with 7 acres in 'the fields of Priestende called Lapersdon' (i.e. Lobbersdown).[42] The Priestend fields lay between Moreton and Weston, from the Cuttle Brook on the east to Lobbersdown Hill in the south-west corner of the parish, and probably originated in Bishop Alexander's grant of 4 carucates to the church in c. 1146.[43]

Early deeds give many furlong and other field names, but except for East Field and West Field recorded at Old Thame in about 1150[44] they throw little light on the field system. The fact that in 1348 the bishop had 208 acres of arable in one course and 252 acres in another may indicate that a two-course rotation was still practised in Old Thame.[45] The evidence in the 14th century is insufficient to say how far consolidation of strips had gone, but there was certainly some although much of the open-field land still lay in ½-acre strips at the end of the century.[46] Thame Abbey, for one, had certainly been consolidating its holdings since the mid-12th century. At that time it made an exchange of land with the men of Moreton and in c. 1190 another exchange is recorded.[47] A late-13th- or early-14th-century account of the abbey's Moreton estate, which was attached to its Home Grange, shows that consolidation was by then well advanced. In one furlong (stadium) there were 36 lands ('rugges'), in another 38 lands, and in a third 13 butts.[48] Later in the 15th century, references to 7-acre strips described as contiguous (conjuncti) occur.[49]

A terrier of the mid-15th century (1441-53) of Attington lands held by the Abbey and Drew Barantyne also shows some consolidation. Attington Field contained 477½ field acres and was divided into three inclosures separated by ditches. The first South Close (141½ a. and 1 gore), lying between Attington village and Copcourt, contained 8 furlongs, varying in size from 13½ to 42 acres. The second inclosure was a little close called North Close, containing over 92 acres. It lay between Attington and Horsenden Hill. There were 7 furlongs in it varying in size from 1¾ to 23 acres. The third inclosure, 'the other great close', was called West Close; it lay between Attington village and the London–Tetsworth road and contained 70 acres, 3 roods in 12 furlongs, varying in extent from 1½ to 23 acres. There was also a number of furlongs, totalling 35¼ acres, described as lying outside the West Close, of which over 5 acres belonged to Tetsworth Grange (i.e. the abbey's farm in Tetsworth). Although much of the land was held by the ten tenants of the abbot and Drew Barantyne in scattered ½-acre strips, there were many blocks of 2 to 4½ acres, and much of the abbot's demesne was held separately and had been so held since the 'foundation' (i.e. 1139). In Broke furlong in the North Field Thame had 19 out of 20 acres separate all the year except from 1 August to 25 March; in 'Le Combes' furlong 20 acres of separate land. The abbot held in all 214 acres, 3 roods and Drew Barantyne had 180 acres, 2 roods. There was also a piece of pasture called Mede acre lying between Wallingford Way and Tetsworth Field. This was divided into 13 lots of which the abbot held 5⅔ and Barantyne 7½ lots.[50]

Considerable changes occurred in the last quarter

[32] Rousham Arch. N 75, N 151, N 152.
[33] See above.
[34] Cal. Pat. 1216-25, 457.
[35] Wool from Thame and Notley abbeys is listed in an Italian merchants' guide to commercial practice (1315) where it is highly priced: W. Cunningham, Growth of English Industry and Commerce, 633.
[36] E 179/161/9.
[37] e.g. E 179/161/17.
[38] Ibid.
[39] E 179/161/30.
[40] E 179/161/41.
[41] Rot. Hund. (Rec. Com.), ii. 820-2.

[42] Rousham Arch. N 303.
[43] See p. 199.
[44] Rousham Arch. N 1; cf. ref. to West Field in Old Thame in 1309: N. 31, 269. For Attington names see Thame Cart. ii. 174-92.
[45] Queen's Coll. MS. 366, f. 60.
[46] Rousham Arch. Charters, passim; e.g. 3½ a. in the North Weston field lay in 6 separate furlongs in 1397: Rousham Arch. N 249.   [47] Thame Cart. i. 44, 47.
[48] Ibid. ii. 195. This document has been identified as relating to Moreton from the field names.
[49] Rousham Arch. N 187, 249.
[50] Thame Cart. ii. 174-92.

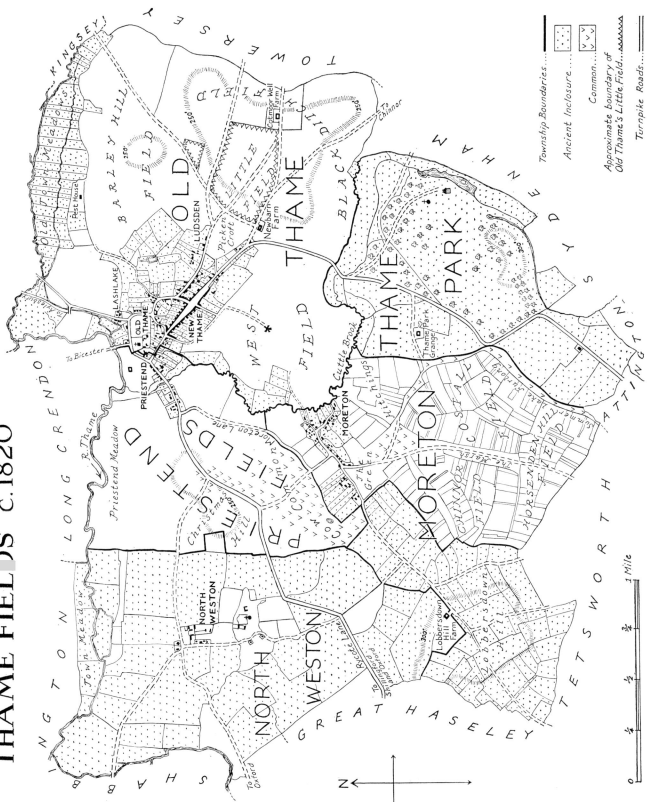

THAME FIELDS C.1820

Map illustrating early inclosure and open fields in Thame and its hamlets before general inclosure. Based on Richard Davis's map (1797), a late-18th-century map of Moreton, Thame inclosure award and map (1826), and North Weston tithe award and map (1847).

of the 15th century, when Geoffrey Dormer, wool stapler, was building up a large estate. In 1473 he acquired Baldington manor in Thame[51] and Attington manor at about the same time. From then on he steadily accumulated land in all the Thame fields, mostly by purchases of a few acres at a time.[52] In 1498 his manor comprised 7 messuages and over 700 acres of arable, meadow, and pasture.[53] In 1509 his son, Geoffrey Dormer, acquired the lease of the bishop's demesne manor of New Thame, and continued to buy up more land.[54] By 1552 Baldington's manor was said to comprise 2,200 acres, and although this figure cannot, perhaps, be taken at its face value it may be accepted that the property was unusually large for this part of the country, and that the emphasis laid on meadow and pasture (1,100 a.) has some significance.[55] The Dormers were noted inclosers elsewhere,[56] and had almost certainly been inclosing at Moreton and Attington at the end of the 15th century or in the early 16th century. Geoffrey Dormer was presented, for instance, in 1481 for inclosing a common pasture at Moreton to the great inconvenience of the other tenants.[57] In 1481 his Attington manor had three times as much pasture as arable, and early 16th-century deeds state that the Dormer manor was commonly called Attington pasture and that its appurtenances were 'meadows, leasurs, and pastures'.[58] In this connexion, furthermore, the names Dormer Leys farm and Dormer Leys Great Ground are also significant. The information given in a 1557 lease that the manor had formerly been leased to Owen Robotham, a butcher, suggests that the rich meadow pastures were being used to fatten beasts for the Thame and Oxford markets.[59] Again, in 1592 when Baldington manor was sold, 30 acres of 'inclosed several ground' were mentioned and other new closes are recorded about the same time.[60]

Thame Abbey or its lessees were certainly active inclosers: its estate valued in 1535 at £19 6s. 8d. in Thame, at £46 16s. in Moreton, and at £21 6s. 8d. in Attington, then all leased out, consisted mainly of pasture and meadow closes.[61] Some of these dated from the late 15th century or before: in 1477–8 the abbey was leasing three pasture closes to tenants for £4 each, a high price compared with the rent of £10 it was receiving for the Home Grange at Moreton; in 1480 the abbot was presented for encroaching on the lord's common in Moreton called 'Somerlake' and 'Redelond', and in 1535 'le Reddlands' are listed as inclosed pasture.[62] Other inclosed pastures in Moreton and Thame were listed and the name of Shepecott farm testifies to the abbey's one-time interest in the wool trade.[63] In 1544 the bishop leased Sheplease meadow for £4 a year.[64]

Land in the south-west at 'Chelyngdon' had also been inclosed by 1490, when 7 acres there were said to be 'several at all times', though men might go through with cattle by licence.[65] On the eastern boundary there had been inclosure at Cotmore Wells, for it was probably the 'Cotnour', where 11 acres were inclosed for pasture and a messuage destroyed in 1493; and inclosure of commons was reported in Old Thame in 1503.[66] At North Weston inclosure may have been completed in the 16th century: in 1538 Sir John Clerke, lord of the manor, obtained a pardon for depopulation ('ruins, decays, and voluntary devastations') and inclosure for pasture both at North Weston and in New Thame,[67] and in 1542 Nicholas Clerke's lease of North Weston manor to Sir John Williams included 2,900 sheep and cattle.[68]

Inclosures such as these and the high price of corn produced the discontent which led to the agrarian rising of 1596. An armourer from Thame was one of the ringleaders and Lord Norreys of Rycote was one of those especially singled out for attack.[69]

Inclosure at Priestend and Old Thame continued into the 17th century. In 1623 every tenant who had land in a certain part of Priestend Field was ordered by the homage to make a quickset hedge round his holding.[70] In the same year the leys which had become widely scattered and intermixed were redivided and allotted on a permanent basis.[71] The stints at this date are interesting on account of the large number of sheep allowed; the holder of a yardland could put on the commons 60 sheep, 8 cattle, and 6 horses.[72] The result was that there were complaints of the commons being overburdened.[73] More extensive inclosure took place in 1651 when some 23 tenants agreed to exchange their strips and to fence off their land for pasture in Lobbersdown Field, one of the Priestend fields.[74] The chief promoter of the scheme was Edward Wray, lord of the manor. The tenants' reasons are of interest: they complained that the field, about 2 miles from Priestend, was too far away to be manured, and so should be laid down to pasture; they also claimed that inclosure with ditches and hedges would increase the supply of wood, which was very scarce. Other tenants conspired to throw down the inclosures and combined in 'a violent manner', but eventually agreed with the majority. Common rights were abandoned and a certain amount of common was set aside for cottagers. The agreement was confirmed by Chancery decree and enrolled.[75]

The period was undoubtedly one of great prosperity for the country's yeoman farmers in general and Thame farmers were no exception: John Woodbridge, yeoman of North Weston, for example, left

[51] See above, p. 172.
[52] e.g. Rousham Arch. N 338, 345, 351, 352, 357, 372, 383.
[53] Ibid. N 382*.
[54] e.g. Ibid. N 394, 396, 397, 399, 400, 401.
[55] Ibid. N 414.
[56] e.g. see above, p. 134.
[57] d.d. Bertie c 16 (uncat.): ct. roll Jan. 1481.
[58] C.P. 40/876/, m. 444; Rousham Arch. N 418, N 442.
[59] Rousham Arch. N 418.
[60] Ibid. N 442.
[61] Valor Eccl. (Rec. Com.), ii. 213; cf. L. & P. Hen. VIII, xxvii, p. 103.
[62] Bodl. MS. Rolls Oxon. 141; d.d. Bertie c 16 (uncat.): ct. roll, Jan. 1481; Valor Eccl. ii. 213.
[63] Valor Eccl. ii. 213; other pastures were 'le Oxelease' and 'cowshippinge mede'.
[64] Linc. Chapter Acts, 1536–47 (L.R.S. xiii), 132. 'Dygged more', leased to a butcher, may have been converted arable: ibid. 95–97.
[65] Rousham Arch. N 303, N 377.
[66] Dom. of Incl. 351; d.d. Bertie c 16 (uncat.): ct. roll, 1503.   [67] L. & P. Hen. VIII, v. 13.
[68] d.d. Bertie b 6 (uncat.).
[69] Cal. S.P. Dom. 1595–7, 317.
[70] d.d. Bertie b 3 (uncat.): ct. roll. Cf. a presentment in 1631 for keeping 'in several' a close belonging to West Field (Old Thame): MS. Top. Gen. c 43, p. 6.
[71] d.d. Bertie b 3 (uncat.): ct. roll.
[72] Ibid.
[73] For complaints of overburdening at earlier dates (e.g. Jan. 1481) see d.d. Bertie c 16.
[74] O.R.O. Thame doc. (uncat.).
[75] Ibid. July 1651.

goods valued at over £1,739 in 1647;[76] in 1662 the tenant of Thame Park Grange left about half that sum;[77] and in 1699 the tenant of Old Thame manor farm paid £400 for a renewal of the lease.[78] This prosperity is reflected in the hearth-tax returns of the 1660's. Moreton appears to have been a village of small yeoman farmers or husbandmen with houses taxed on two hearths or less, but in North Weston, Old Thame, and Priestend there were many substantial farmhouses taxed on four hearths and more.[79] New Thame also had its farmhouses, but here wealth may have come more from a combination of trade and farming. The tax returns also reveal some of the effects of inclosure: North Weston, for instance, has shrunk in size and only 10 persons were listed there for the tax of 1662, when the fullest returns were made.[80] Attington had virtually disappeared; only Richard Cornish, the tenant of part of the manor, paid tax either in 1662 or 1665.[81]

Information about conditions in the early 18th century is provided by a survey made in 1728 of the Earl of Abingdon's estate in Old and New Thame and in Priestend. He was one of the successors to Lord Williams's manors. He owned 1,487 acres in Old Thame and 831 acres in Priestend; the old value of the farmlands in Old Thame is given as £878 4s. 2d. and its real value in 1728 was estimated at £1,075 16s. 2d.; the old value of Priestend lands was £668 and the new £769 12s. 6d.[82] Five-sixths of Old Thame was arable. All the field land was described as good on the whole. It was usually let at 10s. an acre, but the bailiff noted that the times being now so bad for farming the tenants begin to scruple at that price. He recommended that one source of increased rent would be to inclose those meadowlands which still remained common, as this part was the better land and the inclosures would be of particular value to the town 'for the convenience of keeping horses, as well others as their own'.[83] There were about 60 copyholders and 10 leaseholders with land in Old Thame: nearly half of these held small holdings of between 10 and 36 acres, and about a third held under 5 acres. One leaseholder, the tenant of Thame farm, held as much as 486 acres of which 424 acres (or 12 yardlands) were open-field arable.[84]

Part of Moreton was included in the survey (4 copyholds), but the rent of land there, which was partly a poor clay, was only about 8s. an acre.[85] At Priestend a higher proportion of land, three-sevenths, was meadow and pasture. Part of Lobbersdown Hill, where Priestend inclosures lay, was described as 'a parcel of land lying together' of which the soil was naturally poor and had been made worse by over-ploughing. The land was used as pasture and rented at 20s. an acre, but the bailiff considered it worth no more than 12s.[86] Stints were very much reduced compared with the figures given in 1623: in 1728 only 20 sheep were allowed to the yardland, and 4 cows and 4 horses.[87] The rotation practised in the

Priestend open fields was two crops and a fallow. The yield was good as the soil was good, although badly drained. The rent was 10s. an acre, but the bailiff considered that the acre must be a small one or the rent very low, for similar, but inclosed land, was let for 20s. an acre and the common difference between field and inclosed land was reckoned as a third. Meadowland was rented at 40s. an acre and was 'very good'. The land was tenanted by 33 copyholders, 1 leaseholder, and 1 freeholder. Eleven tenants held between 30 and 70 acres, and the rest under 30 acres. Rents ranged from 4s. to £2 a year.[88]

There is no comparable description of Attington and North Weston, but the North Weston estate was sold for £4,000 in 1749. The hamlet's field was completely divided into closes by this time and over half of it was estimated to be pasture and meadow.[89] Attington, also completely inclosed and mostly pasture and meadow,[90] was largely farmed by the Cornish family. Richard Cornish had been the only substantial tenant in the 1660's, and in 1754 a Cornish was the only 40s. freeholder.[91] In 1785 members of the family were tenants of the main estate (the former Abbey manor) and paid ⅙ of the total land tax for their freeholds.[92] Their house, Dormer Leys Farm, is the only one shown on Davis's map of 1797.[93]

Variations of soil and of farming practice in the various parts of the parish are reflected in the land-tax valuations at the end of the 18th century and at the beginning of the 19th century. North Weston and Thame Park had higher valuations (£160 and £127 respectively) than the open-field hamlet of Moreton (£61 12s.) and the partly uninclosed Priestend (£93 6s.). In North Weston the two landowners had 6 tenant farmers between them. Thame Park was owned and farmed by the Wenmans and there were only 3, and later 2, tenant farmers occupying Wenman land outside the Park. In other parts of the parish the land was mostly in the hands of small tenant-farmers. Several like the Loosleys, Hedges, Barnards, and Eustaces occupied land in several hamlets and had in fact fair-sized farms. There were still some men, however, who held only a yardland or a half-yardland.[94] One of the largest farms in the parish was Manor farm at North Weston, which was leased by the Revd. Thomas Plaskett, whose views and experience were frequently cited by Arthur Young. Plaskett used a 5-course rotation and grew turnips, swede and rape, but only one-third of North Weston was under plough at this time (i.e. 1809). Plaskett himself kept a flock of 300 sheep of the New Leicester breed, and milking cows were no doubt also kept, for, as Young remarked, the land round Thame was good for dairy farming.[95]

Davis's map of 1797 shows that it was mainly the pasture land that was inclosed and that the arable was still open-field land.[96] Another 18th-century map shows that there had been some consolidation

[76] Lee, *Thame*, 158 n.
[77] Ibid. 159 n.
[78] d.d. Bertie 25 (uncat.).
[79] *Hearth Tax Oxon.* 43–44, 46–49.
[80] E 179/164/504.
[81] Ibid.; *Hearth Tax Oxon.* 52.
[82] MS. Top. Oxon. c 381, ff. 60–81.
[83] Ibid. ff. 67–79.
[84] Ibid. ff. 60–81; tenants with no field land are not included as it is assumed they were townsmen.
[85] Ibid. ff. 73–74, 79.   [86] Ibid. f. 66.

[87] Ibid. Reduction in stint had probably been progressive. At Old Thame the stint of 80 sheep to the yardland had been reduced to 40 in 1648: MS. Top. Gen. c 44, f. 110.
[88] Ibid. ff. 60–66.   [89] d.d. Bertie b 5 (uncat.).
[90] Davis, *Oxon. Map* (1797).
[91] *Hearth Tax Oxon.* 52; E 179/255/4; *Oxon. Poll*, 1754.
[92] O.R.O. Land tax assess.
[93] Davis, *Oxon. Map* (1797).
[94] O.R.O. Land tax assess.
[95] Young, *Oxon. Agric.* 13, 127, 178, 260, 272, 305.
[96] Davis, *Oxon. Map* (1797).

of strips in Moreton field: groups of 3 or 4 acres were common and there were 30 acres in the largest block, the Earl of Abingdon's.[97] Pasture and meadow were scarce judging from the lease in 1795 of Balliol College's small property, which specified that a yearly rent of £5 must be paid for each acre converted to arable. In 1817 the high price of corn led to this rent being increased to £20 an acre.[98] Although Attington had been long inclosed inclosure of the old Thame, Priestend, and Moreton fields did not begin until 1823 and was not completed before 1826, but in the preceding years many tenants were in fact cultivating part of the open fields separately in 'hitches'.[99] There had also been some further inclosure of meadowland and some land had been taken in from the waste since 1797, but there remained 2,180 acres in the open fields, old inclosure amounting to 2,857 acres. In addition to the open-field arable and meadow 150 acres of waste were allotted. Priestend and Moreton each had three open fields and Old Thame had four; West Field, Barley Hill Field (a division of West Field), and Black Ditch Field, and Little Field, which had developed out of East Field.[1]

To meet the expense of inclosure the commissioners sold 126½ acres, 80 acres of which Miss Wykeham bought. Two of the chief allottees were the Earl of Abingdon, lord of Thame and Priestend manors, and Miss Wykeham, who held Moreton manor and the prebendal tithes. They received 4½ and 5½ acres respectively for manorial rights (equal to 1/10 of the waste). Miss Wykeham was allotted 532 acres for the impropriate tithes, and about 185 acres for her freehold estate in Moreton. The Earl of Abingdon received 110½ acres for his freehold estate and another 62 acres for the copyhold estates of 9 tenants, which had come into his hands since the inclosure Act. The vicar received some 113 acres for his vicarial glebe and Thame tithes. Allotments were made to about 57 other persons in respect of 39 Abingdon leasehold and copyhold estates (797½ a.) and 23 freehold estates (c. 400 a.). Of these the trustees of James Meadowcroft, one of the Abingdon estate tenant-farmers, received 272 acres, and Joseph Way received 137 acres. About 22 allottees, among them Balliol College and Thomas Philip Wykeham, were awarded between 10 and 50 acres. The other allotments were under 10 acres and included 2½ acres for Moreton poor and 6 acres for the Thame churchwardens.[2]

A survey of the Earl of Abingdon's estate in 1827 shows the position immediately after inclosure. The land is described as 'in hand' or 'out on lives'. Thus in 1827 1,503 acres in Thame and Priestend were leased for lives as against 388 acres 'in hand', and the annual values are given as £2,130 and £678. In North Weston, as a result of earlier inclosure, all Lord Abingdon's land (220 a.) was in hand, and was worth £278 a year. The totals are 609 acres in hand and 1,680 acres on long leases or for lives.[3] By 1844, however, many of these leases had fallen

in and the major part (1,413 a.) of Lord Abingdon's land was let on yearly tenancies at a total rent of £2,372. The 958 acres valued at £1,750 a year, still let on leases for lives, produced £44 16s. in quit rents. In spite of these changes in the form of tenure there were still a large number of very small holdings, even amongst the tenants who paid rack-rents. Lord Abingdon owned only 4 farms over 200 acres. Fifteen of his tenants held between 51 and 100 acres, and only three had 100 to 200 acres.[4] This was roughly the position in the parish as a whole. The 1851 census showed that most farms were between 100 to 250 acres, but that many still had under 100 acres. There were three large farms of over 250 acres and one of 870, employing 37 labourers.[5]

By the late 19th century there were only 19 substantial farmers in the parish[6] and one at Attington, and by the early 20th century most holdings under 100 acres had disappeared. The North Weston farms of the Abingdon estate were all over 200 acres in 1913 and another North Weston farm was 325 acres.[7]

The outstanding advantage of inclosure was that it enabled farmers for the first time to put to the best use the mixed soils of the area. Kimmeridge Clay, Portland Beds, Lower Greensand, and Gault made a variety of farming possible, but the suitability of the district for grazing and dairying could now for the first time be fully exploited. Along the river towards Waterstock the clay, modified by sand and gravel, produces some of the best grazing in the county and the meadows along the Cuttle Brook are of almost equal value. After inclosure therefore the trend was towards a conversion from arable to pasture. In 1844 the proportion of pasture to arable was already 13·9 and by 1914 three-quarters of the farmland in the parish was permanent pasture.[8] The new emphasis on dairying and stockbreeding was greatly assisted by the opening of improved communications, especially those with London.[9] Until 1865 butter and cheese were the main products of the dairies, but the rinderpest disease that broke out in that year caused London buyers to seek suppliers farther afield. Thame farmers very largely turned over to the production of milk, which was sent by rail to London from Aylesbury and Tiddington stations[10] until motor transport superseded the railways in the 20th century. All types of farmers were encouraged by the formation of such societies as the Thame Agricultural Society in 1855 and the Heavy Horse Society in 1914, and advance was made, particularly on the larger farms, in the breeding of stock.[11] Another characteristic of 19th-century farming in the Thame area, as elsewhere, was the increased use of machinery of improved types. Threshing mills were replaced by the steam threshing machine, while iron ploughs, harrows, drills, and so on came into general use.[12] This change combined with the turn over to pasture and the amalgamation of farms bore hardly on the agricultural labourer. Less labour was needed and unemployment resulted. It was

97 B.M. Add. MS. 34, 557 A. Lord Charles Spencer who is named on the map was the 2nd son (1740–1820) of the 3rd Duke of Marlborough: *D.N.B.*
98 Balliol Coll. Mun. Moreton leases A 17, 26.
99 O.R.O. Incl. award (1826).
1 Ibid. In 1747 there was a Pounder's Bush Field in Priestend: Brown and Guest, *Thame*, 42, 176.
2 O.R.O. Incl. award.
3 MS. Top. Oxon. b 210, f. 15.
4 Bodl. G.A. Oxon. b 92 (21): *Sale cat.*

5 H.O. 107/1726/2.
6 Kelly, *Dir. Oxon.* (1887–1903).
7 Bodl. G.A. Oxon. b 92 (22, 23): *Sale cats.* Cotmore Wells was only 91 a. in 1885: d.d. Hobbes c 26 (uncat.).
8 G.A. Oxon. b 92 (21): *Sale cat.*; Orr, *Oxon. Agric.* map facing p. 201.
9 See above, p. 163.
10 Orr, *Oxon. Agric.* 28; Brown and Guest, *Thame*, 275.
11 Brown and Guest, *Thame*, 198, 220.
12 Ibid. 218–20.

noted in the report of the Poor Law Union in 1892 that where one farm had employed ten regular men it then employed two only although it had been amalgamated with two other farms.[13]

In the 20th century farming continued on the whole to be of a very varied and individual character, but mixed farms with the emphasis on sheep and cattle and occasionally horse-breeding prevailed.[14] The rich pastures along the River Thame are still (1959) given over purely to grazing. In 1935 on the arable land a four- or five-course rotation was almost universal; wheat, oats, barley, and leguminous crops were those mainly cultivated, but there were notable exceptions. By 1952 one farmer used a three-course rotation, another no rotation at all, using dung instead; one grew sugar beet, another kale; one grew crops only for fodder, one sold half his crops, one sold only wheat and so on. As a consequence of government subsidies the land put down to wheat has tended to increase, and root crops and barley have diminished.[15] In 1952, however, most of the land (76 per cent.) was still permanent or convertible pasture and grass. The total number of cattle to the 100 acres had risen from 28 in 1914 to 42 in 1952; cows and heifers had risen from 11 to 18.[16] The number of sheep fell from 51 to 33, and fewer pigs were kept than in 1914 although the efforts of the Pig Marketing Board had done something to encourage the small local farmer.[17] Thame farms were of moderate size: in 1952 out of 22 holdings in the parish and 3 in Attington 7 were farms of over 150 acres and 8 were over 100 acres. About half were occupied by tenants.[18] Since the First World War Thame Show has become the second largest single-day show in the kingdom, but its social importance is its chief aspect.[19] The County Agricultural Show, which is of far greater value to farmers, was held every ten years at Thame before 1939.[20]

MILLS. There was one mill worth 20s. a year on the bishop's Thame estate in 1086.[21] By 1225 there were two mills on his Thame manor, worth £17 10s. 10d. a year,[22] but as his manor extended over several villages it is not certain that they were both in Thame. Peter the miller, recorded in the survey of about this time, was a Thame man who had to make 1 quarter of malt from the bishop's own grain as well as pay various agricultural dues.[23] In 1279 the bishop is said to have a mill and two weirs in Thame, and Thame Abbey presumably had another mill as it had a miller among its tenants.[24] By 1509 both of the bishop's mills were farmed out for £5 a year;[25] the same rent was paid for them in Queen Elizabeth's time when the estate was held by the Norreys

family.[26] In 1594 the homage of Old Thame said that the lord's malt mill was an ancient mill and that the greater part of Thame town had used the mill for grinding their barley, but whether they did so of their own choice was not known.[27] The tenants of Old Thame were said to have been accustomed to use the lord's water-mill and it was maintained that they would wish to do so in the future if the miller did his duty by them.[28]

The water-mill in Old Thame on the Aylesbury road seems to have been called Lashlake.[29] The tenants in the first half of the 18th century were the Cripps family, millwrights of Haddenham (Bucks.), who also held Thame windmill.[30] They held the water-mill together with the malt millhouse and one acre of land on a 99-year lease for £10 a year.[31] The Earl of Abingdon agreed in the lease to assign timber for the repair of the mill; the tenant was to keep the earl's spaniel or greyhound at the millhouse when it was sent.[32] This mill continued in use until the 20th century.[33] By 1920 it was driven by water and steam.[34] In 1924 it ceased working and shortly after was converted into Thame Mill Laundry.[35]

Bernard Cripps of Kingsey (Bucks.) built the windmill in Barley Hill Field in the early 17th century.[36] It was still held by his descendent John Cripps of Haddenham in 1739, when it was apparently granted to Thomas Juggins.[37] It may have been one of the mills recorded in the first half of the 19th century,[38] but was not in use later.[39]

There was another mill in West Field which was first recorded in 1594 when Robert Dormer was ordered to move his mill in the West Field.[40] It was marked on maps of 1797 and 1880.[41] It ceased to function at the end of the century and the buildings were later incorporated in the isolation hospital.[42]

LOCAL GOVERNMENT. Parish government in the Middle Ages was conducted through the three-weekly courts for Moreton, North Weston, Old Thame, and Priestend respectively, and through the fortnightly portmanmoot for New Thame. Views of frankpledge at which each township was represented by its own tithing-men were held monthly. Immediately above these courts was the hundred court of the Bishop of Lincoln for the hundred of Thame. All were subject to the bishop's officers, and the sheriff's officers were excluded as the bishop had return of writs, pleas *de vetito namii*, and the assize of bread and ale.[43] The bishop also had a prison at Thame.[44]

A few rolls survive of the manorial courts or 'halimots'.[45] Among the offences reported are the usual ones of unrepaired houses, unscoured ditches,

[13] O.R.O. Thame Union Min. Bk. 1892.
[14] Orr, *Oxon. Agric.* 19, 33.
[15] Brown and Guest, *Thame*, 273–4; local inf.
[16] Orr, *Oxon. Agric.* plates facing pp. 212, 213; local inf.
[17] Orr, *Oxon. Agric.* plate facing p. 225; Brown and Guest, *Thame*, 275; local inf.
[18] Inf. the Clerk, Thame U.D.C. As North Weston was transferred to Great Haseley in 1932 a comparison of these figures with earlier ones is profitless.
[19] Inf. the Secretary, Thame Show Cttee.
[20] Brown and Guest, *Thame*, 198.
[21] *V.C.H. Oxon.* i. 402.
[22] Queen's Coll. MS. 366, f. 25.
[23] Ibid. f. 24.
[24] *Rot. Hund.* (Rec. Com.), ii. 820.
[25] *Thame Gazette*, 21 May 1889; manorial accounts.
[26] d.d. Bertie c 27 (uncat.): undated rental.
[27] Ibid. c 15 (uncat.): Mar. ct. (1594).

[28] Ibid.: Oct. ct.   [29] H.O. 107/1726/10.
[30] d.d. Bertie c 24 (uncat.): leases.
[31] Ibid. MS. Top. Oxon. c 381, f. 74.
[32] d.d. Bertie c 24 (uncat.): lease of 1717.
[33] See Kelly, *Dir. Oxon.* (1854, 1869, 1887, 1903).
[34] Ibid. (1920).
[35] Inf. Mr. W. Guest.
[36] Rousham Arch. N 463.
[37] d.d. Bertie c 24 (uncat.): lease of 1739.
[38] Kelly, *Dir. Oxon.* (1854, 1869).
[39] Ibid. (1887, 1891).
[40] d.d. Bertie c 16 (uncat.): ct. roll 1594.
[41] Davis, *Oxon. Map* 1797; O.S. Map 25", xli. 3.
[42] Inf. Mr. W. Guest.
[43] *Rot. Hund.* (Rec. Com.), ii. 820.
[44] See above, p. 115.
[45] e.g. there are records of courts in the years 4, 8, 23, 29 Hen. VI and 20 Edw. IV: d.d. Bertie c 16 (uncat.).

and trespass in 'separate' pastures. On one occasion a licence to marry a widow was obtained for 6s. 8d. In the reign of Henry VI *nativi* living outside the manor were reported on several occasions.[46]

New Thame began and remained a seignorial borough[47] and never acquired any corporate privileges. Its chief officer in the medieval period was the Bishop of Lincoln's bailiff, apparently appointed by him.[48] By the 15th century, if not earlier, there were two bailiffs and two under bailiffs.[49] New Thame was divided into four quarters and the tithing-men for each quarter made presentments at the view of frankpledge. At the great view on St. Luke's Day (18 Oct.) the bailiff, and sometimes other officers, presented those who had broken the assizes. On one occasion as many as 82 men and women were presented for breaches of the assize of ale,[50] on another occasion 63, and 10 for breaches of the assize of bread, 16 for selling meat above price and 5 innkeepers for the same. Seven cobblers, 4 bakers, and 4 chandlers were also presented for overcharging.[51] In addition to these common offences, nuisances on the highway and cases of assault, sometimes with dagger or lance, were presented. The highest total amount received at any view was 73s. 4d. in 1436.[52] This total included fines and a sum known as 'St. Luke's pennies', so named after the day on which the court was held. These pence were paid by some burgesses (1d. each) for the right to merchandise for a year without payment of toll. The numbers paying fluctuated from year to year and sums received varied between 5s. 7d. in 1439 and 1s. 8d. in 1472.[53] Among the suitors of the court who made default in their suit were often to be found the abbots of Thame and Notley, the Vicar of Thame, and local gentry such as the Marmions and these too were among those who paid Luke's pence. As in other town courts the inhabitants were commonly presented for raising the hue unjustly, and for allowing unringed pigs to wander in the streets. But the most common presentments were for throwing putrid offal from shops into the streets, for selling bread underweight, for exposing bad meat for sale, and breaking the assize of ale. Bakers, victuallers, and fishmongers in the north quarter figure particularly prominently.[54] In Henry VII's reign there first appears the presentment of a man for allowing common players of cards and other illicit games to play contrary to the statute and another was presented for keeping suspected men and women in his house.[55] As at the view of frankpledge the tithing-men of each of the four quarters made presentments. The fortnightly portmanmoot court was competent to hear pleas of detinue, trespass, and breach of contract, but the great majority of pleas recorded on the rolls are for debt.[56] The slowness and cumbersomeness of the procedure may be seen in a court of 1433. One case

concerned a debt for woollen cloth bought three years previously and another for russet cloth bought nine years previously.[57]

Pleas about tenements do not occur as a rule. These were heard before the royal justices, but on one occasion a fine was paid for permission to acquire more land in the town to enlarge a burgage tenement. The new tenant made fidelity to the bishop and was admitted tenant according to 'the custom of the borough'. She was to hold for ever at a rent of 2d. a year.[58] As the burgess had the important right of being able to devise as well as sell his burgage freely disputes over burgage property must have arisen frequently.[59] Disputes over wills would have been heard in the peculiar court.[60]

A change in procedure had been introduced by Henry VII's reign, which suggests that autocratic control of the town was increasing. The tithing-man for each quarter now presented in company with a burgess. The business of the court, however, was much reduced and courts appear to have been held less frequently. At a court of 17 May 1503 fines amounted to 6d. only compared with sums of round 3s. commonly received in the reign of Henry VI, and no court after this one was held until 22 July.[61] There is nothing about burgess customary law in the surviving rolls except for one archaic survival. Burgesses often cleared themselves of a charge of debt by resorting to the method of compurgation. There are many cases of a burgess waging his law six-handed or four-handed—i.e. supported by the oaths of five or three of his neighbours.[62]

No 16th-century portmanmoot records have survived, and it is therefore uncertain when the court finally came to an end, but it is likely that it coincided with the break up of the bishop's manor in 1559.[63]

Town affairs like those of the parish as a whole were now being largely conducted in the vestry. There the churchwardens were elected and overseers of the poor nominated. In 1560 there is a record of 'highways men' being chosen 'following the consent of the parishioners'.[64] Three were chosen for New Thame and one each for Old Thame, Priestend, and Moreton. The churchwardens' accounts for this period reveal that their business was not always confined to church affairs. The wardens were usually among the leading men of the town and were also the holders of civil office. It is therefore not surprising to find the warden paying 5s. in 1543 for having the moot-hall clock mended, or that they should have later used the proceeds derived from the sale of church goods for the paving of the town.[65]

Despite the growing importance of the vestry, however, view of frankpledge courts and manorial courts continued to be held by the bishop's successors to the lordship of the 'liberties'. Some records of courts baron for Old Thame, Priestend, North

[46] e.g. d.d. Bertie ct. 5 June 1451.
[47] See above, p. 178.
[48] There is no evidence on the surviving rolls for any election of bailiffs by the court. The earliest known bailiff is John le Brun (occ. 1275–1300): Rousham Arch. N 7.
[49] Ibid. N 345, N 347.
[50] d.d. Bertie c 16 (uncat.): Oct. 1433.
[51] Ibid. Oct. 1461. In a court of 1502 7 bakers of white bread were presented besides the more usual traders.
[52] d.d. Bertie c 16 (uncat.).
[53] Ibid.
[54] Ibid.
[55] Ibid. ct. roll 1501–2.
[56] e.g. in a court of 1433–4 there were 9 pleas of debt and

no other business; in a court of 1461–2 there were 11 pleas of debt and 1 of detinue (ibid.).
[57] Ibid. Oct. 1433.
[58] Ibid. Oct. 1437.
[59] For fines see *Oxon. Fines*, 6, 184, 205.
[60] It was argued, for example, as late as 1733 that a will was invalid as it had been proved in the archdeacon's court which did not have jurisdiction in Thame: Oxf. Archd. Oxon. c 164, f. 129. For the peculiar jurisdiction in general see below, p. 201.
[61] d.d. Bertie c 16 (uncat.).
[62] Ibid.
[63] See above, p. 171.
[64] Lee, *Thame*, 533–4.
[65] Lupton, *Extracts*, 15; see below.

Weston, and Moreton have survived.[66] Their main business was the admission of tenants but from time to time they made regulations about the management of the open fields and officers such as fieldsmen, hogsherds, haywards, and mole-catchers were appointed. Records of the view of frankpledge for New Thame or rather for 'New Thame cum membris', as the title had become, also exist for the 17th century. The court, apart from enforcing the tithing system, was mainly concerned with the upkeep of the roads, and the enforcement of sanitary rules about the streets and market-place. At the October court for 1649 nineteen jurors headed by Robert Robotham, an important burgess, and John Bennett were listed. Presentments included killing bulls unbaited (the offenders were mostly men from neighbouring villages), bloodshed, killing sheep and calves in the shambles contrary to the regulations, and emptying paunches in the shambles. The court ordered also that no inhabitant of New Thame should erect any new tenement or take any inmate into his house unless the landlord was prepared to guarantee the parish against any consequent expense.[67] At this and other views of this period it was repeatedly ordered by the courts that no stalls or booths should be placed on Market Hill, but only on the south-west side beginning from 'the end of the stocks' next the 'Lion' up to the corner of Mr. Powell's house.[68]

The town officers were elected at the October courts. They appear to have varied and the explanation may be that some were not annual appointments. In 1676 there were 2 sealers of leather, 2 constables, 4 tithing-men, 2 ale-tasters, 2 flesh-tasters, and 2 scavengers.[69] Officers were also elected to the liberties; at Old Thame court, for example, in 1608 2 scourers of watercourses, 2 meat-tasters, and 4 tithing-men were elected.[70]

Throughout the 18th century and into the 19th the churchwardens, overseers of the poor, the surveyors of highways, and the constables continued to be the main parish officers acting through the vestry.[71] The first big change took place in 1835 when the Thame Poor Law Union and Board of Guardians came into being.[72] Although with the decline of the manorial courts, the liberties of New Thame, Old Thame, Priestend, and Moreton practically ceased to be units of local government, separate overseers and waywardens for each continued to be responsible for registration of births, marriages, and deaths, vaccination, poor-rate assessment, and sanitation.[73] In 1858–9 the parish officers were 2 churchwardens, 3 guardians, 6 overseers (Thame 4, Priestend 2), 10 surveyors (New Thame 2, Old Thame 2, Moreton 2, Priestend 2, Thame Park 1, North Weston 1), 2 petty constables, and 1 high constable.[74]

After the adoption in 1871 of the Local Government Act of 1858 the Local Board was set up and became automatically the Urban District Council in 1894.[75] Step by step the U.D.C. acquired the full

powers of the parish council. Thus in November 1895 it was given power by the Local Government Board to appoint and revoke the appointment of Assistant Overseers and in March 1896 it was allowed to appoint two trustees for the non-ecclesiastical portion of the Thame charities.[76] The council numbered fifteen, five members retiring each year. Of the first council five were farmers, four were in trade, and three were professional men. T. S. Sutton, a grocer, was the first chairman and was chairman again four times in the next six years. Henry Birch was chairman from 1878 to 1882 and Samuel Lacey from 1887 to 1893.[77] Later it became the custom for the chair to be taken by seniority.

Throughout the century the chief concern of the local authorities was the care of the poor; in the second half of the century sanitation became a major consideration, and also the maintenance of the highways and housing.

POOR RELIEF. The foundation of the Quatremain almshouses,[78] and the many payments for the support of the poor and sick entered in the churchwardens' accounts are evidence for the care taken of the poor in the medieval period.[79] The Elizabethan Poor Law Act of 1601, however, opened a new era in poor relief. Eleven leaves of Thame's first rate-book survive. They cover two months in 1604 and six in 1609. There were between 80 and 90 ratepayers paying 2d. to 1s. a month. Total receipts averaged 35s. to 36s., but usually 16 or more persons were behind with their payments. The number of persons receiving relief, which averaged nearly $3\frac{1}{2}d.$ a person a week, varied from 28 to 33. The total expended for the year was £23 or £24.[80]

Voluntary bequests for the relief of the poor continued to be made alongside the official relief. They included seven cottages to be used as poor houses and to be administered by the churchwardens and also funds to provide clothing.[81] With the building of the County House of Correction in 1720, completed after a bequest of £250 from Francis Clerke of North Weston,[82] a notable advance was made in dealing with the problem of the able-bodied poor. In 1723, however, the churchwardens and inhabitants of Thame complained that the keeper had ceased to employ the poor and in 1726 £100 was spent in converting part of the House of Correction into a workhouse.[83] In 1733 the churchwardens petitioned the court again. They charged the deputy keeper of the House of Correction with allowing the prisoners to go at large, letting part of the prison to lodgers, and with other offences. The keeper had lived at Aylesbury for the past three years.[84] As a result of this complaint the master of the workhouse was appointed keeper of the bridewell also.[85] The workhouse management was 'contracted out' to a 'sober person' who undertook to employ the poor in spinning and other work.[86]

In 1776 a determined effort was made to put the

[66] North Weston 1520–61: d.d. Bertie c 13; Priestend 1595–1846: ibid. b 1, b 3, c 5, c 13, c 14, c 15; Old Thame 1560–1702: ibid. b 1, c 154.
[67] MS. Top. Gen. c 3: Oct. 1649.
[68] Ibid. Thame cts. *passim.*
[69] Ibid. Oct. 1676.   [70] Ibid.
[71] Chwdns' accts. and vestry mins. 1765–1840; 1841–95: d.d. Par. Thame c 4.
[72] O.R.O. Th. Union mins. 18 Sept. 1835.
[73] Ibid. 1836, 1841, 1862, 1875.
[74] *Thame Gazette,* 13 Apr. 1858, 12 Apr. 1859.

[75] U.D.C. Th. Dist. Loc. Bd. Min. Bk. 15 Sept. 1871.
[76] Ibid. 12 Nov. 1895; 20 Mar. 1896.
[77] Ibid. U.D.C. mins. *passim.*
[78] See below, p. 217.
[79] Lupton, *Extracts,* 20, 21, 22.
[80] MS. Top. Oxon. c 5.   [81] See below, p. 218.
[82] d.d. Bertie b 5: abstract of title, p. 2.
[83] O.R.O. Cal. Q. Sess. viii, p. 113.
[84] Ibid. p. 133.
[85] Ibid. pp. 134–5.
[86] *Oxf. Jnl.* 5 Feb. 1763.

care of the poor on a sound basis. Articles of agreement were drawn up between the churchwardens, the four overseers, and twelve inspectors, including the vestry clerk and the keeper of the bridewell: churchwardens and overseers could individually commit to the workhouse but the case was later to come before a full meeting; any person who could contribute to the poor rate could inspect the workhouse and the inmates might lay complaints; the keeper was to be fined 20s. for each case of neglect substantiated before the committee. He was to provide all clothes, schooling for the children, and pay rents, &c. for the poor living outside. He was also to pay all incidental expenses connected with poor strangers except any legal expenses and the cost of their removal. His salary was to be £480 a year and he was to have all the profits arising from work done in the workhouse. Apprenticeships were to be approved by a committee, who allowed an extra 20s. for clothing for each apprentice put out to work. In cases of smallpox the keeper was to provide for 15 inmates only.[87]

In 1776 £666 was expended on the poor, £26 on the rent of the workhouse, which accommodated 30 and was now said to be too small, and £14 on litigation and resettlement of paupers.[88] When the new bridewell at Oxford was opened in 1787 the justices closed the Thame one and put it up for sale in 1788.[89] It was bought by the parish for a workhouse in 1790.[90]

By 1803 the problem of poor relief had increased alarmingly: £3,762 was raised by a rate of 11s. 6d. in the £ but £4,413 had been expended. The Speenhamland system was in use and 260 persons were given out-relief and 56 in-door relief. In addition to these permanent paupers and their families 140 persons received occasional relief.[91] The population of Thame in 1801 was 2,293.[92]

The Poor Law Amendment Act of 1834 was adopted by Thame in 1835 and the first meeting of the guardians took place in September 1835.[93] Under the Act Thame became one of the three districts of the newly established Poor Law Union which consisted of 27 Oxfordshire and 8 Buckinghamshire parishes. The Thame district comprised Thame, Tetsworth, Emmington, Aston Rowant and Kingston Blount, Sydenham, and Towersey (Bucks.). The population of Thame at that time was 2,885 and that of Thame Union 5,243.[94] The guardians were mainly occupied in their first year of office with the plans for the new workhouse. It was built on ground adjoining the Prebendal at a total cost of £8,871. It was to have accommodation for 350 but at first be furnished for about 235.[95] The total cost of the workhouse was £11,438. Between 1840 and 1881 a number of improvements were made. These included the separation of the male and female infirmary wards and the conversion of part of one wing into a chapel.[96]

The guardians showed marked generosity and humane consideration for the personal dignity and material welfare of those needing relief and for the officers of the institution. For the first Master and Matron they proposed a joint salary of £150, but the Poor Law Commissioners thought this too high. £110 was fixed. In August 1838 it was resolved that allowances to paupers receiving or entitled to relief should be determined according to the circumstances of each case without reference to existing allowances, and the allowance to aged and infirm paupers and widows was increased by 6d. a head a week; in November 1838 the guardians represented to the Poor Law Commission that the price of bread in their Union was 19½d. an 8 lb. 11 oz. loaf, while the general price of labour was 9s. 8d. a week and they requested an order as to the manner in which poor industrious labourers in employment, with large families, were to be dealt with under existing conditions.[97] In August 1840 they requested that the Local Government Board should allow them to take into the workhouse parts of large families of able-bodied labourers whose earnings were insufficient for supporting their families; but this was regarded by the Board as not being in the best interests of the Union. Women were not to be forced to wear their hair short and inmates were to be free from any distinguishing mark outside the workhouse. The original dietary was improved, women were instructed in knitting, and children's schooling was advanced.[98]

The suitable employment of able-bodied paupers was all along one of the greatest problems. In accordance with the advice of the Assistant Poor Law Commissioner a mill for grinding corn was adopted, but for six years oakum picking, also advised, was repeatedly rejected as unhealthy and demoralizing. At last in 1843 it was agreed that able-bodied men should pick 4 lb. of oakum a day and women, for whom no other work could be found, 2 lb. a day.[99]

The extent of the problem in the 1830's and 1840's may be gauged from the following figures. During the first quarter of 1836, before the new workhouse was built, there were permanently relieved 116 aged and infirm, orphans and bastards from Thame itself and 214 from the rest of Thame Union. During the last quarter of 1836 when the new workhouse came into use there were 23 inmates from Thame and 93 from the rest of the district, but by 1838 numbers had risen to 156 and 380 respectively. In 1847 accommodation was provided for an additional 40 and 410 became the official limit. The next year was the most critical. On 5 January there were 398 inmates and the guardians reported there would soon be more applicants than they were empowered to receive. A number of special measures were adopted and parishes were empowered to establish Emigration Funds, Thame itself being sanctioned to raise £50. In July the guardians began to meet fortnightly instead of weekly and by February 1849 the number of inmates had fallen to 260.[1] The Census of 1851 recorded that out of a total of 201 inmates 56 paupers were from Thame and of these only 21 were adult. The adult paupers for the district were drawn almost entirely from three classes of workers: agricultural labourers (58), lacemakers (20), and servants (20). There were five resident staff in the House.[2]

The relief of vagrants in the 1840's threatened the

---

[87] d.d. Hobbs c 21: agreement with workhouse keeper.
[88] Ibid.
[89] O.R.O. QSM. 11/2: Trin. Sess. 1788.
[90] d.d. Par. Thame c 4.
[91] *Poor Abstract*, pp. 404–5.   [92] *Census*.
[93] O.R.O. Th. Union Min. Bk. 1835–7.

[94] *Census*, 1841.
[95] O.R.O. Th. Union Min. Bk. 1835–7.
[96] Ibid. 1840–2, &c.   [97] Ibid. 1835–7, 1836–40.
[98] Ibid. 1837–40.   [99] Ibid. 1842–4.
[1] Ibid. 1835–7, &c. to 1847–50.
[2] H.O. 107/1726/2.

efficient conduct of the House and was considered by the guardians to be unjust to the rate-payers, particularly to the Thame rate-payers. No vagrants were relieved before 1841, but in that year the Local Government Board suggested that they be taken in and kept 'six hours next day in working time'. Consequently 961 were relieved in 1844 and numbers had risen by 1847 to 2,790. The Thame guardians accordingly urged that more stringent rules and regulations on 'this important subject' should be adopted. They also made between 1850 and 1853 many strong references to the depressed state of agriculture in the district and the difficulties of rate-payers in meeting expenses. They finally drew up a petition to both Houses of Parliament arguing that present local burdens pressed with undue severity on agricultural interests.[3]

In the second half of the century the workhouse was apparently well administered and the inmates were well conducted. In 1856 Henry Gibbons of Thame, himself a guardian, inspected the workhouse and commented on it favourably in his diary.[4] In 1897 the Local Government Board inspector criticized the out-relief policy, observing that 1 in 18 received relief at Thame compared with 1 in 29 in Buckinghamshire, 1 in 28 in Oxfordshire as a whole, and 1 in 28 throughout England. It was answered on behalf of the Thame Guardians that Thame was an agricultural district and had no 'residential' population, and that relief was administered in as kindly a spirit as possible.[5]

The changed pattern of Poor Relief brought about by pensions, national insurance, and labour exchanges resulted in the abolition of the Unions and of the closing of Thame workhouse in 1935.[6] The functions of the guardians relating to poor relief passed to Public Assistance Committees set up by county and borough councils.

HIGHWAYS, STREETS, AND LIGHTING. The first evidence for any steps to deal with the paving of the town occurs in 1550 after the Highways Act of Edward VI, when part of the money realized from the sale of church goods was used by the churchwardens and 'other honest men' for this purpose. They spent £37 13s. 3d. in 1550 on paving the market-place round the market cross and in making a new causeway at Town's End. In the next year the wardens spent £48 17s. 2d. for digging and carting stone and gravel, possibly for the roads, and over £3 on paving the space round the common well. Over £33 was spent by the warden of Old Thame on materials and labour for the highway from Crendon Bridge past the Vicarage and up the lane by John Stribblehill's door (the present Thame–Long Crendon road). The highways from Priestend Elm 'along the street by Etherigg's' (the present Lower High Street presumably), and so through 'Alyn's lane' (Southern Road) were also paved. In 1552 the way at Town's End towards London was mended for 10s.[7] Lee states that the work continued and that a total of at least £120 was spent by 1560.[8]

The 'highways men' or waywardens of the liberties

came under the control of the Bullingdon Highway Board in 1862, but the town waywardens remained under the vestry until 1871, when the Thame Board of Health was instituted and took over the care of the roads.[9] The board was itself superseded by the Urban District Council in 1894.[10] At first the council was anxious to retain responsibility for all roads, but expense led them to ask the County to define as much road as possible as 'main' road so that it might become the County's responsibility. The Kingsey limestone pit was finally closed in 1890 and thenceforward flints and granite were regularly imported for road-making, and in 1894 steam rolling was first used. The stone sets of the High Street pavements were replaced with Victoria stone in 1888 and the north side of Upper High Street was finished in 1890 by S. Lacey at his own expense. The removal of the cattle market to North Street in 1951 was followed by the transference of the traders' stalls from Cornmarket to the old cattle market.[11]

The streets were first lit by gas in 1842, but this must have been an experiment for it was not until 1849, when W. Jacques persuaded 'the respectable inhabitants' to agree to a 2d. rate to defray the cost, that the lighting became permanent.[12] Electricity was introduced in 1926 being taken in bulk from Aylesbury at the Thame boundary.[13] The town had already been linked with Aylesbury trunk telephone in 1909.[14]

SANITATION. The surviving 17th-century rolls of the view of frankpledge for New Thame show that the court's main business was the enforcement of sanitary regulations.[15]

Regulations about keeping the streets clean and free of obstacles were strict. Any inhabitant who had been warned by the scavengers to put in order the gutter running from his house to the main channels must do so before mid-summer on pain of a fine of £5 10s. This order, however, was made at an October court. Each house-owner was to mend the part of the main water-course in the middle of the street which was before his own house, cleanse the gutters and keep clean the ground between his house and the main water-course; no one was to allow any dunghills, heaps of stones or timber, &c. to be on the street above ten days; everyone dwelling in Sheep and Hog streets was to move dirt from his door every Wednesday; no garbage or entrails were to be emptied into the street; no one was to winnow any grain in the main street, and no one was to dig gravel in the highway at Town's End any nearer the town than the existing pits. The scavengers were to give warning every ten days about clearing the streets. The market cross was to be cleaned every week; no one was to throw filth into either of the two ponds at Town's End (Whitehound's Pond and Butts Pond) or in the ditches in Rookes Lane or adjoining ditches. Another court ordered that no skins or other noisome objects should be left on 'the kerb or on the common pump' in the shambles.

Modern advances in public sanitation were not introduced at Thame until after the adoption of the

[3] O.R.O. Th. Union Min. Bk. 1850–3.
[4] Brown and Guest, *Thame*, 213. Cf. report of Thame Board in *Thame Gazette*, 18 Aug. 1896.
[5] *Thame Gaz.* 27 Apr. 1897.
[6] Brown and Guest, *Thame*, 270.
[7] Lupton, *Extracts*, 18, 21, 22, 23, 25.
[8] Lee, *Thame*, 522–3.
[9] U.D.C. Th. Dist. Loc. Bd. Min. Bk. Oct. 1871. There

are Local Bd. and U.D.C. mins. for Sept. 1871–1959. A draft of mins. for Oct. 1878–Dec. 1888 is at the O.R.O.
[10] U.D.C. mins. 1888–1959.
[11] Inf. the Clerk, U.D.C.
[12] Seymour Diary, cited Brown and Guest, *Thame*, 193. For later developments see U.D.C. mins. *passim*.
[13] U.D.C. mins. 1926.
[14] Ibid. 1909.   [15] MS. Top. Gen. c 43–45.

Local Government Act of 1858. This was the outcome of a medical report by Dr. Buchanan of the Privy Council Medical Department and the violent local controversy which followed.[16]

In 1871 there were 16 deaths from scarlatina and Dr. Lee of Thame called in Dr. Buchanan. The latter found scarlatina decreasing, but reported most scathingly upon the sanitation of the town: there was no place either at the workhouse or elsewhere to which contagious sickness could be removed and there was almost no sanitary government in Thame. The guardians of the Thame Union, as the nuisance authority, employed relieving officers as sanitary inspectors, and they had from time to time dealt with such nuisances as were brought to their notice, but the power to disinfect vested in the guardians had not been used. By the Sewage Utilization Act 1868 the vestry was the sewer authority of the town, but there were no sewers, no provision for excrement or refuse removal, and all manner of nuisances arose from want of these. Dr. Buchanan made many inquiries; but of those questioned 'none had heard of a vestry'; furthermore, the vicar was ill and could not be seen, and the parish clerk could not be discovered.[17]

Down both sides of the broad main street and in some bystreets ran roughly constructed open gutters, which received all manner of liquid house slop and other filth, notably washings from slaughter houses near the market. The gullies led into various ditches some of which ran into the Thame but most were stagnant. The middle 30 ft. of the main street was under the jurisdiction of the Highway Board, but the channels were vested in the waywardens who appeared to have no power of regulating what should enter into them. Dr. Buchanan concluded that unless the inhabitants speedily made a beginning of proper sanitary government it would be necessary to ask the Secretary of State to compel them.

In defence of the town Dr. Reynolds of Thame maintained that the health of the town was better than that of any other of equal size in the kingdom and if drainage was so imperfect typhoid would have resulted. Letters appeared in *The Lancet* and *Public Opinion*.

The Local Board of Health, just elected, ordered wells to be cleaned, and some to be covered and fitted with pumps.[18] In one month 89 notices to abate nuisances were served, 36 complied with and legal proceedings ordered against defaulters. But the Local Government Board wanted a proper system of sewers and a careful examination of the water-supply. These projects were delayed until 1893–5 when the Local Government Board and the Thames Conservancy threatened penalties for river pollution. Catch-pits at Cuttlebrook Ford proved so inadequate that under-draining with a sewage farm and pumping station had to be adopted. In 1898 Messrs. Taylor & Sons drew up the scheme, which cost £7,271, and John Jackson of Plaistow did the work. By 1900 the pumping machinery was installed and most of the houses were connected with the sewers.

But a new difficulty arose—rain water failed to flush the sewers and distribute the sewage over the farm. A new water-supply had to be provided.[19]

WATERWORKS. Apart from the flushing of the sewers the quality of the drinking water had long caused anxiety because it was obtained from some 150 shallow wells, 10–30 ft. deep and easily contaminated. The first boring at Horsenden Hill which would give sufficient fall without the use of a water-tower failed to tap the Lower Greensand. A second boring to reach the Portland Beds along the Kingsey Road found a plentiful supply of uncontaminated water of moderate hardness at Pillmore Arch in Towersey (Bucks.), and a water tower, holding 60,000 gallons, was built off Park Street in 1905. Public pumps were then removed.[20]

FIRE SERVICE. An adequate water-supply solved the chief Fire Service difficulty. The first fire-engine had been provided in 1817 by public subscription,[21] but not until 1878 was a proper brigade formed under H. H. Smith. This was voluntary, but the Town Surveyor took charge and council employees were expected to assist when the voluntary force, for any reason, was not available.[22] In 1881 the brigade won first prize in competition at Aylesbury.[23]

To provide enough water the open drains at the sides of the High Street were dammed with boards specially kept at the engine-house and the pumps in the houses were worked until enough water had accumulated. By 1880 an underground drain had been made from the Whitehound Pond to a storage tank at the junction of Upper High Street and North Street.[24] The modern fire station at Nelson Street was built in 1937.[25]

MARKET AUTHORITY. The council's desire to become the market authority was closely connected with the sanitation of the town. As early as 1881 the council had unsuccessfully tried to obtain a lease of the tolls from Lord Abingdon so that it could control the Market,[26] but it was only in 1927 that Lord Bertie sold the market rights to the council for £1,000.[27]

The acquisition of the market rights meant that the council could levy a toll for the sale of goods and charge stallage for the erection of stalls.[28] In 1760 the tolls were leased by the Earl of Abingdon for £25 16s. and this was still their value in 1899.[29] In 1935 the Urban District Council extended the right to charge stallage to the parking of motor-cars in the market place on market days.[30]

In 1939 the decision was taken to remove the cattle market from the open street. Improvements were necessary and the Government had powers to close street cattle markets, but owing to the war and consequent restrictions permission for the new buildings in North Street was not obtained until 1950 and then a loan of £34,997 was granted. A further £1,566 was loaned in 1953 for a poultry shed.[31]

HOUSING. Since 1918 the borrowing powers conferred by the various Housing Acts have made the provision and maintenance of houses one of the chief services. Town planning is, however, regulated by

[16] *Thame Gazette*, 20 June 1871, July 1871.
[17] Ibid.
[18] U.D.C. Th. Dist. Loc. Bd. Min. Bk. 1871.
[19] Ibid.
[20] U.D.C. min. bk.
[21] List of subscribers printed by J. H. Marshall, Aylesbury (1818).
[22] U.D.C. min. bk.

[23] *Thame Gazette*, 1881.
[24] U.D.C. min. bk.
[25] Ibid.
[26] Ibid.
[27] Ibid.
[28] Ibid.
[29] d.d. Bertie b 5 (uncat.).
[30] U.D.C. mins.
[31] Ibid.

the County Development Committee. About a third of the town's houses are now council houses. Earlier loans, as those for sewerage and water, have been repaid, but in the list of balances of loans since 1941, outstanding on 31 March 1957, housing came easily first. They were as follows: waterworks, £13,166; sewerage, £5,561; markets, £28,616; allotments, £594; and housing, £297,778.[32]

The council is also responsible for the town's recreation grounds. In 1895 the trustees of the recreation ground in Southern Road, which was held on lease from the Hon. Francis Bertie, handed over the ground to the council and in 1951 the council accepted Elms Park as a gift from Mr. and Mrs. Leonard Purser, to be maintained as a park and recreation ground.[33]

The town has no powers of educational administration and is too small to adopt the Library Act of 1892, but the general district rate of 1s. 2d. in the £ in 1872 has risen to 26s. in the pound.[34]

POLICE. The election of petty constables by Courts Leet was discontinued by Act of Parliament in 1842. Instead they were appointed by special sessions of justices from lists submitted by overseers in consultation with the vestry.

In 1852, in accordance with the Superintending Constables Act 1850, Robert Hitchman of the Metropolitan Police was appointed Superintending Constable of the Bullingdon Petty Sessional Division and as such superintended the petty constables at Thame. He resided at Wheatley and provided his own horse and light cart for conveying prisoners. He was also Inspector of Weights and Measures.[35]

Since 1787 Thame had been without a lock-up,[36] and after 1835 the refractory ward at the workhouse had sometimes been used for detaining prisoners, but the guardians forbade this in 1841.[37] However, in 1854 a police station was built at Thame on the present site by Giles Holland, the local builder, at a total cost of £654, shared equally by Oxfordshire and Buckinghamshire. The Superintending Constable was paid a salary of £10 a year with free residence and freedom from taxes, the two counties again sharing the cost.[38]

In 1857 Oxfordshire adopted the County Police Act and Thame was included in the 'A' Division, comprising Headquarters, Bullingdon, Henley, and Watlington.[39] One piece of evidence given to the Select Committee investigating the need for that Act asserted that the Thame petty constables drove vagrants over the border into Buckinghamshire to get rid of them.[40]

Not until 1859, however, was it resolved that the Chief Constable of Oxfordshire should arrange with the Chief Constable of Buckinghamshire that the keeper of the lock-up at Thame be superseded by one of the Oxfordshire police.[41] In 1865 the Buckinghamshire moiety of the lock-up house or branch police station at Thame was purchased by Oxfordshire for £200. In 1869 the establishment was one sergeant and three men. In 1959 it was one inspector and three men.[42]

After the County Court Act (1846) Thame became the head of a County Court district. Sittings were sometimes monthly, sometimes bi-monthly, being held in the Spread Eagle Assembly room until 1861 when the present County Court was built.[43]

Thame has all along been in the Petty Sessional Division of Bullingdon and today (1959) Petty Sessions are held at the County Hall, Oxford on alternate Thursdays and at Thame County Court on the second and last Tuesday in every month.[44]

CHURCH.[45] Since Thame was an ancient manor of the Bishop of Dorchester, there can be little doubt that it had a church early in the Anglo-Saxon period and that this was the mother church for the neighbouring chapelries of Sydenham, Tetsworth, and Towersey (Bucks.).[46] Wulfhere, King of Mercia (657–74), may have been in this church when, as his charter says, he swore 'on the altar' at Thame.[47]

Between 1070 and 1086 the see of Dorchester was moved to Lincoln, and the bishops of Lincoln thus became the lords of Thame. By 1146 the church had been given to Lincoln Cathedral and formed into a prebend, henceforth known as the prebend of Thame.[48] The donor was probably Bishop Alexander (1123–48), who endowed the prebend with land from his Thame manor. Because it belonged to a prebend Thame and its chapels between the 12th and the 19th centuries formed an ecclesiastical peculiar.

In the 13th century a vicarage was endowed and the prebendaries presented to it, except during the second half of the 14th century, when the prebend was held by foreign cardinals and presentations were made by their English agents; and in 1537 when the prebendary granted to Bishop Longland his right of presentation.[49]

The prebend was one of the richest in Lincoln Cathedral, being valued at £35 in 1254, at £112 in 1291, and at £82 12s. 2½d. net in 1535.[50] The prebendary received the greater part of the ecclesiastical income from the parish, the great tithes and the tithes of wool and hay from Thame, Sydenham, Tetsworth, and Towersey.[51] He also held a large estate: 4 carucates of land in Thame which had been granted to the church in free alms by Bishop Alexander and

[32] Ibid.
[33] Ibid.
[34] Ibid.
[35] O.R.O. *List and Rules of Superintending constables for Petty Sessional Division.* (Oxon. 1852), 40.
[36] O.R.O. QSM. 11/2: Trin. Sess. 1788. For the bridewell see ibid. Cal. Q. Sess. viii. 109, 184, 233, 238–40. For the bishop's medieval prison see above, p. 115.
[37] Th. Union min. bk. May 1841.
[38] O.R.O. QSM. 11/16, Epiph. Sess. 1855.
[39] Ibid. Cal. Q. Sess. 1854–9, p. 223.
[40] *First Report from the select cttee. on Police with mins. of Evidence,* 1853.
[41] O.R.O. Oxon. Co. Police mins. 17 Sept. 1859. There are Police minute bks. from 1856.
[42] Ibid. 18 Feb. 1865.
[43] Kelly, *Dir. Oxon.* (1869); *Thame Gazette, passim.*

[44] Inf. the Clerk, U.D.C.
[45] This section, written by Mrs. Hester Jenkins, is based to a considerable extent on notes made by Mr. W. Guest.
[46] See above, p. 170; *V.C.H. Bucks.* iv. 107. Lee, *Thame,* 231.
[47] *Cod. Dipl.* ed. Kemble, v, nos. 987, 988.
[48] *Reg. Antiquiss.* i. 199.
[49] For list of medieval presentations see MS. Top. Oxon. d 460.
[50] Lunt, *Val. Norw.* 278; *Tax Eccl.* (Rec. Com.), 30; *Valor Eccl.* (Rec. Com.), ii. 168.
[51] *Rot. Graves.* 225. Attington is not specifically mentioned, but its inclusion in Thame would have been understood. The greater part of it (314 a.) was tithe free as it formed the demesne of Thame Abbey, but the great tithes of the rest belonged to the prebend (inferred from the evidence of the tithe award, 1848).

which owed service neither to the bishop nor to the king,[52] and ⅓-fee in Tetsworth.[53]

From the late 11th to the 13th century part of the church's revenue had gone to Eynsham Abbey, for Bishop Robert Bloet c. 1095 granted the abbey the demesne tithes of some of his manors, including Thame and Great Milton.[54] These tithes, and a bordar with 2 acres, were confirmed to the abbey in 1109,[55] and in the 13th century the cellarer of Eynsham was receiving the tithes, then valued at 5 marks.[56] In about 1267, in return for the appropriation of Brize Norton church, the abbey gave up its Thame tithes, which became merged with those belonging to the prebend.[57]

In 1547 the prebend was lost to the cathedral when the last prebendary, George Heneage (d. 1549), who had been a resident canon of Lincoln, sold the prebend to Sir John Thynne and Edward Kelway.[58] In 1549 the sale was confirmed by the bishop and by the dean and chapter on condition that the chapter continued to receive an annual pension of £7 from Thame.[59] In 1550 Thynne and Kelway exchanged the prebend for lands in Devon and Somerset with Sir Edward Seymour, second son of the Duke of Somerset.[60]

Somerset and Sir John Williams were probably both involved in the alienation of the prebend, for in 1548 Thynne, who was Somerset's steward, had granted Williams a large part of the prebend.[61] In 1553 he and Seymour confirmed the division: Williams was to have almost all the land belonging to the prebend and the tithes of North Weston, while Seymour was to have the rest of the tithes, the prebendal house with a few acres, and the advowson of the vicarage.[62]

The land which Williams acquired apparently became merged with Thame manor and descended with it to his heirs, the Norreys and Bertie families.[63] In 1625 Edward Wray and his wife, who were then holding Thame manor, granted the tithes of North Weston to William Clerke, who was lord of North Weston manor.[64] After that they followed the descent of the land, so that in effect land in North Weston was free from great tithes.[65]

The other part of the prebend, which Seymour had kept, and which became known as the rectory, he sold probably in the 1550's to Sir John Thynne of Longleat (Wilts.),[66] and from this time until the late 18th century it descended in the Thynne family.[67] Thynne died in 1580, having settled Thame rectory on his eldest son.[68] This Sir John Thynne died in 1604, and the rectory was inherited by his eldest son Sir Thomas Thynne,[69] but was held for life by the latter's younger brother John in satisfaction of a £100 pension, and then by his son John.[70] This was probably the John Thynne of Egham (Surr.), who presented to the vicarage in 1665 and 1675 and died in 1698, heavily in debt,[71] leaving a widow Jane. She still held the Thynne part of the prebend in 1704.[72] By 1606 this branch of the Thynne family had leased the prebend to two Thame families, the Hesters and Stribblehills.[73] The Stribblehills continued as lessees for the rest of the century.[74]

In the late 17th century the rectory returned to the main branch of the Thynne family. Sir Thomas Thynne, later Viscount Weymouth,[75] died without sons in 1714, and while the title descended to his great-nephew Thomas Thynne, 2nd Viscount Weymouth (d. 1751), he is said to have left Thame rectory to John Carteret, the husband of his granddaughter Frances Worsley.[76] Carteret, later to become Earl Granville, presented to Thame vicarage in 1722, 1751, and 1761, and died in 1763.[77] His son and heir died without children in 1776, leaving part of his estates,[78] including the rectory, to his nephew Henry Frederick Thynne, who became Lord Carteret.[79] Thus the rectory returned to the Thynne family, but Lord Carteret sold it, probably in 1786, to John Blackall (d. 1803), lord of Great Milton manor,[80] and his son separated the rectory and the advowson. The latter descended to the Blackalls' heir Walter Long, and was bought by Richard Barry Slater, a High Wycombe doctor,[81] who in 1841 had the livings of Sydenham, Tetsworth, and Towersey separated from that of Thame.[82] On his death the advowson of Thame was vested in five trustees, named the Peache Trustees after the Revd. Alfred Peache.[83] They were the patrons in 1958.

---

[52] *Rot. Hund.* (Rec. Com.), ii. 820.
[53] *Feud. Aids*, iv. 181, 197; see above, p. 149.
[54] *V.C.H. Oxon.* ii. 65.
[55] *Eynsham Cart.* i. 36. For confirmation by Henry II see *Reg. Antiquiss.* i. 83–84. They are described as tithes of wool, cheese, grain, and cattle.
[56] *Eynsham Cart.* i. 225, 307.
[57] Ibid. 246; ii. 170–1. The abbey was to receive 12 marks a year from the prebendary until the appropriation took effect.
[58] C.P. 25(2)/62/493/Hil. 1 Ed. VI. For Heneage see *Linc. Chapter Acts, 1536–47* (L.R.S. xiii), pp. vii–viii.
[59] *Linc. Chapter Acts, 1547–59* (L.R.S. xv), 33–34.
[60] E 326/B 10575; Lee, *Thame*, 140, which contains a summary, pp. 138–40, of deeds at Longleat. This Seymour was evidently Somerset's son by his first wife. For royal presentations in 1550 which apparently had no effect see *Cal. Pat.* 1549–51, 236, 360.   [61] Lee, *Thame*, 139.
[62] Ibid.; d.d. Bertie b 6, 1553 indenture.
[63] The prebend is listed among the Earl of Berkshire's property: C 142/399/153.
[64] C.P. 25(2)/473/Trin. 1 Chas. I; see also ibid. Trin. 4 Chas. I.
[65] d.d. Bertie b 5, Tithe commutation summary; Bodl. Tithe award.
[66] Lee, *Thame*, 139; C.P. 25(2)/196/East. 3 Eliz. which is dated 1561, though Thynne had been patron of the vicarage since 1557: Oxf. Dioc. d 105, p. 172.
[67] The chapter sued Thynne for the pension of £7 from the prebend which it had reserved in 1548. Thynne refused

to pay because he held only half the prebend: C 3/111/28, where it is said to be £7 3s. 4d. For Thynne see *D.N.B.*
[68] C 142/195/118. For the family see *Collins's Peerage*, ed. Sir E. Brydges, ii. 499 sqq.
[69] C.P. 25(2)/339/Mich. 3 Jas. I; see Lee, *Thame*, 139, for provisions of this 150-year lease, which may never have taken effect.
[70] C 142/765/47; Lee, *Thame*, 140. For 17th-cent. deeds about the prebend see C.P. 25(2)/616/Mich. 1653; C.P. 43/282/127; C.P. 43/323/50.
[71] P.R.O. Inst. Bks.; C 5/325/45. For this branch of the family see *Collins's Peerage*, ii. 502.
[72] Lee, *Thame*, 140.
[73] *Oxon. Peculiars*, 175, 176, 177.
[74] For the suit of Frances, widow of John Stribblehill of New Thame, against the Thynnes and the new lessees see C 5/299/48 (1699); C 5/217/37 (1699); C 5/325/45 (1700).
[75] For him see *D.N.B.*
[76] *Par. Coll.* iii. 317. For relationship see *Complete Peerage*, vi. 90.
[77] P.R.O. Inst. Bks. For him see *D.N.B.*
[78] *Complete Peerage*, iii. 68.
[79] His elder brother became the 1st Marquess of Bath.
[80] O.R.O. Land tax assess.; for Blackalls see above, p. 124.
[81] C.P. 25(2)/1513/Hil. 10 & 11 Geo. IV; Lee, *Thame*, 148.
[82] *Return of Benefices United and Disunited*, H.C. 227, p. 6 (1872), xlvi.
[83] Lee, *Thame*, 148; Oxf. Dioc. c 2049, Presentations.

The lay rectory of Thame and Sydenham, the tithes of which brought in about £1,000 a year in the 1820's,[84] but not that of Tetsworth, was sold to Miss Wykeham (later Baroness Wenman) of Thame Park in 1825.[85] By the inclosure award of 1826 the great tithes of Thame and Sydenham—except for those of Thame Park, which as the ancient demesne of Thame Abbey was tithe free, and of North Weston—were commuted for 693 acres, the equivalent of ⅛ of the arable and ⅛ of the meadow land.[86] In 1836 Baroness Wenman sold the prebendal house, with its estate of 14½ acres, for £950 to Charles Stone of Thame.[87] The rest of the rectory lands, with responsibility for the chancel, descended with Thame Park to the Wykeham-Musgraves.[88] In 1958 the lay rector was Mr. F. Bowden, the owner of Thame Park.

As the church was a prebend of Lincoln the parish, with its chapelries, was in the Middle Ages an ecclesiastical peculiar, for Bishop Robert de Chesney (1148–66) freed prebendal parishes from the jurisdiction of the bishop and the archdeacon.[89] The bishops of Lincoln did not visit Thame,[90] but they instituted to the vicarage, and the fact that in 1519 Thame church was one of the centres where the clergy met to hear the constitutions for church reform also shows that the bishop preserved some rights.[91] When the bishop came to Thame he was accorded the privilege of having the church bells rung in his honour.[92] The prebendary of Thame, like the other prebendaries of Lincoln, had ordinary archidiaconal jurisdiction in his parish,[93] and probably held the chapters which the churchwardens attended.[94] Cases of appeal could go to the Chapter of Lincoln, which inducted to the vicarage.[95] Every three years the dean on behalf of the chapter was allowed to visit,[96] and the church bells were rung for him also.[97] In spite of the formation of the see of Oxford in 1542 and the alienation of the prebend from the cathedral in 1547, Thame remained in the jurisdiction of the dean and chapter. They appointed a commissary for all their Oxfordshire, Buckinghamshire, and Northamptonshire peculiars, who visited every year, swore in churchwardens, granted marriage licences, inducted clerks, granted letters of administration, and proved wills.[98] The dean still had the right to visit every three years, although it is not clear how often he did so.[99]

The peculiar records, beginning in 1584, show that the visitations were held in Thame church and were attended by the minister and churchwardens of Thame and its chapels.[1] In about 1675 the vicar and wardens of Great Milton began to attend the visitations at Thame, and from this time the two peculiars were united.[2] So little control did the bishops of Lincoln or Oxford have that in the 18th century it was not clear whether the Lincoln peculiars were in Lincoln or Oxford diocese. Although it was generally believed that the bishop had the right of visitation, no bishop was known to have visited the peculiars before the 19th century.[3] About episcopal institution there was a diversity of practice: in 1545 the Bishop of Lincoln instituted to Thame vicarage, and it was then stated that the parish, although in Oxford diocese, was in his jurisdiction.[4] Later in the 16th century and in the early 17th century the Bishop of Oxford instituted;[5] but in the second half of the century the Bishop of Lincoln again began to institute and it was said that Thame lay in his diocese.[6]

In spite of an opinion given in 1745 by Bishop Sherlock of Salisbury that episcopal rights in the peculiars should belong to the Bishop of Oxford,[7] when the living of Thame fell vacant in 1751 Bishop Secker of Oxford and Bishop Thomas of Lincoln each wrote to Lord Granville, the patron, asking for the presentation of the next vicar. After considering the arguments on both sides, Lord Granville sent it to the Bishop of Lincoln, who was able to institute.[8] The matter, which concerned all the peculiars, continued to be pursued by the bishops of Oxford, who in 1769 were said by an official of the Bishop of Lincoln to have been 'nibbling at and plaguing' the Bishop of Lincoln for 200 years and to have sometimes 'by surprise usurped upon the bishop and dean and chapter'.[9] In 1795 the Bishop of Lincoln again instituted to Thame,[10] and in 1800 the Vicar of Thame considered him his diocesan, an opinion which drew a sharp retort from Bishop Randolph of Oxford.[11]

Although in 1802 the Bishop of Oxford began to visit Great Milton[12] confusion continued as to which diocese Thame was in: sometimes it was listed in Lincoln diocese, sometimes in Oxford diocese.[13] From 1819 it appears to have been visited by the Bishop of Lincoln,[14] and in 1841 he instituted to the

[84] MS. Top. Oxon. c 3, f. 97b.

[85] d.d. Hobbs c 24, Additional abstract of title.

[86] O.R.O. Incl. award; *Return of Land in lieu of Tithes*, H.C. 159, p. 55 (1867), liv. About 532 a. were in Thame and 161 a. in Sydenham.

[87] As n. 85 above.

[88] Oxf. Dioc. b 41; Brown and Guest, *Thame*, 235. In 1890 W. A. Wykeham-Musgrave was claiming all the chancel stalls for the use of his family: Oxf. Dioc. c 2050.

[89] *V.C.H. Lincs.* ii. 80; H. Bradshaw, *Lincoln Cathedral Statutes* (revised C. Wordsworth), i. 309–10.

[90] e.g. *Visit. Dioc. Linc. 1517–31*, i. 119 n.

[91] Ibid. 148, 149.

[92] d.d. Par. Thame c 5, f. 61. For an earlier bitter dispute over pews which necessitated the appointment in 1622 of a commission see Oxf. Dioc. b 20, f. 120.

[93] Bradshaw, op. cit. ii (1), 154.

[94] d.d. Par. Thame c 5, ff. 56b, 62b. They were sometimes held at Tetsworth.

[95] Bradshaw, op. cit. ii (2), 169–70. For two inductions, one in the Lincoln chapter house and one in the choir, see *Linc. Chapter Acts, 1536–47* (L.R.S. xiii), 45–46, 113.

[96] Bradshaw, op. cit. ii (2), 288–9. When the prebend was vacant its custody fell to the chapter: ibid. 291.

[97] d.d. Par. Thame c 5, f. 77.

[98] Oxf. Dioc. c 652, f. 79b; c 655, ff. 53, 60b, 61; c 656,

f. 185. For examples of appointments of commissaries see ibid. c 649, ff. 47, 49.

[99] Ibid. c 655, f. 41b. In 1607 Bishop Chadderton said that no visitation had been held in the prebends for many years: Bradshaw, op. cit. ii (2), 641.

[1] The most important peculiar records are Oxf. Dioc. c 18 (1584–1640, intermittent); Oxf. Archd. Oxon. c 162 (1676–1719); c 163 (1723–35). The first covers only Thame, the last two Thame and Great Milton. Misc. papers are ibid. c 164.

[2] See above, p. 139.   [3] Oxf. Dioc. c 649, f. 1.

[4] Linc. Reg. xxvii, f. 199d.

[5] Oxf. Dioc. d 105, pp. 172, 198 (1557, 1559); c 264, f. 113b (1629).

[6] Oxf. Archd. Oxon. c 164, f. 121 (1675); for a similar opinion of 1676 see Oxf. Dioc. c 649, f. 85.

[7] Oxf. Dioc. c 649, f. 14; c 652, ff. 69–71, 79–80.

[8] Ibid. c 653, ff. 45–55b.

[9] Ibid. c 654, f. 67.

[10] Lee, *Thame*, 147.

[11] Oxf. Dioc. c 655, f. 47b.

[12] See above, p. 139.

[13] *Rep. of Comm. on Eccl. Revenues*, H.C. 54 (1835), xxii (Oxford); *Return of Courts Granting Probate*, H.C. 177, p. 50 (1829), xviii (Lincoln).

[14] d.d. Par. Thame c 4, 1819, 1828.

vicarage.[15] Yet by 1800 the Bishop of Oxford was licensing curates and in 1838 he began to visit the parish.[16] The struggle came to an end with the legislation of the 1830's and 1840's[17] and with the end of the chapter's jurisdiction (see below).

The Chapter of Lincoln upheld the Bishop of Lincoln's rights in their Oxfordshire peculiars, for when he instituted they inducted,[18] whereas when the Bishop of Oxford instituted the Archdeacon of Oxford inducted. The chapter's rights in the peculiars were evidently not questioned until the late 18th century, when the bishops of Oxford began to doubt whether the peculiars had any legal basis. In 1801 the chapter definitely refused to put the question to arbitration and threatened to resist any legal action taken by the Bishop of Oxford.[19] Jurisdiction in Thame peculiar continued to be exercised by the chapter's official, and when it came within the archdeacon's jurisdiction is not clear.[20] The court of the peculiar proved wills until the Court of Probate Act of 1857.[21]

The formation of a prebend at Thame had important consequences for the parish. A prebendal house was built near the church and from there the prebendary's large estate was administered in his absence. When in residence the prebendary assisted at the services in the parish church: his seat in the chancel was opposite the vicar's seat.[22] The richness of the prebend made it much coveted and twice in the 13th century its disposal led to violent conflicts. On the first occasion, in 1241, the king's clerk John Maunsel, a well-known pluralist, was provided to the prebend by the Pope at the instance of Henry III,[23] while Bishop Grosseteste collated Master Simon de London. In order to get possession Maunsel was said to have seized and held the church by force, but eventually he resigned it and was given another benefice.[24] After a vacancy in 1292, the prebend was the subject of a violent dispute between Master Thomas de Sutton, nephew of Bishop Sutton, and the papal provisee, Edward de St. John, which led to the disturbances of 1293-4 and the desecration of the church.[25] Eventually after legal proceedings Sutton obtained the prebend.[26]

During much of the 14th century the prebend was held by foreign cardinals, who farmed the parish,

perhaps sometimes to local men, as was the case in 1378.[27] From the late 14th century the prebendaries were usually distinguished Englishmen, many of whom became bishops. Some of these took a close interest in the parish, by giving gifts to the church,[28] or, as was the case with Adrian de Bardis (1480–1518) and Richard Maudely (1519–31), by making improvements in the chancel.[29] The latter left in addition a bequest for memorial services in the church and may have been buried in it.[30]

There was a vicarage by the time of Bishop Grosseteste (1235–53), who wrote that the prebend was a desirable one because there was a perpetual vicar to relieve the prebendary of most of the cure.[31] The vicar was to receive the oblations of the mother church; he was to have a house and croft on the south side of the church and a virgate of glebe; the tithe of hay from North Weston; a mark from Sydenham for its hay; and a ½-mark from Thame Abbey. In his house he was to keep two chaplains, a deacon, and a subdeacon to help him serve the church, and he was to provide books and ornaments. The vicar was to name the chaplains of the chapels (Sydenham, Tetsworth, and Towersey), who were to receive the income from their altars and have the land belonging to the chapels.[32] The small tithes are not mentioned in this ordination, which was partly superseded by one of 1274: this reserved to the prebendary the great tithes and those of wool and hay, and implied that the vicar had the small tithes from the parish and its chapelries.[33]

In 1291 the vicarage was valued at £8 and in 1535 at £18.[34] At that time it was therefore a rich vicarage, but after the Reformation it became a poor one. The profits of the altar virtually ceased and in 1707 it was worth only £43.[35] In 1810 the living was valued at £170, but the vicar claimed that by the time he had paid for services in the chapels he had no more than £100 left.[36] At the inclosure award in 1826 the small tithes of Thame and Sydenham were commuted for 148 acres, and 32½ acres were allotted for glebe.[37] The value of the living—£300 in 1831[38]—was decreased in 1841 when Thame was separated from its chapelries.[39] From this time the endowment of the living came from about 112 acres of glebe,[40] most of which was sold in 1921,[41] and the small tithes of

[15] MS. Top. Oxon. c 3, f. 29.
[16] Oxf. Dioc. c 327, p. 201; b 41.
[17] 6 & 7 Wm. IV, c. 77; 7 Wm. IV & 1 Vict. c. 71; 1 & 2 Vict. c. 106, § 108; 10 & 11 Vict. c. 98. By 13 & 14 Vict. c. 94, § 24 the ecclesiastical commissioners were empowered to frame schemes for the abolition of peculiars. For a full statement on the dean and chapter's right to exercise ecclesiastical jurisdiction over their prebends see Linc. Dioc. R.O. A/4/12.
[18] Oxf. Dioc. c 653, f. 55; c 649, ff. 58–61, 84–85b.
[19] Ibid. c 655, ff. 60, 131–131b. The most important papers on this question, which affected all the Lincoln peculiars in Oxon., are c 649 passim and c 655, ff. 33–61b. For other correspondence see Bodl. Oldfield's Subject Index to Cuddesdon Palace Mun. See also Oxon. Peculiars, pp. viii–x.
[20] Return of Eccl. Courts, H.C. 232, p. 26 (1828), xx. It was visited by the archdeacon in 1853 but not in the 1860's: Oxf. Archd. Oxon. c 44.
[21] Return of Courts Granting Probate, H.C. 177, p. 50 (1829), xviii; Returns of Eccl. Courts, H.C. 205, pp. 156, 227, 340 (1830), xix.
[22] Lee, Thame, 20. For the prebendal house see above, p. 167.
[23] Cal. Pat. 1232–47, 257. For Maunsel see D.N.B.
[24] For this see Reg. Antiquiss. i. 181–3; Matthew Paris, Chron. Major. (Rolls Ser.), iv. 152–4; Robert Grosseteste, ed. D. A. Callus (1955), 163–4.

[25] See above, p. 160.
[26] J. Le Neve, Fasti, ed. T. D. Hardy, ii. 220.
[27] Cal. Close, 1377–81, 165. For list of prebendaries see Le Neve, Fasti, ii. 220–1 and Lee, Thame 134–8.
[28] See below, p. 210.
[29] See below, pp. 207, 208.
[30] Lee, Thame, 137–8, 171. In 1526 he had a violent dispute with a monk of Thame Abbey whom he claimed owed him money: Visit. Dioc. Linc. 1517–31, ii. 212.
[31] Monumenta Franciscana (Rolls Ser.), i. 186.
[32] Oxf. Archd. Oxon. c 141, pp. 125–6, taken from Linc. Reg. Longland's Memoranda. These are evidently copies from an ordination of Grosseteste's time, made on a presentation to the vicarage by Master Simon de Valentiis (probably the same as Simon de London).
[33] Rot. Graves. 225. It is evident from the tithe award (1848) that the vicar had the small tithes of part of Attington also.
[34] Tax. Eccl. (Rec. Com.), 30; Valor Eccl. (Rec. Com.), ii. 168. [35] Oxf. Archd. Oxon. b 41, f. 133.
[36] Account of Benefices, H.L. (1818), xviii; Oxf. Dioc. c 446, f. 187.
[37] O.R.O. Incl. award; 67½ a. were in Sydenham and 80½ a. in Thame.
[38] Rep. of Comm. on Eccl. Revenues, H.C. 54 (1835), xxii.
[39] See above.
[40] d.d. Bullingdon c 36, pp. 36, 40.
[41] Brown and Guest, Thame, 202.

North Weston. In the 19th century the vicar augmented his income by letting the churchyard at £2 a year, and 200 to 300 sheep were sometimes kept there.[42]

The tithes of North Weston had long been separate from those of the rest of the parish. Part of North Weston had been tithe-free since at least the late 17th century, and by the mid-18th century the small tithes on the rest had been commuted for a modus of about £3 7s., far less than their real value. In 1844, when tithe commutation was being discussed, the vicar tried to break this modus, and finally agreed to accept a tithe rent-charge of £30, which he considered less than half the real value of the tithes.[43] Accordingly in 1848 they were commuted for this sum.[44]

As is shown by the ordination of the vicarage, the vicars of Thame, with several clerks serving under them, must have held an important position. Little is known about the early priests of Thame, and with the exception of Elurich, clerk, and Wlwrich, priest, of uncertain date,[45] and Peter, clerk of Thame, who occurs in the mid-12th century, their names are not known until the mid-13th century.[46] In the 14th and 15th centuries the names of Thame vicars frequently occur in local charters, as do those of the chaplains assisting them, of whom otherwise there would be no record,[47] such as John Elys (fl. 1440), a member of the prominent Thame family of landowners and merchants.[48] A few of the vicars were local men, notably Richard Elys (1340–61), a member of the same family,[49] and John de Towersey (instituted 1378), who was probably the same as the John Lucas who in 1389 gave land to Thame Abbey, perhaps for a chantry, and a chalice to Thame church.[50] Towards the middle of the 15th century it became usual for the vicars to be university graduates; an Oxford graduate was Master John Atherton or Aldersonne (1478–1503), whose brass was once in the church.[51]

Churchwardens' accounts, beginning in 1442, have been preserved and provide a rich store of information about medieval church life.[52] In the 15th century there were evidently four wardens, two from New Thame and two from Old Thame,[53] who collected and spent the church's revenue. Their income came mainly from receipts from the Whitsun Ales, one in New Thame and one in Old Thame and

Priestend,[54] from the rent of the church land,[55] from contributions from the parishioners to the rood light at Easter and Christmas,[56] from receipts from the church play,[57] from the waste of the torches at a funeral, and from occasional bequests. For any major work on the building special contributions were given by the parishioners.[58]

The wardens were responsible for the upkeep of the church fabric (except for the chancel). This included buying supplies and paying workmen, lighting the church, keeping the vestments clean and in repair, keeping the lamps and brasses clean, repairing the organ, keeping the parish records, and keeping the church books in repair: in 1443, for example, they paid an Oxford bookbinder 5s.[59] Constant expenses were the upkeep of the bells and of the clock, the bellman and the keeper of the clock both receiving regular payments.[60] A salary was paid to the organist,[61] and later to the parish clerk, who appears in the 15th century but who first received a salary in the 16th—£1 a year in the 1520's and £4 by 1560.[62] The sexton or sacristan was paid for the work he did.[63]

The 16th century saw many changes in Thame church. Ceremonies and ritual connected with the old faith were abolished. The yearly service held for the benefaction of the church, at which bread was distributed to the poor, came to an end,[64] and so did the endowment of chantry priests. Sir John Clerke's bequest in 1539 to provide a priest to say mass for him for six years was probably the last of the kind at Thame.[65] The many separate lights or altars of which some had their own wardens and possessions,[66] the chief being the altar of St. Christopher with its guild, were taken down and their possessions sold.

The chantry or guild of St. Christopher was founded in 1447 in St. John's aisle by Richard and Sibyl Quatremain of North Weston. It was to be served by a chaplain who would say daily services for the royal family and the members of the guild. The members were to elect the wardens, who were to form a corporate body with the power of acquiring land.[67] The chantry priest, who received £8 a year, besides saying the chantry services, in the 16th century acted as assistant to the vicar.[68] When in 1550 the guild, which had been well endowed,[69] was dissolved and its property sold to Sir John Williams,

[42] Ibid. 203.

[43] d.d. Bertie b 5, Tithe documents. The vicar unsuccessfully claimed the tithe of hay on the basis of the ordination in Grosseteste's time. He had also brought a suit against the landholders for this tithe, but this had been dismissed in 1818: ibid. [44] Bodl. Tithe award.

[45] These two presumably preceded the ordination of the vicarage. Their names occur in a note in what appears to be an early 12th-cent. hand on the fly-leaf of an 11th-cent. book of canons which is supposed once to have belonged to Dorchester Abbey (now Bodl. MS. 718): Mary Bateson, 'The Supposed Latin Penitential of Egbert' &c., E.H.R. ix. 320–6. Salter's view (V.C.H. Oxon. ii. 3) that the notes were in an early 11th-cent. hand cannot be accepted.

[46] Thame Cart. i. 41. For list of medieval vicars see MS. Top. Oxon. d 460.

[47] Rousham Arch. N, passim. Richard, clerk of Attington, occurs in the late 12th cent.: Thame Cart. i. 100.

[48] Rousham Arch. N 314; for the family, see above, p. 180.

[49] Rousham Arch. N 115, N 125, N 135, N 149, N 158.

[50] Cal. Pat. 1388–92, 128; Lee, Thame, 33; see also Rousham Arch. N 206, N 238.

[51] Lee, Thame, 99. For him see ibid. 142 n.; Emden, O.U. Reg. i.

[52] The earliest accounts, 1442–1524, are now d.d. Par.

Thame c 5 (some of the leaves have been cut out). They have been printed to 1472 in Berks. Arch. Jnl. vii sqq.; for details see Oxon. Bibliography (O.H.S. n.s. xi), no. 3874. The accounts 1524–1750 are lost, but there are extracts 1529–60 and a few 17th-cent. ones in H. Lupton, Extracts from the Accounts of Thame (Thame, 1852). Lee, Thame, 25 sqq. has extracts 1442–1648 and has seen the accounts up to 1750: ibid. 152–64. The accounts 1769–1840 are d.d. Par. Thame c 4.

[53] The accounts 1442–96 are only for New Thame; those from 1497 are for both.

[54] e.g. Lee, Thame, 26.   [55] See below, p. 218.

[56] d.d. Par. Thame c 5, f. 62; Berks. Arch. Jnl. viii. 51.

[57] For the day it was given see Lee, Thame, 52.

[58] Berks. Arch. Jnl. viii. 24–27.

[59] Ibid. 72.   [60] Ch. Bells Oxon. 420; Lee, Thame, 76.

[61] d.d. Par. Thame c 5, ff. 54b–55, 59b.

[62] Ibid. ff. 32, 75b; Lee, Thame, 76.

[63] d.d. Par. Thame c 5, ff. 47b, 56.

[64] Lee, Thame, 56, 57, 58.

[65] Ibid. 321 n. 2.   [66] See below, p. 207.

[67] Cal. Pat. 1446–52, 180–1. See also above, p. 173.

[68] Subsidy 1526, 253; Lee, Thame, 423.

[69] For a list of its property see Lee, Thame, 420–3; for court rolls of the guild see d.d. Bertie c 16; for litigation see C 1/55/71–73; L. & P. Hen. VIII, xii(2), pp. 41–42.

he promised to pay £6 a year to a priest or chaplain, to be appointed by him and his heirs, who would help the vicar.[70] The arrangement does not seem to have been permanent, but the poet William Forrest, a former monk of Thame Abbey may have been appointed by him.[71] The chantry's main endowment, however, went to the grammar school and the almshouses.[72]

During the troubled years of the mid-16th century there were probably six vicars, five of them between 1537 and 1559. At the beginning of the century was John Parker (1504–36 or 1537), who was accused first of buying counterfeit money,[73] an indication perhaps of the increasing financial difficulties of the clergy in a period of rising prices and debased currency. In 1533 he was accused of using seditious words against the king.[74] His successor, Master William Goodrich (1537–41), also had difficulties. In 1537 to the complaint of Thomas Stribblehill that the feast of St. Thomas Becket had been kept in the church, the vicar replied that his parishioners 'would have it so'. In the same year there had been a public dispute at a church ale between Robert Johns, a churchwarden, who deplored the harsh treatment of the leaders of the Pilgrimage of Grace, and two members of the Stribblehill family, who supported the government's policy. Johns also advised the selling of the church jewels and plate to avoid their confiscation.[75] The sale of the plate some years later aroused opposition, some parishioners alleging that the wardens had divided the proceeds, £300, amongst themselves.[76]

Changes were also taking place in the services, as is shown by the purchase in the 1540's of a large bible, a hymnal, two English psalters, and the paraphrases of Erasmus.[77] The two fellows of Magdalen College, who in 1553 were interpreting the scriptures at Thame without having been called to the ministry, may be typical of the confusion of the period.[78] With the restoration of Roman Catholicism by Queen Mary changes were again made in the church services, and furniture,[79] and the May ales were revived.[80]

In November 1559 Lord Williams was buried in Thame church with what was probably one of the most elaborate ceremonies ever held there.[81] The fact, however, that in his will he made no provision for services for his soul but instead left money to the almshouses and school shows that a new era had arrived.[82] From 1560 onwards various English books, including a bible, a book of homilies, a communion book, the Book of Common Prayer, and other service books were bought,[83] and the Anglican method of

communion, in which the congregation took part, replaced the Roman Catholic one.[84] A custom which appears in the early 17th century was the renting of the north porch of the church for 10s. or more a year.[85]

During over a hundred years, beginning in 1559, in contrast with the earlier part of the century, Thame had only three vicars.[86] Of these most is known about Thomas Hennant (1629–65). He was on intimate terms with the local gentry, having married a Petty, and was respected in the town.[87] The churchwardens in 1630 granted him the Church House for life in return for his work in keeping the church accounts.[88] Services were stopped for a period when the church was occupied by parliamentary soldiers.[89] Although Hennant had Puritan sympathies,[90] he was left undisturbed at the Restoration. On his death in 1665, he was buried in the chancel.[91] He was succeeded by Hugh Willis (1665–75), headmaster of the grammar school and a onetime royalist,[92] who had to contend with the growing nonconformity in his parish.[93]

The later 17th and 18th centuries were evidently a more stable time in the history of the church, when disputes about pews and about church rates replaced doctrinal disputes.[94] Most of the five vicars who held the living between 1675 and 1841 were resident, and were often assisted by licensed 'lecturers',[95] but because of the small value of the vicarage they started the practice of holding another living as well. William Clerke (1675–1722) was perpetual curate of Long Crendon, and his successor Samuel Thornbury (1722–51) was Rector of Stoke Talmage.[96] A non-resident and probably elderly vicar was Sampson Letsome (1751–61), who had been chaplain to Lord Granville, the patron,[97] and John Newborough (1761–95) was also Vicar of Aston Rowant.

Until about 1720 there were usually four churchwardens. After that there were two, usually one each from New Thame and Old Thame, although occasionally one was chosen from North Weston, Thame Park, Moreton, or Priestend.[98] By about 1770 they were receiving and spending between about £60 and £100 a year, of which perhaps a third came from a rate, for there was rarely a year in which a rate was not levied.[99] Most of the rest of their income came from the church lands and the charities which they administered. Most of their income was therefore spent on charitable payments and on the upkeep of the church and churchyard. In the 18th century the dog-whipper received £1 a year; from the 1820's the organist received 2 guineas; the clerk and the sexton, received an occasional pound or two from the war-

---

[70] *Cal. Pat.* 1550–3, 11; Bodl. MS. ch. Oxon. 3875.
[71] For him see Lee, *Thame*, 401 sqq.; Lupton, *Extracts*, 17. [72] See below, pp. 215, 217.
[73] *L. & P. Hen. VIII*, x, p. 489; see also viii, p. 295. He had acquired Thame in exchange for South Benfleet (Essex) and an unusual Chancery case shows that he and his predecessor had agreed to divide the income of the two vicarages, at least for a year: C 1/345/26.
[74] *L. & P. Hen. VIII*, vi, pp. 192–3, 411, 494; vii, p. 201.
[75] Ibid. xii(2), pp. 143–4. For the consequences of this advice see above, p. 194 and below, p. 210.
[76] *Chant. Cert.* 115–16.
[77] Lupton, *Extracts*, 13, 17, 19, 20.
[78] Macray, *Magd. Reg.* ii. 122, 131.
[79] See below, p. 207.
[80] Lupton, *Extracts*, 25, 26–27, 29.
[81] For description see Lee, *Thame*, 427–30.
[82] *Account of Ld. Williams and his Will* (Thame, 1873).
[83] Lee, *Thame*, 76, 77, 78, 79.

[84] Ibid. 77, 79.
[85] Ibid. 81.
[86] For post-Reformation vicars see ibid. 143 sqq.
[87] For pedigree see Wood, *Life*, i. 35.
[88] Lee, *Thame*, 87 n.
[89] See above, p. 182. The register has a gap for the years 1642–5: Lee, *Thame*, 66.
[90] Wood, *Life*, i. 124.
[91] Ibid. ii. 28.
[92] Lee, *Thame*, 144, 485.
[93] See below, p. 212.
[94] Lee, *Thame*, 188, 189, 192.
[95] Oxf. Archd. Oxon. c 164, f. 136; Lee, *Thame*, 195 n. For list of curates see ibid. 149–51.
[96] Lipscomb, *Bucks.* i. 215; Oldfield, *Clerus Oxon.*
[97] Oxf. Dioc. c 653, ff. 50, 112.
[98] For method of appointment of wardens see Lee, *Thame*, 151–2, 160 n.; for list see ibid. 152–64.
[99] d.d. Par. Thame c 4: chwdns' accts. 1769–1840.

dens, but do not seem to have had a fixed salary. Another regular expense was the churchwardens' feast on Easter Monday or at the visitation. In 1816 the vestry decided that no more than £10 was to be spent on it and named five different inns at which it was to be held in succession. By this time the income and expenses of the wardens had risen and amounted sometimes to £200 or £300 a year.

At this period the vicar was Timothy Tripp Lee (vicar 1795–1840), a member of a Thame family,[1] and from 1814 headmaster of the grammar school. He lived in the parish and in 1830 wrote that he had been there constantly for 35 years without a month's absence.[2] Sometimes on Sundays he had to give several services, for two Sunday services were held in Thame and one in each of the three chapels, and with eleven children to support he did not have the money to pay a regular curate.[3] At this time he was being helped by his son Frederick, who was an un-licensed preacher. Frederick had established a Sun-day evening lecturership which was well attended, visited the sick, and held Sunday schools. In spite of a petition from about 100 Thame householders the bishop refused to license him.[4]

With the separation of Sydenham, Tetsworth, and Towersey from Thame in 1841[5] the number of services at Thame was able to be increased. In 1854 two services with sermons were held on Sundays and another on Wednesday evening, and by 1866 three full services were held every Sunday; communion services were held fifteen times a year.[6] In spite of having congregations of about 600, James Prosser (vicar 1841–72), a Hebrew scholar, was described as 'a man whose pronounced calvinistic views some-what emptied the church', and whose theological ideas incurred criticism.[7] He was also criticized for the scale on which he rebuilt the vicarage in 1841 at a cost of about £2,000 even though the conservatory which was to have been a 'principal feature' of the building was finally omitted.[8] The size of this house and the view expressed in 1838 that the old vicarage was 'a very small house' provides an interesting comment on the rising material standards of the time. Prosser was noted for his generosity to his parishioners. In his later years the care of the parish proved too much for him. In 1871 a memorial circu-lated 'to secure an effective ministry', deplored the fact that within the last 30 years four large dissenting chapels had been built, and Prosser was forced to resign.[9]

Later developments in the history of the church were the introduction of a choir; the starting of an evening school and monthly Bible and communion classes;[10] the building of the mission church in Chinnor Road in 1884, as the town spread towards the station, and its enlargement in 1898; and the building of the Parochial Church Hall in Nelson Street. It was begun in 1913, but for lack of funds was not completed until 1928.[11]

In the Middle Ages there was a chapel, dedicated to St. James, attached to North Weston manor-house. The right of presentation belonged to the lord of the manor,[12] who no doubt paid the chaplain. The chapel was in existence at least by about 1390, when Guy Quatremain was baptized there[13] by the lord's chaplain,[14] and it was probably used for marriages and burials also.[15] In 1526 Richard Birde was curate there, and the curacy was worth more than that of Tetsworth.[16] In the late 17th and early 18th centuries it was used by the Clerkes of North Weston, several of whom were buried there, and occasionally by other people, for marriages and burials.[17] It also served as a chapel of ease for the village until the Clerkes sold the manor in 1755, the preacher receiving about £20 a year.[18]

In the Middle Ages there were two churches attached to Thame Abbey: the abbey church, which was pulled down when the abbey was dissolved, and a chapel at the abbey gates, dedicated to the Blessed Virgin, the oblations of which were worth 3s. 4d. in 1535.[19] In the late 17th and 18th centuries it was used as a private chapel by the Wenman family, and after its restoration in 1836 regular services were held there, 'sweetly and efficiently sung by a chap-lain and a band of surpliced choristers'.[20] The last regular service was held in 1916, when the Wyke-ham-Musgraves were leaving Thame Park, although the family continued to be buried there. A baptismal service was held in 1949 for the son of the owner, Mr. F. Bowden.[21]

The church, dedicated to the *BLESSED VIRGIN MARY*, is a cruciform building consisting of chan-cel, a clerestoried nave, north and south transepts, north and south aisles, a central tower, and south porch with a room above.[22]

The earliest parts of the present building date from the early 13th century.[23] The chancel (60 ft. long) retains four of the original six lancet windows in its north wall and an original north door. The tower arches are of bold Early English design. The transepts, although since reconstructed, were originally of the same period and one lancet window remains in the west wall of the north transept. The nave arcades are also Early English. Later in the 13th century the

[1] Lee, *Thame*, 147, 635 sqq.
[2] Oxf. Dioc. c 664, f. 71.
[3] Ibid. c 659, f. 182; c 446, f. 187; c 664, f. 71b.
[4] Ibid. b 41. For Lee's difficulties with the bishop, see ibid. c 664, ff. 71–79; for his life see Bodl. 11125 e 1, pp. 18–19.   [5] See above, p. 200.
[6] Wilb. Visit.; Oxf. Dioc. c 332.
[7] Brown and Guest, *Thame*, 202, 214.
[8] Oxf. Dioc. b 70; Brown and Guest, *Thame*, 214.
[9] Ibid. 202–5. See below, p. 212.
[10] Ibid. 203; Oxf. Dioc. c 344.
[11] Brown and Guest, *Thame*, 235; Char. Com. file 109, 360.
[12] C.P. 25(2)/34/229/Mich. 34 Hen. VIII.
[13] W. F. Carter, *Quatremains of Oxon.* 18.
[14] Nicholas Sherewynd: Rousham Arch. N 242, N 250. The chapel land is mentioned in 1397: Rousham Arch. N 249.
[15] For the medieval brass of a priest once there see Lee, *Thame*, 289–90.

[16] *Subsidy 1526*, 253.
[17] Ibid. 289, 290, 311, 314. It was last used by the Clerkes in 1750, when Diana Clerke was baptized.
[18] *Par. Coll.* iii. 316; and see above, p. 170.
[19] Lee, *Thame*, 392; *Valor Eccl.* (Rec. Com.), ii. 213. For the buildings see above, pp. 169, 170.
[20] Lee, *Thame*, 397, 398; Lupton, *Thame*, 56.
[21] Brown and Guest, *Thame*, 268; for an unsuccessful attempt to get it consecrated see Oxf. Dioc. c 2049, 1917 letters; inf. the vicar.
[22] There is a very elaborate account of the history of the building up to 1883 in Lee, *Thame, passim.* A report by J. O. Scott on the state of the fabric in 1888 also gives an account of its history (Oxf. Dioc. c 2049). There is a pre-restoration drawing of the exterior of the church from the south-east printed in Lee, *Thame*, frontispiece. See also plates facing pp. 171, 208.
[23] Skelton says the date 1138 was on the tower (*Oxon. Thame Hund.* 7), but this cannot have been the date of building.

fifth and sixth lancets in the north wall of the chancel were replaced by a three-light window. The restored east window is rather later in date and so are the three reticulated windows in the south wall of the chancel which, it is assumed, replaced six lancets. Externally, the Early English buttresses remain unaltered although the string course has been dropped in places so as to pass under each of the 'Decorated' windows.

In the 14th century the aisles appear to have been widened. The fact that the aisle wall encroaches on the lancet window in the north transept shows that the original aisle must have been somewhat narrower.

of the east window; the rebuilding of the north wall and the insertion of a new north window and the making of a new roof. The present east and north windows, each of five lights and both restored, are of this period. The wardens themselves purchased and paid for the materials. They bought freestone at Taynton and ordinary stone at Headington. The latter was supplied by John Beckley, the principal mason employed. He received 7 marks for 'the reryng of the ii syde walls wyt corbeltabul and hascheler abowte ye same ile'. John East of Finchhampstead was the carpenter who made the roof and put it up. John Plummer of Abingdon covered the roof and

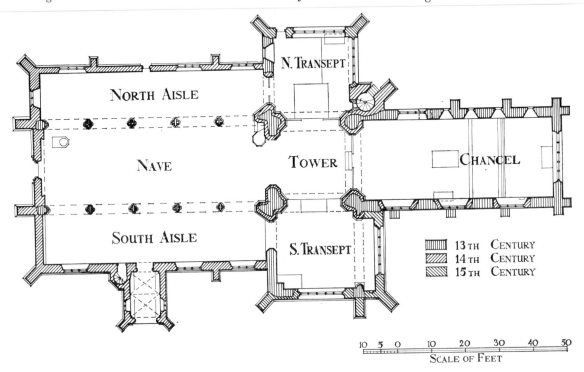

NORTH AISLE

NAVE

SOUTH AISLE

N. TRANSEPT

TOWER

S. TRANSEPT

CHANCEL

	13 TH CENTURY
	14 TH CENTURY
	15 TH CENTURY

10 5 0 10 20 30 40 50

SCALE OF FEET

The windows of the south aisle are good examples of the period. The vaulted porch has a room above with a fireplace and is reached by a staircase. The need for more light and height was met at the end of the 14th century or early in the next by raising the nave walls so as to provide a clerestory. The original steeply pitched roof, the marks of which could be seen until recently on the tower,[24] became flat-pitched and acquired a parapet. The new roof rested inside on stone corbels. The buttresses against the outside of the west wall were built at this time to buttress the nave arcade, as the weight of the clerestory caused a tilt of the nave piers to the west. Two upper stages were added to the tower, raising it to a height of 95 ft., and the tower piers were built round with ashlar to support the additional weight, and that of the bells, so encroaching on the first arch of the nave. The ringing chamber of the tower has a timber roof supported on stone corbels. It is decorated with carved bosses and painted.

In 1442 the reconstruction of the north transept was begun. Full details of the work have been preserved in the churchwardens' accounts.[25] The new work included the taking down and 'setting up' again

made the rain-water pipes. Lead was supplied by William Plummer of Wycombe. Four local masons, John Lawrence, Richard Sharpe, John Walkeleyne, and John Warren were also employed. The total cost of rebuilding the transept was £28 15s. 3d.

It was presumably about this date that the south transept was reconstructed. The north and east windows of five lights are similar to those in the north transept. The east wall was rebuilt farther to the east, the respond and arch belonging to it marking the position of the original wall. The raising of the walls, as was the case with the north transept, meant the substitution of a flat roof with a parapet for the former high-pitched roof. This aisle was dedicated to St. John, and when the Quatremains founded the guild of St. Christopher in 1447 they endowed a chantry chaplain to celebrate divine service daily in this aisle.[26] The tombs of the Quatremains were placed before the new altar.

In 1456 the substantial sum of 42s. 8d. was paid for new leading the steeple.[27] For many years now the tower had had a clock. It was first mentioned in 1442, and in 1465 a floor was constructed beneath, in case the weight fell.[28] Early in the next century in

[24] Inf. Mr. W. Guest.
[25] Berks. Arch. Jnl. vii. 116–19, viii. 24–30.
[26] Lee, Thame, 46 (foundation deed).
[27] Ibid, 44; d.d. Par. Thame c 5, f. 37b.
[28] Lee, Thame, 47.

1529 the tower was rough-cast by Michael Spendler.[29] Work during this period also included the building of two organ lofts, perhaps above the rood screen, between 1477 and 1480[30] for one and perhaps two new organs; and the construction of a door to the loft above St. John's aisle (i.e. the south transept) in 1524 so that the loft might be used as an almery.[31] The loft over the north transept was repaired or enlarged in 1548 when boards were purchased to make the loft 'over Master Dormer's aisle' (i.e. the north transept).[32] Although the lofts in both transepts have since been removed the position of the original floors can still be seen.

The date when the chancel walls were raised and a low roof with parapets replaced the earlier steeply pitched one is uncertain. Sir Gilbert Scott thought that this change was effected late in the 14th or early 15th century,[33] but the presence on the north and south parapets of the arms of Adrian de Bardis, Prebendary of Thame from 1480 to 1501, may indicate that the alteration was made at his expense. His arms in stained glass were also formerly visible in the chancel windows.[34]

The religious changes of Edward VI's and Mary's reigns were reflected in the church building. In 1548 the 'pargitor' was paid for 39 days' work in 'white lynyng' the church,[35] and the pulpit and a desk for the bible were mended.[36] The work of washing out the medieval wall decorations[37] was thoroughly done. Only the traces of a *pieta* on the south-east pier of the tower and stencilled decoration on the soffit of the north window in the north transept were visible in 1959. In 1551 the 'timber work' about the high altar was pulled down. This must have been the canopy of carved wood over the high altar[38] and a communion table and two forms were made.[39] No record of the destruction of the medieval stone reredos exists, but that also may have taken place at this date. The side altars were also pulled down: these included the altars of St. John the Baptist and of St. Christopher in the south transept; of the Most Blessed Trinity in the north transept; of 'our Lady', which appears to have stood where the pulpit now is; of 'All Hallows', standing against the screen separating the north aisle from the north transept; the altar of All Souls, which apparently stood under the arch separating the south aisle from the south transept, where there was also a screen of carved oak; and an unlocated altar of St. Michael.[40]

With the restoration of the Roman Catholic service and ritual in Mary's reign changes were again made in the furnishing of the church. In 1556 a cross and a new rood of Mary and John were bought; in the following year, the rood-loft was mended and a rood-light made and an image of Our Lady for the high altar was purchased.[41] In 1560, however, the rood-

loft and the altars were again taken down.[42] In 1562 a table of commandments was painted; a desk was made in the body of the church for reading the lessons; the clock was mended at great expense,[43] and in 1589 a new pulpit was made,[44] possibly the existing one, with sounding board, which was formerly a three-decker. A new Jacobean communion table was provided in 1625[45] and is still in use; in 1637 in accordance with the injunction of Archbishop Laud it was enclosed by rails.[46]

Little seems to have been done to the fabric in the later 16th and 17th centuries. Payments for rough-casting the church were made in 1564 and 1566;[47] the chancel was probably put in order after about 1609, when it was reported out of repair;[48] the west window of the nave was rebuilt in 1672–3: it has the date 1673 inscribed on the exterior and 1672 and the names of the churchwardens on the interior;[49] and at the end of the century the great south gallery was built at the expense of the master and scholars of the free school and was appropriated to the school in 1693.[50]

By the early 18th century the chancel was in a very dilapidated condition[51] and in 1707 Thomas, 1st Viscount Weymouth, the holder of the prebend, repaired it. This event was once commemorated by an inscription with his arms in the east window.[52] The flat plaster ceiling, which was described in 1888 as being so low that it cut off the top of the east window and chancel arch, must have been inserted at this date; the walls were panelled 'in common deal'; and a classical altar piece erected.[53] In 1792 a new plaster ceiling was put up in the body of the church, semicircular in the nave, and flat in the two side aisles.[54]

Some major repairs were executed in the first half of the 19th century; in 1828 the tower was reroofed and leaded; in 1838 the wall of the north aisle was rebuilt at a cost of £330, the architect being George Wilkinson;[55] and in 1843–5 a series of internal alterations was carried out at a cost of nearly £400 by the architect H. B. Hodson.[56] The nave and aisles were reseated; the font was placed at the crossing of the nave; the prayer desk, which had faced south, was turned to the west; the two Quatremain tombs were moved from their original position and a number of remains of archaeological interest were destroyed or concealed.

In 1889 a thorough restoration was begun. J. O. Scott made a report on the fabric in 1888.[57] He described the church as one of the few large churches which had been left practically unrestored. In addition to necessary repairs to the roof and walls, the 15th-century nave roof was uncovered, the transept ceilings were raised to clear the tower arches, and the chancel was restored at the cost of W. A. Wykeham-Musgrave.[58] This presumably included the removal

[29] MS. Top. Oxon. c 3, f. 196.
[30] Lee, *Thame*, 48–49.
[31] d.d. Par. Thame c 5, f. 78*b*.
[32] Lee, *Thame*, 59.
[33] Oxf. Dioc. c 2049.
[34] Lee, *Thame*, 126.
[35] Ibid. 58.
[36] Ibid. 59.
[37] Ibid. 58–59.
[38] Ibid. 69, 19.
[39] Ibid. 70.
[40] Ibid. 19–23.
[41] Ibid. 73–74.
[42] Ibid. 76.
[43] Ibid. 77.

[44] Ibid. 78.
[45] Ibid. 81.
[46] Ibid. 87.
[47] Ibid. 78.
[48] *Oxon. Peculiars*, 175–7.
[49] Lee, *Thame*, 176.
[50] Oxf. Archd. Oxon c 164, f. 74.
[51] Lee, *Thame*, 167–8, from report of 1707 to Bishop of Lincoln.   [52] Ibid. 168.
[53] Oxf. Dioc. c 2049, Scott's rep.
[54] d.d. Par. Thame c 4: chwdns' accts.
[55] Ibid.
[56] Lee, *Thame*, 179–81; cf. Oxf. Dioc. c 2049, Scott's rep.
[57] Oxf. Dioc. c 2049, Scott's rep.
[58] Brown and Guest, *Thame*, 235. The estimate for restoring the church was £1,800: MS. Top. Oxon. c 105, f. 214.

from the east window of the disfigurement reported by Scott—a large circle in the tracery, divided by very late mullions and transomes. All plaster was removed from ceilings and walls, and all the galleries were taken down. In addition to the Jacobean school gallery there was a singing gallery at the west end of the nave, and other private galleries had been erected in the south transept, at the west end of the north and south aisles, and at the east end of the north aisle. The Wenmans had once had a gallery under the tower arch, but this had already been removed.[59] The restoration of the aisles followed: the south aisle in 1893 and the north aisle in 1897, when the north porch which had been used as a vestry was removed. The total cost was over £3,000.[60]

In 1937–8 the stonework of the body of the church, particularly the north window of the north transept, was repaired under the direction of T. Lawrence Dale, the estimated cost being £1,000. In 1949 the lay rector, Mr. F. Bowden, paid for the restoration of the exterior of the chancel.[61] The south transept, which had been rearranged in 1908,[62] was again refurnished and dedicated as a chapel of St. Christopher in 1954. The architect was J. M. Surman.[63] Gas lighting was first installed in 1840.[64] It was replaced in 1947 by electric light.[65] A new heating system was installed in 1958 by the Southern Gas Board at a charge of nearly £1,000, the money being raised locally.[66]

There was a considerable amount of carved woodwork in the medieval church. Permanent seats were made as early as 1449 in the 'north quarter', and other seats were made and erected by a carpenter from Chilton in the same year.[67] The church still retains a 14th-century screen to the north transept, and a 16th-century chancel screen. The latter has linen-fold panelling below and carved columns above, showing Renaissance influence. A modern screen was erected in 1925 in the west entrance to the north transept in memory of Mary J. Lee, the wife of Dr. H. G. Lee.[68]

Some of the chancel stalls, with a seat for the prebendary on the south and the vicar on the north, were the gift of Prebendary Maudely in 1529,[69] and others were bought by the churchwardens from Thame Abbey in 1540.[70] The choir-stalls under the tower were constructed in 1908 out of the Jacobean gallery once in the south aisle.[71]

The present organ was erected in 1873 in the north transept by Conacher & Co. of Huddersfield at a cost of £300.[72] The churchwardens' accounts show that the church had 'a pair of old organs' as early as

1448. It was probably these that were sold in 1478 and replaced by new ones made by John, organ-maker.[73] The accounts contain various references to them,[74] and new ones were no doubt again bought in 1523 when the old ones were sold to the Rector of Stanton St. John for £10 13s. 4d.[75]

In the early 18th century the church had no organ. Rawlinson says this was because the soldiers of the Earl of Essex had pulled the organs down during the Civil War and 'went tooting about the town with the pipes'.[76] In 1819 £105 raised by subscription was paid to Mr. Brycedon for a new organ,[77] and this was replaced by another in 1842.[78]

The earliest monument in the church is the effigy of a priest now set in the wall of the south transept. It dates from the first half of the 13th century,[79] and probably commemorates one of the prebendaries of Thame.

Thame church is rich in brasses: the two oldest, both on altar tombs, are in the south transept, or the Quatremain aisle. The first is to Thomas Quatremain of North Weston and his wife Katharine (both d. 1342), and to their son Thomas (d. 1398) and his wife Joan. It shows two men in armour (one mutilated) with their wives at the side. Almost all the long inscription is now missing.[80] The second brass is to Richard Quatremain, Esq. (d. 1477) and his wife Sybil (d. 1483). An English verse inscription records Richard's foundation of St. Christopher's chantry.[81] Around the sides of the stone tomb are niches for statues and eight carved panels, each containing a central shield of arms with two shields above. A third brass on an altar tomb, which was once in the south transept[82] but is now in the north transept, is to Geoffrey Dormer (d. 1502/3), merchant of the staple of Calais,[83] his two wives and their 25 children.[84] His coat of arms and merchant's mark are depicted.

There are three other brasses of about the same period to Thame merchants: they are dressed in fur-trimmed gowns and have purses attached to their belts. One is to a man, his wife, and nine children. Another is to Christopher Bridgeman (d. 1503), his wife Maud and their twelve children.[85] The third is to Walter Prat (d. 1508), his wife Isabel and their six children.[86] A similar brass to John Benett (d. 1498) with a verse inscription was mostly there until the early 19th century.[87] The mutilated inscription is now on a wall in the south transept.[88]

Later brasses are to Sir John Clerke (d. 1539) (see below); to John Galey, gent. (d. 1543) (mutilated and on the chancel floor); and to Edward Harris

[59] Lee, *Thame*, 175. For private pews see Oxf. Dioc. c 18, f. 186; Oxf. Archd. Oxon. c 163, *passim*; c 164, f. 77; Oxf. Dioc. b 20, f. 120.
[60] Brown and Guest, *Thame*, 235.
[61] Oxf. Dioc. c 2049, Faculty.
[62] Brown and Guest, *Thame*, 235.
[63] Oxf. Dioc. c 2049, Faculty.
[64] Par. Rec. Chwdns' accts.
[65] Oxf. Dioc. c 2049, Faculty.
[66] Inf. the vicar.   [67] Lee, *Thame*, 41.
[68] Oxf. Dioc. c 2049, Faculty.
[69] Lee, *Thame*, 63.
[70] Lupton, *Extracts*, 13.
[71] Brown and Guest, *Thame*, 235.
[72] Lee, *Thame*, 659.
[73] Ibid. 48–49; and see 20 n.; *Berks. Arch. Jnl.* xix. 85, 86.   [74] e.g. d.d. Par. Thame c 5, f. 52b.
[75] Lee, *Thame*, 52.
[76] *Par. Coll.* iii. 317.   [77] d.d. Par. Thame c 4, 1819.
[78] Par. Rec. chwdns' accts.

[79] Inf. Mr. H. M. Colvin.
[80] For inscription and family see Carter, *Quatremains*, 16–17. The brass incorrectly stated that the younger Thomas d. 1396. For more details of Thame brasses see *Par. Coll.* 310–16; Lee, *Thame*, *passim*; W. R. Barker, 'Monumental Brasses in the Churches of Thame . . .', *Jnl. of Oxf. Univ. Brass-Rubbing Soc.* 1898, i. 137 sqq. For illustrations see MS. Top. Oxon. b 220, ff. 245–251b; for rubbings see Bodl. MS. Rubbings Oxon. Thame 1–10. Parts of many of the brasses are missing.
[81] See above, p. 203.
[82] MS. Top. Oxon. b 220, f. 249.
[83] For him see above, p. 172.
[84] Five boys have been lost.
[85] The effigies of the children have gone but the inscription gives all their names.
[86] For the inscription, see *Par. Coll.* iii. 314.
[87] Illustrated in MS. Top. Oxon. b 220, f. 249b.
[88] MS. Top. Oxon. d 196, f. 352: clipping from *Thame Gaz.* 17 Jan. 1905.

THAME CHURCH

Showing the tomb of Lord Williams and his wife and (left) the Clerke family monuments

(d. 1597), the first headmaster of Thame Grammar School. The last was erected by his pupil and heir William Ballowe.

In 1582 there were two brass inscriptions which are now missing: one was to John Aldersonne, vicar (d. 1503),[89] the other to Henry Bowler (undated), his wife Elizabeth (d. 1555/6) and their ten children.[90] There may also have been at one time a brass to members of the Marmyon family.[91]

In the centre of the chancel is the splendid altar tomb of Lord Williams of Thame (d. 1559) and his first wife Elizabeth, executed in Chellaston marble and surrounded by an iron railing. On it are his alabaster effigy, dressed in full armour, and that of his first wife Elizabeth. Around all the sides are the coats of arms of Williams, Moore, Wentworth, and other families to whom he and his daughters were related by marriage.[92]

In his will Lord Williams provided that he was to be buried in Thame church and that part of the proceeds of the sale of 'Leistropp' manor were to be used for his funeral and the making of his tomb.[93] He also provided for the upkeep of his tomb. In 1661 the Warden of New College found it 'very much mangled, and broken', for it had been damaged by parliamentary soldiers during the Civil War.[94] The estimate of £32 14s. of Mr. Jackson, sculptor (probably the Oxford craftsman John Jackson), for its repair was considered too high and the work given to William Bird of Oxford, who was paid £20 for making a new unicorn (called a lion) a greyhound, and other stone work. Richard Hawkins received £13 6s. 2d. for painting and gilding.[95] The horn of the unicorn has since been broken off.

On the chancel wall there is a brass inscription to Viscount Bertie of Thame (d. 1919), lord of Thame manor and Lord Williams's descendant. The only other memorials to lords of the manors are to the Clerkes of North Weston. The brass to Sir John Clerke (d. 1539) has already been mentioned.[96] There are three shields on the Purbeck marble tomb with the arms of Clerke and above there is a funerary surmounted by a ram's head, the crest of the Clerkes. On the chancel floor is the gravestone, with a long Latin inscription on brass, surmounted by the arms of Clerke impaling Carr, father-in-law of Sir John Clerke, Bt. (d. 1667), and on the chancel wall is a white marble monument to his widow Philadelphia (d. 1698).

Many families of Thame gentry have memorials dating from the 17th century onwards.[97] There are monuments with arms to Rebecca (d. 1631), daughter of John Petty of Stoke Talmage and wife of John Ellis, Rector of Wheatfield, and to Elizabeth (d. 1683), daughter of Maximilian Petty and wife of William Burte, headmaster of Thame school 1631–47. There is a tombstone to Thomas Bryan, gent. (d. 1643); a monument to John Stribblehill, gent. (d. 1692) and to his widow Frances (d. 1722), daughter of Thomas Carter of North Weston; a

tombstone to Edward Leaver, gent. (d. 1697); a monument with arms to Richard Leaver, gent. (d. 1723); an inscription to Thomas Messenger, gent. (d. 1712); a monument to Philip Herbert, Esq. (d. 1749) of Kingsey, M.P. for Oxford; one with arms to William Simons (d. 1764); a tombstone to Harry Style, gent. (d. 1798); and to Richard Smith, Esq. (d. 1808).

Eighteenth and early 19th-century professional men, commemorated mostly by inscriptions or ledgerstones, are Matthew Wilkins (d. 1722), lawyer; Henry Warner (d. 1750/1), attorney; Matthew Loder (d. 1763), surgeon; Edward Rose (d. 1776), attorney; Henry Reynolds (d. 1806), solicitor (by Brine, London); and Sackville Bale Lupton (d. 1840), surgeon.[98]

The only monument to a vicar is that to Timothy Tripp Lee (d. 1840), who was also headmaster of the grammar school. The tombstones of the vicar Samuel Thornbury (d. 1751)[99] and of the nonconformist minister John Nott (d. 1702)[1] are no longer visible. There is a tombstone to William Newborough (d. 1787), Minister of Long Crendon (Bucks.).

Besides Edward Harris and Lee (see above) the following headmasters of the grammar school are commemorated: Richard Boucher (d. 1627), by a monument in the chancel; Thomas Middleton (d. 1694); and the Revd. Alfred Edward Shaw (d. 1921).

There are also memorials to a number of tradesmen and craftsmen: a monument with arms to Robert Heath (d. 1694/5), mason, from whom are probably descended the Revd. Robert Heath (d. 1743) and Robert Heath (d. 1765), to whom there are inscriptions; inscriptions to William Peck, senior (d. 1717), ironmonger; to Edward Phillips (d. 1719), draper; to Samuel Wollaston (d. 1741), apothecary;[2] tombstones to Thomas Haynes (d. 1731), bodice maker; and to John Kent (d. 1737), hatband maker. The tombstone to Richard Cowley (d. 1710), apothecary (*pharmacopola*), is no longer visible.[3]

Other 18th-century inhabitants commemorated are Thomas Crewes (or Crews) (d. 1721/2), Robert Crews (d. 1731/2), and Thomas Crews (d. 1769); Stephen Cook, senior (d. 1707); John Rose (d. 1726/7); Thomas Bayley (d. 1747/8) and his wife; and Edward Burnard (d. 1777). There are 19th-century memorials to Thomas Prickett (d. 1816); Charles Theophilus Dorrington (d. 1821); Thomas Hedges (d. 1847), his wife and daughter, by Bedford, London; and there is a brass to Arthur Conyers (d. 1884). Memorials to the Lee family include a marble monument with arms to Timothy Newmarch Lee (d. 1794), father of the vicar Timothy Tripp Lee; memorials to the vicar's sons Frederick Lee (d. 1841), curate at Thame, and Richard Lee (d. 1882), surgeon; to Dr. Herbert Grove Lee (d. 1909), for 20 years people's churchwarden and his son Douglas Cameron Lee (d. 1938). Other 20th-century inscriptions are to Mrs. F. Eales Shrimpton (d. 1932) and to Constance (d. 1938), wife of Sir Ralph Pearson.

There are war memorials to the dead of the South

---

[89] For its possible position see Barker, op. cit. 151.
[90] Lee, *Thame*, 99.
[91] Ibid. 174 n.
[92] For detailed description see Barker, op. cit. 155–9.
[93] *Some Account of Lord Williams . . . and his Will* (Thame, 1873), 19, 22. For arrangements for keeping the tomb clean see below, p. 217 and Lee, *Thame*, 481.
[94] Ibid. 170 n.
[95] Ibid. 480–2; for Bird see R. Gunnis, *Dict. of British Sculptors, 1660–1851*.

[96] For him see above, p. 173. For inscription see Lee, *Thame*, 95.
[97] The tombstone to Vincent Barry, Esq. (d. 1666) on the floor of the south transept is now concealed.
[98] Lupton, *Thame*, 84. For details of monuments up to c. 1880 and of families commemorated see Lee, *Thame, passim*.
[99] Lee, *Thame*, 117; for him see above, p. 204.
[1] On the west wall of the exterior of the church.
[2] For the family see above, p. 182.
[3] Lee, *Thame*, 117.

African War (1899–1902) and of the First and Second World Wars.

It is likely that the church was once rich in glass and that much of it was destroyed by the parliamentary soldiers who were quartered in the building. Rawlinson mentions some armorial glass in the chancel windows in his day.[4] In 1958 there was no ancient glass, but there were modern stained-glass windows commemorating Harry Lupton, surgeon (d. 1861), and H. W. Reynolds, surgeon (d. 1875), both by Clayton and Bell; Jane Chard (d. 1883); Job and Sarah Shrimpton, erected in 1890 by their children; Winifred Lee (d. 1923), by Morris and Co.[5] The east window, designed by F. E. Howard, is in memory of the parishioners killed in the First World War.[6]

The church was richly furnished in the Middle Ages. An inventory made in 1448 lists vestments and altar furnishings of great richness, of damask, silk, and velvet, many embroidered with gold. There were also a number of crosses, chalices, and candlesticks. Many of the church's possessions were the gifts of local magnates and clergy or distinguished visitors: the prebendaries Nicholas Bubwith, John Wakering, and William Kynwolmarsh had given vestments; Thomas Nash, Rector of Chinnor, had given a chalice, and the vicars John Lucas (1378–1416) and John Derman (1416–?)[7] a chalice and a vestment; other gifts were from Lady Joan Beauchamp and Sir Robert Marney.[8] In addition each of the side altars had its own vestments and plate.[9] Later in the 15th century and in the 16th century the churchwardens' accounts record further gifts.[10]

During the reign of Edward VI most of the plate and the other treasures were sold. In 1547 they were put in the custody of 'divers honest men of the town'. Two of them were churchwardens, and one was the chantry priest, John Collins.[11] In 1547 they sold brass candlesticks to a London brasier; the next year they received £38 10s. 2d. for church plate; in 1549 the great cross fetched £21 4s.; and there were further extensive sales in 1550 and 1551.[12] At least £185, of which £70 was for bells, was obtained. There must also have been other sales for the inhabitants, probably in 1553, listed church property (including four chalices, two crosses, and the foot of the great cross), which had been sold over the last five years for over £300. This sum, they said, had then been divided among the sellers, while the church was left with almost nothing.[13]

The church remained very poorly furnished, for in 1630 its only plate was a brass pot.[14] It seems to have been after 1630, therefore, that the present fine Elizabethan plate was acquired. It consists of a silver-gilt chalice with paten cover of 1569 and inscribed '1570' and 'NT', probably for New Thame, and an-

other and smaller chalice and paten cover of 1570.[15] The church possesses two other pieces of old plate which it was given early in the 18th century: a large paten engraved 'MH 1705' with the arms of Holt impaling those of Stribblehill, the gift of Martha Holt;[16] and a jug-shaped flagon of silver gilt, the gift in 1715 of Thomas Carter, Esq. The remaining plate is late 19th or 20th century.[17] The church once owned two large silver candlesticks, said to have been given by a member of the Thynne family, the lay rectors, but in the late 18th century these disappeared and were replaced by less valuable ones.[18]

The known history of the bells begins in 1448, when there was a ring of five large bells and another bell in the tower not forming part of the ring. The churchwardens' accounts frequently mention the buying, recasting, and repairing of bells.[19] In 1627 the wardens bought a new 'stock' ring of six from Ellis Knight's Reading foundry, and these bells remained in use until 1876 except that in 1664 the tenor was recast.[20] By 1875 two of the bells were cracked, and the vestry decided after protracted discussion, to recast the cracked bells and rehang all instead of adopting Richard Lee's proposal to buy new ones. Lee raised a fund to recast the six bells, but in 1876 eight new bells were rehung in the old frame, an event commemorated by a brass tablet on one of the tower piers. In 1881 when the bells were again taken down it was discovered that all were in fact new and contained no 'old bell metal'. They were rehung in 1884, with a new oak frame and floor, at a cost of £120 borne by S. Lacey.[21] Besides the ring of eight, there was also in the church in 1958 a sanctus bell, probably of the 17th century.[22]

ROMAN CATHOLICISM. A few adherents of the old religion remained in Thame after the Reformation. The earliest recorded recusants belonged to the Etherege family.[23] Dr. George Etherege of Thame was Regius Professor of Greek at Oxford under Queen Mary and was of her faith.[24] He was deprived under Elizabeth, and was living in Thame in 1564 when the sheriff was ordered to summon him before the Ecclesiastical Commissioners; Etherege had already twice disobeyed the summons of the commissioners concerning 'sundry notorious disobediences in causes of religion'.[25] Subsequently he lived in Oxford, practising medicine and 'educating several sons of the nobility in their ancient faith'. In 1577 he was listed as a leading Oxford recusant;[26] but in the same year he was also returned under Thame, with his wife, his son Thomas, and two maids.[27] In 1592 Mary, wife of Thomas Etherege, gent., was the only Thame recusant returned,[28] but in 1606 she and her husband and their son George were presented by the churchwardens for not coming to church or receiving

[4] Par. Coll. iii. 313.
[5] Oxf. Dioc. c 2049, Faculty.
[6] Ibid. Faculty (1921).
[7] Lee, Thame, 32 incorrectly reads his name Dormer.
[8] Ibid. 30–33.
[9] Ibid. 33–35.
[10] e.g. ibid. 42; d.d. Par. Thame c 5, f. 55b; Lupton, Extracts, 16.　　[11] Lupton, Extracts, 18.
[12] Ibid. 19–22.
[13] Lee, Thame, 532; Chant. Cert. 115–16.
[14] Lee, Thame, 83.
[15] It has been suggested that the smaller set once belonged to one of Thame's chapels, Sydenham, Tetsworth, or Towersey: Evans, Ch. Plate.
[16] Ibid.; Lee, Thame, 535; and see p. 622 for family.

[17] Evans, Ch. Plate.　　[18] Lee, Thame, 173.
[19] Ch. Bells Oxon. 415 sqq., where there is a full history of the bells, including many extracts from the churchwardens' accts.
[20] Ibid. 425. For rubbings of inscriptions see MS. Top. Oxon. c 3, ff. 434–6.
[21] Oxf. Dioc. c 2049, application for a faculty and other papers; Brown and Guest, Thame, 234–5.
[22] Ch. Bells Oxon. 413–14.
[23] Acts of P.C. 1550–2, 382, 387.
[24] Ibid. 1552–4, 333. For him see D.N.B. and Wood, Athenae, i. 546–8.
[25] Acts of P.C. 1558–70, 168.
[26] C.R.S. xxii. 97.
[27] Ibid. 112.　　[28] Ibid. xviii. 259.

communion,[29] and at the same time George Etherege, gent., lately of Thame, was fined for recusancy.[30] At least one branch of the family continued to live in the region,[31] but there is no later record of their being recusants.

Others fined for recusancy in the early 17th century were George Hashett (or Haslett), brewer, Thomas Stones of Moreton, and John Greene of North Weston.[32] Two of these were among the fourteen people presented by the churchwardens between 1606 and 1609 for not coming to church or not receiving communion at Easter.[33] Slightly later the Maynes, sometimes reported as of Priestend, sometimes as of Moreton, were another Roman Catholic family. John Mayne, gent., his wife Dorothy, and their children were listed as recusants at various dates between 1623 and 1635.[34]

The Wenmans of Thame Park are on no recusant lists, but Agnes, the first wife of Sir Richard Wenman, was the daughter of Sir George Fermor of Easton Neston (Northants.), and therefore a member of a leading recusant family.[35] When Father John Gerard, the Jesuit, was staying with Elizabeth Vaux at Great Harrowden (Northants.) in 1599 they were visited by a relative of Mrs. Vaux, a lady who lived in Oxfordshire and 'was married to a knight with a large estate, who hoped one day to become a baron', and this lady is thought to have been Agnes Wenman.[36] As her husband was a Protestant she was unable to keep a priest in her house, but she regularly performed certain prescribed religious duties.[37] After the Gunpowder Plot in 1605 both Sir Richard and his wife were questioned and it was alleged that Lady Wenman had corresponded with Mrs. Vaux about the conspiracy, and Sir Richard claimed that Mrs. Vaux had tried to 'pervert his wife'.[38] Nothing was proved against either of the Wenmans and after the death of Agnes Wenman in 1617[39] there was no further report of recusancy at Thame Park until the 18th century.

At the same period Margaret, the wife of Sir William Clerke of North Weston, and the daughter of Sir John Bourne, Secretary of State to Queen Mary, was fined as an Oxford recusant in 1603.[40] Her father was a strong opponent of the new religion.[41] In 1604 a Roman Catholic priest was reported to be with 'Lady Clark at Weston nigh unto Thame'[42] and according to local tradition Catholic services were held at North Weston, either in the chapel or in the manor-house, until 1624,[43] the year of Lady Clerke's death.

There is little further record of Roman Catholicism in Thame until 1766, when the 7th Viscount Wenman married a Roman Catholic, the Lady Eleanor Bertie, a daughter of the 3rd Earl of Abingdon.[44] In 1767 there were only five 'papists' in the parish: Lady Eleanor, her sister, her two maids, and a hatter's wife.[45] From this time probably until 1800, the year of Lord Wenman's death, a Roman Catholic chaplain lived at Thame Park and mass was said in the chapel there. Father Bernard Stafford, alias Cassidy, the superior of the Residence of St. Mary, lived there and was buried in the chapel in 1788.[46] He was followed by a secular priest and then by another Jesuit, William Hothersall.[47]

After the 'reign of terror' in France a large number of Roman Catholic clergy fled to England and in 1796 about 50 from Brittany were housed in the 'Mansion House',[48] and the government grant for their maintenance was supplemented by local collections. The Marquess of Buckingham[49] made contributions, and Richard Smith, the father-in-law of the vicar, Timothy Tripp Lee, generously allowed them £250 a year for four years.[50] They had a temporary chapel in the house, where mass was said. Two of these *emigré* priests were buried in Thame churchyard in 1796 and 1797. The survivors eventually returned to France after a public thanksgiving at which the sermon was preached by the vicar.[51] The house was closed in 1802.[52]

No more is known of Roman Catholicism in Thame until 1912 or 1913, when Colonel Harman Grisewood allowed the use of the prebendal chapel for public Roman Catholic services and Thame had a resident priest, Father Randolph Traill.[53] The present church, St. Joseph's in Brook Lane, was dedicated in 1922.

In 1958 the Roman Catholic community, including no doubt some who lived in neighbouring parishes, numbered 270.[54]

PROTESTANT NONCONFORMITY. Even the established church in Thame was Puritan in character in early Stuart times, and conditions were distinctly favourable for the growth of dissent. Some of the leaders of Thame society had puritan leanings and were sympathetic to the parliamentary cause. The vicar Thomas Hennant (1631–65) and the headmaster of the grammar school William Burte (1631–47) were thought by Anthony Wood to show greater kindness to the parliamentary soldiers than to the royalist. They had both married members of the

[29] *Oxon. Peculiars*, 174–5.
[30] Salter, *Oxon. Recusants*, 21.
[31] Lee, *Thame*, 527.
[32] Salter, *Oxon. Recusants*, 25, 26, 29.
[33] *Oxon. Peculiars*, 175–8. Besides the Ethereges there were Tomsonn Gregorie, Thomas Cobbett, Marion Arnold, Thomas Keene, Eleanor Parsloe, the wives of William Carter and of William Jesoppe, and William Wenlow and his wife.
[34] Salter, *Oxon. Recusants*, 38, 42, 51; Stapleton, *Cath. Miss.* 8.
[35] For pedigree see Lee, *Thame*, 435.
[36] John Gerard, *The Autobiography of an Elizabethan*, trans. P. Caraman (1956), 169. Richard Wenman had been knighted in 1596 and was not raised to the peerage until 1628. Agnes Fermor was a distant cousin of the Vaux family: ibid. 255.
[37] Ibid. 169.
[38] *Cal. S.P. Dom.* 1603–10, 204, 259, 266, 267, 268, 271.
[39] For her see *D.N.B.* under Thos. Wenman.
[40] See above, p. 173.

[41] For Bourne's religious policy see *V.C.H. Worcs.* ii. 47–48.
[42] Salter, *Oxon. Recusants*, 16; A. Wood, *City of Oxford*, iii (O.H.S. xxxvii), 225.   [43] Lee, *Thame*, 308 n.
[44] Stapleton, *Cath. Miss.* 251.
[45] Oxf. Dioc. c 431, f. 91.
[46] Stapleton, *Cath. Miss.* 251–2; Lee, *Thame*, 398. For Stafford see H. Foley, *Records of English Province*, iv. 625 where he is said to have died in 1778.
[47] C.R.S. xxii. 281; Stapleton, *Cath. Miss.* 252. For him see ibid. 233.
[48] For this episode see Stapleton, *Cath. Miss.* 252–4; Lee, *Thame*, 656–7; MS. Top. Oxon. d 41, ff. 387–92b (an article by F. G. Lee in the National Review); and F. X. Plasse, *Le clergé français réfugié en Angleterre* (1886), ii. 44–46.   [49] *Complete Peerage*, ii. 408 n.
[50] MS. Top. Oxon. d 41, f. 392b.
[51] Ibid. f. 392.
[52] Plasse, op. cit. ii. 242.
[53] Kelly, *Dir Oxon.* (1920).
[54] *Catholic Dir.* (1958).

Petty family,[55] and Charnell Petty at least was dubbed by Wood 'an old puritan'.[56] The Pettys were related to the Cromwells, Hampdens, Ingoldsbys, and Wallers,[57] and consequently moved among families of which many members were strongly puritan. After the Restoration there were Quakers, Presbyterians, Independents, and members of the Countess of Huntingdon's Connexion.[58] The Compton Census of 1676 recorded that there were 100 'utter' dissenters.[59]

The continued strength of nonconformity in Thame in the 18th century is demonstrated by the numerous meetings of gentlemen and ministers from Oxfordshire and Buckinghamshire to pass resolutions in favour of the repeal of the Test Act. During the century there was always at least one dissenting congregation, and by the end of the century the Wesleyans had founded a chapel.[60] From the 1820's, when the Baptists became established, there were at least three chapels, and in addition in the first half of the century a number of private houses were registered for worship for unknown denominations.[61] Among the sects at this time were Primitive Methodists and Particular Baptists. The progress made by the nonconformist movement may be judged by the success of its Sunday schools: the roll of 1833 gives 185 Anglican pupils and 234 belonging to the three dissenting Sunday schools (i.e. Congregationalist, Wesleyan, and Baptist).[62] Some children from neighbouring villages were probably included in the nonconformist group. In 1854 the vicar estimated that about a third of the parish was nonconformist and in the 1880's the proportion was probably greater.[63] In this century nonconformity, which had once had a distinctly Calvinistic character, was of a more general Evangelical type, although still strongly opposed to the established church.

So the town was divided into two camps: the rivals would not deal with the same tradesmen, and a dual system of shops grew up.[64] Churchwardens were suspected of trying to restrict the various charities to church people[65] and nonconformists sometimes tried to elect one of their own number as a churchwarden.

Nonconformists co-operated in matters other than opposition to the church: Baptists lent their choir to the Wesleyans for Sunday school anniversaries;[66] Wesleyans their Sunday school to the Congregationalists before they had one of their own;[67] all rallied to the support of the British School, founded in 1835, and the annual Temperance Festival, held from 1841 to 1898.[68] Sometimes combined weekday services were held in different chapels in turn.[69] Nonconformity in Thame was reinforced towards the end of the century by the Salvation Army. By

1958, however, only the Congregationalists, Baptists, and Methodists survived.

PRESBYTERIANS. In its early days Thame nonconformity drew much of its inspiration from the Buckinghamshire movement, and a common opposition to the Anglican church drew the sects together to such an extent that organized separate churches were slow to develop. As late as the 1690's Presbyterians and Independents formed one community and the minister was paid from a Common Fund to which both contributed.[70]

The earliest notice of nonconformist activity in the town occurs in 1669, when an assembly of about 200 Presbyterians and Anabaptists was reported to be meeting in the house of John Burton.[71] One of their 'teachers' was George Swinnock, ejected Vicar of Great Kimble (Bucks.).[72] He was chaplain to Richard Hampden of Great Hampden, who was noted for his Presbyterian sympathies.[73] Two other 'teachers' were also eminent nonconformist divines from Buckinghamshire. Robert Bennet, ejected from Waddesdon, and Samuel Clarke, ejected from High Wycombe, were connected with Buckinghamshire nonconformity through Lord Wharton of Wooburn,[74] who had been a puritan and an opponent of the penal laws of the Restoration period. This Thame assembly, however, was dissolved by the justices of the peace and it removed to Buckinghamshire.[75] A year later the vicar presented about 90 persons for not receiving the sacrament at Easter and for failing to pay their church dues.[76] Among them were Burton, Atkins, Horn, and Edward Howes, a 'Congregationalist'. The house of the last was the first to be licensed in 1672 as a meeting-house. It was registered again in 1690 along with that of John Nott.[77] On neither occasion was the denomination specified. Nott was an ejected minister with Buckinghamshire connexions: like Swinnock, he had been chaplain to Richard Hampden and had also been the preacher in the chapel at Wooburn.[78] When his licence was renewed in 1692[79] it appeared that the 'constant meeting' he had 'newly set up' in 1690[80] was in a house in New Thame. At the time his congregation could not promise him £15 a year, but he received £10 (later £8) from the Common Fund.[81] Edmund Calamy records in his autobiography that when he was at Oxford in 1691 and 1692 he used to 'help' Mr. Nott.[82] Nott died in Thame in 1702 and was buried in St. Mary's church. In the register he is described as a 'nonconforming minister'.[83] Two other houses were licensed in his time: the house of Samuel Horn in 1692 and that of Stephen King, in New Thame, in 1693.[84]

By 1715 the Revd. Matthew Leeson had a con-

[55] Wood, Life, i. 124; V.C.H. Oxon. i. 476.
[56] Wood, Life, i. 184.
[57] For pedigrees see Lee, Thame, 85, 218. [58] See below.
[59] Queen's Coll. MS. 501 (Provost Smith's Collection, vol. 159: draft of original return to the Compton Census, loose sheet at back of vol.). The return does not appear in Salt MS. 33. [60] See below.
[61] Oxf. Dioc. c 644, f. 192 (1817); c 645, ff. 109. 141 (1828, 1829); c 646, ff. 52, 148 (1846, 1851).
[62] Educ. Enq. Abstract, 756.
[63] Wilb. Visit.; Lee, Thame, 633.
[64] Brown and Guest, Thame, 150.
[65] e.g. see letter of 17 Mar. 1883 from the Congregational minister in MS. Top. Oxon. d 41, f. 436 (from Thame Observer).
[66] Thame Methodist Church, Annual Report, 1884.
[67] Thame Cong. Church, Minutes.
[68] Brown and Guest, Thame, 201.

[69] Thame Cong. Ch., Minutes.
[70] Freedom after Ejection, ed. A. Gordon, 158. Cf. Bicester nonconformity; V.C.H. Oxon. vi. 48–49.
[71] G. Lyon Turner, Original Records of Early Nonconformity, iii. 823. [72] Calamy Rev. 473; D.N.B.
[73] For him see D.N.B.
[74] For them see D.N.B. and Calamy Rev. 49, 119.
[75] Lyon Turner, op. cit. 823. [76] Oxon. Peculiars, 180.
[77] Lyon Turner, op. cit. 833; O.R.O. Cal. Q. Sess. viii. 801. [78] For him see Calamy Rev. 368.
[79] O.R.O. Cal. Q. Sess. viii. 802.
[80] Calamy Rev. 368.
[81] Freedom after Ejection, ed. A. Gordon, 85, 320.
[82] E. Calamy, Hist. Account of my own Life (1829), i. 279.
[83] Lee, Thame, 117.
[84] O.R.O. Cal. Q. Sess. viii. 801, 802. It is possible that in 1692 Nott and Horn were sharing a house; the licence is not clear.

gregation specifically described as Presbyterian with a membership of 100–200, eight being gentlemen and the rest tradesmen, farmers, and labourers.[85] It was for these Presbyterians that in 1728 a licence was sought by Samuel Horn, William Pain, Joseph Howes, John Geary, Robert Carruthers, and Thomas Eeles, the trustees for a building in an orchard lately belonging to the Sun Inn, New Thame.[86] This probably marked the erection of the chapel in Sun Yard, said to have been built by the Geary family,[87] although it may have been already in existence. Matthew Leeson was still minister and was also master of a private school where in 1739 he took as a pupil John Wilkes of later notoriety. Wilkes reported his master to be constantly searching for 'some new heresy', and Leeson became a deist two years after and having been obliged to resign his ministry removed his school to Aylesbury.[88] He was succeeded in 1743 by Thomas Dixon, a member of an old nonconformist family, who was paid £25 a year in salary until he left in 1750.[89] By 1772 the Presbyterian community seems to have died out and in about 1780 the meeting-house was sold or let to the Methodists.[90]

CONGREGATIONALISTS (INDEPENDENTS). The sect flourished at Thame in the second half of the 17th century and had a licensed meeting-house in 1672 belonging to Edward Howes.[91] But the Presbyterians were clearly predominant until the mid-18th century when the ascendancy of the Congregationalists seems to have begun. The date of the foundation of their church is given as 1750,[92] but its early history is not well documented. A letter of 1850 describing the 'rise of the Independent cause in Thame' gives the names of early ministers, of which some are recorded to have preached in Chinnor also. They were Mr. Stumphouse, Mr. Murrain, who kept a school and was 'very moderate in his views concerning divine truths'; Mr. Molland, 'very high' (i.e. Calvinistic); Mr. Hornsby 'coarse but high'; and Mr. Day.[93]

In 1786 'all that messuage or tenement in Hoggherd's Hill', being then the 'Chequer' ale house, with forge attached, was bought by public subscription to be made into a meeting-house for the Countess of Huntingdon's Connexion, a movement closely allied to Congregationalism.[94] There is no further record of this sect and their meeting-house was apparently later used by the Independents.[95] The Independent minister at the end of the century, John Paul, was clearly a man of energy and distinction. In 1799 he was allotted £10 a year by the Hughes Trust on condition that he preached one Sunday a year at the New Road chapel in Oxford, and in 1805 he built the Congregational chapel at Chinnor.[96] In 1810 the

Thame Congregational chapel must have been one of the two dissenting chapels recorded there. It may have been the one where no services were said to be held,[97] for it must certainly have gone out of use before 1821, since in that year a new congregation was founded. 'A small church was (then) formed' in the Independent chapel,[98] and from that date Thame Congregationalism has an unbroken history up to the present day (1959), as is shown by the continuous succession of its ministers, beginning with W. H. Wiffen, who had been assistant to Paul in Chinnor.[99] The chapel used was probably the building in the Cattle Market at the east end of Middle Row (now the offices of Burrows and Bradfield). When it was put up for sale in 1829, after the new chapel had been built it was described as an 'Independent dissenters' chapel . . . substantially erected with bricks and timber, tiled and in good repair', and containing pews and fittings.[1]

The new chapel, built in 1827 at a cost of £1,400,[2] is now the Masonic Hall (14 High Street).[3] In 1838 the chapel was registered for marriages[4] and in 1841, with 35 members, it was included in the newly formed Oxfordshire and West Berkshire Association.[5] It had no burial ground and when Wiffen died in 1844 he was buried in front of it.[6] A year later some stir was caused by the appointment of a Baptist minister, Isaac Doxey, but on inquiry from the Congregational Association the chapel members said they were remaining Independent[7] and in 1851 the chapel was returned as an Independent one. Congregations numbered over 100 in the morning, 30 in the afternoon, and 166 in the evening; there was an attendance of between about 120 and 140 children at the morning and afternoon Sunday schools; and the minister held a small Bible class for female domestic servants.[8] Doctrinal trouble arose in 1860 on the resignation of J. G. Stevenson, appointed two years before. He was accused by James Marsh, a prominent Congregationalist, of not preaching in accordance with the principles laid down in the trust deeds of the chapel (i.e. Calvinistic principles). The majority of the members were willing to have the trust deeds altered,[9] but when it was found that this would be illegal Stevenson resigned. The British School allowed him free use of a room for religious meetings and worship.[10] Chapel membership was more than halved and Marsh offered to reimburse Stevenson for any expenses incurred if he would return to the Congregational Church. He refused unless the trust deeds were altered. Marsh brought the state of affairs before the ministers of the Association and the Home Missionary Board, but both were unable to assist from want of funds. The separatist movement was

[85] Dr. William's Library (London), Evans MS. f. 14.
[86] O.R.O. Cal. Q. Sess. viii. 806.
[87] Lupton, Thame, 22. The chapel was eventually sold by the Revd. J. Geary (Lupton, Thame, 23).
[88] H. Bleackley, Life of John Wilkes (1917), 8–9.
[89] For him see D.N.B.
[90] Summers, Congreg. Chs. 8, 262; Brown and Guest, Thame, 149.   [91] Lyon Turner, op. cit. 833.
[92] Congregational Yearbk.
[93] Summers, Congreg. Chs. 262; Thame Cong. Ch. Letter of 1850.
[94] Thame Cong. Ch. Title deeds.
[95] Jackson's Oxf. Jnl. 4 July 1829.
[96] Thame Cong. Ch. Copy of trust deed; Char. Com. file 132037. The trust still functions. One of its aims was to encourage local preaching and the grant of £10 was made, subject to conditions, to the minister 'for the time being'.

[97] Oxf. Dioc. c 441, f. 28. In 1812 the Congregationalists established a Sick Society; this was so successful that the parish church set up another in opposition: Thame Cong. Ch. 1850 letter.
[98] Evangelical Mag. 1821, xxix. 160.
[99] Thame Cong. Ch. List of ministers.
[1] Jackson's Oxf. Jnl. 4 July 1829.
[2] Lupton, Thame, 22; Oxf. Dioc. c 645, f. 95.
[3] Summers, Congreg. Chs. 264.
[4] Lond. Gaz. 20 July 1838.
[5] Minute books of the Berks. S. Oxon. and S. Bucks. Cong. Assoc. (now Union), penes the General Secretary, Reading.
[6] Lupton, Thame, 22.
[7] Cong. Assoc. min. bks.
[8] H.O. 129/5/156.
[9] Thame Cong. Ch. Notes.
[10] O.R.O. British School, Minutes.

finally ended by the managers of the British School, who in 1862 decided that Stevenson should no longer have the use of the schoolroom as his 'strange doctrine' gave offence to some of the subscribers. By 1865 he had left Thame and was officiating at Shanklin.[11] In spite of these events, by 1868 the Congregationalists had sufficiently recovered to consider the building of a larger and more comfortable chapel with a schoolroom.[12] In 1871 the present chapel was built for 'Protestant Dissenters of the Congregational Denomination called Independents being Pædobaptists'. According to the trust deeds the minister was to be chosen by two-thirds of the members at a special meeting, but no mention was made of 'Calvinistic principles'. Part of the ground was to be used for burials and a house already on the site became the manse. The chapel, built of brick and fronted with stone, cost £2,000 and had 450 seats.[13] It had a vestry and schoolroom below.

The period 1881–5 seems to have been most prosperous for the chapel, with an active membership of up to 81 persons.[14] In 1958 there were 48 members.[15] A memorial hall and vestry were built in 1907 at a cost of £300, of which £200 came from a legacy from Samuel Lacey and a grant from the 20th-century fund. A new manse was built in Southern Road in 1922.[16]

The registers date from 1838, the minutes from 1858,[17] and the members' roll from 1881.

SOCIETY OF FRIENDS. A footnote to a draft copy of the original return to the Compton Census of 1676 states that out of 100 'utter' dissenters recorded 32 were Quakers.[18] No further evidence of the movement had been found until William Wheeler (1800–87), a Thame grocer and a writer of religious poetry,[19] who was one of the leading supporters of the British School and the Thame Temperance Society, founded a Quaker meeting, which met in a small building in his garden at 4 East Street. For many years the group resisted the imposition of church rates. On Wheeler's death the society broke up, but the building still exists and its benches are used by a Baptist Bible society in a nearby room.[20]

METHODISTS. Wesleyan preachers met with hostility from the mob and no headway was made until Wesley himself paid two visits to Thame in 1778 and 1782. He used the former Presbyterian chapel on his first visit and had a crowded and attentive meeting. A case of faith-healing occurred.[21]

In about 1780 the Wesleyans bought or leased the chapel in the Sun Yard. Hitherto they had used two rooms in a cottage next to the present Barclays Bank in Middle Row.[22] The community prospered: its Sunday school, started in 1826, had the largest attendance—90 pupils—of the three dissenting schools being held in Thame in 1833.[23] In 1853 a new chapel was built in Upper High Street at a cost of £1,095. It was to serve '40 members' and had an average congregation of 150. The building was of brick with a stone front and seated 300 persons; it had a schoolroom on the ground floor.[24] It is of interest that the trustees of the new building almost all came from the surrounding villages and not from Thame itself; they consisted of the relieving officer, the minister, two farmers, a number of tradesmen and craftsmen, and a servant.[25] In 1875 the chapel, which had just become free from debt, was badly damaged by fire, and its restoration cost £653.[26]

As with the Congregationalists, the most prosperous period of the sect was in the 1880's. In 1884 there were 180 children on the Sunday-school roll, double the number of 40 years before, although only a minority were members; they were taught by eighteen teachers. By 1950 the number of scholars and teachers had declined to 20 and 6 respectively.[27] In the 1880's Thame was at the head of a circuit that included eight Buckinghamshire villages. In addition to the minister, there were eight lay-preachers in the town.[28] In the 20th century Thame has remained a Methodist centre: membership declined only slightly from 64 in 1900 to 59 in 1958.[29] There is still a resident minister, one of the two on the Thame and Watlington circuit.

PRIMITIVE METHODISTS. Primitive Methodists were also strong in the parish. The house in Moreton registered for worship in 1820 may have been used by them,[30] for their first chapel was Bethel chapel, built in 1839 in Moreton.[31] Of its seven trustees, all labourers except for one farmer, four were from Moreton and three from Drayton (Bucks.).[32] In 1851 attendances of 50 and over were reported in the afternoons and evenings.[33] In 1870 a new chapel was built and was registered for marriages in 1875.[34] When the Primitive Methodists joined the Wesleyans in 1932 Moreton chapel became a Methodist chapel. In 1958 it had a membership of ten and was on the Thame and Watlington circuit.[35]

The second Primitive Methodist Society in the parish, the Society of New Jerusalem Methodists, was formed in Thame itself in 1849. Their meeting-place had 150 seats and was in the poorest part of the town. It was considered a 'blessing to the neighbourhood'; and after its opening fighting and quarrelling decreased.[36] The steward was James Phillips, a Thame grocer, and the congregations, of 100 and over in the afternoon and evening, were said to consist entirely of poor people. The Primitive Methodist chapel built in East Street in 1864 was no doubt the

---

[11] Thame Cong. Ch. Minutes and members' roll; Cong. Assoc. min. bks.
[12] Thame Cong. Ch. Minutes.
[13] Ibid. Trust deeds; Lond. Gaz. 4 Oct. 1872.
[14] Thame Cong. Ch. Members' roll.
[15] Congregational Yearbk.
[16] Thame Cong. Ch. Minutes.
[17] The first minute is no. 520.
[18] See n. 58 above.
[19] W. W[heeler], Original Poetry Consisting of Psalms, Hymns, &c. (1874).
[20] Thame Gazette, 1887; inf. members of Wheeler family, and family genealogical MS. at Thame.
[21] Journal of John Wesley, ed. N. Curnock, vi. 214, 375.
[22] Brown and Guest, Thame, 149.
[23] Educ. Enq. Abstract, 756; see also Thame Methodist Church, Sunday-school registers, 1841–3.

[24] Thame Meth. Ch. Copy of schedule approved by chapel Bldg. Cttee. 17 Dec. 1852.
[25] In 1865 the chapel was registered for marriages: Lond. Gaz. 28 Mar. 1865.
[26] Thame Meth. Ch. Builder's contract, 1876.
[27] Ibid. Annual reports.   [28] Ibid. Circuit Plan, 1882.
[29] Ibid. Annual report; Circuit Plan, 1958.
[30] Oxf. Dioc. c 644, ff. 219–20. It was the house of Joseph Mott and in 1851 Isaac Mott was the chapel's manager.   [31] H.O. 129/5/156.
[32] Thame Meth. Ch. Conveyance. It was not licensed until 1850: Oxf. Dioc. c 647, f. 130.
[33] H.O. 129/5/156.
[34] Thame Meth. Ch. Conveyance; Lond. Gaz. 17 Sept. 1875.
[35] Kelly, Dir. Oxon. (1920); Circuit Plan, 1958.
[36] H.O. 129/5/156.

successor to this room.[37] It probably ceased being used as a chapel in about 1900,[38] and was leased from about 1917 to the County Council. The trustees sold it in 1940.[39]

BAPTISTS. In 1851 there were two Baptist meeting-places in Thame. The larger one, belonging to the Particular Baptists, had started in 1825, when the house of Thomas Juggins, a Thame furrier, was registered.[40] In the same year a Baptist Sunday school was started, and by 1833 it had 70 pupils.[41] In 1851 the chapel, built not long before March 1842, had an average Sunday attendance varying from 34 to 103, according to the time of day.[42] Its minister was Stephen Walker, a Thame grocer, and the building was off the south end of Rook's Lane, where remains of a gallery and baptistry still exist.[43] In 1851 the other Baptist meeting-place had an average attendance of no more than 25 persons. Its date of foundation is not given and nothing further is known about it.[44]

There is no further record of these two groups of Baptists, and it seems possible that they united and used the old Presbyterian chapel in the Sun Yard which had been used by the Methodists until they built a new chapel in 1853 (see above). This Sun Yard building was the Baptist chapel from at least 1860 until 1865,[45] when the present chapel in Park Street was built at a cost of £500.[46] At this time there were 40 members. By 1925 membership had sunk to three, but since then there has been a revival and in 1958 there were 38 members.[47] In addition to the chapel, the Baptists used the former Primitive Methodist chapel in East Street as a church hall.

SALVATION ARMY. Between 1886 and 1897 the Salvation Army made intermittent attempts to establish itself, Herbert Booth, General Booth's son, paying a visit in 1887, and arousing a good deal of opposition. Both the Primitive Methodists and the Wesleyans lent their buildings to the Army on different occasions.[48] The Army later built its own small red brick hall in East Street.

SCHOOLS.[49] Since the 16th century Thame has been renowned for its excellent endowed grammar school for boys, founded in 1559 by Lord Williams of Thame. In the 17th century in particular it was attended by an unusual number of pupils who later made their mark in English history.[50] The history of this school has been summarized up to the 1930's in a previous volume.[51] It became a voluntary controlled school under the 1944 Education Act, and in 1955 had 124 day boys and 46 boarders.[52]

The town also attracted a number of private schools, of which at least two, the County Middle Class School for boys and the Girls' Grammar School, had a considerable reputation in the county in the 19th century.[53] Of the more ephemeral ones mention may be made of a boarding school advertised in the Oxford Journal in 1779, of a school at North Weston manor-house recorded in 1819, of a day and boarding school with 42 boys founded in 1827, and of another for 17 girls in 1832, of a classical and commercial school conducted by a Mr. Scadding in 1836, and of Miss Were's establishment at Montpellier House which is recorded in 1840.[54] In 1854 Billing's Oxfordshire Directory listed four private schools.[55]

No evidence has survived about elementary education in Thame before the 1730's, when the strong interest in education in the country generally after peace had been declared in 1713 found expression in the town. Between 1732 and 1740 five bequests were made for the education of poor children: these included bequests by Matthew Crew and the 2nd Earl of Abingdon.[56] About a hundred years later a committee was formed to establish Schools of Industry,[57] and the British school and the National schools were set up. This interest in elementary education was accompanied by an increase in the activity of Sunday schools. There had been two such schools in 1815 with about 30 boys and 50 girls attending.[58] In 1833 there were four attended by 400 children; a Church of England one with a lending library attached, and three others managed by the Independents, Wesleyans, and Baptists respectively.[59]

The Market House School, whose early history has been described in a previous volume,[60] was held in a room over the market-house, rented from the Earl of Abingdon for £2 a year.[61] The school was still in existence in 1833, when it had 54 pupils, 24 educated freely and the rest paid for by their parents, but did not survive long after this, for in 1837 its endowment was transferred to the National school.[62]

In 1837 a British school, later known as the John Hampden School, was built in Brick-kiln Lane on land given by Sarah Richmond. It was paid for and supported out of subscriptions, a government grant, and a legacy of £500 in 1839 by Charles Dorrington.[63] It consisted of a boys' room and a girls' room with a master's house between, and was for long known as the Thame Royal British School because of the patronage of the Duchess of Kent. Later it was called Park Street School.[64] Subscribers at the time of its foundation were allowed to nominate one pupil for every annual subscription of 5s. 6d., and the children paid 1d. a week, or 2d. and 6d. in the top

[37] Thame Meth. Ch. Conveyance.
[38] Kelly, Dir. Oxon. (1891, 1903).
[39] Thame Meth. Ch. Deeds.
[40] Oxf. Dioc. c 645, f. 62. [41] Educ. Eng. Abstract, 756.
[42] H.O. 129/5/156. For the date of building see action brought in 1842: Jackson's Oxf. Jnl. 5 Mar. 1842.
[43] Kelly, Dir. Oxon. (1854).
[44] H.O. 129/5/156. The fact that its minister was Thomas Juggins suggests that the Baptists had once been united but had split into two groups.
[45] Lupton, Thame, 22–23; Kelly, Dir. Oxon. (1864).
[46] Thame Baptist Church Deeds.
[47] Baptist Handbooks.
[48] Brown and Guest, Thame, 201–2.
[49] For further details about the schools see J. H. Brown and W. Guest, History of Thame, 90–92, 111, 146, 205–9; J. H. Brown, A Short History of Thame School; Some Account of Ld. Williams of Thame (Thame 1873). For Lord Williams see above, p. 171.

[50] Brown, Thame School, 76.
[51] V.C.H. Oxon. i. 475–7.
[52] Inf. Oxon. Educ. Cttee.
[53] See below.
[54] Oxf. Jnl. 3 July 1779; 9 Jan. 1836; 7 Jan. 1837; Educ. Enq. Abstract, 756; Jas. Dugdale, The New British Traveller (1819), 115; Oxf. Jnl. 11 Jan. 1840; Billing, Dir. Oxon. (1830).
[55] Billing, Dir. Oxon. (1854).
[56] See V.C.H. Oxon. i. 489; 8th Rep. Com. Char. 547–8.
[57] Oxf. Jnl. 25 June, 12 Nov. 1836.
[58] Educ. of Poor, 732.
[59] Educ. Enq. Abstract, 756.
[60] See V.C.H. Oxon. i. 489.
[61] 8th Rep. Com. Char. 548–9.
[62] Char. Com. f. 70169; ibid. unrep. vol. xlvi. 284.
[63] O.R.O. Thame British Sch. mins.; Lupton, Thame, 22.
[64] O.R.O. British Sch. mins.; Pub. Elem. Sch. Ret. 498; Kelly, Dir. Oxon. (1887, 1903, 1920).

classes. Children from all the surrounding villages attended. Those under five years of age were not admitted. At first gardening, knitting, reading, writing, and arithmetic were taught. The school was undenominational and so the pupils were to attend their own churches on Sundays.[65] From the 1850's the school took boarders; there were six in 1872 and later twelve. An infants' class had been started in 1869.[66] Like the National school, it found difficulty after 1865, when it became subject to government inspection, in meeting the Board of Education's requirements, but it was never declared inefficient. A classroom was added in 1852, and further extensions were made in 1900.[67] Numbers rose from an average of 117 boys and 40 girls in 1846 to 256 children in 1903.[68] The school became a junior and infants' school in 1929 and the seniors were transferred to the Church of England school.[69] In 1947 it ceased to be a voluntary school, and was maintained by the county until 1950, when it was recognized as a primary school. There were 208 juniors and 125 infants in 1954.[70]

The Thame National School Society was formed in 1836 in order to provide the poor of the parish with 'a religious, moral and suitable education'.[71] The Earl of Abingdon gave an acre in the old Hog Fair for the site and Mr. Abraham, a London architect, then working at Thame Park, made a plan and elevations for the schools free of cost.[72] The school was opened in 1838 and like the British school it consisted of a boys' department and a girls' department, separated by a master's house. Infants were taught in rented premises until 1842, when a separate stone building was added, partly paid for by a government grant and the National Society.[73] There were usually a master, a mistress, and an infant mistress.[74] From the 1850's to the 1920's the school was taught by a master and a mistress.[75] In 1837 the endowment of the Market House School was transferred to the National school. In 1881 the income, which had remained constant, was regulated by a Scheme of the Charity Commissioners, under which half went to the maintenance of the school and half to prizes, scholarships, and grants to encourage children to stay at school.[76] The school was inspected from 1867 and until the end of the century found it difficult to reach the required standard. In 1896 it was declared inefficient, but in 1900 when a new classroom had been added the school manager was congratulated on the school premises and a Higher Principle grant was recommended.[77] There was an average attendance of 170 children in 1887 and of 199 children in 1890.[78] Until 1891 fees ranged from 2d. to 6d. a week, and from 1878 tradesmen's children

paid more than those of labourers'; there were 26 charity children who received free education.[79] In 1929 the school became a senior school with 130 seniors and 24 infants; juniors were transferred to the John Hampden School in the same year and all infants were transferred in 1933. In 1945 the school became a secondary modern school with voluntary controlled status from 1949. There were 160 seniors in 1950.[80]

Moreton Church of England school was built in 1860 through the efforts of the vicar on land given by Lady Wenman and with the help of funds given by her and by the government.[81] It was supported for some years by Lady Wenman.[82] In 1873 the school had 54 children.[83] Numbers were never very large: although the school was built for 55 children, there were only 22 in 1891, when it was called a National school.[84] It closed some time after 1920 and the money obtained from the sale of the building was used to endow a Moreton charity.[85]

Of the boys' private schools, the Mansion House School was opened in 1808–9 by John Jones, a former master of the Market House School, and continued for about 20 years.[86] In 1840 it was taken over by L. D. Hunt, and extensive alterations were made which included new classrooms, boarding accommodation, two halls, a gymnasium, and swimming bath, and the school was reopened as the Oxford County School.[87] In 1868 James Marsh, at one time a master of the British school, became headmaster and the school was amalgamated with Howard House School,[88] a private school which he had opened in 1854 at Cuttlebrook House. At this school instruction of a 'sound commercial character' was given for low fees. By 1866 he had 120 pupils, of whom 80 were boarders.[89] The combined schools advertised under the joint names of the Oxford County Middle Class School and Howard House School, and promised 'a practical commercial education'. Boys were prepared for the universities, the Civil Service, and especially for professional and business careers. There was a preparatory department.[90] Marsh's son J. W. Marsh succeeded him in 1883 but committed suicide in 1888 because of financial difficulties.[91] The school was then taken over by T. Gardner and in 1894 by C. H. Hills. In 1900 it became a preparatory school and in 1908 it was transferred to London.[92]

There were two large private schools for girls in the 19th century, one opened by a Miss Todd in 1841 at 40 Upper High St. and another started next to the Wesleyan Chapel in 1849.[93] The former was advertised regularly in the *Thame Gazette* until 1894, when it apparently came to an end. The latter was

[65] *Oxf. Jnl.* 12 Nov. 1836; O.R.O. British Sch. mins. and subscription bk.
[66] O.R.O. British Sch. mins.
[67] Ibid.; *Vol. Sch. Ret.* 26.
[68] Ibid.; *Vol. Sch. Ret.* 26.
[69] Inf. Oxf. Educ. Cttee.
[70] Ibid.
[71] Lupton, *Thame*, 120.
[72] Ibid. 121.
[73] O.R.O. Thame National Sch. mins.: copy of indenture 1838 and plans; *Vol. Sch. Ret.* 26.
[74] Billing, *Dir. Oxon.* (1854).
[75] Ibid.; Kelly, *Dir. Oxon.* (1864, 1869, 1887–1920).
[76] O.R.O. National Sch. mins.; cf. *Ret. of Sch.* 216; and see *V.C.H. Oxon.* i. 489.
[77] O.R.O. National Sch. log bk.
[78] Kelly, *Dir. Oxon.* (1887); *Ret. of Sch.* 216.
[79] O.R.O. National Sch. log bk.

[80] Inf. Oxon. Educ. Cttee.
[81] Lupton, *Thame*, 109; *Sch. bldg. grnts.* 106.
[82] Lupton, *Thame*, 109.
[83] Brown and Guest, *Thame*, 206.
[84] Kelly, *Dir. Oxon.* (1891).
[85] See below, p. 219.
[86] *8th Rep. Com. Char.* 549–50. For Mansion House see above, p. 167.
[87] *Thame Gazette*, 30 Oct. 1888; and see prospectus.
[88] Brown and Guest, *Thame*, 208.
[89] *Thame Gazette*, 11 and 31 Mar. 1868. It is likely that Cuttlebrook House School was the successor of the Priestend boarding school with sixteen boarders recorded in the 1851 census.
[90] Brown and Guest, *Thame*, 208.
[91] Ibid.
[92] Ibid.; Kelly, *Dir. Oxon.* (1920).
[93] *Thame Gazette*, 17 Apr. 1888.

acquired by Mrs. J. Pearce, formerly a mistress at the National school, in 1870. In 1877 the school moved into the old grammar school buildings, formerly used by the Lord Williams's School, and the name was changed to the Girls' Grammar School.[94] A preparatory department for boys was opened when Miss Gillett was principal in 1888.[95] In 1889 Miss Dodwell and her partners acquired the school and later in 1908 they moved into the extensive buildings recently vacated by the Oxford County School for Boys.[96] In 1917 a limited liability company was formed to manage the school with Miss Hockley and Miss Messenger as principals.[97] The school was recognized and inspected from 1907, and was accepted under the 1902 Act as providing secondary education for this part of the county. Until the Geddes economy measures of 1921 the County Education Committee subsidized the school by an annual grant of £125 and made grants for natural science and domestic science equipment.[98] At first boarders outnumbered day pupils: in 1917 there were 77 boarders, but in 1943 it ceased to be a boarding school. From 1921 only 'county scholars' from Buckinghamshire and Oxfordshire who paid fees attended, and by 1948 there were 110 county scholars, 30 fee payers and 35 in the preparatory department. In 1948 the two principals retired and the school closed.[99] Thame girls then went to the temporary girls' secondary school at Water Eaton and later to Holton Park, Wheatley.[1]

Rycotewood College for Rural Crafts was founded in 1938 by Capt. C. Michaelis of Rycote Park to provide free education for three or four years for boys from any county, but preferably from Oxfordshire. His intention was to foster good craftsmanship, especially in cabinet-making. The boys received free board, clothes, and medical attention, and the school was housed in the old work-house, which was adapted for the purpose. During the Second World War the work-house was requisitioned by the War Department and the school was housed in temporary premises in Thame. In 1948 the trust expired and the County Council took over the school; Capt. Michaelis generously transferred the old work-house at a peppercorn rent and on de-requisition it was re-equipped. In 1950 the college returned and was reorganized as a County College for rural crafts with a secondary technical course attached. Numbers rose from 24 in the war period to nearly 75 in 1950.[2] In 1959 a new block of buildings was added. By then there were 110 students in residence. Courses were being given in agricultural engineering and pre-apprenticeship cabinet-making and building.[3]

CHARITIES. Richard Quatremain and his wife founded an almshouse for six 'poor men' in connexion with the guild of St. Christopher, which they founded in 1447.[4] In 1548 after the chantry had been dissolved the almshouses were apparently spared: three beadsmen and three beadswomen were then receiving 11d. a week each—a total of £8 16s. 4d. a year.

The chantry certificate was marked 'Continuatur quosque to the poore'.[5] An account roll for the years 1548–50 shows that the receipts from the property of the dissolved guild amounted to £41 17s. for the two years and notes that Sir John Williams was then the owner. Payments included 6d. a week to each of the five poor men and one woman, amounting to £15 3s. for the year. An additional 1d. a week was paid to the poor men for bread and a sum of 5s. was spent on their smocks, and 22s. 1d. on the repair of the almshouses.[6] It is likely that it was the influence of Sir John Williams, one of the commissioners for the suppression of the chantries, that secured the continuance of the institution. He and the inhabitants of Thame petitioned the crown to this end and when Sir John was granted in 1550 the property of the dissolved guild he agreed to pay £10 13s. 9d. a year to support 'six paupers'.[7] In 1575 the endowment consisted of lands in Long Crendon (Bucks.) and certain 'candle rents', together producing £23 5s. a year, and the almshouse buildings.

The deed of 1575 by which Lord Williams's executors regulated the future management of the grammar school founded by him made arrangements for the almshouses also. The property of both school and almshouses was vested in the Warden and Scholars of New College, the warden was visitor to both, and the schoolmaster acted as secretary and housekeeper to the almshouses. To the original endowment of the almshouses was added land in New Thame, Sydenham, and East Hendred (Berks.), producing £7 4s. 9d. for normal maintenance, and land in New Thame producing £2 13s. 4d. for gowns for the almspeople. The almspeople, to be chosen by Lord Norreys and his heirs (the earls of Abingdon), were to be old and of good character, and 'in spirit a pauper'. They were to attend the parish church at morning and evening service daily, and on Sundays and festivals were to sit in seats in the chancel around Lord Williams's tomb, for the 'dressing' and cleaning of which 2s. was to be paid quarterly to the parish clerk out of the income of the almshouses. In addition to the usual pension the oldest almsman was to receive 4s. a year for cleaning the water-course between the almshouse and the privy.[8]

In the early 19th century the almshouses had a reputation for drunkenness and immorality, in which the inmates were allegedly encouraged by the conduct of the inhabitants of the houses on the other side of Church Row. The moral condition of the almshouses had improved by 1860, though the inmates were thought to be unfortunate in their living conditions. Six years later their houses were stated to be 'poor, it might be said miserable, places' inside.[9] In 1860 an almswoman who had been acting as nurse was said to be too old to continue to do so. Each of the six almspeople received £19 10s. a year in weekly payments; these payments together with gowns and various occasional gifts amounted to an annual distribution of about £22 a head. Although the endowment of the almshouses was in theory separate from that of the school, there was no attempt

[94] Ibid.; O.R.O. National Sch. mins. 1870.
[95] *Thame Gazette*, 17 Apr. 1888.
[96] Inf. Miss Hockley; Kelly, *Dir. Oxon.* (1920).
[97] Inf. Miss Hockley.
[98] Ibid.
[99] Ibid.
[1] Inf. Oxon. Educ. Cttee.
[2] Ditto. For the work-house building see above, p. 165.

[3] *Rycotewood Coll. prospectus.*
[4] *Cal. Pat.* 1446–52, 180–1; *Par. Coll.* iii. 316; for him see above, p. 173.
[5] *Chant. Cert.* 49.
[6] d.d. Bertie c 16 (uncat.).
[7] *Cal. Pat.* 1550–3, 11.
[8] *Some Acct. of Lord Williams* (Thame, 1873), 51 sqq.
[9] Char. Com. file 70169.

to distribute the combined income in exact proportions. In addition to the income from property and rents there was also interest of £189 a year from a fund started in 1798 out of surplus income. The almshouses received, in fact, rather less than the income from the property with which they had been endowed, not taking into account the interest from accumulated capital.[10]

Under a Scheme of 1874 of the Endowed Schools Commission the almshouses were sold and the almspeople were to receive £33 6s. 8d. a year in place of all the former allowances and residence. The charity was placed under the new board of governors established for the school. In 1927–8 £150 was received from invested capital and £60 from the school foundation; of this, £200 was spent in weekly payments to the six almspeople and 10s. in cleaning the founder's tomb.[11]

CHURCH LANDS. By the 15th century the rent from land held by the church formed an important part of the churchwardens' income and was regularly entered in their accounts.[12] Some of the land which the church held after the Reformation had been acquired in the Middle Ages. Land in Buttwell Leys, for instance, had been given for a light.[13] It was said in 1612 that this land had anciently been given for the use of the church. In 1821 it amounted to about 8 acres let at £8 a year which was spent on the repair of the church. In 1821 there was also about 1½ acres in Priestend Field, the rent of 30s. from which was used for the same purpose, and the churchwardens also received for the use of the church a rent-charge of 6s. 8d. which apparently derived from the 15th century or earlier. John Collins, by deed of 1558, gave to the churchwardens for the maintenance of church services a house and garden opposite White Hound Pond; by 1821 the house was in ruins and the land was let for £2 2s. a year. One-sixth of the income from the property given by Nicholas Almond by deed of 1634 was for the repair of the church, but the money was not being used for this purpose in 1821.[14] By 1880 the church had ceased to receive any rent from the land in Priestend Field; the land in Buttwell Leys, then reckoned at 6 acres, yielded £19 a year, the land given by Collins, part of which was let to the Local Board and used for the fire-engine shed, was producing £4 2s., and these rents together with the rent-charge and £2 10s. from Almond's charity were used jointly for the repair of the church and the maintenance of services.[15] Under the Charity Commissioners' Scheme of 1881 these endowments formed part of the Thame Parochial Charities, and under an Order of 1896 were distinguished as the Ecclesiastical Charities, the income being administered by trustees separate from those then appointed to administer the parochial charities in general. The income of the Ecclesiastical Charities in 1948 was £31, excluding the share of a little over £3 from Almond's charity.[16]

PAROCHIAL CHARITIES.[17] By a Scheme of 1881 the Charity Commissioners consolidated the ecclesiastical charities and the charities for the poor (ex-

cluding Lord Williams's Almshouses and Stephen John Johnson's charity), and regulated their application under a new board of trustees.[18] The ecclesiastical charities were the Church Estate and John Collins's charity.[19] There were two charities founded solely for distributions of money to the poor of Thame generally: Thomas Cannon by will of unknown date left £35 to provide a groat each for 30 poor widows annually, and in 1715 the capital was used, together with that of Adkyns's and Stonell's charities (see below), to buy a rent-charge of £7 10s. out of which about £1 was being distributed to the poor in cash in 1880;[20] Friday Street Cottages (also known as the Poor Houses) were bought in 1698 with £40 given by various donors, the income to be distributed in money, but by the 19th century they were normally used for housing poor persons rent-free and it was only after the cottages had been destroyed by fire in 1868 and the site sold (for £50, yielding £1 11s. 2d. in 1880) that regular distributions in cash were resumed.[21] Bread charities were founded by Robert Hall, who by will dated 1655 left a rent-charge of 10s.; by Thomas Funge, who by will dated 1766 left £600 stock producing £18 16s. 10d. in 1880; by Eustace May, who by a deed of 1793 gave a rent-charge of £8; and by Sophia Bull, who by will dated 1801 left £250 stock producing £11 2s. 8d. in 1880. These four charities were being distributed roughly in accordance with the donors' wishes in 1880.[22] The other bread charities, those of William Peck (£10 by will of c. 1717) and Robert Funge (£10 at unknown date) had lapsed by 1776, when the vestry authorized the churchwardens to recover the charity money in arrears; £10 recovered in respect of each charity was, together with £120 recovered for Phyllis Burrows charity (see below), invested in stock in 1782. For a few years thereafter Peck's and Funge's gifts were distributed in bread, but by 1821 were being used as part of Phyllis Burrows charity.[23]

There was an unusually large number of clothing charities. Joan Robotham by will dated 1595 left £10 for the use of the township of New Thame; by 1687 this sum had grown with accumulated interest to £50 and with a further sum of £160, given by a deed of that year by Martha Burrows to provide suits of clothing for seven poor persons (any residue to be distributed among the same seven persons in cash), was invested in land at Piddington. The combined charity was known as the Piddington Estate, the rents from which were to be distributed according to the intentions of the donors in the proportion one to three. By 1821, when the estate comprised a house and garden, a close, and about 10 acres of land, all let for £25 a year, about £15 was spent on gowns for 20 poor women and about £10 was distributed to the poor in sums of 5s. By 1880 the rent had fallen to £21, of which £11 15s. went on gowns and £9 5s. on doles.[24] Before 1821 the restriction of Joan Robotham's charity to New Thame had lapsed, and Martha Burrows's was confined to women. George Benson by a deed of 1641 gave £120 to buy a £6 rent-charge to be spent on suits of clothing for eight

---

10 Ibid.
11 Ibid. G 59.
12 For early accounts see above, p. 203, n. 52.
13 *Cal. Pat.* 1549–51, 45.
14 *8th Rep. Com. Char.* H.C. 13, pp. 550–1 (1823), viii.
15 Char. Com. files 33587, 33673.
16 Ibid. G 59.
17 Unless otherwise stated, the following comes from *8th Rep. Com. Char.* 551–9.
18 Char. Com. file G 59.
19 See above.
20 Char. Com. file 33673.
21 Ibid. 19263, 33673.
22 Ibid. 33673.
23 *8th Rep. Com. Char.* 557; d.d. Par. Thame c 4 (chwdns' accts.).
24 Char. Com. file 33673.

poor persons. Except that it was confined to men by before 1821, the charity was still being so distributed in 1880.[25] William Adkyns by will dated 1691/2 gave £30 for suits of clothes for two poor persons, and in 1715 the capital was used together with that of Cannon's and Stonell's charities to buy a rent-charge of £7 10s., out of which £1 4s. was being spent on clothing in 1880.[26] Richard Leaver, perhaps in 1723, left by will to trustees his property known as the 'Blue Man' in Friday Street, the rent to be used to provide suits for two poor men and two poor women; the cloth was to be bought yearly from a draper belonging to the Church of England and not from a dissenter. By 1820 the rent was £12 and three coats and eighteen gowns were given away.[27] Phyllis Burrows by will proved 1728 gave £100 to provide shirts and shifts for the poor; this sum had accumulated to £120 by 1782 when with Peck's and Robert Funge's charities the capital was invested in stock, the whole interest from which was being used in 1821 for the purposes specified by Phyllis Burrows. By 1866 the charity was carried in one account with Martha May's,[28] and in 1880 £7 7s. was spent on clothing for the poor.[29] Martha May by will dated 1811 gave £700 stock, the interest to be distributed in clothing. About 120 poor women received shifts or petticoats in 1821, and in 1880 £21 was distributed in this way.[30]

There were two apprenticing charities, founded by John Hart, who by will dated 1664 gave a rent-charge of £10, and by Lettice Stonell, who by will dated 1713 gave £100, Lettice Stonell's gift being invested, with those of Adkyns and Cannon (see above) in 1715 in a rent-charge of £7 10s. Between 1803 and 1819 Hart's charity, with occasional assistance from Stonell's, enabled eleven boys to be apprenticed. In 1880 £10 was spent on apprenticing three boys for unusually low fees.[31] In the early 19th century boys were apprenticed for premiums of up to £5 out of Stonell's charity, but by 1819 it had become impossible to place a boy for so small a premium and the trustees did not feel authorized to spend more on a single boy. The Charity Commissioners, however, appear to have dispelled this hesitation: the money was allowed to accumulate, and by 1880 £5 6s. a year was being spent on apprenticing.[32] Nicholas Almond, by a deed of 1638, gave the property later known as 111 High Street for various purposes: one-sixth of the income was for the maintenance of the parish church, one-sixth for the maintenance of roads and bridges in Thame, two-sixths for poor widows, lame and old people, and two-sixths for apprenticing. The property was let for £6 c. 1780, from which £1 went to the surveyors of the highways, £2 18s. 6d. to apprenticing, and the remainder to purposes not specified by the donor. By 1821 the rent had risen to £11, from which £1 was still spent on highways, but there was 'no specific appropriation of any other part of the rent'. Thereafter the charity was distributed in accordance with the donor's intention; by 1880 the rent was £15.[33]

The trustees of the parochial charities, under the Scheme of 1881, also administered Thomas Reed's charity, but this was not included as one of the parochial charities because it benefited only Moreton.[34] Following the Local Government Act of 1894,[35] a separate body of trustees was set up in 1896 to administer the distribution of the ecclesiastical charities, but the property of ecclesiastical and non-ecclesiastical charities continued to be administered together. The trustees of the parochial charities also administered the property of Sophia Susannah Ray's charity from 1916, and of the Moreton Welfare Fund from 1952. Under the Scheme of 1881 the parochial charities proper were divided into three branches—ecclesiastical, educational, and poor's. Each of these was accounted for separately, except that Almond's charity (the one-sixth share for roads and bridges continuing to be paid to the local authority, who received £3 2s. 10d. in 1948) had its own account, as did the charities not part of the parochial charities but administered by the trustees.[36]

The rent-charge forming the endowment of Hall's charity was redeemed for £20 stock in 1933, the 'Blue Man' (Leaver's charity) was sold in 1918, and 111 High Street (Almond's charity) in 1920. The income of the parochial charities excluding the ecclesiastical charities was nearly £140 in 1948: of this sum £20 went to the educational branch account; after various charges and the payment to the local authority from Almond's charity the rest of the expenditure took the form of donations to hospitals and welfare organizations and gifts in cash and kind.[37]

OTHER CHARITIES. Thomas Reed by will dated 1770 left land in Thame the rent from which was to be distributed to poor persons living in the liberty of Moreton. The rent about 1790 was £2 12s. 7½d., and in 1821 £3 10s., which was distributed in sums of from 1s. to 5s.[38] Under a Scheme of 1881 the property was administered by the trustees of the Thame Parochial Charities but continued to be used specifically for Moreton. In 1948 the income of the charity was £5 11s. 3d., and this sum was given to the Moreton Coal Club.[39] Stephen John Johnson gave, shortly before his death in 1878, £100 to the minister and deacons of Thame Congregational Church. Under a deed of 1879 the money was invested in stock and the interest distributed to poor widows of Thame over sixty. In 1932 22 widows each received 5s.[40]

The Victoria Cottage Hospital received £180 in trust under the will of Miss Sophia Susannah Ray (proved 1916), and £500 in trust under the will of Philip J. D. Wykeham (proved 1924) subject to the life-interest of his wife, who died in 1937.[41]

MORETON WELFARE FUND. The proceeds of the sale of the Moreton Church of England school were invested in £200 stock as the endowment of a charity, authorized by the Charity Commissioners in 1952, for promoting the 'physical, moral, mental and spiritual welfare of the inhabitants of Moreton'. The trustees were those of the Thame Parochial Charities. The income in 1954 was £5.[42]

[25] Ibid.
[26] Ibid.
[27] *8th Rep. Com. Char.* 556–7.
[28] Char. Com. file 70169.
[29] Ibid. 33673.
[30] Ibid.
[31] Ibid.
[32] Ibid.

[33] Ibid.
[34] Ibid. G 59; see below.
[35] 56 & 57 Vic. c 73.
[36] Char. Com. file G 59.
[37] Ibid.
[38] *8th Rep. Com. Char.* 559.
[39] Char. Com. file G 59.
[40] Ibid.
[41] Ibid. 93337, 104172.
[42] Inf. the Trustees.

WATERSTOCK

THE ancient parish covered only 653 acres.[1] It lay in a bend of the River Thame which bounded it on the north and west; on the east its boundary followed a brook and then continued with several right-angled turns along what was probably the line of furlongs in the open fields.[2] Large hedgerow elms still mark its course. The Draycott road also marked a part of the eastern boundary. The Thame–Oxford road and the main London–Oxford road which it joins, formed the southern boundary of the parish.

In 1886 the parish was enlarged by the addition of Tiddington Mead (11 a.), formerly in Albury parish, by Draycott village, and by 250 acres from the Oxfordshire part of Ickford parish.[3] Thus Waterstock's eastern boundary mainly followed the Ickford road. In 1954 Draycott village with 60 acres was transferred to Tiddington-with-Albury, and Waterstock's acreage was reduced to 903 acres.[4]

The soil is gravel and loam on Kimmeridge Clay and alluvial soil is found in the meadows bordering the Thame.[5] The parish is low-lying and is mostly within the 200-foot contour, is liable to floods in the north-west and rises to 225 feet in the south-east only.

The main approaches to the village have probably always been from the south by the road leading from the Thame–Oxford road, or from the east by the Tiddington–Ickford road.[6] It is possible that the first of these was the 17th-century 'Gysgire'.[7] In the early 17th century there are several documentary records of Lincroft Bridge near some leyground[8] and to Lincroft which is shown on a 17th-century sketch map.[9] The name, in fact, goes back to the 12th century.[10] There does not seem to have been a stone bridge over the Thame until in 1790 Diana Ashhurst built the present Bow Bridge and a carriage road over Little Mill Meadow to connect with Curson's carriage road from Waterperry House and bridge over Back Ditch.[11] The bridge has a single brick arch and solid outcurving parapets with a stone coping.

Waterstock's nearest station is at Tiddington. The Wycombe and Oxford railway, running except for one short stretch to the south of the parish boundary, was opened in 1864.[12] It absorbed 15 acres of Hedges Great Ground, which was paid for at the rate of £200 an acre.[13]

The village stands near the river about 200 feet up, and centres round its church and manor-house.[14] Long ownership in one family has resulted in a well preserved village, mainly composed of 17th- and 18th-century farm-houses and cottages, built of local brick. It has never been large, but except for a short period in the 19th century it seems to have been more populous in the Middle Ages than it has

ever been since.[15] Eighteen householders were listed for the hearth tax of 1662 and in the 18th century about fifteen to seventeen houses were recorded.[16] In 1665 there were four substantial farm-houses with two to six hearths apiece besides the big house and smaller houses. Many of these houses still survive. The oldest dwellings in the village are four timber-framed Elizabethan or early Jacobean cottages: they are of brick construction, and are built in pairs on opposite sides of the road. Their hipped roofs of thatch are swept down at the ends over one-story extensions. They have irregularly spaced casement windows that are mostly leaded. Two of the ancient farm-houses in the village street are still used as such: Home Farm and the adjoining Park Farm. The first is L-shaped and dates mainly from the 17th and 18th centuries. The 17th-century wing is at right angles to the road and consists of two stories; it is timber-framed with brick infilling and the tiled roof is half-hipped at the end fronting on the road. The north-west elevation of this wing has a timber-framed gable to the right hand, a rectangular chimney-stack to the left hand, and one gabled dormer window. The wing to the north-west is built of 18th-century brick and has a tiled roof. The farm has an ancient thatched barn and a 17th-century granary which is built of brick and timber. Park Farm is a house of two builds: it stands back from the road and appears to be of 18th-century date, although it may incorporate some of an older building. The west front has three bays and is of ashlar stone. Members of the Bull family have been tenants of both these farms for several generations.[17] The farm-house, once Church Farm, lies opposite the church, but it is now three cottages. It dates from the early 18th century and is a two-story house of rubble facing north. It has casement windows, mostly of four lights with mullions and transoms of wood and leaded panes; a six-panelled door and a low stone wall separating it from the street. The schoolhouse (now two cottages) and the cottage for a schoolteacher next door also date from the 18th century. The school has a beam with the date 1751 on it.[18]

There have been some 19th- and 20th-century additions: some cottages of red brick with slate roofs, the stone pump-house at the entrance to the manor, dated W.H.A. 1898, and a war memorial that was erected on the small green after the First World War. The pond which used to be at the cross roads has been filled in,[19] but the stream running beside the road to Home Farm remains. No council houses have been built in the village.

The manor-house has experienced a number of rebuildings. Nothing of the medieval house now survives, but as it was successively lived in by several

[1] *Census*, 1841; the *Census*, 1851–71, gave the area as 653 a. and the survey of 1881 gave it as 678 a.: O.S. *Area Bk.* (1882).
[2] O.S. Map 6″, xxxiv, xl (1886).
[3] O.R.O. L.G.B.O. 19610, 19618.
[4] O.R.O. R.O. 616.
[5] *V.C.H. Oxon.* i, map between pp. 4–5.
[6] O.S. Map 6″, xxxiv, xl (1886).
[7] Oxf. Archd. Oxon. b 41, f. 135.
[8] e.g. ibid.
[9] d.d. Ashhurst d 9.

[10] *Oseney Cart.* iv. 405.
[11] d.d. Ashhurst d 8. For the Cursons of Waterperry see *V.C.H. Oxon.* v. 298.
[12] E. T. MacDermot, *Hist. G.W.R.* ii, 595.
[13] d.d. Ashhurst d 10: contemporary note.
[14] O.S. Map 1 : 2,500, xl. 4 (1881). For name see below, p. 224.   [15] See below, p. 225.
[16] See below, p. 225.
[17] Inf. Mr. C. R. Bull, Waterstock.
[18] See below, p. 230.
[19] Bodl. Tithe award map (1848).

The Entrance Front

The Staircase

WATERSTOCK. THE 18TH-CENTURY MANOR-HOUSE BEFORE ITS
DEMOLITION IN 1953

important families of Oxfordshire gentry it must have been a house of some size. The Bruleys inhabited it in the 13th and 14th centuries and the Danvers family in the 15th century.[20] John Danvers and his wife were given papal licence to have a portable altar to be used for the saying of mass for themselves and their household.[21] At the end of the century Thomas Danvers brought distinction to the village: he was a member of three parliaments and also actively assisted in the foundation of Magdalen College, for he was the friend of Bishop Waynflete and the new learning.[22] It was from his Waterstock house that Danvers wrote in 1494 to President Mayhew of Magdalen College telling that he was busy with the affairs of the college and other learned institutions, and that he was in communication with the king and the king's mother Margaret, Countess of Richmond.[23] The windows of the house were decorated with heraldic glass, for in his account of the painted glass still there in the 17th century, Anthony Wood mentions the arms of Danvers and the related families of Bruley and Verney.[24] Later the house was occupied by the Caves and then by the Crokes.[25] Some details of the building in Sir George Croke's day are known. It was by then one of the larger houses in the county and was taxed on 23 hearths in 1665.[26] The arms of Croke and related families as well as of Danvers were in the windows of the upstairs drawing-room, the great and little parlours and the hall.[27] Plot shows the house on his map of Oxfordshire, and in his account of unusual trees cultivated in the county he mentions the abele tree grown by Sir George Croke, that 'learned and curious botanist', who was one of the earliest members of the Royal Society.[28]

The Crokes were strong supporters of the parliamentary cause and when General Ireton wrote from Waterstock on 16 April 1646, about his preparations for the siege of Wallingford,[29] it may be supposed that he had his headquarters at the house of George Croke, a friend of Baxter and Hampden.[30] This house was pulled down in 1695 and was replaced by a red-brick one in the time of Sir Henry Ashhurst.[31] The new house, begun in 1695, was being completed in 1696 when Mr. Thomas Hodges, joiner, of St. Dunstan's, Stepney, was commissioned to wainscot the hall and passage-way leading to the south-west part of the mansion. He undertook to use 'good dram stuff'; to make and fix handsome stone mouldings round the windows of the hall, and 'breaks' in the cornice over each of the windows; to make and fix a seven-penny cornice round the hall; make doors of eight or ten panels with six-inch stone moulding round the door cases, 'pullexions to be laid into both sides'. He was to be paid 3s. a yard for most of the work, but 2s. 4d. for the wainscot in the passage.[32] In 1787 Sir Henry Ashhurst, the eminent judge, took down this building, and erected a new mansion of

stone rather higher up the slope above the church. The foundation stone was laid in 1787 and the family moved in in 1791.[33] According to a manuscript memorandum among the family papers the architect was 'Sir Richard Coucerell', presumably an error for S. P. Cockerell (1754–1827).[34] The south-east and entrance front were of five bays with the centre bay and its pediment slightly projecting. The entrance on the ground floor was by a double six-panelled door in a Doric surround with sidelights and a stilted arched fanlight. On the first floor there was a central Venetian window with engaged Ionic columns. There was a string-course at the first floor level and a modillioned cornice and a hipped roof of slate. The wall swept up in the north-east corner to a square garden-house. Sir Henry Ashhurst improved and enlarged his garden by taking part of the churchyard in exchange for certain undertakings to the rector,[35] and it was perhaps in his day that the bricks from the old house were used for making the walled garden. It was, however, in 1807–8, in the time of his son W. H. Ashhurst, that the grounds were laid out 'under the direction of Sir John Hopper' (presumably the architect Thomas Hopper is meant).[36] The ornamental water shown on the tithe map of 1848 may belong to this date.[37] The 18th-century house was pulled down in 1953, owing to the expense of its upkeep,[38] after the servants' quarters, a square stone building of two stories attached to the main house by a corridor, had been converted in 1953 by Major and Mrs. Ruck-Keene into a modern dwelling. Their house is of four bays and has a one-story extension to the left hand. The stone cartouche of arms, formerly over the central door of the stable courtyard, is above the entrance door; a marble mantlepiece, moved from the old mansion, is in the drawing-room; and the staircase is a copy, on a reduced scale, of the Georgian staircase of the old mansion. The builders were Hinkins & Frewin Ltd. of Oxford. The stables, built in the form of a courtyard, and lying to the south-east of the old mansion and the present house, remain. They are built of stone and are probably contemporary with the 1787 house. They are entered through stone gate-piers.

The only other gentleman's house in the village is the Rectory. It was repaired in 1787 by Mrs. Ashhurst, the mother of Sir Henry, for the new rector, R. B. B. Robinson.[39] In the main it is an 18th-century stone house of two stories, but an older wing remains. The south-west front is of three bays. The 19th-century bay window extending from the ground floor to the second floor was added before 1857.[40] The veranda with pent roof across the front is also later. The house had a well-laid-out garden with some fine trees, which include a female gingko.[41]

Away from the village street and approached by a road across the fields is the picturesque mill-house on

[20] See below, p. 223.
[21] Cal. Papal L. 1431–47, 233.
[22] Macnamara, Danvers Family, 156–7.
[23] Ibid. 162–3.
[24] Par. Coll. iii. 323–7.
[25] See below, p. 223. For Edward Cave see Par. Coll. iii. 324.
[26] Par. Coll. iii. 321–2, 324–7.
[27] Hearth Tax, Oxon. 45.
[28] Plot, Nat. Hist. Oxon. (1705), 175.
[29] Cal. S.P. Dom. 1645–7, 419.
[30] For Sir George see Sir Alexander Croke, Genealogical History of the Croke Family, ii. 556–7, additions, 377.

[31] Ibid. 559.
[32] d.d. Ashhurst d 9.
[33] Ibid. d. 10: a late 19th-cent. note. Bricks on the site of the old house have been dug up in recent times. For a view see plate facing p. 221.
[34] d.d. Ashhurst d 10: late 19th-cent. notes.
[35] Ibid. d 10.
[36] Ibid. d 10: late 19th-cent. note.
[37] Bodl. Tithe award.
[38] Inf. Mrs. Ruck Keene.
[39] MS. Top. Oxon. b 220, f. 135b.
[40] Par. Rec. Plan of 1857.
[41] Inf. the Rector, the Revd. G. S. S. Gillott.

an island in the Thame. It is in origin a 15th-century house, but has been rebuilt in the Elizabethan period. Its plan is L-shaped: it is timber-framed with brick filling, and has two stories. In the south front there is one half-hipped gable to the left hand, and two gabled dormer windows to the centre and right. The casement windows and entrance door are irregularly spaced. Inside, one of the timber beams has the initials of Sir Henry Ashhurst carved on it and the date 1693. All the timber used is uncut tree trunks. The oldest part of the house is the stone walling in the south-west corner.

The village has been associated with a number of families of interest who held the lordship and resided at the manor-house.[42] The Ashhursts who were resident from 1691 to the mid-20th century may, perhaps, be specially mentioned. An event of minor importance, but of some local interest, occurred in 1695 when Sarah Smith, the sister-in-law of the vicar, Charles Hinde,[43] married in Waterstock church White Kennett,[44] then Vicar of Ambrosden, but later to be distinguished by high preferment in the church and as the author of *Parochial Antiquities in the counties of Oxford and Bucks.*[45]

MANOR. An estate, assessed at 5 hides, at *WATER-STOCK* was held freely by the Saxon Alwi in the time of the Confessor. In 1086 it was held by Sawold 'of the fee of St. Mary of Lincoln'.[46] This Sawold should perhaps be identified with the Sawold who was one of the bishop's knights and held 4 hides of the manor of Thame.[47] As later evidence shows that Waterstock was a member of Thame manor throughout the Middle Ages the identification seems highly probable, and it must be supposed that the Domesday scribes duplicated the entry relating to Sawold.[48] In the early 16th century the bishop still received a relief of 50s. on the death of the lord of Waterstock.[49]

In the earliest list of the bishop's knights in 1166 the holder of the fee is not named.[50] A Richard Foliot, however, had land in neighbouring Waterperry in about 1190,[51] and the family had held land in Waterstock at an earlier date, for Richard's father, possibly Bartholomew Foliot,[52] had granted it to Oseney Abbey.[53] The Foliots' relatives, the Chesneys, were overlords of Albury, another neighbouring parish.[54] As one of them was Robert de Chesney, Bishop of Lincoln (1148–66), it is not unlikely that Bishop Robert enfeoffed the Foliots with Waterstock. Bartholomew Foliot, a knight, and known to

have had a tenant there in 1218,[55] was certainly in possession of the manor in 1235 or 1236, when he presented to the church,[56] and perhaps as late as 1250.[57] He had been succeeded by Sir William Foliot, probably by 1255 and at latest by 1268.[58] The latter was dead by 1276 when his widow Agnes claimed a house and ½-virgate in Waterstock as her dower.[59] William Foliot's heir was Katherine, his daughter apparently by his first wife,[60] who carried the estate to the Bruley family through her marriage with Sir Henry Bruley, knight of the shire for Oxfordshire in 1297. It remained in the family for five generations. Sir Henry was returned in 1279 as lord of Waterstock[61] and as the holder of a ½-fee in 1305.[62] He was presumably dead by 1315, when Katherine settled the manor on her second son John, to be held of her during her lifetime at a rent of £50 and after her death for a rose.[63] Her heir was her eldest son (or grandson) William, who inherited the family manor of Aston Bruley in White Ladies Aston (Worcs.)[64]

John Bruley was lord of the manor in 1316 and 1327.[65] The date of his death is uncertain and his heir according to the herald's pedigree was John.[66] He appears to have been succeeded at Waterstock, however, by a Thomas Bruley: in 1346 John Bruley was returned as holding the manor, 'sometime held by Thomas Bruley'.[67] It is likely that this Thomas was John Bruley's younger brother whom he had presented to the rectory, and that he acted as guardian to John II when he was a minor.[68] John II, who was probably the husband of Bona Fitzellis and collector of the subsidy in Oxfordshire in 1350,[69] may have been dead by 1361, when Thomas Bruley is said to have presented a certain Thomas atte Fortheye on the death of the rector Thomas Bruley,[70] but it is more probable that John was still patron and that the appearance of 'Thomas' as patron is the result of a scribal error.[71] By 1372 at all events John II was dead and his heir John III was a minor.[72] The boy may never have succeeded, as in 1380 Waterstock was in the possession of William and Agnes Bruley.[73] The suggestion that William Bruley was John's son is hardly possible and he was more probably a cousin, a descendant of Henry, the youngest brother of John (I) Bruley.[74] There seems little doubt that his wife Agnes was his cousin and the descendant of William Bruley, John I's eldest brother or nephew.[75] The fine made by Agnes and William in 1380 implies that Agnes had a claim to Waterstock in her own right: they settled the pro-

42 For them see below.
43 See below, p. 227.
44 Hearne, *Remarks*, viii. 400; Par. Reg.
45 *D.N.B.*; *V.C.H. Oxon.* v. 25–26.
46 *V.C.H. Oxon.* i. 403. For Sawold and the hidage of Waterstock see above, p. 114.
47 e.g. *Feud. Aids*, iv. 167, 182, 198.
48 See above, p. 114.
49 Queen's Coll. MS. 366, f. 38b.
50 *Red Bk. Exch.* (Rolls Ser.), 374–6.
51 *Oseney Cart.* iv. 405.
52 Ibid. 388. For Bartholomew Foliot see also Farrer, *Honors*, iii. 235 (c. 1165–82).
53 *Oseney Cart.* iv. 405.
54 See *V.C.H. Oxon.* v. 9.
55 *Fines Oxon.* 59.   56 *Rot. Grosse.* 446.
57 He witnessed a charter dated c. 1250: *Boarstall Cart.* 98.
58 *Rot. Hund.* (Rec. Com.), ii. 38; *Rot. Graves.* 220.
59 Macnamara, *Danvers Family*, 221.
60 Ibid. 222.

61 *Rot. Hund.* ii. 821. For him see Moor, *Knights of Ed. I*, i (Harl. Soc. lxxx), 152.
62 Queen's Coll. MS. 366, f. 34b. Macnamara wrongly dates the list of tenants as made in 1300: *Danvers Family*, 57. Cf. *Bk. of Fees*, 40 for the ½-fee in 1209–12.
63 C.P. 25(1)/189/16/117, dated as 1315 by Macnamara, op. cit. 222.   64 *V.C.H. Worcs.* iii. 559.
65 *Feuds. Aids*, iv. 167; E 179/161/9.
66 *Visit. Oxon.* 186.
67 *Feud. Aids*, iv. 182.
68 See pedigree in Macnamara, *Danvers Family*, 224 and list of medieval presentations in MS. Top. Oxon. d 460.
69 *Visit. Oxon.* 44; *V.C.H. Bucks.* iv. 81; *Cal. Fine R.*, 1347–56, 269.
70 Linc. Reg. ix, f. 276d.
71 Cf. Macnamara, op. cit. 224–5.
72 Linc. Reg. x, f. 355d.
73 C.P. 25(1)/191/23/13.
74 See pedigree in Macnamara, op. cit. 224.
75 Ibid. Agnes's correct pedigree is given in *Genealogist*, N.S. xx. 157.

perty first on the heirs of their bodies; secondly on the heirs of Agnes by a second marriage; and thirdly on the collateral heirs of William.[76]

William Bruley, knight of the shire for Oxfordshire in 1395, outlived his wife and their son John, who had married Maud Quatremain, sister and co-heiress of Richard Quatremain of Rycote.[77] Before 1423, however, he had enfeoffed his granddaughter Joan and her husband John Danvers, of Epwell in Swalcliffe and later of Colthorpe in Banbury, with Waterstock manor.[78] Danvers, who represented the county in three parliaments, and built up a large landed estate, was returned as lord in 1428[79] and appears to have died shortly after 1448.[80] His widow Joan married as her second husband Sir Walter Mauntell of Nether Heyford (Northants.) and they presented to Waterstock church in 1467 and 1469.[81] Much of John Danvers's property went to his sons by his first wife, but Thomas, his eldest son by Joan Bruley, succeeded to his mother's lands.[82] He married twice, first a daughter of James Fiennes, Lord Saye and Sele, and secondly Sybil Fowler, member of a family with whom the Danvers family was already connected by marriage.[83] Danvers died in 1502,[84] leaving the manor for life to his widow, who lived until 1511[85] and outlived both the next heir, her brother-in-law Sir William Danvers (d. 1504) of Thatcham (Berks.)[86] and the latter's son John (d. 1508).[87] The infant son of John Danvers, also called John, was his father's heir, but he died in 1517 and his heirs were his four sisters.[88] One of these died, and by an arrangement presumably made between the three survivors, Waterstock passed to Elizabeth, the second eldest, and her husband Thomas Cave of Stanford (Northants.).[89] He obtained licence to take possession of his wife's lands in 1522.[90] By a fine of 1528 the manor and advowson were settled on Thomas and Elizabeth with remainder to the heirs of Elizabeth should Thomas and Elizabeth have no issue.[91] The Cave family, who acquired in the same way the neighbouring manor of Tiddington,[92] became by this marriage lords of Waterstock for almost a hundred years. Sir Thomas was knighted in 1553

and died in 1558.[93] One of his younger sons, Edward,[94] appears also temporarily to have held Waterstock. He was living in the manor-house in 1574[95] and was probably the Edward Cave of Bampton who presented to Waterstock church between 1576 and 1580.[96] However, Roger Cave, Sir Thomas's son and heir, who married Margaret Cecil, sister of Lord Burghley, held the manor at his death in 1586 and settled it in tail male on his four sons.[97] The eldest, Sir Thomas Cave, succeeded, and in 1610 he and his brother Sir William sold Waterstock to George Croke, the grandson of John Croke of Chilton (Bucks.), the purchaser of Studley Priory.[98] Sir George, who became a noted judge, was buried at Waterstock in 1642, leaving his wife Mary a life interest in the manor.[99] Since their son died young, Croke's heir was his nephew George Croke, son of Henry Croke (d. 1642), Rector of Waterstock.[1] He married Jane, daughter of the parliamentary leader Sir Richard Onslow,[2] and was knighted in 1660. According to Wood, he 'ran out his estate' and got into debt.[3] On his death in 1680 Waterstock, by then encumbered by mortgages,[4] was divided between his two daughters, Elizabeth, wife of Sir Thomas Wyndham, Bt., of Trent (Som.),[5] and Sarah, who later married Henry Wigmore.[6]

In 1691 they sold the manor for nearly £16,000 to Sir Henry Ashhurst, Bt.,[7] who already owned the neighbouring Emmington manor. His descendants lived in Waterstock until the mid-20th century and were prominent in the life of the county. Sir Henry, who served in Parliament for many years, was, like his father Henry Ashhurst, a London merchant and a friend of Richard Baxter,[8] but he settled at Waterstock and died there in 1711. He was succeeded by his son Henry, who died childless in 1732, when the title lapsed.[9] The estate was inherited by the latter's niece Diana, the wife of Thomas Henry Ashhurst (d. 1744), a distant cousin and a member of the Lancashire branch of the family.[10] Their son Sir William Henry Ashhurst (d. 1807), a well-known judge,[11] was succeeded by his son William Henry Ashhurst, M.P. (d. 1846),[12] and his grandson John Henry Ashhurst

[76] C.P. 25(1)/191/23/13.
[77] Macnamara, op. cit. 225. For Maud see W. F. Carter, *The Quatremains of Oxon.* 58–59; for William see Macnamara, op. cit. 225.
[78] Linc. Reg. xvi, f. 142; cf. C.P. 25(1)/292/66/86.
[79] *Feud. Aids,* iv. 198.
[80] Macnamara, op. cit. 101. He was certainly alive in 1441: *Cal. Papal L.* ix. 233. For his career see Macnamara, op. cit. 95–101.
[81] Macnamara, op. cit. 101; Linc. Reg. xx, ff. 244d, 246d.
[82] For Thomas see Macnamara, op. cit. 155–70; J. C. Wedgwood, *Hist. of Parl.* (*Biographies*), 256–7; above, p. 221.
[83] Macnamara, op. cit. 155. For Sybil see also below, p. 228.
[84] For his will see ibid. 167–9; for his tomb see below, p. 228.
[85] C 142/26/52. For her will see Macnamara, op. cit. 171.
[86] C 142/24/62. For his will see Macnamara, op. cit. 178–9.
[87] C 142/24/62(2), 63. For his will see Macnamara, op. cit. 186–7. He died in 1508: C 142/32/36.
[88] C 142/32/36; Macnamara, op. cit. 187.
[89] For the Caves see Bridges, *Northants.* i. 579–80; Sir A. Croke, *Genealogical Hist. of Croke Fam.* (1823), i, table 22.
[90] *L. & P. Hen. VIII,* iii (2), p. 892.
[91] C.P. 25(2)/51/366/Mich. 20 Hen. VIII.
[92] *V.C.H. Oxon.* v. 11 and vi, Corrigenda.
[93] W. A. Shaw, *Knights of England,* ii. 67; Bridges, *Northants.* i. 579.
[94] *V.C.H. Oxon.* v. 11.

[95] *Visit. Oxon.* 44, 154; cf. Req. 2/78/105.
[96] Dunkin MS. 439/2, f. 276b; Kennett, *Paroch. Antiq.* ii. 414.
[97] C 142/213/148.
[98] C.P. 25(2)/339/East. 8 Jas. I. For Croke see *D.N.B.*; Croke, *Hist. of Croke Fam.* i. 561–605; *V.C.H. Oxon.* v. 63, 76.
[99] d.d. Ashhurst c 5, abstract of title.
[1] Croke, op. cit. i. 556, 601.
[2] d.d. Ashhurst c 5, no. 9; *Par. Coll.* iii. 322; and above, p. 221.
[3] Wood, *Life,* ii. 136; Wood, *Fasti.* ii. 139. For him see Foster, *Alumni,* and Kennett, *Paroch. Antiq.* ii. 492.
[4] For mortgages see d.d. Ashhurst c 5 and d 6, *passim;* C.P. 25(2)/587/Trin. 1653; 588/Trin. 1654; 709/East. 28 Chas. II; C 5/169/29.
[5] G.E.C. *Baronetage,* iv. 57; cf. C.P. 25(2)/710/Mich. 32 Chas. II.
[6] d.d. Ashhurst c 5, abstract of title; C.P. 25(2)/863/Trin. 2 Wm. & Mary.
[7] d.d. Ashhurst c 4; c 5, abstract of title.
[8] F. J. Powicke, 'The Revd. Richard Baxter and his Lancs. Friend Mr. Henry Ashhurst,' *Bull. John Rylands Libr.* xiii. 323–5. d.d. Ashhurst c 1 is a book of his business letters. For his father see *D.N.B.*
[9] G.E.C. *Baronetage,* iv. 151. For Ashhurst genealogy see Burke, *Land. Gent.* (1937, &c.); Wood, *Life,* ii. 137 n. For family see also d.d. Ashhurst b 1, d 9.
[10] For them see *V.C.H. Lancs.* iv. 100.
[11] See *D.N.B.*
[12] For him see W. R. J. Williams, *Parl. Hist. of Oxon.* 79; below, p. 225.

(d. 1885). The son of the last, William Henry, died in 1929[13] and his daughter, Gladys Mary Ashhurst, J.P., was the last member of the family.[14] On her death in 1949 Waterstock passed to her nephew, Major Henry W. A. Ruck-Keene who now (1959) lives at Waterstock.

ECONOMIC AND SOCIAL HISTORY. Nothing is known of any early settlement at Waterstock, but the name, meaning 'water place', indicates an Anglo-Saxon origin. In 1086 it was assessed at 5 hides, 3 of which were in demesne, with 2 ploughs and a mill worth 9s. 5d. There were 5 serfs, the only inhabitants mentioned, and 36 acres of meadow. The jurors declared that there was sufficient land for 5 ploughs, and a marginal note states that there had been that number in King Edward's time, 3 of them on the demesne. The value of the estate had appreciated from 20s. to no less than 50s.[15]

By 1279 the servile element in the population had disappeared, and there had been considerable tenurial development. The lord of the manor had 10½ virgates in demesne, together with a fishery and a mill. His tenants held a further 12 virgates. Among them were 8 virgaters who each paid 5s. rent and services to the same value, and 2 cottagers who paid 6s. and rendered services worth 2s. There were also 5 free tenants, 4 of whom held a total of 4 virgates and paid rent amounting to 6s. 8d., while a fifth held a ½-virgate of one of the others in socage.[16]

The 14th-century tax assessments support the impression given by the hundred rolls of a village with few tenants, all of whom had small holdings. In 1306, for instance, out of 17 persons taxed only 3, including Henry Bruley, lord of the manor, were assessed at more than 2s.[17] In 1327 of 25 taxed for the $\frac{1}{20}$th 10 paid 2s. and over. The total assessment was £2 7s.[18] Under the new assessment of 1334, the total rose to £3 2s. 4d. for the $\frac{1}{15}$th.[19]

Only 51 persons over fourteen were listed in the poll tax of 1377,[20] possibly as a consequence of the Black Death and subsequent economic changes. The returns for the subsidy of 1523 indicate that there had been a concentration of wealth since the early 14th century and perhaps some decline in population. There were eleven contributors to the total tax of £1 7s. 8d. The only gentleman in the list, presumably the tenant of the manor, was the only man of means, with goods worth £17 compared with the better-off yeomen with goods worth £8 and £7.[21]

Glebe terriers of 1601 and 1609 give the earliest details of the field system.[22] These show that there were three arable fields grouped round the village. To the south lay Conygere Field, which was renamed South Field in the later terrier. The old name survived in the Warren close and field of 17th- and 18th-century indentures and the Warren of the 1848 tithe award map.[23] To the east was Gravelly Field, said to

have been called so on account of its soil, but renamed East Field in 1609. To the north of this lay the North East or Hamm Field, as it was anciently called.[24] In addition there was Lincroft in the north-west, an island of some 40 acres of ley ground that was divided into two series of 2-acre strips. South of Lincroft lay the small 2-acre glebe meadow, Moor meadow, and the Cowleys.[25]

The earliest recorded inclosure was made in about 1530 when some pasture was inclosed to form West Field.[26] Further inclosure apparently took place between 1601 and 1609, for the later terrier was said to have been made 'since the inclosure'.[27] It is not clear what had been done, for the glebe lands still lay unconsolidated in ½-acre strips in each of the common fields. But the South Field was now in two parts—apparently a new division of the old Conygere Field, the parsonage having 7 ½-acres in one field and another 7 in the other. This could be an indication of a change from a 3- to a 4-field system of cultivation. There were 2½ glebe acres in each of the other fields. The later terrier also shows that all three arable fields were hedged, and this may have been done since 1601, when there is no mention of other than private hedges. There is specific mention of the new hedge in North East Field.[28]

It is clear that considerable inclosure of demesne land took place in the 17th and 18th centuries. An instance of this may have occurred in 1618, when George Croke was given permission to convert 180 acres of arable to pasture.[29] In 1663 Sir George Croke mortgaged the Windmill Ground of 105 acres to Edward Honywood, a London citizen and ironmonger. This land was said to be inclosed and to have been at one time converted into tillage but later laid down for pasture.[30] The year before when it had been leased for 21 years, together with the Mill Close of 10 acres, the rent was £133.[31] In 1676 'further pastures' of 92 acres adjoining Windmill Field were in the occupation of two of Croke's tenants.[32] As late as 1749 part of Windmill Field (adjoining Mill Close) was said to have been 'lately' inclosed, although perhaps this should not be taken too literally.[33] In 1680 Lincroft, which had earlier been divided up into strips, was said to be in the occupation of Sir George Croke himself.[34] In 1676 he had mortgaged a number of closes and meadows, all said to be demesne land, which formed a fairly compact block of land in the north of the parish. The aggregate of their rents was £202.[35] In the same year he had mortgaged other land, mainly meadow, situated in the southern part of the parish, which produced £199 rent.[36] It seems likely that most if not all of these lands were inclosed.

In the latter half of the 18th century there was one landowner, the Ashhurst family, in Waterstock, and four principal tenants.[37] In 1749 the Ashhursts had leased lands to Stephen Radford at a rent of £200.

---

[13] For him see E. Gaskell, *Oxon. Leaders* (c. 1900).
[14] Many of her papers are in d.d. Ashhurst c 10–11, c 15–17.
[15] *V.C.H. Oxon.* i. 403.
[16] *Rot. Hund.* (Rec. Com.), ii. 821.
[17] E 179/161/10.
[18] E 179/161/9.
[19] E 179/164/7.
[20] E 179/161/41.
[21] E 179/161/198.
[22] Oxf. Archd. Oxon. c 142, ff. 75, 79.
[23] d.d. Ashhurst d 6; Bodl. Tithe award.
[24] Oxf. Archd. Oxon. c 142, ff. 75, 79.
[25] Oxf. Dioc. c 449; d.d. Ashhurst d 9; Bodl. Tithe award and map.

[26] Oxf. Archd. Oxon. c 142, f. 75.
[27] Ibid. f. 79.
[28] Ibid. ff. 75, 79.
[29] B.M. Add. Ch. 39971 (27).
[30] d.d. Ashhurst d 6 (uncat.): deed of 1680.
[31] Bodl. MS. ch. Oxon. 413.
[32] d.d. Ashhurst d 6 (uncat.): indenture of 1690; cf. C 5/169/29.
[33] Bodl. MS. ch. Oxon. 4150.
[34] d.d. Ashhurst d 6: mortgage indenture.
[35] Ibid.: 1681 mortgage assignment.
[36] Ibid.: 1683 deed.
[37] O.R.O. Land tax assess.

By the terms of his lease he was permitted to plough Windmill Field, together with some neighbouring land, a third at a time. Each third could be maintained as arable for five years and used for five crops only and was then to be returned to pasture, the whole to remain pasture for the last five years of the term. He was also allowed to cultivate other fields for five years, but at the end of that time he was to sow grass and to reconvert to pasture under penalty of £5 an acre for neglect.[38] A Radford remained as tenant until at least 1832.[39] A second tenement was leased for 21 years in 1760 to Humphrey Eaton.[40] His main arable land lay in Thameswhy Ground immediately to the north of the Oxford–Thame road and consisted of 30 acres which he had to plough in 10-acre lots for four years and four crops of corn, which meant that over a period each third lay fallow one year in three. He could plough other lands for the first five years of his term, but in the fifth they were to be sown with grass. He was to pay £223 rent, and £10 less in the last year of the term. Eatons held the farm until at least 1821, after which it apparently passed to the Parsons family.[41] Of the other two tenements assessed in 1785 much less is known.[42]

As elsewhere in the neighbourhood there may have been an increase, though a small one, in population in the last quarter of the 18th century. The first official census of 1801 recorded 114 inhabitants.[43] Earlier returns of the number of houses in the parish gave 16 in 1768 and 15 thirty years earlier.[44] If these figures are accurate there would appear to have been little change in population since the second half of the 17th century. Eighteen householders were listed for the hearth tax of 1662 and 55 adults over 16 were returned for the Compton Census of 1676.[45]

Arthur Young gives some account of farming at Waterstock at the beginning of the 19th century. He describes the land as all grass, which seems to have been an exaggeration, and as for the most part inclosed pasture.[46] The grass lands were good and mostly let, the meadows for 50s. and the pasture for 40s. an acre.[47] Two tons of hay were taken from every acre at the first crop, and one at the second, although it was considered bad for the land to take a second crop.[48] W. H. Ashhurst appears as a progressive dairy farmer. He had planted cabbages (for cattle food), when these were still uncommon in Oxfordshire, and had brought in short-horn cattle, which were fed on hay, not straw, in the winter. The butter was sent under contract to London.[49]

In the first half of the 19th century there were four and, after 1821, three tenant farmers, Ashhurst keeping the smallest acreage in his own hand.[50] James Parsons, who farmed 158 acres at a rent of £257, went bankrupt in 1832. He was mainly a cattle farmer, but he also kept some sheep and raised crops of wheat, barley, oats, and beans. He had a malt-mill and granary which, together with other effects, were valued at £55 8s. 6d.[51]

The 1848 tithe-award map gives the first comprehensive view of Waterstock. To the west along the bank of the Thame lay a belt of meadow and grassland which broadened out to occupy the whole of the north-west corner of the parish, while the arable land was concentrated mainly in the north-east and south. The total acreage was 653, of which 269 acres were arable and 348 meadow and pasture. Three tenants occupied farms of 244, 208, and 166 acres respectively.[52]

For most of the latter half of the 19th century there were two tenant farmers. A document of 1876 gives details of the farming methods imposed by the landlord. The tenant was to cultivate the arable according to a 'five-field system of husbandry', $\frac{3}{5}$ in wheat, barley, or oats, $\frac{1}{5}$ left fallow for turnips and vetches for feeding sheep and horses, and $\frac{1}{5}$ in clover, beans, or pulse. Not more than two white straw crops were to be grown in succession and even then they were not to be of the same kind. The tenant was to consume on the farm all hay, turnips, straw, fodder, and chaff produced there, and to spread all dung on the fields. At least twice in a summer he was to cut the thistles on the pasture lands.[53]

In 1885, when W. H. Ashhurst took over the Waterstock estate on the death of his father, there were two farms of 206 and 326 acres, the tenants paying rents of £412 and £630 respectively.[54] Ashhurst probably kept about 116 acres in his own hand, as his father had done.[55] On the estate were 20 cottages, their rents ranging from £2 5s. to £2 12s.

There were three farms in 1939, Home farm and Park farm in the village, and Lower farm on the Thame–Oxford Road,[56] and the same number in 1959. At both dates mixed farming was practised.

The presence of gravel had long been known and in an 18th-century lease Sir George Croke had reserved his rights to dig for it in return for proper compensation.[57] In 1924 Highways Construction were permitted to dig gravel for two years at a rent of £10 an acre plus royalties. The workings lay just to the north of the village and the contractors were allowed to lay a light railway to connect them with a siding on the G.W.R. line south of the Oxford–Thame Road.[58]

During the first 30 years of the 19th century the population had risen fairly steadily from 114 in 1801 to a peak of 142 in 1831. It then fluctuated until a new peak of 147 was reached in 1861. Thereafter there was a steady decline until in 1901—despite the addition of Draycott to the parish—there were only 108 persons.[59] This trend was continued in the 20th century, and by 1951 there were 96 persons in the civil parish.[60]

MILLS. A mill at Waterstock is mentioned in both Domesday Book and the hundred rolls.[61] In 1528 there was said to be both a water- and a horse-driven mill.[62] In indentures and fines of the 17th and 18th

[38] Bodl. MS. ch. Oxon. 4150.
[39] O.R.O. Land tax assess.
[40] Bodl. MS. ch. Oxon. 4152.
[41] O.R.O. Land tax assess.   [42] Ibid.
[43] V.C.H. Oxon. ii. 222.
[44] Oxf. Dioc. d 560; Secker's Visit.
[45] E 179/255/4; Compton Census.
[46] Young, Oxon. Agric. 12, 217.
[47] Ibid. 217.   [48] Ibid.
[49] Ibid. 173, 273–4.
[50] O.R.O. Land tax assess.

[51] d.d. Parsons d 7.
[52] Bodl. Tithe award.
[53] d.d. Ashhurst d 10 (uncat.).   [54] Ibid.
[55] d.d. Ashhurst d 11 (uncat.).
[56] Kelly, Dir. Oxon. (1939).
[57] Bodl. MS. ch. Oxon. 4141.
[58] d.d. Ashhurst d 8; d 10.
[59] V.C.H. Oxon. ii. 222; and see above, p. 220.
[60] Census, 1931, 1951.
[61] V.C.H. Oxon. i. 403; Rot. Hund. (Rec. Com.), ii. 821.
[62] C.P. 25(2)/51/366.

centuries two water grist mills and one windmill are commonly mentioned. It is unlikely, however, that there were two water-mills under separate roofs. In 1676 the water grist mill with a little meadow was worth £30 a year.[63] In 1697 Sir Henry Ashhurst leased to Richard Lamboll, formerly of Thame, for 21 years and at an annual rent of £50 the corn and water-mills under one roof, a dwelling-house, and two portions of meadow containing 6 acres, as well as the corn and windmills under one roof on Windmill Ground, together with Mill Close containing about 10½ acres. Sir Henry reserved to himself and his tenants the right of pulling up the floodgates every year from 1 May to 10 October, if floods threatened their property.[64] In 1725 there was a similar lease to Richard Lamborne of Lamborn (Berks.) for a further 20 years and at the same rent.[65]

The mill was built on a small island in the Thame, the water passing over weirs on both sides, the larger weir on the west or Waterperry side providing the water for the mill race—it was apparently this weir which was rebuilt in 1846 by John Collins of Wolvercote at a cost of £150.[66] By 1957 the mill and millhouse had been converted into a modern dwelling. No trace remains of the windmill.

CHURCH. The earliest evidence for the existence of Waterstock church, a rectory in Cuddesdon deanery, dates from about 1190, when the parish had its own priest Elias.[67] The first recorded presentation was made in 1235 or 1236 by Bartholomew Foliot, the lord of the manor.[68] Since then the descent of the advowson has followed that of the manor. In 1372, during the minority of John Bruley, Robert Woubourne of Milton was patron, and in 1380 John Salveyn for an unexplained reason. In the 15th century the Danvers family succeeded the Bruleys as patrons; in 1467 and 1469 Joan, the widow of John Danvers, and her second husband Sir Walter Mauntell presented; in 1517, during the minority of John Danvers, William Boughton presented, and in 1528 Danvers's three sisters and their husbands did so. The advowson passed with the manor to one of these, Elizabeth and her husband Thomas Cave, and remained with the family until George Croke bought it in 1610. The presentation of 1551 was sold, however, to a group which included John Smith, Provost of Oriel College,[69] and in 1576 the queen presented by lapse.[70] In 1691 manor and advowson were bought by Sir Henry Ashhurst, who came from a family with Puritan sympathies.[71] In 1709, in order to preserve 'serious godliness' in the parishes of which he was patron (Waterstock and Emmington), he made arrangements, if his son should die without

sons, for trustees to choose two ministers 'that believe and preach the old doctrinal articles commonly called Calvinistical'. The trustees included several well-known Presbyterian divines and Edmund Calamy, the historian of nonconformity. The lord of the manor was to present one of the two selected ministers to the living.[72] At each vacancy each trustee was to receive 20s. with which to buy a 'book of divinity'. Although Sir Henry's son died without sons, it is not clear if this method of choosing a rector was ever used. The advowson remained with the Ashhursts until the death of Miss Ashhurst in 1949. The patrons in 1957 were her executors.

There have twice been attempts in the 20th century to unite the livings of Waterstock and Waterperry, but though held together, they remain separate benefices.[73]

In the Middle Ages the rectory was a rather poor one, worth £4 in 1254 and £5 6s. 8d. in 1291.[74] By 1535 its value had risen to £10 16s. ½d.[75] In the early 17th century it was said to be worth £100,[76] but soon after this it was impoverished by an arrangement made sometime before 1659 between the rector and the lord of the manor. The lord, who owned the whole parish except the glebe, agreed to pay the rector a modus of £40 a year instead of tithes.[77] Accordingly, the value of the rectory, derived from this £40 and the glebe, rose little between the mid-17th and the mid-19th centuries. In 1716 it was worth £55, in 1806 only £64 10s.,[78] and in 1847, when the question of commuting the tithes was raised, J. H. Ashhurst claimed that on the basis of this composition the parish was tithe free.[79] The Tithe Commissioners, on the other hand, considered the modus 'absolutely void'[80] and in 1848 the tithes were commuted for £250.[81]

The small glebe was first mentioned in 1341[82] and its earliest terriers date from 1601 and 1609.[83] In 1806 it consisted of 12 acres, the greater part of which lay next to the rectory.[84] In 1790 the rector had given Sir William Henry Ashhurst, who was rebuilding the church, ¾-acre of glebe in return for a promise that in the future the lord of the manor would be responsible for the upkeep of the chancel.[85]

Medieval rectors, in spite of the comparative poverty of the living, held it as a rule for many years. They never exchanged it for a better one and most of them died at their posts.[86] Examples are Master John de Hadenham (c. 1235–68); Thomas Bruley (1326–61), probably a younger brother of the lord of the manor, who acted as feoffee for Waterperry manor;[87] John Kent (1423–67), who acted as feoffee for the Danvers family;[88] and Master John Brown (1469–99), who is portrayed in one of the church

[63] d.d. Ashhurst d 6: 1683 indenture.
[64] Bodl. MS. ch. Oxon. 4142; d.d. Ashhurst d 8.
[65] Bodl. MS. chs. Oxon. 4145, 4146.
[66] d.d. Ashhurst d 10.
[67] Oseney Cart. iv. 405.
[68] Rot. Grosse. 446. For medieval presentations see MS. Top. d 460.
[69] Oxf. Dioc. d 105, p. 141.
[70] O.A.S. Rep. 1919, 245.
[71] See above, p. 223.
[72] Bodl. MS. ch. Oxon. 4257. Among the other trustees were Richard Mayo, a London minister, and his son; William Tongue and Samuel Rosewell, 2 London Presbyterians; Matthew Henry, a Chester minister, and his son (for all these see D.N.B.); and Michael Pope, a Bristol minister.
[73] d.d. Ashhurst d 10, 1914 and 1925 letters. In 1951 they were considered as united: Census, 1951: Eccl. Areas.
[74] Lunt, Val. Norw. 306; Tax. Eccl. (Rec. Com.), 31.

[75] Valor Eccl. (Rec. Com.), ii. 171.
[76] Dunkin MS. 439/2, f. 176.
[77] d.d. Ashhurst d 10, 1847 case. The arrangement was said to be ancient in 1659.
[78] Oxf. Dioc. c 155, f. 48; c 449, f. 55.
[79] d.d. Ashhurst d 10, 1847 case.
[80] Ibid. 1847 decision.   [81] Bodl. Tithe award.
[82] Inq. Non. (Rec. Com.), 134.
[83] Oxf. Archd. c 142, pp. 75–82. For an exchange of less than an acre with manor lands see d.d. Ashhurst d 10, 1666 indenture.
[84] Oxf. Dioc. c 449, f. 55.
[85] Bodl. MS. ch. Oxon. 4154.
[86] For a list of rectors see Macnamara, Danvers Family, 226; for a corrected list of medieval ones see MS. Top. Oxon. d 460.
[87] Cal. Inq. p.m. xiii, p. 127.
[88] C.P. 25(1)/292/66/86.

windows.[89] It seems likely that these clerks were resident. Proof of residence in 1405 comes from an account of a robbery. The rector's church and house were then broken into and coverlets, sheets, jewels, and household utensils worth 20 marks belonging to him and the churchwardens were stolen.[90]

In the early 16th century the wills of Sir Thomas Danvers (d. 1502), who was a generous benefactor to the church building,[91] and of his widow Sibyl (d. 1511) show the close connexion between the church and the family living at the manor-house. They were both buried in the church and both left instructions for services to be said for them there. Two Oxford scholars were to say daily mass for Sir Thomas, and on the eight principal feasts these masses were to be said in Waterstock; two Oxford scholars were likewise to say services for Dame Sibyl, but only once a year in Waterstock on the day of her anniversary.[92] The rector at the time of their death, Robert Wright (1501–16), to whom Sir Thomas left a bequest of 13s. 4d., was a witness of Sibyl's will.[93] He was probably dead by the time of the episcopal visitation of about 1520, when the church was found to be comparatively well cared for: the only faults noted were that the font was kept unlocked and some windows were broken.[94]

Later in the century the parish had some highly educated rectors, but they only held the living for short periods. Richard Bruern (1551–9), who may have had to resign it as he did his Oxford professorship because of immorality,[95] was succeeded by Thomas Bruern (d. 1561), once a Fellow of Brasenose College.[96] John Tatham, rector in 1576, was Rector of Lincoln College;[97] and John Rider, who was perhaps rector in 1580, was a well-known lexicographer who became a bishop.[98]

In the early 17th century, when George Croke was patron, he gave the living to two of his nephews: Charles Croke (rector in 1616), who was later chaplain to Charles I;[99] and Henry Croke (1618–42), also Canon of Lincoln and Wells, who may, like other members of the Croke family, have been more sympathetic to Puritanism. The inventory of his goods at his death indicates that he was of a scholarly character: his Waterstock house had a 'study chamber', and there were books there to the value of £40.[1]

After the Restoration the living was held for nearly 50 years by Charles Hinde (1677–1725), described by Hearne as 'the pettifogger of Waterstock'.[2] He was presented by Sir George Croke and was clearly on excellent terms with Croke's successor, Sir Henry Ashhurst. He shared the interest of his most dearly beloved patron in the history of the church building. Hearne also relates that he was regretful that the old village custom of holding 'prones (homilies) and

wakes' had ceased.[3] Hinde was succeeded by Edward Lewis (1726–84), an author and a strong opponent of Roman Catholicism, who also held the other Ashhurst living of Emmington.[4] He lived at Waterstock, but on Sundays he went to Emmington while a curate from Oxford, who received £20 or £25 a year, took the services at Waterstock.[5] Throughout the century two services and one sermon were given on Sundays, and the sacrament was administered four times a year.[6] In the second half of the century the rector said prayers, which anyone could attend, on Wednesdays, Fridays, and saints' days at the Ashhursts' house.[7]

On Lewis's death a characteristic 18th-century arrangement was made. The antiquary John Gutch served the church with a curate from 1785 to 1789 and kept the living warm for the son of the Rector of Albury, who was at that time a student at Oxford.[8] The young R. B. B. Robinson (rector 1790–1826)[9] duly succeeded, and lived at Waterstock in the Rectory which the Ashhursts had rebuilt for him. They also presented him to Emmington.[10] From this time the parish almost always had a resident rector. To this fact and to the piety of the Ashhursts may perhaps be attributed the fact that no papists and no protestant nonconformists were recorded in the 18th or 19th centuries.

During the century the number of communicants increased steadily. In 1738 there had been less than 20; in the early 19th century there were between 30 and 40; in 1854 over 50 and over 60 in 1878.[11] James H. Ashhurst (1856–96), a younger son of W. H. Ashhurst and Rural Dean of Cuddesdon, brought a new fervour into the religious life of the parish. He increased the number of communion services from the four of 1854 to over twelve a year; continued the Sunday school, gave religious instruction in the day schools; and held a well-attended night school in winter. In his time nearly everyone in Waterstock went to church.[12]

The church of *ST. LEONARD* is a stone building of various dates comprising a chancel, nave, north aisle, western tower, and north and south porches. The early medieval church was rebuilt at the end of the 15th century by Thomas Danvers and his first wife, a daughter of James Fiennes, Lord Saye and Sele[13]. An inscription below the arms of Danvers which was in a window in the north aisle and which was recorded by Anthony Wood indicates that they began the work by rebuilding the nave. The inscription ran: 'Orate pro animabus . . . filiae Jacobi Finys, qui istam ecclesiam fecerunt anno gratiae MCCCCLXXX.'[14] A north aisle dedicated to St. Ann was being built in 1501, for Thomas Danvers directed in his will, dated November 1501, that the

[89] See below, p. 229.
[90] Cal. Pat. 1408–13, 460–1.
[91] See below, p. 228.
[92] Macnamara, Danvers Family, 167–9, 171–3.
[93] Ibid. 167, 173.
[94] Visit. Dioc. Linc. 1517–31, i. 138.
[95] For him see D.N.B.
[96] Brasenose Reg. (O.H.S. lv), 8; O.A.S. Rep. 1920, 244.
[97] For him see A. Clark, Lincoln Coll. 49.
[98] O.A.S. Rep. 1920, 246; for him see D.N.B.
[99] For him see Sir A. Croke, Genealogical Hist. of the Croke Family (1823), i. 506–10; Wood, Fasti, i. 423–4.
[1] MS. Wills Oxon. 13: inv. of H. Croke (d. 1642). For him see Croke, op. cit. 552–4, 556; Foster, Alumni.
[2] Hearne, Remarks, iii. 123.
[3] Ibid. viii. 400.

[4] For him see D.N.B.; d.d. Ashhurst d 14: 1676 conveyance.
[5] Oxf. Dioc. c 652, ff. 75–76; d 560. One curate was said to be 'in daily expectation of much better things'.
[6] Secker's Visit.; Oxf. Dioc. d 554, d 557, d 565.
[7] Oxf. Dioc. d 557; c 327, p. 94.
[8] Ibid. c 327, p. 94.
[9] For his father Christopher Robinson see V.C.H. Oxon. v. 14.
[10] Oxf. Dioc. c 327, p. 94; MS. Top. Oxon. b 220, f. 135b; Oxf. Dioc. c 449, f. 55.
[11] Secker's Visit.; Oxf. Dioc. d 549, p. 63; Wilb. Visit.; Oxf. Dioc. c 344.
[12] Oxf. Dioc. c 332, c 344.
[13] Macnamara, Danvers Family, 155.
[14] Par. Coll. iii. 322.

'aisle' be finished 'in as goodly hast as it may be and covered with lead'.[15] A new chancel, which he had begun, was also to be finished under the supervision of his second wife Sybyl Brecknoke (neé Fowler).[16] He directed that he should be buried in the chancel 'before St. Leonard'. His monument, described by Wood, no longer exists.[17]

The windows of the new building were filled with painted glass mostly of 15th and early 16th-century date. Nothing further is known of the history of the fabric until 1692, when Sir Henry Ashhurst was given permission to take over part of the north aisle (28 ft. by 12 ft.) as a 'dormitory' or burial place for his

the foundation; the south wall of the nave was repaired, two new windows and a door being inserted in place of the old ones; the plaster ceiling was removed so as to open up the nave roof, and a battlemented cornice was added. The gallery erected at the west end at some unknown date was abolished. A new chancel arch was built; a new east window, copied from one at Great Milton church, was inserted and the chancel ceiling was raised so as to show the point of the window. The chancel and north aisle were reroofed, the north wall of the aisle having been made 3 feet higher. A new vestry and a south and a north porch were built. The church was

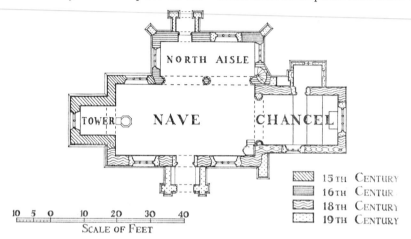

NORTH AISLE

TOWER   NAVE   CHANCEL

10 5 0   10   20   30   40
SCALE OF FEET

15TH CENTURY
16TH CENTURY
18TH CENTURY
19TH CENTURY

family on condition that he kept it in repair and beautified it.[18] The fabric was apparently neglected in the first half of the 18th century, for in 1758 the archdeacon ordered that elder bushes and banks of rubbish should be moved from 'the foundation of the walls of the church'; that part of the walls and tower should be repointed, the pavement of church and chancel should be laid and made even, and a new door should be made on the north side.[19] In 1789 the church was again reported out of repair and in 1790 nave and chancel were rebuilt by Sir W. H. Ashhurst.[20] Early 19th-century drawings of the church and an account of the same period record that the chancel had an east window of three lights without tracery and no side windows; that there were two windows in the south wall of the nave, each of three round-headed lights under a square label and that the nave had a flat ceiling with a cornice; that the north aisle with its perpendicular windows and the west tower of three stories with a parapet and small bellcote had been left in their original state except for the addition of the clock on the east face of the tower.[21]

In 1845 chancel, nave, and tower all needed repair. The estimated cost was about £30.[22] No major repairs were executed until a thorough restoration was carried out during 1857–8 under the direction of the architect G. E. Street. The builder was George Wyatt of Oxford. The church was under-pinned, a brick gutter put round it and the earth removed from

repaved, Minton tiles being used for the chancel, and it was reseated and refurnished. Parishioners gave a new pulpit, lectern, prayer desk, altar rails, and font. The medieval font, 'plain and round', had to be replaced as it no longer held water. Thomas Willement did three painted windows (i.e. the east and west windows and a small one in the chancel); Castell of London painted the Belief, the Lord's Prayer and the Commandments, and three texts for the back of the altar for use on festivals. The total cost, including the gifts of furniture, windows, and the two new porches, was about £1,500.[23]

Further alterations were made later in the century. In 1861 the east window in the north aisle was given by Mrs. Ashhurst and in 1872 the painted reredos of the Last Supper and altar dado, consisting of panels with painted figures of saints and prophets, was given by the Revd. J. H. Ashhurst.[24] In 1888 a new belfry floor was made and a clock was placed in the tower.[25]

There was another restoration in 1930. The roof was stripped and covered with slates; the church was refloored and put in 'complete order'.[26] Electric light has since been installed.

The chief glory of the medieval church was its painted glass. Only that in the three top lights of the Ashhurst window in the north aisle has survived the various restorations, but Anthony Wood visited Waterstock in May 1668, and has left a detailed record.[27] In the chancel window were the arms of

[15] Macnamara, *Danvers Family*, 167–8: his will.
[16] For her see ibid. 155–6, 170–4; and for pedigree see Bodl. G.A. Oxon. 4° 687, 321–2.
[17] *Par. Coll.* iii. 321.
[18] d.d. Ashhurst d 10, Faculty.
[19] Oxf. Archd. Oxon. d 13, f. 51b. For seats being out of repair in 1726 see ibid. c 116.
[20] Ibid. c 109, ff. 300–1.

[21] MS. Top. Oxon. b 220, ff. 135–6: drawing from south and account of *c.* 1810; ibid. a 69, no. 571: Buckler drawing from NE. (1822).   [22] d.d. Ashhurst d 10.
[23] Par. Rec. MS. notes; d.d. Ashhurst d 8, Papers on restoration; MS. Top. Oxon. d 92, f. 189b.
[24] Par. Rec. MS. notes.   [25] Ibid.   [26] Ibid.
[27] Wood, *Life*, ii. 136; *Par. Coll.* iii. 321 sqq.; Bodl. G.A. Oxon. 4° 687, 321–4.

France and England quartered, and the arms of the Bruley, Quartermain, and Danvers families. In the north window of the nave were the figures of two men 'all in blew', each kneeling before a desk, one a clergyman the other a layman, and the pictures of three saints above them.[28] This window was commissioned, according to the inscription underneath, by Master John Brown, once rector of the church, in memory of himself, his father Thomas Brown, and his mother. Master John Brown (rector 1469–99) and his father may be identified with the figures in two of the surviving fragments.[29] The other surviving fragment is 13th-century glass. The rest of the glass described by Wood was probably commissioned by Thomas Danvers or his two wives, either for the windows of the nave after it was rebuilt in 1480 or for the north aisle after 1501. The armorial glass included the arms of many families with which the Danvers were allied by marriage, those for instance of Brancastre, Pury, Verney, Fowler, and Brecknoke. There were also painted figures of Thomas Danvers and his two wives, and over them the pictures of three female saints, identified by Wood as Barbara, 'Trinitas', and Anna; a figure of Thomas Danvers, esquire (presumably one commissioned before his investiture as a knight in 1501);[30] and of John Danvers, esquire.

There was formerly an inscription which ran: 'Orate pro animabus Johannis Danvers et domine Johanne et heredis Johannis Bruly et Matildae Quatermayne uxoris sue quondam patronorum istius ecclesie.' There were also inscriptions to the following: Henry Danvers and his wife Beatrice, the daughter of Sir Ralph Verney; Richard Danvers of Prestcote; Sir John Fray and his wife Agnes; William Fowler and his wife Cicely; and William Danvers and his wife Anne. Anne died in 1531[31] and seems to have been the last of the Danvers family to be commemorated. Wood also describes a figure of a bishop with his crozier resting on his shoulder, wearing his mitre and 'praying'. The last figure had an inscription beneath with the names of George Neville, Archbishop of York (1464–76), William Waynflete, Bishop of Winchester, a friend of Thomas Danvers, and Thomas Danvers himself. Another figure of a bishop surmounted the archiepiscopal arms of York quartering Montague, Monthermer, and Neville.[32] In the east window of the north aisle were the arms of Croke and Bennett. As this is the only glass commemorating the Croke family recorded by Wood, all the rest being in the windows of the manor-house, it is possible that the available window space was filled by 1610, when George Croke became lord of the manor.[33] The Ashhurst window in the north aisle seems to have been mostly inserted just before 1852. It is mentioned in Gardner's directory for that year, but not in the architectural guide of 1846. Forty-three shields fill three lights and illustrate the genealogy of the Ashhurst family from Adam de Ashhurst, 'sans date', to John Henry Ashhurst,

1848. Most of the shields in the east light have Ashhurst in the dexter and the sinister half is left blank for the use of posterity.[34] Later in the century an oval panel painted with an achievement of arms and the inscription 'John Warner and Elizabeth Ashhurst married 29th April 1755', was inserted in the middle of the east light. It is signed W. Peckitt 1769 and is contemporary with some of his glass in New College chapel.[35] The last marriage commemorated was in 1881: the work was inferior and the enamel has already faded. The church also has some wall-paintings: these were noted in 1887, but are no longer visible.[36] Between the north and south doors are the matrices of two brasses, one an early 15th-century half-effigy of a man, the other possibly of a priest.[37] In the centre aisle is a marble gravestone with the remains of an inscription in Lombardic letters: + WILLIAM : DE : LA : BA . . . . . . MERCI. It was probably to William de la Beche.[38]

The principal monument, with arms, in the church is to Sir George Croke, Justice of the King's Bench and lord of the manor (d. 1641/2). The inscription has been ascribed to Matthew Hale.[39] It was moved from the chancel in 1858 to the north aisle. A black marble gravestone to Dame Mary, his widow (d. 1657), and another to Charles Hinde, rector (d. 1725), were also moved from the chancel and are also in the north aisle. There are memorial tablets to the following: the rector's son Francis Hinde of London (d. 1720) and his wife; Dame Frances Allin (d. 1743), daughter of Sir Henry Ashhurst; Edward Lewis, rector (d. 1784) and his wife; Sir William Henry Ashhurst (d. 1807); Robert Robinson, Rector of Waterstock and Emmington (d. 1826) and his wife; and William Henry Ashhurst, Esq., M.P. (d. 1846).

The Edwardian inventory records one chalice.[40] The church now possesses two Elizabethan silver chalices, one hall-marked 1569 and the other 1570 with the maker's mark AK; both have lost their paten covers. There is a large silver paten with foot dated 1715 and bearing the initials C.J. for Joseph Clare, and a silver flagon of 1863. There is a 16th-century pewter paten, and a pewter tankard flagon.[41]

A medieval bell inscribed *Sante Nicholae si* was recast by Gillett of Croydon in 1888, and so were two bells dated 1616 and 1664 and originally made by Henry Knight and Richard Keene respectively.[42]

In 1697 the south side of the churchyard was said to be too narrow, so that the graves lay exposed 'to the scandal of the Christian church'. Since part of the Ashhursts' house stood within the north side of the churchyard, Sir Henry Ashhurst gave some land on the south in exchange. He also promised to build a 'handsome' churchyard wall of stone coped with brick and a 'handsome' pair of gates with iron bars.[43]

In 1858 the boundary wall on the north side of the churchyard was replaced by an iron railing set in stone and a new south gate was made at a cost of £38.[44]

The registers date from 1580.[45]

[28] *Par. Coll.* iii. 323.
[29] See list of medieval rectors in Macnamara, *Danvers Family*, 226.
[30] Ibid. 164.
[31] Ibid. 181. For the related families see ibid. *passim* and W. F. Carter, *Quatremains of Oxon. passim.*
[32] Bodl. 1373, l 64, 90.
[33] See above, p. 223.
[34] For an account of the glass see Lamborn, *Arm. Glass*, 165.

[35] For Peckitt see *D.N.B.*
[36] Bodl. G.A. Oxon. 4° 697: newspaper cutting, 1887.
[37] MS. Top. Oxon. d 196, ff. 391, 393.
[38] Ibid. f. 392.   [39] Gardner, *Dir. Oxon.* (1852).
[40] *Chant. Cert.* 117.
[41] Evans, *Ch. Plate.*
[42] *Ch. Bells Oxon.* 431–2.
[43] d.d. Ashhurst d 8: 1697 indenture.
[44] Ibid. d 10; Papers on restoration.
[45] Those up to 1812 are in d.d. Par. Waterstock c 1–2.

SCHOOLS. No information about schooling in the village has been found before the 19th century. There was a day school by 1805 and in 1808 ten children were being taught to read there.[46] A Sunday school with 13 children, supported by Mrs. Ashhurst, was set up in 1808.[47] Between 1815 and 1818 another day-school was opened and in 1818 there were 18 children attending the two day-schools and 16 attending the Sunday school.[48] The situation was much the same in 1833, when the schools were described as a day school for 7 girls, supported by the squire, an infant school with about 10 boys and girls, who were paid for by their parents, and the Sunday school with 16 boys and 7 girls.[49] It is difficult to follow the fortunes of these schools, but it is probable that there was some continuity between them and the school of 1854, described as 'complete for week and Sunday', and the Church of England school that existed in 1871.[50] The Church school was a mixed school run on National Society lines; it had an average attendance of 25 at the end of the 19th century.[51] The school was apparently reorganized in 1903–4, for Waterstock Church of England School was said to have been opened in 1904.[52] Lack of numbers led to its being closed in 1916 and the children later went to Tiddington school.[53]

[46] Oxf. Dioc. c 327, p. 242; d 707; c 433.
[47] Ibid. d 707; c 433.
[48] Ibid. c 433; *Educ. of Poor*, 732.
[49] *Educ. Enq. Abstract*, 757.
[50] *Wilb. Visit.*; *Elem. Educ. Ret.* 320.
[51] Kelly, *Dir. Oxon.* (1887, 1891, 1903).
[52] *List of Sch.* 530; *Vol. Sch. Ret.* 36.
[53] Inf. Oxf. Educ. Cttee (1956).
[54] She was a Bennett: Sir A. Croke, *Genealogical Hist. of*

NONCONFORMITY. None recorded.

CHARITY. By will proved in 1631 Ambrose Bennett, of London, no doubt a relative of Lady Mary Croke,[54] charged certain lands in Rotherhithe with a rent of £8 a year for the benefit of the poor of Waterstock at Lady Day and Michaelmas.[55] At the end of the century the money was not paid for several years and the churchwardens and overseers of Waterstock, and of two other parishes which had received similar bequests, exhibited a bill against John Bennett in Chancery. In 1704 he promised to make regular payments.[56] These were regularly made throughout the 18th century and accounts were kept from 1707 of the distribution of the money. In 1823 20 poor people benefited, the sums granted varying between 5s. and 12s. according to the size of individual families.[57] In 1877 the rent-charge was redeemed for £267 stock.[58] The income in 1923 and again in 1937 was £6 13s. 4d.[59] but the method of its distribution at that time cannot be ascertained.

The parishioners of Waterstock have the right to send almspeople to Croke's almshouses in Studley.[60]

Croke Fam. (1823), ii. 565.
[55] P.C.C. 29 St. John. It was made in 1630, not 1636, as in *8th Rep. Com. Char.* 560.
[56] Bodl. MS. ch. Oxon. 4255; ibid. 4258 is an extract from the will.
[57] *8th Rep. Com. Char.* 560–1; Oxf. Dioc. d 555.
[58] Char. Com. file 18064.
[59] Ibid. Accts. file.
[60] *V.C.H. Oxon.* v. 76.

TAX ASSESSMENTS OF THE VILLAGES AND HAMLETS OF DORCHESTER AND THAME HUNDREDS, 1306-1523

	1306[a] a 30th		1327[b] a 20th		1344[c] a 15th	1377[d] Poll tax	1523[e] Lay subsidy	
	£ s. d.	Contributors	£ s. d.	Contributors	£ s. d.	Contributors	£ s. d.	Contributors
Chislehampton .	1 7 0¼	16	2 11 6	21	3 0 3	57	12 2	9
Clifton Hampden .	1 10 0¾	16	2 17 6	33	2 17 2	79	1 12 10	17
Dorchester[f] . .	3 10 0*		4 9 10	39	3 19 8	215	6 18 10	47
Burcot . .	1 2 10¾	10	2 7 2	17	2 15 6	41	17 6	14
TOTAL . .	4 12 10¾		6 17 0	56	6 15 2	256	7 16 4	61
Drayton St. Leonard	1 10 0 *		4 0 10	25	2 1 3	72	2 18 2	16
Stadhampton . .	(1 0 4)	14+	2 13 7	28	1 17 9	63	1 7 4	24
South Stoke . .	1 1 8	21 }						
Woodcote . .	13 5¾	13 }	4 4 0	40	3 11 2	194	9 6 6	39
TOTAL . .	1 15 1¾	34 }						
Milton, Great[g] } Little }	5 11 7†	44+	6 6 6	72	8 2 10	242	{ 4 4 0 { 1 8 8	22 / 15
Ascot . .			2 2 0	24	2 15 8	48	12 10	6
TOTAL . .			8 8 6	96	10 18 6	290	6 5 6	43
Thame, Old . .	6 1 10	39+	5 3 6	50	3 7 9	128	4 8 10	22
New .	6 3 2†	55+	6 7 11	67	9 2 8	325	15 15 6	78
Priestend[h] .						83 }	1 3 2	17
Attington .	16 10	11	2 2 4	16 }	4 18 11	{ 27 }		
Moreton .	1 8 4	21	2 5 6	20 }		{ 69	2 15 10	13
Tetsworth .	1 13 6	24+	2 16 10	27	3 19 3	110	2 8 10	26
Weston, North .	1 19 5	23	3 2 11	27	2 14 6	49	15 4	7
TOTAL . .	18 3 1		21 19 0	207	24 3 1	791	27 7 6	163
Waterstock . .	1 3 2	17	2 7 0	25	3 2 4	51	1 7 8	11

+ Mutilated: number of names incomplete.

* Mutilated: rubric and all names missing.

† Mutilated: rubric and some names missing.

( ) Mutilated: the total given is the sum of the surviving payments.

[a] E 179/161/10.

[b] E 179/161/9. The 1316 tax assessment is mutilated for these hundreds and has not been included in the tables. On these Edwardian taxes, see J. W. Willard, *E.H.R.* xxviii. 517–21; xxix. 317–21; xxx. 69–74.

[c] E 179/161/17 (the earliest Oxfordshire example of the 1334 assessment). Cf. E 164/7 (tax levied in 1415) for another example of the assessments fixed in 1334.

[d] E 179/161/41.

[e] E 179/191/198.

[f] Dorchester included Fifield in Benson as well as Overy in its early 14th- and 16th-century tax assessments.

[g] For assessments of Coombe and the Chilworths, also in Great Milton parish, see *V.C.H. Oxon.* vi. 318.

[h] Priestend is almost certainly included in the assessment of Old Thame in the early 14th cent.

INDEX

NOTE. The following abbreviations have been used: abp., archbishop; Abr., Abraham; acct., account; admin., administration; adv. (advs.), advowson(s); Alex., Alexander; Alf., Alfred; And., Andrew; Ant., Anthony; archd., archdeacon; Art., Arthur; b., born; Baldw., Baldwin; Bart., Bartholomew; Ben., Benjamin; Bern., Bernard; bldg., building; bnss., baroness; bp., bishop; Brig-Gen., Brigadier-General; bro., brother; bt., baronet; *c.*, circa; can., canon; Capt., Captain; Cath., Catherine; cent., century; ch. (chs.), church(es); ch. bldg., church building; ch. hist., church history; chap. (chaps.), chapel(s); char. (chars.), charity (charities); Chas., Charles; chpl., chaplain; civ. par., civil parish; civ. war, civil war; clk., clerk; Co., Company; Col., Colonel; coll., college; Compt. cens., Compton census; const., constable; ct. (cts.), court(s); ctss., countess; cttee., committee; cur.(s.), curate(s); d., died; Dan., Daniel; dau., daughter; Dav., David; dchss., duchess; depop., depopulation; dom. arch., domestic architecture; Dot., Dorothy; ec. hist., economic history; Edm., Edmund; Edw., Edward; Eliz., Elizabeth; est. (ests.), estate(s); f., father; fl., flourished; Fr., Father; Fred., Federick; Gab., Gabriel; Gen., General; Geo., George; Geof., Geoffrey; geol., geology; Gil., Gilbert; Gr., Grammar; grddau., granddaughter; grds., grandson; Greg., Gregory; hd., head; Hen., Henry; Herb., Herbert; ho. (hos.), house(s); hon., honor; hosp., hospital; How., Howard; Humph., Humphrey; hund. (hunds.), hundred(s); incl., inclosure; Jas., James; Jon., Jonathan; Jos., Joseph; jr., junior; jurisd., jurisdiction; Kath., Katharine; kt., knight; Laur., Laurence; Lawr., Lawrence; ld., lord; ldy., lady; Len., Lennard; Leon., Leonard; Lew., Lewis; Lond., London; Lt., Lieutenant m., married; Magd., Magdalen; maj., major; Maj-Gen., Major-General; man., manor; man. ho., manor house; Marg., Margaret; Mat., Matthew; Max., Maximilian; mchss., Marchioness; med., medieval; Mic., Michael; mkt., market; mod., modern; mon., monumental; mqss., marquess; Nat., Nathaniel; Nic., Nicholas; noncf., nonconformity; occs., occupations; Osw., Oswald; Oxf., Oxford; P.N., Place Names; par. (pars.), parish(es); par. govt., parish government; pec., peculiar; Pet., Peter; Phil., Philip; pk., park; pncss., princess; poor rel., poor relief; pop., population; preb., prebendary; pres., president; princ., principal; profssns., professions; prop., property; Prot. noncf., Protestant nonconformity; prov., provost; prss. (prsses.), prioress(es); quad., quadrangle; r., rector; R.C., Roman Catholic; rcty., rectory; Rcty. (Recties.), Rectory (Rectories) (building); rds., roads; Reg., Reginald; Revd., Reverend; Reyn., Reynold; Ric., Richard; riv., river; rlwy., railway; Rob., Robert; Rog., Roger; Rom. Cathm., Roman Catholicism; s., son; Sam., Samuel; sch. (schs.), school(s); Seb., Sebastian; Sim., Simon; sis., sister; soc., society; soc. conds., social conditions; Sol., Solomon; sr., senior; st., street; Steph., Stephen; Theoph., Theophilus; Thos., Thomas; Tim., Timothy; top., topography; v., vicar; vct. viscount; vctss., viscountess; Ven., Venerable; Vic., Vicarage (building); vics., vicars; vill., (vills.), village(s); Vinc., Vincent; w., wife; Wal., Walter; ward. (wards.), warden(s); wd. (wds.), wood(s); wid., widow; Wm., William; yeo. fam., yeoman family.

Abbott, Rob., v. of S. Stoke, 106
Abingdon, earls of, 18, 43, 50, 115, 161, 186, 215, 217; *and see* Bertie, Jas., Montagu, Willoughby; ests. in Burcot, 66; in Chislehampton, 12; in Dorchester, 48, 50, 51, 64; in Drayton, 73, 76, 77, 78, 79; in Tetsworth, 150, 151; in Thame, 191, 192, 193, 198; in N. Weston, 174; surveys of, 191, 192; fam. of, 4, 166, 176, 200
Abingdon (Berks.), 8, 27, 28, 29, 31, 179, 180; Christ's Hosp. at, 21, 27; Guild of the Holy Cross at, 21, 27, 40, 152; Prot. noncf., 38; rds., 5, 6, 27, 30, 65, 66
Abingdon Abbey (Berks.), 28, 30, 119; abbots of, 27, 29, 37, 133; *and see* Aldred, Coventry, Faritius, Hendreth, Hugh, Ingulf, Nic. of Culham, Rainald, Rathanus; grange of, 29; prop. of, 30, 31, 32, 35, 36
Abingdon Bridge, 27, 30
Abingdon Poor Law Union, 34, 35
Abingdon races, 31
Abingdon Rural Sanitary Council, 35
Abingdon School, hdmaster of, *see* Woods
Above Hill (Woodcote), 93
Abraham, Rob., architect, 169, 216
Adam, Jas. and Rob., architects, 95
Adam the glazier, 180
Adam de Ashhurst, 229
Adelaide (Australia), bp. of, *see* Short
Adkyns, John, 154; Wm., 219
Admiralty Storage Depot, *see* Royal Naval Air Station, Culham
Adwell, 98, 160
Ælfhild, 31, 35
Æschwine, bp. of Dorchester, 60
Agincourt, battle of, 120
Agriculture, Board of, *see* Board of Agriculture
Alan, clk. of Tetsworth, and his w. Clarissa, 150, 156
Albury, 172, 220; *and see* Tiddington
Aldenham, Lords, *see* Gibbs

Aldersonne, *see* Atherton
Aldred, abbot of Abingdon, 31
Aldrynton, de, Eliz., *see* Loveday, 19; Hen., 19; Thos, 19
Aldworth fam., 118
Alexander, bp. of Lincoln, 53, 58, 87, 125, 139, 171, 172, 177, 178, 186, 189, 199
Alexander the carpenter, 179
Alexander the smith, 85
Alexander of Burcot (Bridicot), 67
Alexander of Coombe, 129
Algeria, 184
Alice (fl. 1225), wid. (?) of James de Cardunville, 125
Alice the glazier, 180
Allam, Ric., 24, 70
Allen, John, 83; Moses and his w. Mary, 108; Rob., 84
Allin, Dame Frances, *see* Ashhurst
Allnutts Hosp., *see* Goring
Almond, Nic., 218, 219
Almshouses, 112, 230; *and see* Lord Williams' Almshouses, Quatremain Almshouses
Alured (fl. 1086), kt., 114, 174
Aluric (fl. 1086), kt., 114, 126, 130
Alwi (fl. mid-11th cent.), 222
Anabaptists, 144
Andersey Island, in Culham, 27, 28, 31, 36; Anglo-Saxon chap. on, 30, 35; King Offa's residence on, 30; Norman hunting lodge on, 30
Anderson, Thos., 144
Archdale, Abr., 117
Architects, *see* Abraham; Adam; Billing; Blomfield; Blow; Bradfield; Brakspear; Brandon; Bruton; Buckler; Butterfield; Clacy; Clarke; Cockerell; Cranstoun; Dale; Dowbigin; Grayson; Harris; Hayward; Hodson; Hopper; Howard; Rayson; Scott, Sir Geo. Gil.; Scott, Sir Gil.; Scott, J. O.; Smith, Francis; Smith, Wm.; Spiers; Street; Surman; Underwood; Wardell; Wilkinson; Wills; Wyatt
Arden, Hen., 96; Mary, *see* Palmer

Ascot, in Gt. Milton, 81, 90, 92, 115, 117, 130, 187; chapelry, 121, 138; ec. hist., 130, 131, 133; fees, 114; Ho., 121–2; incl., 133–4; mans., 124, 126, 127, 172, 173, Fynes, 126–7, Quatremains, 127; top., 130
Asheley, Nic., r. of S. Stoke and v. of Aston Rowant, 105
Ashfield, Sir Edm., 43, 44, 46, 53, 54, 79; Eliz., m. Wm. Fettiplace, 43; fam., 53
Ashhurst, Diana, w. of Thos. Hen., 220, 221, 223; Eliz., m. John Warner, 229; Dame Frances Allin, 229; Gladys Mary, J.P., 224; Sir Hen. (d. 1711), 221, 222, 223, 226, 229; Sir Hen. (d. 1732), 223; Revd. Jas., 141, 145, 227; John Hen., 223, 224, 229; Susannah, m. Francis Clerke, 173; Thos. Hen., 223; Sir Wm. Hen. (d. 1807), 221, 223, 229; Wm. Hen., M.P. (d. 1846), 221, 223, 229; Wm. Hen. (d. 1929), 224, 225; Mrs. (fl. 1808), 230; fam., 113, 229
Ashhurst, de, Adam, 229
Aston, deanery, 155
Aston Bruley, in White Ladies Aston (Worcs.), 222
Aston Rowant, 160, 196
Astry, Revd. Francis, 143; Ralph and his w. Anne, 144; fam., 118
Athelstan, King of Wessex, 31
Atherton (Aldersonne), Master John, v. of Thame, 203, 209
Atkins, Mr. —, 212
Attehalle, John, v. of Culham, 36
Attington, in Thame, 114, 115, 147, 157, 163, 193; Abbot, 175; burgesses at Thame, 179; Dormer Leys farm, 170, 190, 191; ests., 187, 188; fee, 174–5; fields, 188; incl., 190, 192; man., 175, 190, 191; med. vill., 116, 170, 186; P.N., 186; sch. (with Tetsworth), 159; taxes, 188; tithes, 156; township, 162

CORRIGENDA TO VOLUMES III, V AND VI

Vol. III, plate facing p. 237, *for* 1733 *read* before 1728

Vol. V,   page 4, line 8, *for* 1492 *read* 1592

    ,,   page 326, *s.v.* Cropredy *delete* (Northants.)

Vol. VI, page xv, line 11 from the end, *for* Charlton *read* Chorlton

    ,,   page 9*b*, line 19, *for* atainder *read* attainder

    ,,   page 27*b*, 12 lines from the end, *for* no tclear *read* not clear

    ,,   page 39*b*, line 7, *for* 1868 *read* 1862

    ,,   page 47*b*, last line but one, *for* 19th *read* 20th

    ,,   page 48*b*, line 26, *for* Bornish *read* Cornish

    ,,   page 54*a*, line 41, *for* sunday *read* Sunday

    ,,   page 78*a*, line 31, *for* school-room *read* sick-room

    ,,   page 115*a*, line 22, *for* 1940 *read* 1950

    ,,   page 183*b*, line 10 from the end, *for* 1885 *read* 1897

    ,,   page 194, note 50, *for* Thc two shiclds *read* Othcr fragments

    ,,   page 240*a*, line 28, *for* Abbot *read* Bishop

    ,,   page 254, note 2, *for* Holbeck *read* Holbech

    ,,   page 259*a*, line 2, *for* three *read* two

    ,,   page 284*a*, line 14 from the end, *for* ritual *read* ceremonial

    ,,   page 333, note 57, *for* Peek, *read* Peck

    ,,   page 386, *s.v.* Westminster Abbey, *between* almoner, 240; *and* dean and chapter, *insert* bp. of, 240